"Outstanding . . . . A sensitive, practical approach to sound land management, this book contains a wealth of information. The advice and procedures are concise and achievable for the layman. The drawings are pleasing and clear. This excellent commentary and guide is as useful as it is delightful to read."

—Barbara Webster
Cleveland Museum of Natural History

"Exceptional . . . . Written with a gentle sense of humor, this is a one-of-a-kind book that belongs on the bookshelf of everyone who works with conservation, on their own land or in community projects, by themselves or with children, in scouting or 4-H projects. A truly educational and immensely satisfying book."

—*Popular Handicraft*

"A great guide for teachers and scout leaders."

—Mike Galvin
Pacific Search

"*The Earth Manual* is the most basic of how-to books on nature. With its list of resources for additional information and its step-by-step instructions, it resembles a visit from an ecologically hip county agent. And for a lot of problems involved in ownership of country land, that's precisely the combination you need."

—Bernard Carman
Up Country

"A whole book of gentle advice and easily absorbed wisdom."

—Peter Warshall
Coevolution Quarterly

THE EARTH MANUAL

THE EARTH MANUAL

How to Work on Wild Land Without Taming It

by Malcolm Margolin

Drawings by Michael Harney

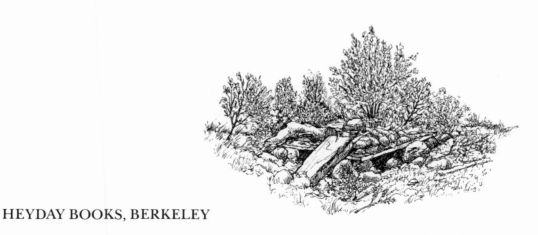

HEYDAY BOOKS, BERKELEY

Special thanks to Huey Johnson, Dick Raymond, and Life Forum for the grant that made writing this book possible.

Library of Congress Cataloging in Publication Data:
Margolin, Malcolm.   The earth manual.
Includes bibliographies and index.
1. Nature conservation—Handbooks, manuals, etc. 2. Wildlife habitat improvement–Handbooks, manuals, etc. 3. Arboriculture–Handbooks, manuals, etc. 4. Soil conservation–Handbooks, manuals, etc. 5. Nature trails—Handbooks, manuals, etc.
I. Title. QH75.M36 1985   639.9   85-80259
ISBN 0-930588-18-5 (pbk.)

Published by Heyday Books P.O. Box 9145 Berkeley, CA 94709

Cover illustration by Carl Buell
Cover and interior design by Sarah Levin

10   9   8   7   6   5   4   3

Contents

Foreword

Between well-trimmed suburban lawns and the vast regions of mountain wilderness, there are millions of patches of land that are semiwild. They may be wood lots, small forests, parks, a farm's "back forty," or even an untended corner of a big back yard—land invaded by civilization but far from conquered. This book is about how to take care of such land: how to stop its erosion, heal its scars, cure its injured trees, increase its wildlife, restock it with shrubs and wildflowers, and otherwise work with (rather than against) the wildness of the land.

Wildness comes in many forms. We recognize it easily in mountain lions and thunderstorms. But there is also wildness in a milkweed seed as it bounces lightly along the ground, in a bee twisting and probing within the womb of a wildflower, in the sunlight as it shatters upon the tree tops and pours down through the branches. Wildness cannot be programmed or created; it can only be accepted, and perhaps gently encouraged. Nothing more.

No matter how many acres you own, no matter how noble your ideas may be, you are not a "master planner" with control over the destiny of your wild land. In truth, you're not even a middle-management executive. If you want to encourage the wildness of your land, the very best you can hope to be is a good-natured, easygoing handyperson who putters around, solves minor problems, and does a few obviously worthwhile acts.

"But surely you must have an overall plan to guide you," people used to insist. So I'd lead them off into the woods.

"This is where the plans are being made," I'd say. "Scattered, scattered everywhere. In millions of leaves, in billions of seeds, in bird songs thrown down like streamers. In fact, everything in the universe is working together, at every moment and in every action planning out the destiny of these woods."

"It sounds like a complicated plan," people would tell me.

And I'd agree. It is complicated. Too many people ignore the complexities and rush off into wild land with their hands full of tools and their heads full of notions. They'd be better off giving their hands and heads a rest and using their bottoms. For sitting. Try it. Sit long, sit hard, sit in enough different places, and you will develop a sure feel for your land. Bits and pieces of the plan will become clear to you. It may take a long time. But once you develop a feel for where your land is heading, this, more than anything else, will give you the knowledge you need to work in harmony with it.

I have sat long and hard on many fine pieces of land throughout the country. But most of my working experience with land came during my three years at Redwood

Regional Park in the hills above Oakland, California. My job consisted largely of running the park's conservation program, and I involved thousands of youngsters from the San Francisco Bay Area in our various projects. We built erosion-control check dams, planted several thousand trees, and constructed ponds and watering holes. We collected, treated, and dispersed hundreds of bags of wildflower seeds. We restored several acres of meadow land, blended eroding firebreaks into the landscape, nursed injured trees back to health, cut hundreds of yards of trail, logged off part of a fire-gutted eucalyptus forest, stabilized a huge gully and slide area, and did all sorts of things to encourage wildlife.

This book is about what we did, how we did it, and how you can do it too—without money, fancy tools, or advanced skills, in fact, without even any kids. These are all projects you can do on wild land by yourself, or sometimes with the help of a friend or two.

I don't want to pretend that working on wild land is always fun. But I expect you'll find it a lot easier than you think. After all, as long as you are working to bring out the wildness of your land, your land will be more than willing to cooperate.

THE EARTH MANUAL

CHAPTER ONE
WILDLIFE

🌿 WILDLIFE. When we come into the woods, the first thing we want to know is, "What kind of animals live here?" Kids in particular ask this question. They expect a bear behind every bush, and when after ten minutes they don't even see a rabbit, they feel cheated. "Hey, man, these ain't the *real* woods. All the animals have been killed here."

Before beginning any wildlife project with a group of youngsters, I found it necessary to prove to them (and perhaps myself as well) that wildlife does indeed exist and that these are the *real* woods. Yet since most wildlife tends to be shy—especially when confronted with a group of jumping, yelling, stomping kids—I learned to "see" the animals I was dealing with mostly through their signs.

Try searching for animal signs sometime—not just casually, but in earnest—and I think you'll be delighted with the results. Animal signs are everywhere, once you learn to focus on them. There's browsed grass and leaves. There are tracks in the mud. There are deer and rabbit pathways through the meadows as well as mouse tunnels, gopher holes, and mole mounds. There are animal droppings—a sure winner if you are leading a group of younger children, since droppings combine two of their favorite obsessions: animals and turds. A pile of feathers shows where a bird was eaten, and perhaps who has eaten it. The litter of half-eaten nuts teaches us that animals are enormously sloppy, inefficient feeders—a fact that younger children are always glad to hear. Holes in trees and dens in the ground show where animals live. Elsewhere are trees that have been girdled by mice and rabbits, or whose bark has been scraped away by deer rubbing off their velvet. Pellets give away an owl's roost. Hawks and vultures overhead are interesting in themselves and also indicators of lots of life down below. A glance beneath stones and logs often exposes a wealth of salamanders, toads, mice, and especially snakes.

If alone, you might try stalking your wildlife like a hunter without a weapon. You can walk a trail for years without ever seeing a fox. Yet make a sincere, strenuous effort to spot one; watch for tracks, droppings, and pathways through the brush; learn everything you can about their habits, hours of activity, and territorial instincts; devote a whole day or more to the task of finding your local fox; and I guarantee that you will succeed. Not only that, but once you get acquainted with one fox, for some mysterious reason you begin noticing other foxes wherever you go.

By doing wildlife projects, you get in closer touch with wild animals and at the same time in closer touch with yourself. Kids seem to take this closeness for granted. They are vitally interested in wildlife from their earliest years.

They grow up on animal stories and animal crackers. Feeding ducks and pigeons are big events. They clutch teddy bears at night while worrying about the lions outside their windows. Kids love animals, they are terrified of animals, they want to hold animals, they want to help animals, they want to be animals, they are intrigued by the sameness between people and animals, and they are equally intrigued by the wonderful otherness too.

But as we grow, most of us have no contact with real wild animals—only with domesticated animals, stuffed animals, zoo animals, cartoon animals, and advertising animals ("Tony the Tiger sez . . ."). Our emotional and fantasy lives quietly mourn the loss.

Another handicap we bear is the weight of "common knowledge"—the mythology that tells us, for example, that foxes, wolves, ferrets, owls, hawks, eagles, and snakes are vicious, bloodthirsty creatures. Anyone who has dealt even in passing with snakes, owls, and hawks knows how unaggressive these creatures can be, while foxes, wolves, and ferrets can be downright charming and affectionate. I wish that wildlife could form an "Animal Lib" group to "tell it like it is." I think they would point up our terrible and profound fear, ignorance, and exploitation of wild creatures.

Wildlife projects will give you the chance to get reacquainted with animals, to deal with them as they really are, to consider their needs, to experience their vitality, and perhaps to rekindle in yourself a sheer childlike delight in their very existence. It would be unspeakably sad and lonely if we were the only animals on the globe. And it's so much fun to have all these other odd creatures along for the ride.

Wildlife Concepts

Before jumping into specific things you can do to foster a healthy, balanced, self-sufficient wildlife population, there are some elementary concepts you should know. These are general wildlife concepts that you should think about whenever you make *any* changes on your land at all.

Wildlife needs

Wildlife needs food, cover, and water. It needs all these things within a fairly compact area—how compact depends on the size of an animal's "territory." If any one of these things is missing, or in short supply, this will limit the number of creatures the land can support.

The next time you look at a piece of land, chant over and over again, like a mantra,

> Food, cover, water;
> Food, cover, water;
> Food, cover, water.

It will help you see the land as an animal might see it. A thick forest may have plenty of cover but no food. An irrigated farm may have plenty of water and enough food to feast Noah's Ark, but if there is no cover, it will be virtually a wildlife desert.

Water is sometimes difficult to judge. If it rains throughout the year, or if there is generally fog or heavy dew, water may not be a major problem. If you think you have a water problem, see pages 189-203 for directions on how to build ponds and watering holes.

Law of the minimum

Averages mean a lot to insurance brokers and baseball players, but they mean absolutely nothing to wildlife. It is not the average condition but the most extreme condition that determines wildlife population. Your land may have enough average rainfall for a sizable quail population. But if every year, or even every two or three years, there is a month-long drought, it is this extreme condition of drought that will determine how many quail can survive. Likewise, all wildlife has to adapt itself to the extremes of food shortage, temperature, water shortage, or the elimination of cover. If you want to help your wildlife, the best areas to focus your attention are at the various extremes—a periodic food shortage in March, for example, a drought in August, or a severe freeze in February might be good places to begin.

Do not restock

Do not worry about restocking on thinly populated land —unless, of course, the animal you're interested in has been totally exterminated from your area. If there is even a remnant, no matter how skinny, suppressed, and discouraged, it will do the restocking for you.

Instead of restocking, what you should be doing is improving the habitat and thus the *carrying capacity* of the land. On good grouse habitat, for example, you can find perhaps one grouse every 3 or 4 acres. On bad habitat you'll be lucky to find one in 200 acres. If you release more grouse in a bad grouse habitat, they'll die off very quickly—within a few weeks even—until their numbers are back to what the habitat can support.

Once you improve the habitat, however, you can take advantage of wildlife population dynamics—a fantastically explosive force. You've undoubtedly read those figures for rabbits or mice—showing how if all the bunnies from one pair of rabbits lived and reproduced, and if all their offspring lived and reproduced, within a few years we'd need periscopes to see each other. It's true for all wildlife.

If the habitat's right, your animals will have far more fun restocking the land than you will—and they'll do a much better job of it too.

Predators

I'm sure it's not necessary to tell you that predators do not wipe out their prey. In national parks where both predators and prey are equally protected, I have never heard of a single case where the existence of the prey was endangered. In fact, despite healthy predation, the most common problem in such protected areas is still overpopulation of deer, rabbits, and other prey animals.

Variety

There is no such thing as the perfect habitat for all wildlife. Every species of animal has its own preferences. If you strip a piece of land of all its vegetation and let it alone, it will eventually go through several stages of weeds, grasses, shrubs, small trees, and big trees until it reaches its climax. At each stage it will be a preferred habitat of different animals. Animals that like fields will be evicted by the eventual arrival of brush. Animals that like shrubs will be made homeless by the forest. If you want a variety of wildlife, the thing to do is to create as many varieties of habitat as you can within the bounds of your natural environment.

When two environments meet, by the way, the wildlife possibilities are multiplied many times over. This is known as the *edge effect*. The edge of a forest is far more fruitful than the center. Other exciting places are the shores of lakes and ponds, the borders of meadow land and brush, and (for birds) the billowy area where the tree canopy meets the sky.

Manage your land for all wildlife

It is important to keep *all* your wildlife in mind, especially when you are dealing with experts who think that *wildlife* means *game animals.* Take, for example, the matter of prescribed burns, where you burn off the forest floor under controlled conditions. Prescribed burns are very fashionable these days. It's the "in" thing to treat Smokey with condescension and burn off a few acres every year. The idea behind burning, as far as wildlife management goes, is that on the charred soil a lush crop of weeds, berries, legumes, and grasses will grow up which are very good for deer, grouse, moose, quail, bear, and various other game animals. This is true. But remember that the same fire is also going to destroy millions of mice, rats, ground squirrels, lemmings, worms, insects, soil organisms, snakes, toads, newts, rodents, amphibians, reptiles, and the predators that depend on them. I'm not saying you should *never* burn, but if you do, keep in mind *all* your wildlife.

Brush Piles

Architecturally, there is not much to building a brush pile. You simply pile up a lot of brush with the idea of providing shelter for small animals. If you want to get more elaborate, you can put heavy logs or rocks on the bottom to prevent the pile from matting down to the ground, thus keeping it open for the entrances and exits of the animals you attract. You should pile the brush as high as you can—at least four or five feet high—and in general try to keep it twice as wide as it is high. If you have some more heavy logs or limbs, throw them on top to compress the pile and keep it from blowing apart, and, *voilà,* you have the perfect brush pile. Members of the American Institute of Architects might blanch when they see it, but your wildlife will love it. A brush pile is nature's very own idea of style, borrowed from the dwellings of muskrats, pack rats, and beavers. It's also a wonderful project for a group of little kids.

Where to get brush

I would not cut down brush especially to make a brush pile, since there is usually lots of material available: dead trees; slash from logging, thinning, pruning, or trail building; old fence posts; or brush from a brush-clearance (meadow-restoration) project. Another good source of brush is a collection of your community's old Christmas trees—a good way of recycling Christmas trees and involving your community in your land.

Where to build brush piles

The best place for a brush pile is where there is lots of food, lots of water, but no shelter. Meadows and clear forests are good places. Remember that the animals you attract will be small and not very far ranging, so that the closer they are to food and water, the better they will survive.

The future of a brush pile

I've always admired the old-car method of berry farming. It works like this. Just drive an old car into a field, desert it, and within a few years it will be totally covered with berries —with no planting, no cultivating, no watering on your part.

The old-car method works equally well for brush piles. You can plant cuttings if you want, but even if you do absolutely nothing, the brush pile will soon be taken over by blackberries, Virginia creeper, bittersweet, wild grapes, and other berries. The seeds are brought by birds who perch on the brush, and, while adding songs to the air, gently perk up their tails and drop a few seeds into the brush pile. The brush itself decays into humus with time, but the big mound of brambles and berries is likely to remain for many years.

Fish brush piles

Brush piles work just as beautifully for fish as they do for birds and animals. A brush pile in the water gives small fish a place to escape to, gives fry a place to hatch and grow up, and gives algae a place to cling to and produce food.

The problem with a fish brush pile, of course, is that brush can float away. But if you can find a still backwater or the edge of a small pond, throw in some brush, stake it or weigh it down, and it will serve your fish population very nicely.

The only thing to watch out for in building a fish brush pile is overenthusiasm. Don't overdo it if you are dealing with an enclosed body of water like a pond or a small lake. A moderate amount of cover will benefit your fish. Too much cover, however, and the fish will overpopulate. Unlike mammals, overpopulations of fish do not usually starve; rather, horror of horrors, they dwarf. Instead of a few dozen healthy trout, you end up with hundreds, even thousands, of trout ignominiously going through life as minnows. So, unless you're into miniaturization, I suggest you go easy on fish brush piles.

Rock piles

Piles of rock are not quite as effective as brush piles, but if you are in a field with lots of rock and no brush, you might pile some of the rocks anyway. Here again, make the pile as big as you can, leave some space at the bottom for entrances and exits, and you will very likely provide a fine home for some animal. Or for some fish if you pile the stones in the water.

Living brush piles

Sometimes you can get natural vegetation to look and act like a brush pile. One good way of doing this is to cut halfway through a tree and let it fall with the lean. (See page 39.) This way it will stay alive for a few seasons, providing browse and shelter for many animals.

Another trick you might consider is multiple layering. You can convert a fairly modest bush into a huge jumble of thickets by staking some of its branches underground. (For detailed instructions on how to layer, see pages 132-134.)

The inhabitants

The animals that live in brush piles are generally secretive. Yet if you place the pile in a good location, you'll be surprised at the activity. You may never see an animal, but tracks, well-worn paths, droppings, songs of birds, peepings and whistlings, the interest of a hawk overhead, and scamperings and rustlings every time you pass are all indications of brush-pile prosperity.

Holes and Dens

Animals simply love to live in holes. They love caves, holes in trees, and dens in the ground. Not long ago humans were among the animals competing for big, clean holes and caves. And what high standards we still have! Nothing worse can be said of a dwelling than "it's an absolute hole." Yet people who can afford it make a separate room which they call a "den," panel it with wood, keep it warm, stuffy, natural, and holelike, and show it off to their friends. If you decide to make a few animal holes around your land, it would be wise to remember this human situation. Not all holes are created equal. A nasty, ticky-tacky hole might do in an emergency, but a good hole is an animal's idea of true wealth. Spend some time making the hole comfortable, well drained, and secure, and it will attract an animal and make it happy for many years.

Den trees

In old forests, you will find lots of dying trees, lots of insects to burrow into the dying trees, and lots of wood-peckers to eat the insects. In the process, woodpeckers make holes for their own nests, and these holes later become dens for owls, squirrels, several kinds of birds, possums, rac-coons, and other creatures.

Without holes to nest in, squirrels will build leaf nests. One look at these clumsy, bulky, inept-looking structures will let you know that the squirrels would much rather have a den. Also, because of exposure to the weather and to predators, squirrels are rarely successful in raising a family in a leaf nest.

One of the best and most satisfying projects I know is to clear out rot from an old tree injury, creating a well-drained cavity in the process. Not only will this keep the tree sound, it will also provide a premium den site. (See pages 63-65.)

Another thing you can do, I suppose, is build wooden boxes, which most definitely attract wood ducks, squirrels, and other animals. If you want to create a sort of shantytown for wood ducks, there are instructions and plans available elsewhere. I find the idea aesthetically silly and condescend-ing toward animals—but the animals don't seem to mind very much, so maybe I'm just being a purist.

One thing you might consider, especially if you have a predominantly second-growth forest of adolescent trees, is to create a dead-tree environment that will attract insects that will, in turn, attract woodpeckers. Unfortunately, there is only one way to create a dead-tree environment: you have to go out and kill trees. This makes for a rather ambiguous —although occasionally necessary—conservation project. The best way of going about it is to find a few larger trees and girdle them. Use a chisel and mallet to cut a wide band around the tree. The band should be about two inches wide and deep enough to remove all the bark and cambium (the green juicy layer just under the bark). The tree will die on its feet and will hopefully remain standing for several years, attracting termites, insects, woodpeckers, and the other lively guests that attend the dying of a tree.

Ground dens

What a woodpecker does in the trees, ground hogs do on the land. Ground hogs (also called woodchucks or marmots) are the housing contractors of the woods, building roomy dens that are later taken over by foxes, skunks, rabbits, snakes, raccoons, possums, and other creatures.

If your land is short of holes, one of the best long-range measures is to encourage ground hogs—as long as you don't encourage them too close to any garden or nursery you're planning to build. Unfortunately, the human race has been so eager to get rid of ground hogs that no one has done any research on how to attract them. I once asked an old-timer how you go about attracting ground hogs, and all I got was one of those long, sarcastic, head-scratching, "What is this world coming to?" sort of stares. The best way I know is to build a few brush piles, under which ground hogs dearly love to build their dens.

Until such time as you can transfer conservation duties to the ground hogs, you might want to build some dens your-self. Build them near cover, near winter food, and near

Culvert den

water, and make sure they are well drained so that you don't drown the animal you will attract.

A good den can be made out of old pipes, drain tiles, or sections of culvert. Lay them down in some inconspicuous place and heap stones, dirt, and brush over them—partly to disguise them, partly to keep the sun from baking the inhabitants. Make sure there are at least two exits and that all the entrances and exits are well disguised with brush or stone.

Another good den can be made from rocks and a piece of old plywood or sheet metal. Simply arrange the rocks on the ground and put the wood or the metal on top to form a roof. Cover everything with lots of earth and rocks, and again remember to provide cover at the entrances and exits.

Building a den is easy. Now comes the hard part. You've got to stay away. Don't keep returning to shine flashlights into the holes or beat on the den with your walking stick. Do the best thing any landlord can do—stay out of your tenants' way. Eventually you'll notice a well-worn path leading up to the entrance. This may be your only reward for a job well-done.

Variations on a Hedgerow

If you have any open meadows, you should definitely consider putting in a few scraggly hedgerows. Meadows and fields have lots of food for wildlife, but lack of cover often keeps animals away. No rabbit in his right mind wants to get caught in the middle of a field.

A hedgerow is a row of thick, bushy plants which provides both shelter and a passageway for animals to get across the field. Any bushy plant will make a good hedgerow, but the best type of plant is one that is both thorny and bears an edible fruit.

How to make a wild hedgerow

If you decide to break up a field with a hedgerow, you should try to avoid a straight line of bushes. It looks artificial. You can learn how to plant a wild-looking hedgerow by watching an animal, even a cat, make its way across a field. It will seldom make a beeline but will run from a bush to a rock, sidle along a fallen log, dash under a fence rail, and zigzag from one clump of weeds to another. In planning your hedgerow, keep this image in mind. There are probably several good sheltered places already in your field. All you have to do is connect them with a brush pile, a log, a pile of stones, and a few shrubs that you can plant. Youngsters, by the way, really enjoy planning out a hedgerow of this type. It's like playing hide-and-seek.

What to plant

In deciding what to plant, keep your eyes open to see what in your neighborhood grows close to the ground in a thick, hedgelike way. You can sometimes get good advice from your local Fish and Game Department, but don't let them sell you on a foreign exotic like lespedeza or multiflora rose (which spreads like crazy), and beware of anything that needs constant pruning to keep it shrubby.

In California there are various shrubs, especially ceanothus or buckthorn, that make good cover and provide some food in the bargain. In other parts of the country, hedgerow materials with a fairly good reputation are Osage orange, high-bush cranberry (*Viburnum trilobum*), bayberry, and various small dogwoods. Spruce is especially good, since it grows close to the ground, has sharp needles that discourage larger predators, and doesn't lose its leaves in the winter.

There are various ways of planting shrubs. You can grow

them from seed and plant them out as you would a tree. Or you can take cuttings and, after treating them properly, plant them out as a hedgerow (see pages 127-143).

Ditches

One place where you can apply the hedgerow concept of cover and passageway is along drainage ditches and gullies, wherever they penetrate into a field. Ditches and gullies often have plenty of water. By planting berries, shrubs, and vines, you can add cover and food, thereby completing the formula for wildlife intensity. And by dense planting you may be able to prevent further erosion along drainage ditches.

Predators

Making hedgerows and planting ditches will help various small animals outsmart their predators. But don't feel sorry for your local foxes and hawks. Any improvement in the health and population of a prey animal is also an improvement for the predator. In fact, if you are one of those sainted, wild souls who manages land especially for eagles, wolves, foxes, or other predators, making hedgerows is one of the best things you can do. Whereas without hedgerows your field can support perhaps only two families of rabbits, it can now support four. These extra two families will produce more than forty bunnies a year, which will make the predators very happy indeed.

Corridors

Another good project to keep in mind is creating the mirror image of hedgerows—namely, corridors through heavy brush. The idea here is to clear out strips to allow animals to penetrate the brush land for browse. Deer, in particular, will benefit. Avoid straight lines and save your-self work by connecting already existing clearings. Also, don't be too concerned with pulling the brush out by the roots. If the corridors are used regularly, any new growth will be trampled or browsed.

Clearings   Some people find it hard to believe that by cutting down trees you can greatly increase your wildlife. Yet it is gener-ally true. Dense forests are very poor wildlife habitats. Create a few openings, however, and you will encourage a much more varied and plentiful wildlife population.

Clearings are very much part of the natural landscape. They are caused by flooding, fire, windstorm, and certain conditions of soil, rainfall, and exposure. What makes them so good for wildlife is that the sun reaches the ground, causing a lush growth of weeds, berry bushes, shrubs, grasses, and fruit trees that would otherwise be shaded out in a forest. Trees at the edge of openings also receive lots of sun, which allows them to spread out and keep their lower branches—thus providing easy-to-get-at food and shelter for many animals.

Indians understood the value of openings in the woods, and throughout the country they were reported to have burned the land periodically to maintain them.

The best time to think about openings is when you're planting trees. Do not plant a thick, unbroken forest. Leave small half-acre or one-acre clearings here and there—say, one every quarter mile or so. If you make lots of small clearings, you will touch the borders of many home ter-ritories and benefit the maximum number of animals.

Another good project is to keep track of your current openings and visit them every year or two with lopping shears and a grub hoe to keep the forest trees from gaining a foothold.

If you are going to clear an opening out of an already established forest, you'd be best off with a sunny exposure (either south or west). You can pile the slash into brush piles. If you want the opening to remain open, be sure to watch the stumps, lest they resprout (see pages 39-40). Another consideration: you might do the felling during the critical food period of late winter and early spring. The buds and twigs of the trees you chop down—especially maple and birch—will provide good emergency browse.

Dusting places

After you make a clearing, a very nice amenity to provide is a place where animals can dust off. Many birds and small mammals are made very happy by dust baths—perhaps it removes parasites, perhaps it serves some other function, or perhaps (a reason orthodox zoologists might find hard to accept) it's just a whole lot of fun. Whatever its purpose, you might want to throw a few handfuls of sand, dry earth, crumbly wood, or sawdust into the middle of a clearing, where it will be well used and appreciated.

Forested openings

Some forest trees tend to darken the ground and eliminate other vegetation. But there are other trees—especially locusts, alders, and aspen—that actually encourage growth beneath them. These trees give a light shade (rather than a heavy shade) and, more important, they encourage nitrification—that is, they foster the bacteria that convert atmospheric nitrogen into nitrogen fertilizer. Not only is the ground beneath these trees full of shrubs, bushes, weeds, vines, and herbs, but these plants are actually more nutritious than the same plants growing somewhere else. You might do well to plant these trees and protect them wherever they are now growing, especially since the lumber industry considers them "weed trees" and on commercial land is doing everything it can to replace them with money-making conifers.

Food   Planting food for wildlife is a delightful switch. For ages wild animals have been used to feed humans; now you have the chance to feed them instead.

Before getting into specific suggestions, let's examine the yearly food cycle of, say, a deer. In the late spring and throughout the summer, there is plenty of green grass, weeds, wildflowers, berries, and fruit. "Livin' is easy," as the song about summertime goes.

In the fall, grains and many seeds ripen, but the big event is the nut harvest. Acorns, beechnuts, hickories, hazelnuts —all fantastically nutritious—are readily available until the first snows. The deer put on a good layer of fat, and they are ready for winter.

In the winter, deer paw through the snow after acorns and eat whatever tough greens they can find (especially wintergreen). By the end of winter, however, they are reduced to eating buds and twigs. They seem to go about it with all the gusto of a starving man eating his boots. Buds and twigs are definitely a last-resort food.

At the beginning of spring (about late February through the first week of April), there is a general food emergency in the woods. Deer and other animals have used up their layers of fat. The ground has been scoured for acorns and nuts. The browse has been pretty well eaten, and the earliest leafy greens have not yet come. If you want to increase your wildlife population significantly, this is the season when you should concentrate your efforts.

What exactly should you plant? It varies from one area to the next. Your local Fish and Game Bureau is usually a good source of specific suggestions. But in general, here are some things you ought to be thinking about.

Nut trees

Planting nut trees, or *mast,* is probably the best thing you can do for your wildlife. It builds them up in the fall and keeps them alive through the winter. Oaks, beeches, hickories, black walnuts, butternuts, hazelnuts, chinquapin, piñon pines, and junipers are among the most valuable nut trees.

You can plant nut tree seedlings or you can collect nuts in the fall and plant them directly in the field. However you do it, you should plant as wide a variety as your environment can support. Do not pin all your hopes on just one species of tree, since nut trees are notoriously unreliable about producing. For five years a tree may be bountiful, then one year it will seem to forget. If you want to assure your animals of a steady diet of nuts, you'll have to plant several different species.

A word about acorns, which are singly the most valuable wildlife mast. Some oaks, as you may know, produce sweet acorns. These are the so-called "white" oaks. The "red" oaks, on the other hand, produce such bitter acorns, so full of tannin, that just looking at them puckers you up. Despite popular opinion, however, the bitter acorns are extremely valuable to wildlife. In the fall animals prefer sweet acorns, which play a major role in fattening them up. But sweet acorns rot quickly. The tannin in the bitter acorns prevents them from rotting, keeping them sound often until the next spring.

Release cutting

Release cutting is a very valuable aid to nut and fruit trees. Most of these are transitional, destined to be overshadowed as a forest progresses toward its climax growth. If, however, you clear around an especially valuable nut or fruit tree, you can "release" it. By doing so you will reap double rewards. The tree will spread out and bear more heavily, while underneath it, shrubs and greens will spring up for even greater wildlife benefit.

Freeze-ripened fruits

There are certain fruits that stay on the tree throughout the winter. In the early winter they are often too bitter or otherwise unpalatable for wildlife. But by late winter the repeated freezing and thawing have made them quite edible —just at the season when they are most needed. Among the plants that generally follow this pattern are Oregon grape, crab apples, mountain ash, high-bush cranberry, hawthorn, staghorn sumac, winterberry, coralberry, and partridgeberry.

Early foods

Another good thing to do is to plant a variety of the earliest foods, foods that are ready to be eaten just at the end of winter. Elms generally have seeds that ripen very early, and so do other plants. Consult your local Fish and Game people, your Soil Conservation District, or (the ultimate revolution!) your own eyes for information about the earliest-ripening forage plants in your area.

Gourmet diets

Even during the spring, summer, and fall, certain animals have very narrow food preferences. Birds, in particular, are often very fussy about what they'll eat. There is no way you can attract acorn woodpeckers without acorns. Here again, you might get local advice from the Fish and Game Bureau or from your local chapter of the Audubon Society about what other foods you might plant—especially in conjunction with reforestation projects, erosion-control plantings, or other such projects.

Artificial feeding

As a matter of theory, I'd avoid artificial feeding of wildlife. In an overbrowsed area, feeding deer will merely aggravate the problem. Feeding waterfowl may convince them to winter further north than usual—with potentially dangerous results. In fact, wildlife theory is now swinging to a hard line that you should *never* give handouts to your wildlife. So much for the theory. When it gets cold and nasty and when the animals you love are obviously having trouble, and you just happen to be sitting on a bale of alfalfa—well, I'll leave you to cope with the "theory" as best you can.

If you decide not to resort to artificial feeding as a regular thing, there are still several abnormal circumstances under which you might consider it:

· For rare, endangered, or threatened species.
· During extreme emergencies. Not necessarily the coldest week of the year, but certainly during the coldest week in fifty years.
· When some act of civilization has deprived your wildlife of its usual food. A logging operation may have cleared out most of the nut trees and replanted the area with nothing but pine. Or perhaps a housing development has gone up in a sheltered valley where elk would regularly congregate during the coldest part of the winter. Under circumstances

like these, you can feel perfectly justified in putting out some food—but once you begin, please keep it up on a regular basis.

The best emergency foods for small animals and birds are corn or chicken feed. For larger animals, corn, hay, or alfalfa will be welcome.

Reading

For wildlife habitat improvement, the more specific the book the more valuable it is. The U.S. Forest Service, state Forestry Divisions, state Fish and Game Departments, and many other organizations have produced books, pamphlets, papers, and articles on how to encourage a certain animal or improve a particular environment. These can usually be found in a college forestry or biology library.

General books that I have found helpful would include:

The Way to Game Abundance, by Wallace Byron Grange. New York: Scribner's, 1949.

This is an absorbing book dealing with the larger issues of cycles, population mathematics, predation, territoriality, and vegetation succession. The issues are all brilliantly covered in intelligent, readable prose. It's a book that examines all the clichés—their clichés ("All predators are bad") and our clichés ("All predators are good") in light of the author's experience. This is a rare book that not only covers the bigger issues but does so in such a manner that you can use the information in a practical way.

The book is also fun to read.

Wildlife Habitat Improvement Handbook. Forest Service Handbook FSH 2609.11. Washington, D.C.: U.S. Forest Service, 1969.

Written for Forest Service personnel, this handbook has sound, practical information and advice. It has especially good chapters on stream improvement (for fish) and on water-hole construction. It also has valuable lists of plants and trees for waterfowl.

The Farmer and Wildlife, by Durward L. Allen. Second revised edition. Washington, D.C.: Wildlife Management Institute, 1970.

This 62-page booklet is aimed at the farmer and his concerns: cultivation, irrigation, and grazing. It focuses on how to reconcile the farmer's interests with those of wildlife and is available free from the Wildlife Management Institute, Wire Building, Washington, D.C. 20005.

American Wildlife and Plants, by Alexander C. Martin, Herbert S. Zim, and Arnold L. Nelson. New York: McGraw-Hill, 1951. Paperback reprint by Dover Books, New York.

This is a big book and very thorough. It covers all major species of birds and mammals, one by one, giving the food habits of each. It breaks down these habits by geographical area, season, and the importance any one food plays in the total diet. Next it turns to the plants, listing major species of grass, herbs, aquatic plants, vines, shrubs, and trees, and telling what animals eat them and where.

CHAPTER THREE
FELLING A TREE

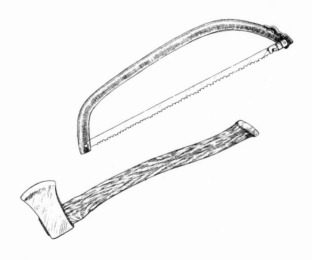

FELLING A TREE. This chapter will tell you how to cut down a tree. Don't be shocked. No matter how much you love trees, there are times when you will have to fell them. And when you do, you will probably discover a secret that most sensitive conservationists try to hide—even from themselves. It's fun to chop down trees! It's fun to look a tree over, plan its fall, and work hard against a real physical objective. There is a definite thrill when, after twenty minutes of sawing, you hear the telltale crack, there is a long, pregnant pause, and the tree slowly, ever so slowly, begins its final journey to the ground. It's very exciting to yell, "Timber!" and backstep rapidly away, all your senses wildly alert. And there is something overpowering and deeply satisfying when the tree hits the ground with a huge crash, the ground shakes, and then a tremendous, complete silence follows.

As a conservation project, I found tree felling hard to beat. Kids just love it. It doesn't matter if the kids are teen-age boys on a macho trip, a group of girls from a parochial high school, or fifth graders on a bird hike. If there is a tree to be chopped down, kids will fight for the privilege. This used to disturb me. Here I was, a hotshot conservationist, supposedly leading the younger generation off to a new, gentle ecological consciousness—yet our spirit was unmistakably that of the Goths about to sack Rome.

I've always been troubled by the spiritual aspects of felling trees, and I don't have any easy solutions. Kids love to chop down trees, and so indeed do I; yet at the same time, I am appalled at the eagerness and heartlessness with which we take on the job. Felling trees is the only project I know where having fun is a problem. I wish I had more of this problem on other projects I've been involved in.

Planning
the Downfall

There are many technical, textbookish reasons for cutting down trees under the guise of "forest management." But most forests need far less managing than professionals pretend. Nevertheless, there are still times when you will want to fell a tree. For example:

Exotics. You might want to rid your land of some foreign exotic (like eucalyptus in California) where it is ecologically inappropriate and where it is crowding out native vegetation and the life systems that native vegetation supports.

Release cutting. You might want to remove competition from around an especially valuable nut- or fruit-bearing tree if you feel that it is being crowded or overshadowed.

Trail building. Most of the time you can work your way

around a tree, but there are rare times when you will have to cut.

Thinning. Sometimes after logging, burning, or over-enthusiastic planting, the land will sprout many thousands of trees growing close together, crowding each other out, and dwarfing each other. Instead of a noble forest, you might find a thicket of toothpicks. Time will take care of the problem, if you're willing to wait a hundred or so years. But if you're impatient, you can thin the forest yourself.

Wildlife cuttings. If you have a uniformly dense forest, you might want to create a few scattered openings where grasses, weeds, legumes, and shrubs can grow. Or, during a severe winter, you might want to fell a tree here and there to give deer, rabbits, and elk (if you're so lucky) some tender buds and twigs to browse on.

Which trees to cut

This will depend largely on why you are cutting them. Let's say you are thinning or making small clearings. You might take your cues from the lumber industry, which divides all trees into roughly two categories: "good" trees (i.e., trees that make money) and "bad" trees (trees that don't make money). Bad trees, needless to say, must be gotten rid of, and if you seek professional advice, you will be urged to chop down "wolf" trees, "weed" trees, trees that are too young, trees that are too old, crooked trees, and so on. The goal of traditional thinning methods is to produce valuable, uniform lumber. Lumber people love uniformity, but that is exactly what you do not want. You want as much diversity as you can get within the bounds of your natural environment. So go easy on professional advice and ignore the traditional rules for thinning (if you happen to know them). Remember that a single, half-rotten, malformed oak tree might have greater wildlife value than an acre of thriving young conifers. As you thin, try to create an authentic environment (whatever that means for your area) and a varied one. Add a touch of craziness here and there, and you will end up with a forest with lots of wildlife, lots of different plants, and lots of interesting trees with unloggable personalities.

Erosion

Whenever you cut a tree, you should be thinking about erosion. What is going to hold the soil together once the tree is down? Don't cut too much at any one time, especially on slopes. Clear in small patches, leaving trees standing (at least temporarily) to hold the soil and serve as windbreaks.

To further minimize erosion, you might try dropping trees perpendicular to the flow of water. Left in place, they will act as check dams, slowing down the water and perhaps preventing the development of gullies.

Clear a work area

Sawing down a tree is hard work, and you must have a comfortable area in which to do it. You most certainly do not want to work in cramped quarters, your body contorted like a pretzel. Clear out a place where you can get a firm footing, and if you're using an ax, remove enough brush so that you can get a free swing. Lop off any lower branches of the tree that are in your way. Then clear out an escape route or two, preferably at 135-degree angles to the direction you expect the tree to fall. Fix the escape routes firmly in your mind.

Looking a tree over

Before felling a tree, walk around it and study it. Check it once more for value. Is it a den tree (one with holes)? Is it a fruit tree? A nut tree? Are there any nests? Is it a rare species?

Then look it over for safety. Be sure to avoid trees with dead branches. Dead branches are called "widow makers," for obvious reasons.

Judging the fall

Now think about where the tree will naturally fall. Which way is it leaning? Stand back and hold your ax out before you by the tip of the handle, with the blade pointing at the tree. The handle will be *plumb,* and by sighting along it, you can determine the lean.

Look at the balance. Too many heavy branches on one side may help pull the tree over to that side. Pay careful attention to the top. If the top is nodding in one direction, that's the way the tree is likely to fall.

Next you should check the trunk at about waist height, where you will be cutting. If you see any rot, or if in fact at any time during the cutting you feel yourself sawing through rot, remember that this will influence the fall toward the weaker side.

Finally, take the wind into account, especially if the tree has lots of foliage. Add these four factors together—lean, balance, rot, and wind—and weighing the lean most heavily, you will get a good idea of where the tree wants to fall.

Once you have figured out where the tree wants to fall, file that information away and begin thinking about what is best for you. Look for a clear space (or *bed* as it's called) into which you can drop the tree where it won't damage anything valuable or get hung up in the branches of another tree. But do not, under any circumstances, consider dropping a tree up a steep slope: it is very likely to hit against the slope and kick back at you.

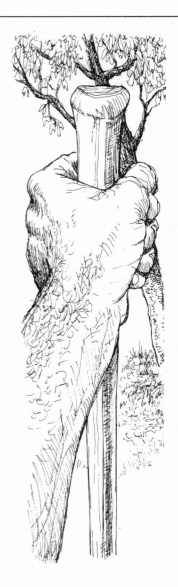

You now know where you want to drop the tree and where the tree wants to fall. Do you both agree? If you and the tree are within forty-five degrees of each other, you can proceed without any special skills or equipment.

Roping

Let's say, however, that you and the tree have very different ideas on where it should fall. If you expect to get your way, you'll need a rope or cable. Tie the rope as high on the tree as you can. Then, as you cut, have someone pull hard and constantly in the direction you want the tree to fall. Needless to say, make the rope long enough so that whoever is pulling does not end up with a tree on top of him. Often it is better to run the rope through a pulley or around another tree and then back beyond the tree you are cutting down.

For a smaller tree, you might dispense with the rope and simply have someone push against it with a forked stick, positioning the stick high on the tree for maximum leverage.

Dropping a Tree

Once you have cleared a work area, determined the direction of the fall, made sure of your escape routes, and perhaps attached a rope or cable, you are ready to cut. In the following pages, I will tell you how to do it. The basic procedures are not very difficult to learn, but please don't consider yourself an expert just because you have read this chapter.

There is no book in the world that is going to teach you how to fell trees with the assurance, grace, and safety of an expert lumberjack. Be prepared for the eventuality that now and then, especially in the beginning, you will mess things up and drop a tree in the wrong direction. When this happens, don't just pass it off as something that *experience* will eventually take care of. *Experience* won't take care of a blessed thing—unless you think deeply and creatively about it as it happens. Learning from mistakes is always a lot harder than moralists pretend—especially when your hands are blistering from an ax, your arms are aching from a hand saw, or perhaps your whole body is dulled from the buzzing and vibrating of a chain saw. Yet if you want to become competent at felling trees, it is under circumstances such as these that you will have to be most alert and thoughtful.

Make a few mistakes, figure out why, and eventually you'll learn the craft. Until then, I hope you'll think of yourself as an apprentice. I especially hope that you'll serve out your apprenticeship deep in the woods—not, for goodness' sake, in your back yard, book in one hand and saw in the other, family and friends crowded around in admiration, while you undertake to drop a 100-foot spruce into a narrow space between your house, a neighbor's house, and some high-voltage power lines.

Small trees

For small trees up to about six inches in diameter, you do not need any fancy, formal cuts. An ax will do the job as well as a saw. Chop a notch into the tree on the side on which you want it to fall. Keep chopping. When you are about three-quarters of the way through the tree, you can usually stand off to one side and push it over into its bed. Pushing with a forked stick is particularly effective.

Tools

The traditional way of felling bigger trees is with an undercut and then a back cut. It is possible to use an ax, but it is also dangerous. The chopping tends to dislodge weak branches, which can fall on your head, and the lack of precision in an ax cut means a certain lack of predictability in how the tree falls. Later on I'll tell you how to use an ax, but if at all possible, do it with a saw. There are various big-toothed hand saws that do the job, but my favorite is a bow saw with a tubular frame. A chain saw makes the job a lot easier but a lot more dangerous.

The undercut

The undercut is made on the side toward which you want the tree to fall. Begin at about waist height with a horizontal cut about one-third the distance through the tree. Then pull out the saw and begin another cut well above the first cut, angling it down until you have cut out a wedge. The inside angle of the wedge should be at least forty-five degrees.

Before going on to the back cut, check what you have done. Make especially sure that the inside edge of the undercut is perpendicular to the direction of the fall. You can check this with a hand-made sighting stick, or with a straight-handled, double-headed ax. Facing the cut, insert the ax head against the inner edge, and the handle will point to the direction of the fall.

Back cut

Once you are comfortably certain that the undercut is correct, you can begin the back cut, or *felling cut.* Go around to the other side of the tree, opposite the undercut side, and saw into the tree about two inches above the base of the undercut. Keep the cut level. Don't angle it down.

Keep sawing, all the while paying careful attention to the *hinge,* the piece of uncut wood between the back cut and the undercut. The tree will topple before the saw cuts all the way through, and how it falls will depend largely on the hinge. As you saw, try your best to keep the hinge uniformly thick. If it is uneven, when the tree begins to fall it may tear

sighting stick

easily from the thin end of the hinge while hanging back on the thick end, perhaps causing the tree to twist in its fall.

In addition to the hinge, you should also keep a very close watch on the *kerf*, the space that the saw leaves behind it as you cut through the tree. This space will give you your only advance warning of how the tree is going to fall. When you get about one-third of the way toward the undercut, you should notice the space getting ever so slightly bigger. Good! This means that the tree is beginning to pull toward the undercut, which is where you want it to go. Keep sawing until you hear the crack. Remove the saw, back off, and—as if I had to tell you—stay alert.

On rare occasions, however, you'll notice that the kerf, instead of getting bigger, is closing up on you. This means that you have misjudged the lean or the balance of the tree and that the tree has no intention whatsoever of falling in the direction of the undercut. Don't just keep sawing in the hope that the tree will change its mind; trees don't change their minds. If you keep sawing, the kerf will eventually close up so tight that it will trap the saw. Before this happens, remove the saw and put tension on the tree with a rope or a forked stick to force it over to the right direction. Or, if you have them (and you should), knock some wedges into the back cut to open up the space. One way is to saw a bit, then, keeping the saw in place, knock the wedges in, saw a bit more, then knock the wedges in a bit further—until as the tree is weakened it's lifted up toward the undercut. If you are going to use this procedure with a chain saw, make certain you use wooden or plastic wedges rather than metal wedges.

There is one more eventuality which is rare indeed but does happen once in a blue moon. Sometimes you find yourself sawing, the hinge growing thinner and thinner, but

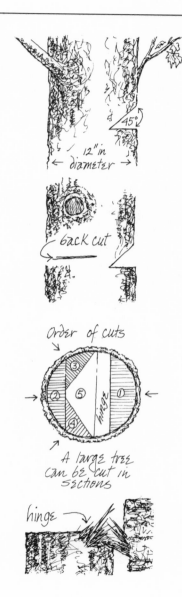

45°

12" in
← diameter →

back cut

Order of cuts

A large tree
can be cut in
sections

hinge →

the tree gives absolutely no indication of which way it is heading. What's happening is that the tree is balanced on its hinge. It may fall one way, it may fall the other way, or—most dangerous of all—without a hinge to guide it, it may slide off its stump and kick out at you. If you ever feel the hinge getting too small for comfort, stop sawing right away and use ropes, a forked stick, or wedges to get the tree down.

Using an ax

I've already told you that dropping a big tree with an ax is dangerous, difficult, and foolhardy—right? If you decide on going ahead anyway, here's how. Make certain, first of all, that you are working with the lean of the tree, that there are no dead branches to get jarred loose, that the consequences of miscalculation are minimal, and that you have your escape routes well prepared.

Then begin chopping an undercut on the side where you want the tree to fall. But instead of making a cut one-third of the way through the tree, you should chop about 50 or even 60 per cent of the way through. Also, unless you're extraordinarily proficient, you won't end up with a neat wedge but with a wide, sloppy cut. This wide cut should have a *focus,* that is, one area running across the tree that is deeper than the rest. Try to leave this focus as clean and even as you can, since it will be serving as a hinge when the tree falls.

When you've completed your undercut, get around to the other side of the tree to begin your back cut, or felling cut. Aim it two or three inches above the focus of the undercut. And do your best to keep the hinge especially thick on both ends. If you give in to the temptation to chop away at the easy corners rather than the bulky middle, you will weaken the edges of the hinge in such a way that when the tree falls it might twist on its eccentric hinge.

Felling with the lean

Sometimes you come upon a tree that is leaning with an exaggerated, theatrical posture off to one side. Trees like this can be easily felled with a single cut on the opposite side of the lean. When you have cut halfway through the tree, it will usually crack and fall, leaving the bottom half attached. You can sever the tree entirely, of course (watch out for the roll). Or you can let it be. The connected part will keep the leaves and twigs alive for a season or two, providing excellent wildlife browse at a level where deer and rabbits can benefit from it.

Lodged trees

Sometimes you cannot get the tree quite into the bed you have made for it, and the tree gets hung up in the branches of another tree. If this happens, you have troubles. There is only one safe way of dislodging it: wrap a cable around the butt end and use a winch, a "come-along," or a truck to pull it free. Sometimes you can "walk" it away, using another pole as a lever. If none of these tricks works, leave it in place. Call it a natural bridge, a deer tunnel, an *Arc de Triomphe,* a half-finished tepee—call it whatever you want, but if you can possibly avoid it, don't try to chop it down. It will only get you into more trouble.

Stumps

After you fell a tree, you are left with a waist-high stump. You might want to level the stump to the ground, for aesthetic reasons if for no other. (If you're using a chain saw, watch out for stones lodged in the base of the tree.)

Whether you level the stump or not, the main thing to beware of is the possibility of crown sprouting. Many trees will wait for a few months after you've chopped them down; then, after you've safely forgotten about them, they suddenly come out with a circle of little sprouts or suckers arranged in a ring around the old stump. Instead of one tree, you'll have a dozen. It's like Hydra.

Your wildlife, of course, will probably rejoice at all the tender young sprouts and buds so close to the ground. If, however, you are making a trail or creating a clearing, you may not be quite as happy. The officially recommended way of treating a stump is with any of several poisons on the market. Some of them don't seem to work very well, others seem to work too well, and all of them are dangerous and unpleasant to handle. If you don't want to use them, you'll have to resign yourself to maintenance. Return every four or five months for a few years to lop off the suckers; eventually the root system will get the message and will give up.

Safety

I was usually pretty cool and unconcerned about safety, even when I was dealing with kids. I could, I suppose, have given them a long, dull lecture about safety, nagged at them, and spied on them; and if I had kept a sharp lookout, I suspect that I would have had the experience of watching them get hurt. Nagged-at kids always seem to be the ones who get hurt. On the other hand, I like to feel that happy kids enjoying lots of freedom and responsibility are far less likely to have accidents.

But when it came to felling trees, my suave, cool attitude dissolved. Sometimes I'd go out on a clear morning with a group of kids, very much aware of being warm and alive, of our friendliness, our good spirit, our feelings of adventure— conscious of ourselves as a community of humans about to have fun and serve the needs of our wild land. Then I'd look at the saws and axes in the hands of a group of fourteen-year-olds, and I'd get scared out of my wits.

There were seven precautions that I always took and I suggest you do the same—whether for a group of kids, friends, or for yourself.

· Avoid windy days.
· Stay away from steep slopes.
· Take along a first-aid kit and make sure you have a vehicle nearby.
· Issue hard hats and insist that they be worn. I had expected some resistance about hard hats. I thought that adolescents would feel toward them the way they sometimes feel toward seat belts. But I was wrong. They love hard hats; it's a symbol that they are doing dangerous, adult work. They not only wore them faithfully in the woods, but they wore them during lunch, paraded around in them, modeled them happily, and more than once tried to take them home at the end of the day.
· Keep the groups small—under five kids. When you are dropping trees, you have to spread out to avoid dropping them on each other. More than five kids will be so spread out that you won't be able to keep track of them.
· Never fell trees alone.
· Learn to stop early. Felling trees is hard work. Whether you are using saws or axes, you soon develop sore muscles and blisters. After a while—sometimes after a very short while—you find yourself holding your body in strange ways to avoid straining already tired muscles. Soon you begin holding your ax or your saw gingerly to avoid breaking blisters. When you notice this, stop the logging right then.

These are my seven safety rules, and I followed them scrupulously. They worked for me, yet I was still never very easy about felling trees with kids. On one hand I wanted to give them maximum freedom—that's what wild lands mean to me. I wanted them to have fun, take chances, and attack problems with imagination, with spirit, and without any adult hovering over them anxiously. On the other hand I wanted them to be safe and do things "properly." This put me in a double bind. Usually, I sinned in the direction of freedom. The kids made out very well this way—no one ever got hurt and the kids were quite happy—but at the end of the day I was usually a total wreck.

Reading

The U.S. Forest Service has a variety of booklets about logging, many of them aimed at the farmer with a small wood lot and not too technical. There are a number of them, for the different areas around the country. The best of those I've seen are listed below.

Northeastern Loggers' Handbook, by Fred C. Simmons. Handbook No. 6. Washington, D.C.: U.S. Department of Agriculture, 1951.

This is a 160-page book, clearly illustrated and written for "the young or inexperienced woodman." Since it is aimed at the logging industry, you'll find sections about logging trucks, road construction, cable logging, etc., that are not very useful but are interesting nevertheless.

There are very good sections on the use and care of axes, saws, and other tools; on how to fell trees; on overcoming unfavorable leans; and (if you're interested) on limbing and bucking the tree into usable logs.

It's well illustrated and simply, plainly written.

Axe Manual of Peter McLaren, by Peter McLaren. Philadelphia: Fayette R. Plumb, 1929.

This is a real oldie, but if you happen to spot it in some fusty old bookstore, grab it. It dates back to the pre-chainsaw days when the ax was the woodsman's bread and butter. McLaren was "America's Champion Chopper," and the book gets right down to the nitty-gritty of how to hold the ax, how to make the chips fly easily, the different kinds of cuts you can make, wedges you can improvise out of log sections, and lots of other very useful information for people who still use an ax. There is also a good section on the care and sharpening of axes and on how to refit handles. It was published by the makers of Plumb axes.

CHAPTER THREE
THE MULCH MYSTIQUE

THE MULCH MYSTIQUE. Stripped of its mystery, mulching is a very simple act. You locate a bunch of organic matter, like straw, leaves, lawn clippings, or wood chips; you collect it from where it's not wanted; and you spread it out someplace else where it will do some good.

Mulching is a very simple project—dull and repetitive if you take it too seriously or keep at it too long, but lots of fun for yourself or for groups of younger children who can roll in the mulch, horseplay in it, and throw it at each other while (incidentally, it seems) doing a piece of important work. Not only can it be fun, but if you think deeply about mulch, it can be a perceptually liberating experience as well.

These may sound like exaggerated claims, but there is something about mulching that generates fanatic devotion. Enthusiastic mulchers—and there is no other kind—insist that with the magic of mulching, their vegetable gardens no longer need weeding, watering, or fertilizing as ordinary gardens do. Yet they grow king-sized cauliflowers, luxuriant lettuces, peas that ripen weeks before their neighbors', and squashes that stay firm long past the first frost. When I first heard about mulching, it sounded very interesting, very seductive, and very far-fetched. I didn't believe it!

In fact, for many years I had the vague idea that mulching was an exotic invention of organic gardeners. Or, to be more precise, the invention of a single organic gardener, an eccentric New York escapee named Ruth Stout who settled in Connecticut, wrote a book and several articles about mulching, and has become, so to speak, the *grande dame* of mulch.

But recently I have learned a lot more about mulching—especially about mulching on wild lands—and I've discovered that mulching was invented long before Ruth Stout. In fact, it was invented long before the human race. Mulching is a marvelous process invented by plants—a process by which wild plants have survived and prospered for eons. Without watering, without weeding, and without fertilizing.

The mulching process is actually very easy to understand. Every kid who has walked through the autumn woods, swishing and kicking the piles of dry leaves, knows something about mulch. Someday, attack one of those big piles of leaves, and as you scrape away at the various layers, your eyes, fingers, and nose will tell you everything you have to know about mulch.

The topmost layer consists of dry, fresh-fallen leaves—whether the broad leaves of deciduous trees that fall all at one time or thin pine needles that drop throughout the year. Brush these dry leaves aside and beneath them you will find the older leaves—matted, moist, and half decomposed.

Like an archeologist, keep digging down through time. The leaves will get more and more decayed until finally you reach the *leaf soil,* or *humus*—the thoroughly rotted leaves and twigs that earthworms and moles have already begun to mix with the mineral soil underneath.

There are more lessons to be learned from leafing through good soil than leafing through many a book. You can see how the area beneath a well-mulched tree lacks weeds and competing grasses, their seeds buried under tons of leaf litter. Dig your fingers under the humus and you can feel how the thick layer of leaves acts as a blanket, keeping the earth from freezing too deeply in the winter and from baking in the summer. Feel how squishy and sponge-like the leaf mold is—a perfect texture for absorbing and holding water while allowing air to circulate. And you can easily understand how the leaf fall is actually a recycling of nutrients: the natural nitrates and other more exotic minerals that the roots have mined from the lower parts of the soil go into the leaves, and at the end of the growing season, they are returned to the soil for use again in the following years.

These are very important concepts, and they help one to understand that mulching is a natural process rather than some magic, hocus-pocus piece of untidy mystification. But as you dig down into the leaf mold, I think you will discover something more amazing. This world of decaying leaves is, in itself, a marvelous thriving environment of incredible complexity and beauty. If you are lucky, you may stumble upon the giants of this environment: the salamanders, mice, and moles that tunnel through the humus. You are more likely to find the larger bugs, such as centipedes and pill bugs. But look closely, with a lens if possible, and you will *definitely* see a thriving, teeming world of creeping, crawling, humping, wiggling, thrashing, squirming beasties—thou-

sands of them to the square foot. Some are barely visible
motes gliding over a leaf edge; others are incredibly fierce
and dramatic, like miniature dragons in a Chinese parade.
This is a rich, full world—yet it is only a hint of the fantastic
microscopic universe hidden to our eyes.

I feel that there is as much wonder, beauty, and mystery in
this terribly alive environment as there is in the unexplored
jungles of the Amazon. When I am with kids, I try to
communicate this wonder to them, to make them realize
that when we mulch a tree, we are not merely doing some
mundane agricultural act that will benefit the tree and improve the soil. We are creating a natural environment that is
very wonderful, very complicated, and forever beyond our
understanding.

If you are dealing with youngsters, I urge you to get them
to help you dig around in the humus. Most kids love to dig in
dirt, and this is the most interesting dirt in the world—dirt
crawling with decay, earthworms, and bugs. But some kids
unfortunately are standoffish; they think that dirt and bugs
are bad. This is tragic. Do your best to help them overcome
it. If the kids are too fastidious to dig around with you, try
anyway. The knowledge that they have met some adult,
however crazy, who likes dirt may someday help them in
their quests to become healthy, accepting human animals.

To mulch or not to mulch?

Before you begin collecting spoiled hay, rotten manure,
and other such goodies, take a long, slow look at your forest
floor. You can learn more about the health of your forest
from the depth of the humus at your feet than from the
height of the trees above your head.

If the layer of leaf mold and humus is thick, rejoice! Your
forest is in natural, healthy condition and you do not need

mulch—in fact, if your forest is in such good condition, you do not need this book.

On the other hand, if you are restoring a piece of abused land, you are probably not so fortunate. Fire may have burned the leaf mold away; people, vehicles, or cattle may have pulverized or compacted it; or you may have just planted a new forest where the trees have not yet begun to build up their mulch beds.

Any bare—or balding—piece of land can benefit from mulching. Placing mulch around a tree is both helpful and natural. Other places that can use mulch, urgently at that, are bare slopes or disused road beds (see pages 90-91) and around trees suffering from compacted soil (see pages 69-70).

What kind of mulch?

The longer you mulch, the more prejudices and stubborn attitudes you will probably develop, until you eventually become so crotchety, opinionated, and impossible that everyone will consider you an expert.

My own preference was rotten horse manure. I adored The Stuff and attributed all sorts of magical properties to it. I knew of a stockpile behind a deserted stable, and I cherished this bit of knowledge the way a prospector might cherish the location of his gold mine.

Yet, to be honest about it, any vegetable matter will do as a mulch. Some, of course, are better than others. Some are more acid, others more base. Some have more nitrogen than others. Some rot faster and others more slowly. If you are raising vegetables, delicate flowers, or exotic shrubs, you might worry about these fine points. But for general wildland management, any organic matter is better than bare ground. What you use will probably depend on what you can get. One word of warning, though: do not use an inflammable mulch in a high-fire-hazard area. Dry sawdust in particular has been known to ignite by spontaneous combustion.

Here is a list of some of the more commonly available mulches, and a few comments:

Hay. Look for "spoiled hay," that is, hay that has been ruined by rain and is no longer good for animal feed. The farmer's woe can be your delight. You can often get spoiled hay free for the hauling. It makes a fast-rotting, excellent mulch. It is easy and pleasant to handle, and it is the best mulch you can get for erosion control (see pages 90–91).

Leaves. Obviously the most natural mulch for trees. Before collecting them from city streets or parks, think about how to compress them in the back of your truck. Some sheets of plywood and a few stones might help.

Oak leaves and pine needles have a reputation for making the soil acid. I generally wouldn't be too concerned about this, but if you mulch often with these leaves, an application of lime won't hurt any.

Lawn clippings. This is perfectly good stuff, and city parks departments will often give it to you free. Don't lay it on much thicker than six inches, because bigger piles of green lawn clippings sometimes heat up ferociously as they decay.

Sawdust. Personally, I hate sawdust. I find it hard to handle and boring to shovel, it looks dull and sodden when wet, it tends to blow away when dry, and it makes me sneeze. Other people use it regularly, and some people even prefer it. Different strokes for different folks, as they say. If you live near a sawmill, you may get it free and help reduce air pollution at the same time.

One occasional problem with sawdust is that sometimes

the first application creates a nitrogen deficiency in the soil. It seems that the organisms that digest cellulose use up lots of nitrogen, which they borrow from the soil. Once the sawdust starts to rot, however, the organisms die off and return the nitrogen to the soil, so the problem is short-term. If a recently mulched tree shows signs of nitrogen starvation (look for a yellowing of the leaves), add some sort of nitrogen-rich compost or fertilizer.

Wood chips. Wood chips are another of my favorites. They don't decay as fast as sawdust and have none of sawdust's drawbacks. They are often available from utility companies or anyone else with a chipper.

Old Christmas Trees. Why not? Returning a Christmas tree to the soil would be an excellent Christmas present for your land. And soliciting Christmas trees from the community is a fine way of getting people involved.

Dry weed stalks and hay. If you are planting trees in the middle of an old pasture, you might bring along a sickle or scythe and cut weeds and hay right fom the site. Don't worry about weed seeds. They won't stand a chance if you make the mulch deep enough.

Agricultural and food processing wastes. Depending upon your local agriculture and industries, you might get buckwheat hulls, ground corncobs, rice or wheat stalks, crushed sugar cane, peanut hulls, spent brewery hops, cocoa bean hulls, or well-rotted manure. Look around, become mulch conscious, and remember: *any* organic material (no matter how weird it smells) is better than bare soil.

Applying the mulch

There's really not much to it. If the soil is hard and compacted, you might rototill the area first. Otherwise, just dump the stuff around the tree. Don't even dig up the weeds and grasses; unless the sod is exceptionally thick, bury them! If the mulch is deep enough, the weeds and grasses below will rot and add to the mulch.

After you've dumped the mulch and spread it around a bit, you must rake it away from the tree trunk. If you leave it piled around the trunk, the millions of little beasties will soon arrive to nibble away at the bark. Spread the mulch so that most of it is under the *drip line*—the area underneath the outermost branches of the tree. If the material is light, you can throw some sticks, branches, or logs over it or wet it down so that it won't blow away. For erosion-control mulching on steep slopes, see pages 90-91.

Afterwards

After you've mulched, there is nothing else to do. Nothing. Please don't cultivate the ground with the idea of working some of the mulch into the soil. If the mulch has not yet decomposed, cultivating won't do any good and might even steal moisture and nutrients away from the roots. If the mulch has decomposed, then it is soil, organic soil, and the earthworms will have an absolutely ecstatic time mixing it with the mineral soil underneath. If you want your share of ecstasy, there is nothing better you can do than watch the earthworms.

Mulching with youngsters

As far as the land is concerned, mulching is always a very successful project. But I've found that many city kids who come to the park are severely puzzled by it all. Nature for them is often a still life. Their idea of a beautiful forest is some sort of Rousseau-ian painting of eternally perfect trees and clean green lawns upon which romp Bambi-like

animals who never defecate or die. Their idea of a worthwhile conservation project is to pick litter. But now, instead
of making the woods clean-clean-clean, pretty-pretty-
pretty, they find themselves following a madman through
the forest, spreading garbage under the trees, and making
homes for millions of yucky, ugly wiggling things. If this
wasn't shocking enough, the magic mulch they are being
asked to handle turns out to be old horse manure!

I always try to treat kids with respect. Their fears and
prejudices are very real to them and very important. I've
learned that no matter how clear my own vision may be, I
cannot force them to *see* when seeing is too threatening to
everything they have been taught.

If you find yourself with a group of kids who are too
fastidious to handle mulching, try to explain what it is all
about as clearly and gently as possible. Tell them what you
feel, let them absorb intellectually what they can, and then
go on to something else. No matter how sure you are of your
own sensibilities, you cannot force them on anyone else—
especially children.

As you have probably guessed, I've had some difficulties
with mulching projects. But I've also had a lot of fun. Many
youngsters have really gotten behind throwing the mulch
around. One common reaction has been to treat the whole
business of spreading manure and making earthworm houses
as something hilariously funny. I've seen kids giggle for
hours over it. In fact, they have occasionally made ruthless
fun of me for liking such things, but they were so obviously
happy and were so obviously thinking, feeling, and experiencing that being made fun of seemed more like a reward
than an insult.

Reading

I haven't found any books specifically devoted to mulching on wild lands. The following books deal with garden mulching, and they will certainly give you many good ideas.

How to Have a Green Thumb Without an Aching Back, by Ruth Stout. New York: Cornerstone Library, 1955.

This is a classic of a book, available in paperback and always in print. I expect it is one of the few modern books that will be in print 500 years from now. It's thoroughly wise, eccentric, individual, and very funny. It makes wonderful reading, even for nongardeners—just as Izaak Walton's *The Compleat Angler* is a delight even to those who never fish.

Handbook on Mulches. Handbook No. 23. Third printing. New York: Brooklyn Botanic Garden, 1970.

Like other handbooks in this series, this is a hodgepodge of articles by different authors. Some are very helpful, some really excellent, and some rather esoteric. There's a very good section on sawdust mulching. It can be ordered by sending $3.05 to Brooklyn Botanic Garden, 1000 Washington Avenue, Brooklyn, N.Y. 11225.

Soil Animals, by Friedrich Schaller. Ann Arbor: University of Michigan Press, Ann Arbor Science Library, 1968.

This readily available paperback was written for the layperson by a German zoologist. It deals mostly with microscopic animals and will turn you on to an utterly fascinating world. There's a good section on how soil animals turn leaves into humus, with lots of information about earthworms and all sorts of strange facts about the way the animals breathe, eat, feel, smell, and mate. It reads like a combination of a college biology text and *Ripley's Believe It or Not.*

CHAPTER FOUR
BE YOUR OWN
TREE DOCTOR

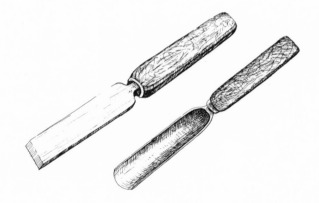

BE YOUR OWN TREE DOCTOR. This chapter describes several different things you can do to cure a sick tree or heal an injured one. But before you do anything, I hope you'll stop to consider that on wild land, diseases and wounds play valuable roles. There is nothing *bad* about a diseased tree. In fact, sick, dying, and dead trees are necessary to a balanced environment.

Let's say, for example, that you have an oak tree that's infested with oak moths. It is obviously a sick tree, and, according to professional foresters and landscapers, it must be sprayed at once. But if you look at it without prejudice, if you really make an effort to see the tree as it is, you will see much more than just a sick tree. You will see a healthy, thriving, vibrant colony of oak moths—wiggling, spinning, and fluttering, totally admirable and unspeakably, joyously alive.

Oak trees can generally withstand two or more years of severe moth attacks without being seriously affected. But let's imagine the very worst—namely, that the tree will die. If this is the only tree shading your back yard, you might very well be alarmed at the prospect. But in the wilds, is the death of a tree really so terrible? Dead trees house woodpeckers, small birds, owls, squirrels, raccoons, and possums. Tear away the loose bark from a dead tree, and out crawl termites, beetles, and flies from among colorful explosions of slime mold and other fungi. Once I found a sleepy, confused bat underneath a flap of bark. Indeed, sometimes it seems that a "dead" tree is more gloriously alive than a healthy tree. The death of a tree means that tree matter gets transformed into termite matter. In a balanced environment, death is not The End but an ongoing process—and a very lively process at that.

In working with youngsters, I found that they have very powerful feelings about disease, injuries, and death. They'll scarcely notice a forest full of twittering, fluttering birds; but they'll never fail to gather around the body of a dead finch or injured pigeon to stare, commiserate, and wonder. Whether it's a bird or a tree, kids seem to have an open and admirable curiosity about something dead or dying. They have a wonderment about death which I think is basically a wonderment about life. It was a pleasure not to fill their heads with sanctimonious, anxious thoughts, but instead to share in their wonder.

The death of trees in the wilds is to be expected, and it is not especially to be mourned. A dead tree is not a tragedy, and a sick tree is not an emergency that calls for sprays and poisons. If a tree is naturally troubled, it would be condescending to meddle in its fate. We should beware of foisting our own images of health and prosperity onto the environment.

Yet there are times when caring for trees is necessary—
especially when you are undoing the damage done by people. I was constantly treating injuries caused by jackknives,
automobile bumpers, bulldozer blades, snowplows, bad
pruning (especially by utility companies and road crews),
soil compaction, barbed wire, or cows with itchy heads. In
short, there is plenty of opportunity for tree doctoring
on wild lands—as long as it's in the spirit of *undoing* rather
than *doing*.

This section deals with how to treat wounds, gouges,
tears, and other physical injuries to a tree. Treating an
injured tree will help it considerably, but there is rarely
anything urgent about it. Most trees are remarkably hardy
and remarkably slow. They are slow to mature and slow to
die. We have all known trees that were rotten through and
through, riddled with holes and crawling with bugs. Every
fall the tree would be given up for dead, and every spring it
would delight us with a burst of brave new leaves. Most trees
are very persistent, so relax. Wait until you're in the mood
for a leisurely, intimate, craftsmanlike communion with a
tree. The tree will wait, and so can you.

*Treating an
Injured Tree*

Why treat a wound?

When you come across a freshly wounded tree, you may
find sap and resin oozing out and you will think, Good grief,
the poor tree is bleeding to death! Don't worry. Trees rarely
bleed to death—otherwise the maple sugar industry would
have dried up long ago.

The problem with wounds generally is that they are places
where moisture can gather. And rot sets in wherever there's
moisture. So the principle behind treating tree injuries is to
eliminate any place where water might collect.

First aid

If you catch the injury fairly soon, before rot sets in, you can simply give the tree a little first aid.

If the injury is in the form of a jagged stub, cut the stub off, following the instructions for pruning on pages 150-151.

If the injury is a wound directly on the trunk or against a major branch, use your jackknife to trace an elongated, pointed ellipse—like a football standing on end—around the whole wound. The knife should be cutting through firm bark all along its path.

Next clean the area within the ellipse. Remove all the bark, fibers, and shreds. You can use a broad stroke of the jackknife, a broad chisel, a paint scraper, or a file.

Whatever tool you use, get the area within the ellipse down to smooth bare wood. Don't leave islands of bark within the ellipse, no matter how sound the bark looks. Remember: smooth! Pretend you are a drop of water sliding down the trunk or splashing directly onto the wound. Gravity is pulling you down. Is there any place you can stop and rest? If so, that place must be removed.

Next use your knife to bevel the edges of the ellipse outward. Look at what you have done. Between the bark and the exposed wood you'll notice a thin, juicy layer. This is the cambium, the tree's point of greatest aliveness. This is the part of the tree that grows and will form the *callus* or scar tissue that, over the next several years, will creep over the wound, covering it and protecting the tree from rot.

You can then apply a dressing if you want to. (It's not essential.) Cover the edge of the ellipse with orange shellac to prevent the cambium from drying out. Shellac is a tree's very own dressing, made by pine trees specifically to seal their own wounds. Then swab on the tree paint—unpleasant, asphalty stuff that will help seal out moisture. It's available in most garden shops.

After you have applied the dressing, look over your work. You have turned an ugly wound into a neat scar. Congratulate yourself on a fine, craftsmanlike job. Over the years, if you watch for it, you will notice the callus forming over the scar, closing it off until the wound has completely disappeared.

Surgery

If the wound has been neglected for a long time and rot has set in, it's too late for first aid. You'll now have to perform a bit of tree surgery.

By tree surgery I do not mean that you should fill cavities with cement. This business of filling cavities is not tree surgery—it's more like tree dentistry. Frankly, I join with the wrens, the wood ducks, the squirrels, and the bees in rejoicing every time I see a hole in a tree. In fact, many tree surgeons have concluded that cement fillings are often harmful. Cement is rigid, while a tree is always bending and swaying. No matter how carefully the cement is put in, it will often crack, and cracks are ideal places for rot to get started.

To treat a rot-infested wound, you must first get rid of all the punky, rotten wood. But before doing anything, probe. With a brace and bit, drill a few test holes into the rotten wood and keep drilling until you hit solid wood. Be especially sure to probe downwards, which is how rot usually spreads. Does the rot extend deep into the tree? If so, wish the tree good luck, pack up your tools, and go on to something else. You can literally spend days cleaning out a large cavity and never get to the bottom of it.

If, however, you hit solid wood within six inches or a foot of the entrance, you can begin to clean out the rotten wood.

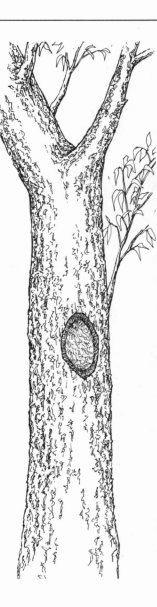

The best tool for the job is a woodpecker's bill—attached to the woodpecker, of course. Otherwise, use a wood-carving gouge. If the wood is really rotten, you can just shovel it out, using the gouge as a spoon. Don't feel you're hurting the tree: rotten wood is no more alive than are dried, fallen leaves. Dig in as far as you can, using the palm of your hand as a hammer against the gouge. Work the hole down to solid wood. Then smooth the inside as best you can, again eliminating shreds and pockets where water can collect. Without the special equipment that a tree surgeon has, you'll never get the inside of the cavity perfectly smooth. So leave perfection to the gods and the masochists, and do the best you can.

After you have gotten rid of the rot, you are left with a cavity. Now you *must* provide drainage. Otherwise, the hole will collect water and become a small pond—picturesque, but "rot city" nevertheless. If the hole is a small one, you can simply slope it outwards so that the water drains through the mouth of the hole. If the cavity is deep, however, you will have to drill a hole from the outside of the tree, angling it up toward the bottom of the cavity. Make sure the drainage hole hits the cavity at its lowest point. It is considered good practice to knock a length of pipe or copper tubing into the hole to prevent the tree from sealing it up within a few years.

Finally, you can apply the dressing. Professionals disinfect the cavity with bichloride of mercury, but I find it much too dangerous for my own comfort. Instead, I use denatured alcohol, which seems to do a fairly good job. (Also, at the end of the day I clean my tools with the alcohol so that I will not carry an infection to the next tree I work on.) If the tree is particularly valuable to you, you might then smear a layer of tree paint throughout the cavity, being careful not to plug up the drainage hole. But as long as the sides of the cavity are smooth and the hole is well-drained, I don't think that tree paint is necessary.

Cleaning out a rot-infested wound has a double benefit. It stops the spread of rot, thus helping to keep the tree sound. It also creates an airy, well-drained cavity—a Waldorf-Astoria of a cavity—for which some lucky animal will be profoundly grateful.

When I was working with youngsters, we tore down a lot of unnecessary barbed-wire fences. This was an especially good project for groups of older, tougher kids. They felt they were doing something useful, something easy to understand, and (best of all) something destructive. In case you've forgotten, kids just love to destroy. And what better thing is there to destroy than a barbed-wire fence? We all hate fences, all fences, but especially barbed-wire fences. Among us we have all ripped thousands of pairs of pants and gotten millions of nasty scratches from sneaking under or over barbed wire. I think of this project as The Ripped Shirt's Revenge.

That we hate barbed wire and that it looks so ugly are reasons enough to remove it. But there's more. By tearing it down, you will be saving the lives of hawks and owls, who often get tangled up and maimed while hot after a rabbit or a mouse. Finally, all along the fence line you will most probably find (and save) trees suffering from barbed-wire strangulation because they were used as fence posts.

There is, however, one circumstance in which I temper my hatred of barbed-wire fences. Sometimes, by protecting the ground beneath it from grazing animals and by providing a perch for many birds who drop seeds, a barbed-wire fence transforms itself into a hedgerow of interesting vege-

Barbed-Wire Wounds

tation. This creates a valuable wildlife habitat, especially in otherwise open meadows. In such a case, I would leave the fence in place, although I'd still walk its length to check for injured trees.

Removing the fence

There is only one way to handle barbed wire—carefully and with gloves. And make sure you have thick gloves. The scratches you get from rusty barbed wire have a way of staying around for a long time, itching, threatening to get infected, and sometimes carrying out their threat.

First, detach the wire from the posts—usually with a pair of pliers. As you detach the wire, begin rolling it around something, a stick or a piece of the fence post, perhaps. If, instead of rolling it, you just bunch it, the consequences will be dire. After a few hundred feet, you will find yourself with a tangled heap of barbed wire that will dwarf you, your truck, and your powers of invention. You can't leave it behind because it's too ugly; you can't drag it over the ground because it keeps getting caught up in everything; you can't load it into the truck because it's too springy; and you certainly cannot untangle it in anything less than a month. Hassling with balls of snarled barbed wire is a most discouraging (and painful) way to spend an afternoon. So keep rolling it. When the spool gets too big, cut the wire and begin another spool.

After taking care of the wire, you can remove the fence posts. Dig them out using bars, sledgehammers, and shovels. Used fence posts are salable or tradable if they're made of metal or some weathered, durable wood.

Finally, after you have done battle with the wires and the posts, you can return like a medic to treat the wounded trees.

Unstrangling your trees

Barbed wire wrapped around a tree is something like a hanging, except that the noose does not tighten. Instead, the noose stays fixed, while over the years the tree expands until circulation gets cut off. The tree almost invariably dies. This is a sad and gruesome death—all because someone was too lazy to knock in an extra fence post.

If the wire is recent, you can probably pull it off easily with pliers. If the wire is embedded in the bark, however, stuck in by resins and sap, you will have to be more careful. Grab one end firmly with the pliers and pull steadily away. Don't wiggle or make a sharp bend in the wire; otherwise the wire may break off. Just pull steadily and hard at a shallow angle until something happens. If you're having a good day, that something will be the release of the wire.

Let's say, however, that you're not having such a good day and the wire breaks off so that you no longer have a place to grab it. If the wire was merely stapled to one side of the tree (rather than wrapped completely around it), I would leave it in place. The tree will suffer from this piece of wire, but it will suffer even more from your gouging to get the wire out.

But if the wire was wrapped entirely around the tree, you will have to remove it, or at least sections of it, to save the tree's life. Dig in at several places with a chisel to expose parts of the wire. Break the wire with a sharp blow of the chisel, grab one strand at a time with the pliers, and yank out what you can from each side of the gouge. It is not necessary to get all the wire out. Just get out enough to prevent complete girdling of the tree and to keep some circulation going. After you're through, treat your gouges as wounds, apply a coat of tree paint (not essential but helpful), and hope for the best.

Afterwards

There is a joyful surge of energy that comes after a day of ripping down barbed-wire fences. You have taken a major step in uncivilizing a piece of land. You have liberated it, removed the signs of its bondage, and begun to heal its scars. You will soon begin to see your land in a brand new way, without its fragmentation into pastures and old property lines.

At the beginning of the day you were fresh and clean, while the land was crisscrossed with barbed wire. By afternoon the land will look almost reborn—but you may very well be crisscrossed by nicks and scratches. Barbed wire dies, but it dies fighting. Please treat yourself (and whoever happens to be helping you) at least as well as you have treated your trees: use soap, hot water, and proper first aid for everyone's cuts.

Bulldozer Dirt Piles

Here is a project where you tag along after a bulldozer, trying to undo some of its damage.

In the tree-planting chapter that comes later, I emphasize how necessary it is to transplant a tree with its crown (or root collar) at ground level. If the tree is planted too deep in the ground, its roots suffocate and its trunk rots.

Bulldozer operators on the whole don't seem to understand this. Wherever they have been doing road work, trail work, or grading, you can be sure to find dirt piled around the bases of trees—just as if this were the very best possible place for it.

When you come upon trees drowning in dirt, pull out your shovel and start digging. Keep at it until the area around the tree is back to ground level. You should do this for any tree, but it is especially important for conifers and for white oaks, tulip trees, lindens, and beeches, all of which suffer easily from trunk rot.

Soil compaction around trees is a very serious and persistent problem. It happens when the soil is compressed by bulldozer treads, vehicles, foot traffic, cattle hoofs, or careless agricultural practices.

Whatever the reason, trees suffer because air cannot penetrate through the compressed soil and water cannot seep through. Or if water does seep through, it doesn't drain properly.

There's no easy cure for compacted soil, but there is a lot you can do to help get the healing process started.

Compacted Soil

How to recognize compacted soil

If you're not sure whether or not your soil is compacted, try this test. Dig a hole two or three feet deep. Then fill it with water. How long does it take the water to drain? If it takes a long time—say, twelve or more hours—your soil is either compacted or fantastically clayey. In either case, the treatment is the same.

Treatment

First break up the upper parts of the soil. Cultivate it as deeply as you can. Hoes, picks, mattocks, and muscle power will do the job, but a rototiller or tractor (if you have one) will do it with less complaining.

Then lay a thick bed of mulch over the soil. Lay it on like a blanket. Don't work it into the soil. Just let it sit and rot. (See pages 53-54).

The best long-range cures for compaction are earthworms, gophers, moles, ground squirrels—and time. Time will pass at its own rate, without any help from you. You can plant earthworms under the mulch, but if you don't, they'll probably arrive anyway. I don't know how or from where, but they'll arrive. Moles, gophers, and ground squirrels are marvelously independent. People who hate them can't seem to get rid of them, and people who want them can't seem to attract them. But maybe you'll be lucky.

In any case, all you can really do is keep mulching and wait. The mulch will rot from above, the tree's roots will break up the earth below, and the earthworms will happily mix it all together. It will be geological ages before the soil gets back to "virgin condition" of good tilth and high organic content—but once you break up the compaction, cover it with mulch, and keep away whatever caused the compaction in the first place, you have begun a soil-building process that will continue by itself until the next ice age.

Feeding a Tree

If the soil is compacted, if the tree has been surrounded with asphalt, or if the leaves have been raked away every year, the tree may be a victim of starvation.

The only permanent cure for starvation is mulch (see pages 47-56). But mulch (like other natural processes) is often slow. If you are restoring a piece of land that has been badly abused and the trees are in trouble, you might want to give them an emergency shot of fertilizer to keep them going until the mulch begins to act.

How to identify a starving tree

If the tree is in obvious difficulty, riddled with disease, crawling with insects, sporting dead branches and "stag horns," suffering from *tip dieback*, and looking generally beaten, forget it. It has already dug too deeply into its reserve strength. Try to think of it as picturesque, if you can, and let it die in peace. Plant some other trees around it to take its place.

If the tree is merely nonvigorous—listless, sort of droopy, and depressed looking—it can benefit from a dose of fertilizer. The signs of a sick tree are subtle. If you're in doubt, compare it with a tree that you think is healthy. Look especially for a slight yellowing of the leaves, smaller annual growth, and a very slow rate of callusing over wounds.

What kind of fertilizer

Chemical fertilizers are fast-acting and are probably the best thing for a starving tree. If you are an organic gardener, please don't sulk. I use chemical fertilizers as medication, not food. I would not give a tree a steady diet of chemical fertilizer any more than I'd give a person a steady diet of penicillin. Mulch takes a long time to add its nutrients to the soil, however, and until it does I think a starving tree will appreciate a shot of fertilizer to keep it going.

Any general-purpose garden fertilizer will do the job. But if the leaves are yellowed, you might want to use a high-nitrogen fertilizer—say, 10-8-8 or 10-6-4 or something along those lines.

For a slower-acting but safer fertilizer, you can use more or less equal parts of phosphate rock, granite dust, and cottonseed meal. Mix these together with a large amount of compost (necessary to help break down the rock powders) and dig the mixture into the ground, approximating as best you can the following instructions.

How to apply the fertilizer

Don't just broadcast the fertilizer over the ground. If you do, you'll encourage a thick, lush growth of weeds and grasses under the tree—a marvelous green carpet for those who like to lie under a tree watching the clouds, but not much use to the tree.

There is a special technique for fertilizing trees. Use bars, crowbars, or especially long bolts sharpened at one end to punch holes underneath the outermost branches of the tree (the drip line), which is where most of the feeding roots are. The holes should be about two feet deep and about two feet apart.

Weigh out the proper amount of fertilizer and pile it onto a newspaper. Use three pounds of chemical fertilizer for every inch of trunk diameter on trees six inches or wider. If the tree is between three inches and five inches, use only two pounds per inch. If in doubt, use too little. After you've weighed out the fertilizer, distribute it evenly among the holes you've made. Do not fill the holes much more than halfway. If you have too much fertilizer, dig more holes. The more holes you dig, the better off you'll be, as long as they're deep enough and within a couple of feet of the drip line.

Finally, fill the holes with dirt, stomp the dirt down hard, and water the ground thoroughly. If you cannot get water to where you're working, save the fertilizer for just before a good, soaking rain.

Many people consider early spring to be the best time to apply fertilizer. And while I personally remain skeptical, many nursery experts I know refuse to fertilize in the summer because they do not want to force new growth just before the autumn frosts.

Afterwards

After you have treated a sick tree, do not expect the tree to thank you with any dramatic gestures of gratitude. It won't turn dark green overnight, grow ten feet in a single year, or do anything else exhibitionistic. Don't take it personally. Trees are very slow. They get sick so slowly that you scarcely notice it. A sick tree can live on stored nourishment for years before visibly suffering. When a tree starts to get better, the process is equally slow. A tree does not put all its energy into new growth; it leaves such spendthrift behavior to the weeds. Instead, trees store nutrients, create a reserve, and gradually build themselves up again.

No wonder they live so long.

Reading

Here are some helpful books about tree care.

The Care and Feeding of Trees, by Richard C. Murphy and William E. Meyer. New York: Crown Publishers, 1969.

A very useful book, but it is definitely oriented toward ornamental trees rather than forest trees. Nevertheless, it does give lots of information, especially on fertilizing, pruning, and treating injuries. It also has good drawings.

Tree Maintenance, by P. P. Pirone. New York: Oxford University Press, 1959. Fifth edition, 1978.

This book has gone through a number of printings and editions, and is *the* textbook and reference work on tree care. It is dull but ever-so-thorough. It gives descriptions of many individual trees, covering their preferences and idiosyncracies. There are very good sections on planting, fertilizing, and treating wounds. The book describes mostly "street trees," but it is still valuable for forest use. It's available in most larger libraries.

The Care and Repair of Ornamental Trees, by A. D. Le Sueur. Revised edition. London: Country Life, 1949.

This book is very British, very "ornamental," and very unavailable. It's also outdated, with a section, for example, on how to treat tree injuries caused by the German bombings. Yet it is a thoroughly knowledgeable and intelligent book—written with great care—and one of the few tree books that I find myself browsing through just for the fun of it. I don't suggest you make a special search for it, but if you happen to stumble across a copy somewhere, grab it!

Tree Disease Concepts, by Paul D. Manion. Englewood, New Jersey: Prentice-Hall, 1981.

This is a college text in forest pathology, written to provide students with an "introductory treatment of concepts of tree diseases." Not so much a field guide to identifying specific diseases, nor a list of "cures," this is a book that discusses soil conditions, weather damage, air pollution, fungi, nematodes, and other agents of harm to trees. A comprehensive, as well as readily comprehensible, book.

CHAPTER FIVE
EROSION CONTROL

EROSION CONTROL. A visitor from outer space might have a good laugh at how we handle—or don't handle —erosion. Our homes have locks on the door, latches on the window, insurance policies in the dresser drawer, and we support a huge police and prison system—largely to protect a few cameras, watches, and other gewgaws. Meanwhile, outside our windows, every rainstorm carries away thousands of tons of valuable topsoil upon which we depend for our very survival. Our scale of values is pathetically confused, when you stop to think about it. With modern assembly-line methods, we could replace a stolen tape deck in minutes. Yet it takes nature almost a thousand years to rebuild one inch of topsoil.

Some people, especially farmers, have a fatalistic attitude toward erosion. Land erodes, they feel, just as people grow old, automobiles sputter and stall, and apple trees eventually give out. But land is not like that. It does not have to erode. In fact, a healthy land adds humus and builds up its fertility every year. Individual plants and animals die, giving up their lives to help build a healthy, vital, growing soil for future generations of plants and animals. This nourishing of the soil is what makes death meaningful and even beautiful. Think about that for a moment, and don't accept erosion as a "fact of life."

Another conceptual trap you can fall into is the "Grand Canyon argument." Erosion built the Grand Canyon, so the argument goes, implying that erosion is a natural process that should not be interfered with. But erosion is "natural" only in desertlike areas where there is too little rainfall to maintain a thick growth of vegetation. When the rain does come, it is often in raging torrents that wash away the sparsely vegetated soil and create the dramatic canyons and badlands of the American West. Elsewhere, however, erosion is usually unnatural, the result of human misuse of the land.

On the whole, I feel that erosion control was the most important work I did at Redwood Park. In fact, I have an almost missionary zeal whenever I think of erosion control. But there is one thing I should not gloss over. Fighting erosion is a hard, heavy battle; and, as with any other worthwhile battle, there's a good chance that *you* will lose. Water erosion is a strong, persistent enemy. It's a fascinating enemy too: crafty, treacherous, sneaky, unforgiving, unforgetting, mindless, and merciless. Supposedly you can make a pact with the devil, but not with erosion.

In this chapter there are instructions for building check dams, contour trenches, and wattles. Follow these instructions and you'll have good reason to expect success. Most of the time. But there is also a good chance that an exceptionally heavy rain, exceptionally unstable soil, or a minor fault in construction will allow the water to wash your structure right away. When that happens, what are you left with? If you and whoever works with you did not enjoy the experience of working together, you are left with nothing. Less than nothing! But if the experience of building and planting was warm, cooperative, compassionate, and friendly, the project was a success whether the check dams hold or not.

As an engineering venture, you should build your structures as if they were going to last forever. Perhaps they will. But as a spiritual venture you should treat the whole thing as if success or failure of the structures is totally irrelevant. Make sure the process is human and loving, have fun, and open your eyes to the here and now. Saving soil is important, but not at the expense of losing a group of kids or a group of friends.

In the following sections I tell you what deeds you must do to fight erosion. But before you put on your coat of armor and rush out of the house, let's stop for a minute to examine the nature of the beast. Here is a model of a typically eroding watershed.

How Erosion Happens

To begin at the beginning, drops of rain fall down. Plip, plip, plip. They hit the ground at a speed of about thirty feet a second. If your land is healthy and the raindrops fall onto a thickly carpeted meadow, a wonderful thing happens. It is something you have to see to appreciate fully. The next time it begins to rain, try to forget everything your mother taught you about "catching your death of cold," lie down on your belly, nestle your chin into the grass, and get a frog's-eye view of how raindrops fall. You'll see how the raindrops

hit the individual blades of grass, causing them to bend
down. This bending absorbs the energy of the raindrop,
and the raindrop slides gently off the blade of grass, which
immediately springs up again, waiting to catch another raindrop. Perhaps it's just my own sense of humor, but the sight
of hundreds of blades of grass bowing down and popping
back up like piano keys strikes me as one of the merriest
sights in the world, and I've spent embarrassing amounts of
time crawling through wet meadows in the rain, witnessing
the wonderful antics of the blades of grass.

After the energy of the raindrop is taken up by the grass,
the raindrop slides gently to the ground. On a healthy
meadow with lots of humus, the ground is spongy and
absorbent and the raindrop quickly sinks out of sight.

A similar thing happens in a forest. As every kid knows,
the best place to run when a sudden rain comes is under a
tree—unless, of course, there is thunder and lightning. The
leaves of the tree break the raindrops into a fine mist. What
moisture does fall through the canopy is easily absorbed by
the understory, the leaf litter, and the humus, and it too
sinks gently into the ground.

But let's say that the ground has been logged, grazed,
burned, cultivated, or otherwise disturbed. There are now
bare patches of earth. When the raindrops hit a bare spot,
they strike full force, like tiny hammers, and splatter the
soil. This splattering breaks up clods of earth into fine
particles. The raindrops hold the fine particles in suspen-
sion. As the water sinks into the soil, these fine particles get
filtered out and soon clog up and seal the passageways
through which the water would ordinarily flow. The clogging and sealing effect is very important: clear water perco-
lates through the soil ten times faster than muddy water.
After a brief time the soil becomes crusty and impenetrable,

and the water can no longer sink in. Instead it forms puddles on the surface.

On flat land, the puddles loiter around, grow bigger, and form temporary ponds. The soil structure is damaged somewhat, but there is no real erosion.

On slopes, however, the water flows downhill over the surface of the ground, evenly, like a sheet. It carries dirt particles dislodged from the tops of hills and deposits them below, creating what is known as *sheet erosion*.

Probably the worst thing that can happen at this point is that the flow of water becomes channelized, either because of the topography of the land or because of an accidental occurrence like a furrow, a tire rut, or a cow path running downhill. The water gathers speed and the particles of dirt act like sandpaper. The water soon cuts a small trench or rill, which it may eventually widen and deepen into a gully.

As you can see, a gully is really the result of erosion—not the cause. Yet once the gully gets established, it brings about many severe problems. With each rainstorm, it gets deeper and deeper until it may even cut below the level of the ground water, draining it and lowering the water table.

We now have the beginning of a vicious cycle. As you probably know, much deep-rooted vegetation depends more on ground water than on surface water from the rain. As the water table is lowered—both from lack of rainwater penetration and from the draining action of gullies—vegetation over the watershed becomes more meager and scruffier. In some places fields of thick grasses are replaced entirely by sagebrush and chaparral, with scraggly growth and much exposed soil. Less ground water leads to scruffy vegetation, which leads to more bare soil, which leads to more splatter, more soil clogging, less water penetration, more runoff, and a further deepening of the gully. As the

water table

① ② gully ↓ ③ ④ ⑤ ⑥

a gully can eventually lower the watertable

gully deepens, it drains the water table still more, producing a further loss of vegetation, more exposed soil, more splatter, and so on for another downward cycle.

Meanwhile, as the gully gets deeper, the earth along its banks begins to cave in. Soon the gully sends out fingers that spread over the meadow, eating steadily away at the soil.

Within a few years, thousands of tons of topsoil are washed away, along with thousands of tons of subsoil. Where does it all go? Eventually, the gully probably drains into a stream. On a healthy watershed, a good cover of vegetation absorbs water, holds it like a sponge, and releases it gradually into the stream. The stream runs steadily and cleanly. But on an eroding watershed, the water runs off the surface with a heavy load of suspended silt, swoops through the gullies, and flushes out into the stream after every rainstorm. Instead of a clear, even-flowing stream, there is now an intermittent dry creek given over to flash floods. The silt kills whatever life there is in the stream and acts like sandpaper to cut into the stream bed and banks, causing further damage.

Sound dismal? It is! Yet this is exactly what is happening to thousands of small watersheds around the country. You should be aware of this process, but if your land has a few gullies, please don't get depressed. Fight back! Gullies can be stopped, and even if the "vicious cycle" has begun, there is a lot you can do to reverse it. That's what this chapter is about: how you can stop erosion without a lot of money, bulldozers, or a detachment from the Corps of Engineers.

So far I've given you a model of a typically eroding watershed, a model which should help you to conceptualize what is happening on your own land. If all you are going to do is think about erosion, you can stop here. But if you are going to *do* something about it, you will need a gut-level feeling for how erosion is happening on your land. This feeling, more than anything you read, will tell you where to plant, where to mulch, where to build check dams, and where to stay out of the way. It will prevent you from building a matchstick structure to stop a raging torrent, and it will save you the trouble of building a Hoover Dam to control a trickle.

In short, you've got to get wet! You've got to go out in the rain, lie belly down on your meadows, squish soil and mud through your fingers, look at the color of your water, and poke at the sides of your gullies to see how solid they are. Water is amazing stuff, and to see what it does, you've got to get intimately acquainted with it. Intimately! Right through to your socks.

A firsthand understanding of how your land is (or isn't) eroding will have its side benefits. It will get you out in the rain, which is sort of magical in its own right. It will also give you an appreciation for the strength, determination, and beauty of the erosion process. If you are going to fight erosion, it's much better to fight a beautiful enemy that you admire rather than an ugly enemy you hardly know.

One more thing. The Soil Conservation Service is an excellent ally in fighting erosion. You will find them by looking in the phone book under U.S. Government, Department of Agriculture. Personally, I think the Soil Conservation Service is one of the few good things the government is now doing. I've called upon them for various meadow, forest, stream, and gully problems. They have sent me (free!) grassland experts, stream experts, and soil engineers —persons who knew their subject well and who not only gave me advice but usable advice at that. My own good experiences with the Soil Conservation Service may have been accidental, but by all means give them a try.

Fighting Erosion with Plants

Later on in this chapter, I'll explain how to build structures that will stop erosion and hold your soil together. Building these structures can be fun and they can be effective, but please don't take them too seriously. The Army Corps of Engineers seems to view erosion-control structures as monuments, and in many places their cement bulwarks are even more prominent and obtrusive than the original erosion. Don't make that mistake. The structures I recommend are merely temporary, even rinky-dink, devices to hold the soil together until a permanent vegetative cover can get established.

The only successful and lasting way to fight erosion is with plants. One of the nicest things about using plants is that plants *want* to fight erosion. In fact, they want to fight erosion even more than you do, and what's more, they know how to do it. Take a blade of grass, for example. Grass depends upon topsoil for its survival, and over the last several million years it has developed ways of holding on to and increasing the earth's supply of topsoil. Grass intercepts raindrops; it forms a tough, tangled mat that prevents raindrops from flowing downhill; its fibrous roots embrace the soil and hold it together. Decaying roots create passageways through which water can penetrate, while transpiration allows the grass to pump water out of the soil before the soil gets waterlogged. At the end of its life, grass falls to the ground, decays, and becomes humus, which is the best of all possible elements in the topsoil. Plants depend upon a healthy soil and they have learned how to serve and preserve that soil. Every time you drop a seed into the ground, you are introducing an ally with millions of years of genetic experience in fighting erosion and tremendous willingness to put that experience to use.

Temporary cover

The first thing you should think about when you are faced with an erosion problem is a temporary (or emergency) cover. You will eventually want to plant a permanent cover of native plants that will perpetuate themselves and restore the soil. But if you have a lot of bare land and an immediate danger of erosion, you have to act fast. You need some sort of temporary vegetation just to hold things together until the permanent vegetation can get established.

There are certain plants that have a special capacity for stopping erosion. I wish I could tell you exactly what you should plant on your land—I know it would make your life easier—but I can't. There are too many variables. I know that in the hills above Oakland I can get good results with a mixture of rye, barley, trefoil, mustard, and a few other minor flowers. But I doubt if this information will help you if you are in Indiana, Georgia, Vermont, or Alaska.

All I can do is give you some general advice about what you should look for in an emergency cover plant. For the specifics you'll need local guidance from your Soil Conservation Service, county agricultural extension agent, your local hermit and organic gardener, or your local seed dealer (who often has a special "erosion control mix"). Or you can look into some of the books I recommend at the end of this chapter which give a species-by-species run-down of many valuable erosion-control plants and tell where they can be used.

The ideal erosion stopper is a plant that:

· Germinates quickly and easily;
· Grows fast *before* the first heavy rains;
· Has a dense, fibrous root system;

· Is frost resistant;

· Is temporary—make sure the recommended "wonder plant" isn't some horrendous weed that will take over everything in sight;

· Is a mixture. Don't depend on one plant, no matter how good its reputation. And make certain that at least one element of the mixture is a legume (member of the pea family). Legumes do for soil what yogurt does for the intestines—they foster lots of beneficial microorganisms that do much of the real heroics in creating healthy soil.

How to plant a temporary cover

The best way to establish a temporary cover is first to dress the ground with a light sprinkling of very well-rotted manure or compost. You might want to work it into the soil a little bit with a hoe and then rake it some—but not too deeply. If you have erosion, you want to disturb the soil as little as possible. Once you've prepared the soil, simply broadcast the seeds a day or two before you expect rain.

Fertilizers and exotics

What if you are dealing with a huge area, or if you don't have enough manure or compost for even a small area? Here's what you do. Scratch the surface of the ground slightly with a rake. Then spread the seed before you expect a rain. Wait until the seed has germinated and growth is under way, then carefully add an appropriate chemical fertilizer. (The Soil Conservation Service or a local seed dealer will tell you how much seed to scatter and what kind of fertilizer is "appropriate.")

Aside from chemical fertilizer, there is another bitter pill you may have to swallow. Some of the most effective plants for erosion control are exotic grasses and clovers. Call me a native-plant chauvinist, but I normally avoid foreign exotics. I have very high standards about not using them. For that matter, I have very high standards about not forcing growth with chemical fertilizers. Yet when the soil is bare and the rains are due, I am faced with a clear choice: I can either hang on to my standards, or I can hang on to my topsoil. Standards can be replaced, rationalized, or even forgotten within a week. Topsoil takes thousands of years to form. Whenever I've had to make a choice, I've opted in favor of topsoil.

If you do decide to use an exotic, there are special guidelines you should follow. Make sure the exotic has been around for a long time and is well tested in your area. Make especially certain that it won't escape and spread all over the place.

After seeding

If your land is relatively flat, you can seed and forget. But what if you're working on a steep slope where the soil is so unstable that you're afraid it will wash away, or where the land is so hard that you think the seeds might simply float down the hill? In such cases you'll have to devise some way of holding the seeds and earth in place—at least until the seeds germinate, roots work their way into the soil, and green stuff rises up like flags of victory to tell you everything is going well.

Willow stakes

In the following sections I describe several structures that will hold the soil together for a while. You can use any materials to build these structures, but if you use willow cuttings (see pages 134-139), you will reap an extraordinary advantage. Not only will they serve a mundane mechanical function as posts or stakes, but they will very likely sprout, send down roots, help bind the soil, and carry on an exuberant and useful existence of their own. Willows are especially valuable wherever you're dealing with moist land and bad drainage.

In addition to willows, there are other cuttings you can use for living stakes or posts. In our part of California, for example, elderberries and "mule fat" sprout easily from cuttings. Under hard conditions they may last for only one or two seasons—but while they last they'll do a lot of good.

Black locusts

The black locust is not an insect; it's a tree with a fine reputation for erosion control. It establishes itself on poor, dry sites, has a spectacular rate of growth and a good root structure, and adds a lot of nitrogen to depleted soil. It is not unusual for a three-year-old locust to be fifteen feet tall (thank goodness it's not an insect!) with a root system spreading twenty-five feet.

You can plant locusts as seedlings or from root cuttings (see pages 129-132). For erosion control, plant them close together—say, five feet by five feet, or even three feet by three feet in really bad places.

Permanent vegetation

Temporary vegetation is meant to give out, and even willows and locusts are not usually climax species. You should plan for what you hope the permanent vegetation will be. Find out what was there before the land was misused. Decide whether the land can support its climax vegetation, or whether you should begin further down the line of succession. I can't advise you what to plant—it varies from one area to another, and in fact sometimes from one acre to the next—but by studying uneroded, undisturbed land in your neighborhood, you should be able to figure it out.

The best time to plant permanent vegetation is just as soon as the temporary vegetation has stabilized things— usually toward the end of the first rainy season.

It may sound silly and quixotic to you, but if you are going to control erosion, you must begin by fighting raindrops. Raindrops hammer insistently at your land, and to prevent damage there are two things you must do. First, you've got to make sure there is something waiting to intercept the raindrops before they hit bare soil: vegetation, if possible, or some sort of mulch. Secondly, once the raindrops fall, you've got to stop them, corral them, and let them sink into the ground. If, perhaps with trenches, brush mats, or wattles, you can get the raindrops to sink into the ground wherever they fall, there will be no runoff, and thus no erosion.

Conquering the Splatter

How to recognize sheet erosion

Sheet erosion, according to the people who measure such things, causes 80 per cent of all topsoil losses. Gullies cause only about 20 per cent. Yet a gully stands out like a wound, screaming for attention, while sheet erosion happens so gradually, almost invisibly, that it's hard to detect. You think everything is all right until one day you wake up and realize that your topsoil is gone. Sheet erosion is very insidious.

Is your land suffering from sheet erosion? Looking for sheet erosion is a little bit like searching for a snake. If you merely walk around, sniffing flowers and lackadaisically enjoying whatever strikes your eye, you are unlikely to see a snake. But if you make a special effort to find one, turning over logs and stones, looking hard between the blades of grass and around bushes, you will probably find several snakes in a few hours.

The same is true of sheet erosion. You have to go out into your fields with nothing else on your mind except looking for sheet erosion. Don't get waylaid by flowers, butterflies, or ripe strawberries. Keep your mind on your task. Climb to the top of a hill, forget about the view, and look down at the soil. Here is what you should be looking for.

Bald spots. This is the most obvious sign to watch for on the hilltops and slopes, often with a build-up of fertile soil down below.

Exposed roots. Roots of trees, shrubs, and other plants do not *grow* out of the ground. If the roots are exposed, it is because the soil has been washed away.

Stains on old fence posts. These sometimes show that the soil was once deeper than it now is.

Exposed rock. If you feel that your meadows have been getting rockier and rockier each year, unless your land is a gathering spot for meteorites, this is a sign that the soil is being washed away.

Mulch

Once you discover sheet erosion, don't waste too much time either admiring it or bemoaning it. Get the right mixture of seeds, put them in a wide, shallow basket, and go skipping across your meadows like Ceres strewing the seed.

In most places you can seed and forget. But if the soil is loose and unstable or if it is so hard that you're afraid the seed will wash off, or if the slope is exceptionally steep, you should apply a mulch after you've seeded. A light covering of mulch does wonders. It cushions the impact of the raindrops, like those blades of grass, and allows the water to settle in gradually. It creates a network of little dams on the ground that impound the water and prevent it from getting a running start down the hill. It absorbs water. And as it decays, it adds organic matter that eroding land usually needs so desperately.

When you mulch, follow the suggestions on pages 50-54. But remember this important difference: underneath the mulch are seeds, and you want to encourage, not smother, their growth. So keep the mulch covering thin—no more than an inch or two—and avoid any mulch that tends to mat down.

Straw is far and away the best mulch you can get for erosion control, but other mulches also work very well.

Brush mats

Brush mats are for really nasty places—places where you want to use a mulch but where the slope is so steep that you're afraid a loose mulch will wash down the hill. Believe me, an eroding hillside with a huge pile of soggy mulch at its base is a nightmarish sight. The way to avoid it is to use brush as your mulch and tie the brush together into mats.

To make a brush mat, first lay two wires parallel to each other on the ground, about two feet apart. Lay the brush over the wire. If you use fir boughs or pine boughs, pile them very thin; otherwise, they'll smother the seed. If you use sparser chaparral brush, you can make the mats as much as six inches thick.

After you arrange the brush over the wires, bring the wires back over the top of the brush. Use baling wire to connect the upper and lower strands of wire. Pull them tightly together and tie them off, making a connection every six inches or so. The loose ends can be twisted tight with pliers.

You now have a brush mat that will hold together very

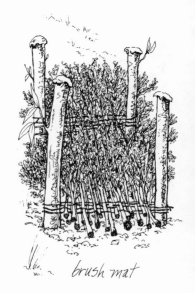

brush mat

effectively, even on quite steep slopes. If you want to be extra safe, you can stake your brush mats down to the ground—preferably with sproutable, rootable stakes.

Contour trenches

Here is still another technique you can use in addition to mulching. If by some chance you don't have any mulch, you can sometimes use this technique *instead* of mulching.

Contour trenches are simply ditches that you dig along a hillside, following a contour and running perpendicular to the flow of water. They catch water and allow it to sink into the ground before it can get a running start down the hill. Contour trenches are particularly valuable on hardened soil—like old logging roads—where water penetration is painfully slow.

To make contour trenches, first gather all your friends and issue them picks, mattocks, and shovels. When the moaning and groaning stop, begin digging several short trenches five or six inches deep and no more than about two or three feet apart. Keep this project short! Digging ditches on a hard-packed, heavily eroded slope is nobody's idea of great fun.

Brush wattles

Simple seeding, mulching, brush mats, and contour trenches will take care of 98 per cent of your sheet erosion problems. For those rare times when you have an exquisitely nasty and persistent problem with sheet erosion, you can resort to brush wattles.

Begin by making a series of contour trenches at least eight inches deep, preferably deeper. As you remove the dirt, somehow get it out of the area. Next, lay some brush in the trenches. Stagger the brush along the trench so that it all interlocks, like strands within a rope. As you build up the brush, stomp it hard so that it packs into the trenches. If it keeps springing up, you can try packing it down with some dirt. The last several pieces of brush that you lay in the trench should stick up above the level of the land. To help keep the brush in place, knock in stakes (preferably stakes capable of growing) just behind the trench on the downhill side. Space the stakes one foot, or at most two feet, apart. If you have lots of long, limber branches, you should weave them between the stakes to form a wattle fence.

What you're left with is admittedly a weird structure, and one that is hard to build—especially on a steep, unstable slope where you are most likely to need it. It has, in fact, only one redeeming feature: it works! The water running downhill sinks into the trenches. Silt suspended in the water also gets caught in the trenches and builds up within the protruding branches of the brush and behind the wattle fence. A wattled slope soon forms little terraces of relatively stable silty soil—excellent places for plants to get a start.

Gullies

Patrick Henry (of "liberty or death" fame) once said, "Since the achievement of our independence, he is the greatest patriot who stops the most gullies." I used to think this statement a bit outlandish, but the more I've gotten to know about land, gullies, and patriotism, the more I've come to agree.

Rills

The easiest way of stopping a gully is to catch it early. Whenever you see small rills (or channels), get right to work. Use a mattock or a hoe to break them up. Work in some compost or rotted manure, if you can, and rake the area smooth. Then treat the area as you would for sheet erosion

—seed it, mulch it, or possibly use brush mats or contour trenches.

Gully monsters

A neglected rill may grow up to be a monster gully. In the next several pages, I'll tell you how to go about fighting and conquering gullies. It's a long, complicated fight, but very much worth the trouble. We no longer have fire-eating dragons, but we do have land-eating gullies to fight. Just to make sure you can find your way through the following instructions, here is an outline of the battle plans:

· Stabilize the gully bottom. The bottom is more important than the sides. If the gully continues to dig deeper, no matter what else you do, the sides will cave and slump. You've got to prevent the gully from getting any deeper, and you should even attempt to build up the bottom.
· Grade the walls of the gully to their *angle of repose*—the angle at which they will no longer slump or slide.
· Stop or reduce the flow of water entering the gully.
· Plant an immediate cover of grasses and legumes that will hold everything together for a season or two.
· Plant a permanent cover of native shrubs, trees, vines, and grasses that will eventually stabilize the area, perpetuate themselves, build up soil fertility, encourage wildlife, and completely restore the land.

Check dams

The way to stabilize the gully bottom and build it up again is with check dams. Please don't be intimidated by the thought of building a dam. You're not going to be competing with Grand Coulee or Aswan. In fact, your check dams won't even hold any water. They are merely obstructions that will slow the water down. And the best of all possible obstruc-

wattle fence

tions (as we all know from our various misadventures in life) is a big mess. Basically that is what a check dam is: a big mess of brush or perhaps straw packed into the bottom of the gully, with a simple structure to hold it all in place.

Why a check dam works

I think we all have an intuitive sense of why a check dam works: a slow-moving stream carries far less silt and does far less damage than a raging torrent. But to understand how dramatically true this is, you might want to consider a few hard-core engineering facts. If you reduce the speed of the flow of water by one-half, here (according to certain laws of hydraulics) is what happens:

· The erosive or cutting capacity of the water is reduced about four times.
· The quantity of silt that can be carried is reduced about thirty-two times.
· The size of particle that can be transported by pushing or rolling is reduced about sixty-four times.

As you can see, by slowing down the flow of water, you reduce the amount of damage it can do, and you very spectacularly reduce the amount of silt it can carry. If there is lots of silt suspended in the water, once you slow the water down, most of the silt will be dropped—thus building up the bottom of the gully again.

One year later

The principles of check dam architecture

There are many possible designs and materials for building check dams, but whichever one you choose must adhere to certain architectural principles of check dam construction.

Head-to-toe alignment. The most effective way of building check dams is to build them in a series where the base of the upper dam is on a level with the top of the lower dam. This will eventually stabilize the whole gully bottom and will create a series of steps or terraces.

head-to-toe alignment

Smallness. "The bigger they are, the harder they fall" applies particularly to check dams. For most gullies, the check dams should be no more than about two feet high. Anything much higher than two feet will necessitate anchors, *deadmen,* and other retaining-wall features. Several small dams are far more effective and easier to build than a few big dams.

Digging it in. The dam must be dug into the walls of the gully, not just laid genteelly up against them. Unless the dams are dug far enough in, water will sweep around them.

Notching. A notch is a place where the water can flow over the dam. This is essential. Without one, the silt builds up behind the dam, the water flows on top of the silt, and instead of being led through the notch, it may start eating away at one of the slopes. Eventually, it may make a new channel around the dam. I've seen many erosion-control dams standing proudly and nobly on dry land while gullies flowed merrily around them.

Apron. Once the silt builds up behind the dam, the water flows through the notch like a waterfall. You'll need an apron to catch it before it digs out a pool and undermines the dam. The easiest apron is a bed of stones where the water can simply knock itself out and flow tamely to the next check dam.

Building a check dam

There are several possibilities for building very good check dams: a rock dam, a wire dam, a stake dam, a pole dam, and a plank or slab dam. Which one you choose to build will probably depend more upon the materials you can scrounge up than upon anything else. I built mostly pole check dams because we had plenty of poles. Whichever one you decide on, remember to follow the general principles already laid out.

Grading the slopes

After you build the check dams, your next step is to break down the steep gully walls to their *angle of repose*. To my ears, "angle of repose" is one of the most beautiful phrases in the language. Unfortunately, it's far easier to say it than to do it. I know of no easy way of breaking down steep, cliff-like slopes. Professionals sometimes use dynamite and bulldozers, so I've been told, but all the bulldozer operators I've ever met are scared to death of working along the rim of a sizable gully. When it comes to grading gully slopes, the machine age has deserted you, my friend, and what you are left with, wonder of wonders, is your hands! So get together a collection of picks, mattocks, shovels, and digging bars, round up everyone you know who owes you a favor, and get on with it. Knock off the sharp edges, and wherever you can, gentle out the steep slopes.

As you are working, you'll be knocking tons of earth down into the gully bottom. The first rains will dissolve this earth, spread it out, and deposit it behind the check dams to raise the bottom. You can help this process along, and also prepare the bottom for planting, by breaking up whatever heavy clods fall into the bottom. If you have any water, you might also wet the dirt down to compact it and further ready it for planting.

Once the slopes have been graded to their angle of repose, you should treat them for sheet erosion, with seed, mulch, or the other devices recommended in the previous section.

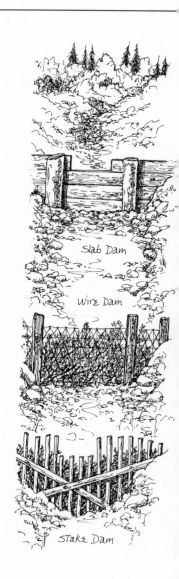

Slab Dam

Wire Dam

Stake Dam

Limiting the water flow

You now have to make certain that as little water as possible enters the gully. Where is the water coming from that originally carved it out? You must find that water, even if it means going out in the middle of a rainstorm.

You can usually restrict the flow by treating the area above the gully head for sheet erosion. Contour trenches generally work quite well, and as a last resort brush wattles are nearly infallible. Whatever treatment you use, make sure you extend it far up the slope.

Occasionally an expert will appear in your life and suggest that you divert the flow of water away from the gully. He will urge you to build a "diversion ditch," perhaps with an "entrapment compound." He will probably pull out a pencil and paper and make a few fancy diagrams. When you meet such an expert, the first thing you should do is grimace, pound your chest, jump up and down, and point excitedly to the sky. If this doesn't scare him off, grab your hat and run. As you can guess, my own experience with "diversion" has been disastrous. Diversion does not solve any problem; it just moves the problem somewhere else.

Planting

Once you've stabilized the bottom of the gully, graded the slopes, and reduced the flow of water, you have completed the mechanical aspects of controlling the gully.

Now you should plant. Use the previously mentioned routine of temporary planting followed by permanent planting. Don't plant anything in the bottom until the silt has collected into terraces. Then you can plant moisture-loving trees right in the silt, where they'll usually thrive.

Maintenance

Remember the little Dutch boy who put his finger in the dike, held back the ocean, and became a culture hero to all five-year-olds? I don't suggest you spend all next spring with your finger in a check dam, but the Dutch-Boy Principle still holds: small leaks can be easily plugged. Sometimes all that is necessary is for you to shove a few pine boughs in at the right place. If you do, silt will continue to collect. If you don't, the leak will often get bigger and bigger, bringing the whole dam down. You should also check to see that the mulch is still in place, the grass has germinated well, and no heavy flow of water is entering the gully. Visit your check dams as often as you can during the first one or two seasons to see how well they are holding up and to solve minor problems before they grow.

Culverts

Culverts are pipes that bring water under a road or trail. They are responsible for thousands of gullies in every state. Road engineers have a strange idea that if they install these culverts at a steep pitch, the water will flow through them very fast and keep the culverts clean of debris. Road engineers really love "self-cleaning" or "self-maintaining" culverts. But as I've already mentioned, the fast flow of water increases its erosive powers many times over. And often at the dump end of the culvert you will find a huge gully.

If there is already a gully, you have no choice but to try to repair it as outlined above. But if you can catch the problem early, the best thing you can do is dump a lot of rocks, broken asphalt, or cement rubble under where the culvert lets out. This will break the force of the water, acting much like an apron beneath a check dam. If you do this wherever you have a culvert, you will save a lot of aggravation and a lot of soil as well.

Afterwards

I don't want to minimize the fact that controlling a gully is hard work. But it is necessary work, and in the long run extremely satisfying.

Once you have brought a gully under control, watch it closely and uncritically. You may be in for a surprise. Some of the most beautiful places I know are old, stabilized gullies. When you are fighting a gully, you are primarily fighting erosion damage. But you are also creating a shady, potentially lovely, miniature canyon which will collect moisture, support many plants, and become a wonderful refuge for wildlife. Turning a barren gully into a lush pocket of life is the nearest a human being can come to an oyster, which turns its injuries into pearls.

Streams   If you have erosion problems along your stream, keep in mind that these problems are almost invariably the end result of sheet erosion, gullying, faulty road construction, overgrazing, and other abuses throughout the watershed. This section will tell you a few things that you can do to help alleviate the sufferings of an eroding stream or creek. Do what you can, but always remember that working directly on a stream is only a stopgap measure. The ultimate healing must take place throughout your whole watershed. If you ignore this advice and concentrate your efforts on the stream, your watershed will continue to go downhill— literally—and each year you will find yourself having to build bigger and uglier structures in your stream, stonewalling its banks, sandbagging, jettying, deflecting, and diverting, until eventually (with the best of intentions) you have converted a living stream into a grotesque plumbing problem. In the end you will hate your stream for being so ungrateful to you, and your stream will hate you for being such an oppressor. So avoid the Army Corps of Engineers nightmare. Remember that a living stream—like all living things—is bound to be rebellious. Respect its rebelliousness. Do a few light projects to help your stream along, but if the stream doesn't respond, don't force it. You are trying to assist your stream, not defeat it. Keep your stream projects modest, and by all means concentrate most of your erosion-control efforts on the watershed around the stream.

Bank erosion

Streams can erode in two directions: they can dig increasingly deeper channels for themselves (channel erosion), or they can eat away at the banks. If your problem is bank erosion, there are several steps you might take.

First of all, stop all physical injuries to the banks. In particular, stop grazing animals (cows, horses, and sheep) from breaking down the banks to get to the water. You may have to fence off parts of the stream and, if necessary, even build a watering trough away from the stream's edge.

Next, you can build deflectors. Deflectors are basically piles of stone placed upstream from an eroding bank to absorb the force of the water. But you can't just dump some stones into the stream and hope they'll do the job. You've got to build a deflector as carefully as you would any other structure. First, dig some of the stones into the bank; otherwise the water will nibble, nibble, nibble, all day and all night, never resting until it eats its way around the stones and eventually leaves them stranded midstream as an ineffectual island. Next, lay the other stones out from the bank a couple of feet into the channel. Mortar the stones

rock deflector

together if the stream is dry. Or if the stones are all sizable, you can move them around so that they are stable, using smaller stones to chink the cracks. Or, if all you have are smaller stones the size of footballs, you can try corralling them with logs dug into the bank.

Finally, you should plant the banks heavily. Willows, planted as stakes along the banks, are particularly good. (See pages 134-139).

Channel erosion

Another serious problem with an eroding stream, similar to that encountered in gullies, is that it often cuts deeper and deeper into its channel, causing the banks to slump and eventually draining and lowering the water table.

I once spent a lot of time building well-crafted pole check dams in the streams of Redwood Park. The idea was to slow down the water, get the silt to build up in the stream bed, and raise the water level of the creek. It sounded good to me and to the several erosion-control engineers I talked with. The stream, however, had different ideas. The first rainy winter it rose up, flexed its muscles, and knocked down every one of my well-crafted check dams.

In gullies, of course, pole check dams work quite well. In a stream they also work very well for a season or two, collecting big and impressive baskets of silt. But it doesn't do a bit of good. You can't get trees and grasses to grow in the middle of a stream as you can in a gully, and most assuredly in two, three, four, or five years, your dams will collapse and their fine collection of silt will be washed downstream.

While pole check dams do not hold up, the hydraulic principles are still valid; namely, as you slow down the flow of water, its erosive power is cut drastically. You can, if you want, construct permanent, well-made rock check dams.

But I have come to prefer a more casual approach. Every year before the first fall rains, I'd gather an ax, a shovel, a strong bar, and a couple of strong kids, and we'd set out for a walk along the stream. When we came to rocks or fallen logs lying along the bank, we'd pry them into the stream. Then we'd arrange them into small, *temporary* check dams. We'd key a few rocks well into the bank (otherwise the water would sweep around the rocks and eat away at the bank), we'd make the rough equivalent of a notch to handle the overflow, and we'd arrange some stones beneath the notch to act as an apron.

Check dams such as these are very makeshift, guaranteed to last no more than a season or two. But you are not worried about permanence. You do not want future generations to gaze in wonder at your check dams. Make them small, tight, and frequent. What you are trying to do is break up a swiftly flowing stream into several pools, slowing the water down so that it will do less damage to the stream bed. Every year you will have to rebuild your makeshift dams, but that's all right, since the permanent cure for your stream's problem lies elsewhere, throughout the watershed. Until then, like an earth doctor, I suggest you give your stream not only annual checkups but annual check dams— dozens of little stone check dams to help it along until the watershed regains its good health.

Reading

In other areas of conservation there is pitifully little information. Not so with erosion control. The 1930s were dust bowl years, gully years, and Civilian Conservation Corps years. The CCC, the Forest Service, and the Soil Conservation Service all published loads of erosion-control pamphlets and books. Every field worker who developed a new style of check dam—and there were hundreds—published a description of it. Sometimes the check dams collapsed within a few years, but the publications live on to clog our minds. The problem I've had with erosion-control literature is wading through it all for what seems sound, relevant, trustworthy, and useful. Here are some of the books I have found especially handy for small-scale erosion-control projects.

Handbook of Erosion Control in Mountain Meadows, by Charles J. Kraebel and Arthur F. Pillsbury. California Forest and Range Experimental Station: U.S. Forest Service, 1934.

For most people this is probably an impossible book to get hold of, but by all means try your best. It's the most thoroughly practical book I know, with lots of simple suggestions for controlling gullies. There are excellent diagrams and a strong emphasis on using native materials.

A Study of Early Gully-Control Structures in the Colorado Front Range, by Burchard H. Heede. Paper No. 55. Rocky Mountain Forest and Range Experiment Station: U.S. Forest Service, 1960.

This publication is a review of several Civilian Conservation Corps structures, examined twenty-five years after they were built. It shows which ones stood up, which ones failed, how they failed, and why they failed. It's very instructive. Here is your chance to learn from someone else's mistakes.

Grass in Soil Erosion Control, by Layman Carrier. SCS-TP-4. Washington, D.C.: Conservation Service, 1936.

This pamphlet gives a short list of various grasses and discusses their erosion-fighting values.

Results of and Recommendations for Seeding Grasses and Legumes on TVA-CCC Erosion Control Projects, by J. H. Nicholson and John E. Snyder. Norris, Tennessee: Tennessee Valley Authority, 1938.

This list of grasses and legumes rates them according to where they will grow, what their moisture and soil needs are, how well they bind the soil, and how well they build up soil fertility.

Trees and Shrubs for Erosion Control in Southern California Mountains, by Jerome S. Horton. California Forest and Range Experiment Station: U.S. Forest Service, 1949.

Giving a plant-by-plant list of several species of tree and bush, this book tells where to plant them, when to plant them, and even how to plant them. It also has detailed diagrams of various erosion-control structures. It's too bad this valuable book is so limited in geographical area. You might check to see if your own Forest and Range Experiment Station has a similar publication.

The Stream Conservation Handbook, edited by Nathanial P. Reed. New York: Crown Publishers, 1974.

This book claims that "the primary objective of stream improvement is the restoration and enhancement of trout habitat." It was written for fishermen, many of whom are beginning to band together into groups like Trout Unlimited to maintain their streams. The big-stream scale of this book will probably make it not very handy for small landholders. But if you do happen to have a fishing creek, it will tell you what you have to know to keep it fishable.

CHAPTER SIX
THE SEED BAG

Species: Layia Platyglossa
(Tidy tips)
Date Collected: 6|4|94
Place: West facing slopes
   ...of Pinehurst Knob
Environment: Dry,
Rocky, well-drained
soil, grassy, sparse
   vegetation

🌱THE SEED BAG. During the month or two when most California plants go to seed, I would wander over the meadows collecting bags and bags of seeds—wildflower seeds, tree seeds, grass seeds, shrub seeds, vine seeds, even thistle seeds. My seed collection was the envy of every squirrel and gopher in the state.

Not only did I collect seeds myself, but I also involved hundreds of youngsters in the activity. Sometimes the seeds we collected would get planted at once. Other times I'd extract them, dry them, store them, and treat them before giving them back to others to plant. It all sounds terribly complicated, but it isn't. I've been fairly successful without being a botanical genius. I think anyone else can be equally successful, even if he or she has never so much as put a radish seed in the ground. That's what this chapter is all

about: a step-by-step procedure that will enable anyone—
i.e., you—to begin collecting seeds and growing wild plants
from them.

"But why bother?" you may ask. Don't wild plants take
care of reproduction themselves—the less interference from
us the better?

There are many frivolous reasons for collecting wild
seeds. Who can resist trying to increase a stock of baby-blue-
eyes or trilliums simply for the joy of it? But there are
practical reasons too. In fact, the more seeds you have, the
more uses you find for them. Seeds have proved indispens-
able to me in erosion-control work for revegetating gullies,
washed-out roads, unstable slide areas, and on hillsides
where the soil was getting dangerously thin. After a fire it
was a pleasure to have several pounds of wildflower seeds to
give to the charred soil. I used seeds to help repair trail
damage, to increase wildlife forage, to replace edible plants
I'd been eating, and to landscape buildings with native
plants. I'd spread the seeds of certain lupines, clovers, and
vetches in places where I wanted to improve the soil's fertility; I'd carefully collect and treat the seeds of rare plants to
help ensure their survival; and I was always trading seeds
with other wild-seed buffs. Trading seeds turned out to be
unexpected fun. How much can *you* wheel and deal for a
half-pound sack of fawn lily seeds?

You can even earn money collecting seeds. You won't get
rich, not by any means, but wild plant seeds are definitely
salable. Try local garden clubs, native-plant societies, highway departments, or dealers. (For a partial list of wild-seed
dealers, write to the National Arboretum, Washington, D.C.)

But while there's a chance you might sell a few seeds, I
assume that you're far more likely to be collecting seeds for
your own use. Let me give you one piece of advice (which

you'll probably ignore): don't overcollect! Collecting seeds can be addicting: once you start, it's hard to stop. Collecting is fun, but planting seeds is hard work. You can't just scatter them lovingly over the earth. If that's all you're going to do, why not stay home and let nature do the job for you? If you really want to grow native plants, you may have to work the ground like a garden. You may even be wise to germinate the seeds in flats, transplant the young plants into pots or cans, and later (sometimes much later) plant them out in the field. Bear this in mind, and limit your collecting to what you can handle.

For me the whole seed experience has been more than just a practical pursuit; it has been an aesthetic and spiritual adventure as well. I used to think that the flower season was over once the soft, fragrant petals dropped. Now I keep my eyes open and watch the falling petals give way to another kind of beauty—the geometrical, architectural beauty of seed pods and seeds.

Throughout the hot, dry, withering California summer —when the flowers were gone and everything in nature seemed to have died—I'd go out with youth groups to collect these seeds, treat them, watch over them, and think about the life contained within them.

Seeds are very beautiful and very mysterious. In the following sections I describe the specific techniques for collecting, treating, and planting them. It's certainly important to understand these techniques, and by using them I expect you'll have great success in getting wild plants to grow. But there is something beyond success. The longer I have been dealing with seeds, the more I have gotten fleeting perceptions of their beauty, their power, and their mystery. Over the years, as my intimacy with seeds has increased, these fleeting, flickering perceptions have been growing stronger and steadier—until I have come to value these expanding perceptions almost as much as I value the thousands of wildflowers I have grown.

Collecting and Extracting Seeds

You may feel that you don't know very much about wild plants, you hardly know one wildflower from another, and you haven't the foggiest idea what their seeds look like. Join the crowd. There are 20,000 wild plants in the United States, and everybody—even the expert who drops Latin names—feels somewhat inadequate to the task.

Yet there are several dozen seeds that you do know, even now. You know acorns, chestnuts, maple wings, and pine cones. You probably know rose hips, several berries, May apples, sunflower seeds, milkweed seeds, and lots more. You undoubtedly know enough to get started right away.

As for learning more about seeds, there's only one way. You've got to go out and observe. It's easy and it's fun. Fix your attention on a flower (stake it out if necessary), return every few days, and you will see the seeds develop, ripen, and eventually scatter. Or when the plant is flowering, concentrate on its leaves, which will identify it after the flowers have fallen away. You'll be amazed to find how common flowers you've always vaguely known produce those barbed and corkscrewy seeds you've been pulling out of your socks since childhood. You'll also come to appreciate, I think, that in their own way seeds and seed pods are as beautiful as the flowers they come from.

When to collect seeds

The best time to collect seeds is when they're dry and ripe. A ripe seed no longer depends on the mother plant for nourishment, and it's ready to enter the world—"a little plant in a box with its lunch," as someone once described it.

To test for ripeness, crush a seed. If it gives off a milky or gelatinous substance, it's not yet ripe.

How to collect seeds

Big seeds (especially nuts) can often be collected directly off the ground as long as they're not wet, moldy, or wormy. But most seeds must be collected while the pod or capsule is still attached to the plant. The idea is to collect the seeds just as the capsules are beginning to open but before the wind steals the seed—a period often lasting several weeks. For most flower seeds, you simply run your hand up the stem, using your fingers as a comb, to collect both seeds and capsules. Be sloppy! Let lots of seeds get away. You don't want to strip an area completely.

For grass seed you might imitate the Indians, who grabbed a handful of stalks, bent them over a basket, and shook out the seeds.

Although it's best to collect ripe seeds, there are times when this is tedious. Some plants, like mustard, ripen in such a way that on any one stalk there are dozens of green pods to every ripe pod. In such cases you should wait until the pods or capsules are as nearly ripe as possible. Then pick the entire seed stalks, lay them out on newspapers in the sun, and wait. In a few days most of the pods will have opened, and you can shake the seeds out. Or, as an alternative, you can collect the whole stalks, put them upside down in paper bags, hang the bags in a dry, warm place, and the seeds will separate from the pods.

There are a few seeds that *must* be collected when the pods are green. Certain lupines and vetches, for example, do not have seed pods which open gradually. The pods explode— bang!—and shoot the seeds considerable distances.

For plants like these, collect the seed pods when they are still green, with a section of stem attached to each pod. (The unripened seeds must still draw nutrients from the stem.) Lay the seed pods out on newspapers in the sun and cover them with a layer of cheesecloth or screen. After several days the sounds of battle will fade, the cheesecloth will stop jumping, and the seed is ready to be collected.

Labeling

I generally collect seeds in paper bags, and as I collect I write relevant information right on the bag. Here's an example:

Species: Layia platyglossa (Tidytips)
Date Collected: 6/4/74
Place: West-facing slope of Pinehurst Knob
Environment: Dry, rocky, well-drained soil;
  open, grassy, sparse vegetation.

Proper labeling is *very* important. I know how corny and highschoolish that sounds, but it's true, nevertheless. Nothing is more frustrating and wasteful than to come upon a bag of fascinating seeds, bursting with vitality, and not to know what they are. You don't know where to plant them, when to plant them, or how to treat them. Avoid this tragedy: label your seeds carefully!

A side benefit of labeling, by the way, is that it trains your observation and increases your knowledge of the environment. Certain of our flowers grow only on rocky, serpentine soil. I never would have discovered this if I hadn't had a blank space on a label to fill in. Now, wherever I find patches of these flowers, I kick the ground and, sure enough, I find serpentine rocks. By observing the placement of such flowers throughout the park, I'm beginning to get a picture of the geology of the area—something I find delightful since I'm totally intimidated by geology.

Extracting

After you've collected the seeds, you'll have to extract them from their pods, capsules, fruits, cones, or whatever kind of container they come in. The purpose of extracting is to separate the seeds from other materials that might absorb moisture and cause rot. If you're at all compulsive or perfectionistic, this isn't the job for you. Without a ridiculous amount of effort or equipment, you'll *never* get the seeds perfectly clean. And when you throw away the chaff, pulp, or cones, you'll *always* be throwing away lots of perfectly good seeds. Reconcile yourself to waste, and look at it this way: nature often produces millions of seeds to get one plant that will survive. However wasteful you may be, you are many times more efficient than that.

For many seeds it's enough to crush the pods or capsules by hand, put everything in a bag, and shake the bag vigorously. The seeds fall to the bottom while the chaff remains on top.

If the bag-shaking procedure doesn't work out too well, you can play around with colanders, strainers, and screens of varying meshes. Or try tossing the seeds in the wind to see how well they'll winnow. (An electric fan is probably better than the wind for winnowing, but it's hardly as picturesque.)

Another trick for round or smooth seeds is to dump the mix onto a blanket and then tilt the blanket until the seeds roll or slide off, leaving behind the angular pieces of capsules.

For fleshy fruit like berries and rose hips, soak the fruit in warm (not hot!) water until you can crush the pulp. The seeds will sink to the bottom and the pulp will rise to the top.

Dry the seeds at once, unless you're going to plant them immediately.

Cones

Pine cones, fir cones, and other cones present special problems in both collecting and extracting. The cones you find on the ground are usually open and the seed has long since fallen away—or been eaten by birds and squirrels. The fat, closed cones that are full of seeds are usually swinging 50, 100, or even 200 feet above your head.

Professional seed collectors sometimes use rifles to shoot the cones down from especially desirable trees, but I assume you'll find this too impractical or too noisy, you don't have a rifle, you don't have a hard hat, or you're a lousy shot. There are ways of getting around this. First off, keep your eyes out for squirrel caches in the corners of old buildings and elsewhere. (If you feel guilty about stealing from the squirrels—and you should!—leave them some store-bought nuts.) Also watch for logging operations nearby, or do your own thinning at a time when the cones are ready to be collected. Or keep an eye out for trees that grow on the edge of clearings. These trees often have low branches that may bear cones within reach. A final trick is to check paved roads. At certain times you can sweep the seeds off the road as they fall from the trees. Or you can sometimes collect the cones by standing on the roof of your car or truck, or by setting up a ladder from a truck bed. You should collect cones when the bracts are just opening or loosening their hold on the seed.

The next problem is to extract the seeds from the cones. Put the cones in a warm room, or in the sun, for several days or even a couple of weeks. The scales will often open and you can shake the seeds out.

Sequoia Cone and seed

If the scales don't open, you'll have to bake the cones in the oven. Use a low temperature, not more than 110 to 120 degrees Fahrenheit. Turn the cones over now and then, and eventually most of them will open.

Baking cones sounds strange, I know, but it's really very natural. Many species of pine hold on to their seeds until after a forest fire. The fire clears the ground, lays a bed of ashes, and the heat of the fire liberates the seed, which falls into this hospitable bed. In the absence of a forest fire, your oven will provide the heat necessary to liberate the seeds. A nice dividend of baking cones is the delicious smell of pine, redwood, or whatever that will fill your kitchen.

By the way, if your oven doesn't go down to 110 or 120 degrees, you can try a trick I learned from an amateur yogurt maker. Turn the oven off completely and run a light bulb on an extension cord into the oven compartment. The cord will prop the door open slightly to provide good ventilation, and the bulb will supply enough heat to pop the cones.

If you are going to plant your seeds immediately after collecting them, you might want to skim through this section. But at least glance at the paragraphs headed *Treatment* so that you'll know what to do if your seeds stubbornly refuse to germinate.

Drying, Storing, and Treating Wild Seeds

Drying

If you're going to store the seeds for more than a month or two, you must keep them dry. Spread them out in shallow layers in a dry, well-ventilated room and turn them over every day or so. Remove any seeds that look moldy.

Or, better yet, dry the seeds in the sun. The sun will kill insect eggs and fungi.

Douglas Fir
Cone and seed

Storing

In most cases, seeds can be kept in paper bags or manila envelopes (not plastic bags!) in a dry, relatively cool place.

If you're going to keep the seeds for longer than a few months, the *ideal* way to do it for most Temperate Zone (nontropical) seeds is to pack them in airtight containers and store them in a refrigerator or some other cool place. Do not pack them in airtight containers, however, unless you are absolutely certain that they have been dried properly. Otherwise they'll rot.

The best general advice I can give about drying and storage is this: be careful, but not overscrupulous. Most seeds are remarkably hardy—evolution has made certain of that—and they'll usually survive whatever minor ineptitudes you inflict upon them.

Treatment

Most seeds germinate without any particular difficulty. But quite often you'll come upon a plant with an especially stubborn seed. Paradoxically, in many plants the *failure* to germinate easily is an important survival trait. Take the case of a plant that flowers in August and whose seed ripens in September. The seed falls to the ground, and if it were to germinate immediately, the tender young shoot would be killed by the winter frost. The seed must stay dormant until the conditions are right. Dormancy consists of a thick coat in some seeds, or certain chemical *germination blocks* in others. Through time the seed undergoes experiences that wear away the thick coat or break down the germination blocks. The seed may sit in acid soil for many months; it may be subjected to the cold damp of winter, perhaps the heat of summer, and often periods of alternate freezing and thawing. In other words, there are lengthy, risky processes in nature that break down the seed's dormancy and induce germination at (hopefully) the right time—and it is such processes that we are imitating with our various treatments.

At the end of this chapter I mention several books that give lists of wild seeds and suggest various treatments to help get them to germinate. Depending on the species, the books might recommend *hot water, scarification, sulfuric acid,* or *stratification.* Here is what those terms mean.

Hot water. Boil about four cups of water to every cup of seeds. When the water boils, turn the heat off, wait a couple of minutes (until the temperature drops to about 180 degrees Fahrenheit), and add the seeds. Let the water return to room temperature and let the seeds soak at room temperature for another few hours.

Scarification. Cut into the seed coat with a knife or prick it with a pin. For small seeds, rub between two sheets of sandpaper. The idea is to break through the seed's thick coat so that moisture can enter.

Sulfuric acid. Soak the seed in concentrated sulfuric acid for the recommended number of hours (usually two to four). Use enough acid to cover the seeds. Concentrated sulfuric acid is corrosive, dangerous stuff, so be careful. When you're through soaking the seed, pour the acid off and save it for the next batch. Wash the seeds thoroughly in lots and lots of cold water. (If, by the way, you can't get any concentrated sulfuric acid, you might try soaking the seeds in battery acid. Battery acid is diluted sulfuric acid, so you'll have to soak the seed for longer than the books recommend.)

Stratification. Put the seeds into a moist (not wet!) medium. Sand is best. Pack the seeds sparsely so that each seed comes in contact with some of the medium and refrigerate for the recommended period of time (usually about three months).

The best container for the seeds (although not necessarily for your refrigerator) is a wooden box covered by waxed paper to prevent rapid drying. I've heard of people using jars but I've never gotten good results this way. If you live in a cold climate, you would do very well to put the moist sand into flats or boxes and leave them outside all winter in a sheltered place. In either case, check them every so often to make sure that the medium is still damp and water them every month or so. *Almost all tree seeds seem to benefit from stratification.* In fact, most nuts, acorns, maple wings, etc., cannot be dried and must be stored in this fashion.

As you try your hand at stratification, sulfuric acid, scarification, or hot water, I hope you'll bear in mind that seed treatment is not an exact science. If at first you don't succeed, experiment! Also remember: after you treat the seeds, they're ready and raring to go. You should plant them at once, so plan accordingly. In other words, don't treat seeds in November if you're not going to plant them until March.

Planting   If you want to be very efficient, and if you have lots of time and energy, you can plant seeds in seed beds or flats and raise them artificially before putting them out in the field. This is very good practice for trees, shrubs, and many hardy perennials. There are many ways of doing it, using seed beds, cold frames, etc.; any beginner's guide to gardening will tell you how. But as you follow the gardening instructions, please keep in mind this important difference. Garden plants are often exotic, specially bred plants that are very finicky. They usually need exceptionally fertile soil. Wild plants do not need such fertility. In fact, if you pamper them too much in the nursery, they'll grow lush, wanton vegetation that will make it hard for them to adjust to their ultimate fate in the wild.

Direct planting

The seeds of annuals and biennials, as well as those perennials you don't want to fuss with, can be planted directly where you want them to grow. Choose locations that approximate the places where you found the parent plants. Clear a small patch of ground, spade it, rake it free of lumps, compress it somewhat, press in the seed, and cover lightly with soil (sifted soil or sand, if possible). Don't bury the seed too deeply, and *don't plant the seeds too thickly.*

Waiting

This is the roughest part. After you plant your seeds, you wait to see what comes up. Did you pick the pods too early? Leave them out in the sun too long? Store them too wet? Plant them too late? You wait and you wait, and it's really quite exciting.

Sometimes everyone around you is growing poppies by the zillion. You take all sorts of care and precautions, but you can't seem to get a single poppy to pop. Do poppies hate you? Examine that possibility. If you feel all's well between you and the poppies, then all I can say is, Wait!

Some seeds stay in the ground a year, or even two years, before germinating. Others (biennials) come up one year in vegetative form, the second year in flowering form. Some, like trilliums, are virtually unrecognizable for several years. So wait! It's happened time and again that the seeds we planted years before—and had long given up on—suddenly one spring weekend explode all over the place.

It's worth waiting for.

Reading

Wildflower propagation and gardening with native plants are subjects that seem to encourage locally written, privately published books that are often quite good. Be sure to check with your local library.

Also, don't hesitate to ask for information from local botanic gardens, garden clubs, and especially native plant societies. People there are helpful, knowledgeable, and usually delighted to see a new face.

Here are some books on seeding that I have found especially helpful.

Collecting and Handling Seeds of Wild Plants, by N. T. Mirov and Charles J. Kraebel. Forestry Publication No. 5. Washington, D.C.: Civilian Conservation Corps, 1939.

Available in forestry and agriculture libraries, its forty-one pages can easily be photocopied. This is an extremely valuable book that covers the collecting, handling, treating, and planting of wild seeds, as well as other means of propagation, instructions for setting up a nursery, and methods of cultivation. This book was written primarily for CCC people in the field, and it's especially strong for California and the West.

Handbook of Wild Flower Cultivation, by Kathryn S. Taylor and Stephen F. Hamblin. New York: Macmillan, 1963.

This is an excellent book with lots of general, easy-to-digest information on how to propagate wildflowers. There are some very good hints for most common flowers. The book seems especially oriented toward New England.

Growing Woodland Plants, by Clarence and Eleanor G.

Birdseye. New York: Oxford University Press, 1951. Re-issued in a Dover paperback edition, 1972.

This book covers eastern wildflowers along with exceptionally good sections on growing native ferns and orchids. Beside seeds, it deals with other methods of propagation like root division, tubers, and cuttings. Its most valuable feature, however, is the care it takes to describe the soil conditions preferred by each plant.

Seed Propagation of Native California Plants, by Dara Emery. Leaflets of the Santa Barbara Botanic Garden, vol. 1, no. 10. Santa Barbara, California, 1964.

Very accurate, but also very local. This was my seed bible at Redwood Park, since it tells how to handle the seeds of just about every California native plant.

Collecting Forest Tree Seeds and Growing Your Own Seedlings, by Bernard S. Douglas. Portland, Oregon: U.S. Forest Service (Pacific Northwest Region), 1975.

This 32-page pamphlet covers only conifers, but it covers the subject well. Written primarily for geneticists, Christmas tree farmers, reforesters, and others with high-volume demands, it nonetheless gives practical guidance for collecting seeds, storing and treating them, putting them out in nursery beds, caring for the seedlings, and lifting and transplanting them.

Collecting, Processing, and Germinating Seeds of Western Wildland Plants, by James A. Young. Oakland, California: U.S. Department of Agriculture (Agricultural Research), 1981.

An excellent pamphlet on how to collect, thresh, clean, store, protect, and germinate seeds from wild plants. Great information, especially on timing the collecting and drying of seeds for longer storage. Despite the title, this booklet is every bit as useful for the eastern U.S. as for the western. It is available free from the Science and Education Administration, Renewable Resource Center, 920 Valley Rd., Reno, Nevada 89512.

CHAPTER SEVEN
PLANT MIDWIFERY

PLANT MIDWIFERY. One of my favorite projects was to get together with a group of kids and spend the morning running around in the woods, helping the plants to reproduce. In case you've forgotten your own childhood obsessions, nothing intrigues a youngster quite like the mysteries of reproduction.

"C'mon," I'd yell. "Let's go out and see how the plants make babies."

Seeds, of course, are the major means of reproduction, but there are other ways—ancient ways by which plants have reproduced themselves long before they evolved the newfangled techniques of pollen, flowers, and seeds.

We notice, for example, how some trees send suckers from beneath the ground—and this is our inspiration for collecting root cuttings.

We discover a tree that has fallen over, and wherever its branches touch the ground, new trees are springing up. This is our inspiration for layering and stem cuttings.

Such expeditions into the woods to study natural reproduction are necessary if we are to relate honestly to the plant kingdom when we take cuttings. They help remind us that vegetative reproduction is not some sort of gimmick invented by modern gardeners but a natural process of plants. Our role in propagation is to watch closely, understand what we can about the needs of plants, and quietly help the plants fulfill those needs. We are not plant producers but plant midwives.

How do these projects turn out? I have had many successes and some failures. I could, I suppose, moan and groan about the failures, but I'd much rather celebrate the successes. Accepting failures without feeling bad is hard for many people—especially schoolchildren. They think they must be 90 per cent right to get an A, and unless they get an A they are not quite good enough. Nothing in nature is 90 per cent right. A redwood tree produces millions of seeds to get one or two trees that will survive. Why should we make standards for ourselves that are so different from anything else in nature?

Once you get into it, I think you'll find that collecting cuttings is fun. In fact, it can be addictive. When the primitive regions of the mind discover that you can lop off a branch, stick it in the ground, and end up with a tree— watch out! I know people who, when the urge is upon them, run around with knives and baggies in their pockets, eyeing every bush and flower, as excited as kleptomaniacs in Woolworth's.

If the cutting mania takes you over, go with it! You'll probably try to reproduce every plant in sight, and in a few months you'll learn more than this or any other book will ever teach you.

In wild forests acts of growth and reproduction are happening all the time, freely and openly. The complex, awesome dance of creation is always going on. When I'd enter the woods with my crews of little earth mothers and earth fathers to take cuttings, it was with the spirit that we were not the owners or even the guardians of the forest, but that we, too, had come to join the dance.

It's a common sight to find a fallen tree with its network of roots clawing the air. Or to come upon a road or stream whose eroding banks expose the naked roots of the trees. Or in the course of transplanting a tree to leave behind dozens of severed roots. These are sad sights, but you can turn them into an advantage. Cut off some of these roots, handle them properly, and with little effort you can create a whole forest of trees.

Root Cuttings

I know that poplar, black locust, sumac, sassafras, most shrubs of the poppy family, and many conifers will gladly reproduce this way, and I suspect that many other trees and bushes will too.

Collecting root cuttings

You can collect your cuttings almost anytime at all. But the best time is from late fall through the winter, when the roots are relatively inactive—and when perhaps you are relatively inactive too.

The ideal root cutting to look for is one that is young but not too skinny. A skinny root has too little food reserve to do all the hard work necessary to turn itself into a complete plant. A good cutting is at least as thick as a pencil and from about two to four inches long.

As you cut through the roots (lopping shears or hand snips are fine), be clean and decisive. No ripped or jagged ends, please. The perfect root cutting will be moist, firm, of good color, and free from rot. It may have a light green layer just under the skin. If it has hair roots clinging to it, do your best to keep these roots moist—although this will not always be possible.

Polarity

As you are cutting, you'll have to record which end of the root is nearest the crown of the tree. This end will eventually produce the stem, while the lower end will send out rootlets. If you plant a root cutting upside down, it will get confused and die. The conventional way of recording which end is up is to cut straight across at the crown end and to slant the cut on the root-tip end of the cutting.

Wintering

Root cuttings do best when planted in warming soil. Thus if you collect them during the fall or winter, you should store them until the following spring.

First tie them into bundles like stalks of asparagus. Then bury them in moist sand or sawdust. Keep them in a shed, a garage, or in a cellar. The ideal storage temperature is 40 degrees Fahrenheit, but as long as they aren't subjected to prolonged freezing or prolonged warmth, I wouldn't be too fussy. Keep them covered and leave them alone, except to check every so often that they are still moist.

Darkness

Roots, the gentle, sensual, feet-mouths of plants, hate light. That's why they grow down rather than up. Scientifically, I don't know whether it makes any difference, but from the moment I collect them until the moment I return them to the ground, I respect their fear of light and do my best to keep them in darkness.

Getting ready

In early spring, as soon as the ground has thawed, your root cuttings will be ready for planting. Pull them out of the sand or sawdust, untie the bundles, and lay them out on a damp newspaper in a dimly lit room to examine them. If nothing has happened, just put them aside for planting. Many of the cuttings, however, will probably have a crown of buds around the top and perhaps a dangle of rootlets at the bottom. Decide which is the strongest bud and (as much as it may pain you) flick the other buds off. Leave the rootlets intact, and be sure to keep them moist until planting time. That's important: don't let those fragile rootlets dry out for even a minute.

Planting

If you want to be extra sure your cuttings will survive, you can plant them in containers or in good garden soil. Water them, weed them, and tend them for a year until they're ready for transplanting in the wild. Any good gardening book will tell you how to do it: follow the instructions for planting bulbs.

Or you can do what I do, which is to put the root cuttings directly into the field at an auspicious time of the year and let them fend for themselves. Think of your cuttings as temporarily decapitated bare-root seedlings (which is exactly what they are) and follow the instructions on pages 159-168). Remember especially to plant the cutting right side up. Leave the top of the cutting about one inch *below* the surface of the soil.

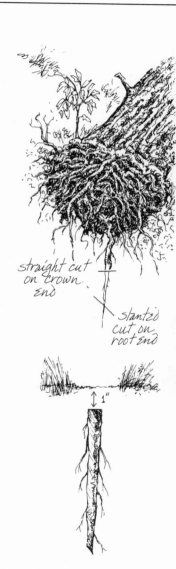

straight cut
on crown
end

slanted
cut on
root end

1"

Afterwards

Your cuttings will certainly appreciate some attention during their first six months. Deep watering, a gift of mulch once the stem has broken ground, and protection from nibblers are not necessary, but they will make life easier for your cuttings. They'll also give you an excuse to partake of the struggle of the bud as it bursts through the soil and reaches hungrily toward the sky.

Layering   We've all seen how ivy, blackberry canes, and the branches of many shrubs touch the ground and take root. This, basically, is what layering is all about. You bend a branch and bury a portion of it. The buried part grows roots while the tip of the branch takes off like a kid running away from home. You can either leave the new plant in place or return several months later to dig it up and transplant it somewhere else.

Layering is a natural, effortless, and almost foolproof way of reproducing many plants. You don't need any skills, special tools, or a saintly commitment to water, weed, shade, or cultivate. In fact, you can lay this book down, grab a trowel, walk out into your backyard, do some layering, and be back in your easy chair before a cup of tea gets cold. Several months later, your negligible effort will result in a new plant. It's that easy! I hope you'll try it soon.

When to layer

Almost any woody plant will layer successfully, as long as its branches are flexible enough to be bent into the ground. Probably the best time to layer is in the early spring, before the explosion of buds. Use the dormant branches of the previous year's growth. Spring soil is warm and moist, and roots just love warmth and moisture.

If the dormant branches are too stiff and woody to be bent into the ground, it will be best to wait until summer. Use the new growth that is almost mature but still pliable. Summer layering will work well as long as nature or a hose can keep the soil moist enough to promote rooting.

Preparing the branch

Take the branch you are going to layer gently in your hand, and make a sharp bend about eight to twelve inches from the tip.

If the underside of the bend has cracked from the bending, that's fine. If it hasn't, you should create a wound. You can either cut the underside with a knife (some nursery people cut as much as halfway through the stem), or you can rub off some of the bark that has crumpled from the bending. Wounding, while it's not 100 per cent necessary, does serve a purpose. The branch tip will still draw the water and minerals it needs from the tree's roots, since these flow through the inner parts of the branches. But the foods and growth hormones manufactured by the leaves pass through the outermost parts of the stem. Instead of going back to nourish the mother tree, they are interrupted by the wound you've made. They begin to accumulate there, and eventually they stimulate the growth of roots.

Burying the branch

Next, use a shovel, a trowel, a mattock, or a pick to dig up the earth and bury the bend of the branch. Use a forked stick, a bent wire, or even a stone to prevent the branch from springing up again. Cover the bend to a depth of three to six inches and stomp the earth over it once or twice lightly.

This will usually be enough, unless the ground is exceptionally clayey. If so, you might wish to dig fairly deep and work in some compost to lighten the soil and make it more congenial to rooting.

The final step is to put a stake next to the new tip and tie the tip lightly to it to make it grow upright.

The nicest thing about layering is that unless you are up against brutal summer droughts, you don't have to do another blessed thing.

Transplanting

If you want to transplant the new creation, return in about seven to twelve months. Cut the connections with the mother plant and then treat the new plant as you would any other tree or shrub. Dig it up carefully, following the instructions on pages 176-186. Be sure to follow *all* the instructions, especially in regard to pruning the plant back a bit.

Another possibility for a layered plant is mentioned on page 12. You can leave the newly rooted shoots in place. Don't even bother to sever the connections. That way you can convert a modest bush into a complete tangle. Subscribers to *Garden Beautiful* won't think much of this accomplishment, but your wildlife will be delighted by the tangled living brush pile you've created.

Willow Stakes

One of the first things the early settlers did when they claimed a piece of land was to put up a fence. To make the fence, they'd fell some relatively valueless tree, like a willow, perhaps, and cut it into posts. After driving the posts roughly into the ground with a maul, they'd set the log rails on top of the posts, and there would be a crisp, clean-looking fence — for a couple of months at least.

Now if you've ever dealt much with fences, you know that the major problem is usually decay. But if the fence is made of willow posts, there is another very different sort of problem. After a few months the fence posts begin to sprout. Thick, turgid buds appear and spread up and down the posts. The buds burst into leaf, and soon the fence begins to grow—no longer a fence but a living, vigorous row of willow trees.

Many river trees like willows, cottonwoods, and poplars have this marvelous, persistent ability to sprout. It's an important part of their survival, I suspect. Many of these trees have long, whiplike, or brittle branches that break off in winter and float downstream. The heavier end eventually settles somewhere in the wet mud and sends out roots, and a new tree begins growing.

This remarkable rooting ability, which proved so disconcerting to early fence builders, can be a great boon to us. A willow branch pounded into the ground will grow anywhere —yes, anywhere—as long as there is enough year-round moisture. Willows will root in the most barren and unstable of soils, which makes them the most valuable tree I know for erosion control. (See pages 87-88).

Cottonwoods and poplars can also be rooted if you follow the instructions I'm going to give. But in addition to water they need a richer, "river bottom" type of soil if they are to prosper.

When to plant

The best time to plant willow cuttings is in the fall or very early spring—when we call the tree *dormant*. Actually, only the leaves are dormant. The roots continue to grow all winter from stored energy, and when the buds burst in the spring, the new leaves will have a healthy system of roots to provide them with moisture and minerals.

There is a way of planting willows when they are in leaf. The danger, of course, is that the leaves will transpire moisture faster than the growing roots can provide it and the tree will dry out. You can prevent this by clipping off all the leaves along the stake except one or two, and by continuing to trim off leaves all summer long. It's a lot of trouble, and it's a bit risky, but if you can plant only during the leafy season, you might give this method a try.

Collecting and preparing willow branches

To get cuttings from a living tree while preserving the health of the tree, follow the instructions for pruning on pages 147-153. Any willow will give equally good cuttings, so don't worry too much about the species.

After you collect the branches, cut them into convenient lengths for planting. Don't try to chop them up while you're in the middle of a tangle of willows, but drag the branches out to a clear area where you can set up a chopping block and have enough room to work.

The cuttings should be at least eighteen inches long and at least a half-inch thick. Anything this size or bigger—even up to ten or twelve feet long—will grow, but the bigger the cutting, the deeper you will have to plant it, so beware.

One thing that determines the length of the cuttings is the water table. If you're planting on land that is wet year-round, you can use shorter lengths. In our part of California, where it gets dry in the summer, I usually have to cut the stakes five feet long or more so that I can pound them deep enough to reach moist soil.

To cut a branch, lay it over a chopping block and use a sharp ax. At the thicker end (the end toward the trunk), make a point. At the narrow end (toward the tip of the branch), make a flat, straight cut.

It is very important to note which is the butt end. If you plant the willow upside down, the sap will flow in the wrong direction and the cutting will die.

Preparing a hole

If the ground is soft and moist, you can just pound the stake into the ground without any preparation.

If the ground is rocky, however, you might strip the bark too badly by pounding, so you must first prepare a hole— much the same idea as countersinking a hole for a screw. For smaller stakes, you can pound a digging bar or even a crowbar into the ground, wiggle it around a bit, pull it out, and insert the cutting. For really big cuttings, you may have to start the hole with a shovel or a post-hole digger (if you've got one), then use the digging bar after you're a foot or so down.

The ground at the bottom of the hole should be moist, wet, or even flooded. If you are planting in winter or spring, remember that the water table is probably much higher than it will be later in the year, so dig deeper than you think is necessary.

Pounding the cutting in

This step is a mind boggler. I would definitely recommend it as therapy to those "nature lovers" who tip-toe across lawns, who cannot bear to see a tree pruned, and who otherwise insist that plants are very fragile, delicate pieces of creation. You take your carefully shaped cutting, insert its pointed end into your carefully made hole, and just pound the hell out of it. A heavy wooden mallet is the best tool. Or have someone hold a piece of wood on the flat head of the stake while you pound away with a sledgehammer. The idea is to knock the stake deeply into the ground without splitting the top too much. Split stakes grow, but they tend to dry fast, rot, or (if they live very long) develop badly.

The cutting should have at least half its length under

ground, and even two-thirds or more of its length can be buried. If you don't plant it deep enough, there will be too much leaf and too little root.

Browsing

Cattle are notorious for browsing young willows. They'll desert a pile of hay, a bed of straw, the shade of an oak tree, or a field of alfalfa and come running whenever they see a young willow. If there are cattle present, you'll have to fence off the planting.

Wildlife browsing should not be too severe, unless you happen to have an overabundance of hungry deer at the end of a long, hard winter. If this is the case, you'd be best off planting bigger, taller, thicker cuttings, which are less tasty and which can withstand browsing somewhat better.

Have faith

The first time I planted willows, I felt utterly depressed. After a full, hard day's work, I stood there with a group of youngsters looking at what we had done. It was a weird, desolate scene. Everywhere around us we saw dead-looking sticks pounded into the ground. It reminded me of an empty drive-in theater, or a municipal parking lot with hundreds of parking meters all over the place. We were all very tired, cold, and discouraged. The kids kept asking me if I thought these stakes would grow, and I said, "Of course"—but only because that was what I was expected to say.

Later that spring the kids returned to the area to camp. What they saw, as they told me later, was so exciting that they couldn't fall asleep that night. The "parking meters" were covered with thick, juicy buds just beginning to burst into leaf.

Since then I've found willow cutting to be one of the easiest, surest, and most rewarding of all projects.

Knowing how to take hardwood cuttings is a valuable skill if you are dealing creatively with wild land. Most wild plants are totally unavailable from commercial nurseries. You can often get Japanese, Chinese, or Canadian maples far more easily than you can get the species of maple that is growing (or should be growing) in your own backyard.

Hardwood Cuttings

Taking hardwood cuttings is one of the easiest ways of reproducing plants. (*Hardwood* means that the wood is fully matured, or hard.) You simply cut off a dormant shoot, store it through the winter, and plant it in the spring. I know this technique works well with dogwood, ninebark, catalpa, hazelnut, honeysuckle, elderberry, and snowberry; and it's valuable for other species too.

I've found this to be an especially good project for school children, by the way, since it conveniently corresponds to the school year. The students can take cuttings in November, see them through the winter, plant them in April, and enjoy the results by June. Instead of a final exam and a grade, they'll have dozens of living plants to reward them for their efforts.

Biologically, taking hardwood cuttings is a lot like layering. The difference is that you detach the shoot immediately rather than wait until the roots have formed. Instead of feeding off the parent, the shoot feeds off its own reserves. It's not as safe and sure a method as layering, but it's often more convenient.

How rooting takes place

Why is it that a severed shoot produces roots? Some plants, like willows and poplars, have dormant root begin-

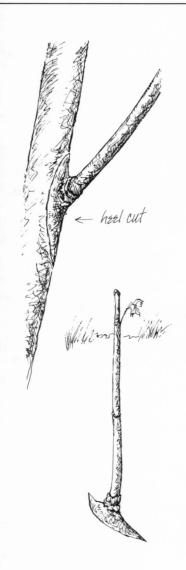

← heel cut

nings all along their stems. They are exceptionally easy to root. Knock them into the ground, and the dormant roots wake up fighting.

Most other plants, however, aren't quite so eager. What happens is this. Under the bark is the green, juicy layer of cambium. When a shoot is lopped off, the cambium within the shoot responds to the injury in two ways. First it covers the wound with a callus, or scar tissue. Next, if the moisture and temperature are at all encouraging, the cambium begins to produce roots at the point of injury. It won't produce these roots, however, until it first makes the callus. Keep this sequence in mind, since it explains why we treat hardwood cuttings the way we do.

Taking the cuttings

Pruning and trail clearing are excellent sources of hardwood cuttings. The best time to collect them is in late fall and early winter. This gives the callus a chance to grow before spring.

Choose dormant shoots from the previous season's growth. Crown sprouts or water sprouts are acceptable—as long as they are fairly typical-looking shoots at least as thick as a pencil. Those that will survive best, however, are regular branches and twigs that have been growing in the sun and are therefore generally richer in stored food than shaded branches or fast-growing sprouts.

After you collect the shoots, you should cut them into sections four to twelve inches long with at least two nodes to each section. Make the top cut an inch or less above one node and make the lower cut at a slant just below the bottom node. Make certain that the cuts are clean too: you don't want your cuttings to look as if you had chewed them off the parent tree.

Heels

Some plants root better if you take them with a *heel*—a small section of the larger branch to which your cutting is attached. As you can imagine, taking a heel damages the tree from which you are cutting it. So generally I take heels only from branches I've already pruned.

Storing the cuttings

You'll now have to store the cuttings until spring. Tie them in bundles, if you want, and bury them in moist (not wet) sand at a cool temperature. The ideal temperature range (if you can do it) is in the low forties—warm enough to form a callus but not quite warm enough to make the leaves sprout.

While your cuttings are cooling their heels, so to speak, you should check them frequently to make sure the sand is still moist and the buds are not swelling. Ordinarily, swelling buds are a cause for great joy—but not now. If you notice this happening, lower the temperature. Otherwise, the shoots will burst into leaf long before the roots have developed enough to support those leaves.

As you check your cuttings, you might also pause to think about what they are going through underneath the moist sand. All its life the cambium has been geared toward producing stem, stem, and more stem. Now it must change. It must totally realign its inner resources and begin to produce roots. Everything looks peaceful and quiet underneath your sand, but the changes are enormous—the sorts of enormous changes that go on inside a cocoon as a caterpillar slowly transforms itself into a butterfly.

Planting

Within about six weeks the callus will have formed. Some-times you can see a scabby white growth. Often it's just a thin, transparent covering.

To be honest, hardwood cuttings look a bit disappointing. "You mean this stick is going to grow?" a kid once asked me. "It's not a stick," I replied. "It's a magic wand."

You can plant the cuttings as soon as the ground thaws. Follow the instruction on planting bare-root seedlings, pages 159-168. Insert the cutting deeper into the hole, however, so that the top bud is just peeking out above the surface of the soil. Stomp the ground hard to pack the earth against the stem, and you are done. With average luck you can return a few months later and report to your friends a heartwarming tale: Local Cutting Makes Good!

Reading

There are dozens, perhaps even hundreds, of books on plant propagation. They all seem to cover the same range of subjects: softwood cuttings, hardwood cuttings, seeds, divi-sions, grafting, etc. Some books cover the field better than others, but they are all basically sound. If in doubt, choose the one with the most helpful pictures. I mean it.

Among the many books I've looked at, the ones I've found most valuable and practical have been these:

Propagation for the Home Garden. Handbook No. 103. Revised edition. New York: Brooklyn Botanic Garden Record, 1984.

This short manual (76 pages) with lots of photos and sketches is the most useful book I know on plant propagation. It tells you most of the important things you should know about propagation and gives many useful hints without drowning you in expert-oriented details. If you can't get it in your local bookstores, you can order it by sending $3.05 to Brooklyn Botanic Garden, 1000 Washington Avenue, Brooklyn, N.Y. 11225.

Plant Propagation: Principles and Practices, by Hudson T. Hartmann and Dale E. Kester. Third edition. New York: Prentice-Hall, 1975.

This is a heavy, 700-page book with lots of information, aimed mostly at professional nursery operators. The book is especially valuable, however, because in addition to telling you what to do, it also tells you *why* you are doing it, with long, somewhat technical excursions into plant anatomy, biology, and chemistry. If you want to know more about such things, this book is a good place to turn.

Use of Vegetation for Erosion Control in Mountain Meadows, by C. J. Kraebel and Arthur Pillsbury. Technical Note No. 2. California Forest Experimental Station: U.S. Forest Service, 1933.

I don't know where you'll ever get hold of this one—only bigger forestry libraries are likely to have it—but if you do manage to get a copy, you'll find that it has a thorough section on willow stakes. It tells you not only how to plant them but where and why, with lots of diagrams.

Also, *Growing Woodland Plants* by Clarence and Eleanor Birdseye, mentioned on pages 122-123, has lots of good advice on propagating wild plants by cuttings.

CHAPTER EIGHT
PRUNING

PRUNING. Pruning trees and shrubs is usually a light, easy job. It demands a bit more sensitivity and judgment than most other projects in this book, and it can even be artistic (a bit like sculpting)—but don't let that scare you away. Simply think about what you're doing and, if you are doing it with friends or with kids, avoid anyone who seems overly gung-ho. Otherwise, at the end of the day you might find, as I have, a few pathetic, suffering stubs sticking out of the ground, an enormous pile of slash, and some over-worked kid with sweat on his brow and an infuriating grin on his face.

While I have run into an occasional mad hacker, most people I've dealt with have been quite the opposite. Most of us are timid snippers, very much afraid of hurting the tree. We seem to think that trees might be like people and that

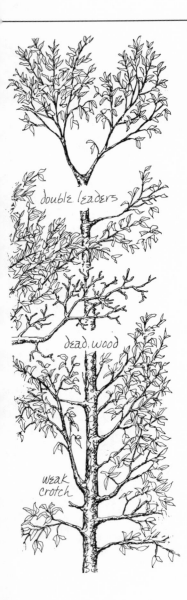

double leaders

dead wood

weak
crotch

cutting off a branch may be something like cutting off a human arm, leg, or finger. But this is hardly the case. Trees have a certain polymorphous vegetative ability that people lack. If you put a branch into the ground, it will grow roots. If you put roots into the ground, they will grow stems. If you saw off a weak limb, the whole tree will be strengthened and growth will be spurted elsewhere. If you decapitate a pine, it will grow two heads. If you chop a tree right down to the ground, it will often produce dozens of crown sprouts, each striving madly to become a tree.

There is something very crazy, marvelous, and irresponsible about vegetative growth, especially when you compare it with the careful, conservative growth of humans. I think it's important to understand this difference. The idea that trees are like people leads us to think of trees as an inferior sort of life. Understanding their truly remarkable nature, however, leads us closer to the truth: as wonderful as we are, in many ways we are actually inferior plants.

Why prune a wild tree?

I assume, heaven forbid, that you are not going to shape, coif, or barber your wild trees. I am certainly not going to tell you how to shape a bush to look like a dancing elephant, nor will I even tell you how to jazz up an unproductive apple tree you might have in your backyard. A well-pruned tree is perfectly appropriate for a formal garden or a backyard, but it would be as out of place in the wilds as a poodle dressed in a knitted jacket and vinyl booties.

Your attitude toward wild trees should be laissez faire—or at least fairly lazy. Yet there are many times when you will have to prune, such as when you are:

· Collecting cuttings;
· Building and maintaining trails;

- Reducing foliage on newly transplanted trees;
- Gathering willow stakes for replanting; or
- Repairing the butchering job usually done by highway departments and utility companies along their rights of way.

In short, if you *have* to prune, here's how to do it in such a way as to leave the tree strong and attractive.

Tools

There are basically only two pruning tools: a wide-toothed saw for bigger branches, and lopping shears for twigs.

Unless you are hopelessly hung up on the "right tool for the right job" mystique, these two tools will serve you very well. Look closely at the fancy arsenal that professional tree people lug around and you will see that all their equipment is just so many variations of these two basic tools.

When to prune

It's probably better to prune a tree when it's dormant, but this is not quite necessary. Just try to avoid the extremes of heat and cold—as much for your sake as for the tree's.

How to begin

If you are repairing damage to a tree, or if you are clearing a trail, you don't have any choice as to which branches you must remove. So go right ahead and do what has to be done.

But if you are reducing foliage on a newly transplanted tree, taking cuttings, or gathering willow stakes, you can prune the tree almost any way you want. Don't just hurl yourself at the tree and begin cutting. Pruning a tree is a very big event—not in your life, perhaps, but certainly in the life of the tree. Plan it out beforehand. Put your tools

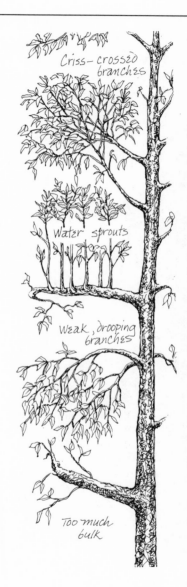

Criss-crossed branches

Water sprouts

Weak, drooping branches

Too much bulk

down as far away from you as possible and sit down near the tree. Look it over, see what it's like, and get to know it. What is its general shape? How is it balanced? Are its leaves scattered all along the branches or are they growing mainly at the tips? Move around a bit and study the tree from all sides. After a while you will feel thoroughly easy and intimate with the tree; then you can begin the cutting.

I would, as a general policy, put health before beauty, and I would first cut off any branches that are traditionally considered weak: water sprouts, crisscrossed branches, weak crotches, dead wood, double leaders, branches with lots of bulk but little foliage, shaded branches, crown sprouts, and drooping branches.

If the health cut brings you to a good place, then by all means stop there. If not, where you go next will depend largely on your artistic judgment and what your *feel* for the tree is. My own preference is to simplify: that is, keep the general shape and balance but make it more sparse.

Another thing you might do is to *head* the tree. Leave the major branches intact and cut away on the outermost parts of the tree—as if you were trimming a hedge. This is especially valuable for newly transplanted trees, since it keeps the foliage closer to the trunk and reduces the distance that the sap and nutrients must be circulated.

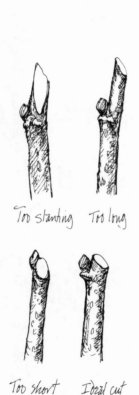

Too slanting   Too long

Too short   Ideal cut

How to cut a big branch

The most important thing to remember is DON'T LEAVE A STUB! Once you've cut off the foliage, the sap will no longer flow out to the stub. The stub will die, rot, and often carry the rot back into the heart of the tree.

The idea of cutting a big branch is to cut it flush with the trunk, or flush with the major branch to which it is attached. Don't try to do it with a single cut. You'll run into trouble if you do. If you cut from below, the saw will bind as the branch begins to weaken. If you cut from above, the branch may very well tear off a strip of bark as it falls.

The proper way of cutting a big branch is with three cuts, as shown on this page. The first two cuts will bring down the branch, and the third cut will take off the stub.

Once the branch has been cut off flush against the trunk, inspect the scar to make sure there are no shreds of bark or pockets that might catch water. Then, if you want, cover the wound with tree paint.

Cutting off twigs

Small twigs (under one-half inch) do not have to be cut off flush with the next major branch, they do not need tree paint, and in fact they do not need any special care at all.

If, however, you want to make the perfect cut, the tree will certainly benefit. Use lopping shears to make a slanting cut just above a node. (A node is a place where a leaf or a bud joins the stem.) The cut will heal over quickly and growth will resume at the node.

If you are dealing with kids, by the way, you'll find that they have a tendency to cut off quite sizable branches with the lopping shears, until they have bent the lopping shears out of shape. There's not much you can do about this; it is simply the way kids are made and the way lopping shears are made. Put them together and you get bent lopping shears. I don't have any solution, but I thought I'd warn you anyway.

When to stop

I usually like people who get carried away by what they're doing, but not when they're pruning. Knowing when to stop is urgent. Make sure you have a plan, carry out the plan, and

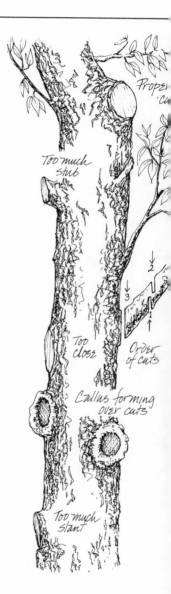

Proper 'Cu

Too much stub

Too close

1
2
3

Order of cuts

Callus forming over cuts

Too much slant

then stop. Don't keep snipping away until the tree looks "perfect." If kids are doing the work, or if you're still learning how to prune, the trees you finish will often look ragged, chopped, and impoverished—as if they just stepped out of a barbers' college. Don't feel bad. It will take the tree a few weeks to recover from the insult, heal over its wounds, and begin to make itself beautiful again. Trees want to be beautiful, and they have the power to make themselves beautiful. It's the expression of their vegetative urge. If you've made any aesthetic mistakes, the tree will repair them within a year. Sculptors should be so lucky!

Reading

There are many good books about pruning, although they deal mostly with ornamental and orchard trees rather than with wild trees.

Sunset Pruning Handbook, by Roy L. Hudson. Menlo Park, California: Sunset Books, 1952. Revised edition, 1972.

The older editions of this book had lots of excellent pictures and drawings. You could learn a lot just by looking at the pictures.

The new edition does away with most of the pictures and has instead a very helpful tree-by-tree description of how to prune.

The ideal book would be a combination of these two.

The Pruning Book, by Gustav Wittrock. Emmanus, Pa.: Rodale Press, 1971.

This is a competent book that covers the subject well. It's not too exciting, but maybe pruning isn't supposed to be. The fact that it's published by Rodale Press will undoubtedly recommend it to organic gardeners.

The Pruning Manual, by Everett Christopher. New York: Macmillan, 1954.

This is a reworking of *The Pruning Book*, written by Dr. Liberty Hyde Bailey in 1898. A classic, it deals almost exclusively with fruit trees. It also has a fairly good section on tree biology as it relates to pruning—very valuable if you're the sort of person who asks why as well as how.

CHAPTER NINE
PLANTING TREES

PLANTING TREES. The challenge of tree plant-
ing, as I see it, is not to find volunteers who will help you out.
That's easy. Tree planting is by far the most popular of all
conservation projects. Nor is it especially challenging to
plant a tree in such a way that it will grow. That's also easy.
The real challenge is to overcome the weighty, pious expec-
tations that surround tree planting and to turn it into a
fresh, sensual, fun-loving act.

One way I found to make it fun, especially for kids, was to
make it easy. I always gave kids fewer trees than I felt they
could handle. At the end of the day they were still full of
energy and perhaps disappointed that I didn't have any
more trees to give them. It was a far better way to end the
day than with a group of cranky, blistered kids who wished
they had never come.

The other thing I did was to avoid every possible cliché. I think we've all had it up to here with tree planting sentimentality. Never once in dealing with kids did I dangle before them the image of grateful unborn generations thanking us for our selfless act. Instead, I would assemble the kids and give them what must have been the craziest speech they ever heard. "Be quiet, please. You've got to be quiet. It's lunchtime. The trees are eating. Sh-sh-sh! The trees in the forest are always eating. It's always lunchtime. No wonder the trees are so fat. Just look at the bellies on them. They eat all day long, all night long, every day of the year. Eat, eat, eat. Millions of mouths, always eating. No wonder trees don't move and run around and jump. They don't have time. All they have time to do is eat. The earth is like a huge banquet table, and all their lives they sit at the table, eating, eating, growing, growing, swelling, swelling."

I would then talk about how the trees were breathing, breathing, breathing, always breathing, millions of noses breathing in and out. I would talk about drinking, digesting, circulating, and communicating. "That bee over there is bringing a sackful of genetic messages from one tree to another."

With my fingers I would explain how trees grow—how they grope and strain at the tips of their branches and at the wiggly ends of their roots. We'd look at trees and notice how the branches writhe and strain and how the leaves spread out submissively before the sun.

The purpose of this sort of presentation was not so much to teach kids facts but rather to shake them up, to make them see, perhaps to impress upon them the stark, wonderful, awesome fact that trees are *alive*.

Sometimes, when I sensed that the kids were really with me, I would suggest that we imitate the trees. We would become a forest. Our legs would be roots, our torsos trunks, our arms branches. We'd adopt various positions, experimenting around, until each of us had achieved a sense of his or her own treedom: some were slender and graceful as willows, some squat and gnarled like mountain junipers, some straight and ambitious like redwoods, some muscular like beeches, some loose and expansive like elms. When we had found our tree personalities, we'd hold still. Like trees, we did not move; yet we were very much alive, aware of our environment and in strangely intimate contact with each other. "Think tree thoughts," I'd suggest. Once we began to think tree thoughts, and perhaps even receive tree thoughts from the forest around us, I knew that we were ready to do the job of planting trees.

But is it really necessary to go through an awareness struggle just to plant a tree? Of course not—otherwise few trees would ever get planted. (In fact, I've worked on professional tree-planting crews where I've seen whole forests planted by men whose awareness hardly extended beyond their next pay check.) If you put a tree into the ground with any reasonable amount of care, it will grow. That's part of the aliveness of the tree: it has a will to grow. As tree planters we are merely the servants—and, at our best, the admirers—of that will.

Bare-Root Seedlings

A bare-root seedling is a skinny creature that has been plucked naked out of the earth. You cannot go to a nursery and buy one bare-root seedling any more than you can go to a supermarket for a single toothpick. You buy them in large numbers (the minimum order from a California state nursery is 500). They are easy to plant, easy to come by, and they are cheap. State and industrial nurseries will be glad to sell them to you. They are the best way I know to reforest big areas quickly and cheaply.

To plant or not to plant

Despite the many virtues of trees, making a forest is not always a good idea. Take, for example, the case of Grass Valley, a piece of land near Oakland that consists mostly of rolling California meadows. It is a rich, varied environment of snakes, gophers, mice, grasses, and wildflowers—a sort of green, magical place over which vultures hang and hawks glide. There are wooded canyons nearby that shelter deer who browse the meadows at dawn and foxes who stalk mice at night. Perhaps one day it will again support eagles.

Each spring, along with the wildflowers, come thousands of Boy Scouts to camp in Grass Valley. As a "conservation project" they invariably bring along Monterey pines to plant here. I am utterly appalled at all the eager, earnest, mis-guided hard work that goes into planting these trees and the false sense of accomplishment the kids get as they collect their merit badges. To me these orchards of struggling, out-of-place, ecologically senseless trees are nearly as un-welcome as a tract development.

The idea I want to get across is simply this: planting trees can actually be destructive where the trees will succeed a natural, thriving environment. I would never plant trees on meadows, bogs, chaparral, or on valuable wildlife habitats like old orchards, hedgerows, or bramble thickets unless I had some very compelling reason (erosion control or wild-life problems, perhaps).

In the absence of really pressing reasons, I hope you will plant trees only to *re*forest. That is, plant forests only on land which once held forests in the past. There are millions

bare root
seedling

of acres of forest land that have been logged, farmed, grazed, or mined that can urgently use reforestation.

What trees to plant

Before ordering your hundreds of bare-root seedlings, here are some questions you should ask about your land: What species of trees were on it before it was cleared? Can the soil support such trees again? If not, what native trees once grew here that prepared the land for the climax forest?

If you don't know how to ask these questions directly of the land, you'll have to ask them of people. Agricultural extension agents, soil conservation agents, and state foresters can give you free advice. Sometimes it's even good advice, if you discount their pro-lumber, pro-agriculture, pro-game-animal prejudices. Don't let them talk you into some Australian exotic that grows ten feet a year, and steer clear of the latest, genetically improved, straight-from-the-lab hybrid "supertree," developed by a university "especially for your type of land." Make sure you insist on native stock whose adaptability and vigor are guaranteed by thousands of years of evolutionary struggle.

Also, try to plant a variety of native trees on your land, although here again you may have to fight expert advice. In the state of Washington, for example, you'll probably be urged to plant solid unbroken rows of Douglas firs—just the way Weyerhaeuser and the U.S. Forest Service are doing it. This sort of monocultural "tree farm" produces good timber, but it is disastrous to wildlife and an insult to the ecological integrity of the land. Plus you run the risk of losing the whole plantation from a single disease, insect attack, or unusual change of weather. The original forests of Washington had western hemlock, spruces, alders, willows, cottonwoods, larches, true firs, and many other minor trees, in addition to Douglas firs. If I lived in that area, I would try to re-create this original variety as closely as possible. I might even give greater weight to the deciduous hardwoods, since they provide a better wildlife habitat than conifers.

There is a trick to planting a variety of trees, however. If you plant them mixed up, one or two species will quickly grow up, overshadowing and killing the others. If, for example, you were to plant redwoods, live oaks, and buckeyes together, you would end up in thirty years with a sparse redwood forest. To allow the oaks and buckeyes the sun they need, I'd plant them in blocks (or groves) of at least twenty trees.

Spacing

How far apart should you plant your trees? Here again, the commercial foresters have got it all figured out. If you space the trees six feet by six feet or perhaps six by eight under good conditions of light and moisture, the trees will grow tall and straight, prune themselves neatly of lower branches, and produce the optimum amounts of cellulose fiber per acre per year. To which my own reaction is, yeccchhh!

You may plant them close together (say, five by five or even four by four) if you feel the trees are puny or the environment is hostile. You should also plant them close together for erosion control where you want a thick mat of roots to form. You can always thin later.

If you expect most of the trees to survive, however, plant them further apart. Ten by ten or even twelve by twelve is good spacing. These trees will keep their lower branches, which make for good wildlife cover, and there will be enough space between the trees for herbaceous plants, berries, and "volunteer" trees.

Another advantage of wide spacing is that trees with low branches will always be unattractive to loggers—an important survival factor in any forest you plant.

If you decide to adopt the closer commercial spacing, I hope you'll leave clearings here and there for wildlife.

Whatever you decide about spacing, remember that these numbers (eight by eight or six by six) are only rough guides. Please don't plant the trees in straight rows, each tree exactly eight feet or six feet from its nearest neighbors. Imitate nature. Be an anarchist.

Ordering your trees

Order from a nearby nursery, one that is within the same genetic "seed zone," and preferably at the same altitude, as your land.

Try to get trees between five inches and nine inches tall. Trees smaller than five inches often get crowded out by weeds—a truly ignoble fate. Trees bigger than nine inches usually have a shaggy, luxuriant root system that makes planting very difficult.

Arrange delivery of the trees as close to the planting day as you dare. If the trees arrive too early, you'll have a storage problem. (Of course, if they arrive too late, you won't have any trees.) If your tree-planting program extends over many weeks or months, you can often have the nursery stagger the deliveries.

Here is a chart to help you decide how many trees you'll need:

Spacing	Trees per Acre
4×4	2720
5×5	1740
6×6	1200
7×7	900
6×8	900
8×8	680
6×12	600
8×10	540
10×10	440
12×12	300
14×14	220

By the way, you don't have to rent a twenty-foot van to pick up your thousand bare-root seedlings. You don't even need a pickup truck. A shopping cart will more than do the job. You'll be amazed, and probably disappointed, at how little space one thousand tightly wrapped trees take up.

Bare-root seedlings come in bundles, usually fifty trees to each bundle. The roots are packed in moss, excelsior, or some other moist, absorbent material, and they are wrapped in plastic or waxed wrapping paper to keep the moisture in.

If you're going to use them within three or four days, simply keep the trees out of the sun in a cool, moist place, and they'll stay alive and vigorous.

Heeling in

If, however, you are going to keep the trees for longer than a few days, you'll have to "heel them in." Dig a long V-shaped trench in the shade. Make sure the walls of the trench are moist (not puddly wet!). Break open the bundles and arrange the seedlings along the length of the trench, leaning them against one wall of the V. Make sure you keep those roots moist! The roots should all be below ground level. They should not be bunched, turned upwards, or too intimately intertwined. They should just be hanging naturally along the wall of the trench. Also make sure the stems are separated from each other. This is important, because if you pack them too closely together, the little devils begin to generate heat and can actually smolder. Bury the roots, moistening the soil and tamping it in as you go along to remove air pockets. Make sure that the stems are above ground and that none of the foliage has been buried.

The trees are now temporarily planted, and if you keep the soil moist, they will last very well for three weeks or a month.

When and how to plant

The best times to plant bare-root seedlings are in early spring, as soon as the ground thaws, or very early fall, well before the ground freezes. Choose a cloudy, foggy, or rainy day if you can.

heeling in

Along the Pacific Coast, where it rains all winter, we've found November through March to be the best months for tree planting.

A strong person can plant 100 trees in about three hours, easily and well.

If you are working with friends or groups of kids, have everyone bring a bucket, pail, or large coffee can. Fill the bottom of each container with wet moss, wet wood chips, wet soil, anything wet—except water. (You don't want water because it will wash off the bits of soil still clinging to the tree roots and leave them more "bare" than necessary.) Then hand out the trees.

Now comes the single most important thing to remember: THE ROOTS MUST BE KEPT MOIST AT ALL TIMES. Etch that

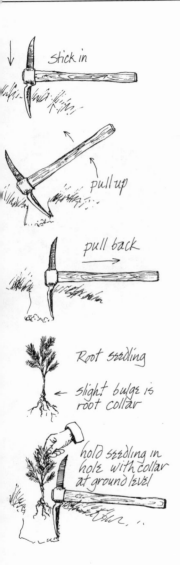

stick in

pull up

pull back →

Root seedling

← slight bulge is root collar

hold seedling in hole with collar at ground level

thought into your consciousness; tattoo it on your arm if need be. Trees feed through their tiniest hair roots, and these must be kept moist if the tree is to stay alive. If you expose the roots to the air on a hot, sunny day for even one minute, the tree will almost certainly die. Even on a rainy day a tree whose roots are exposed for only two minutes will have its survival chances reduced by about 40 per cent.

You and your volunteers now spread out over the field to create a new forest. Your first question will be, "Where is the best place to plant a tree?" One place is probably as good as another, but here are a couple of tricks that might prove mildly beneficial.

Most trees, and especially bare roots, suffer from the hot sun. A spot on the north or east side of a stump, boulder, or other object may give them a slight boost.

A second thing you might keep in mind is moisture. If your tree loves moisture, or the area seems dry, plant in dips and hollows. If the tree loves good drainage, plant on small hillocks.

Each planter will need a planting tool. My favorite is the so-called Western planting tool, or *hodad*. Other good tools are planting bars, mattocks, or narrow shovels.

Here are the actual steps in planting the tree:

· Scalp the sod if there is any.
· Plunge the tool deep and straight into the ground.
· Lift up on the handle.
· Pull the handle back to open a slit.
· Peer into the hole you just made. It should be reasonably moist but not filling up with water.
· Remove one (and only one) tree from the bucket. As you are moving it quickly from bucket to hole, notice how the roots hang down. When you plant it, you will want the roots to hang down just that way, naturally.

· Insert the tree into the hole with a wiping motion. Don't cram it in, or the roots will bunch up.

· Now pull the tree up to its proper height. The root collar should be at soil level and the roots should hang freely.

· Pull out the tool and let the earth plop and settle around the roots.

· Next plunge the tool into the ground away from the tree and ram the soil hard against the roots.

· Withdrawing the tool, stomp hard at the base of the tree to press the soil down around the roots.

· Pull at one leaf. If the leaf comes off in your hand, the tree is tightly planted. But if you can pull the tree out of the ground by a single leaf, it is too loose—so return to step one and plant it all over again in a different place.

· Give the tree a second stomp, wish it good luck, and move on.

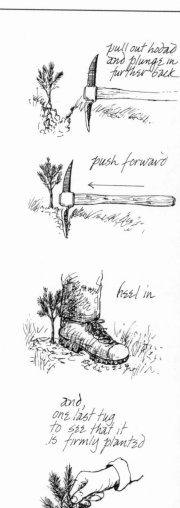

Mistakes

Here is a checklist of the most common mistakes that cause newly planted trees to die:

Dried roots. Somewhere in the storing or planting, those tender little hair roots dried out.

"J" roots and bunched roots. This happens when the hole is too shallow (a common problem if you're working with youngsters). The roots are either turned up at the ends ("J-rooted") or scrunched up in a tangled ball at the bottom.

Wrong depth. If the tree is planted too deep, with the root collar buried, the tree may suffocate or suffer rot. If the collar is too exposed, the roots may dry out.

Air pocket. This happens when the tree is planted too loosely.

Occasionally you will get a bundle of trees with outrageously lush roots. This is common with two-year-old seedlings that have never been transplanted in the nursery.

Remember not to J-root them or bunch the roots into the hole. The ideal solution is to dig a deeper hole, but if this is too demanding, you'd be well off to prune the roots to a more convenient length. Cut them off cleanly with a knife. I don't recommend this, mind you. I just mention root pruning as a lesser evil than J-rooting.

Afterwards

You've planted your land, and as far as I'm concerned, you're through. Mulching? Watering? Deer and rodent control? Fertilizing? If you want to go through the effort, that's fine indeed. Any effort you make will most likely increase your trees' chances of survival. As for me, I feel that bare-root planting is simply a once-over treatment for a large area. Under ideal circumstances, I expect no more than 80 per cent survival, and I overplant accordingly. In rough situations I'm not at all ashamed of 15 per cent survival.

I plant a tree as well as I can, and when I'm done, I turn my back on it. I view myself as a marriage broker: I introduce the trees to the environment in the best circumstances possible, but after the introduction, it's up to them to work out a satisfactory relationship.

Container-Grown Trees

Some day, go to your local arboretum and think about what's happening there. You'll probably find loblolly pines from the Caribbean, white pines from New England, ponderosa pines from Colorado, bristlecone pines from California, South American pines, Asian pines—trees from all over the world growing, indeed thriving, right next to each other. For me, it's an inspiration: here I am, fretting, worrying, and chewing my fingernails about whether I can grow redwoods on prime redwood land, and these people are growing trees thousands of miles from their native environments.

Of course, they don't do it the way I described in the previous section—with bare-root seedlings. If the founders of an arboretum had planted their area with a grab bag full of bare-root exotics, no matter how carefully they did it, 90 per cent of the trees they planted would have probably been wiped out within a year. Bare-root seedlings are for re-foresting huge areas cheaply and easily, using native stock which stands a good chance of "taking," and which requires no further care to survive.

But let's say that you are planting a more difficult area. Or a smaller area, like a school yard or an empty lot, where you want to be certain that each tree you plant survives. Or perhaps you have a lot of time and energy to devote to preparing the ground, planting the trees carefully, and caring for them later on. In such cases you'd be better off doing what arboretum planters or landscapers do—plant trees that have been grown in containers.

In this section I'm going to explain how to plant a container-grown tree with virtually 100 per cent likelihood of its survival. I'm going to give you a lot of fussy advice about how to prepare the planting area, dig the hole, break the tree loose from its container, what sort of soil to backfill the hole with, how to mulch, how to water, and how to stake and tie the tree so that it won't blow over. I hope you'll view these instructions as you would items on a supermarket shelf: just because they're being offered doesn't mean you've got to take them. If you were to plant a potted tree next to a bare-root seedling and walk off, leaving them both to fend for themselves, the potted tree would be more likely to survive. After all, it still has its root ball intact, a friendly mass of soil to which its roots can cling and draw nourishment throughout the trauma of "transplant shock." In other words, this is not how you *must* plant every container-grown tree, but the more suggestions you follow, the better off your tree will be.

There's one more thing that I really want you to understand. Too many people get so carried away by the poetry of planting a tree that they ignore the hard-work aspects of it—until halfway through the project, when blisters rise higher, spirits ebb lower, and everyone wishes he or she were home watching TV. There is ground that has to be cleared, deep, wide holes that have to be dug, and perhaps soil, mulch, and buckets of water that have to be hauled to the site. If you have lots of trees to plant, line up as many volunteers as you can. And if you're working with kids, remember: chipping away at a hard piece of ground with too heavy a tool is *no* kid's idea of a good time—even if it is for a good cause.

When and where to plant

You have a lot more latitude with a container-grown tree than with a bare-root seedling. If you're going to take care of it later—that is, mulch and water it regularly—you can plant it almost anywhere and in almost any season (except in the heat of summer and, of course, when the ground is frozen solid).

If, however, you are going to leave it pretty much to its fate after planting, you should follow more closely the instructions for bare-root seedlings in the previous section.

Choosing a tree

Again, you have a much wider choice of species—witness the arboretum—although as a matter of ecological ethics I would still plant only native stock.

One thing to be cautious about, however, is the age of a tree. If you can help it, avoid a tree that's more than three or four years old. Older trees have more difficulty adapting to a new environment. There's also a good chance that an older tree may be *root bound*. This happens when the roots grow too big in an enclosed space. Instead of growing outward and downward, they reach the sides of the container and begin to spiral. If you ever discover this condition while you're planting, do not just put the root-bound tree in the ground and hope for the best. It's likely that the roots will never straighten themselves out properly, even in good soil. The tree may look healthy for several years, but as the crisscrossed, intertwined roots grow thicker, they inevitably choke each other and cut off circulation to the whole tree. The tree actually strangles itself. It's gruesome to contemplate. The best you can do for such a tree as you're planting it is to break the ball of earth apart, untangle and comb out the roots by hand (making sure the roots are always moist), and plant the tree as a bare root. Prune the top branches as severely as you dare, give it as much mulching, watering and attention as you can afford, and you just might save it.

Another thing you can do for a tree is to harden it gradually to its new environment. Don't take a tree from a cool, moist, shady nursery, for example, and plant it on a hot, dry, exposed hillside without preparing the tree for its fate. In such cases you'd be wise to move the tree gradually, giving it a little more sun and exposure each day, and spreading the change out over as many weeks as you can.

Prepare the hole

There's an old saying that claims you'll make out better planting a fifty-cent tree in a ten-dollar hole than planting a ten-dollar tree in a fifty-cent hole. Pay heed!

As you dig the hole, you should segregate the soil. The

top layer of sod, if there is one, can be skimmed off. (You might want to keep it for your compost heap.) As you begin digging, you should carefully pile the topsoil next to the hole. If you eventually reach rocky subsoil, shovel it away from the planting site.

The hole should be about twice as wide as the diameter of the container and perhaps half again as deep as the depth of the container—unless by some unheard-of good fortune you're digging into good, loamy soil, in which case you can make the hole much smaller.

Now that you've laboriously dug a nice, deep, wide hole, a hole you can be proud of, you should begin to fill it. You are going to replace some of that rocky subsoil you may have removed with the best topsoil you have. Use the topsoil you took out of the upper parts of the hole if there's enough, or add your own special concoction of compost and loam. If you don't have any superblend available, do the best you can—perhaps mixing some well-rotted manure or a handful of peat moss with the subsoil. Using whatever you can, build up the hole, moistening and tamping the soil as you fill, until the hole is the same depth as the container.

At the risk of belaboring this point, let me say once more that the soil you put into the bottom of the hole is very important. If it's too sandy or coarse, water will drain too rapidly from the roots. If it's too clayey, the roots will get waterlogged.

Planting the tree

Once you've prepared the hole, try to get the tree out of its container without crumbling the ball of soil. It helps greatly if you water the tree the day before the planting.

The way I've always done it is to cut the can away from the soil by snipping through the upper rim with wire cutters, running slits down the sides, and pulling the can away. If you want to save the container, you'll have to run a long knife or machete along the inner walls of the can, bang a bit on the bottom and sides to loosen the soil, and carefully slide the soil ball out.

Some nurseries now sell trees in biodegradable containers made of peat moss or tarpaper. In that case, simply plant the tree in the ground, container and all (according to the instructions), and the container will quickly decay.

Once the tree is out of its container, you should work quickly. Lower the root ball into the hole. The root collar should be level with the surrounding land.

Now fill in the sides of the hole with the best soil you've got. Again, you can use the topsoil you shoveled out of the hole, or more of that wonderfully rich compost loam concoction you've brought along for the occasion. No commercial fertilizers, please; you'll burn the roots.

Fill the sides of the holes, pressing, moistening, and tamping the soil in place as you go to eliminate air pockets.

When you get to within an inch or two of the surrounding land, arrange the earth into a bowl with the tree as an island in the middle. The bowl will collect water during future waterings or rainstorms.

Watering the tree

Add water slowly, letting it sink in before adding more. After a lot of hard work, this long drink should be a leisurely, restful step—both for you and for the tree.

For a long time I resisted adding anything except pure water. Lately, however, I've begun to use vitamin B-1, available in most garden stores under various brand names. I may be experiencing the enthusiasm of a recent convert, but as near as I can see, vitamin B-1 is virtually a "wonder drug," greatly reducing transplant shock and apparently strengthening the entire tree.

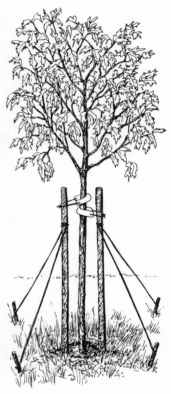

Mulch

I've been telling you so many things you should do, it's now a pleasure to tell you something you shouldn't do. Do not clear a big circle around the tree.

Perhaps someone once taught you that you must clear a circle to remove competing vegetation that might rob your tree of water and nourishment. But what they forgot to mention is that the circle of bare earth will bake and crack in the summer and freeze solid in the winter.

If you think that competition will be a problem, instead of clearing, lay a thick bed of mulch around the tree. The mulch will also help retain moisture, and it will add organic matter to the soil. Follow the instructions on pages 53-54, remembering especially not to lay the mulch up against the stem lest rot set in.

Screening, staking, and guying

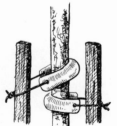

I've lost many trees through deer browsing, mouse nibbling, rabbit chomping, cattle grazing, antler rubbing, and people stomping—all because I seldom put up any sort of protective screen around the trees. I'll probably lose a lot more trees in my lifetime, too, because I am generally reluctant to put up a screen. It's part laziness, mostly aesthetics.

But if you really want to protect a tree and don't care how imprisoned it looks, you can knock three or four stakes around the tree and then wrap a piece of screen around the stakes.

As for supporting a tree, you'll probably never run into this problem. With trees under four feet tall it's unnecessary and pretentious. If the tree's over four feet tall, you shouldn't be planting it except as an instant landscaping adventure or perhaps as an emergency transplant from an area where it's being threatened.

If the situation arises where you have to support the tree, there are various ways to do it with stakes and guy wires. Check periodically to make sure the supports are taut enough to hold the tree up without cutting into the bark. Also, if you stake a tree, make sure later on that the ground hasn't settled, leaving the tree dangling by its stakes. Remember to remove the stakes within a year, or at most, two years.

Transplant shock

You plant the tree, you do all the hard work, and at last the tree is in the ground. A week passes by, and you go out to examine your pride and joy. The tree looks just awful. The leaves are droopy, and the tree looks sad and out of place. This is a condition known as transplant shock. Don't worry. You are probably in a greater state of shock than the tree.

If, however, the tree is suffering grotesquely and if it doesn't show any new growth at the tips, you can often help it along with a shot of vitamin B-1 and some courageous pruning. Cut away as much as one-third of the foliage, with an eye toward making the tree more compact (see pages 149-152). This will reduce transpiration (the loss of moisture from the leaves) until the roots have a chance to establish themselves.

Another thing you might do to help the tree along is to erect some sort of temporary screen or other cover to give the tree partial shade from the sun.

Other than vitamin B-1, pruning, and shading, there's not much else to do for a tree suffering from transplant shock. Don't inflict overdoses of water, fertilizer, and *angst* on a tree that's already got enough problems adjusting to a new environment. Have faith, and most likely the tree will eventually respond.

Transplanting Wild Trees

In this section I'll tell you how to dig up wild trees and transplant them. The process is very easy to understand. You simply dig around and under the tree until you've freed the roots with a ball of soil attached. You wrap the root ball in burlap or canvas to prevent it from falling apart, transport the tree, and replant it somewhere else.

For a very small tree the whole operation may take no more than two people, two shovels, and about twenty minutes. To move a bigger tree you can figure on a whole day's struggle with several of your strongest friends and some equipment.

My advice on this project is: aim small. It's a lot more satisfying to move a small tree easily and well than to fight all day with a tree bigger than you can handle. In such fights both you and the tree tend to lose.

Where to get wild trees

I am afraid, frankly, that the information on how to transplant wild trees might be misused and that some people will raid the forest for trees. Please don't. Even if you think the tree won't make it in the woods, let it be. The determination isn't yours; survival decisions are best left to evolution, environment, and natural accident.

There are other places where you can legitimately get wild trees. Every time a road is widened, a lot cleared, or a trail built, trees are being destroyed. Find out where the bulldozers are going. Call local contractors. Contact your city, county, or state highway departments. Or monitor your own trail-building activities. Think of the instructions in this section as a way to rescue trees from human "development."

The ideal tree to transplant

If you have a lot of trees to choose from, pick one that is growing in moist soil in a clear, open place. Such a tree will be likely to have a compact, fibrous root structure, which means you can get away with a relatively small root ball. A tree that is growing in bad soil or in heavy competition with other trees will often have a long, spreading, searching root system that makes digging it up very difficult.

Whatever you do, be sure to watch out for trees that are really suckers and crown sprouts—that is, shoots growing out of an old stump. If you start digging one of these, you may find yourself with a six-inch tree and a thirty-foot root system.

Also try to avoid species of trees that send down long taproots. This is especially common with trees and shrubs that grow in dry places.

Some trees that are extremely easy to transplant are maples, buckeyes, horse chestnuts, catalpas, hackberries, hawthorns, ashes, honey locusts, apples, sycamores, poplars, pears, pin oaks, willows, Osage oranges, and elms. I wouldn't avoid trees not listed here, however. Moving them is not easy, but still very possible.

When to move a tree

The ideal time to move a deciduous tree is when it's dormant. Of course, only the leaves are really dormant. The roots grow all winter, probably happy that they don't have any leaves overhead to make demands.

Evergreens are (by definition) always in leaf. The best time to move them is in the early fall so that the roots will establish themselves before the soil freezes. Next best time is in early spring, just as soon as the ground thaws.

Of course, if you're out to rescue trees, you may have no choice about the "ideal" time: a bulldozer may have made the decision for you. Even if you're way out of season, go ahead anyway. Just be more careful, dig a bigger ball, water the tree often after you transplant it, prune it back more severely than you might, add vitamin B-1, and you'll most likely make out fine.

Checking for disease

Before moving a tree, inspect it thoroughly. Examine the leaves, buds, branches, and stem. When you dig, be aware of the soil around the roots. Look the tree over for signs of insects, larvae, galls, slime, rot, fungi, or anything that looks unhealthy. Avoid moving a weakened tree, since it will not transplant well and you don't want to spread any infection or infestation.

Preparing the soil

If the soil is too dry when you move a tree, the ball will crumble. If the soil is too wet, *you* will probably crumble. (You have no idea what "heavy" is all about until you've spent an afternoon struggling with a sodden ball of soil.)

The best way of handling this is to wait until two days after a heavy rain. Or, if the soil is fairly dry, water the tree thoroughly about two days before you are going to move it.

How big a ball

After a while you'll develop a sense of what size ball you'll need for each species and habitat of tree. The rule of thumb is to dig under the drip line (the outermost branches), which is where most of the feeding roots are concentrated. But if you distrust your thumb, you can refer to this handy, official table:

Caliber* (inches)	Diameter of Ball (inches)	Weight of Ball (pounds)
less than 1	14	115
1–1¼	16	175
1¼–1½	18	250
1½–1¾	20	340
1¾–2	22	450
2–2½	24	600
2½–3	28	815
3–3½	32	1,400
3½–4	36	2,000

*Caliber means the diameter of the tree at a point about six inches above ground level.

This table was written in the 1930s by the American Nurserymen's Association. Everyone who moves trees seems to have a copy of it tucked away somewhere. Everyone calls it The Guide and considers it the final authority. And, to let you in on a trade secret, everyone cheats like crazy on it.

You can get away with a smaller-than-recommended ball if:

· The tree is one of those listed previously as an easy-to-move species;
· You are moving it from an "ideal" habitat (moist, loamy soil and little competition);
· You are moving it at an ideal time;
· The tree is an evergreen, most of which have fairly compact root systems;
· You are going to take extra good care of the tree after it's transplanted; or
· You are willing to take a risk.

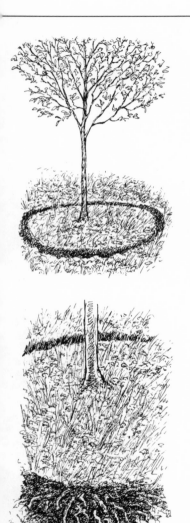

In any case, I generally use this guide and the drip line merely as crude estimates, and I proceed on a trial-and-error basis. If as I dig I come upon no roots whatsoever, I assume that all the roots must be within the ball and the ball is probably too big. If, however, I find myself cutting through several major roots without many hair roots, then the hair roots are probably all outside the ball and the ball is too little. A just-right ball is somewhere between these two extremes —lots of fiber and a few middle-sized roots.

Tree roots that have been left behind, by the way, can often be used as root cuttings (see pages 129-132).

Root pruning

If you have six months' or a year's warning before moving a tree, there's a procedure you can follow that will increase the tree's chances and will allow you to reduce the size of the root ball significantly.

Dig a trench around the tree as if you were going to remove it, except that the trench might be closer than recommended. Do not undercut the tree, however. Saw cleanly through the many large roots you will come across. Then fill the trench again with a rich, compost-filled loam, tamping the earth down and moistening it as you fill. Water the tree well and leave it alone. The tree will begin to develop hair roots within the area defined by the trench, thus preparing itself to be moved.

If by some miracle you have two years' warning before moving a tree, you can do the root pruning in two stages, cutting alternate sections of the trench each year.

One word of warning, though: don't root prune any tree in the heat of summer. And don't root prune an evergreen in the dead of winter.

Lifting a small tree

To lift a small tree (one whose diameter is under 1½ inches, say), all you need is a friend and two pointed spades. If the soil is soft enough, you plunge the spades into it and score a deep circle around the tree. If the soil is rocky, you may have to dig a trench. Then, using both spades on opposite ends of the circle or trench, pull on them like levers, slipping them under the tree as you pull and lifting the ball up. Handle the tree gently out of the hole, place the burlap or canvas underneath, pull away the spades, and fasten the cloth tightly around the ball.

Lifting a medium-sized tree

Here's how to lift a medium-sized tree, with a diameter of up to about 2½ inches.

The easiest way to do it is with power equipment like a back hoe, which is not so outrageous as it sounds. When we've rescued trees from road crews and bulldozers, we've often found our "enemies" more than willing to cooperate with us. A skilled back hoe operator can very gently dig out a tree, lift it, and nestle it down onto a piece of burlap which you've laid out on the bed of a truck.

If back hoes are out of your reach, you can, of course, do it by hand—or rather hands, because you'll need at least three or four strong, willing people for the job. First dig a trench at the appropriate distance and to the appropriate depth. Then round off the ball with the back of a shovel, tapering it inward at the bottom. Keep working at the bottom until the ball collapses into the hole.

Usually you will have to wrap the ball before removing it from the hole. Use two shovels on one side (or two shovels and a plank) to tip it as you shove the burlap halfway

underneath. Repeat the operation on the opposite side of the ball, pulling the burlap through, wrapping it around the ball, and finally tying it.

Once the burlap is in place, holding the ball together, you can begin to pry the ball out of its hole. Shovels and planks will usually do the trick, especially if you create a slope on one side to move the tree onto. If you find that you've gotten into something bigger than you can handle easily, you'll have to dig out an inclined plane, slide a platform down the plane and under the ball, and pull it out this way. When building an inclined plane, you might want to water it heavily so that the tree will slide up it on a bed of mud.

Once you get the burlap around the ball, you can temporarily fasten it in place with nails. Then wind some sort of cord around the ball and tie it tight. If you are inept at knot tying, use several smaller lengths of rope so that if one section happens to slip loose the whole thing won't unravel.

Instead of burlap, it is also very common to build a box for the roots out of planks and plywood. If you do so, make certain that the corners of the box will hold together under the tugging and straining necessary to get the box out of the hole. I usually use corner braces. Also, if the plywood is thinner than three-quarter inch, reinforce it wherever you see it beginning to bulge out of shape.

The advantage of wooden boxes is that they hold the roots and soil together much more safely than burlap—especially for larger trees. The disadvantage is that boxes are generally much heavier than balls, and to get one out of its hole you will almost definitely have to build an inclined plane and perhaps use a winch.

Moving a big tree

If you have to, you can move a tree as tall as twelve feet with a trunk diameter of four inches or more.

You'll need plenty of equipment—ropes, winches, flat-bed trucks, pulleys, chains, etc. A back hoe is a real blessing. If you have enough equipment, moving a big tree can be an elegant piece of engineering. If you don't, it can be a frustrating ordeal.

Because of all the equipment you'll need, instructions for big-tree moving are out of the range of this particular book. If you want to try it anyway, hunt up a copy of *Transplanting Trees and Other Woody Plants*, mentioned at the end of this chapter. It has lots of diagrams and valuable information.

Bare rooting

Up to now I've used a curious fiction that how-to books often toy with—namely, that everything will go smoothly. Now, time out for reality. You gently insert the shovels and planks underneath the root ball, you lift it tenderly to slip the burlap underneath, and the root ball falls apart. Or perhaps the burlap splits or the solid, reinforced box you made shatters under the strain of pulling and tugging. Instead of a neat, compact ball, you are faced with a tangle of naked roots screaming for attention.

Whatever you do, don't scream back. Quickly wrap the roots in damp burlap to keep them moist. Wrap them separately, one piece of burlap for each major root. If you try to pull all the roots together and stuff them into one piece of burlap, you'll injure them.

Actually, it is quite possible to transplant a tree without any soil ball at all. In fact, many—maybe even most—nursery people do not even bother with heavy soil balls if they are moving a deciduous tree while it is dormant. They just dig the tree out of the ground, knocking the soil off the roots and wrapping each root in burlap as they progress. Instead of a root ball they end up with something that looks like an octopus in bandages, but the tree usually survives.

If you do transplant a tree bare rooted, either by necessity or choice, remember not to let the roots dry out even for one minute, and don't forget your vitamins—vitamin B-1 to be precise. Also, a large bare-rooted tree might be unsteady, so you may have to stake it for a year or two.

Transporting the tree

When you move a tree, make sure it is secured so that it doesn't become damaged or destroyed by knocking around in the back of a truck. It might be wise to tie a lasso around the branches and bring them closer to the trunk.

Also, don't do what I once did—speed proudly along the highway with a load of uncovered trees in an open pickup truck. They all got windburned on the side facing the wind.

And remember to keep the ball moist if you're driving a long way.

Planting

Follow the instructions for planting container-grown trees in the previous section, keeping in mind the following suggestions.

Keep the tree out of the ground for as short a time as you can manage. If you're handling a big tree, it would be wise to dig the hole first, then dig up the tree. Try to plant the tree in an environment, altitude, and exposure similar to that from which it came.

It's also important, I feel, to orient the tree properly. Make sure the side of the tree that was originally facing north is facing north again. Otherwise, branches, leaves, and bark that developed in the shade will suddenly be exposed to the sun at a time when the tree can least handle such changes. If you have trouble telling east from west, bring along a compass and tag the tree before you pull it out of the ground.

If the ball is wrapped in burlap, you can loosen the burlap and leave it on. It will deteriorate very fast. Canvas and wood won't, however, so they should come off. Simply reverse the procedure by which you got them on.

Pruning

When you transplant a wild tree, you have got to prune. The foliage must be reduced by at least one-third to help compensate for the loss of roots. Follow the instructions on pages 149-152, remembering especially to *head* the tree. That is, as you prune make the tree more compact rather than sparser. Prune as drastically as you dare, but remember, whatever you do, don't prune the *leader*. (The leader is the topmost center spire of certain trees.)

Guying, staking, and aftercare

Again, follow the instructions in the section about container-grown trees.

One good thing to do, especially for evergreens, is to wash off the leaves periodically (but not on hot, sunny days). The leaves will absorb some of the moisture, and this helps reduce transpiration.

Transplant shock for wildlings can be severe, and their survival rate is lower than for nursery-grown trees. But don't let this scare you off. If you have planted them well, if you prune them back enough, if you care for them devotedly, most of the trees you transplant will pull through very well.

Reading

Most garden books have helpful sections on tree planting. Especially valuable is *Tree Maintenance* by P. P. Pirone, referred to on page 73. Also, for bare-root seedlings and general forest planting, check with your state division of forestry. They often put out very specific guides to the trees and conditions of your area.

Transplanting Trees and Other Woody Plants, by A. Robert Thompson. Tree Preservation Bulletin No. 1. Washington, D.C.: U.S. Department of the Interior, 1940. Revised in 1954.

This is another of the CCC bulletins that was exceptionally well done, with lots of basic and practical information. It has many sketches, many knowledgeable hints, and a generous section on how to move big trees. You can still get it by sending thirty-five cents to the Superintendent of Documents, U.S. Printing Office, Washington, D.C. 20401. It will answer most of your questions, except the big one: "Why isn't the government publishing stuff like this today?"

CHAPTER TEN
PONDS AND WATERING HOLES

PONDS AND WATERING HOLES. I've made several small ponds. The one I'm least proud of operated on a float-valve system and looked hauntingly like the tank of a toilet.

But, come to think of it, all the ponds I made were in one way or another artificial. Ponds are not a natural feature of the Oakland Hills, and I've been asked whether building them isn't a "development"—the sort of thing I'm usually opposed to. My excuse, in case you're interested, is this: Since people have been overbuilding, overfarming, and generally misusing the soil, they have severely lowered the water table. Streams which once flowed year 'round now dry up in the summer. By making artificial watering holes and ponds I am merely helping to restore the water conditions to what they were before the arrival of destructive technology.

So much for the excuse. The truth is I enjoy ponds the way some people seem to enjoy instant cake mixes. You buy the mix in a dull, squarish box, empty out an unpromising powder, add water, and as if by magic you end up with a cake.

That is sort of what it's like building a pond. Begin with some dry land, add water, and stand back! You'll soon get dragonflies, cattails, reeds, rushes, sedges, red-winged blackbirds, frogs, newts, quail, doves, and other assorted wildlife. Damselflies, as pretty as their name, stake out territories. Striders, boatsmen, and whirligig beetles appear from nowhere.

Adding water to dry land is the best piece of magic I know. I hope you'll try it soon.

Basically, the way you go about making a small pond is to dig a hole in the ground, seal the hole so that it won't leak, and then fill it with water. This is not as easy as it sounds, since water is a most rebellious substance. If you turn your back on a pile of rocks, you can be pretty sure the rocks won't run off. In fact, rocks will sit dutifully in one place until the next geological age. Not so with water! Water will run downhill, flow over obstacles, flow under obstacles, push things out of its way, sink into the ground, or, as a last resort, it will simply evaporate. Water seems to have a headstrong mind of its own. No wonder kids enjoy it so much.

I found no other project (except chopping down trees) that would involve a group of kids as completely as building a pond or a watering hole. While there is a lot of hard work to be done, there is also the chance to get muddy, dirty, and wet while having a cover story for Mother: "We were helping the man build a wildlife pond." Nothing ends the day as merrily as a rowdy, no-holds-barred mud and water fight. In fact, one problem I've had with this project is that water fights would often end the productive phase of the day long before I wanted it to be over.

Yet I not only loved to see the kids get wet, I encouraged it. In fact, I encouraged them to get acquainted with water on all its levels. To me, water is the most amazing stuff in the world. Try to see it through fresh eyes sometime. Take a glass of water in your hand and pretend it's something brand new—a new element brought back by astronauts from the moon, perhaps. You are a scientist, and you have to describe it for the first time to an eager world. Put your finger in it and describe how it feels to someone who has never felt water. Withdraw your finger and describe how the water closes up over the finger hole and instantly forms a placid surface. Pour it from one container to another and describe the sound it makes. Try to explain the riddle of how it can be both transparent and visible at the same time—how it distorts and reflects, yet how at the same time you can see through it. Watch it drip, spray, flow, turn silvery, cohere, adhere, freeze, boil, and do a thousand amazing tricks. Spend ten minutes playing around with water, and you'll find it to be the most peculiar stuff imaginable. If you happen to be with a group of receptive kids, perhaps you can communicate what a wonderful substance water really is. And if the mood is right, perhaps you can go on to explain the profound secret that our schools, jobs, governments, and all our institutions conspire to keep hidden from them, a secret we can learn from poets and artists: namely, that when seen freshly, all the common things around us are crazy, inexplicable, and totally miraculous.

Unlike tree planting, where you have to wait twenty years for a forest to grow, the satisfactions you get from building a pond are immediate. I remember working once with a group of kids to catch water from a spring and pipe it downhill to a sheltered place. It took us three days. When we finally hooked up the last section of pipe and the water came trickling through, a cheer went up so loud and joyful you'd have thought we had just won an Olympic event.

The next day we returned to the watering hole to see if it was filling up and holding water.

"How long do you think it will be before it will attract animals?" they asked me.

"A few months," I answered, as if I knew what I was talking about. I was wrong! I looked, and in the middle of the watering hole was a clear impression of a raccoon track. We stared at it for a long time. You'd have thought we had found the Hope Diamond in our watering hole. The track, of course, is long since gone. But it has left a permanent impression in my mind and the minds of the kids.

Water Sources

To build a pond, you'll need a steady source of water, a site capable of holding the water, and perhaps the plumbing to get the water from its source to the pond site. The problem is usually in finding and developing a steady source of water, so let's begin there.

Potholes

The handiest source of water is ground water that is close to the surface. All you have to do is dig until you reach it.

A marsh that remains wet for nine or ten months of the year is your best bet. But before digging into such a marsh, you must make certain that there are no rare creatures whose survival is favored by intermittent water. In our part of California, for example, there are several native frogs that burrow into the mud as the marshes dry out. Once these areas are converted to year-round watering holes, an introduced species of bullfrog moves in and takes over, pushing out the natives. In most areas, making a pothole will be a positive asset to your wildlife, but to make absolutely sure, check with your local state college or some other wildlife authority.

The best way to learn how to make a pothole is from alligators. As the marshes in the Everglades begin to dry out, alligators dig small ponds by thrashing wildly about. During the dry seasons, these alligator ponds support an unbelievable concentration of alligators, turtles, snakes, fish, and birds. They literally teem with life.

If your land doesn't have any alligators, you'll have to do the work yourself. Grab a shovel and dig down to the water level. Dig deep enough the first time so that you won't have to disturb the pond again, even when the water table sinks in the heat of the summer. As you dig out the pothole, follow the instructions in the section of the chapter entitled *Containers* (pages 196-201), especially the instructions in regard to sloping the banks and providing shade, wind shelter, and animal cover.

Another thing you can learn from the alligators, by the way, is to keep your pothole fairly small. If you were to build a big pond, the evaporation would be greatly increased. This could lower the water table for the surrounding area.

On the whole, you should consider your pothole a temporary pond—one that you may have to dig out every year or two. This adds up to some work, but I think it's worth it. A small pothole will keep your marsh alive and vigorous during the dry spells in late summer. It may be just what you need to turn an intermittent marsh into a real swamp.

Springs

Another natural source of water is a dripping spring, as long as it drips all year round—especially in dry times, which is when you really need the water.

A good place to look for springs or seepages is along the

banks of road cuts. If the dripping water is naturally collected somewhere below the spring, I wouldn't do anything
further. Nature has made you a perfect watering hole. If the
drippings disappear into the ground, however, you can
turn to the next section on containers to learn how to seal
the ground so that the water will build up into a little
watering hole.

Some springs release lots of water, but instead of dripping, the water spreads out over a mossy rock. One thing
you can do is to wedge a stick or two in strategic places to
lead the water away from the rock and drop it in a place
where you can better use it.

The ancients used to think that gods, spirits, and genies
lived in springs. Whether this is true or not, springs are
certainly temperamental creatures. Hurt a spring's feelings
and it will stop running. When this happens, you're left
feeling very helpless, and it is easy to believe that deep
within the earth a genie is slapping his knee and laughing
indecently at your plight.

To avoid insulting a spring, you should do everything
quietly and gently, moving as little earth as possible. Also
make certain that you do not create any back pressure on
the spring. Genies hate back pressure! As long as the water
is dripping down into a container, the spring will continue
to function. But if you should try to build up a container to
the level of the spring outlet, the back pressure will often
clog the pores through which the water flows, and the water
will seek other outlets.

Seeps

Sometimes instead of a flowing or a dripping spring you
will find a wet spot on a hillside. You may not see any water,
but the ground will be moist and there will be sedges, rushes,
or maybe even cattails. You know there is water, but how can

you make that water available to wildlife? Get a hand trowel, sit next to the seep, and begin near the bottom. Dig a long, narrow hole, like a tunnel, angling it upwards. Do it gently, easily. Every time you take out a scoop of earth, pause for a few moments to see if water will begin to collect and flow down your tunnel. Once the flow begins, stop working and go home for the day. The next day you can return. Has the flow increased? If so, you should stop digging. If the flow has decreased or stopped, however, you'll have to dig some more. Eventually you should get a nice flow, even from an amazingly short tunnel. Push some gravel gently into the hole to keep it from collapsing. Or, for a more permanent arrangement, insert a length of pipe with holes drilled along the bottom. You're now through. You've turned a seepage into a first-class spring.

Rainfall-catching devices

In certain areas of the country you might consider trapping the rainwater as it falls. The idea is based on water-catching systems in dry areas where rainwater flows off a roof into gutters, down a drainpipe, and into a barrel, where it's held for future use. Keeping this model in mind, you might be able to take advantage of natural run-off which you can funnel into a tank or cistern. Or you might make what is known as a "gallinaceous guzzler" to catch dew and condensation. Since I haven't had any experience here, I won't presume to give you advice. The Forest Service handbook mentioned on page 25 has what look like excellent diagrams and suggestions.

Public water supply

If you have a water line running through or near your property, you might consider tapping into it. Personally, I feel ambivalent about using public water supplies for a wildlife pond. On the one hand, it seems unnatural, it offends my sense of wild-land aesthetics, and I'm dubious about how chlorine and other added chemicals affect the balance of pond life. On the other hand, it's easy to get at, plentiful, dependable, and ever so tempting. I'll leave you to work out the pros and cons. I've used municipal water for a pond, and despite my doubts about the source, I was very happy with the result.

If you do decide to use the public water supply, you'll have to deal with the chlorine in it. Chlorine evaporates in about twenty-four hours, so that the day after you fill your pond there will be virtually no chlorine present. To minimize later damage, you should keep the pond level high by adding new water gradually and often. That way the incoming chlorinated water will never be more than a small percentage of the total standing water. If, instead, you let the pond level go way down and then turn on the tap full force, the sudden inflow of chlorine will wipe out a lot of the algae and microlife upon which a healthy pond environment depends.

Containers

Once you are sure of your source of water, you can begin developing a site for your pond.

Dig in or build up

There are two different ideas about how to make a pond. There are those who simply make holes in the ground, and there are those who build walls or dams. I've tried both ways, and unless I lose my sanity completely, I don't think I'll ever again build a pond on the dam principle. Whenever I've done it, I've spent dozens of boring days getting the walls properly compacted and graded, building elaborate spillways, and contending with leakages and cave-ins. I had to keep the walls well covered with sod while stopping the growth of trees whose roots might open up ways for the water to escape. Every time I saw a crayfish, a gopher, a mole, a badger, or any burrowing animal, instead of rejoicing, I'd fret. I even became suspicious of earthworms. An elevated wall that contains water is totally unnatural, and everything in nature will work day and night to destroy it: rain, wind, trees, frost, and animals. Build a dam or a wall and you'll be fighting your land, which is exactly the attitude you want to get away from. So take my advice: avoid berms, retaining walls, dams, and other above-ground structures. Instead dig yourself a humble hole. You'll be a lot happier.

Where to dig a hole

The best place to dig a hole is on level ground that holds water naturally. Clay soil is usually fairly watertight. To find out how well your ground holds water, dig a test hole, fill it with water, and watch what happens. If the soil is exceptionally dry, you may have to refill it two or three times. If after the second or third refill the water stays around for several hours, you're in good shape and can build a pond. As time goes on, the pores in such soil will probably seal themselves, and the site will be relatively impermeable.

If, however, the soil is well drained everywhere you look, don't give up. Instructions on how to stop leaks follow later in this chapter.

If you have a wide choice of locations, you might get fussy and look for a place with shade and shelter from the wind. Shade keeps the water cool, reduces evaporation, and discourages the rapid proliferation of algae that takes place in the full sun. Shelter from the wind is desirable since ruffled water evaporates much faster than calm water. If you cannot find a ready-made, shady, sheltered spot, do your best to create one by strategic planting of trees.

Digging a hole

What can I say about digging a hole? It's simply hard work. So get in there with a pick and shovel, get the job done, and promise yourself (and your helpers) a nice reward when you're through. Wheelbarrows are handy, since you'll want to move the loose soil far enough from the pond so that the first rains won't wash it back in. As you dig, slope the sides of the pond gently so that any small animals that fall in can scramble back out again.

How big? That depends, of course, on your flow of water. If you are dealing with a drip, drip, drip, a small "guzzler-type" watering hole of less than one square foot would be appropriate. If you have unlimited water, you can dig as deep and as wide as your muscles and will power will let you.

If you are planning to establish a pond environment with a few fish and some water plants, you should make certain that parts of the pond are at least two feet deep. This will help keep the pond at a fairly constant temperature and will give fish a cool place to escape to. Totally shallow water heats up during the day, gets cold at night, and freezes solid for a good part of the winter.

Erosion

Whenever you are dealing with water, you should think about possible erosion. Standing water won't cause any problems, but moving water definitely will. So study carefully the places where the water enters your pond and where it might overflow.

The water entering the pond can usually be taken care of

without much difficulty. Provide a rock for the water to fall over, and this will break the force.

The most serious erosion problems occur at the overflow point. Find the lowest point along the banks of your pond, either by eyeballing it (which can be misleading) or by using a line level.

If you expect overflow to be a rare event, simply make certain that the lowest point is well vegetated, preferably with a thick sod.

If you expect frequent overflow, you should make sure that whatever route the water takes is solidly protected. A bed of rocks (riprap) is very good. It will slow the water down and give it a chance to sink into the ground.

Whatever you do, don't let a gully get started at the pond's outlet. If you see one forming, rush (don't walk) to the chapter on erosion control (pages 77-105) and deal with the problem immediately. Not only will the gully cause a lot of damage to the area surrounding the pond, but it will eventually undermine your pond and drain it.

Leaks

If your pond begins to leak, or if you started with well-drained land that won't hold water very well, there are several things you can do:

Mucking. Very often you can stop a ground leak by mucking up the water. Simply stand in the middle of your pond with a pick, a mattock, or a hoe and make a big, muddy mess. An Irish setter, if you can borrow one, will do the job beautifully. As I discuss in the chapter on erosion control, dirty water clogs the pores in the ground and penetrates only one-tenth as fast as clean water. A couple of episodes of mucking are usually enough to clog up most leaks.

Compacting. This is hard work, but it is a natural way of

stopping leaks. Let the water drain out of the pond and plow up the bottom. Plow it as deep as you can—at least one foot. A rototiller is good if you can get one; otherwise, use mattocks and picks. Rake out all the rocks, roots, and other vegetation you find. Then compact the bottom.

The way this was done in "the good old days" was with livestock. A herd of cattle, oxen, or horses was driven back and forth until the pond bottom was as hard as pavement. If you can't borrow a herd of animals for the occasion, do a lot of stomping and pounding with the butt end of a four-by-four. As you can imagine, compacting is practical only for small areas.

Adding clay. The usual reason for leaks is sandy or rocky soil. You can usually correct this by adding clay. Mix the clay with the soil to as great a depth as possible and then compact it as well as you can. You can usually get ordinary clay locally, by digging it out of the ground.

A special kind of clay that is used for sealing ponds is bentonite. Bentonite is also used as a base for finger paints, and you can often find it sold in arts-and-crafts supply houses. It is a very fine, powdery clay with a microscopic structure that looks like an accordion. Add water, and each accordionlike particle expands many times its size. If you mix it in with the soil at the bottom of the pond, it will expand until it seals the pores. Bentonite is almost foolproof, but like other "foolproof" things, it has a serious drawback. It has a slimy, creamy texture—like finger paint. So if you use it, dig it in very deep and then dress the surface with dirt or rocks to keep all that slimy stuff underground.

Last resort. If you've tried everything and the pond still keeps leaking, I guess all that's left is modern technology. Concrete, fiberglass, and various plastics should work, but

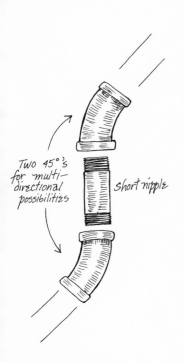

Two 45°'s for multi-directional possibilities

Short nipple

since I've never been that desperate, I don't have much to say about them.

If the water drips directly from the source into the hole, you can skip this section. Skip it with joy.

Plumbing

If you have to move water from one place to another, however, you'll need plumbing. Even if you don't know a street el from a union, don't worry. Plumbing a pond is a lot easier than plumbing a house. In fact, house plumbing has given the whole trade a terrible reputation. It usually involves crawling around on your belly in wet, smelly places, handling clumsy, oversized tools in cramped quarters, struggling with corroded connections of galvanized or even cast-iron pipe, and doing everything according to a complicated system of codes.

Plumbing a pond, on the other hand, is much easier. The only hard part is burying the pipeline, which amounts simply to ditch digging. The rest is easy if you follow these three hints:

· Use plastic pipe. Steer clear of galvanized pipe unless you have all the right dies, taps, wrenches, vises, reamers, and cutters. Plastic pipe is a little more expensive, but you don't need any special tools. In fact, plumbing with plastic pipe is only slightly more difficult than playing with Tinkertoys. You can cut the pipes with a hacksaw, and instead of threading you simply glue them together. If you bury the plastic pipe carefully so that the sun doesn't crack it, plastic pipe is said to be immortal.

· Leaks always happen at the joints. Before burying the pipe, mark the joints with stakes or a pile of stones. Thus if you do manage to make a botch of the job, you won't have to dig up the whole pipeline to find out where you goofed.

· Water flows downhill. Remember this, please. Meditate upon it if necessary. You'd be surprised how often people forget this simple fact when they are doing plumbing. If you are tapping into a high-pressure line, you can run your pipes any old way. But if you are dealing with gravity flow from a cistern or a spring, try to keep your pipes running *continuously* downhill. Otherwise you'll eventually create clogs, jams, and troubles I wouldn't wish on anyone.

Bearing these three hints in mind, you are ready to do your own plumbing. Even if you've never done any plumbing at all, I think you can do a perfectly fine job on everything except tapping into a major water line, which should be done by someone with experience and tools.

Arrivals and Transplants

For a week or so after you've built your pond, visit it daily. It's foolish to tell you this, frankly, because for the week or so after you've built your pond, virtually nothing can keep you away. But you should be on hand to make sure that water is flowing into the pond, to catch small leaks before they get bigger, and to appreciate the marvelous things that water will do.

Within a day or two after you turn on the valve to let the water flow, your pond will have life. Insects like boatsmen, striders, and dragonflies come immediately. A few months later there will be reeds, rushes, and sedges. Within a year you can expect cattails in the pond and the seedlings of water-loving trees like willows and alders along its borders.

Cover

No matter how big or small your pond is, it needs cover to protect the wildlife that will use it. Quail, raccoons, and other small animals will appreciate a nearby hedgerow or brush pile to protect them from predators. Try to provide at least two escape routes.

Fish

It might be a good idea to add a small, hardy native fish to your pond to help eat the mosquito larvae and eggs. In California we have a fish called a mosquito fish, and everyplace else seems to have a fish called a mosquito fish too. They may all be different species of fish for all I know, but they all do the job. Unfortunately, they often work overtime, eating the eggs and larvae of frogs, toads, turtles, and other interesting animals your pond might otherwise support. I leave you to work out the mosquito fish dilemma as best you can.

If your area has a small algae-eating minnow (you can find out from your state university), this might make a good addition to your pond.

For ponds over, say, 150 square feet, you can try out a predator fish to keep the minnows or mosquito fish under control. A bluegill is probably best. I would definitely avoid exotic fish, *especially goldfish*, which tend to take over.

Trees

If the pond is at all sizable, the area around it will be moist enough to support some valuable trees. Your wildlife will especially appreciate any of the swamp oaks—water oak, willow oak, nuttall oak, cherry-bark oak, swamp red oak, and pin oak, all of which have nutritious and plentiful acorns.

Easy does it

What about turtles, frogs, crayfish, freshwater clams, pond lilies, and other spectacular forms of pond life? I urge you to go easy here. Be especially aware of "aquarium mania," a disease common among aquarium buffs. They no sooner get a two-quart fishbowl than they begin stocking it with every imaginable fish, plant, bubbling device, crustacean, and amphibian. The results of this disease are fatal—not to the aquarium buff, but to the creatures that get thrown willy-nilly into the fishbowl.

In short, if you go in for heavy stocking of your pond, you will have to cope with many failures and be responsible for the death of many small creatures. So go lightly, add little, and let the water relate to your land. Visit your finished pond as you might visit your grown child: not as its creator but as its guest and admirer, willing to help out in an emergency but otherwise careful not to interfere. Appreciate what is happening, keep your senses alive, and you'll be surprised and delighted with the vigorous life that will appear spontaneously around your pond.

Reading

Except for the U.S. Forest Service *Wildlife Habitat Improvement Handbook* (mentioned on page 25), with its section on rain-catching contraptions, I haven't found any really useful books on building small ponds and watering holes.

## CHAPTER ELEVEN

HAPPY TRAILS TO YOU

🌿 HAPPY TRAILS TO YOU. Making a trail might go against your idea of what unspoiled land should be. In a sense you'll be working against nature. No matter how proud you may be of your trail, nature will treat it contemptuously. It will do everything possible to wash it away, cover it with rocks and branches, and vegetate it into obscurity.

Yet if your land has thick brush or undergrowth, you will, of course, need a trail just to get around. But even on relatively open land there's a very good reason to make a trail. In fact, if you hike frequently over your land, you're going to make a trail, whether you like it or not. You'll make a trail just as surely as a deer makes a trail, a cow makes a trail, even a mouse makes a trail. Your body will break through brush. Your big fat boots with their Vibram soles will disturb and compress the soil. Erosion will follow in

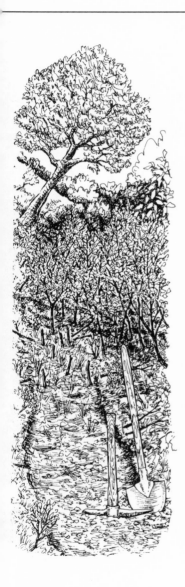

your footsteps. Think about it. As long as you are destined to make a trail one way or another, you might consider making one properly and deliberately—a trail that will be pleasant to hike along and will cause minimal damage from erosion and trampled vegetation.

Another good reason for making a trail is that it's exciting—and sometimes even fun. Especially with kids, trail building seems to connect with the rich fantasy life of being a pioneer and explorer. It doesn't matter how small the woods happen to be. Land without a trail is "the impenetrable jungle."

"Are we the first people ever to set foot here?" kids would ask as I'd lead them into the forest to help me build a trail.

"It could be," I'd answer, and for the rest of the day the kids would be alert. It's almost as if they expected to stumble upon an Indian burial ground, pirate's gold, a mountain lion's den, the home of Tarzan and Jane, or perhaps even a dinosaur left over from a previous age.

Of course, no one ever found a dinosaur, and sometimes the fantasy would come crashing down with the discovery of a not-so-ancient beer can. But that's not really very important. As long as the kids are alert, looking, and wondering— as long as they *feel* that they are in a brand new place— they'll turn up plenty of things.

I've had joyful times working with kids, but trail making, more than most other projects, points up one of the greatest drawbacks—namely, the quality of work you can expect. I have lots of craftsmanly ideas about what the perfect trail should look like. It should look accidental rather than "built." It should be simple yet varied, unobtrusive yet clearly visible. I want all the scars hidden and the trees and shrubs along the sides pruned with consummate sensitivity.

These fantasies about the ideal trail are as likely to be

fulfilled as a kid's fantasies about finding a dinosaur. Kids' work is bound to be sloppy and half done. That is the nature of kids. So we have a tacit agreement. The kids tolerate my artsy ideas and I tolerate their sloppiness. Nature, needless to say, tolerates everyone and sets about in good time to repair and obscure whatever aesthetic mistakes any of us make.

Planning the work

There are some parts of trail making that are fun and other parts that involve hard work. I've always had a marvelous time hacking my way through the brush, following the route I had previously laid out. If there were no other considerations, I'd happily hack my way right to the end of the trail. At the end of the day I'd feel like a member of the Explorers' Club who had reached his goal. But on the following days I'd feel more like a member of a chain gang. After you've hacked through the brush, what is left is the hard work of grading, digging, and struggling with the drainage problems. My advice is to move slowly. After you've staked out the route, do one section at a time as completely as possible. That way every day you will have a taste of the hard work as well as a taste of the trailblazer's exhilaration.

Planning the trail

Before you plunge into the woods with a machete in your hand and a crazy gleam in your eye, let's think about what you want in a trail.

Firebreak. You might want your trail to double as a firebreak or a place where crews can maintain a fire line. In some places, especially California, this is an important consideration. There are all sorts of esoteric things you must take into account in building a firebreak: prevailing winds, inflammability of different types of vegetation, conditions of the crown, availability of water, accessibility to trucks, visibility from the air, and more. Your local fire department can give you the lowdown. Listen to them eagerly, but I hope you'll keep this perspective in mind: you are building a trail first, a fire line second. In other words, do not make the perfect fire line (which is usually ugly) and hope to use it as a trail. It will make a poor trail. Instead, concentrate on making a good trail, adapting it wherever possible to its secondary function as a firebreak or potential fire line.

Loop. Consider making a loop trail. This won't always be possible or necessary, and it will involve extra work, but it's a lot more exciting to return along a different route from the one you arrived on.

Bypass fragile places. If you are expecting heavy public use of a trail, do not build it right through especially beautiful and fragile areas. Bypass them and create spur trails to serve them. This is sort of sneaky, I know. And it will add footage to your trail building. But it's the best way I know of protecting fragile areas while still making them accessible.

Easy or hard? If the trail is primarily for your own private use, it doesn't matter very much whether it's easy or hard. Your body will soon accustom itself to the steepness and ruggedness of any trail if you hike it often, and you'll scarcely notice the difference. If the trail is open to the public, however, I'd make it as easy as possible. I know that some backpackers intentionally seek out the toughest trails and race along them, covering as much distance as possible. For them hiking is a sort of athletic event. There is nothing wrong with this, and in fact it can be quite exhilarating. But not everyone wants to run an obstacle course. For most people a tough trail gets in the way of their enjoyment. In

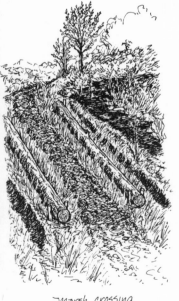

Marsh crossing

thinking about where to put a public trail, I would stick to places where you can maintain an easy grade.

Surveying

Your first real work is to lay out the route for your trail. You know where the trail begins, you know where it ends, and you are now going to figure out the best way of connecting the beginning with the end.

Your basic criteria will be to: keep the trail varied, winding, and interesting; maintain a fairly steady grade; avoid traversing steep slopes; stay away from loose duff and rock rubble; and skirt marshes and wet spots.

Naturally, you won't be able to attain all these goals. If you *must* traverse a steep slope, go through a marsh, or cross a talus bed, I'll show you how to do it later in this chapter. But do your best to avoid these difficult situations. An extra day or two spent surveying for an easy trail route may save you a week of hard work once the trail building starts.

Depending on how much work you're willing to do, you can put a trail almost anywhere. But there is one never-to-be-broken rule you must follow: NEVER HEAD A TRAIL STRAIGHT UP A HILL! Not only is it tiring, but if a person can hike straight up, water can wash straight down, which will lead to a chronic and nasty erosion problem.

The most popular method of laying out a trail is the "wandering-cow method." That is how the streets of Boston were supposedly designed. The city founders let their cows wander over the land and then built the streets to follow the cow paths. The result is gentle, winding, organic streets full of interest and surprise.

If you don't have a cow of your own, or if your cow refuses to wander, you will have to take over the job yourself. It's not

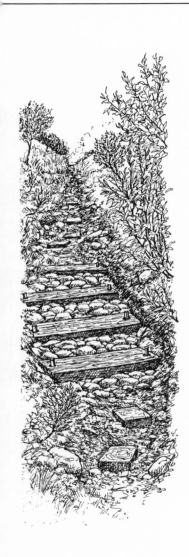

at all a bad job. All you have to do is think like a cow, feel like a cow, amble like a cow. Wander contentedly and unhurriedly from the beginning of the trail to the end. Anytime you have to make a decision, choose the course of least resistance. If it seems as if you had a fairly nice walk with no impossible obstacles, *voilà*, you have just mapped out a perfect trail.

The wandering-cow method will work in almost all cases. But let's say you're building a trail through thick chaparral or dense forest. You are forever over your head in nasty bushes, you can't see more than fifty feet in any direction, and you're lost from the minute you enter the forest. No cow in her right mind is going to wander through stuff like this. At least not contentedly.

One way of laying out a trail through dense forest or brush is to find a friend who will stand at the end of the trail and yell his fool head off while you walk steadily toward his voice.

Or sometimes you can go to the end of the trail and run a flag up the tallest tree to serve as a guide. Or you can float a batch of helium balloons—if you can find a convenient source of helium.

However you do it, surveying a trail through brush or dense understory can be physically hard work. Be sure to take along gloves, a long-sleeved shirt, and tough dungarees. Also bring a canteen and your favorite brush-cutting tool. If you've never used a machete, I suggest you try one. It takes a while to learn how to take care of it, keep it sharp, and use it effectively. (Try cutting a branch from below rather than hacking down at it from above.) But once you learn how to use it, you'll find a machete to be a very amenable tool. You'll eventually be using it as gracefully and unconsciously as you now use a spoon or a pencil.

In surveying a trail, of course, you'll need something to mark the trail with. Use ribbons, plastic ribbons if possible, which you can tie to trees and bushes along the way. You might want to pick up two or more different colors. Use one color to mark the various experimental passes you make and the other color to mark out the final route you have chosen.

Switchbacks

Before going any further, let me tell you what I think about switchbacks. As I've already said, you *never* head a trail straight up a hill. But let's say you're at the bottom of a hill; how do you get to the top? The traditional way of doing it is with a system of zigzags called switchbacks.

In theory, switchbacks are perfectly fine. They look very fancy and professional. The only problem with them is that they don't work. Ever! No sooner do you build a switchback than people begin cutting across it, creating slides and gullies straight down your hill. To counter this you can, I suppose, put up signs that say, "Keep on the Trail." Or you can put up educational signs that explain what terrible damage cutting across the trail does. The purpose of these signs is to change human behavior. Lots of luck! I personally think you'd be better off accepting human behavior and changing the design of your trail to eliminate switchbacks—or at least reduce their number.

One way to minimize switchbacks is to make the zigzags much longer. Instead of making six short zigzags, try doing it with only two or three more leisurely ones.

Another way to eliminate switchbacks is to make the trail extremely steep. Not straight up and down the hill, but still at an outrageous angle. You can even build steps. This will make for uncomfortably steep hiking, but over short dis-

outsloping

insloping

outsloping with
water bars

tances it may be better than switchbacks that are doomed
to fail.

Clearing

I won't insult you by giving you the "standards" for how
wide, how steep, how high, how many rest stops, etc. Such
things depend on your taste and the usage you expect from
your trail. My own preference is to make the trail narrow
through open forests and meadows. In thick undergrowth
or chaparral, however, I widen the trail considerably—
partly to give a view, partly to give grasses and wildflowers a
chance to spring up along the sides of the trail, but mostly to
avoid the hassles of continually maintaining a narrow trail
against the ambitions of invading brush.

Most of the actual work of clearing a trail is fairly easy.
You move along rapidly. Use lopping shears and a saw to
clear away the vegetation, keeping in mind the instructions
for pruning. You might also remember that growth is stimu-
lated when the tip of a branch is pointed up, and that growth
tends to be suppressed when the branch is pointed down.
Consequently, when trimming the shrubs along the trail's
edge, I often leave more down-facing branches than I otherwise might.

Grading and sloping

After you've got the vegetation cleared away, use shovels
and mattocks to clear the ground, remove rocks, and smooth
the tread. As you smooth, think continually about drainage.
Your trail will eventually get compacted with use, and the
water, instead of being absorbed, will run off. If it runs off in
many places, there won't be much damage. The problem is
that sometimes the water gets channelized and washes down
the trail to create a trough. In time the stream of water breaks

through the trail's edge, causing all sorts of damage to the trail and to the land below.

There are many things you might do to minimize erosion damage while you are building the trail. For example:

Outsloping. By sloping the trail *gently* away from the hillside, water will be drawn off the trail continually. It will never collect, and you will solve most drainage problems before they begin.

Insloping. If the edge of the trail is fragile, or the slope very steep, you might have to slope the trail in toward a hillside. Water will now gather and flow along the inner bank. This water must be gotten rid of frequently; otherwise, it will become a raging torrent. The best ways of getting rid of it are with a wide, rock-filled depression that cuts across the trail (a swale), or by leading it away wherever the trail makes a bend.

Thank-you-ma'ams. With such a beautiful name, you'd expect a thank-you-ma'am to be at least a hybrid rose. Sorry, but it's nothing more than a trench dug diagonally across the trail. It works well for an emergency, but it tends to fill in after a season or two.

Water bars. A water bar is a log buried in the trail, usually diagonally, that diverts the water from the center of the trail to the edge.

Special problems

Once you've cleared the tread and attended to the drainage, that's all there is to it—90 per cent of the time. Unless, of course, you run into special problems like crossing marshes, crossing talus slopes, traversing very steep slopes, or having to build steps. Throughout this chapter there are drawings that show you how to handle these situations. Handle them in a deliberate, craftsmanlike manner—and if you can

possibly help it, handle them as infrequently as you can. In other words, try to route the trail away from problem areas.

Clean up

It's been said that great artists hide their art. Well, great trail builders hide—no, not their trails, definitely not their trails—but their trail building.

· Loose earth can be thrown downhill, and the first rains will wash it away. Just don't throw it in piles, but spread it out.
· The slash can be pulled off the trail and piled into brush piles for animals (see pages 9–12).
· Some of the prunings can be collected and used as cuttings to make new plants (see pages 134-142).
· Small trees and shrubs in the middle of the trail can be dug up and transplanted (see pages 176-186).
· Disturbed soil should be treated for erosion (see pages 89-93).
· And bare ground should be replanted with grass and wildflower seeds.

I hate to sound like a nag, but for goodness' sake, clean up after yourself!

Afterwards

Your trail is now ready for use. You wait and watch the weather. No, you are not waiting for a perfect, clear, sunny day when you can don your *lederhosen*, put a sprig of edelweiss in your hat, and walk out whistling a happy tune. Quite the opposite. You are waiting for a cold, wretched rainstorm. When it happens, put on your rain gear, grab a shovel, and hike along the trail. Keep your nose to the ground. What is the water doing? Is it flowing off the trail in

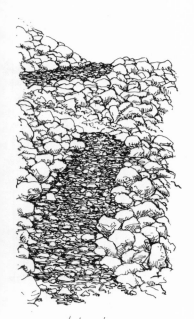

talus slope: trail built out, not cut into slope

many places? Fine! You may now lift your nose and enjoy the view. If it is channelizing, however, you'll have to break up the channels right away. You can do it temporarily with a few thank-you-ma'ams, but be sure to return later to build something more permanent—like a water bar or a decent outslope.

The trail is now built. Of course, every year during the spring and summer you'll have to do some light clearing. You will be especially alert for damage after long periods of rain. But by and large your work is finished. You have built the trail, and it is now time to let the trail help build you. Go hiking often and bring friends. You're undoubtedly proud of your craftsmanship. You want to show your friends all the tricks you've learned and all the difficulties you've overcome. You point out a particularly elegant example of outsloping. But your friends aren't looking. They really don't care. Instead they are gawking at the trees, gawking at the flowers, gawking at the birds. And that's exactly as it should be. Congratulations! Your trail is a success!

Reading

Believe it or not, I haven't found many good books about making trails. For that matter, I haven't found many bad books either. With the exception of the two fine books listed below, there doesn't seem to have been anything written on the subject.

AMC Field Guide to Trail Building and Maintenance, by Robert D. Proudman. Boston: Appalachian Mountain Club, 1977.

The author was the Appalachian Mountain Club's trail

supervisor, and this book is based on considerable research and first-hand experience. It covers everything from designing trails, laying them out, building them, and maintaining them to management problems such as easements, insurance, and other legal considerations. Well illustrated with photos and drawings, this book is detailed, helpful, and has a fine (yet not finicky) sense of the craft of trail building. A first-rate book.

Trail Planning and Layout, by Byron L. Ashbaugh and Raymond J. Kordish. Information Education Bulletin No. 4. New York: National Audubon Society, revised edition, 1971.

This book covers mostly self-guiding nature trails, but it has some ideas and techniques you can use for other trail building as well. Copies may be ordered from the National Audubon Society, Nature Center Planning Division, 950 Third Avenue, New York, N.Y. 10022. The price is $3.00.

## CHAPTER TWELVE

WORKING WITH KIDS

WORKING WITH KIDS. This chapter is for teachers, youth leaders, and those of you who would like to get a volunteer conservation program going. Perhaps you'd like to collect a group of kids, walk out with them to where the beautiful and miraculous are spread out before you like a feast, and do some honest, helpful work. Here is an account of how I got the conservation program at Redwood Park together, the mistakes that I made, and how I think it might be done better.

Who are your volunteers? If you're beginning a conservation program from scratch, a lot of them are going to be Boy Scouts. In fact, Boy Scouts are actively looking for conservation projects, and once they hear you have a creative and successful program going, your phone won't stop ringing.

Before going on to other volunteers, let me get the Boy Scouts off my chest. A lot of conservationists have dealt with Boy Scouts and been profoundly disappointed. A troop calls in asking for a project, arrives at the proper time and in the proper uniform, does a halfhearted piece of work, and disappears. The kids get merit badges, a few trees get put into the ground, a few bags of litter get picked, but the whole experience lacks a sense of excitement or significance.

The program at Redwood Park was different, and the difference lay in this: I never took the Boy Scouts at their word. They came looking for merit badges, and indeed I made certain that they got merit badges. But I also made certain that they got something else—namely, as rich and human an experience as we could squeeze out of the situation at hand.

By and large, I had the most fun with school kids, especially high school students from loosely structured schools. You'll have to go looking for them and deal with school administrators, but in the San Francisco Bay Area this wasn't any problem. Many of the schools I worked with provided transportation to the park and gave the kids course credit in natural science or physical education for stomping around the woods.

In dealing with schools, be sure you get volunteers, not conscripts. Avoid whole classes that have come merely because the teacher told them to. Before I learned this lesson thoroughly, I often found myself facing thirty-six hostile teen-agers who had just slunk out of a school bus. In the immortal words of one teacher, I was expected to "put these damn kids to work and teach them something about the ecology." But no one ever told me how. Then one day, as I found myself looking into thirty-six teen-age smirks, I knew exactly what I wanted to do. I did what any other gentle, basically sane naturalist would have done in such a situation. With a loud and joyful "whoopee," I turned my back and ran away.

"C'mon," I yelled. "The ecology lecture is this way." And I took off like a madman—up slopes and down slopes, across meadows and through forests. Most of the kids followed me close behind, tripping, rolling, stumbling, shouting, and— best of all—laughing. We left the teachers far behind. We splashed through the stream and drank water from a fresh brook. We ate miner's lettuce underneath a big oak tree. We talked and joked, and when we got back to the bus I asked the kids, "Did you learn anything about the ecology?"

"Yeah," said one kid. "It's fun." Since that day, whenever I found myself with a group of conscripts, I did my best to have fun and left the productive work for another day.

Another place to look for volunteers is among 4-H Clubs, Girl Scouts, Brownies, Cub Scouts, YMCAs, and fraternal organizations like DeMolay.

In addition to volunteer labor, I had terrific success in getting volunteer expertise. The Soil Conservation District and my local agricultural extension agent proved invaluable. I was also lucky in that several universities and colleges are within an hour's drive of Redwood Park. By knocking at doors I got the foremost experts in the country to advise me on wildlife problems, watershed management, erosion-control engineering, meadow-land ecology, and so on.

When I first came to Redwood Park there was already a conservation program which I stepped into. One of my first acts was to beef it up with a lot of recruiting. I attended Boy Scout meetings and spoke to school administrators and other youth leaders. Throughout these speeches I kept emphasizing what I felt was the most important thing about the program: it was not designed to get free labor out of kids but to give them an educational experience.

There's something important I'd like to add about the spirit of recruiting. It has to be honest. The temptation to exaggerate is enormous. I was offering an interesting, for many kids an enjoyable, day in the woods. Sometimes, though, instead of "interesting," I found myself substituting "fascinating." For "enjoyable" I would talk about "ecstatic." Instead of describing how we planted trees or collected seeds, I found myself muttering nonsense about Saving the Ecology. Why I did it, I don't know. Afterwards, I would feel just terrible, like an encyclopedia salesman, perhaps. I've worked with groups that were promised ecstasy, enlightenment, and The Salvation of Mother Earth. We had a rather disappointing time. On the other hand, groups who were told frankly, "We'll walk around a bit, look at how plants grow and how water flows, do a couple of hours' work, get to know each other, and maybe we'll really hit it off"—these groups tended to enjoy themselves much more. The moral is obvious: recruit, but recruit honestly. To the extent that we represent the beginnings of a new consciousness, unless we're honest we've lost it all, right at the start.

Once you get your volunteers lined up, you have to figure out the best project for them. Throughout the book I've described many of my favorite projects and the sorts of kids who seem to enjoy them best. But let me repeat something I've said before: DO NOT MAKE THE PROJECTS TOO DIF-FICULT. A project cannot be too hard for them, either physically or conceptually. When I first took the conservation job at Redwood Park, I used to talk a lot about native California grasses. These were perennial bunch grasses which, under the pressures of grazing, gave way to the

European annuals that now dominate the grasslands. I'd
explain how the annuals have failed to hold the land against
invading brush, especially when fire was also controlled. I'd
then discuss the ecology of chaparral and the limitations of
coyote brush, the influence of gopher erosion, the adjust-
ment of wildlife, and the theory of fire-climax ecology.
Then I'd explain my scheme for restoring the native perennial grasses, and off we'd march, me and a group of open-
mouthed kids who didn't have the vaguest idea what I was
talking about, and for whom this conservation project, like
the rest of their lives, was a profoundly muddled piece of
adult mystification that demanded bodily discomfort.

In short, I had a lot of fairly sophisticated land-manage-
ment ideas and some ambitious projects in mind that I was
never able to do because they were beyond the comprehen-
sion of most of my volunteers. For most kids, grass is grass,
and that's all there is to it.

I've also learned to avoid projects that are physically too
difficult, like pick-and-shovel work. There's no way in the
world you can convince a group of kids that digging a
trench is fun, educational, or rewarding.

When it comes to difficulty, by the way, don't trust the
kids' estimates of what they can handle. I found that many
of them have rather grandiose ideas, and they'd come to me
with huge, earth-moving projects. They seemed almost
relieved when I would reduce their schemes to more manageable proportions. I found it best to be firm at the beginning and then give the group a free hand later on.

Sometimes hard physical work is unavoidable, like certain
erosion-control projects, or burying pipeline to a pond. In
such cases I often adopted a policy of outright, up-front
bribery. I'd choose a group of the biggest kids I could find
and explain that this was a terrible project but that the work

simply had to get done. In return, I'd promise something
extra special for the group. I usually gave them free camp-
ing privileges and trucked them off to a swimming hole at
the end of the day.

Whether a project was easy or hard, one thing I did offer
was a humane experience. When kids came to the park, I
did not want it to be "just another day" in their lives. I feel
very sorry for the busloads of city kids who get dragged out
into the woods by their teachers, lectured at, told facts, and
quizzed the next day. I also feel sorry for the large numbers
of alert kids for whom "ecology" no longer means the relationship between butterflies and milkweed but has come to
mean poison, pollution, and catastrophe. My own approach
with kids was to stress basic sensual and physical experiences, to swing on rope swings and play in water, to spend as
much time as we could in immediate sensations that go
beyond interpretation.

I tried to give a lot to the kids who came to the park, and
the main thing I had to offer was myself. I know how
egotistical and platitudinous that sounds, but since it's true
I'll say it anyway. I remember when I was a kid how mysterious the adult world seemed, and how grateful and amazed I
was when any adult stepped out of his or her role as teacher,
mail carrier, uncle, or whatever and made authentic human
contact with me. That's what I tried to do. I avoided the
stereotyped nature walks, and instead I offered kids intimacy and a frank sharing of my own sensibilities. I did not
merely say, "This is a live oak." I tried to tell them something
about what I was seeing and feeling in the presence of that
live oak. Many kids would respond to this approach with an
openness about their own feelings. Often we'd make real
contact, become friends, and the kids would return again
and again. During my three years at Redwood Park I sus-

pect it was these bonds of friendship more than anything else that made the conservation program so alive and so much fun.

Reading

Nature Study for Conservation, by John W. Brainerd. New York: Macmillan, 1971.

This book was sponsored by the American Nature Study Society and has an introduction by Roger Tory Peterson. It covers things that kids might study, like mapping, seed experiments, a wildlife census, vegetative surveys, etc. On the surface it is a conventional, textbookish presentation about how to introduce kids to nature. But beyond that it is an excellent, sensitive book by a man who has obviously had lots of experience teaching kids—and who has learned from his experience.

Working with Nature, by John Brainerd. New York: Oxford University Press, 1973.

This second book by John Brainerd passes from merely studying nature to working with it—either with kids or by yourself. The book seems to suffer from being over-organized—both in the way the material is presented and in its general feeling toward land. Yet there are some very worthwhile suggestions on various aspects of land management, water management, vegetative management, and wildlife management. There's even a unique chapter entitled "Rock Management," with instructions for removing rock from outcroppings, breaking it up, moving boulders, and building stone fences.

Further Help

There are two potentially valuable sources of advice and expertise—your local agricultural extension agent (often listed as the County Farm and Home Adviser) and the Soil Conservation District (an agency of the U.S. Department of Agriculture). I say *potentially* because what you get from either agency depends largely on who's running it in your area.

Agricultural extension agents, like doctors, seem more and more to be getting away from home visits. But they are accessible by telephone. In fact, all day long their telephones are ringing with calls from people who want to know why their lettuce is wilting, why their roses are dropping off, why their lawns are being attacked by brown spots, and how to can peaches, build nesting boxes for wrens, or plant avocado pits. Agricultural extension agents are expected to be omniscient, and needless to say, they are not. Competent and helpful, if you're lucky, but definitely not omniscient. If you feel that your local agent is not answering your question very well, ask to be referred to someone else—a state forester, a fish and wildlife agent, or perhaps a local nursery operator.

The Soil Conservation District, on the other hand, is far more likely to send someone out to your land—as long as you can convince them that what you are doing is in some way related to conservation of soil. In the areas of pond building or erosion control, they may even supply you with free engineering advice.

A possible source of money for your projects is the Agricultural Stabilization and Conservation Agency, also part of the U.S. Department of Agriculture. This is the agency that for the last few decades has been paying farmers to keep land idle and keep food off the market, thus "stabilizing" the economy. Less well known are its conservation functions. For certain projects like reforestation, erosion control, and water conservation, there is a cost-sharing plan in which the government foots part of the bill. The catch is that if your project is approved, it must be executed according to strict standards: you may find out that the forest you had in mind is considerably different from what the agency had in mind. Nevertheless, if you have a large piece of land on which you are planning to do a lot of work, by all means get in touch with your local agent to see where you agree and what you can work out.

Index

Assembly Language for the PC,
Third Edition

*John Socha
and
Peter Norton*

Brady Publishing

New York   London   Toronto   Sydney   Tokyo   Singapore

About the Authors

John Socha is known in the PC industry for his writing and his software products. In the early days of the IBM PC, he wrote a column for the now defunct magazine *Softalk*, in which he published such programs as ScrnSave (the first screen saver) and Whereis (the first program to find files on hard disks). After the demise of *Softalk*, John concentrated on finishing his Ph.D. in Physics and writing The Norton Commander, which became a best-selling software product. He is also the coauthor of the best-selling book *PC-World DOS 5 Complete Handbook* and the author of *Learn Programming* and *Visual Basic 2 with John Socha*. John grew up in Wisconsin, earned a B.S. degree in Electrical Engineering from the University of Wisconsin, and an M.S. and a Ph.D. in Applied Physics from Cornell University. He now runs a software company called Socha Computing that develops Windows and Macintosh utility software in Kirkland, Washington.

Entrepreneurial software developer Peter Norton is the author of more than a dozen technical books. His first book, the best-selling classic *Inside the IBM PC*, was published in 1983, and was followed later in the year by another Brady book, his immensely popular guide to DOS.

Born in 1943 and raised in Seattle, Washington, Mr. Norton attended Reed College in Portland, Oregon, where he majored in physics and mathematics. He completed his education at the University of California at Berkeley where he received a Bachelor of Arts in mathematics. During the Vietnam War he served in the U.S. Army and taught emergency medicine to combat medics. He received a priestly teaching certificate after studying for five years in a Zen Buddhist monastery. Mr. Norton held a variety of positions in the computer industry before he created the Norton Utilities software program in 1982. He subsequently founded his own company, Peter Norton Computing, Inc., to develop and market his software. During the last decade, he has written many popular columns for computer magazines. In 1990 he sold his company to Symantec Corporation and devoted himself to the Norton Family Foundation, a fund that provides financial assistance to arts organizations in the Los Angeles area. He currently lives in Santa Monica, California, with his wife Eileen and their two young children Diana and Michael.

Credits

Publisher
Michael Violano

Managing Editor
Kelly D. Dobbs

Editor
Tracy Smith

Production Editors
Bettina Versaci
Tom Dillon

Developmental Editor
Perry King

Editorial Assistant
Lisa Rose

Book Designer
Michele Laseau

Cover Designer
HUB Graphics

Production Team
Katy Bodenmiller
Christine Cook
Lisa Daugherty
Carla Hall-Batton
Dennis Clay Hager
Howard Jones
John Kane
Loren Christopher Malloy
Sean Medlock
Tim Montgomery
Roger Morgan
Linda Quigley
Michelle Self
Susan Shepard
Angie Trzepacz

Contents

Introduction

Why Learn Assembly Language?

There are now more reasons than ever to learn assembly language. Even programmers who only use a high-level language like C/C++ or Pascal can benefit from learning assembly language.

When we wrote the first edition of this book, several years ago, programmers and companies were actually writing entire programs in assembly language. For example, Lotus 1-2-3 before release 2 was written entirely in assembly language. These days, very few programs are written entirely in assembly language. Even 1-2-3 has now been rewritten in C, and many programmers are moving on to C++, which is a very powerful descendent of the C programming language. So if people are not writing large programs in assembly language, then why would you want to learn and use assembly language?

Knowing assembly language will make you a better programmer, even if you never actually write any assembly-language subroutines or code for your programs. Many of the idiosyncrasies you will find in C/C++ or Pascal programs have their roots in the microprocessor and its design. When you learn assembly language, you are really learning about the architecture of your computer. This insight should make many of the artifacts of computer languages clear to you. For example, you will see why an integer has a value range of −32,768 to 32,767, and you will learn all about bytes, words, and segments.

Assembly language programs are at the heart of any PC compatible computer. In relation to all other programming languages, assembly language is the lowest common denominator. It takes you closer to the machine than the higher-level languages do, so learning assembly language also means learning to understand the 80x86 microprocessor inside your computer.

This knowledge about the microprocessor is also very useful in the world of Microsoft Windows, as you will see in Chapter 33, which discusses protected-mode and Windows programming. You will learn about some features of Windows programming that you probably won't find in any other book. This is because there are programming techniques that you can do and learn about in assembly language that you would not normally learn about in a high-level language.

At some time or other most programmers write or modify some assembly language code. This is even true for Microsoft Windows programs. The most common reason to use assembly language is for speed. Computers, modern C/C++ and Pascal compilers are very fast; compiled code runs very quickly. But there are times when even compiled C/C++ or Pascal code won't be fast enough. Very often in these cases you can write a small amount of assembly-language code to perform the work in the inner loop.

Compilers have also improved significantly since we wrote the first edition of this book. Years ago you *had* to use an assembler, such as Microsoft's Macro Assembler, to add assembly-language code to your programs. But almost all compilers these days support *in-line assembly*, which allows you to add a few lines of assembly-language code directly to your program, between lines of C/C++ or Pascal code. This makes it much easier to use small amounts of assembly language in your programs. You will learn how to use in-line assembly in Chapter 31.

There are also other cases which require programmers to write larger amounts of code in assembly language. If you are writing a device driver for DOS or Windows, or almost any other operating system (except for Windows NT), you will probably have to write the device driver in assembly language. For example, Windows has a very powerful mechanism called a Virtual Device Driver (also known as a VxD) that allows you to alter the way devices work inside Windows for all Windows and DOS programs running under Windows. These VxDs must be written in assembly language.

The Approach We Use

Like most introductory books on assembly language programming, this book shows you how to use the instructions of the 80x86 microprocessor. But we will go much farther and cover *advanced* material that you will find invaluable when you start to write your own programs.

By the time you finish reading this book, you will know how to write large assembly language programs and how to use assembly language in your C/C++ programs and Windows programs. Along the way, you will also learn many techniques that professional programmers use to make their work simpler.

These techniques, which include modular design and step-wise refinement, will double or triple your programming speed and help you write more readable and reliable programs.

The technique of step-wise refinement, in particular, takes a lot of the work out of writing complex programs. If you have ever had that sinking, where-do-I-start feeling, you will find that step-wise refinement gives you a simple and natural way to write programs. It is also fun!

We will also try to show you how comments can help you write better programs. Well-written comments explain *why* you are doing something, rather than *what* you are doing. In well-written code it should be obvious what the code is doing, but it certainly may not be clear why you are doing something.

This book is not all theory. We will also build a program called Dskpatch (for Disk Patch), and you will find it useful for several reasons. First, you will see step-wise refinement and modular design at work in a real program and you will have an opportunity to see why these techniques are so useful. Also, Dskpatch is a general-purpose, full-screen editor for disk sectors—one that you can continue to use both in whole and in part long after you have finished with this book.

Organization of This Book

We have chosen an approach to teaching assembly language that we think will get you up to speed as quickly as possible without overwhelming you with details. With this approach you will be able to learn a lot about the 80x86 instructions before you have to learn about using an assembler. We have also chosen to write most of the sample programs for DOS because it is a lot easier to write small programs in DOS than to write the same program for Windows. The concepts and techniques you learn will also apply to programs you write in other operating environments, so if you want to program for Windows, you might read Parts I and II, then skip to Chapters 31 and 33.

This book is divided into four parts, each with a different emphasis. Whether or not you know anything about microprocessors or assembly language, you will find sections that are of interest to you.

Part I focuses on the 80x86 microprocessor. You will learn the mysteries of bits, bytes, and machine language. Each of the seven chapters contains a wealth of real examples that use a program called Debug, which comes with DOS. Debug will allow us to look *inside* the 80x86 microprocessor nestled deep in your PC as it runs DOS. Part I assumes only that you have a rudimentary knowledge of programming languages and know how to work with your computer.

Part II, Chapters 8 through 16, moves on to assembly language and how to write programs for the assembler. The approach is not complicated, and rather than cover all the details of the assembler itself, we will concentrate on a set of assembler commands needed to write useful programs.

We will use the assembler to rewrite some of the programs from Part I, and then move on to begin creating Dskpatch. We will build this program slowly, in order for you to learn how to use step-wise refinement in building large programs. We will also cover techniques like modular design that help in writing clear programs. As mentioned, these techniques will simplify programming by removing some of the complexities normally associated with writing assembly-language programs.

In Part III, which includes Chapters 17 to 28, we will concentrate on using more advanced features found in PCs. These features include moving the cursor and clearing the screen. We will also discuss techniques for debugging larger assembly-language programs. Assembly-language programs grow quickly and can easily be two or more pages long without doing very much (Dskpatch will be longer). Even though we will use these debugging techniques on programs larger than a few pages, you also will find them useful with small programs.

Part IV covers a number of advanced topics that will be of interest to you when you start to write real programs. The first two chapters cover details about COM programs, memory, and segments. Then there is a chapter on writing directly to screen memory for very fast screen displays. Next, there is a chapter on writing assembly-language procedures that you can use in your C/C++ programs. You will learn how to write general-purpose routines entirely in assembly language for any memory model, and you will also learn how to use in-line assembly. There is a lot of material in this chapter that is very difficult to find elsewhere. Next is a chapter on RAM-resident programs, complete with a program called DISKLITE that adds a disk light to your screen. Finally, you will find a chapter on protected-mode and Windows programming that will show you some interesting details about the way Windows works on an 80386 or better microprocessor.

What Is on the Disk?

The disk included with this book contains most of the code examples you will find in this book in a directory called CHAPS. We have included a more advanced version of Dskpatch in a directory called ADVANCED. Appendix A discusses both of these directories.

Appendix B contains a complete listing of the Dskpatch program we will build in this book. Appendix C contains listings for some general-purpose libraries for C and C++ programs that you'll find on the disk at the back of this book.

The set of libraries for C and C++ programs allows you to write quickly to the screen and support a mouse. This code is the code that we used to write the Norton Commander, which means we had to deal with issues that other authors who have not written commercial software have never encountered. It also means that these libraries have been thoroughly tested by hundreds of thousands of users. All of this code is included on the disk at the back of this book, and you'll find complete listings of this code in Appendix C.

What You Will Need
to Use the Examples

There are a few tools you will need in order to use the examples in this book. For all the examples in Part I, you need nothing more than the Debug program that comes with DOS. In Part II you will need a simple text editor, such as the Edit program in DOS 5 or later, and an assembler, such as Microsoft's Macro Assembler (MASM) or Borland's Turbo Assembler (TASM). All of the examples in this book have been tested on various versions of MASM and TASM. In Chapters 31 and 33, however, you will need MASM 6 (or later) or TASM to assemble the examples.

Finally, to compile some of the C examples in Chapter 33, you will need QuickC for Windows, Borland C++, or Microsoft C 6.0 or later. All of these C compilers support in-line assembly and allow you to compile Windows programs.

Dskpatch

In our work with assembly language, we will look directly at disk sectors and displaying characters and numbers stored there by DOS in hexadecimal notation. Dskpatch is a full-screen editor for disks and it will allow us to change these characters and numbers in a disk sector. By using Dskpatch you could, for example, look at the sector where DOS stores the directory for a disk and you could change file names or other information. Doing so is a good way to learn how DOS stores information on a disk.

You will get more out of Dskpatch than just one program, though. Dskpatch contains about 50 subroutines. Many of these are general-purpose subroutines you will find useful when you write your own programs. Thus, not only is this book an introduction to the 80x86 and assembly-language programming, it is also a source of useful subroutines.

P A R T I

Machine Language

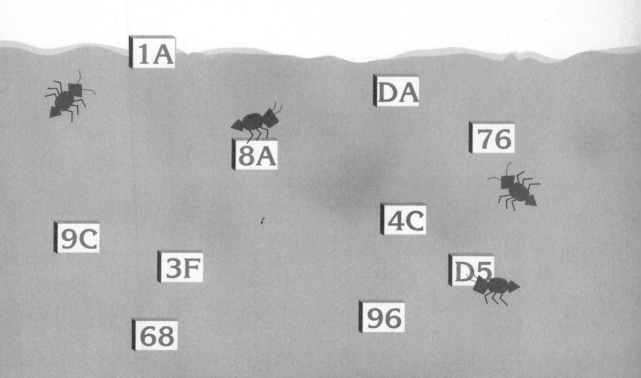

Learning Debug and Computer Arithmetic

In this chapter you are going to learn how the computer handles arithmetic. This is a fundamental concept for assembly-language programs. It has a significant impact on all programs you will write, whether in C, assembly language, or any other computer language.

Topics Covered

In this chapter you will start working with the microprocessor inside your computer right away. You will use a program called Debug to start working with computer arithmetic. It is a good starting point because Debug is at the heart of almost all assembly-language programs. We will continue to use Debug in all the chapters in this book, which will allow you to write and run very simple programs.

A Brief History of Intel Microprocessors

Before looking at assembly language, a few words are in order about microprocessors. Currently (as of 1992) there are four main microprocessors used in PC compatible computers: the 8088, 80286, 80386, and 80486 microprocessors (and Intel is working on the next generation, which will be called the Pentium). The 8088 microprocessor was first used in the original IBM PC and is the slowest, least powerful microprocessor. Very few computers are built with the 8088 microprocessor.

Next came the 80286 in the IBM AT, which was about four times faster, and the first computer capable of running IBM's OS/2. The 80286 is also the minimum microprocessor required to run Windows 3.1. Most computers are currently built around the faster 80386 or 80486 microprocessors, which also have additional capabilities that Windows can use.

The 80286, 80386, and 80486 are *supersets* of the 8088 microprocessor, which means any programs written for the 8088 microprocessor will run on any of the others. Almost all programs written for MS-DOS or PC-DOS, as opposed to Windows, are written using just 8088 features so they will run on all MS-DOS computers. In this book we will be covering mostly the 8088 instructions so the programs you will write will work on all MS-DOS computers. However, later in the book you will find some coverage of Windows programming in the *protected mode* of the 80286 and better microprocessors, which is used by operating systems such as Windows and OS/2. Because there are so many different microprocessors used in PCs, we will refer to the entire family as 80x86 microprocessors.

Counting the Computer Way

For your first foray into assembly language you will learn how computers count. That may sound simple enough. After all, you count to 11 by starting at one and counting up:

1, 2, 3, 4, 5, 6, 7, 8, 9, 10, 11.

A computer does not count that way. Instead, it counts to five like this: 1, 10, 11, 100, 101. The numbers 10, 11, 100, and so on are binary numbers, based on a numbering system with only two digits, 1 and 0, instead of the ten associated with our more familiar decimal numbers. Thus, the binary number 10 is equivalent to the decimal number we know as two.

We are interested in binary numbers because they are the form in which numbers are used by the 80x86 microprocessor inside your PC. But while computers thrive on binary numbers, those strings of ones and zeros can be long and cumbersome to write out. The solution? Hexadecimal numbers—a far more compact way to write binary numbers. In this chapter, you will learn both ways to write numbers: hexadecimal and binary. As you learn how computers count, you will also learn how they store numbers—bits, bytes, and words. If you already know about binary and hexadecimal numbers, bits, bytes, and words, you can skip to the chapter summary.

Counting with Hexadecimal Numbers

Since hexadecimal numbers are easier to handle than binary numbers—at least in terms of length—we will begin with hexadecimal (hex for short), and use DEBUG.COM, a program included with DOS. You will use Debug here and in later chapters to enter and run machine-language programs one instruction at a time. Like BASIC, Debug provides a nice, interactive environment. But unlike BASIC, it doesn't know decimal numbers. To Debug, the number 10 is a hexadecimal number—not ten. Since Debug only speaks in hexadecimal, you will need to learn something about hex numbers. But first, let's take a short side trip and find out a little about Debug itself.

Using Debug

Why does this program carry the name Debug? *Bugs*, in the computer world, are mistakes in a program. A working program has no bugs, while a nonworking or "limping" program has at least one bug. You can find mistakes and correct them by using Debug to run a program one instruction at a time and by watching how the program works. This is known as *debugging*, hence the name Debug.

According to computer folklore, the term debugging stems from the early days of computing—in particular, a day on which the Mark I computer at Harvard failed. After a long search, technicians found the source of their troubles: a small moth caught between the contacts of a relay. The technicians removed the moth and wrote a note in the log book about "debugging" the Mark I.

From here on, in interactive sessions like this one, the text you type will be in boldface against a gray background to distinguish it from your computer's responses, as follows:

C>**DEBUG**

Type the gray text (DEBUG in this example), press the Enter key, and you should see a response similar to the ones we show in these sessions. You won't always see exactly the same responses because your computer probably has a different amount of memory from the computer on which we wrote this book. (We will begin to encounter such differences in the next chapter.) In addition, notice that we use uppercase letters in all examples. This is only to avoid any confusion between the lowercase letter l (el) and the number 1 (one). If you prefer, you can type all examples in lowercase letters.

Now, with those few conventions noted, start Debug by typing its name after the DOS prompt (which is C> in the following example).

C>**DEBUG**

The hyphen you see in response to your command is Debug's prompt symbol, just as C> is a DOS prompt. It means Debug is waiting for a command. To leave Debug and return to DOS, just type Q (for *Quit*) at the hyphen prompt and press Enter. Try quitting now, if you like, and then return to Debug.

`-Q`

`C>DEBUG`
`-`

Now we can get down to learning about hex numbers.

Doing Hex Arithmetic

We will use a Debug command called H. H is short for *Hexarithmetic*, and as its name suggests, it adds and subtracts two hex numbers. Let's see how H works by starting with 2 + 3. We know that 2 + 3 = 5 for decimal numbers. Is this true for hex numbers? Make sure you are still in Debug and, at the hyphen prompt, type the following screened text:

`-H 3 2`
`0005  0001`

Debug prints both the sum (0005) and the difference (0001) of 3 and 2. The Hexarithmetic command, shown in Figure 1-1, always calculates the sum and difference of two numbers, as it did here. So far, the results are the same for hex and decimal numbers: 5 is the sum of 3 + 2 in decimal, and 1 is the difference (3 − 2). Sometimes, however, you can encounter a few surprises.

For example, what if you typed H 2 3, to add and subtract two and three, instead of three and two? If you try it you get FFFF, instead of −1, for 2 − 3. Strange as it may look, however, FFFF is a number. In fact, it is hex for −1.

`-H 2 3`
`0005  FFFF`

We will come back to this rather unusual −1 shortly. But first, let's explore the realm of slightly larger numbers to see how an F can appear in a number.

7

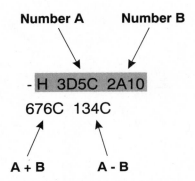

Figure 1-1: The Hexarithmetic command.

To see what the Hexarithmetic command does with larger numbers, try nine plus one, which would give you the decimal number 10.

```
-H 9 1
000A  0008
```

Nine plus one equals A? That's right: A is the hex number for ten. Now, what if we try for an even larger number, such as 15?

```
-H 9 6
000F  0003
```

If you try other numbers between ten and fifteen, you will find 16 digits altogether—0 through F (0 through 9 and A through F), see Figure 1-2. The name hexadecimal comes from hexa- (6), plus deca- (10), which, when combined, represent 16. The digits 0 through 9 are the same in both hexadecimal and decimal; the hexadecimal digits A through F are equal to the decimals 10 through 15.

Why does Debug speak in hexadecimal? Soon you will see that you can write 256 different numbers with two hex digits. As you may already suspect, 256 also bears some relationship to the unit known as a byte, and the byte plays a major role in computers and in this book. You will find out more about bytes near the end of this chapter, but for now we will continue to concentrate on learning hex, the only number system known to Debug and hex math.

Decimal	Hex digit	
0	0	
1	1	
2	2	
3	3	These digits are the
4	4	same for both decimal
5	5	and hex.
6	6	
7	7	
8	8	
9	9	
10	A	
11	B	These digits are new
12	C	hexadecimal digits.
13	D	
14	E	
15	F	

Figure 1-2: Hexadecimal digits.

Converting Hexadecimal to Decimal

Thus far, you have learned single-digit hex numbers. Now, let's see how you represent larger hex numbers and how you convert these numbers to decimal numbers.

Just as with decimal numbers, you can build multiple-digit hex numbers by adding more digits on the left. Suppose, for example, you add the number 1 to the largest single-digit decimal number, 9. The result is a two-digit number, 10 (ten). What happens when you add 1 to the largest single-digit hex number, F? You get 10 again.

But wait—10 in hex is really 16, not 10. This could become rather confusing. We need some way to tell these two 10s apart. From now on we will place the letter h after any hex number. Thus, you can tell that 10h is hexadecimal for 16 and 10 is decimal ten.

Now let's look at how to convert numbers between hex and decimal. You know that 10h is 16, but how do you convert a larger hex number, such as D3h, converted to a decimal number without counting up to D3h from 10h? Or, how is the decimal number 173 converted to hex?

You cannot rely on Debug for help, because it cannot speak in decimal. In Chapter 10, we will write a program to convert a hex number into decimal notation so that our programs can talk to us in decimal. But right now, we will have to do these conversions by hand. We will begin by returning to the familiar world of decimal numbers.

What does the number 276 mean? In grade school, you learned that 276 means you have two hundreds, seven tens, and six ones. Or, more graphically as follows:

```
2    * 100  =  200
 7   *  10  =   70
  6 *   1  =    6
_____
276         =  276
```

Well, that certainly helps illustrate the meanings of those digits. Can we use the same graphic method with a hex number? Of course.

Consider the number D3h mentioned earlier. D is the hexadecimal digit 13, and there are 16 hex digits, versus 10 for decimal, so D3h is thirteen sixteens and three ones. Or, presented graphically as follows:

```
D  → 13 * 16  =  208
 3 →  3 *  1  =    3
_____
D3h           =  211
```

For the decimal number 276, you multiply digits by 100, 10, and 1; for the hex number D3, multiply digits by 16 and 1. You would multiply four decimal digits by 1000, 100, 10, and 1. Which four numbers would you use with four hex digits? For decimal, the numbers 1000, 100, 10, and 1 are all powers of 10, as follows:

$$10^3 = 1000$$
$$10^2 = 100$$
$$10^1 = 10$$
$$10^0 = 1$$

You can use the same exact method for hex digits, but with powers of 16, instead of 10, so the four numbers are as follows:

$16^3 = 4096$
$16^2 = 256$
$16^1 = 16$
$16^0 = 1$

For example, you can convert 3AC8h to decimal by using these four numbers. (See Figure 1-3 for more examples.)

```
3      →  3 * 4096 = 12288
 A    → 10 *  256 =  2560
  C  → 12 *   16 =   192
   8→  8 *    1 =     8
─────────────────────────
3AC8h           = 15048
```

```
7      →   7 * 16 = 112
 C    →  12 *  1 =  12
─────────────────────────
7Ch          =      124
```

```
3      →   3 * 256 = 768
 F    →  15 *  16 = 240
  9  →   9 *   1 =   9
─────────────────────────
3F9h          =    1,017
```

```
A        → 10 * 4,096 = 40,960
 F      → 15 *   256 =  3,840
  1    →  1 *    16 =     16
   C  → 12 *     1 =     12
─────────────────────────────
AF1Ch           =      44,828
```

```
3        →  3 * 65,536 = 196,608
 B      → 11 *  4,096 =  45,056
  8    →  8 *    256 =   2,048
   D  → 13 *     16 =     208
    2→  2 *      1 =       2
─────────────────────────────────
3B8D2h            =       243,922
```

Figure 1-3: More hexadecimal to decimal conversions.

Now let's discover what happens when we add hex numbers that have more than one digit. For this, we will use Debug and the numbers 3A7h and 1EDh, as follows:

```
-H 3A7 1ED
0594  01BA
```

So you see that 3A7h + 1EDh = 594h. You can check the results by converting these numbers to decimal and doing the addition (and subtraction, if you wish) in decimal form; if you are more adventurous, do the calculations directly in hex.

Five-Digit Hex Numbers

So far, hex math is quite straightforward. What happens when you try adding even larger hex numbers? Try a five-digit hex number, as follows (See Figure 1-4 for more examples):

```
-H 5C3F0 4BC6
  ^ Error
```

```
      1                 1                 1
     3A7               F451               C
   + 92A             + CB03             + D
   -----             ------             ----
     CD1              1BF54              19


     1 1 1 1           1 1
     BCD8              BCD8
   + FAE9            + 0509
   -------           -------
    1B7C1             C1E1
```

Figure 1-4: More examples of hexadecimal addition.

That is an unexpected response. Why does Debug say that you have an error here? The reason has to do with a unit of storage called the *word*. Debug's Hexarithmetic command works only with words, and words happen to be long enough to hold four hex digits, no more.

You will learn more about words in a few pages, but for now, remember that you can work only with four hex digits. Thus, if you try to add two four-digit hex numbers, such as C000h and D000h (which should give you 19000h), you get 9000h instead. Debug keeps only the four rightmost digits of the answer.

```
-H C000 D000
9000  F000
-
```

Converting Decimal to Hex

So far you have only seen the conversion from hex to decimal. Now let's look at how to convert decimal numbers to hex. As mentioned earlier, in Chapter 10 you will create a program to write the 80x86's numbers as decimal numbers; in Chapter 23, you will write another program to read decimal numbers into the 80x86. But, as with decimal-to-hex conversions, you will begin by doing the conversions by hand. Again, start by recalling a bit of grade school math.

When you first learned division, you would divide 9 by 2 to get 4 with a remainder of 1. We will use the remainder to convert decimal numbers to hex. See what happens when you repeatedly divide a decimal number, in this case 493, by 10?

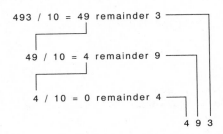

The digits of 493 appear as the remainder in reverse order—that is, starting with the rightmost digit (3). You saw in the last section that all you needed for a hex-to-decimal conversion was to replace powers of 10 with powers of 16. For a decimal-to-hex conversion, can you divide by 16 instead of 10? Indeed, that is the conversion method. For example, find the hex number for 493. You can divide by 16, you get the following:

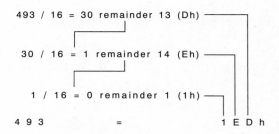

1EDh is the hex equivalent of decimal 493. In other words, keep dividing by 16, and form the final hex number from the remainders. That's all there is to it. Figure 1-5 gives more examples of decimal to hex conversions.

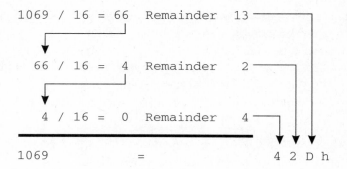

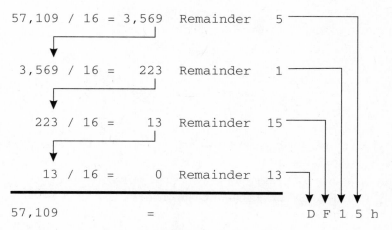

Figure 1-5: More examples of hexadecimal conversions.

Working with Negative Numbers

If you recall, there is still an unanswered puzzle in the number FFFFh. We said that FFFFh is actually −1. Yet, if you convert FFFFh to decimal, we get 65535. How can that be? Does it behave as a negative number?

Well, if you add FFFFh (alias −1) to 5, the result should be 4, because 5 − 1 = 4. Is that what happens? Use Debug's H command to add 5 and FFFFh, and you see the following:

```
-H 5 FFFF
0004  0006
-
```

Debug *seems* to treat FFFFh as −1. But FFFFh won't always behave as −1 in programs we will write. To see why not, let's do this addition by hand.

When adding two decimal numbers, you will often find yourself *carrying* a one to the next column, as follows:

```
  ¹ ¹
    9 5
+   5 8
  ─────
  1 5 3
```

The addition of two hex numbers isn't much different. Adding 3 to F gives 2, with a carry into the next column, as follows:

```
  ¹
    F h
+   3 h
  ─────
  1 2 h
```

Now, watch what happens when you add 5 to FFFFh.

```
    1  1  1  1
    0  0  0  5  h
+   F  F  F  F  h
   1  0  0  0  4  h
```

Since Fh + 1h = 10h, the successive carries neatly move a 1 into the far left position. If you ignore this 1, you have the correct answer for 5 − 1: namely, 4. Strange as it seems, FFFFh behaves as −1 when *you ignore this overflow*. It is called an overflow because the number is now five digits long, but Debug keeps only the last (rightmost) four digits.

Is this overflow an error, or is the answer correct? Well, yes and yes. You can choose either answer. Don't the answers contradict each other? Not really, because you can view these numbers in either of two ways.

Suppose you take FFFFh as equal to 65536. This is a positive number, and it happens to be the largest number you can write with four hex digits. In this case FFFFh is called an *unsigned* number. It is unsigned because you said all four-digit numbers are positive. Adding 5 to FFFFh gives you 10004h; no other answer is correct. In the case of unsigned numbers, then, an overflow is an error.

On the other hand, you can treat FFFFh as a negative number, as Debug did when you used the H command to add FFFFh to 5. FFFFh behaves as −1 as long as you ignore the overflow. In fact, the numbers 8000h through FFFFh all behave as negative numbers. For *signed* numbers, as here, the overflow is not an error.

The 80x86 microprocessor can view numbers either as unsigned or signed; the choice is yours. There are slightly different instructions for each, and we will explore these differences in later chapters as we begin to use numbers on the 80x86. Right now, before you can learn to actually write the negative of, say, 3C8h, we need to unmask the bit and see how it fits into the scheme of bytes, words, and hex.

Bits, Bytes, Words, and Binary Notation

It is time to dig deeper into the intricacies of your PC—time to learn about the arithmetic of the 80x86: binary numbers. The 80x86 microprocessor, with all its power, is rather dumb. It knows only the two digits 0 and 1, so any number it uses must be formed from a long string of 0s and 1s. This is the *binary* (base 2) number system.

When Debug prints a number in hex, it uses a small program to convert its internal numbers from binary to hexadecimal. In Chapter 5, we will build such a program to write binary numbers in hex notation, but first we need to learn more about binary numbers themselves.

Let's take the binary number 1011b (the b stands for binary). This number is equal to the decimal 11, or Bh in hex. To see why, multiply the digits of 1011b by the number's base, 2:

Powers of 2:

$2^3 = 8$
$2^2 = 4$
$2^1 = 2$
$2^0 = 1$

So that:

```
1 * 8   =   8
0 * 4   =   0
1 * 2   =   2
1 * 1   =   1
─────────────
1011b  =  11   or   Bh
```

Likewise, 1111b is Fh, or 15. 1111b is the largest unsigned four-digit binary number you can write, while 0000b is the smallest. Thus, with four binary digits you can write 16 different numbers (see Figure 1-6). There are exactly 16 hex digits, so you can write one hex digit for every four binary digits.

Binary	Decimal	Hexadecimal
0000	0	0
0001	1	1
0010	2	2
0011	3	3
0100	4	4
0101	5	5
0110	6	6
0111	7	7
1000	8	8
1001	9	9
1010	10	A
1011	11	B
1100	12	C
1101	13	D
1110	14	E
1111	15	F

Figure 1-6: Binary, hex, decimal for 0 through F.

A two-digit hex number, such as 4Ch, can be written as 0100 1100b. It's comprised of eight digits, which we separate into groups of four for easy reading. Each one of these binary digits is known as a bit, so a number like 0100 1100b, or 4Ch, is eight bits long.

Very often, we find it convenient to number each of the bits in a long string, with bit 0 farthest to the right. The 1 in 10b then is bit number 1, and the leftmost bit in 1011b is number 3. Numbering bits in this way makes it easier for us to talk about any particular one, as we will want to later on.

A group of eight binary digits is known as a *byte*, while a group of 16 binary digits, or two bytes, is a *word*, see Figure 1-7. We will use these terms frequently throughout this book, because bits, bytes, and words are all fundamental to the 80x86.

Now you can see why hexadecimal notation is convenient. Two hex digits fit exactly into one byte (four bits per hex digit), and four digits fit exactly into one word. The same cannot be said for decimal numbers. If you try to use two decimal digits for one byte, numbers larger than 99 cannot be written, so you lose the values from 100 to 255—more than half the range of numbers a byte can hold. If you use three decimal digits you must *ignore* more than half the three-digit decimal numbers because the numbers 256 through 999 cannot be contained in one byte.

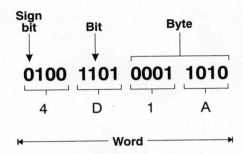

Figure 1-7: A word is made out of bits and bytes.

Two's Complement—An Odd Sort of Negative Number

Now you are ready to learn more about negative numbers. We said before that the numbers 8000h through FFFFh all behave as negative numbers when you ignore the overflow. There is an easy way to spot negative numbers when you write them in binary. The binary forms for positive and negative numbers are as follows:

```
Positive numbers:
    0000h  0000 0000 0000 0000b
     .      .
     .      .
     .      .
    7FFFh  0111 1111 1111 1111b

Negative numbers:
    8000h  1000 0000 0000 0000b
     .      .
     .      .
     .      .
    FFFFh  1111 1111 1111 1111b
```

In the binary forms for all the positive numbers, the leftmost bit (bit 15) is always 0. For all negative numbers, this leftmost bit is always 1. This difference is, in fact, the way that the 80x86 microprocessor knows when a number is negative: It looks at bit 15, the *sign bit*. If you use instructions for unsigned numbers in your programs, the 80x86 will ignore the sign bit, and you will be free to use signed numbers at your convenience.

These negative numbers are known as the *Two's Complement* of positive numbers. Why complement? Because the conversion from a positive number, such as 3C8h, to its two's-complement form is a two-step process, with the first being the conversion of the number to its *complement*.

We won't need to negate numbers often, but we will do the conversion here just so you can see how the 80x86 microprocessor negates numbers. The conversion will seem a bit strange. You won't see why it works, but you will see that it does work.

To find the two's-complement form (negative) of any number, first write the number in binary, ignoring the sign. For example, 4Ch becomes 0000 0000 0100 1100b.

To negate this number, first reverse all the zeros and ones. This process of reversing is called *complementing*, and taking the complement of 4Ch, we find that:

$$0 0 0 0 \quad 0 0 0 0 \quad 0 1 0 0 \quad 1 1 0 0$$

becomes:

$$1 1 1 1 \quad 1 1 1 1 \quad 1 0 1 1 \quad 0 0 1 1$$

In the second step of the conversion, add 1:

```
                            1  1
 1 1 1 1   1 1 1 1   1 0 1 1   0 0 1 1
+                                    1
 ─────────────────────────────────────
 1 1 1 1   1 1 1 1   1 0 1 1   0 1 0 0
                            −4Ch = FFB4h
```

The answer, FFB4h, is the result you get if you use Debug's H command to subtract 4Ch from 0h.

If you wish, you can add FFB4h to 4Ch by hand, to verify that the answer is 10000h. And from our earlier discussion, you know that you should ignore this leftmost 1 to get 0 (4C + (−4C) = 0) when you do two's-complement addition.

Summary

This chapter has been a fairly steep climb into the world of hexadecimal and binary numbers, and it may have required a fair amount of mental exercise. Soon, in Chapter 3, we will slow down to a gentler pace—once you have learned enough to converse with Debug in hex. Now take a breath of fresh air and look back on where you have been and what you have found.

We started out by introducing Debug. In chapters to come, you will become intimate friends with Debug but, since it does not understand your familiar decimal numbers, you began the friendship by learning a new numbering system, hexadecimal notation.

In learning about hex numbers, you also learned how to convert decimal numbers to hex, and hex numbers to decimal. You will write a program to do these translations later, but first you had to learn the language yourself.

Once we covered the basics of hexadecimal notation, we were able to wander off for a look at bits, bytes, words, and binary numbers—important characters you will encounter frequently as you continue to explore the world of the 80x86 and assembly-language programming.

Finally, we moved on to learn about negative numbers in hex—the two's-complement numbers. They led you to signed and unsigned numbers, where you also witnessed overflows of two different types: one in which an overflow leaves the correct answer (addition of two signed numbers), and one in which the overflow leads to the wrong answer (addition of two unsigned numbers).

All this learning will pay off in later chapters, because you will use your knowledge of hex numbers to speak with Debug. Debug will act as an interpreter between you and the 80x86 microprocessor waiting inside your PC.

In the next chapter, you use the knowledge you have gained so far to learn about the 80x86. We will rely on Debug again, and the use of hex numbers, rather than binary, to talk to the 80x86. You will learn about the microprocessor's registers—the places where it stores numbers—and, in Chapter 3, you will be ready to write a real program that will print a character on the screen.

You will also learn more about how the 80x86 does it's math. By the time you reach Chapter 10, you will be able to write a program to convert binary numbers to decimal.

Doing Arithmetic with the 80x86

In this chapter you will learn how to build your first programs. These programs will be one-line programs that add, subtract, multiply, and divide two numbers. These programs use instructions inside the 80x86 microprocessor.

Topics Covered

$\mathbf{K}$nowing something of Debug's hex arithmetic and the 80x86's binary arithmetic, you can begin to learn how the 80x86 does its math. It uses internal commands called *instructions.*

Using Registers as Variables

Debug, your guide and interpreter, knows much about the 80x86 microprocessor inside your PC. We use it to delve into the inner workings of the 80x86. You begin by asking Debug to display what it can about small pieces of memory called *registers*, in which you can store numbers. Registers are like variables in BASIC, but they are not exactly the same. Unlike the BASIC language, the 80x86 microprocessor contains a fixed number of registers, and these registers are not part of your PC's memory. Ask Debug to display the 80x86's registers with the R, for *Register*, command as follows:

```
-R
AX=0000  BX=0000  CX=0000  DX=0000  SP=FFEE  BP=0000  SI=0000  DI=0000
DS=3756  ES=3756  SS=3756  CS=3756  IP=0100   NV UP DI PL NZ NA PO NC
3756:0100 E485          IN      AL,85
-
```

You will probably see different numbers in the second and third lines of your display. Those numbers reflect the amount of memory in a computer. You will continue to see such differences, and later you will learn more about them.

For now, Debug has certainly given you a lot of information. Concentrate on the first four registers, AX, BX, CX, and DX, all of which Debug says are equal to 0000, both here and on your display. These registers are the *general-purpose* registers. The other registers, SP, BP, SI, DI, DS, ES, SS, CS, and IP, are special-purpose registers that we will deal with in later chapters.

The four-digit number following each register name is in hex notation. In Chapter 1, you learned that one word is described exactly by four hex digits. Here, you can see that each of the 13 registers in the 80x86 is one word, or 16 bits long. This is why computers based on the 80x86 microprocessor are known as 16-bit machines. (The 80386 and above microprocessors also have a 32-bit mode, where the registers can be 32 bits long, but currently only Windows NT really uses the 32-bit mode of these processors.)

We mentioned that the registers are like BASIC variables. That means you should be able to change them, and you can. Debug's R command does more than display registers. Followed by the name of the register, the command tells Debug that you wish to view the register and then change it. For example, you can change the AX register as follows:

```
-R AX
AX 0000
:3A7
-
```

Look at the registers again to see if the AX register now contains 3A7h.

```
-R
AX=03A7  BX=0000  CX=0000  DX=0000  SP=FFEE  BP=0000  SI=0000  DI=0000
DS=3757  ES=3756  SS=3756  CS=3756  IP=0100   NV UP DI PL NZ NA PO NC
3756:0100 E485         IN      AL,85
-
```

It does. Furthermore, you can put any hex number into any register with the R command by specifying the register's name and entering the new number after the colon. From here on, we will be using this command whenever you need to place numbers into the 80x86's registers.

You may recall seeing the number 3A7h in Chapter 1, where you used Debug's Hexarithmetic command to add 3A7h and 1EDh. Back then, Debug did the work for you. This time, we will use Debug merely as an interpreter so we can work directly with the 80x86. We will give the 80x86 instructions to add numbers from two registers: we will place a number in the BX register and then instruct the 80x86 to add the number in BX to the number in AX and put the answer back into AX. First, you need a number in the BX register. This time, let's add 3A7h and 92Ah. Use the R command to store 92Ah into BX.

Using Memory in the 80x86

The AX and BX registers should, respectively, contain 3A7h and 92Ah, as you can verify with the R command:

```
AX=03A7  BX=092A  CX=0000  DX=0000  SP=FFEE  BP=0000  SI=0000  DI=0000
DS=3756  ES=3756  SS=3756  CS=3756  IP=0100   NV UP DI PL NZ NA PO NC
3756:0100 E485         IN      AL,85
```

27

Now that you have these two numbers in the AX and BX registers, how do you tell the 80x86 to add BX to AX? By putting some numbers into your computer's memory.

Your IBM PC probably has at least 640K of memory—far more than you will need to use here. We will place two bytes of *machine code* into a corner of this vast amount of memory. In this case, the machine code will be two binary numbers that tell the 80x86 to add the BX register to AX. Then, we will *execute* this instruction with the help of Debug.

Where should you place the two-byte instruction in memory? And how will you tell the 80x86 where to find it? As it turns out, the 80x86 chops memory into 64K pieces known as *segments*. Most of the time, you will be looking at memory within one of these segments without really knowing where the segment starts. You can do this because of the way the 80x86 labels memory.

All bytes in memory are labeled with numbers, starting with 0h and working up. Remember the four-digit limitation on hex numbers? That means the highest number the 80x86 can use is the hex equivalent of 65535, which means the maximum number of labels it can use is 64K. Even so, experience tells you that the 80x86 can call on more than 64K of memory by being a little bit tricky. It uses two numbers, one for each 64K segment and one for each byte, or *offset*, within the segment. Each segment begins at a multiple of 16 bytes, so by overlapping segments and offsets, the 80x86 effectively can label more than 64K of memory. In fact, this is precisely how the 80x86 uses up to one million bytes of memory. (As you will see in a later chapter, a simple variation on this scheme allows the 80286 and above microprocessor to access more than a single megabyte of memory.)

The addresses (labels) you will use are offsets from the start of a segment. You will write addresses as a segment number, followed by the offset within the segment. For example, 3756:0100 will mean that you are at an offset of 1.00h within segment 3756h, see Figure 2-1.

In Chapter 11 you will learn more about segments and why the segment number is so high. For now, you can trust Debug to look after the segments for you so that you can work within one segment without having to pay attention to segment numbers. For the time being, we will refer to addresses only by their offsets. Each of these addresses refers to one byte in the segment, and the addresses are sequential, so 101h is the byte following 100h in memory.

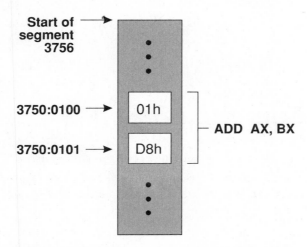

Figure 2-1: Instruction begins 100h bytes from the start of the segment.

Written out, the two-byte instruction to add BX to AX looks like this: ADD AX,BX. We will place this instruction at locations 100h and 101h, in whatever segment Debug starts to use. In referring to your ADD instruction, we will say that it is *at* location 100h, since this is the location of the first byte of the instruction.

Debug's command for examining and changing memory is called E, for *Enter*. Use the following command to enter the two bytes of the ADD instruction.

```
-E 100
3756:0100  E4.01
-E 101
3756:0101  85.D8
-
```

The numbers 01h and D8h are the 80x86's machine language for the ADD instruction at memory locations 3756:0100 and 3756:0101. The segment number you see will probably be different, but that difference won't affect your

29

program. Likewise, Debug probably displayed a different two-digit number for each of your E commands. These numbers (E4h and 85h in our example) are the old numbers in memory at offset addresses 100h and 101h of the segment Debug chose—that is, the numbers are data from previous programs left in memory when you started Debug. (If you just started your computer, the numbers will probably be 00.)

Addition, 80x86 Style

Now your register display should look something like this:

```
AX=03A7  BX=092A  CX=0000  DX=0000  SP=FFEE  BP=0000  SI=0000  DI=0000
DS=3756  ES=3756  SS=3756  CS=3756  IP=0100    NV UP DI PL NZ NA PO NC
3756:0100 01D8           ADD       AX,BX
```

The ADD instruction is neatly placed in memory, just where you want it to be. You know this from reading the third line of the display. The first two numbers, 3756:0100, give you the address (100h) for the first number of the ADD instruction. Next to this, you see the two bytes for ADD: 01D8. The byte equal to 01h is at address 100h, while D8h is at 101h. Finally, since you entered your instruction in *machine language*—numbers that have no meaning to us, but the 80x86 will interpret as an add instruction—the message ADD AX,BX confirms that you entered the instruction correctly.

Even though you placed the ADD instruction in memory, you are not quite ready to run it through the 80x86 (*execute* it). First, you need to tell the 80x86 where to find the instruction.

The 80x86 finds segment and offset addresses for instructions in two special registers, CS and IP, which you can see listed in the preceding register display. The segment number is stored in the CS, or *Code Segment*, register, which we will discuss shortly. If you look at the register display, you can see that Debug has already set the CS register for you (CS=3756, in our example). The full starting address of your instruction, however, is 3756:0100.

The second part of this address (the offset within segment 3756) is stored in the IP (*Instruction Pointer*) register. The 80x86 uses the offset in the IP register to actually find our first instruction. You can tell it where to look by setting the IP register to the address of your first instruction—IP=0100.

The IP register is already set to 100h because Debug sets IP to 100h whenever you first start it. Knowing this, we have deliberately chosen 100h as the address of the first instruction and have thus eliminated the need to set the IP register in a separate step. It is a good point to keep in mind.

Now, with the instruction in place and the registers set correctly, we will tell Debug to execute our one instruction. We will use Debug's T (*Trace*) command, which executes one instruction at a time and then displays the registers. After each trace, the IP should point to the next instruction. In this case, it will point to 102h. Since we have not put an instruction at 102h, the last line of the register display will show an instruction left over from some other program. Ask Debug to trace one instruction with the T command as follows:

```
-T
AX=0CD1  BX=092A  CX=0000  DX=0000  SP=FFEE  BP=0000  SI=0000  DI=0000
DS=3756  ES=3756  SS=3756  CS=3756  IP=0102    NV UP DI PL NZ AC PE NC
3756:0102 AC          LODSB
-
```

The AX register now contains CD1h, which is the sum of 3A7h and 92Ah. The IP register points to address 102h, so the last line of the register display shows some instruction at memory location 102h, rather than 100h. Figures 2-2 and 2-3 summarize the before and after of running the add instruction.

We mentioned earlier that the instruction pointer, together with the CS register, always points to the next instruction for the 80x86. If you typed T again, you would execute the next instruction, but don't do it just yet—your 80x86 might head for limbo.

Instead, what if you want to execute the ADD instruction again, adding 92Ah to CD1h and storing the new answer in AX? For that you need to tell the 80x86 where to find its next instruction, which you want to be the ADD instruction at 0100h. Can you just change the IP register to 0100h? Try it by using the R command to set IP to 100, and look at the register display as follows:

```
AX=0CD1  BX=092A  CX=0000  DX=0000  SP=FFEE  BP=0000  SI=0000  DI=0000
DS=3756  ES=3756  SS=3756  CS=3756  IP=0100    NV UP DI PL NZ AC PE NC
3756:0100          ADD     AX,BX
```

That's done it. Try the T command again and see if the AX register contains 15FBh. It does.

31

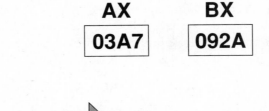

Figure 2-2: Before executing the ADD instruction.

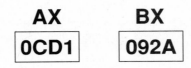

Figure 2-3: After executing the ADD instruction.

You should always check the IP register and the instruction at the bottom of an R display before using the T command. That way, you will be sure the 80x86 executes the instruction you want it to.

Now, set the IP register to 100h once again and make certain that the registers contain AX = 15FB, BX = 092A. Now you will try subtraction.

Subtraction, 80x86 Style

We are going to write an instruction that will subtract BX from AX. After two subtractions, you will have 3A7h in AX—the point from which you started before your two additions. You will also see an easier way to enter two bytes into memory.

When you entered the two bytes for your ADD instruction, you typed the E command twice: once with 0100h for the first address, and once with 0101h for the second address. The procedure worked, but as it turns out you can actually enter the second byte without another E command if you separate it from the first byte with a space. When you have finished entering bytes, pressing the Enter key will exit from the Enter command. Try this method for your subtract instruction:

```
-E 100
3756:0100  01.29  D8.D8
```

The register display (remember to reset the IP register to 100h) should now show the instruction SUB AX,BX, which subtracts the BX register from the AX register and leaves the result in AX. The order of AX and BX may seem backwards, but the instruction is like the BASIC statement AX = AX – BX except that the 80x86, unlike BASIC, always puts the answer into the first variable (register).

Execute this instruction with the T command. AX should contain CD1. Change IP to point back to this instruction, and execute it again (remember to check the instruction at the bottom of the R display first). AX should now be 03A7.

Negative Numbers in the 80x86

In the last chapter, you learned how the 80x86 uses the two's-complement form for negative numbers. Now, you will work directly with the SUB instruction to calculate negative numbers. Put the 80x86 to a test, to see whether you get FFFFh for −1. If you subtract one from zero and, if correct, the subtraction should place FFFFh (−1) into AX. Set AX equal to zero and BX to one, then trace through the instruction at address 0100h. Just what you expected: AX = FFFFh.

While you have this subtraction instruction handy, you may wish to try some different numbers to gain a better feel for two's-complement arithmetic. For example, see what result you get for −2.

Bytes in the 80x86

All of your arithmetic so far has been performed on words, hence the four hex digits. Does the 80x86 microprocessor know how to perform math with bytes? Yes, it does.

Since one word is formed from two bytes, each general-purpose register can be divided into two bytes, known as the *high byte* (the first two hex digits) and the *low byte* (the second two hex digits). Each of these registers can be called by its letter (A through D), followed by X for a word, H for the high byte, or L for the low byte. For example, DL and DH are byte registers, and DX is a word register, see Figure 2-4.

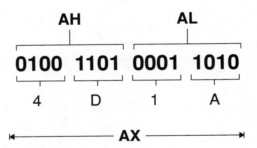

Figure 2-4: The AX register split into two byte registers (AH and AL).

To test byte-sized math with an ADD instruction, you enter the two bytes 00h and C4h, starting at location 0100h. At the bottom of the register display, you will see the instruction ADD AH,AL, which will add the two bytes of the AX register and place the result in the high byte, AH.

Next, load the AX register with 0102h. This places 01h in the AH register and 02h in the AL register. Set the IP register to 100h, execute the T command, and you will find that AX now contains 0302. The result of 01h + 02h is 03h, and that value is in the AH register.

Suppose you had not meant to add 01h and 02h. Suppose you really meant to add 01h and 03h. If the AX register already contained 0102, could you use Debug to change the AL register to 03h? No. You have to change the entire

AX register to 0103h because Debug only allows us to change *word* registers. There isn't a way to change just the low or high part of a register with Debug. But, as you saw in the last chapter, this isn't a problem. With hex numbers, a word can be split into two bytes by breaking the four-digit hex number in half. Thus, the word 0103h becomes the two bytes 01h and 03h.

To try this ADD instruction, load the AX register with 0103h. Your ADD AH,AL instruction is still at memory location 0100h, so reset the IP register to 100h and, with 01h and 03h now in the AH and AL registers, trace through this instruction. This time, AX contains 0403h: 04h, the sum of 01h + 03h is now in the AH register.

Multiplication and Division, 80x86 Style

You have seen the 80x86 add and subtract two numbers. Now you will see that it can also multiply and divide—clever processor. The multiply instruction is called MUL, and the machine code to multiply AX and BX is F7h E3h. We will enter this into memory, but first a word about the MUL instruction.

Where does the MUL instruction store its answer? In the AX register? Not quite; we have to be careful here. As you will soon see, multiplying two 16-bit numbers can give a 32-bit answer, so the MUL instruction stores its result in two registers, DX and AX. The higher 16 bits are placed in the DX register; the lower, into AX. We will write this register combination as DX:AX, from time to time.

Back to Debug and the 80x86. Enter the multiply instruction, F7h E3h, at location 0100h, just as you did for the addition and subtraction instructions, and set AX = 7C4Bh and BX = 100h. You will see the instruction in the register display as MUL BX, without any reference to the AX register. To multiply words, as here, the 80x86 always multiplies the register you name in the instruction by the AX register, and stores the answer in the DX:AX pair of registers.

Before you actually execute this MUL instruction, do the multiplication by hand. The three digits 100 have the same effect in hex as in decimal, so to multiply by 100h simply add two zeros to the right of a hex number. Thus, 100h * 7C4Bh = 7C4B00h. This result is too long to fit into one word, so we will split it into the two words 007Ch and 4B00h.

Use Debug to trace through the instruction. You will see that DX contains the word 007Ch, and AX contains the word 4B00h. In other words, the 80x86 returned the result of the *word-multiply* instruction in the DX:AX pair of registers (see Figures 2-5 and 2-6). Since multiplying two words together can never be longer than two words, but will often be longer than one word (as you just saw), the word-multiply instruction *always* returns the result in the DX:AX pair of registers.

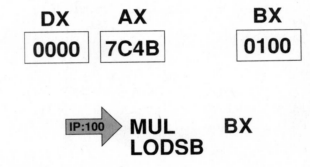

Figure 2-5: Before executing the MUL instruction.

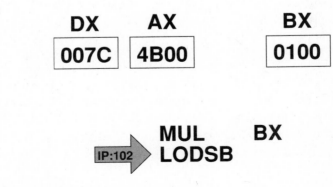

Figure 2-6: After executing the MUL instruction.

What about division? When you divide numbers are divided, the 80x86 keeps both the result and the remainder of the division. To see how the 80x86's division works, first place the instruction F7h F3h at 0100h (and 101h). Like the MUL instruction, DIV uses DX:AX without being told, so all you see is DIV BX. Now, load the registers so that DX = 007Ch and AX = 4B12h; BX should still contain 0100h.

Again, let's first calculate results by hand: 7C4B12h / 100h = 7C4Bh, with 12h left over. When you execute the division instruction at 0100h, you find that AX = 7C4Bh, the result of your division; and DX = 0012h, which is the remainder (see Figures 2-7 and 2-8). (We will put this remainder to use in Chapter 10, when we write a program to convert decimal numbers to hex by using the remainders, just as in Chapter 1.)

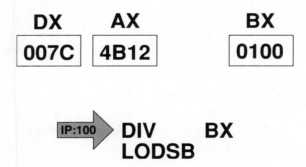

Figure 2-7: Before executing the DIV instruction.

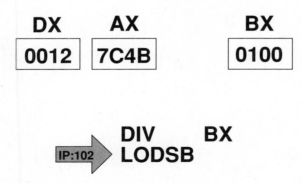

Figure 2-8: After executing the DIV instruction.

37

Summary

It is almost time to write a real program—one to print a character on the screen. You have put in your time learning the basics. First take a look at the ground that you have covered, and then we will move on.

You began this chapter by learning about registers and noticing their similarity to variables in BASIC. Unlike BASIC, however, the 80x86 has a small, fixed number of registers. We concentrated on the four general-purpose registers (AX, BX, CX, and DX), with a quick look at the CS and IP registers, which the 80x86 uses to locate segment and offset addresses.

After learning how to change and read registers, we moved on to build some single-instruction programs by entering the machine codes to add, subtract, multiply, and divide two numbers with the AX and BX registers. In future chapters we will use much of what you learned here, but you won't need to remember the machine codes for each instruction.

You also learned how to tell Debug to execute or trace through a single instruction. You will come to rely heavily on Debug to trace through your programs. Of course, as programs grow in size, this tracing will become both more useful and more tedious. Later on you will build on your experience and learn how to execute more than one instruction with a single Debug command.

Let's turn back to real programs and learn how to make a program that speaks.

Printing Characters

In this chapter you will build several real programs. You will start with a one-line program that displays a single character on your screen. Then you will turn this into a two-line program that displays a character and stops running, all by itself. Finally, you will build a program that displays a whole string of characters on your screen.

Topics Covered

You now know enough to do something solid, so roll up your sleeves and flex your fingers. We will begin by instructing DOS to send a character to the screen. Then move on to even more interesting work—building a small program with more than one instruction, and from there, learning another way to put data into registers from within a program. Now, onto getting DOS to speak.

INT—Using DOS Functions

We will add a new instruction, called INT (for *Interrupt*) to your four math instructions ADD, SUB, MUL, and DIV. INT is something like a subroutine call in any other programming language. We will use the INT instruction to ask DOS to print a character, A, on the screen for us.

Before you learn how INT works, let's run through an example. Start Debug and place 200h into AX and 41h into DX. The INT instruction for DOS functions is INT 21h—in machine code, CDh 21h. This is a two-byte instruction like the DIV instruction in the last chapter. Put INT 21h in memory, starting at location 100h, and use the R command to confirm that the instruction reads INT 21 (remember to set IP to 100h if it isn't already there).

Now you are ready to execute this instruction, but you cannot use the trace command here as you did in the last chapter. The trace command executes one instruction at a time, but the INT instruction calls upon a large program in DOS to do the actual work.

You don't want to execute each of the instructions in the entire DOS "subroutine" by tracing through it one instruction at a time. Instead, you want to *run* your one-line program, but stop before executing the instruction at location 102h. You can do this with Debug's G (*Go till*) command, followed by the address at which you want to stop. The command is as follows:

```
-G 102
A
AX=0241  BX=0000  CX=0000  DX=0041  SP=FFEE  BP=0000  SI=0000  DI=0000
DS=3970  ES=3970  SS=3970  CS=3970  IP=0102    NV UP DI PL NZ NA PO NC
3970:0102 8BE5          MOV     SP,BP
```

DOS printed the character A, and then returned control to your small program. (Remember, the instruction at 102h is just data left behind by another program, so you will probably see something different.) Your small program is, in a sense, two instructions long, the second instruction being whatever is at location 102h. It looks something like the following:

```
INT     21
MOV     SP,BP              (Or whatever is on your computer)
```

This random second instruction will soon be replaced with one of your own. For now, since it isn't anything you want to execute, you told Debug to run your program, stop execution when it reached the second instruction, and display the registers when it was done.

How did DOS know that it should print the A? The 02h in the AH register told DOS to print a character. Another number in AH would tell DOS to execute a different function. (You will see others later, but if you are curious right now, you can find a list of functions in Appendix D that will be used in this book.)

As for the character, DOS uses the number in the DL register as the ASCII code for the character to print when you ask it to send a character to the screen. You stored 41h, the ASCII code for an uppercase A.

In Appendix D, you will find a chart of ASCII character codes for all the characters your PC can display. The numbers are in both decimal and hex notation. Since Debug can only read hex, here is a good chance for you to practice converting decimal numbers to hex. Pick a character from the table and convert it to hex on your own. Then, verify your conversion by typing your hex value into the DL register and running the INT instruction again (remember to reset IP to 100h).

You may have wondered what would have happened if you had tried the trace command on the INT instruction. Suppose that you had not executed the G 102 command and, instead, traced a short distance through it to see what happens. If you try this yourself, don't go too far—you may find your PC doing something strange. After you have traced through a few steps, exit Debug with the Q command. This will clean up any mess you have left behind.

```
-R
AX=0200  BX=0000  CX=0000  DX=0041  SP=FFEE  BP=0000  SI=0000  DI=0000
DS=3970  ES=3970  SS=3970  CS=3970  IP=0100    NV UP DI PL NZ NA PO NC
3970:0100 CD21            INT    21
-T

AX=0200  BX=0000  CX=0000  DX=0041  SP=FFE8  BP=0000  SI=0000  DI=0000
DS=3970  ES=3970  SS=3970  CS=3372  IP=0180    NV UP DI PL NZ NA PO NC
3372:0180 80FC4B          CMP    AH,4B
-T

AX=0200  BX=0000  CX=0000  DX=0041  SP=FFE8  BP=0000  SI=0000  DI=0000
DS=3970  ES=3970  SS=3970  CS=3372  IP=0183    NV UP DI NG NZ AC PE CY
3372:0183 7405            JZ     018A
-T

AX=0200  BX=0000  CX=0000  DX=0041  SP=FFE8  BP=0000  SI=0000  DI=0000
DS=3970  ES=3970  SS=3970  CS=3372  IP=0185    NV UP DI NG NZ AC PE CY
3372:0185 2E              CS:
3372:0186 FF2EAB0B        JMP    FAR [0BAB]                CS:0BAB=0BFF
-Q
```

Notice that the first number of the address changed here, from 3970 to 3372. These last three instructions were part of DOS, and the program for DOS is in another segment. In fact, there are many more instructions that DOS executes before it prints a single character. Even an apparently simple task is not as easy as it sounds. Now you can understand why you used the G command to run the program to location 102h. If you had not used the G command, there would have been a torrent of instructions from DOS. (If you are using a different version of DOS, the instructions you see when you try this may be different.)

Exiting Programs—INT 20h

Do you remember that your INT instruction was 21h? If you changed the 21h to a 20h, you would have INT 20h instead. INT 20h is another interrupt instruction, and it tells DOS we want to exit our program so DOS can take full control again. In our case, INT 20h will send control back to Debug, since we are executing our programs from Debug, rather than from DOS.

Enter the instruction CDh 20h, starting at location 100h, then try the following (remember to check the INT 20h instruction with the R command):

```
-G 102

Program terminated normally
-R

AX=0000  BX=0000  CX=0000  DX=0000  SP=FFEE  BP=0000  SI=0000  DI=0000
DS=3970  ES=3970  SS=3970  CS=3970  IP=0100   NV UP DI PL NZ NA PO NC
3970:0100 CD20          INT    20
-G

Program terminated normally
-R

AX=0000  BX=0000  CX=0000  DX=0000  SP=FFEE  BP=0000  SI=0000  DI=0000
DS=3970  ES=3970  SS=3970  CS=3970  IP=0100   NV UP DI PL NZ NA PO NC
3970:0100 CD20          INT    20
```

The command G, with no number after it, executes the entire program (which is just one instruction now, because INT 20 is an *exit* instruction), and then returns to the start. IP has been reset to 100h, which is where we started. The registers in this example are 0 only because we started Debug afresh.

You can use this INT 20h instruction at the end of a program to return control gracefully to DOS (or Debug). Next, you put this instruction together with INT 21h and build a two-line program.

Putting the Pieces Together— A Two-Line Program

Starting at location 100h, enter the two instructions INT 21h, INT 20h (CDh 21h CDh 20h) one after the other. (From now on, we will always start programs at location 100h.)

When you had only one instruction, you could "list" that instruction with the R command, but now you have two instructions. To see them, use the U (*Unassemble*) command, which lists part of a program in memory:

```
-U 100
3970:0100 CD21          INT     21
3970:0102 CD20          INT     20
3970:0104 D98D460250B8  ESC     09,[DI+0246][DI+B850]
3970:010A 8D00          LEA     AX,[BX+SI]
3970:010C 50            PUSH    AX
3970:010D E82A23        CALL    243A
3970:0110 8BE5          MOV     SP,BP
3970:0112 83C41A        ADD     SP,+1A
3970:0115 5D            POP     BP
3970:0116 C3            RET
3970:0117 55            PUSH    BP
3970:0118 83EC02        SUB     SP,+02
3970:011B 8BEC          MOV     BP,SP
3970:011D 823E0E0000    CMP     BYTE PTR [000E],00
```

The first two instructions are recognized as the two instructions which were just entered. The other instructions are remnants left in memory. As your program grows, you will fill this display with more of your own code.

Now, fill the AH register with 02h and the DL register with the number for any character (just as you did earlier when you changed the AX and DX registers), then simply type the G command to see your character. For example, if you place 41h into DL, you see the following:

```
-G
```

```
A
Program terminated normally
-
```

Try this a few times with other characters in DL before we move on to other ways to set these registers.

Entering Programs

From here on, most of our programs will be more than one instruction long. To present these programs, we will use an unassemble display. The last program would appear as follows:

```
3970:0100 CD21          INT     21
3970:0102 CD20          INT     20
```

So far, you have entered the instructions for your programs directly as numbers, such as CDh, 21h. But that is a lot of work, and, as it turns out, there is a much easier way to enter instructions.

In addition to the unassemble command, Debug includes an A (*Assemble*) command, which allows you to enter the mnemonic, or human-readable, instructions directly. So rather than entering those cryptic numbers for your short program, you can use the assemble command to enter the following:

```
-A 100
3970:0100 INT 21
3970:0102 INT 20
3970:0104
-
```

When you have finished assembling instructions, all you have to do is press the Enter key, and the Debug prompt reappears. Here, the A command told Debug that you wished to enter instructions in mnemonic form, and the 100 told Debug to start entering instructions at location 100h. Since Debug's assemble command makes entering programs much simpler, we will use it from now on to enter instructions.

MOVing Data into Registers

Although we have relied on Debug quite a bit, we won't always run programs with it. Normally, a program would set the AH and DL registers itself before an INT 21h instruction. To do this, you will learn another instruction, called MOV. Once you know enough about this instruction, you can take your small program to print a character and make a real program—one that can be executed directly from DOS.

Soon, the MOV instruction will be used to load numbers into registers AH and DL. But let's start learning about MOV by moving numbers between registers. Place 1234h into AX (12h into the AH register, and 34h in AL) and ABCDh into DX (ABh in DH, and CDh in DL). Now, enter the following instruction with the A command:

```
396F:0100 88D4          MOV     AH,DL
```

This instruction *moves* the number in DL into AH by putting a copy of it into AH; DL is not affected. If you trace through this one line, you will find that AX = CD34h and DX = ABCDh. Only AH has changed. It now holds a copy of the number in DL.

Like the BASIC assignment statement AH = DL, a MOV instruction copies a number from the second register to the first, and for this reason we write AH before DL. Although there are some restrictions, which you will find out about later, you can use other forms of the MOV instruction to copy numbers between other pairs of registers. For example, reset IP and try the following:

```
396F:0100 89C3         MOV     BX,AX
```

You have just moved words, rather than bytes, between registers. The MOV instruction always works between words and words, or bytes and bytes; never between words and bytes. It makes sense, for how would you move a word into a byte?

We originally set out to move a number into the AH and DL registers. Let's do so now with another form of the MOV instruction, which is as follows:

```
396F:0100 B402         MOV     AH,02
```

This instruction moves 02h into the AH register without affecting the AL register. The second byte of the instruction, 02h, is the number we wish to move. Try moving a different number into AH. Change the second byte to another number, such as C1h, with the E 101 command.

Now, put all the pieces of this chapter together and build a longer program. This one will print an asterisk, *, all by itself, with no need to set the AH and DL registers. The program uses MOV instructions to set the AH and DL registers before the INT 21h call to DOS. The instructions are as follows:

```
396F:0100 B402         MOV     AH,02
396F:0102 B22A         MOV     DL,2A
396F:0104 CD21         INT     21
396F:0106 CD20         INT     20
```

Enter the program and check it with the U command (U 100). Make sure IP points to location 100h, then try the G command to run the entire program. You should see the * character appear on your screen, as follows:

```
-G
*
Program terminated normally
-
```

Now that you have a complete, self-contained program, you can write it to disk as a COM program, so you will be able to execute it directly from DOS. We can run a .COM program from DOS simply by typing its name. Since your program doesn't yet have a name, you need to give it one. The Debug command N (*Name*) gives a name to a file before you write it to disk. Type the following command to give the name WRITESTR.COM to our program.

```
-N WRITESTR.COM
```

This command does not write a file to the disk, though—it simply names the file that will be written with another command that you will use below.

Next, you must give Debug a byte count, telling it the number of bytes in the program so it will know how much memory you want to write to your file. If you refer to the unassemble listing of your program, you can see that each instruction is two bytes long (this won't always be true). There are four instructions, so your program is 4 * 2 = 8 bytes long. (You could also put Debug's H command to work and use hexarithmetic to determine the number of bytes in your program. Typing H 108 100 to subtract the first address after your program, 108, from 100 will produce 8.)

Once you have your byte count, you need somewhere to put it. Debug uses the pair of registers BX:CX for the length of your file, so putting 8h into CX tells Debug that your program is eight bytes long. Finally, since your file is only eight bytes long, you also need to set BX to zero. Once the name and length of the program is set, write it to disk with Debug's W (for *Write*) command, as follows:

```
-W
Writing 00008 bytes
-
```

You now have a program on your disk called WRITESTR.COM, so exit Debug with a Q, and look for it. Use the DOS Dir command to list the file:

```
C>DIR WRITESTR.COM

 Volume in drive C has no label
 Directory of  C:\
```

```
WRITESTR COM        8 08-28-92  10:05a
       1 File(s)            8 bytes
                      663552 bytes free
```

C>

The directory listing tells you that WRITESTR.COM is on the disk and that it is eight bytes long. To run the program, type *Writestr* at the DOS prompt. You will see a * appear on the display.

Writing a String of Characters

As a final example for this chapter, you use INT 21h, with a different function number in the AH register, to write a whole string of characters. You will have to store the string of characters in memory and tell DOS where to find the string. In the process, you will also learn more about addresses and memory.

You have already seen that function number 02h for INT 21h prints one character on the screen. Another function, number 09h, prints an entire string, and stops printing characters when it finds a $ symbol in the string. To put a string into memory, start at location 200h, so the string won't become tangled with the code for your program. Enter the following numbers by using the instruction E 200:

48	65	6C	6C
6F	2C	20	44
4F	53	20	68
65	72	65	2E
24			

The last number, 24h, is the ASCII code for a $ sign, and it tells DOS that this is the end of your string of characters. You will see what this string says in a minute, when you run the program, which you should enter as follows:

```
396F:0100 B409        MOV    AH,09
396F:0102 BA0002      MOV    DX,0200
396F:0105 CD21        INT    21
396F:0107 CD20        INT    20
```

200h is the address of the string you entered, and loading 200h into the DX register tells DOS where to find the string of characters. Check your program with the U command, then run it with a G command:

```
-G
Hello, DOS here.
Program terminated normally
```

Now that you have stored some characters in memory, it is time to meet another Debug command, D (for *Dump*). The dump command dumps memory to the screen somewhat like U lists instructions. Just as when you use the U command, simply place an address after D to tell Debug where to start the dump. For example, type the command D 200 to see a dump of the string you just entered.

```
-D 200
396F:0200   48 65 6C 6C 6F 2C 20 44-4F 53 20 68 65 72 65 2E   Hello, DOS here.
396F:0210   24 5D C3 55 83 EC 30 8B-EC C7 06 10 00 00 00 E8   $]CU.10.1G.....h
   .
   .
   .
```

After each pair of address numbers (such as 396F:0200 in the example), you see 16 hex bytes, followed by the 16 ASCII characters for these bytes. On the first line you see most of the ASCII codes and characters you typed in. The ending $ sign you typed is the first character on the second line; the remainder of that line is a miscellaneous assortment of characters.

Wherever you see a period (.) in the ASCII window, it represents either a period or a special character, such as the Greek letter pi. Debug's D command displays only 96 of the 256 characters in the PC character set, so a period is used for the remaining 160 characters.

You can use the D command in the future to check numbers entered for data, whether those data are characters or ordinary numbers. (For more information, refer to the Debug section in your DOS manual.)

Your string-writing program is complete, so you can write it to the disk. The procedure is the same one you used to write WRITESTR.COM to disk, except this time you have to set your program length to a value long enough to include the string at 200h. The program begins at line 100h, and you can see from the memory dump just performed that the first character ( ]) following the $ sign that ends our string is at location 211h. You can use the H command to find the difference between these two numbers. Find 211h – 100h and store this value into the CX register and set BX to zero. Use the N command to give the program a name (with the .COM extension so you can run the program directly from DOS), then use the W command to write the program and data to a disk file.

That's it for writing characters to the screen, aside from one final note—DOS never sends the $ character. This occurs because DOS uses the $ sign to mark the end of a string of characters. That means you cannot use DOS to print a string with a $ in it, but in a later chapter, you will learn how to print a string with a $ sign or any other special character.

Summary

The first two chapters brought you to the point where you could work on a real program. In this chapter, you used your knowledge of hex numbers, Debug, 80x86 instructions, and memory to build short programs to print a character and a string of characters on the screen. In the process you also learned some new things.

First you learned about INT instructions—not in much detail, but enough to write two short programs. In later chapters, you will gain more knowledge about interrupt instructions as you increase your understanding of the 80x86 microprocessor tucked under the cover of your PC.

Debug has, once again, been a useful and faithful guide. We have been relying heavily on Debug to display the contents of registers and memory, and in this chapter we used its abilities even more. Debug ran your short programs with the G command.

You also learned about the INT 20 exit instruction as well as the MOV instruction for moving numbers into and between registers. The exit instruction (INT 20) allowed you to build a complete program that could be written to the disk and run directly from DOS without the help of Debug. The MOV instruction gave you the ability to set registers before an INT 21 (print) instruction, so you could write a self-contained program to print one character.

Finally, we rounded out the chapter with the INT 21h function to print an entire string of characters. We will use all these instructions heavily throughout the rest of this book, but as you saw from using the Debug assemble and unassemble commands, you won't need to remember the machine codes for these instructions.

Now you know enough to move on to printing binary numbers. In the next chapter you will build a short program to take one byte and print it on the screen as a string of binary digits (zeros and ones).

Printing Binary Numbers

In this chapter you will learn several new things that you will use to build a small program that displays a number on your screen in binary notation. The tools you will use are the RCL (rotate carry left) instruction, the carry flag, the ADC (add with carry), and the LOOP instruction.

4

Topics Covered

In this chapter you will build a program to write binary numbers to the screen as strings of zeros and ones. You have most of the knowledge you need, and your work here will help solidify ideas you have already covered. This chapter also adds a few instructions to those you already know, including another version of ADD and some instructions to help repeat parts of your program. Let's begin by learning something completely new.

Rotating Numbers through the Carry Flag

In Chapter 2, when you first encountered hex arithmetic, you found that adding 1 to FFFFh should give you 10000h, but does not. Only the four hex digits to the right fit into one word; the 1 does not fit. You also found that this 1 is an overflow and that it is not lost. Where does it go? It is put into something called a *flag*—in this case, the *Carry Flag*, or *CF*. Flags contain one-bit numbers, so they can hold either a zero or a one. If you need to carry a one into the fifth hex digit, it goes into the carry flag.

Go back to the ADD instruction of Chapter 3 (ADD AX,BX). Put FFFFh into AX and 1 into BX, then trace through the ADD instruction. At the end of the second line of Debug's R display, you will see eight pairs of letters. The last of these, which can read either NC or CY, is the carry flag. Right now, because your ADD instruction resulted in an overflow of 1, you will see that the carry status reads CY (*Carry*). The carry bit is now 1 (or, as we will say, it's set).

To confirm that you have stored a seventeenth bit here (it would be the ninth bit for a byte addition), add one to the zero in AX by resetting IP to 100h and tracing through the ADD instruction again. The carry flag is affected by each ADD instruction, and this time there shouldn't be any overflow, so the carry should be reset. The carry does become zero, as indicated by the NC, which stands for *No Carry*, in the R display.

You learn about other status flags later in this book. If you are curious, you can find information about them right now under Debug's R command in your DOS manual.

Let's review the task of printing a binary number to see how the carry information could be useful. You will print only one character at a time, so you want to pick off the bits of your number, one by one, from left to right. For example, the first character you would want to print in the number 1000 0000b would be the one. If you could move this entire byte left one place, dropping the one into the carry flag and adding a 0 to the right side, then repeat the process for each succeeding digit, the carry flag would pick off your binary digits. You can do just this with a new instruction called RCL (*Rotate Carry Left*). To see how it functions, enter the short program as follows:

```
3985:0100 D0D3          RCL     BL,1
```

This instruction *rotates* the byte in BL to the left by one bit (hence the ,1) through the carry flag. The instruction is called rotate, because RCL moves the leftmost bit into the carry flag, while moving the bit currently in the carry flag into the rightmost bit position (0) as in Figure 4-1. In the process, all the other bits are moved or rotated to the left. After enough rotations (17 for a word, 9 for a byte) the bits are moved back into their original positions and you get back the original number. Place B7h in the BX register, then trace through this rotate instruction several times. Converting your results to binary, you will see the following:

```
Carry       BL register
  0       1 0 1 1   0 1 1 1     B7h      We start here
  1       0 1 1 0   1 1 1 0     6Eh
  0       1 1 0 1   1 1 0 1     DDh
  1       1 0 1 1   1 0 1 0     BAh
                 .
                 .
                 .
  0       1 0 1 1   0 1 1 1     B7h      After 9 rotations
```

In the first rotation, bit 7 of BL moves into the carry flag; the bit in the carry flag moves into bit 0 of BL; all other bits move left one position. Succeeding moves continue rotating the bits to the left until, after nine rotations, the original number is back in the BL register.

You are getting closer to building a program to write binary numbers to the screen, but you still need a few other pieces. Let's see how you can convert the bit in the carry flag into the character 0 or 1.

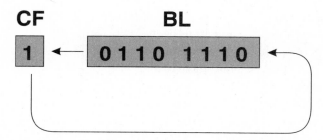

Figure 4-1: The RCL BL,1 instruction.

Adding the Carry Flag to a Number

The normal ADD instruction, for example, ADD AX,BX, simply adds two numbers. Another instruction, ADC (*Add with Carry*), adds three numbers: the two, as before, *plus* one bit from the carry flag. If you look in your ASCII table, you will discover that 30h is the character 0 and 31h is the character 1. So, adding the carry flag to 30h gives the character 0 when the carry is clear, and 1 when the carry is set. Thus, if DL = 0 and the carry flag is set (1), executing the following instruction adds DL(0) and 1h (the carry) to 30h ('0'), which gives 31h ('1').

```
ADC   DL,30
```

With one instruction you have converted the carry to a character that you can print.

At this point, rather than run through an example of ADC, wait until you have a complete program. After you have built the program you will execute its instructions one at a time in a procedure called *single-stepping*. Through this procedure you will see both how the ADC instruction works and how it fits nicely into your program. First, you need one more instruction which you will use to repeat your RCL, ADC, and INT 21h (print) instructions eight times—once for each bit in a byte.

Looping—Repeating a Block of Code

As mentioned, the RCL instruction is not limited to rotating bytes; it can also rotate entire words. We will use this ability to demonstrate the *LOOP* instruction. LOOP is similar to the FOR-NEXT command in Basic, but not as general. As with BASIC's FOR-NEXT loop, you need to tell LOOP how many times to run through a loop. You do this by placing your repeat count in register CX. Each time it goes through the loop, the 80x86 subtracts one from CX; when CX becomes zero, LOOP ends the loop.

Why the CX register? The C in CX stands for *Count*. You can use this register as a general-purpose register, but as you will see in the next chapter, you can also use the CX register with other instructions when you wish to repeat operations.

Here is a simple program that rotates the BX register left eight times, moving BL into BH (but not the reverse, because you rotate through the carry flag):

```
396F:0100 BBC5A3      MOV     BX,A3C5
396F:0103 B90800      MOV     CX,0008
396F:0106 D1D3        RCL     BX,1
396F:0108 E2FC        LOOP    0106
396F:010A CD20        INT     20
```

The loop starts at 106h (RCL BX,1) and ends with the LOOP instruction. The number following LOOP (106h) is the address of the RCL instruction. When you run the program, LOOP subtracts one from CX, then jumps to address 106h if CX is not equal to zero. The instruction RCL BX,1 (Rotate Carry Left, one place) is executed eight times here, because CX is set to eight before the loop.

You may have noticed that, unlike the FOR-NEXT loop in BASIC, the LOOP instruction is at the end of our loop (where you would put the NEXT statement in BASIC). The start of the loop, the RCL instruction at 106h, has no special instruction like FOR has in BASIC. If you know a language like Pascal, you can see that the LOOP instruction is somewhat akin to the REPEAT-UNTIL pair of instructions, where the REPEAT instruction just labels the start of the block of instructions to loop through.

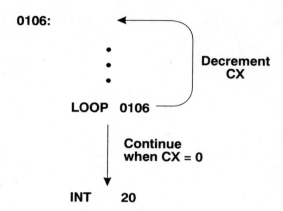

Figure 4-2: The LOOP instruction.

There are different ways you could execute your small program. If you simply type G, you won't see any change in the register display, because Debug saves all the registers before it starts carrying out a G command. Then, if it encounters an INT 20 instruction (as it will in your program), it restores all the registers. Try G. You will see that IP has been reset to 100h (where you started), and that the other registers don't look any different, either.

If you have the patience, you can trace through this program, instead. Taking it one step at a time, you can watch the registers change at each step, as follows:

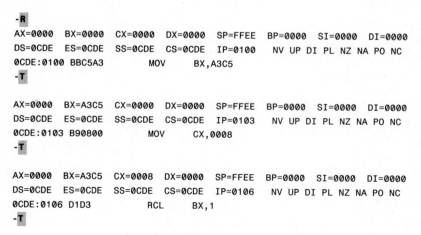

```
-R
AX=0000  BX=0000  CX=0000  DX=0000  SP=FFEE  BP=0000  SI=0000  DI=0000
DS=0CDE  ES=0CDE  SS=0CDE  CS=0CDE  IP=0100   NV UP DI PL NZ NA PO NC
0CDE:0100 BBC5A3        MOV     BX,A3C5
-T

AX=0000  BX=A3C5  CX=0000  DX=0000  SP=FFEE  BP=0000  SI=0000  DI=0000
DS=0CDE  ES=0CDE  SS=0CDE  CS=0CDE  IP=0103   NV UP DI PL NZ NA PO NC
0CDE:0103 B90800        MOV     CX,0008
-T

AX=0000  BX=A3C5  CX=0008  DX=0000  SP=FFEE  BP=0000  SI=0000  DI=0000
DS=0CDE  ES=0CDE  SS=0CDE  CS=0CDE  IP=0106   NV UP DI PL NZ NA PO NC
0CDE:0106 D1D3          RCL     BX,1
-T
```

```
AX=0000  BX=478A  CX=0008  DX=0000  SP=FFEE  BP=0000  SI=0000  DI=0000
DS=0CDE  ES=0CDE  SS=0CDE  CS=0CDE  IP=0108    OV UP DI PL NZ NA PO CY
0CDE:0108 E2FC          LOOP    0106
-T
AX=0000  BX=478A  CX=0007  DX=0000  SP=FFEE  BP=0000  SI=0000  DI=0000
DS=0CDE  ES=0CDE  SS=0CDE  CS=0CDE  IP=0106    OV UP DI PL NZ NA PO CY
0CDE:0106 D1D3          RCL     BX,1
                          .
                          .
                          .
-T

AX=0000  BX=C551  CX=0001  DX=0000  SP=FFEE  BP=0000  SI=0000  DI=0000
DS=0CDE  ES=0CDE  SS=0CDE  CS=0CDE  IP=0108    NV UP DI PL NZ NA PO CY
0CDE:0108 E2FC          LOOP    0106
-T

AX=0000  BX=C551  CX=0000  DX=0000  SP=FFEE  BP=0000  SI=0000  DI=0000
DS=0CDE  ES=0CDE  SS=0CDE  CS=0CDE  IP=010A    NV UP DI PL NZ NA PO CY
0CDE:010A CD20          INT     20
```

Alternatively, you can type G 10A to execute the program up to, but not including, the INT 20 instruction at 10Ah. The registers will then show the result of your program.

If you try this, you will see CX = 0 and either BX = C551 or BX = C5D1, depending on the value of the carry flag before you ran the program. The C5 your program's MOV instruction put into BL at the start is now in the BH register, but BL doesn't contain A3, because you rotated BX *through* the carry. Later, you will see other ways of rotating without going through the carry. Let's get back to the goal of printing a number in binary notation.

Building a Program to Display a Binary Number

You have seen how to strip off binary digits one at a time and convert them to ASCII characters. If you add an INT 21h instruction to print your digits, your program will be finished as you can see in the following program. The first instruction sets AH to 02 for the INT 21h function call (recall, 02 tells DOS to print the character in the DL register). The program is as follows:

```
3985:0100 B402          MOV     AH,02
3985:0102 B90800        MOV     CX,0008
3985:0105 B200          MOV     DL,00
3985:0107 D0D3          RCL     BL,1
3985:0109 80D230        ADC     DL,30
3985:010C CD21          INT     21
3985:010E E2F5          LOOP    0105
3985:0110 CD20          INT     20
```

You have seen how all the pieces work alone; here is how they work together. You rotate BL (with the instruction RCL BL,1) to pick off the bits of a number. Pick a number you want printed in binary and load it into the BL register; then run this program with a G command. After the INT 20h instruction, the G command restores the registers to the values they had before. BL still contains the number you see printed in binary.

The ADC DL,30 instruction in your program converts the carry flag to a 0 or a 1 character. The instruction MOV DL,0 sets DL to zero first, then the ADC instruction adds 30h to DL, and then finally adds the carry. Since 30h is the ASCII code for a 0, the result of ADC DL,30 is the code for 0 when the carry is clear (NC) or 1 if the carry is set (CY).

If you want to see what happens when you run this program, trace through it. Keep in mind that you will need to be a bit careful in single-stepping through it with the T command. It contains an INT 21h instruction and, as you saw when you first encountered INT 21h, DOS does a great deal of work for that one instruction. That is why you cannot use T on the INT 21.

You can, however, trace through all the other instructions in this program except the final INT 20, which won't concern you until the very end. During your tracing, type G 10E each time you loop through and reach the INT 21h instruction. Your G command, followed by an address, will tell Debug to continue running the program until IP becomes the address (10E) you entered. That is, Debug will execute the INT 21h instruction without your tracing through it, but stops before executing the LOOP instruction at 10E so you can return to tracing through the program. (The number you type after G is known as a *breakpoint*; breakpoints are very useful when you are trying to understand the inner workings of programs.) Finally, terminate the program when you reach the INT 20h instruction by typing the G command by itself.

Stepping over INTs with the Proceed Command

Whether or not you have tried out the instructions to trace through the program, you have seen that an instruction like G 10E allows you to trace *over* an INT instruction that starts at, say, 10Ch. But that means each time you want to trace over an INT instruction, you need to find the address of the instruction immediately following the INT instruction.

As it turns out, there is a Debug command that makes tracing through INT instructions much simpler. The P (*Proceed*) command does all the work for you. To see how it works, trace through the program, but when you reach the INT 21h instruction type P, rather than G 10E.

We will make heavy use of the P command in the rest of this book, because it is a nice way to trace over commands like INT, which call on large programs such as the routines inside DOS.

That is all we will cover about printing binary numbers as strings of zeros and ones for now. Here is a simple exercise for you to practice on—see if you can modify this program to print a *b* at the end of your binary number. (Hint: The ASCII code for b is 62h.)

Summary

This chapter provided a chance to catch your breath a bit after your hard work on new concepts in Chapters 1 through 3. So where have you been, and what have you seen?

You had your first encounter with flags and had a look at the carry flag. This was of special interest because it made the job of printing a binary number quite simple. It did so as soon as you learned about the rotate instruction RCL, which rotates a byte or word to the left, one bit at a time.

Once you learned about the carry flag and rotating bytes and words, you learned a new version of the add instruction, ADC. You used this later to build your program to print a number in binary notation.

This is where the LOOP instruction entered the scene. By loading the CX register with a loop count, you could keep the 80x86 executing a loop of instructions a number of times. You set CX to 8, to execute a loop eight times.

That is all you needed to write your program. You will use these tools again in the following chapters. In the next chapter we will print a binary number in hexadecimal notation, just as Debug does. By the time we finish Chapter 5, you will have a better idea of how Debug translates numbers from binary to hex. Then, we will move on to the other end of Debug—reading the numbers typed in hex and converting them to the 80x86's binary notation.

Printing Numbers in Hex

In this chapter you will learn some new tools needed to build a program that displays a binary number in hexadecimal notation. You will learn about the zero flag, as well as several other flags. You will learn how to use the CMP (compare) instruction to set these flags, and the JZ (jump if zero) conditional jump instruction to control your program. Finally, you will learn about Boolean logic and the AND instruction.

Topics Covered

The program in Chapter 4 was fairly straightforward. You were lucky because the carry flag made it easy to print a binary number as a string of 0 and 1 characters. Now we will move on to printing numbers in hex notation. The work will be a bit less direct and we will begin to repeat ourselves in our programs, writing the same sequence of instructions more than once. But that type of repetition won't last forever. In Chapter 7 you will learn about procedures or subroutines that eliminate the need to write more than one copy of a group of instructions. First, you learn some more useful instructions and see how to print numbers in hex.

Comparing Numbers

In the last chapter you learned something about status flags and examined the carry flag, which is represented as either CY or NC in Debug's R display. The other flags are equally useful, keeping track of the *status* for the last arithmetic operation. There are eight flags altogether, and you will learn about them as they are needed.

Other Status Flags

Recall that CY means the carry flag is 1, or set, whereas NC means the carry flag is 0. In all flags 1 means *true* and 0 means *false*. For example, if a SUB instruction results in 0, the flag known as the Zero Flag would be set to 1— true—and you would see it in the R display as ZR (*Zero*). Otherwise, the zero flag would be reset to 0—NZ (*Not Zero*).

Look at an example that tests the zero flag. You will use the SUB instruction to subtract two numbers. If the two numbers are equal, the result will be zero, and the zero flag will appear as ZR on your display. Enter the following subtract instruction:

```
396F:0100 29D8          SUB     AX,BX
```

Now, trace through the instruction with a few different numbers, watching for ZR or NZ to appear in the zero flag. If you place the same number (F5h in the following example) into both the AX and BX registers, you will see the zero flag set after one subtract instruction, and cleared after another, as follows:

```
-R
AX=00F5  BX=00F5  CX=0000  DX=0000  SP=FFEE  BP=0000  SI=0000  DI=0000
DS=0CDE  ES=0CDE  SS=0CDE  CS=0CDE  IP=0100   NV UP DI PL NZ NA PO NC
0CDE:0100 29D8         SUB     AX,BX
-T

AX=0000  BX=00F5  CX=0000  DX=0000  SP=FFEE  BP=0000  SI=0000  DI=0000
DS=0CDE  ES=0CDE  SS=0CDE  CS=0CDE  IP=0102   NV UP DI PL ZR NA PE NC
0CDE:0102 3F           AAS
-R IP
IP 0102
:100
-R
AX=0000  BX=00F5  CX=0000  DX=0000  SP=FFEE  BP=0000  SI=0000  DI=0000
DS=0CDE  ES=0CDE  SS=0CDE  CS=0CDE  IP=0100   NV UP DI PL ZR NA PE NC
0CDE:0100 29D8         SUB     AX,BX
-T

AX=FF0B  BX=00F5  CX=0000  DX=0000  SP=FFEE  BP=0000  SI=0000  DI=0000
DS=0CDE  ES=0CDE  SS=0CDE  CS=0CDE  IP=0102   NV UP DI NG NZ AC PO CY
0CDE:0102 3F           AAS
```

If you subtract one from zero, the result is FFFFh, which is −1 in two's-complement form. Can you tell from the R display whether a number is positive or negative? Yes—another flag, called the Sign Flag, changes between NG (*Negative*) and PL (*Plus*), and is set to 1 when a number is a negative two's-complement number.

Another new flag you will be interested in is the Overflow Flag, which changes between OV (*Overflow*) when the flag is 1 and NV (*No Overflow*) when the flag is 0. The overflow flag is set if the sign bit changes when it shouldn't. For example, if you add two positive numbers, such as 7000h and 6000h, you get a negative number, D000h, or −12288. This is an error because the result overflows the word. The result should be positive, but isn't, so the 80x86 sets the overflow flag. (Remember, if you were dealing with unsigned numbers, this would not be an error and you would ignore the overflow flag.)

Try several different numbers to see if you can set and reset each of these flags, trying them out until you are comfortable with them. For the overflow, subtract a large negative number from a large positive number—for example, 7000h − 8000h, since 8000h is a negative number equal to −32768 in two's-complement form.

Using the Status Bits—Conditional Jumps

Now you are ready to look at a set of instructions called the *conditional jump* instructions. They allow you to check status flags more conveniently than you have been able to so far. The instruction JZ (*Jump if Zero*) jumps to a new address if the last arithmetic result was zero. Thus, if you follow a SUB instruction with, say, JZ 15A, a result of zero for the subtraction would cause the 80x86 to jump to and start executing statements at address 15Ah, rather than at the next instruction.

The JZ instruction tests the zero flag, and, if it is set (ZR), does a jump. The opposite of JZ is JNZ (*Jump if Not Zero*). Let's look at a simple example that uses JNZ and subtracts one from a number until the result is zero, as follows:

```
396F:0100 2C01          SUB     AL,01
396F:0102 75FC          JNZ     0100
396F:0104 CD20          INT     20
```

Put a number like three in AL so you will go through the loop a few times, then trace through this program, one instruction at a time, to see how conditional branches work. We put the INT 20h instruction at the end so typing G by accident won't drop off the end of your program; it's a good defensive practice.

Using CMP to Compare Numbers

You may have noticed that using SUB to compare two numbers has the potentially undesirable side effect of changing the first number. CMP (*Compare*) allows you to do the subtraction without storing the result anywhere and without changing the first number. The result is used only to set the flags, so you can use one of the many conditional jump instructions after a compare. To see what happens, set both AX and BX to the same number, F5h, and trace through this instruction, as follows:

```
-A 100
0CDE:0100 CMP AX,BX
0CDE:0102
-T
```

```
AX=00F5  BX=00F5  CX=0000  DX=0000  SP=FFEE  BP=0000  SI=0000  DI=0000
DS=0CDE  ES=0CDE  SS=0CDE  CS=0CDE  IP=0102     NV UP DI PL ZR NA PE NC
0CDE:0102 3F              AAS
```

The zero flag is now set (ZR), but F5h remains in both registers.

To use CMP to print a single hex digit. Create a set of instructions that uses flags to alter the flow of your program, as LOOP did in the last chapter, in a manner similar to BASIC's IF-THEN statement. This new set of instructions will use the flags to test for such conditions as less than, greater than, and so on. You will not have to worry about which flags are set when the first number is less than the second; the instructions know which flags to look at.

Printing a Single Hex Digit

Start by putting a small number (between 0 and Fh) into the BL register. Since any number between 0 and Fh is equivalent to one hex digit, you can convert your choice to a single ASCII character and then print it. Look at the steps needed to do the conversion.

Character	ASCII Code (Hex)	Character	ASCII Code (Hex)
/	2F	<	3C
0	30	=	3D
1	31	>	3E
2	32	?	3F
3	33	@	40
4	34	A	41
5	35	B	42
6	36	C	43
7	37	D	44
8	38	E	45
9	39	F	46
:	3A	G	47
;	3B	H	49

Figure 5-1: Partial ASCII table showing the characters used by hex digits.

The ASCII characters 0 through 9 have the values 30h through 39h; the characters A through F, however, have the values 41h through 46h (see Figure 5-1).

71

The problem is that these two groups of ASCII characters are separated by seven characters. As a result, the conversion to ASCII will be different for the two groups of numbers (0 through 9 and Ah through Fh), so you handle each group differently. A BASIC program to do this two-part conversion looks like this:

```
IF  BL < &H0A THEN
    BL = BL + &H30
ELSE
    BL = BL + &H37
END IF
```

The BASIC conversion program is fairly simple. Unfortunately, the 80x86's machine language doesn't include an ELSE statement. It is far more primitive than BASIC is, so you will need to be somewhat clever. Here is another BASIC program, this time one that mimics the method you will use for the machine-language program.

```
BL = BL + &H30
IF  BL >= &H3A THEN
    BL = BL + &H7
END IF
```

You can convince yourself that this program works by trying it with some choice examples. The numbers 0, 9, Ah, and Fh are particularly good because these four numbers cover all the *boundary* conditions, which are areas where we often run into problems.

Here, 0 and Fh are, respectively, the smallest and largest single-digit hex numbers. By using 0 and Fh, you check the bottom and top of the range. The numbers 9 and 0Ah, although next to each other, require two different conversion schemes in the program. By using 9 and 0Ah, you confirm that you have chosen the correct place to switch between these two conversion schemes.

The machine-language version of this program contains a few more steps, but it is essentially the same as the BASIC version. It uses the CMP instruction, as well as a conditional jump instruction called JL (*Jump if Less Than*). The program to take a single-digit hex number in the BL register and print it in hex is as follows:

Notice that we just wrote 0Ah for the number A, rather than AH, so we wouldn't confuse the number Ah with the register AH. We will often place a zero before hex numbers in situations like this that could be confusing. In fact, since it never hurts to place a zero before a hex number, it is a good idea to place a zero before all hex numbers.

```
3985:0100 B402        MOV    AH,02
3985:0102 88DA        MOV    DL,BL
3985:0104 80C230      ADD    DL,30
3985:0107 80FA3A      CMP    DL,3A
```

```
3985:010A 7C03          JL      010F
3985:010C 80C207        ADD     DL,07
3985:010F CD21          INT     21
3985:0111 CD20          INT     20
```

The CMP instruction, as you saw before, subtracts two numbers (DL – 3Ah) to set the flags, but it does not change DL. So if DL is less than 3Ah, the JL 10F instruction skips to the INT 21h instruction at 10Fh. Place a single-digit hex number in BL and trace through this example to get a better feeling for CMP and our algorithm to convert hex to ASCII. Remember to use either the G command with a breakpoint or the P command when you run the INT instructions.

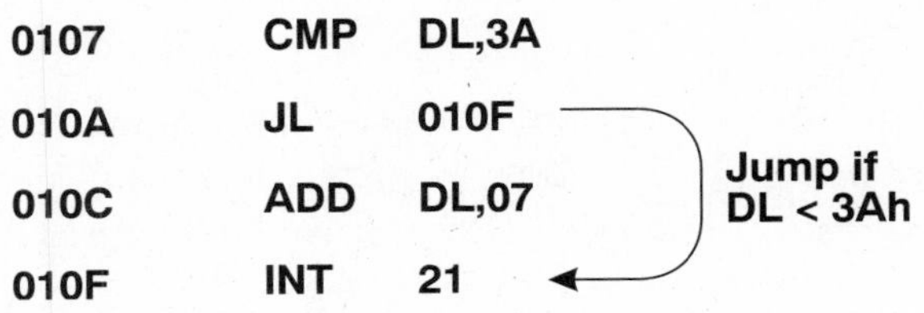

Figure 5-2: The JL instruction.

Using Rotate To Get the Upper Nibble

The program works for any single-digit hex number, but we need a few more steps to print a two-digit hex number. We need to isolate each digit (four bits, which are often called a *nibble*) of this two-digit hex number. In this section, you will see that you can easily isolate the first, or higher, four bits. In the next section, you will encounter a concept known as a *logical operation*, which you will use to isolate the lower four bits—the second of the two hex digits.

To begin, recall that the RCL instruction rotates a byte or a word to the left through the carry flag. In the last chapter you used the instruction RCL BL,1, where the number one told the 80x86 to rotate BL left by one bit. You can rotate by more than one bit if you want, but you cannot simply write the instruction RCL BL,2. For rotations by more than one bit, you must place a rotate count in the CL register.

Although RCL BL,2 isn't a legal 8088 instruction, it works just fine with the 80286 and above processors found on most of today's computers. Since there are still some PCs with the older 8088s, it is best to write your programs for the lowest common denominator—the older 8088.

The CL register is used here in much the same way as the CX register is used by the LOOP instruction to determine the number of times to repeat a loop. The 80x86 uses CL for the number of times to rotate a byte or word, rather than the CX register, because it makes no sense to rotate more than 16 times. The eight-bit CL register is more than large enough to hold your maximum shift count.

How does all this tie in with printing a two-digit hex number? The plan is to rotate the byte in DL four bits to the right. To do so, you will use a slightly different rotate instruction called SHR (*Shift Right*). Using SHR, you will be able to move the upper four bits of your number to the rightmost nibble (four bits).

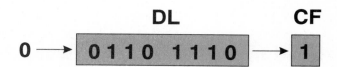

Figure 5-3: The SHR DL,1 Instruction.

You also want the upper four bits of DL set to zero, so that the entire register becomes equal to the nibble you are shifting into the right nibble. If you were to enter SHR DL,1, your instruction would move the byte in DL one bit to the right. At the *same* time it would move bit 0 into the carry flag, while *shifting* a zero into bit 7 (the highest, or leftmost, bit in DL). If you do that three more times, the upper four bits will end up shifted right into the lower four bits, while the upper four bits will all have had zeros shifted into them. You can do all that shifting in one instruction by using the CL register as the *shift count*. Setting CL to four before the instruction SHR DL,CL, will ensure that DL becomes equal to the upper hex digit. To see how this works, place 4 into

CL and 5Dh into DL. Then enter and trace through the following SHR instruction:

```
3985:0100 D2EA        SHR     DL,CL
```

DL should now be 05h, which is the first digit in the number 5Dh. Now you can print this digit with a program like the one used earlier. By putting together the pieces you have so far, you can build the following program to take a number in the BL register and print the first hex digit:

```
3985:0100 B402        MOV     AH,02
3985:0102 88DA        MOV     DL,BL
3985:0104 B104        MOV     CL,04
3985:0106 D2EA        SHR     DL,CL
3985:0108 80C230      ADD     DL,30
3985:010B 80FA3A      CMP     DL,3A
3985:010E 7C03        JL      0113
3985:0110 80C207      ADD     DL,07
3985:0113 CD21        INT     21
3985:0115 CD20        INT     20
```

Using AND to Isolate the Lower Nibble

Now that you can print the first of the two digits in a hex number, let's see how you can isolate and print the second digit. You will clear the upper four bits of your original (unshifted) number to zero, leaving DL equal to the lower four bits. It is easy to set the upper four bits to zero with an instruction called AND. The AND instruction is one of the *logical* instructions—those that have their roots in formal logic.

In formal logic, "A is true, if B *and* C are both true." But if either B or C is false, then A must also be false. If you take this statement, substitute one for true and zero for false, then look at the various combinations of A, B, and C, you can create what is known as a *truth table*. Here is the truth table for ANDing two bits together:

AND	F	T		AND	0	1
F	F	T	=	0	0	0
T	F	T		1	0	1

Down the left and across the top are the values for the two bits. The results for the AND are in the table, so you see that 0 AND 1 gives 0.

The AND instruction works on bytes and words by ANDing together the bits of each byte or word that are in the same position. For example, the statement AND BL,CL successively ANDs bits 0 of BL and CL, bits 1, bits 2, and so on, and places the result in BL. We can make this clearer with an example in binary, as follows:

```
      1 0 1 1 0 1 0 1
AND   0 1 1 1 0 1 1 0
      ─────────────────
      0 0 1 1 0 1 0 0
```

Furthermore, by ANDing 0Fh to any number, you can set the upper four bits to zero, as follows:

```
      0 1 1 1 1 0 1 1     7Bh
AND   0 0 0 0 1 1 1 1  =  0Fh
      ─────────────────
      0 0 0 0 1 0 1 1     0Bh
```

Next you can put this logic into a short program that takes the number in BL, isolates the lower hex digit by ANDing 0Fh to the upper four bits, and then prints the result as a character. You saw most of the details of this program when you printed the upper hex digit; the only new detail is the AND instruction.

```
3985:0100 B402          MOV     AH,02
3985:0102 88DA          MOV     DL,BL
3985:0104 80E20F        AND     DL,0F
3985:0107 80C230        ADD     DL,30
3985:010A 80FA3A        CMP     DL,3A
3985:010D 7C03          JL      0112
3985:010F 80C207        ADD     DL,07
3985:0112 CD21          INT     21
3985:0114 CD20          INT     20
```

Try this with some two-digit hex numbers in BL before you move on to put the pieces together to print both digits. You should see the rightmost hex digit of your number in BL on the screen.

Putting It All Together

There isn't much to change when you put all the pieces together. You need only to change the address of the second JL instruction used to print the second hex digit. The complete program is as follows:

```
3985:0100 B402        MOV     AH,02
3985:0102 88DA        MOV     DL,BL
3985:0104 B104        MOV     CL,04
3985:0106 D2EA        SHR     DL,CL
3985:0108 80C230      ADD     DL,30
3985:010B 80FA3A      CMP     DL,3A
3985:010E 7C03        JL      0113
3985:0110 80C207      ADD     DL,07
3985:0113 CD21        INT     21
3985:0115 88DA        MOV     DL,BL
3985:0117 80E20F      AND     DL,0F
3985:011A 80C230      ADD     DL,30
3985:011D 80FA3A      CMP     DL,3A
3985:0120 7C03        JL      0125
3985:0122 80C207      ADD     DL,07
3985:0125 CD21        INT     21
3985:0127 CD20        INT     20
```

After you have entered this program, you will have to type *U 100*, followed by *U*, to see the entire unassembled listing. Note that you have repeated one set of five instructions twice: the instructions at 108h through 113h, and 11Ah through 125h. In Chapter 7 you will learn how to write this sequence of instructions just once using a new instruction called CALL.

Summary

In this chapter, you learned more about how Debug translates numbers from the 80x86's binary format to a hex format you can read. What did you add to your growing store of knowledge?

First, you learned about some of the two-letter flags you see on the right side of the register (R) display. These status bits give you a great deal of information about the last arithmetic operation. By looking at the zero flag, for example, you could tell whether the result of the last operation was zero. You also found that you could compare two numbers with a CMP instruction.

Next, you learned how to print a single-digit hex number. Armed with this information, you learned about the SHR instruction, enabling you to move the upper digit of a two-digit hex number into the lower four bits of BL. That completed, you could print the digit, as before.

Finally, the AND instruction allowed you to isolate the lower hex digit from the upper. By putting all these pieces together, you wrote a program to print a two-digit hex number.

We could have continued on to print a four-digit hex number, but at this point, we would find ourselves repeating instructions. Before you try to print a four-digit hex number, you will learn about procedures in Chapter 7. Then, you will know enough to write a procedure to do the job. By then you will also be ready to learn about the assembler—a program that will do much of your work. Now, on to reading hex numbers.

Reading Characters

In this chapter you will learn how to read characters from your keyboard. You will build a small program that reads a two-digit hex number from the keyboard.

6

Topics Covered

Now that you know how to print a byte in hex notation, you are going to reverse the process by reading two characters—hex digits—from the keyboard and converting them into a single byte.

Reading One Character

The DOS INT 21h function call we have been using has an input function, number 1, that reads a character from the keyboard. When you learned about function calls in Chapter 4, you saw that the function number must be placed in the AH register before an INT 21h call. To try function 1 for INT 21h, enter INT 21h at location 0100h as follows:

```
396F:0100 CD21          INT     21
```

Place 01h into AH and type either *G 102* or *P* to run this one instruction. All you will see is the blinking cursor. Actually, DOS has paused and is waiting until you press a key (don't do so yet). Once you press a key, DOS will place the ASCII code for that character into the AL register. You will use this instruction later to read the characters of a hex number. Right now, see what happens when you press a key like the F1 key. DOS will return a 0 in AL and a semicolon (;) after Debug's hyphen prompt.

F1 is one of a set of special keys with *extended codes*, which DOS treats differently from the keys representing normal ASCII characters. (You will find a table listing these extended codes in Appendix D.) For each of these special keys, DOS sends *two* characters, one right after the other. The first character returned is always zero, indicating that the next character is the *scan code* for a special key.

To read both characters, you would have to execute INT 21h twice. But in our example, you read only the first character, the zero, and leave the scan code in DOS. When Debug finished with the G 102 (or P) command, it began to read characters, and the first character it read was the scan code left behind from the F1 key, namely, 59, which is the ASCII code for a semicolon.

Later, when we develop the Dskpatch program, you will begin to use these extended codes to bring the cursor and function keys to life. Until then, we will just work with the normal ASCII characters.

Reading a Single-Digit Hex Number

Next you need to reverse the conversion that you used in Chapter 5, when you transformed a single-digit hex number to the ASCII code for one of the characters in 0 through 9 or A through F. To convert one character, such as C or D, from a hex character to a byte, you must subtract either 30h (for 0 through 9) or 37h (for A through F). Here is a simple program that will read one ASCII character and convert it to a byte.

```
3985:0100 B401        MOV    AH,01
3985:0102 CD21        INT    21
3985:0104 2C30        SUB    AL,30
3985:0106 3C09        CMP    AL,09
3985:0108 7E02        JLE    010C
3985:010A 2C07        SUB    AL,07
3985:010C CD20        INT    20
```

Most of these instructions should be familiar now, but there is one new one, JLE (*Jump if Less than or Equal*). In your program, this instruction jumps if AL is less than or equal to 9h.

To see the conversion from hex character to ASCII, you need to see the AL register just before the INT 20h is executed. Since Debug restores the registers when it executes the INT 20h, you will need to set a breakpoint, as you did in Chapter 4. Here, type *G 10C*, and you will see that AL will contain the hex number converted from a character.

Try typing some characters, such as *k* or a lowercase *d*, that are not hex digits to see what happens. You will notice that this program works correctly only when the input is one of the digits 0 through 9 or the uppercase letters A through F. You will correct this minor failing in the next chapter when you learn about subroutines, or procedures. Until then, we will be sloppy and ignore error conditions. You will have to type correct characters for your program to work properly.

Reading a Two-Digit Hex Number

Reading two hex digits isn't much more complicated than reading one, but it does require many more instructions. Begin by reading the first digit, then place its hex value in the DL register and multiply it by 16. To perform this multiplication, shift the DL register left four bits, which places a hex zero (four zero bits) to the right of the digit you just read. The instruction SHL DL,CL, with CL set to four, does the trick by inserting zeros at the right. In fact, the SHL (*Shift Left*) instruction is known as an *arithmetic shift*, because it has the same effect as an arithmetic multiplication by two, four, eight, and so on, depending on the number (such as one, two, or three) in CL (See Figure 6-1).

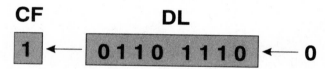

Figure 6-1: The SHL DL,1 instruction.

Finally, with the first digit shifted over, add the second hex digit to the number in DL (the first digit * 16). You can see and work through all these details in the following program:

```
3985:0100 B401        MOV     AH,01
3985:0102 CD21        INT     21
3985:0104 88C2        MOV     DL,AL
3985:0106 80EA30      SUB     DL,30
3985:0109 80FA09      CMP     DL,09
3985:010C 7E03        JLE     0111
3985:010E 80EA07      SUB     DL,07
3985:0111 B104        MOV     CL,04
3985:0113 D2E2        SHL     DL,CL
3985:0115 CD21        INT     21
3985:0117 2C30        SUB     AL,30
3985:0119 3C09        CMP     AL,09
3985:011B 7E02        JLE     011F
3985:011D 2C07        SUB     AL,07
3985:011F 00C2        ADD     DL,AL
3985:0121 CD20        INT     20
```

Now that you have a working program, it is a good idea to check the boundary conditions to confirm that it is working properly. For these boundary conditions, use the numbers 00, 09, 0A, 0F, 90, A0, F0, and some other number, such as 3C.

Use a breakpoint to run the program without executing the INT 20h instruction. (Make sure you use uppercase letters for your hex input.)

Summary

You have finally had a chance to practice what you learned in previous chapters without being flooded with new information. Using a new INT 21 function (number 1) to read characters, you developed a program to read a two-digit hex number. Along the way, we emphasized the need to test programs with all the boundary conditions.

We will wrap up Part I by learning about procedures in the 80x86.

Using Procedures to Write Reusable Code

In this chapter you will learn how to write small, general-purpose pieces of code called procedures that you can use from anywhere in your program. Procedures are something you will use heavily in almost any program you write. In this process you will also learn about the stack, and you will build a new hex-input routine that prevents you from typing invalid digits.

Topics Covered

In the next chapter, we will discuss MASM, the macro assembler, and you will begin to use *assembly* language. But before leaving Debug, you will look at one last set of examples and learn about subroutines and a special place to store numbers called the *stack*.

Writing Procedures

A procedure is a list of instructions that can be executed from different places in a program, rather than having to repeat the same list of instructions at each place they're needed. In BASIC such lists are called *subroutines*, but we will call them *procedures* for reasons that will become clear later.

You move to and from procedures by using a pair of instructions. You call a procedure with one instruction, *CALL*. You return from the procedure with a *RET* instruction.

Here is a simple BASIC program, written in QBasic, that you will later re-write in machine language. This program calls a subroutine ten times, each time printing a single character, starting with A and ending with J, as follows:

```
DIM SHARED A
A = &H41                    'ASCII for 'A'
FOR I = 1 TO 10
    DoPrint
    A = A + 1
NEXT I

SUB DoPrint
    PRINT CHR$(A);
END SUB
```

QBasic is actually much simpler than older versions of BASIC, such as GW-BASIC, that were shipped with versions of DOS before DOS 5.0. Earlier versions of BASIC required line numbers in front of each line of the program, and you had to use the GOSUB and RETURN commands to write the same code. Since the older BASIC looks more like the machine code we will write below, here is the above program rewritten in a primitive version of BASIC, using line numbers.

```
10 A = &H41                    'ASCII for 'A'
20 FOR I = 1 TO 10
30 GOSUB 1000
40 A = A + 1
50 NEXT I
60 END

1000 PRINT CHR$(A)
1010 RETURN
```

In this case the subroutine follows a practice common when BASIC programs needed line numbers, by beginning at line 1000 to leave room for more instructions to be added to the main program without affecting the line number of the subroutine. You will have to do the same with your machine-language procedure since you cannot move machine-language programs easily (this won't be a problem once you start to use the assembler in the next chapter, so it is only a temporary problem). You will put the machine-language subroutine at 200h, far away from the main program at 100h. You will also replace GOSUB 1000 with the instruction CALL 200h, which *calls* the procedure at memory location 200h. The CALL sets IP to 200h, and the 80x86 starts executing the instructions at 200h.

The FOR-NEXT loop of the BASIC program (as you saw in Chapter 4) can be written as a LOOP instruction. The other pieces of the main program (except for the INC instruction) should be familiar. They are as follows:

```
3985:0100 B241        MOV     DL,41
3985:0102 B90A00      MOV     CX,000A
3985:0105 E8F800      CALL    0200
3985:0108 FEC2        INC     DL
3985:010A E2F9        LOOP    0105
3985:010C CD20        INT     20
```

The first instruction places 41h (ASCII for A) into the DL register, because the INT 21h instruction prints the character given by the ASCII code in DL. The INT 21h instruction itself is located some distance away, in the procedure at location 200h. INC DL, the new instruction, *increments* the DL register. That is, it adds one to DL, setting DL to the next character in the alphabet. The procedure you should enter at 200h is as follows:

```
3985:0200 B402        MOV     AH,02
3985:0202 CD21        INT     21
3985:0204 C3          RET
```

Recall that the 02h in AH tells DOS to print the character in DL when you execute the INT 21h instruction. RET is a new instruction that *returns* to the first instruction (LOOP) following the CALL in your main program.

Type G to see the output of this program, then single-step through it to see how it works (remember to use either a breakpoint or the P command to run the INT 21 instruction).

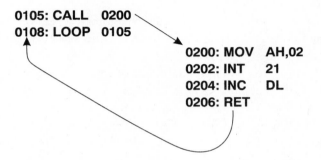

Figure 7-1: The CALL and RET instructions.

How CALL Works: The Stack and Return Addresses

The CALL instruction in your program needs to save the *return address* somewhere so the 80x86 will know where to resume executing instructions when it sees the RET instruction. For the storage place itself, there is a portion of memory known as the *stack*. For tracking what is on the stack, there are two registers that you can see on the R display: the SP (*Stack Pointer*) register, which points to the top of the stack, and the SS (*Stack Segment*), which holds the segment number.

In operation, a stack for the 80x86 is just like a stack of trays in a cafeteria, where placing a tray on the top covers the trays underneath. The last tray on the stack is the first to come off, so another name for a stack is LIFO, for *Last*

In, First Out. This order, LIFO, is precisely what you need for retrieving return addresses after you make *nested* CALLs like the following:

```
396F:0100 E8FD00          CALL    0200
          .
          .
          .
396F:0200 E8FD00          CALL    0300
396F:0203 C3              RET
          .
          .
          .
396F:0300 E8FD00          CALL    0400
396F:0303 C3              RET
          .
          .
          .
396F:0400 C3              RET
```

The instruction at 100h calls one at 200h, which calls one at 300h, which calls one at 400h, where you finally see a return (RET) instruction. This RET returns to the instruction following the *previous* CALL instruction, at 300h, so the 80x86 resumes executing instructions at 303h. But there it encounters a RET instruction at 303h, which pulls the next oldest address (203h) off the stack. So the 80x86 resumes executing instructions at 203h, and so on. Each RET *pops* the topmost return address off the stack, so each RET follows the same path backward as the CALLs did forward, see Figures 7-2 and 7-3.

Try entering a program like the preceding one. Use multiple calls, and trace through the program to see how the calls and returns work. Although the process may not seem very interesting right now, there are other uses for this stack, and a good understanding of how it works will come in handy. (In a later chapter, you will look for the stack in memory.)

PUSHing and POPping Data

The stack is a useful place to store words of data for a while, provided you are careful to restore the stack before a RET instruction. You have seen that a CALL instruction *pushes* the return address (one word) onto the top of the stack, while a RET instruction *pops* this word off the top of the stack, loads it into the IP register, and exposes the word that was lying underneath it. You can do the same thing with the instructions PUSH and POP, which allow you to push and pop words.

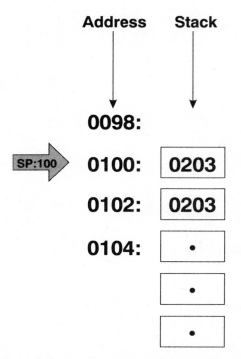

Figure 7-2: The stack just before executing the CALL 400 instruction.

It is often convenient to save the values of registers at the beginning of a procedure and restore them at the end, just before the RET instruction. Then you are free to use these registers in any way you like within the procedure, as long as you restore their values at the end.

Programs are built from many levels of procedures, with each level calling the procedures at the next level down. By saving registers at the beginning of a procedure and restoring them at the end, you remove unwanted interactions between procedures at different levels, making your programming much easier. You will see more about saving and restoring registers in Chapter 13, when we discuss modular design. Following is an example (don't enter it) that saves and restores CX and DX:

```
396F:0200 51         PUSH   CX
396F:0201 52         PUSH   DX
396F:0202 B90800     MOV    CX,0008
396F:0205 E8F800     CALL   0300
396F:0208 FEC2       INC    DL
396F:020A E2F9       LOOP   0205
396F:020C 5A         POP    DX
396F:020D 59         POP    CX
396F:020E C3         RET
```

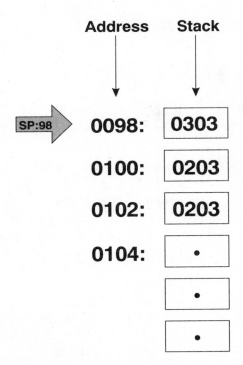

Figure 7-3: The stack just after executing the CALL 400 instruction.

Notice that the POPs are in reverse order from the PUSHes, because a POP removes the word placed most recently on the stack, and the old value of DX is on top of the old CX.

Saving and restoring CX and DX allows you to change these registers in the procedure that begins at 200h, but without changing the values used by any procedure that calls this one. Once you have saved CX and DX, you can use these registers to hold *local* variables—variables you can use within this procedure without affecting the values used by the calling program.

You will often use such local variables to simplify programming tasks. As long as you are careful to restore the original values, you won't have to worry about your procedures changing any of the registers used by the calling program. This will become clearer in the next example, which is a procedure to read a hex number. Unlike the program in Chapter 6, your new program now will allow only valid characters such as A, but not K.

Reading Hex Numbers with More Class

Next, you can create a procedure that keeps reading characters until it receives one that can be converted to a hex number between 0 and Fh. You do not want to display any invalid characters, so you will sift through your input using a new INT 21h function, number 8, that reads a character but does not pass it onto the screen. That way you can *echo* (display) characters only if they are valid. Place 8h into the AH register and run through this instruction, typing an A just after you type G 102.

```
3985:0100 CD21          INT     21
```

The ASCII code for A (41h) is now in the AL register, but the A didn't appear on the screen. Using this function, your program can read characters without echoing them until it reads a valid hex digit (0 through 9 or A through F), which it will then echo. The procedure to do this and to convert the hex character to a hex number is as follows:

```
3985:0200 52            PUSH    DX
3985:0201 B408          MOV     AH,08
3985:0203 CD21          INT     21
3985:0205 3C30          CMP     AL,30
3985:0207 72FA          JB      0203
3985:0209 3C46          CMP     AL,46
```

```
3985:020B 77F6        JA      0203
3985:020D 3C39        CMP     AL,39
3985:020F 770A        JA      021B
3985:0211 B402        MOV     AH,02
3985:0213 88C2        MOV     DL,AL
3985:0215 CD21        INT     21
3985:0217 2C30        SUB     AL,30
3985:0219 5A          POP     DX
3985:021A C3          RET
3985:021B 3C41        CMP     AL,41
3985:021D 72E4        JB      0203
3985:021F B402        MOV     AH,02
3985:0221 88C2        MOV     DL,AL
3985:0223 CD21        INT     21
3985:0225 2C37        SUB     AL,37
3985:0227 5A          POP     DX
3985:0228 C3          RET
```

The procedure reads a character in AL (with the INT 21h at 203h) and checks to see if it is valid with the CMPs and conditional jumps. If the character just read is not a valid character, the conditional jump instructions sends the 80x86 back to location 203, where the INT 21h reads another character. (JA is *Jump if Above*, and JB is *Jump if Below*. Both treat the two numbers as unsigned numbers, whereas the JL instruction used earlier treated both as signed numbers.)

By line 211h, you know that you have a valid digit between 0 and 9, so you just subtract the code for the character 0 and return the result in the AL register, remembering to pop the DX register, which you saved at the beginning of the procedure. The process for hex digits A through F is much the same. Notice that there are two RET instructions in this procedure. (You could have had more, or you could have had just one.) Here is a very simple program to test the procedure:

```
3985:0100 E8FD00        CALL    0200
3985:0103 CD20          INT     20
```

As you have done before, use either the G command with a breakpoint, or use the P command. You want to execute the CALL 200h instruction without executing the INT 20h instruction, so you can see the registers just before the program terminates and the registers are restored.

You will see the cursor at the left side of the screen, waiting patiently for a character. Type *k*, which isn't a valid character. Nothing should happen. Now, type any of the uppercase hex characters. You should see the character's hex value in AL and the character itself echoed on the screen. Test this procedure with the boundary conditions: '/' (the character before zero), 0, 9, ':' (the character just after 9), and so on. Now that you have this procedure, the program to read a two-digit hex number with error handling is fairly straightforward.

```
3985:0100 E8FD00      CALL    0200
3985:0103 88C2        MOV     DL,AL
3985:0105 B104        MOV     CL,04
3985:0107 D2E2        SHL     DL,CL
3985:0109 E8F400      CALL    0200
3985:010C 00C2        ADD     DL,AL
3985:010E B402        MOV     AH,02
3985:0110 CD21        INT     21
3985:0112 CD20        INT     20
```

You can run this program from DOS, since it reads in a two-digit hex number and then displays the ASCII character that corresponds to the number you typed in.

Aside from the procedure, your main program is much simpler than the version you wrote in the last chapter, and you have not duplicated the instructions to read characters. You did add error handling, even if it did complicate the procedure; error handling ensures that the program accepts only valid input.

You can also see the reason for saving the DX register in the procedure. The main program stores the hex number in DL, so you don't want your procedure at 200h to change DL. On the other hand, the procedure at 200h must use DL itself to echo characters. So, by using the instruction PUSH DX at the beginning of the procedure, and POP DX at the end, you saved yourself from problems. From now on, to avoid complicated interactions between procedures, be very strict about saving any registers used by a procedure.

Summary

Your programming is becoming more sophisticated. You have learned about procedures, which enable you to reuse the same set of instructions without rewriting them each time. You have also discovered the stack and seen that a CALL stores a return address on the top of the stack, while a RET instruction returns to the address on the top of the stack.

You learned how to use the stack for more than just saving return addresses. You used the stack to store the values of registers (with a PUSH instruction) so you could use them in a procedure. By restoring the registers (with a POP instruction) at the end of each procedure, you avoided unwanted interactions between procedures. By always saving and restoring registers in procedures that you write, you can CALL other procedures without worrying about which registers are used within the other procedure.

Finally, armed with this knowledge, you moved on to build a better program to read hex numbers—this time, with error checking. The program you built here is similar to one you will use in later chapters, when you begin to develop your Dskpatch program.

Now you are ready to move on to Part II, where you will learn how to use the assembler. The next chapter covers the use of the assembler to convert a program to machine language. You will also see that there will not be any reason to leave room between procedures, as in this chapter, when you put your procedure way up at location 200h.

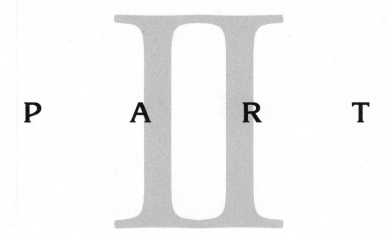

P A R T
II

Assembly Language

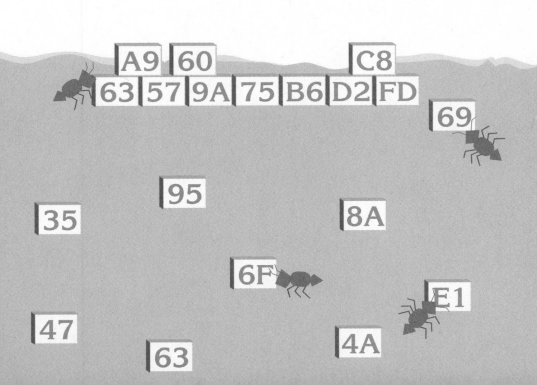

Welcome to the Assembler

In this chapter you will learn how to build programs using either the Microsoft Macro Assembler or the Borland Turbo Assembler. Building programs with the assembler is much easier than building them with Debug. You will learn how to assemble and link programs and how to comment your programs and use labels so they are easy to understand.

Topics Covered

At long last you are ready to meet the assembler, a DOS program that will make your programming much simpler. From now on, you will write mnemonic, human-readable instructions directly, using the assembler to turn your programs into machine code.

This chapter and the next will be somewhat heavy with details on the assembler, but learning these details will be well worth the effort. Once you know how to use the assembler, you will get back on course in learning how to write assembly-language programs.

Building a Program without Debug

Up to this point, you have typed only *DEBUG* and then your program instructions. Now that you are about to leave Debug behind and to write programs without it, you will have to use either an editor or a word processor to create text, or human-readable files containing assembly-language instructions.

Begin by creating a *source file*—the name for the text version of an assembly-language program. You will create a source file for the program you built and named Writestr (short for Write Star) back in Chapter 3. To refresh your memory, here is the Debug version:

```
396F:0100 B402        MOV     AH,02
396F:0102 B261        MOV     DL,2A
396F:0104 CD21        INT     21
396F:0106 CD20        INT     20
```

Use a text editor, such as DOS's Edit, to enter the following lines of code into a file named WRITESTR.ASM (the extension .ASM means this is an assembler source file). Here, as with Debug, lowercase works just as well as uppercase, but we will continue to use uppercase letters to avoid confusion between the number 1 (one) and the lowercase letter l:

```
.MODEL SMALL
.CODE

        MOV     AH,2h
        MOV     DL,2Ah
```

```
INT     21h
INT     20h

END
```

This is the same program you created in Chapter 3, but it contains a few necessary changes and additions. Notice that there is an *h* after each hex number in the program. This *h* tells the assembler that the numbers are in hexadecimal. Unlike Debug, which assumes all numbers are in hexadecimal, the assembler assumes all numbers are decimal. You tell it otherwise by placing an *h* after any hexadecimal number (see Figure 8-1).

The assembler can become confused by numbers, such as ACh, that look like a name or an instruction. To avoid this, always type a zero before a hex number that begins with a letter. For example, type 0ACh—*not* ACh.

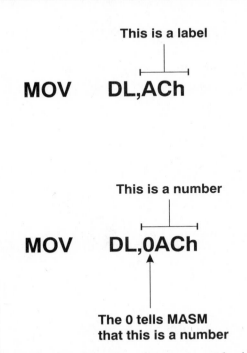

This is a label

MOV   DL,ACh

This is a number

MOV   DL,0ACh

**The 0 tells MASM
that this is a number**

Figure 8-1: Put a zero before hexadecimal numbers starting with a letter, otherwise the assembler will treat the number as a name.

The following program demonstrates what happens when you assemble a program with ACH rather than 0ACH.

```
.MODEL   SMALL
.CODE

        MOV     DL,ACh
        INT     20h


        END
```

The output is as follows:

```
C>ML /C TEST.ASM
Microsoft (R) Macro Assembler Version 6.00
Copyright (C) Microsoft Corp 1981-1991.  All rights reserved.

 Assembling: test.asm
test.asm(3): error A2006: undefined symbol : ACh

C>
```

Definitely not encouraging. But changing the ACh to 0ACh will satisfy the assembler. Also notice the spacing of the commands in the assembler program. We used tabs to align everything neatly and to make the source text more readable. Compare the program you entered with the following:

```
.MODEL SMALL
.CODE
MOV AH,2h
MOV DL,2Ah
INT 21h
INT 20h
END
```

A bit of a mess; the assembler does not care, but we do.

Now let's return to the three new lines in your source file. The three new lines are all *directives* (also sometimes called *pseudo-ops*, or pseudo-operations). They are called directives because they supply information and directions to the assembler, rather than generate instructions. The END directive marks the end of the source file so the assembler knows it is finished when it sees an END. Later on, you will see that END is also useful in other ways. But right now, let's put aside any further discussion of it or the other two directives and focus on the assembler.

Creating Source Files

Even though you have entered the lines of WRITESTR.ASM, there is one more consideration before we move on to actually assemble our program. The assembler can use source files that contain standard ASCII characters only. If you are using a word processor, bear in mind that not all word processors write disk files using only the standard ASCII characters. Microsoft Word is one such culprit. For such word processors, use the non-document, or unformatted, mode when you save your files.

Before you try assembling WRITESTR.ASM, make sure it is still ASCII. From DOS, type:

`C>TYPE WRITESTR.ASM`

You should see the same text you entered, as you entered it. If you see strange characters in your program (many word processors put additional formatting information into the file, which the assembler will treat as errors) you may have to use a different editor or word processor to enter programs. You will also need a blank line after the END statement in your file. The DOS Edit program (available in DOS 5 and later) will work well for creating source files.

You will need to read this note if you are using a version of MASM before 6.0, or Borland's Turbo Assembler.

If you are using an older version of MASM than 6.0, you will need to use a slightly different syntax for assembling files. Instead of using a command like "ML /C WRITESTR.ASM", you will need to use the command MASM followed by the file name (without the .ASM extension), and finally a semicolon: "MASM WRITESTR;".

If you are using Borland's Turbo Assembler, you will need to use a slightly different syntax for assembling files. Instead of using a command like "ML /C WRITESTR.ASM", you will need to use the command TASM followed by the file name (without the .ASM extension), and finally a semicolon: "TASM WRITESTR;".

Now, let's begin to assemble Writestr. (If you are using Borland's Turbo Assembler, type "TASM WRITESTR;" instead of "ML /C WRITESTR.ASM".)

```
C>ML /C WRITESTR.ASM
Microsoft (R) Macro Assembler Version 6.00
Copyright (C) Microsoft Corp 1981-1991.  All rights reserved.

 Assembling: writestr.asm

C>
```

You are not finished yet. At this point, the assembler has produced a file called WRITESTR.OBJ, which you will find on your disk. This is an intermediate file, called an *object file*. It contains the machine-language program, along with a lot of bookkeeping information used by another DOS program called the *Linker*.

Linking Your Program

Right now, you want the linker to take your OBJ file and create an EXE version of it. Link WRITESTR.OBJ by typing the following:

```
C>LINK WRITESTR;

Microsoft (R) Segmented-Executable Linker   Version 5.13
Copyright (C) Microsoft Corp 1984-1991.  All rights reserved.

LINK : warning L4021: no stack segment
LINK : warning L4038: program has no starting address

C>
```

Even though the linker warns you that there is no stack segment, you don't need one right now. After you learn how to add more of the trappings, you will see why you might want a stack segment. You also can ignore the warning about no starting address, which is not important here since you will be creating a COM file (you will see why later).

Now you have your EXE file, but this still isn't the last step. Next, you need to create a COM version, which is just what you created with Debug. Later you will see why you need all of these steps. For now, you will create a COM version of Writestr.

106

For your final step, you will use a program EXE2BIN.EXE. Exe2bin, as its name implies, converts an EXE file to a COM, or binary (bin) file. There is a difference between EXE and COM files, but we won't deal with the differences until Chapter 11. For now just create the COM file by typing the following:

```
C>EXE2BIN WRITESTR WRITESTR.COM
```

```
C>
```

The response did not tell you very much. To see whether Exe2bin worked, list all of the Writestr files you have created so far.

```
C>DIR WRITESTR.*
```

```
Volume in drive C has no label
Volume Serial Number is 191C-8737
Directory of C:\SOURCE\ASM

WRITESTR ASM        73 10-13-92    1:51p
WRITESTR OBJ       107 10-13-92    2:04p
WRITESTR EXE       520 10-13-92    2:07p
WRITESTR COM         8 10-13-92    2:12p
        4 file(s)         708 bytes
                     1179648 bytes free
```

```
C>
```

Type *writestr* to run the COM version and verify that your program functions properly (recall that it should print an asterisk on your screen). The exact sizes DOS reports for the first three files may vary a bit.

The results may seem a little anticlimactic, because it looks as though you are back where you were in Chapter 3. You are not; you have gained a great deal. It will become much clearer when you deal with calls again. Notice that you never once had to worry about where your program was put in memory, as you did about IP in Debug. The addresses were all taken care of for you.

Very soon you will appreciate this feature of the assembler: it will make programming much easier. For example, recall that in the last chapter you wasted space by placing your main program at 100h and the procedure you called at 200h. You will see that using the assembler allows us to place the procedure immediately after the main program without any gap. First, let's see how your program looks to Debug.

Looking at Writestr in Debug

To see how Debug reconstructs your program from the machine code of WRITESTR.COM, read your COM file into Debug and unassemble it, as follows:

```
C>DEBUG WRITESTR.COM
-U
397F:0100 B402        MOV     AH,02
397F:0102 B22A        MOV     DL,2A
397F:0104 CD21        INT     21
397F:0106 CD20        INT     20
          .
          .
          .
```

This is exactly what you had in Chapter 3. This is all Debug sees in WRITESTR.COM. The END and the two lines at the start of your source file did not make it through at all. What happened to them?

These directives do not appear in the final machine-language version of the program because they are for bookkeeping only. The assembler takes care of a lot of bookkeeping at the cost of some extra lines. You will make good use of directives to simplify your job. You will see how they affect your program when you learn about segments in Chapter 11.

Using Comments

Because you are no longer operating directly with Debug, you are free to add more to your program that the assembler sees but won't pass on to the 80x86. Perhaps the most important additions you can make are comments, which are invaluable in making a program clear. In assembly language programs, you place comments after a semicolon, which works like a single quotation mark (') in BASIC or the // in C++. The assembler ignores anything on the line after a semicolon, so you can add anything you want. If you add comments to your brief program you will see quite an improvement—you can understand this program without having to think back and remember what each line means.

```
.MODEL  SMALL
.CODE

        MOV     AH,2h           ;Select DOS function 2, character output
        MOV     DL,2Ah          ;Load the ASCII code for '*' to be printed
        INT     21h             ;Print it with INT 21h
        INT     20h             ;And exit to DOS

        END
```

Using Labels for Code

To round off this chapter, let's take a look at labels, which are another book-keeping feature of the assembler that make programming smoother.

Until now, you had to give a specific address when jumping from one part of a program to another with one of the jump commands. In everyday programming, inserting new instructions forces you to change the addresses in jump instructions. The assembler takes care of this problem with *labels*—names you give to the addresses of any instructions or memory locations. A label takes the place of an address. As soon as the assembler sees a label, it replaces the label with the correct address before sending it on to the 80x86, as in Figure 8-2.

Many programmers believe that well-written code doesn't need comments because well-written code is easy to understand. Not! While you may be able to understand what some code does without comments, you may not be able to figure out why the code is doing what it is. Good comments should therefore say why your code is doing something, not just what it's doing.

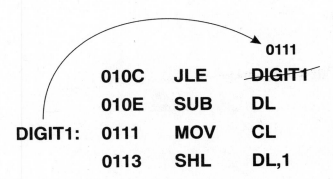

Figure 8-2: The assembler substitutes addresses for labels.

Labels can be up to 31 characters long and can contain letters, numbers, and any of the following symbols: a question mark (?), a period (.), an *at* symbol (@), an underline (_), or a dollar sign ($). They cannot start with a digit (0 through 9), and a period can be used only as the first character.

As a practical example, let's take a look at your program from Chapter 6 that reads a two-digit hex number. It contains two jumps, JLE 0111 and JLE 011F. The old version is as follows:

```
3985:0100 B401        MOV    AH,01
3985:0102 CD21        INT    21
3985:0104 88C2        MOV    DL,AL
3985:0106 80EA30      SUB    DL,30
3985:0109 80FA09      CMP    DL,09
3985:010C 7E03        JLE    0111
3985:010E 80EA07      SUB    DL,07
3985:0111 B104        MOV    CL,04
3985:0113 D2E2        SHL    DL,CL
3985:0115 CD21        INT    21
3985:0117 2C30        SUB    AL,30
3985:0119 3C09        CMP    AL,09
3985:011B 7E02        JLE    011F
3985:011D 2C07        SUB    AL,07
3985:011F 00C2        ADD    DL,AL
3985:0121 CD20        INT    20
```

The function of this program is not obvious. If this program is not fresh in your mind, it may take a while for you to understand it again. Adding comments and labels makes this program much easier to understand as follows:

```
.MODEL  SMALL
.CODE

        MOV    AH,1h      ;Select DOS function 1, character input
        INT    21h        ;Read a character, and return ASCII code in AL
        MOV    DL,AL      ;Move ASCII code into DL
        SUB    DL,30h     ;Subtract 30h to convert digit to 0 - 9
        CMP    DL,9h      ;Was it a digit between 0 and 9?
        JLE    DIGIT1     ;Yes, we have the first digit (four bits)
        SUB    DL,7h      ;No, subtract 7h to convert letter A - F
DIGIT1:
        MOV    CL,4h      ;Prepare to multiply by 16
        SHL    DL,CL      ;Multiply by shifting, becomes upper four bits
```

```
        INT     21h             ;Get next character
        SUB     AL,30h          ;Repeat conversion
        CMP     AL,9h           ;Is it a digit 0 - 9?
        JLE     DIGIT2          ;Yes, so we have the second digit
        SUB     AL,7h           ;No, subtract 7h
DIGIT2:
        ADD     DL,AL           ;ADD second digit
        INT     20h             ;And exit

        END
```

The labels here, DIGIT1 and DIGIT2, are of a type known as *NEAR* labels, because a colon (:) appears after the labels when they are defined. The term *NEAR* has to do with segments, which we will cover in Chapter 11 along with the MODEL, and CODE directives. If you assembled the preceding program and then unassembled it with Debug, you would see DIGIT1 replaced by 0111h and DIGIT2 replaced by 011Fh.

Summary

This has been quite a chapter. In a way, it is as if you have stepped into a new world. The assembler is much easier to work with than Debug, so you can now begin to write real programs because the assembler does much of the bookkeeping for you.

What have you learned here? You began by learning how to create a source file and then you went through the steps of assembling, linking, and converting it from an OBJ file to an EXE, and then a COM file, using a simple program from Chapter 3. The assembly language program you created contained a few directives that you have never seen before, but which will become familiar once you have become more comfortable using the assembler. In fact, you will place MODEL, CODE, and END directives in all of your programs from now on, because they are needed, even though it will not be apparent why until Chapter 11.

Next, you learned about comments. You may have wondered how you survived without comments. Comments add so much to the readability of programs that you should not skimp on them.

Finally you learned about labels, which make our programs even more readable. You will use all of these ideas and methods throughout the rest of this book. Let's move on to the next chapter to see how the assembler makes procedures easier to use.

Writing Procedures in Assembly Language

In this chapter you will learn how to write procedures in assembly language. This is much easier than writing them in machine language. You will also build the WRITE_CHAR and WRITE_HEX procedures, which you will use to build the Dskpatch program.

Files altered: VIDEO_IO.ASM

Disk file: VIDEO.9ASM

Topics Covered

Now that you have met the assembler, it is time to become more comfortable writing assembly language programs. In this chapter, we will return to the subject of procedures. You will see how to write procedures much more easily with the help of the hard-working assembler. Then, you will move on to building some useful procedures, which you will use when you develop your Dskpatch program in later chapters.

You will begin with two procedures to print a byte in hexadecimal. Along the way, you will meet several more directives. But, like MODEL, CODE, and END in Chapter 8, they will be left mostly undefined until Chapter 11, where you will learn more about segments.

The Assembler's Procedures

When we first mentioned procedures, we left a large gap between the main program and its procedures so that we would have room for changes without having to worry about our main program overlapping a procedure. Now you have the assembler. Because it does all the work of assigning addresses to instructions, you no longer need to leave a gap between procedures. With the assembler, each time you make a change, you just assemble the program again.

You built a small program with one CALL in Chapter 7. The program did nothing more than print the letters A through J. It appeared as follows:

```
3985:0100 B241          MOV     DL,41
3985:0102 B90A00        MOV     CX,000A
3985:0105 E8F800        CALL    0200
3985:0108 FEC2          INC     DL
3985:010A E2F9          LOOP    0105
3985:010C CD20          INT     20

3985:0200 B402          MOV     AH,02
3985:0202 CD21          INT     21
3985:0204 C3            RET
```

Let's turn this into a program for the assembler. It will be hard to read without labels and comments, so add those embellishments to make your program far more readable as shown in Figure 9-1.

Listing 9-1 The Program PRINTAJ.ASM

```
.MODEL   SMALL
.CODE

PRINT_A_J        PROC
         MOV     DL,'A'                  ;Start with the character A
         MOV     CX,10                   ;Print 10 characters, starting with A
PRINT_LOOP:
         CALL    WRITE_CHAR              ;Print character
         INC     DL                      ;Move to the next char in the alphabet
         LOOP    PRINT_LOOP              ;Continue for 10 characters
         INT     20h                     ;Return to DOS
PRINT_A_J        ENDP

WRITE_CHAR       PROC
         MOV     AH,2                    ;Set function code for character output
         INT     21h                     ;Print the character already in DL
         RET                             ;Return from this procedure
WRITE_CHAR       ENDP

         END     PRINT_A_J
```

There are two new directives here: PROC, and ENDP. PROC and ENDP are directives for defining procedures. As you can see, both the main program and the procedure that was at 200h are surrounded by matching pairs of the directives PROC and ENDP.

PROC defines the beginning of a procedure; ENDP defines the end. The label in front of each is the name you give to the procedure they define. Thus, in the main procedure, PRINT_A_J, you can replace your CALL 200 instruction with the more readable CALL WRITE_CHAR. Just insert the name of the procedure, and the assembler assigns the addresses without a gap between procedures.

Because you have two procedures, you need to tell the assembler which to use as the main procedure—where the 80x86 should start executing your program. The END directive takes care of this detail. By writing END PRINT_A_J, you tell the assembler that PRINT_A_J is the main procedure. Later, you will see that the main procedure can be anywhere. Right now, however, you are

117

dealing with .COM files, and you will need to place the main procedure first in our source file.

Now you are ready to begin. If you haven't done so yet, enter the program into a file called PRINTAJ.ASM and generate the .COM version, by using the same steps you did in the last chapter. Remember that you need to use different syntax in place of ML if you are using the Turbo Assembler.

```
ML /C PRINTAJ.ASM
LINK PRINTAJ;
EXE2BIN PRINTAJ PRINTAJ.COM
```

If you encounter any error messages that you do not recognize, check that you have typed in the program correctly.

Then give Printaj a try. Make sure you have run Exe2bin *before* you run Printaj. Otherwise, you will end up running the EXE version of Printaj, which will crash when it encounters the INT 20h instruction for reasons you will see in Chapter 11.

When you are satisfied, use Debug to unassemble the program and see how the assembler fits the two procedures together. Recall that you can read a particular file into Debug by typing its name as part of the command line. For example, type *DEBUG PRINTAJ.COM* and see the following:

```
-U
3985:0100 B241        MOV     DL,41
3985:0102 B90A00      MOV     CX,000A
3985:0105 E80600      CALL    010E
3985:0108 FEC2        INC     DL
3985:010A E2F9        LOOP    0105
3985:010C CD20        INT     20
3985:010E B402        MOV     AH,02
3985:0110 CD21        INT     21
3985:0112 C3          RET
```

The program is nice and snug, with no gap between the two procedures, as shown in Figure 9-1.

The Hex-Output Procedures

You have seen hex-output procedures twice before: once in Chapter 5, where you learned how to print a number in hex, and again in Chapter 7, where you saw how to simplify the program by using a procedure to print one hex digit. Now you are going to add yet another procedure to print one character.

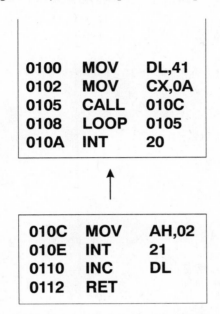

Figure 9-1: MASM assembles separate procedures without a gap.

By using a central procedure to write a character to the screen, you can change the way this procedure writes characters without affecting the rest of the program. It will be changed several times. Enter the following program into the file VIDEO_IO.ASM. The disk that accompanies this book includes the file under the name VIDEO_9.ASM as shown in Listing 9-2.

Listing 9-2 The New File VIDEO_IO.ASM (VIDEO_9.ASM)

```
.MODEL   SMALL
.CODE

TEST_WRITE_HEX   PROC
         MOV     DL,3Fh                    ;Test with 3Fh
         CALL    WRITE_HEX
```

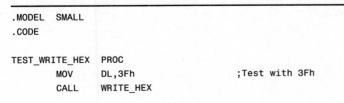

continues

Listing 9-2 continued

```
        INT     20h                 ;Return to DOS
TEST_WRITE_HEX  ENDP


        PUBLIC  WRITE_HEX
;--------------------------------------------------------------------;
; This procedure converts the byte in the DL register to hex and writes ;
; the two hex digits at the current cursor position.                 ;
;                                                                    ;
; On Entry:   DL      Byte to be converted to hex.                   ;
;                                                                    ;
; Uses: WRITE_HEX_DIGIT                                              ;
;--------------------------------------------------------------------;
WRITE_HEX       PROC                        ;Entry point
        PUSH    CX                          ;Save registers used in this
                                              procedure
        PUSH    DX
        MOV     DH,DL               ;Make a copy of byte
        MOV     CX,4                ;Get the upper nibble in DL
        SHR     DL,CL
        CALL    WRITE_HEX_DIGIT     ;Display first hex digit
        MOV     DL,DH               ;Get lower nibble into DL
        AND     DL,0Fh              ;Remove the upper nibble
        CALL    WRITE_HEX_DIGIT     ;Display second hex digit
        POP     DX
        POP     CX
        RET
WRITE_HEX       ENDP


        PUBLIC  WRITE_HEX_DIGIT
;--------------------------------------------------------------------;
; This procedure converts the lower 4 bits of DL to a hex digit and  ;
; writes it to the screen.                                           ;
;                                                                    ;
; On Entry:   DL      Lower 4 bits contain number to be printed      ;
;                     in hex.                                        ;
;                                                                    ;
; Uses:       WRITE_CHAR                                             ;
;--------------------------------------------------------------------;
WRITE_HEX_DIGIT PROC
        PUSH    DX                  ;Save registers used
        CMP     DL,10               ;Is this nibble <10?
        JAE     HEX_LETTER          ;No, convert to a letter
```

```
              ADD      DL,"0"                    ;Yes, convert to a digit
              JMP      Short WRITE_DIGIT         ;Now write this character
HEX_LETTER:
              ADD      DL,"A"-10                 ;Convert to hex letter
WRITE_DIGIT:
              CALL     WRITE_CHAR                ;Display the letter on the screen
              POP      DX                        ;Restore old value of DX
              RET
WRITE_HEX_DIGIT ENDP


       PUBLIC  WRITE_CHAR
;------------------------------------------------------------;
; This procedure prints a character on the screen using the DOS    ;
; function call.                                              ;
;                                                             ;
; On Entry:   DL      Byte to print on screen.                ;
;------------------------------------------------------------;
WRITE_CHAR     PROC
       PUSH    AX
       MOV     AH,2                      ;Call for character output
       INT     21h                       ;Output character in DL register
       POP     AX                        ;Restore old value in AX
       RET                               ;And return
WRITE_CHAR     ENDP

       END     TEST_WRITE_HEX
```

The DOS function to print characters treats some characters specially. For example, using the DOS function to output 07 results in a beep, without printing the character for 07, which is a small diamond. You will see a new version of WRITE_CHAR that will print a diamond in Part III, where you will learn about the ROM BIOS routines inside your IBM PC. For now, we will just use the DOS function to print characters.

The new directive PUBLIC is here for future use. You will also use this directive in Chapter 13 when you learn about modular design. PUBLIC simply tells the assembler to generate some more information for the linker. The linker allows you to bring separate pieces of your program, assembled from different source files, together into one program. PUBLIC informs the assembler that the procedure named after the PUBLIC directive should be made public, or available to procedures in other files.

Right now, Video_io contains three procedures to write a byte as a hex number, as well as a short main program to test these procedures. You will be adding many procedures to the file as you develop Dskpatch. By the end of this book, VIDEO_IO.ASM will be filled with many general-purpose procedures.

The procedure TEST_WRITE_HEX that we have included does just what it says: it tests WRITE_HEX, which uses WRITE_HEX_DIGIT and WRITE_CHAR. As soon as you verify the accuracy of the function of these three procedures, you will remove TEST_WRITE_HEX from VIDEO_IO.ASM.

Create the COM version of Video_io, and use Debug to thoroughly test WRITE_HEX. Change the 3Fh at memory location 101h to each of the boundary conditions you tried in Chapter 5 (use the digits 0, 9, A, and F in different combinations for each of the two digits), then use G to run TEST_WRITE_HEX.

You will use many simple test programs to test new procedures that you have written. In this way, you can build a program piece by piece, rather than building and debugging it all at once. This incremental method is much faster and easier, because you confine bugs to the new code.

The Beginnings of Modular Design

Note that ahead of each procedure in Video_io we have included a block of comments briefly describing the function of each procedure. More importantly, these comments tell which registers the procedure uses to pass information back and forth, as well as what other procedures it uses. As one feature of your modular approach, the comment block allows you to use any procedure by looking at the description. There is no need to relearn how the procedure does its work. This also makes it fairly easy to rewrite one procedure without having to rewrite any of the procedures that call it.

We have also used PUSH and POP instructions to save and restore any registers used within each procedure. We will do this for every procedure we write, except for test procedures. This approach, too, is part of the modular style you will be using.

Recall that we save and restore any register used so we never have to worry about complex interactions between procedures trying to fight over the small number of registers in the 80x86. Each procedure is free to use as many registers as it likes, *provided* it restores them before the RET instruction. It is a small price to pay for the added simplicity. In addition, without saving and restoring registers, the task of rewriting procedures would be mind-rending. You would be sure to lose much hair in the process.

Also try to use many small procedures, instead of one large one. This makes the programming task simpler, although sometimes we will write longer procedures when the design becomes particularly convoluted.

These ideas and methods will all be borne out more fully in the chapters to come. In the next chapter, for example, we will add another procedure to Video_io: a procedure to take a word in the DX register and print the number in decimal on the screen.

A Program Skeleton

As you have seen in this and the preceding chapter, the assembler imposes a certain amount of overhead on any programs you write. In other words, you need to write a few directives that tell the assembler the basics. For future reference, the absolute minimum you will need for programs you write is as follows:

```
.MODEL   SMALL
.CODE

Some_procedure   PROC
          .
          .
          .
          INT    20h
Some_procedure   ENDP

          END    Some_procedure
```

We will add some new directives to this program skeleton in later chapters. You can use it, as shown here, as the starting point for new programs you write. Or, you can use some of the programs and procedures from this book as your starting point.

Summary

You are really making progress now. In this chapter, you learned how to write procedures in assembly language. From now on we will use procedures all the time. By using small procedures, you will make your programs more manageable.

You saw that a procedure begins with a PROC definition and ends with an ENDP directive. We rewrote PRINT_A_J to test your new knowledge of procedures, then went on to rewrite our program to write a hex number—this time with an extra procedure. Now that procedures are so easy to work with, there is little reason not to break programs into more procedures. In fact, you have seen ample reasons in favor of using many small procedures.

At the end of this chapter we talked briefly about modular design, a philosophy that will save you a great deal of time and effort. Modular programs will be easier to write and easier to read. They will also be easier for someone else to modify than programs created with the well-worn technique of spaghetti logic—programs written with very long procedures and many interactions.

Now you are ready to build another useful procedure. Then, in Chapter 11, you will learn about segments. From there you will move on to developing larger programs where you will really start to use the techniques of modular design.

Printing in Decimal

In this chapter you will build a subroutine to display a number in decimal notation. You will use this subroutine later in the Dskpatch program. You will also learn about a few tricks that assembly-language programmers often use in their programs, mostly just for the fun of it. You will learn about the XOR (exclusive or) and the OR instructions, as well as the SI and DI registers.

Files altered: VIDEO_IO.ASM

Disk file: VIDEO_10.ASM

10

Topics Covered

We have been promising that we would write a procedure to take a word and print it in decimal notation. WRITE_DECIMAL uses some new tricks—ways to save a byte here and a few microseconds there. Perhaps such tricks will hardly seem to be worth the effort. But if you memorize them, you will find you can use them to shorten and speed up programs. Through these tricks, you will also learn about two new types of logical operations to add to the AND instruction covered in Chapter 5. First, let's review the process for converting a word to decimal digits.

Reviewing the Conversion to Decimal

Division is the key to converting a word to decimal digits. Recall that the DIV instruction calculates both the integer answer and its remainder. Calculating 12345/10 yields 1234 as the integer answer, and 5 as the remainder. In this example, 5 is simply the rightmost digit. If you divide by 10 again, you will get the next digit to the left. Repeated division by 10 *strips off* the digits from right to left, each time putting a digit in the remainder.

The digits come out in reverse order, but in assembly-language programming, there is a fix for that. Remember the stack? It is just like a stack of lunch trays: The first one to come off the top is the last tray that was set down. If you substitute digits for trays, and place the digits one on top of the other as they come out of the remainder, you will have it. You can pull out the digits in correct order.

The top digit is the first digit in your number and the other digits are underneath it. So, if you push the remainders as you calculate them and print the remainders as you pop them off the stack, the digits will be in correct order, as shown in Figure 10-1.

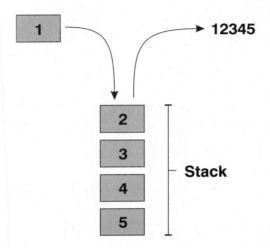

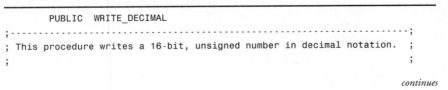

Figure 10-1: PUSHing the Digits onto the Stack Reverses Their Order.

The following program is the complete procedure to print a number in decimal notation. As mentioned, there are a few tricks hiding in this procedure. You will get to them soon enough, but let's try WRITE_DECIMAL to see if it works.

Place WRITE_DECIMAL into VIDEO_IO.ASM (see Listing 10-10), along with the proce-dures for writing a byte in hex. Make sure you place WRITE_DECIMAL *after* TEST_WRITE_HEX, which you will be replacing with TEST_WRITE_DECIMAL. To save some work, WRITE_DECIMAL uses WRITE_HEX_DIGIT to convert one nibble (four bits) into a digit.

Listing 10-1 Add to VIDEO_IO.ASM (Complete listing in VIDEO_10.ASM; see also Listing 10.2)

```
        PUBLIC  WRITE_DECIMAL
;-------------------------------------------------------------------;
; This procedure writes a 16-bit, unsigned number in decimal notation.  ;
;                                                                   ;
```

continues

Listing 10-1 continued

```
; On Entry:       DX      N : 16-bit, unsigned number.              ;
;                                                                   ;
; Uses:           WRITE_HEX_DIGIT                                   ;
;-------------------------------------------------------------------;
WRITE_DECIMAL    PROC
        PUSH     AX                       ;Save registers used here
        PUSH     CX
        PUSH     DX
        PUSH     SI
        MOV      AX,DX
        MOV      SI,10                     ;Will divide by 10 using SI
        XOR      CX,CX                     ;Count of digits placed on stack
NON_ZERO:
        XOR      DX,DX                     ;Set upper word of N to 0
        DIV      SI                        ;Calculate N/10 and (N mod 10)
        PUSH     DX                        ;Push one digit onto the stack
        INC      CX                        ;One more digit added
        OR       AX,AX                     ;N = 0 yet?
        JNE      NON_ZERO                  ;Nope, continue
WRITE_DIGIT_LOOP:
        POP      DX                        ;Get the digits in reverse order
        CALL     WRITE_HEX_DIGIT
        LOOP     WRITE_DIGIT_LOOP
END_DECIMAL:
        POP      SI
        POP      DX
        POP      CX
        POP      AX
        RET
WRITE_DECIMAL    ENDP
```

Notice that we have included a new register, the SI (*Source Index*) register. Later you will see why it has been given that name. You will also meet its brother, the DI, or *Destination Index* register. Both registers have special uses, but they can also be used as if they were general-purpose registers. Since WRITE_DECIMAL needs four general-purpose registers, we used SI, even though we could have used BX, simply to show that SI (and DI) can serve as general-purpose registers if need be.

Before you try out our new procedure, you need to make two other changes to VIDEO_IO.ASM. First, remove the procedure TEST_WRITE_HEX, and insert the test procedure, which follows, in its place as shown in Listing 10-2.

Listing 10-2 Replace TEST_WRITE_HEX in VIDEO_IO.ASM with This Procedure (Complete listing in VIDEO_10.ASM)

```
TEST_WRITE_DECIMAL      PROC
        MOV     DX,12345
        CALL    WRITE_DECIMAL
        INT     20h                     ;Return to DOS
TEST_WRITE_DECIMAL      ENDP
```

This procedure tests WRITE_DECIMAL with the number 12345 (which the assembler converts to the word 3039h).

Second, you need to change the END statement at the end of VIDEO_IO.ASM to read END TEST_WRITE_DECIMAL, because TEST_WRITE_DECIMAL is now your main procedure.

Make these changes and give VIDEO_IO a whirl. Convert it to its .COM version and see if it works. If it doesn't, check your source file for errors. If you are adventurous, try to find your bug with Debug.

Some Tricks and Shortcuts

Hiding in WRITE_DECIMAL are two tricks of the trade garnered from the people who wrote the ROM BIOS procedures you will meet in Chapter 17. (IBM used to print the source code for their ROM BIOS, but that kind of sharing is a thing of the past.) The first is an efficient instruction to set a register to zero. It is not much more efficient than MOV AX,0, and perhaps it is not worth the effort, but it is the sort of trick you will find people using, so here it is. The following instruction sets the AX register to zero.

```
XOR     AX,AX
```

How? To understand that, we need to learn about the logical operation called an *Exclusive OR*, hence the name XOR.

The exclusive OR is similar to an OR (which you will see next), but the result of XORing two trues is true if *only* one bit is true, not if both are true.

XOR	0	1
0	0	1
1	1	0

Thus, if you exclusive OR a number to itself, you get zero:

```
    1 0 1 0  0 1 0 1
XOR 1 0 1 1  0 1 0 1

    0 0 0 0  0 0 0 0
```

That is the trick. You won't find other uses for the XOR instruction in this book, but we thought you would find it interesting.

As a short aside, you will also find many people using another quick trick to set a register to zero. Rather than using the XOR instruction, we could have used the following to set the AX register to zero:

```
SUB     AX,AX
```

Now for the other trick. It is just about as devious as our XOR scheme to clear a register, and it uses a cousin to the exclusive OR—the OR function.

We want to check the AX register to see if it is zero. To do this, we could use the instruction CMP AX,0. But we would rather use a trick: It's more fun, and a little more efficient, too. So, we write OR AX,AX and follow this instruction with a JNE (Jump if Not Equal) conditional jump. (We could also have used JNZ—Jump if Not Zero.)

The OR instruction, like any of the math instructions, sets the flags, including the zero flag. Like AND, OR is a logical concept. But here, a result is true if one *OR* the other bit is true.

OR	0	1
0	0	1
1	1	1

If we take a number and OR it to itself, you get the original number back again:

```
    1 0 1 1  0 1 0 1
OR  1 0 1 1  0 1 0 1
    1 0 1 1  0 1 0 1
```

The OR instruction is also useful for setting just one bit in a byte. For example, we can set bit 3 in the number we just used:

```
    1 0 1 1  0 1 0 1
OR  0 0 0 0  1 0 0 0
    1 0 1 1  1 1 0 1
```

There will be more tricks to play before you are through with this book, but these two are the only ones that are entirely for fun.

The Inner Workings of WRITE_DECIMAL

To see how WRITE_DECIMAL performs its task, study the listing; we won't cover many details here. However, we do need to point out a few more things.

First, the CX register is used to count how many digits you pushed onto the stack, so you know how many to remove. The CX register is a particularly convenient choice, because you can build a loop with the LOOP instruction and use the CX register to store the repeat count. This choice makes the digit-output loop (WRITE_DIGIT_LOOP) almost trivial, because the LOOP instruction uses the CX register directly. You will use CX often when you have to store a count.

Next, be careful to check the boundary conditions here. The boundary condition at 0 isn't a problem, as you can check. The other boundary condition is 65535, or FFFFh, which you can check easily with Debug. Just load VIDEO_IO.COM into Debug by typing *DEBUG VIDEO_IO.COM* and change the 12345 (3039h) at 101h to 65535 (FFFFh). (WRITE_DECIMAL works with unsigned numbers. See if you can write a version to display signed numbers.)

You may have noticed a sticky point here, having to do with the 80x86, not your program. Debug works mostly with bytes (at least the E command does), but you want to change a word. You must be careful, since the 80x86 stores the bytes in a different order. An unassemble for the MOV instruction is as follows:

```
3985:0100 BA3930        MOV        DX,3039
```

You can tell from the *BA3930* part of this display that the byte at 101h is 39h, and the one at 102h is 30h (BA is the MOV instruction). These two bytes are the two bytes of 3039h, but seemingly in reverse order. Confusing? The order is logical, after a short explanation.

A word consists of two parts, the lower byte and the upper byte. The lower byte is the least significant byte (39h in 3039h), while the upper byte is the most significant byte (30h) as you can see in Figure 10-2. It makes sense, then, to place the lower byte at the lower address in memory. (Many other computer architectures, such as the Motorola 680x0 family used in the Apple Macintosh, actually reverse these two bytes, and this can be a bit confusing if you are writing programs on several different types of computers.)

Try different numbers for the word starting at 101h, and you will see how this storage works. Use TEST_WRITE_DECIMAL to see if you got it right, or unassemble the first instruction.

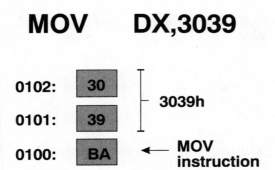

Figure 10-2: The 80x86 Stores Numbers with the Lower Byte First in Memory.

Summary

You added a few new instructions to your repertoire, as well as a few tricks for fun. You also learned about two other registers, SI and DI, that you can use as general-purpose registers. They have other uses that you will see in later chapters.

You learned about the XOR and OR logical instructions, which allow you to work between individual bits in two bytes or words. In your WRITE_DECIMAL procedure, you used the XOR AX,AX instruction as a tricky way to set the AX register to zero. You used OR AX,AX as a devious way to write the equivalent of CMP AX,0 to test the AX register and see if it is zero. Finally, you learned about how the 80x86 stores a word in memory by checking the boundary conditions of your new procedure, WRITE_DECIMAL.

You now have another general-purpose procedure, WRITE_DECIMAL, that you will be able to use in the future for your own programs.

Take a breather now. We've got a few *different* chapters scheduled next. Chapter 11 covers segments in detail. Segments are perhaps the most complicated part of the 80x86 microprocessor, so the chapter may prove to be rather heavy going. Even so, we need to cover the topic for following chapters.

After that, you will make a slight course correction and get back on track by learning what to do with the program Dskpatch. You will do a bit of probing on disks, and learn about sectors, tracks, and other such things.

From there, we can plot a simple course for preliminary versions of Dskpatch. En route, you will get a chance to see how to develop large programs. Programmers don't write an entire program, then debug it. They write sections and try each section before they move on—programming is much less work that way. You have used this approach to a limited extent by writing and testing WRITE_HEX and WRITE_DECIMAL, for which the test programs were very simple. The test programs from here on will be more complex, but more interesting, too.

Segments

In this chapter you will learn about segments, which are very important to assembly-language programs. From here on, you will always build EXE, rather than COM, programs. These programs use at least two segments. You will also learn about the PSP (Program Segment Prefix), about the DOSSEG directive for controlling segment order, about NEAR and FAR calls for working with large programs, and more about how INT instructions work.

Files altered: None

11

Topics Covered

How Memory Is Divided into Segments

The Stack

The Program Segment Prefix (PSP)

The DOSSEG Directive

NEAR and FAR CALLs

More on the INT Instruction

Interrupt Vectors

Summary

In the preceding chapters, you encountered several directives that dealt with segments. Now the time has come to look at segments themselves, and at how the 80x86 manages to address a full megabyte (1,048,576 bytes) of memory under DOS. From this, you will begin to understand why segments need their own directives in the assembler, and in later chapters you will begin to use different segments (thus far, you have used only one).

Let's start at the 80x86 level by learning how it constructs the 20-bit addresses needed for a full megabyte of memory.

How Memory Is Divided into Segments

Segments are about the only part of the 80x86 that you have not covered yet. They are, perhaps, the most confusing part of this microprocessor. In fact, segments are what you call a *kludge* in this business—computerese for a makeshift fix to a problem. The 80386 and 80486 microprocessors have additional addressing modes that are much simpler and do not use segments. Unfortunately DOS does not use this mode (the WIN32s programming kit for Windows does allow you to use this *linear* addressing mode).

The problem, in this case, is being able to address more than 64K of memory—the limit with one word, since 65535 is the largest number a single word can hold. Intel, designers of the 80x86, used segments and segment registers to "fix" this problem, and in the process made the 80x86 more confusing.

So far, you have not had to worry about this problem. You have been using the IP register to hold the address of the next instruction for the 80x86 to execute ever since you met Debug in Chapter 2. Back then, you may recall we said the address is actually formed from both the CS register and the IP register. But we never really said how. Let's find out.

Although the complete address is formed from two registers, the 80x86 does not form a two-word number for the address. If you were to take CS:IP as a 32-bit number (two 16-bit numbers side by side), the 80x86 would be able to address about four billion bytes—far more than the one million bytes it can actually address in DOS. The 80x86's method is slightly more complicated. The CS register provides the *starting* address for the code segment, where a segment is 64K of memory.

As you can see in Figure 11-1, the 80x86 divides memory into many overlapping segments, with a new segment starting every 16 bytes. The first segment (segment 0) starts at memory location 0; the second (segment 1) starts at 10h (16); the third starts at 20h (32), and so on.

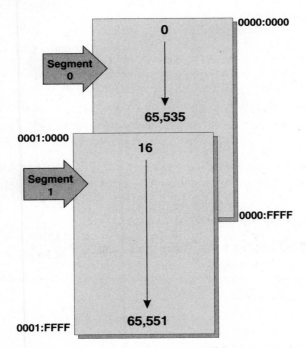

Figure 11-1: Overlapping segments start every 16 bytes and are 65536 bytes long.

The actual address is just CS * 16 + IP. For example, if the CS register contains 3FA8 and IP contains D017, the absolute address is evident as follows.

```
  CS * 16 : 0 0 1 1 1 1 1 1 1 0 1 0 1 0 0 0 0 0 0 0
+ IP      : 1 1 0 1 0 0 0 0 0 0 0 1 0 1 1 1       1
           ─────────────────────────────────────────
            0 1 0 0 1 1 0 0 1 0 1 0 1 0 0 1 0 1 1 1
```

We multiplied by 16 by shifting CS left four bits and injecting zeros at the right, as you can see in Figure 11-2.

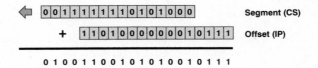

Figure 11-2: The absolute address of CS:IP is CS * 16 + IP.

Now, this may seem like a strange way to address more than 64K of memory—but it works. Soon, you will begin to see how well it really works.

The 80x86 has four segment registers: CS (Code Segment), DS (Data Segment), SS (Stack Segment), and ES (Extra Segment). The CS register you have been looking at is used by the 80x86 for the segment where the next instruction is stored. In much the same way, DS is the segment where the 80x86 looks for data, and SS is where the 80x86 places the stack.

Before we go on, let's look at a short program, which is quite different from any you have seen before. This short program uses two different segments. Enter this program into the file TEST_SEG.ASM as follows:

Listing 11-1 The Program TEST_SEG.ASM
(Not included on disk)

```
DOSSEG
.MODEL SMALL

.STACK                                  ;Allocate a 1K stack

.CODE

TEST_SEGMENT    PROC
        MOV     AH,4Ch                  ;Ask for the exit-to-dos function
        INT     21h                     ;Return to DOS
TEST_SEGMENT    ENDP

        END     TEST_SEGMENT
```

Assemble and link Test_seg, but do not generate a COM file for it. (If you are using MASM 6 or later, you can type "ML TEST_SEG.ASM" to both assemble and link in one step!) The result will be TEST_SEG.EXE, which is slightly different from a COM file.

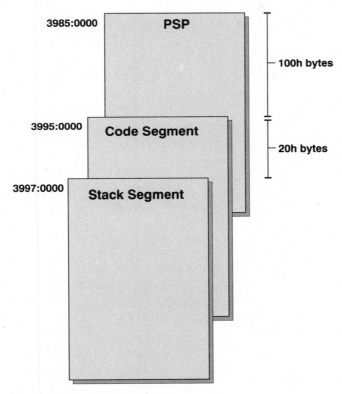

Figure 11-3: Memory layout for TEST_SEG.EXE.

You have to use a method other than INT 20h in order to exit from EXE files. For COM files, INT 20h works perfectly well, but it doesn't work at all for EXE files because the organization of segments is very different, as you will see in this chapter; more on this difference later. From now on you will use INT 21h, function 4Ch to exit programs.

143

When you use Debug on a COM file, Debug sets all the segment registers to the same number, with the program starting at an *offset* of 100h from the start of this segment. The first 256 bytes (100h) are used to store various pieces of information. Although this area does not contain much you will need, we will look at part of this area soon.

Try loading TEST_SEG.EXE into Debug to see what happens with segments in an EXE file.

```
C>DEBUG TEST_SEG.EXE
-R
AX=0000  BX=0000  CX=0004  DX=0000  SP=0400  BP=0000  SI=0000  DI=0000
DS=3985  ES=3985  SS=3997  CS=3995  IP=0000   NV UP EI PL NZ NA PO NC
3995:0000 B44C          MOV     AH,4C
```

The values of the SS and CS registers are different from those for DS and ES as you can also see in Figure 11-3.

The Stack

Two segments are defined in this program. The STACK segment (which is actually the data segment) is where you place the stack (hence, the .STACK), and the code segment (which is actually called _TEXT) is where all your instructions are stored. The .STACK directive tells the assembler to create a 1024 byte stack. (You could create a larger or smaller stack by putting a number after .STACK. For example, .STACK 128 would create a stack 128 bytes long.)

The address for the top of the stack is given by SS:SP. SP is the Stack Pointer, like IP is the instruction pointer for code, and is an offset within the current Stack Segment.

Actually, "top-of-stack" is a misnomer, because the stack grows from high memory toward low memory. Therefore, the *top* of the stack is really at the bottom of the stack in memory, and new entries to the stack are placed progressively lower in memory. Here, SP is 400h, which is 1024 decimal, because you defined a stack area 1024 bytes long. You haven't placed anything on the stack as yet, so top-of-stack is still at the top of the memory you set aside for the stack: 400h.

If you think back to the COM programs in previous chapters, you never declared a stack segment, which raises two questions: Why didn't you have to declare a stack segment for COM programs? And where was the stack in the COM programs? All the COM programs you created had only one segment, and all the segment registers (CS, DS, ES, and SS) pointed to this segment. Since you had just one segment, you didn't need a separate stack segment. As to where the stack was, if you look at the register display for WRITESTR.COM, you will see the stack is at the very end of the segment (SP = FFEE). The stack is as follows:

```
-R
AX=0000  BX=0000  CX=0000  DX=0000  SP=FFEE  BP=0000  SI=0000  DI=0000
DS=3995  ES=3995  SS=3995  CS=3995  IP=0100    NV UP EI PL NZ NA PO NC
3995:0100 B402         MOV    AH,02
-
```

DOS always sets the stack pointer to the very end of the segment when it loads a COM file into memory. For this reason, you do not need to declare a stack segment (with .STACK) for COM files. What would happen if you removed the .STACK directive from TEST_SEG.ASM?

```
C>DEBUG TEST_SEG.EXE
-R
AX=0000  BX=0000  CX=0004  DX=0000  SP=0000  BP=0000  SI=0000  DI=0000
DS=3985  ES=3985  SS=3995  CS=3995  IP=0000    NV UP EI PL NZ NA PO NC
3D90:0000 B44C         MOV    AH,4C
-
```

The stack is now at 3995:0, which is the start of your program (CS:0). This is very bad news. You do not want the stack anywhere near your program's code. Since the stack pointer is at SS:0, it has no room to grow (since the stack grows down in memory). For these reasons, you *must* declare a stack segment for EXE programs.

Always declare a stack segment with .STACK in EXE programs.

Getting back to the two-segment example, notice that the Stack Segment (SS) is segment number 3997 (this will probably be different for you), while our Code Segment (CS) is at segment 3995—two less than SS, or just 32 bytes lower in memory. Since we did not put any data into the stack segment, unassembling starting at CS:0 will show our program (MOV AH,4C and INT 21) followed by whatever happened to be in memory.

```
-U CS:0
3995:0000 B44C          MOV      AH,4C
3995:0002 CD21          INT      21
3995:0004 65            DB       65
3995:0005 2028          AND      [BX+SI],CH
3995:0007 59            POP      CX
3995:0008 2F            DAS
3995:0009 4E            DEC      SI
3995:000A 293F          SUB      [BX],DI
          .
          .
          .
```

You will almost certainly see different instructions after the INT 21h in this Debug listing.

The Program Segment Prefix (PSP)

The "scratch area" is actually called a PSP (Program Segment Prefix) and contains information for use by DOS. In other words, do not assume you can make use of this area.

In looking at the register display, you may have noticed that the ES and DS registers contain 3985h, 10h less than the beginning of the program at segment 3995h. Multiplying by 16 to get the number of bytes you can see that there are 100h (or 256) bytes before your program starts. This is the same scratch area placed at the beginning of a COM file.

Among other things, this 256 byte PSP at the start of programs contains characters typed after the name of the program, starting at 80h from the start of the PSP. For example:

```
C>DEBUG TEST_SEG.EXE And now for some characters you will see in the memory dump
-D DS:80
3985:0080 39 20 41 6E 64 20 6E 6F-77 20 66 6F 72 20 73 6F   9 And now for so
3985:0090 6D 65 20 63 68 61 72 61-63 74 65 72 73 20 77 65   me characters we
3985:00A0 27 6C 6C 20 73 65 65 20-69 6E 20 74 68 65 20 6D   'll see in the m
3985:00B0 65 6D 6F 72 79 20 64 75-6D 70 0D 20 6D 65 6D 6F   emory dump. memo
3985:00C0 72 79 20 64 75 6D 70 0D-00 00 00 00 00 00 00 00   ry dump.........
          .
          .
          .
```

The first byte says you typed 39h (or 57) characters, including the first space after TEST_SEG.EXE. You won't use this information in this book, but it helps show why you might want such a large PSP.

The PSP also contains information that DOS uses when exiting from a program, with either the INT 20h or the INT 21h, function 4Ch instructions. For reasons that are not clear, the INT 20h instruction expects the CS register to point to the start of this PSP, which it does for a COM program but *not* for an EXE program. The exit function (INT 21h, function 4Ch) was added to DOS with the introduction of version 2.00 to make it easier to exit from EXE programs; function 4Ch does not expect the CS register to point to the start of the PSP. You should use INT 21h, function 4Ch from now on to exit programs.

The code for COM files always starts at an offset of 100h in the code segment to leave room for this 256-byte PSP at the start. This is unlike the EXE file, which had its code start at IP = 0000, because the code segment started 100h bytes after the beginning of the area in memory.

In the early days of DOS, most programs were written as COM programs because they were slightly simpler to write. But today, almost all programs are written as EXE programs. So in the rest of this book, we will be working almost entirely with EXE programs. Figure 11-4 summarizes the differences between COM and EXE programs.

The DOSSEG Directive

If you take a look again at TEST_SEG.EXE, you will notice that the stack segment is higher in memory than the code segment. Yet in the source file you defined the stack (.STACK) *before* any of the code (.CODE). So why is the stack higher in memory than the code?

The DOSSEG directive at the start of the program tells the assembler that you want the segments of your program loaded in a very specific order with the code segment appearing first, and the stack last. In Chapter 14 you will see more about DOSSEG and the order of segments when you add another segment to hold data.

Memory layout for .COM programs

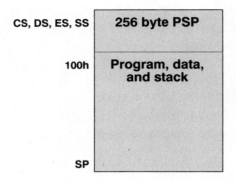

Memory layout for .EXE programs

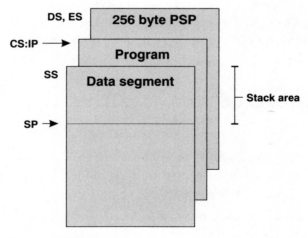

Figure 11-4: COM vs EXE programs.

NEAR and FAR CALLs

The rest of the information in this chapter is purely for your interest, since you won't be making use of it in this book. Skip the next two sections and read them later if you find the going tough or you are anxious to get back to programming.

Let's step back for a minute and take a closer look at the CALL instructions used in previous chapters. Specifically let's look at the short program in Chapter 7, where you first learned about the CALL instruction. You wrote a very short program that looked like the following (without the procedure at 200h):

```
3985:0100 B241        MOV     DL,41
3985:0102 B90A00      MOV     CX,000A
3985:0105 E8F800      CALL    0200
3985:0108 E2FB        LOOP    0105
3985:010A CD20        INT     20
```

As you can see by looking at the machine code on the left, the CALL instruction occupies only three bytes (E8F800). The first byte (E8h) is the CALL instruction and the second two bytes form an offset. The 80x86 calculates the address of the routine you are calling by adding this offset of 00F8h (remember that the 80x86 stores the lower byte of a word in memory *before* the high byte, so you have to reverse the bytes) to the address of the next instruction (108h in the program). In this case you have F8h + 108h = 200h.

The fact that this instruction uses a single word for the offset means that CALLs are limited to a single segment, which is 64K bytes long. So how is it that you can write a program like Lotus 1-2-3 that is larger than 64K? By using FAR, rather than NEAR, calls.

NEAR CALLs are limited to a single segment. In other words, they change the IP register without affecting the CS register. For this reason they are sometimes known as *intrasegment* CALLs.

You can also have FAR CALLs that change both the CS *and* IP registers. Such CALLs are often known as *intersegment* CALLs because they call procedures in other segments.

Going along with these two versions of the CALL instruction are two versions of the RET instruction. The NEAR CALL, as you saw in Chapter 7, pushes a single word onto the stack for its return address. The corresponding RET instruction pops this word off the stack and into the IP register.

In the case of FAR CALLs and RETs, a word is not sufficient because we're dealing with another segment. In other words, you need to save a two-word return address on the stack: one word for the instruction pointer (IP) and the other for the code segment (CS). The FAR RET pops two words off the stack— one for the CS register, and the other for IP.

How does the assembler know which of these two CALLs and RETs to use? When should it use the FAR CALL, and when should it use the NEAR CALL? By putting a NEAR or FAR directive after the PROC directive. By way of example, look at the following program:

```
PROC_ONE        PROC    FAR
                .
                .
                .
        RET
PROC_ONE        ENDP


PROC_TWO        PROC    NEAR
        CALL    PROC_ONE
                .
                .
                .
        RET
PROC_TWO        ENDP
```

When the assembler sees the CALL PROC_ONE instruction, it hunts in its table for the definition of PROC_ONE, which, is PROC_ONE PROC FAR. This definition tells whether the procedure is a NEAR or FAR procedure.

In the case of a NEAR procedure, the assembler generates a NEAR CALL. And conversely, it generates a FAR CALL, as shown in Figure 11-5, if the procedure you're calling was defined as a FAR procedure. In other words, the assembler uses the definition of the procedure that you're *calling* to determine the type of CALL instruction that is needed.

For the RET instruction, the assembler looks at the definition of the procedure that contains the RET instruction. In your program, the RET instruction for PROC_ONE will be a FAR RET, as shown in Figure 11-6, because

PROC_ONE is declared to be a FAR procedure. Likewise, the RET in PROC_TWO is a NEAR RET.

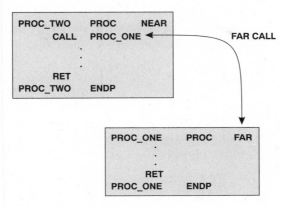

Figure 11-5: The assembler produces a FAR CALL.

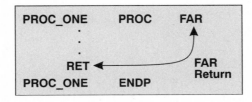

Figure 11-6: The assembler produces a FAR RET.

What happens when you don't put a NEAR or FAR directive after the PROC? The assembler uses the information in the .MODEL directive to determine whether procedures are NEAR or FAR if you don't explicitly declare a procedure as NEAR or FAR. We're using the .MODEL SMALL directive, which tells the assembler that you have only one code segment, so all the procedures are NEAR procedures. There are other .MODEL directives (such as MEDIUM) that tell the assembler to make procedures FAR if they are not explicitly declared as NEAR.

151

More on the INT Instruction

The INT instruction is much like a CALL instruction, but with a minor difference. The name *INT* comes from the word *interrupt*. An interrupt is an external signal that causes the 80x86 to execute a procedure and then return to what it was doing before it received the interrupt. An INT instruction doesn't interrupt the 80x86, but it is treated as if it did.

When the 80x86 receives an interrupt, it needs to store more information on the stack than just the two words for the return address. It has to store the values of the status flags—the carry flag, the zero flag, and so on. These values are stored in the Flag Register, and the 80x86 pushes this information onto the stack before the return address.

Your IBM PC regularly responds to a number of different interrupts. The 80x86 inside your IBM PC receives an interrupt from the clock 18.2 times every second, for example. Each of these interrupts causes the 80x86 to stop what it is doing and execute a procedure to count the clock pulses. Now, envision such an interrupt occurring between the following two program instructions.

```
CMP     AH,2
JNE     NOT_2
```

Assume AH = 2, so the zero flag will be set after the CMP instruction, which means that the JNE instruction will not branch to NOT_2.

Now, imagine that the clock interrupts the 80x86 between these two instructions. That means the 80x86 runs off to carry out the interrupt procedure before it checks the zero flag (with the JNE instruction). If the 80x86 didn't save and restore the flag registers, the JNE instruction would use flags set by the interrupt procedure, *not* from your CMP instruction. To prevent such disasters, the 80x86 *always* saves and restores the flag register for interrupts. An interrupt saves the flags, and an IRET (*Interrupt Return*) instruction restores the flags at the end of the interrupt procedure. The same is true for an INT instruction. After executing the INT 21 instruction, the 80x86's stack will look like this:

```
Top of stack  →   Old IP (return address part I)
                  Old CS (return address part II)
                  Old Flag Register
```

The stack grows into lower memory, so the Old Flag Register is actually highest in memory.

When you place an INT instruction in a program, the interrupt is no surprise. Why save the flags? Isn't saving the flags useful only when an external interrupt comes at an unpredictable time? As it turns out, the answer is no. There is a very good reason for saving and restoring the flags for INT instructions. In fact, without this feature, Debug would not be possible.

Debug uses a special flag in the flag register called the Trap Flag. This flag puts the 80x86 into a special mode known as *single-step* mode. Debug uses this to trace through programs one instruction at a time. When the trap flag is set, the 80x86 issues an INT 1 after it executes any instruction.

The INT 1 also clears the trap flag so the 80x86 won't be in single-step mode while you are inside Debug's INT 1 procedure. Since INT 1 saved the flags to the stack, issuing an IRET to return to the program you are debugging restores the trap flag. Then, you will receive another INT 1 interrupt after the next instruction in your program. This is just one example of when it is useful to save the flag registers. But, as you will see next, this restore-flag feature isn't always appropriate.

Some interrupt procedures bypass the restoration of the flag registers. For example, the INT 21h procedure in DOS sometimes changes the flag registers by short-circuiting the normal return process. Many of the INT 21h procedures that read or write disk information return with the carry flag set if there was an error of some sort (such as no disk in the drive).

Interrupt Vectors

Where do these interrupt instructions get the addresses for procedures? Each interrupt instruction has an interrupt number, such as the 21h in INT 21h. The 80x86 finds addresses for interrupt procedures in a table of *interrupt vectors*, which is located at the bottom of memory. For example, the two-word address for the INT 21h procedure is at 0000:0084. You get this address by multiplying the interrupt number by 4 (4 * 21h = 84h), because we need four bytes (two words) for each vector or procedure address.

Vectors are exceedingly useful for adding features to DOS because they enable you to intercept calls to interrupt procedures by changing the addresses in the vector table. We will use this trick at the end of this book to add a disk light to your computer's screen.

All of these ideas and methods should become clearer as you see more examples. Most of this book from here on will be filled with examples, so there will be plenty to study. If you have been feeling a bit overwhelmed by new information, rest easy. We will take a short breather in the next chapter to get re-oriented and back on course.

Summary

This chapter contained a lot of information. You won't use it all, but you did need to learn more about segments. Chapter 13 covers modular design, and you will use some aspects of segments to make your job easier.

You began this chapter by learning how the 80x86 divides memory into segments. To understand segments in more detail, you built an EXE program with two different segments. You also learned that you need to use INT 21h, function 4Ch rather than INT 20h to exit from EXE programs. This is important since you will be using EXE programs from now on in this book.

You also found that the 100h (256-byte) PSP (Program Segment Prefix) at the start of your programs contains a copy of what you typed on the command line. You won't use this knowledge in this book, but it helps you see why DOS sets aside such a large chunk of memory for the purpose.

Finally you learned more about the DOSSEG, MODEL, .CODE, STACK, NEAR, and FAR directives. These are all directives that help you work with segments. In this book, you will barely use the power of these directives, because our EXE programs will use only two segments. But for programmers who write *very large* programs in assembly language (using the MEDIUM memory model), these directives are invaluable. If you are interested, you will find the details in your macro assembler manual.

At the very end of this chapter you learned more about the roots of the helpful INT instruction. Now, you are just about ready to slow down and learn how to *write* larger and more useful assembly language programs.

Course Corrections— How To Build Dskpatch

In this chapter you will learn more about what is covered in the rest of this book. In particular, you will look at the game plan you will use to build the Dskpatch program that will be the center of attention until Part IV.

Files altered: None

12

Topics Covered

Disks, Sectors, and So Forth

The Game Plan for Building Dskpatch

Summary

We have been poking into a lot of new and interesting places. You may have wondered whether we have been wandering about somewhat aimlessly. We haven't been, of course. You are now familiar enough with your new surroundings for us to plot a course for the rest of this book. We will take a close look at a design for the Dskpatch program. Then you will spend the rest of this book developing Dskpatch, much as you will later develop programs of your own.

We will not present the finished version of Dskpatch all at once; that is not the way we DOS wrote it. Instead, we will present short test programs to check each stage of your program as you write it. To do this, you need to know where you want to go. Hence, our course correction here. Since Dskpatch will deal with information on disks, that's where you will begin.

Disks, Sectors, and So Forth

The information on your floppy disks is divided into *sectors*. Each sector holds 512 bytes of information. A double-sided, double-density 5-1/4" disk formatted with DOS 2.0 or above has a total of 720 sectors, or 720 * 512 = 368,640 bytes (see Table 12-1 for other types of disks). If you could look directly at these sectors, you could examine the directory directly, or you could look at the files on the disk. You cannot—not by yourself—but Dskpatch will. Let's use Debug to learn more about sectors and get an idea of how you will display a sector with Dskpatch.

Debug has a command, L (*Load*), to read sectors from disk into memory where you can look at the data. As an example, let's look at the directory that starts at sector 5 on a double-sided disk (use Table 12-1 to determine what number to use for the directory if you have a different type of disk). Load sector 5 from the disk in drive A (drive 0 to Debug) by using the L command. Make sure you have a 360K (or 1.2M, 720K, or 1.44M) disk in drive A, then enter the following:

```
-L100 0 51
```

Table 12-1 Starting Sector for the Root Directory

Disk Type	Sectors/disk	Directory
5-1/4", 360K	720	5h
5-1/4", 1.2M	2,400	Fh
3-1/2", 720K	1,440	7h
3-1/2", 1.44M	2,880	13h

As you can see in Figure 12-1, this command loads sectors into memory, starting with sector 5 and continuing through one sector at an offset of 100 within the data segment.

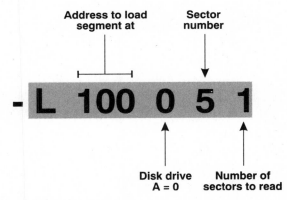

Figure 12-1: DEBUG's Load Command.

To display sector 5, you can use a Dump command as follows:

```
-D 100
396F:0100   49 42 4D 42 49 4F 20 20-43 4F 4D 27 00 00 00 00   IBMBIO  COM'....
396F:0110   00 00 00 00 00 00 00 60-68 06 02 00 00 12 00 00   .......'h......
396F:0120   49 42 4D 44 4F 53 20 20-43 4F 4D 27 00 00 00 00   IBMDOS  COM'....
396F:0130   00 00 00 00 00 00 00 60-68 06 07 00 00 43 00 00   .......'h....C..
396F:0140   43 4F 4D 4D 41 4E 44 20-43 4F 4D 20 00 00 00 00   COMMAND COM ....
396F:0150   00 00 00 00 00 00 00 60-68 06 18 00 00 45 00 00   .......'h....E..
396F:0160   41 53 53 45 4D 42 4C 45-52 20 20 08 00 00 00 00   ASSEMBLER   ....
396F:0170   00 00 00 00 00 00 33 9C-B0 06 00 00 00 00 00 00   ......3.0......
```

159

```
-D
396F:0180  46 57 20 20 20 20 20 20-43 4F 4D 20 00 00 00 00   FW      COM ....
396F:0190  00 00 00 00 00 00 00 00-6F 05 2A 00 80 AF 00 00   ........o.*../..
396F:01A0  46 57 20 20 20 20 20 20-4F 56 4C 20 00 00 00 00   FW      OVL ....
396F:01B0  00 00 00 00 00 00 00 00-72 05 56 00 81 02 00 00   ........r.V.....
396F:01C0  46 57 20 20 20 20 20 20-53 57 50 20 00 00 00 00   FW      SWP ....
396F:01D0  00 00 00 00 00 00 9B 8A-FF 06 57 00 00 C8 00 00   ..........W..H..
396F:01E0  43 4F 4E 46 49 47 20 20-44 41 54 20 00 00 00 00   CONFIG  DAT ....
396F:01F0  00 00 00 00 00 00 1D 82-A1 06 89 00 00 28 00 00   ........!....(..
```

We will use a format much like this for Dskpatch, but with improvements. Dskpatch will be the equivalent of a full-screen editor for disk sectors. You will be able to display sectors on the screen and move the cursor about the sector display, changing numbers or characters as you want. You will also be able to write this altered sector back to the disk. That is why it is called Disk Patch—actually Dskpatch, because you cannot have more than eight characters in the name.

Dskpatch is the motivation for the procedures you will write. It is by no means an end in itself. In using Dskpatch as an example for this book, we will also manage to present many procedures that you will find useful when you attempt to write your own programs. That means you will find many general-purpose procedures for display output, display manipulation, keyboard input, and more.

Let's take a closer look at some of the improvements you will make to Debug's sector dump. The display from Debug only shows the "printable" characters—96 out of the 256 different characters that an IBM PC can display. Why is that? This occurs because MS-DOS was designed to run on many different computers, including computers that used simple computer terminals. The author of Debug chose to show a period for all other characters. Most computers are PC-compatibles, so there is no reason for Debug to continue to restrict its display, but no one at Microsoft ever changed the code.

Dskpatch is for PC compatibles, so you can display all 256 different characters with a bit of work. Using the DOS function 2 for character output, You can display almost all characters. However, DOS gives special meaning to some, such as 7, which rings the bell. There are characters for special codes like 7, and in Part III you will learn how to display them.

We will also make heavy use of the function keys so that you can display the next sector by pressing the F4 key. You will also be able to change any byte by moving the cursor to that byte and typing in a new number. It will be just like

160

using a word processor, where you can easily change characters. More of these details will appear as you slowly build Dskpatch. Figure 12-2 shows what its normal display will look like—a vast improvement over the display from Debug.

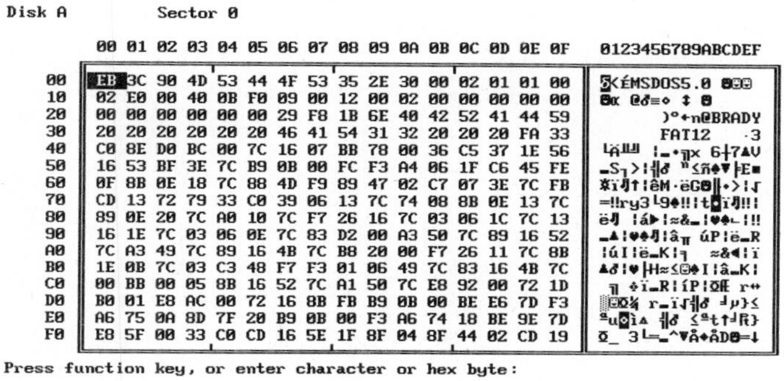

Figure 12-2: Example of Dskpatch's Display.

The Game Plan for Building Dskpatch

In Chapter 13, you will learn how to break your program into many different source files. Then, you will begin serious work on Dskpatch in Chapter 14. At the end, you will have nine source files for Dskpatch that have to be linked together. Even if you don't enter and run all these programs now, they'll be here when you're ready for them, or when you want to borrow some of the general-purpose procedures. In any case, you will get a better idea of how to write long programs as you read through the following chapters.

You have already created several useful procedures such as WRITE_HEX to write a byte as a two-digit hex number and WRITE_DECIMAL to write a number in decimal. Now, you will write some programs to display a block of memory in much the same way Debug's D command does. Start by displaying 16 bytes of memory, one line of Debug's display, and then work toward displaying 16 lines of 16 bytes each (half a sector). A full sector won't fit on

161

the display at one time with the format we have chosen, so Dskpatch includes procedures for scrolling through a sector using the ROM BIOS—not DOS—interrupts. That will come much later, though, after you have built a full-screen display of half a sector.

Once you can dump 256 bytes from memory, you will build another procedure to read a sector from the disk into our area of memory. You will dump half a sector on the screen, and you will be able to use Debug to alter the program, so you can dump different sectors. At that point, you will have a functional, but not very attractive, display, so making it pretty comes next.

With a bit more work and some more procedures, you will rebuild the half-sector display to be much more pleasing aesthetically. It still won't be a full-screen display, so it will just scroll past like Debug's dump did. The full-screen display will come next, and you will learn about the ROM BIOS routines that allow you to control the display, move the cursor, etc. Then, you will be ready to learn how to use more ROM BIOS routines to print all 256 different characters.

Next will come the keyboard input and command procedures so you can start interacting with Dskpatch. About that time you will also need another course correction.

Summary

You have seen enough of the future here. You should have a better idea of where we're headed, so let's move on to the next chapter. Chapter 13 will lay the groundwork for modular design and teach you how to split a program into different source files. Then, in Chapter 14, you will write test procedures to display sections of memory.

Modular Design—Building Programs in Pieces

In this chapter you will learn how to break your programs into more than one file. You will also learn more about modular design, which is the foundation of well-organized programs. Finally, you will take a look at Microsoft's Programmers Workbench, which is a nice environment for building complex programs with many source files.

Files altered: VIDEO_IO.ASM and TEST.ASM

Disk files: VIDEO_13.ASM and TEST13.ASM

13

Topics Covered

Separate Assembling

The Three Laws of Modular Design

Using the Programmer's Workbench

Summary

Without modular design, Dskpatch wouldn't have been much fun to write. Using a modular design greatly eases the task of writing any but the smallest program. This chapter sets some ground rules for modular design which will be followed throughout the rest of the book. Let's begin by learning how to separate a large program into many different source files.

Separate Assembling

In Chapter 10, we added the procedure WRITE_DECIMAL to VIDEO_IO.ASM, and we also added a short test procedure called TEST_WRITE_DECIMAL. Let's take this test procedure out of VIDEO_IO.ASM and put it in a file of its own, called TEST.ASM. Then, you will assemble these two files separately and link them together into one program as shown in Listing 13-1. The TEST.ASM file is as follows:

Listing 13-1 The File TEST.ASM (TEST13.ASM)

```
DOSSEG
.MODEL   SMALL

.STACK

.CODE
        EXTRN    WRITE_DECIMAL:PROC

TEST_WRITE_DECIMAL      PROC
        MOV     DX,12345
        CALL    WRITE_DECIMAL
        MOV     AH,4Ch                   ;Return to DOS
        INT     21h
TEST_WRITE_DECIMAL      ENDP

        END     TEST_WRITE_DECIMAL
```

You have seen most of this source file before, but the EXTRN directive is new. The statement EXTRN WRITE_DECIMAL:PROC tells the assembler two things—that WRITE_DECIMAL is in another, *external,* file, and that it is a procedure. What kind of procedure (NEAR or FAR) depends on the MODEL directive. Since we have used .MODEL SMALL, which defines procedures to be NEAR, WRITE_DECIMAL is in the same segment. The assembler thus generates a NEAR CALL for this procedure. It would generate a FAR CALL if we had placed a FAR after WRITE_DECIMAL. You can use NEAR or FAR in place of the PROC in the EXTRN statement if you wanted to explicitly define the type of procedure, but it is better to let the .MODEL directive define the procedure types.

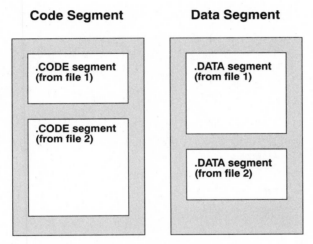

Figure 13-1: LINK stitches together segments from different files.

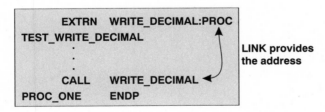

Figure 13-2: LINK assigns the addresses for external names.

These are about the only changes you need for separate source files until you begin to store data in memory. At that point, you will introduce another

167

segment for data. Now, let's modify VIDEO_IO.ASM, and then assemble and link the two files. Remove the procedure TEST_WRITE_DECIMAL from VIDEO_IO.ASM because you have placed it in TEST.ASM and you do not need it in Video_io.

Finally, change END TEST_WRITE_DECIMAL at the end of VIDEO_IO.ASM to just END. Once again you moved the main procedure was moved to TEST.ASM. The procedures in VIDEO_IO.ASM are now *external* procedures. That is, they have no function by themselves; they must be linked to procedures that call them from other files. You don't need a name after the END directive in VIDEO_IO.ASM because your main program is now in TEST.ASM.

When you have finished making these changes, your VIDEO_IO.ASM source file should look something like the following listing. The complete listing is included in VIDEO_13.ASM on the disk.

```
.MODEL   SMALL
.CODE

         PUBLIC   WRITE_HEX
             .
             .
             .
WRITE_HEX        ENDP


         PUBLIC   WRITE_HEX_DIGIT
             .
             .
             .
WRITE_HEX_DIGIT ENDP


         PUBLIC   WRITE_CHAR
             .
             .
             .
WRITE_CHAR       ENDP
```

```
        PUBLIC  WRITE_DECIMAL
             .
             .
             .
WRITE_DECIMAL   ENDP


        END
```

Assemble these two files just as you assembled Video_io before, using ML /c followed by the file name. TEST.ASM knows all it needs to know about VIDEO_IO.ASM through the EXTRN statement. The rest will come when you link the two files.

> ML can assemble more than one file at a time. All you have to do is include all the files you want to assemble after the ML /c. For example, you can assemble both files being used here with this command:
>
> ```
> ML /C TEST.ASM VIDEO_IO.ASM
> ```
>
> You can create the TEST.EXE file directly without creating any of the OBJ files along the way. If you type ML without the /C switch, this tells ML to create an EXE file directly. To see how this works, delete the OBJ files from your disk, then type the following to create TEST.EXE:
>
> ```
> ML TEST.ASM VIDEO_IO.ASM
> ```
>
> When you assemble a program like this, the final program will always have the same name, but with an EXE extension, as the first file name in the list.

Now you should have the files TEST.OBJ and VIDEO_IO.OBJ. Use the following command to link these two files into one program named TEST.EXE:

```
C>LINK TEST VIDEO_IO;
```

LINK stitches the procedures of these two files together to create one file containing the entire program. It uses the first file name you entered as the name for the resulting EXE file, so you now have TEST.EXE.

That's it; you created one program from two source files. The final EXE program is identical in function to the COM version you created in Chapter 10 from the single file VIDEO_IO.ASM, when it contained the main procedure TEST_WRITE_DECIMAL.

We will make heavy use of separate source files from here on. Their value will become clearer as the procedures stack up. In the next chapter, you will write a test program to dump sections of memory in hex. You will usually write a simple test version of a procedure before writing the complete version. Doing so will allow you to see how to write a good final version, as well as to save effort and mental turmoil in the process. There are several other useful ways to save effort. They are called *The Three Laws of Modular Design*.

The Three Laws of Modular Design

These laws are summarized in Table 13-1. They aren't really *laws*, they are suggestions. But we will use them throughout this book. Define your own laws if you like; either way, stick to the same ones all the time. Your job will be much easier if you are consistent.

Table 13-1 The Three Laws of Modular Design

1. Save and restore all registers, unless the procedure returns a value in that register.

2. Be consistent about which registers you use to pass information. For example:

DL, DX	Send byte and word values
AL, AX	Return byte and word values
BX:AX	Return double-word values
DS:DX	Send and return addresses

CX	Repeat counts and other counts
CF	Set when there is an error; an error code should be returned in one of the registers, such as AL or AX.

3. Define all external interactions in the comment header:

- Information needed on entry

- Information returned (registers changed)

- Procedures called

- Variables used (read, written, and so on)

There is an obvious parallel between modular design in programming and modular design in engineering. An electrical engineer, for example, can build a very complicated piece of equipment from boxes that perform different functions, without knowing how each box works inside. But if each box uses different voltages and different connections, the lack of consistency creates a major headache for the engineer who must somehow provide a different voltage for each box and create special connections between boxes. Fortunately for the engineer, there are standards providing for only a small number of standard voltages. So, perhaps only four different voltages need to be provided instead of a different voltage for each box.

Modular design and standard interfaces are just as important in assembly-language programs, and that is why we will lay down the laws (so to speak), and use those laws from here on. As you will see by the end of this book, these rules will make your task much simpler. Let's take a look at these laws in detail.

Save and restore *all* registers, *unless* the procedure returns a value in that register.

There aren't that many registers in the 80x86. By saving registers at the start of a procedure, you free them for use within that procedure. But you must be careful to restore them at the end of the procedure. You will see us doing this in all of the procedures, with PUSH instructions appearing first in each procedure and POPs at the end.

The only exception is for procedures that must return some information to the calling procedure. For example, a procedure that reads a character from the keyboard must somehow return the character. Don't save any registers that are used to return information.

Short procedures also help the register-shortage problem. At times, you will write a procedure that is used by only one other procedure. Not only does this help with the shortage of registers, it also makes the program easier to write and read. You will see more of this as we write procedures for Dskpatch.

Be consistent about which registers you use to pass information.

Your job becomes simpler if standards are set for exchanging information between procedures. Use one register for sending information, and one for receiving information. You will also need to send addresses for long pieces of data. For this you will use the DS:DX pair of registers so that your data can be anywhere in memory. You will learn more about this when we introduce a new segment for data and begin to make use of the DS register.

The CX register is reserved for repeat counts. Soon you will write a procedure to write one character several times so that you can write 10 spaces by calling this procedure (WRITE_CHAR_N_TIMES) with CX set to 10. Use the CX register whenever you have a repeat count or when you want to return some count, such as the number of characters read from the keyboard (you will do this when we write a procedure named READ_STRING).

Finally, set the Carry Flag (CF) whenever there is an error, and clear it whenever there isn't an error. Not all procedures use carry flags. For example, WRITE_CHAR always works, so there is no reason to return an error report. But a procedure that writes to the disk can encounter many errors (no disk, write-protection, and so on). In this case, you will use a register to return an error code. There is no standard here because DOS uses different registers for different functions.

Define *all* external interactions in the comment header.

There is no need to learn how a procedure works if all you want to do is use it. This is why we place a detailed comment header before each procedure. This header contains *all* the information you need to know. It tells you what to place in each register before calling the procedure, and what information the procedure returns. Most procedures use registers for their variables, but some of the procedures use variables in memory. The comment header should say which of these memory variables are read and which are changed. Finally, each header should list other procedures called. An example of a full-blown header with much of this information is as follows:

```
;----------------------------------------------------------------;
; This is an example of a full-blown header. This part would normally   ;
; be a brief description of what this procedure does. For example,      ;
; this procedure will write the message "Sector   " on the first line.  ;
;                                                                       ;
; On entry:     DS:DX   Address of the message "Sector   "             ;
; Returns:      AX      Error code if there was an error               ;
;                                                                       ;
; Calls:        GOTO_XY, WRITE_STRING   (procedures called)            ;
; Reads:        STATUS_LINE_NO          (memory variables read only)   ;
; Writes:       DUMMY                   (memory variables altered)     ;
;----------------------------------------------------------------;
```

Whenever you want to use any procedure you have written, you can just glance at this comment header to learn how to use it. There will be no need to delve into the inner workings of the procedure to find out what it does.

You may discover from time to time that your comment headers don't tell you enough so you can use the subroutine, and you have to actually read the code. When you find yourself doing this, consider rewriting your comment header so it does a better job of explaining how the subroutine works. If you don't rewrite the header, you may find yourself again reading the code.

These laws make assembly language programming easier, and we will be certain to abide by them, but often not on the first try. The first version of a procedure or program is a test case. Frequently, we don't know exactly how to write the program we have in mind, so on these "rough drafts," we will write the program without concern for the laws of modular design. We will just plow through and get something that works. Then we can backtrack and do a good job by rewriting each procedure to conform to these laws.

Programming is a process that goes by leaps and bounds. Throughout this book we will show much, but not all, of the stuttering that went into writing

Dskpatch. There is not room enough to contain all the versions we wrote before we settled on the final version. Our first tries often bear very little resemblance to the final versions you will see. When you write programs, don't worry about getting everything right the first time. Be prepared to rewrite each procedure as you learn more about what you really want.

In the next chapter, you will build a simple test program to print a block of memory. It won't be the final version; we will go through others before we are satisfied, and even then, there will be other changes we would like to make. The moral is: A program is never done . . . but it must be stopped somewhere.

Using the Programmer's Workbench

The Microsoft MASM 6.0 package includes a full programming environment, called the *Programmer's Workbench*. This can make your job of building assembly language programs much easier. In reality, some programmers love the Programmer's Workbench (PWB), and others hate it. Since there are a number of people who don't like PWB, we won't force you to use it in this book; we will continue to use ML and LINK directly. For those of you who feel adventuresome, PWB has a lot to offer.

In this section we would like to give you an introduction to using PWB. We will use PWB to build TEST.EXE so you can see how you might use PWB to build your own assembly-language programs that use multiple files. We will assume that you asked to install PWB when you installed MASM 6—if you didn't, go back and do so now.

When you first start PWB you will see a screen like the one shown in Figure 13-3. At this point you could simply start typing a program, then use the pull-down menus to save the file. But since you already have two files, you will take a different approach.

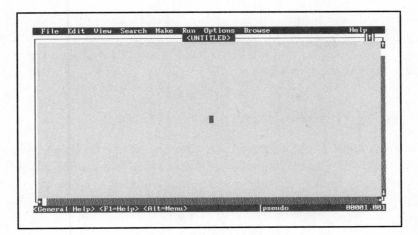

Figure 13-3: Programmer's Workbench when you first start it.

Using PWB's Pull-Down Menus

You are going to create a *program list*, which is a list of files that constitute a program. PWB can use this list of files to automatically create the EXE file, as you will see. Before we go on, a few words about pull-down menus and dialog boxes. PWB makes heavy use of both features, so you will need to know how to use them. To pull down a menu, you have two choices, depending on whether you want to use the keyboard or the mouse.

The keyboard interface centers around the Alt key. When you press the Alt key, PWB highlights the first letter of each menu item, which indicates that you can press Alt+*letter*. For example, you will want to pull down the Make menu, by pressing Alt+M. Once the menu is down, either use the cursor keys and press Enter to select an item from the list, or type one of the highlighted letters you see in the pull-down menu. In either case, you will notice that only one menu item, Set Program List... has a letter highlighted. This happens because all the other menu items are grayed out, which means their options are not available.

175

Using pull-down menus with the mouse is even easier. Simply click the left button on the menu bar at the top of the screen on any of the menu titles, such as Make, and a menu will drop down. You can then click on any of the menu items to select that item.

Setting the Program List

Now pull down the Make menu and select the item Select Program List... You will see the "Select Program List" dialog box, which is a dialog box that allows you to open an existing Program List. You need to create a new program list, which you can do by typing a name and pressing Enter. Type TEST and press Enter.

PWB will display another dialog box asking if you want to create the file "test.mak." Press Enter or click on the <Yes> button—you do want to create a new program list. Now you will now see the dialog box in Figure 13-4.

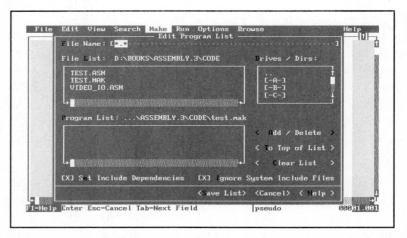

Figure 13-4: Use the Edit Program List dialog box to create and change program lists.

This dialog box is where you actually build program lists, or modify them once you have already built a list. You want to add two files to this program list:

TEST.ASM and VIDEO_IO.ASM, both of which should be visible in the File List window near the top of this dialog box. The steps you can follow to add these two files to the Program List are as follows:

1. Press Tab until the cursor moves to the File List window (probably a single Tab).

2. Use the up and down cursor keys to highlight TEST.ASM, then press the Enter key. You should now see TEST.ASM in the Program List window.

3. Repeat step 2 to add VIDEO_IO.ASM to the Program List.

4. Press Alt+S or click on the `<Save List>` button to save this program list.

PWB will think for a couple of seconds, then you will see the mostly-blank screen that you saw when you first started PWB. It may not seem like you have done much, but you have.

Building TEST.EXE

Pull down the Make menu again and you will notice it is quite different. Now all the items in this menu are enabled. But you will also notice that `test.exe` appears in the Build menu item. This means you can build TEST.EXE simply by pulling down the Make menu and selecting Build. What is even better is that PWB keeps track of which files you have changed, and it only assembles the files that need to be changed.

If you try building TEST.EXE, you will get the following error message:

`LINK : warning L4050: file not suitable for /EXEPACK; relink without`

What does this mean? By default, PWB tells the linker to try to *pack* your EXE file. Packed EXE files are files that have been compressed so they take up less disk space. The problem here is that your program is so small it cannot be packed without actually growing in size. The file grows because LINK has to add a small program to any EXE file it packs to unpack that program when its loaded into memory. Since this unpacker is larger than the entire TEST.EXE program, the LINK failed.

You can tell which Program List is currently selected by looking at the Edit Program List... *item in the Make menu. If you see a name, such as* test *after this item, you know that the Program List with that name is currently selected.*

177

What you have to do is change the way PWB tells LINK to create your EXE file. Pull down the Options menu and select LINK Options.... Then in the LINK Options dialog box press Alt+R or click on <Set Release Options...> to bring up yet another dialog box. Press Alt+E or click on Pack EXE file to make sure this option is not checked (it is checked whenever there is an x in square brackets, such as [X]). You want to make sure it reads the following:

```
[ ] Pack EXE file
```

Finally, click on the <OK> button in each of these dialog boxes (or use the Tab key to move the cursor to the <OK> button, then press Enter). Now select Build from the Make menu. It should work.

To reward you for all your hard work, you will see the final dialog box, like the one in Figure 13-5. You can then elect to run your program.

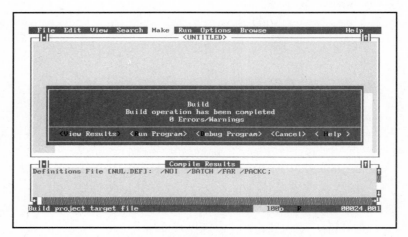

Figure 13-5: Final dialog box when PWB finished building your program.

Editing Files in PWB

If all PWB could do is build programs, it would not be that useful. Fortunately, PWB can do much more for you. For starters, you can edit any of the files in your Program List. An easier way to get to your files, however, is another feature called Browse, which enables you to jump very quickly to any place in your program.

Before you can use the Browse feature, however, you need to enable it. Pull down the Options menu and select the "Browse Options..." item. Once the dialog box appears, press Alt+B to check the "Generate Browse Information" option (so it has [X] next to it) and press Enter. Build your program again by selecting Build from the Make menu. Press Esc when you see the final dialog box saying that the Build operation finished. Whenever you rebuild your program with the Generate Browse Information option checked, PWB keeps a lot of information on your program which it needs for all the items in the Browse menu.

Pull down the Browse menu and select View Relationship. You will see a dialog box that lists two files in it. These are the two files that make up your Program List. Select the file TEST.ASM and press Alt+G (Goto). You will now have the file TEST.ASM visible in an edit window (see Figure 13-6) and you can edit TEST.ASM.

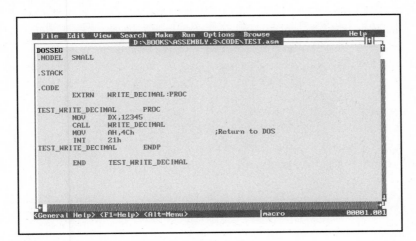

Figure 13-6: TEST.ASM in its own edit window.

Jump to Definitions

Move the cursor to the name WRITE_DECIMAL after the CALL. Now pull down the Browse menu and select "Goto Definition." You will see the dialog box in Figure 13-7, with WRITE_DECIMAL highlighted in the list. This list shows all of the procedures, labels, etc. in your program. Press Enter, and now you are looking at the definition of WRITE_DECIMAL in the file VIDEO_IO.ASM.

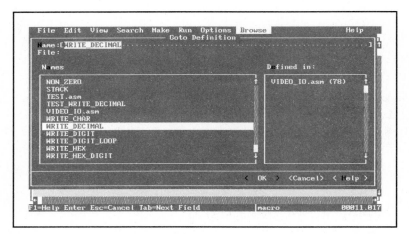

Figure 13-7: This dialog box enables you to jump quickly to any part of your program.

You can easily jump to any definition in any of the files of your project by using this menu item. You can also find all of the places where a particular subroutine is used in other parts of your program by using the Goto Definition... item in the Browse menu.

The information used by the Browse menu comes from the last build you did on your program. It won't reflect any changes you have made to your files since the last time you built your program from *within* PWB. Changes you make outside PWB won't show up inside PWB until you use PWB's Build command again.

Loading the Program List

PWB has one rather rude habit that probably keeps a lot of programmers from using it. When you exit and then start PWB again, it remembers all the files you had opened, but it *does not* remember the last Program List that you were using. You have to explicitly load the Program List each time you start PWB. You do this by using the Set Program List... from the Make menu to select the .MAK file you want to use. Fortunately, there is an easier solution.

There is a little-known switch you can use to have PWB automatically load the last Program list you were using. You can also use the /PL switch (this *must* be in uppercase letters). Type the following:

```
C>pwb /PL
```

There are far more features of PWB than we can show here, but this should give you an idea of how to use PWB. You might want to try using PWB for all the programs in the rest of this book. You can also use Microsoft's wonderful CodeView debugger from within PWB.

For the rest of this book, however, we will mainly show you the details of using ML and LINK to do all the work. There are two reasons for this. First, this will give you a better understanding of all the steps and other tools out there; second, there are many people who detest PWB, and they would not be happy if we used PWB for the rest of this book. To back up that claim, most programmers we know like to use the Brief editor, along with the Make program you will learn in Chapter 15. I personally don't know of any programmers who use PWB.

Summary

This has been a chapter for you to remember and use in the future. We began by teaching you how to separate a program into a number of different source files that can be assembled independently, then stitched together with the linker. We used the PUBLIC and EXTRN directives to inform the linker that there are connections between different source files. PUBLIC says that other source files can CALL the procedures named after PUBLICs, while EXTRN tells the assembler that the procedure you want to use is in another file.

Then we moved on to The Three Laws of Modular Design. These rules are meant to make your programming job simpler, so use them when writing your own programs (just as you will see us use them in this book). You will find it easier to write, debug, and read programs if they conform to these three laws.

Finally, we covered Microsoft's Programmers Workbench, which has a lot of nice features and is nice to work with once you get accustomed to its quirks. In all fairness, many programming systems have quirks, so it is a matter of what you are used to working with and what your co-workers use.

Dumping Memory

In this chapter you will learn how to use the different addressing modes to access memory. You will also learn how to store data in the data segment and how to set DS so it points to this data segment. The changes you will make to your program will allow you to display an area of memory in hex and as characters, much as Debug can display an area of memory.

Files altered: DISP_SEC.ASM, CURSOR.ASM, and VIDEO_IO.ASM

Disk files: DISP_S14.ASM, CURSOR14.ASM, and VIDEO_14.ASM

Topics Covered

From here on, we will concentrate on building Dskpatch in much the same way we originally wrote it. Some of the instructions in new procedures may be unfamiliar. We will explain each briefly as we come across them. (For detailed information, you will need a book that covers all of the instructions in detail. Most reference books that cover any of the 80x86 microprocessors have all the information you should need.)

Rather than cover all the 80x86 instructions, we will concentrate on new concepts, such as the different modes of addressing memory, which we will cover in this chapter. In Part III, we will move even farther away from the details of instructions and begin to see information specific to writing DOS programs that use the screen and keyboard.

Now, you will learn about *addressing modes* by writing a short test program to dump 16 bytes of memory in hex notation. To begin, you need to learn how to use memory as variables.

Using Addressing Modes to Access Memory

You have seen two addressing modes; they are known as the *register* and *immediate* addressing modes. The first mode you learned about was the register mode, which uses registers as variables. For example, the following instruction uses the two registers AX and BX as variables.

```
MOV     AX,BX
```

Then, you moved on to the immediate addressing mode, in which you moved a number directly into a register, as in the following example:

```
MOV     AX,2
```

This example moves the byte or word of memory *immediately* following the instruction into a register. In this sense, the MOV instruction in our example is one byte long, with two more bytes for the data (0002):

```
396F:0100 B80200        MOV     AX,0002
```

The instruction is B8h, and the two bytes of data (02h and 00h) follow this (remember that the 80x86 stores the low byte, 02h, first in memory).

Now you will learn how to use memory as a variable. The immediate mode allows you to read the piece of fixed memory immediately following that one instruction, but it does not allow you to change memory. For this, you will need other addressing modes.

Let's begin with an example. The following program reads 16 bytes of memory, one byte at a time. Each byte is displayed in hex notation, with a single space between each of the 16 hex numbers. Enter the program into the file DISP_SEC.ASM and assemble it. Enter the Listing 14-1 into the new file DISP_SEC.ASM.

Listing 14-1 The New File DISP_SEC.ASM

```
DOSSEG
.MODEL   SMALL

.STACK

.DATA

         PUBLIC  SECTOR
SECTOR   DB      10h, 11h, 12h, 13h, 14h, 15h, 16h, 17h  ;Test pattern
         DB      18h, 19h, 1Ah, 1Bh, 1Ch, 1Dh, 1Eh, 1Fh


.CODE

         EXTRN   WRITE_HEX:PROC
         EXTRN   WRITE_CHAR:PROC
;-------------------------------------------------------------------;
; This is a simple test program to dump 16 bytes of memory as hex   ;
; numbers, all on one line.                                         ;
;-------------------------------------------------------------------;
DISP_LINE        PROC
         MOV     AX,DGROUP               ;Put data segment into AX
         MOV     DS,AX                   ;Set DS to point to data

         XOR     BX,BX                   ;Set BX to 0
         MOV     CX,16                   ;Dump 16 bytes
HEX_LOOP:
         MOV     DL,SECTOR[BX]           ;Get 1 byte
         CALL    WRITE_HEX               ;Dump this byte in hex
```

continues

Listing 14-1 continued

```
        MOV     DL,' '                  ;Write a space between numbers
        CALL    WRITE_CHAR
        INC     BX
        LOOP    HEX_LOOP


        MOV     AH,4Ch                  ;Return to DOS
        INT     21h
DISP_LINE       ENDP


        END     DISP_LINE
```

Try your new program to see how it works. Assemble Disp_sec.

You are ready to link DISP_SEC.OBJ and VIDEO_IO.OBJ and create an EXE file named DISP_SEC.EXE. LINK creates a program by putting the pieces together in the same order as the names on the command line. Since you want the main procedure to appear at the start of the program, the first file name in the LINK command needs to be the name of the file that contains the main procedure (Disp_sec in this case). A semicolon must appear at the end of the list of files, so type the following command:

`C>LINK DISP_SEC VIDEO_IO;`

Linking will always be the same, with more names before the semicolon when you have more files. The main procedure should always be in the first file listed. In general, the preceding step for the files *file1*, *file2*, and so on, is as follows:

`LINK file1 file2 file3 ...;`

Now, run the EXE file. If you don't see the following when you run the program, go back and check carefully for a mistake.

`10 11 12 13 14 15 16 17 18 19 1A 1B 1C 1D 1E 1F`

Now let's see how Disp_sec works. The following instruction uses a new addressing mode known as *Indirect Memory Addressing*—addressing memory through the *Base* register with *offset*, or more simply, *Base Relative*.

```
MOV     DL,SECTOR[BX]           ;Get 1 byte
```

In order to see what this really means, you need to first learn more about segments.

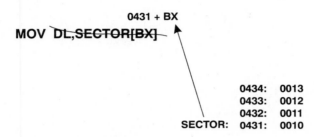

Figure 14-1: Translation of SECTOR[BX].

Using the Data Segment

Looking at Disp_sec, you will see that the label SECTOR appears after .DATA. The .DATA directive declares a data segment that is used for memory variables. (The name of the segment created by .DATA is _DATA.) Any time you want to store and read data in memory, you will set aside some space in this segment. We will get back to memory variables, but first a little more about segments.

The .MODEL SMALL directive creates what Microsoft calls a small memory-model program. Small programs are defined as programs that have up to 64K of code and up to 64K of data. In other words, one segment for code and one segment for data. Since both the data (defined by .DATA) and the stack (defined by .STACK) are data, they are put into a single segment as shown in Figure 14-2.

This *grouping* of the stack and data segments into one segment is handled by a mechanism in the assembler called *groups*. In particular, the assembler creates a group called DGROUP that creates a single segment out of all the segments used for data. So far you have learned the .DATA and .STACK directives. There are several other data directives that create segments in this group (you will see another later in this book). Fortunately, the .MODEL, .DATA, and .STACK directives handle all of this behind the scenes. Knowing some of what happens behind the scenes, however, will come in use later when you look at memory maps to see how programs are put together.

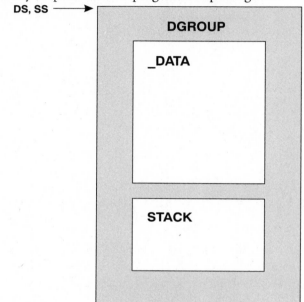

Figure 14-2: Stack and data in one segment group (DGROUP).

Another thing that happens automatically as a result of the DOSSEG directive is that the STACK segment is loaded into memory above the DATA segment. The data segment we created has data in it (10h, 11h, 12h, and so on) that needs to be in the EXE file so it can be copied into memory when the program is run by DOS. The stack, on the other hand, needs to take space in memory, but the stack's memory does not need to be initialized (only SS:SP has to be set). So by putting the stack segment after the data segment, you don't need to set aside space on the disk for the stack (see Figure 14-3).

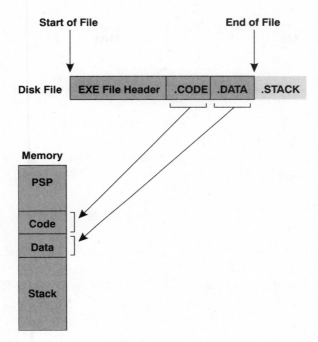

Figure 14-3: The stack segment uses no disk space.

Base-Relative Addressing

It is time to get back to the base-relative addressing mode. The following two lines set aside 16 bytes of memory in the data segment starting at SECTOR, which the assembler converts to an address.

```
SECTOR  DB      10h, 11h, 12h, 13h, 14h, 15h, 16h, 17h  ;Test pattern
        DB      18h, 19h, 1Ah, 1Bh, 1Ch, 1Dh, 1Eh, 1Fh
```

DB, you may recall, stands for *Define Byte*. The numbers after each DB are initial values. When you first start DISP_SEC.EXE, the memory starting at SECTOR will contain 10h, 11h, 12h, and so on. If we wrote the command below the instruction would move the first byte (10h) into the DL register.

```
MOV     DL,SECTOR
```

191

This is known as *direct* memory addressing. But we did not write that. Instead, we placed [BX] after SECTOR. This may look suspiciously like an index into an array, like the following BASIC statement which moves the 10th element of L into K.

```
K = L(10)
```

In fact, the MOV instruction is much the same. The BX register contains an *offset* in memory from SECTOR. So if BX is 0, the MOV DL,SECTOR[BX] moves the first byte (10h here) into DL. If BX is 0Ah, this MOV instruction moves the eleventh byte (1Ah—remember, the first byte is at BX = 0) into DL.

On the other hand, the instruction MOV DX,SECTOR[BX] with BX = 0Ah would move the sixth word into DX, since an offset of 10 bytes is the same as 5 words, and the first word is at offset zero. (For enthusiasts this last MOV instruction is not legal because SECTOR is a byte label, whereas DX is a word register. You would have to write MOV DX,Word Ptr SECTOR[BX] to tell the assembler that you really want to use SECTOR as a word label in this instruction.)

There are many other addressing modes and some will be covered later. All of the addressing modes are summarized in Table 14-1.

Table 14-1 Addressing Modes

Addressing Mode	Format of Address	Segment Register Used
Register	register (such as AX)	None
Immediate	data (such as 12345)	None
	Memory Addressing Modes	
Register Indirect	[BX]	DS
	[BP]	SS
	[DI]	DS
	[SI]	DS

Addressing Mode	Format of Address	Segment Register Used
Base Relative*	label[BX]	DS
	label[BP]	SS
Direct Indexed*	label[DI]	DS
	label[SI]	DS
Base Indexed*	label[BX+SI]	DS
	label[BX+DI]	DS
	label [BP+SI]	SS
	label[BP+DI]	SS
String Commands:		Read from DS:SI
(MOVSW, LODSB, *and so on*)		Write to ES:DI

* Label[...] can be replaced by [disp+...], where *disp* is a displacement. Thus, we could write [10+BX] and the address would be 10 + BX.

Setting DS to Point to Your Data Segment

This discussion has glossed over one minor detail. In Chapter 11 we mentioned that both the DS and ES registers point to the PSP, not to your data segment when DOS starts the program. The first two lines in DISP_LINE set DS so it points to our data segment as follows:

```
MOV     AX,DGROUP               ;Put data segment into AX
MOV     DS,AX                   ;Set DS to point to data
```

The first line moves the segment address for our data group (called DGROUP) that contains .DATA and .STACK into the AX register. The second line sets DS so it points to your data.

There is one sticky point here. If you remember the discussions about the segment registers, we said that the segment used for programs depends on how much memory is already in use. In other words, you cannot know the value of DGROUP until DOS loads the program in memory. How, then do you know what number to load into AX?

There is a small header at the start of each EXE file that contains a list of addresses in your program that have to be calculated. DOS uses this information to calculate the value of DGROUP and update the value in the MOV AX,DGROUP instruction when it loads DISP_SEC.EXE into memory. This process is known as relocation. You will see how DOS does relocation in Chapter 28.

There is another fine point of writing programs for the 80x86 family of microprocessor. Notice that we set the value of DS with two instructions rather than the single instruction, as follows.

```
MOV     DS,DGROUP
```

You need two instructions because you cannot move a number directly into a segment register on the 80x86; first you have to move the segment number into the AX register. Requiring two instructions, rather than one, simplified the design of the original 80x86 microprocessor. This made it less expensive to manufacture but more difficult to program.

Adding Characters to the Dump

You are almost finished writing the procedure that creates a dump display similar to Debug's. So far, you have dumped the hex numbers for one line; in the next step, you will add the character display following the hex display. The new version of DISP_LINE (in DISP_SEC.ASM), with a second loop added to display the characters, is as follows:

Listing 14-2 Changes to DISP_LINE in DISP_SEC.ASM

```
DISP_LINE       PROC
        MOV     AX,DGROUP           ;Put data segment into AX
        MOV     DS,AX               ;Set DS to point to data
```

```
            XOR     BX,BX                   ;Set BX to 0
            MOV     CX,16                   ;Dump 16 bytes
HEX_LOOP:
            MOV     DL,SECTOR[BX]           ;Get 1 byte
            CALL    WRITE_HEX               ;Dump this byte in hex
            MOV     DL,' '                  ;Write a space between numbers
            CALL    WRITE_CHAR
            INC     BX
            LOOP    HEX_LOOP

            MOV     DL,' '                  ;Add another space before characters
            CALL    WRITE_CHAR
            MOV     CX,16
            XOR     BX,BX                   ;Set BX back to 0
ASCII_LOOP:
            MOV     DL,SECTOR[BX]
            CALL    WRITE_CHAR
            INC     BX
            LOOP    ASCII_LOOP

            MOV     AH,4Ch                  ;Return to DOS
            INT     21h
DISP_LINE   ENDP
```

Assemble this, link it to Video_io, and try it. Figure 14-4 shows the output you should see.

```
C>disp_sec
10 11 12 13 14 15 16 17 18 19 1A 1B 1C 1D 1E 1F  ►◄‡‼¶§_‡↑↓←→∟↔▲▼
C>_
```

Figure 14-4: DISP_LINE's output.

Try changing the data to include a 0Dh or a 0Ah. You will see a rather strange display, because 0Ah and 0Dh are the characters for the line-feed and carriage-return characters. DOS interprets these as commands to move the cursor, but we would like to see them as just ordinary characters for this part of the display. To do this, you must change WRITE_CHAR to print *all* characters, without applying any special meaning. You will do that in Part III, but for now, rewrite WRITE_CHAR slightly so that it prints a period in place of the low characters (between 0 and 1Fh), as you can see in Figure 14-5.

195

```
C>disp_sec
10 11 12 13 14 15 16 17 18 19 1A 1B 1C 1D 1E 1F ...............
C>_
```

Figure 14-5: Modified version of DISP_LINE.

Replace the WRITE_CHAR in VIDEO_IO.ASM with the following new procedure in Listing 14-3:

Listing 14-3 A New WRITE_CHAR in VIDEO_IO.ASM (Complete listing in VIDEO_14.ASM)

```
        PUBLIC  WRITE_CHAR
;----------------------------------------------------------------;
; This procedure prints a character on the screen using the DOS  ;
; function call. WRITE_CHAR replaces the characters 0 through 1Fh with ;
; a period.                                                      ;
;                                                                ;
; On entry:      DL       byte to print on screen.               ;
;----------------------------------------------------------------;
WRITE_CHAR      PROC
        PUSH    AX
        PUSH    DX
        CMP     DL,32               ;Is character before a space?
        JAE     IS_PRINTABLE        ;No, then print as is
        MOV     DL,'.'              ;Yes, replace with a period
IS_PRINTABLE:
        MOV     AH,2                ;Call for character output
        INT     21h                 ;Output character in DL register
        POP     DX                  ;Restore old value in AX and DX
        POP     AX
        RET
WRITE_CHAR      ENDP
```

Try this new procedure with Disp_sec, and change the data to various characters to check the boundary conditions.

Dumping 256 Bytes of Memory

Now you have learned how to dump one line, or 16 bytes, of memory. The next step is to dump 256 bytes of memory. This happens to be exactly half the number of bytes in a sector, so you are working toward building a display of half a sector. You still have many more improvements to make; this is just a test version.

You will need two new procedures and a modified version of DISP_LINE. The new procedures are DISP_HALF_SECTOR, which will soon evolve into a finished procedure to display half a sector, and SEND_CRLF, which sends the cursor to the beginning of the next line (CRLF stands for *Carriage Return-Line Feed*, the pair of characters that move the cursor to the next line).

SEND_CRLF is very simple, so let's start with it. Place the following procedure in Listing 14-4 into a file called CURSOR.ASM.

Listing 14-4 The New File CURSOR.ASM (CURSOR14.ASM)

```
CR          EQU     13                      ;Carriage return
LF          EQU     10                      ;Line feed

.MODEL  SMALL
.CODE

            PUBLIC  SEND_CRLF
;-------------------------------------------------------------------;
; This routine just sends a carriage return-line feed pair to the   ;
; display, using the DOS routines so that scrolling will be handled ;
; correctly.                                                        ;
;-------------------------------------------------------------------;
SEND_CRLF       PROC
            PUSH    AX
            PUSH    DX
            MOV     AH,2
            MOV     DL,CR
            INT     21h
            MOV     DL,LF
            INT     21h
```

continues

Listing 14-4 continued

```
        POP     DX
        POP     AX
        RET
SEND_CRLF       ENDP


        END
```

This procedure sends a Carriage Return and Line Feed pair, using the DOS function 2 to send characters. The following statement uses the EQU directive to define the name CR to be equal to 13.

```
CR      EQU     13                      ;Carriage return
```

So the instruction MOV DL,CR is equivalent to MOV DL,13. As shown in Figure 14-6, the assembler substitutes 13 whenever it sees CR. Likewise, it substitutes 10 whenever it sees LF.

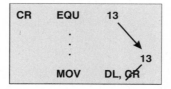

Figure 14-6: The EQU directive lets us use names in places of numbers.

From here on, we will show the changes in our programs so you won't have to check each line to see if it's new or different. Additions to our programs will be shown against a gray background, and text you should delete will be printed with a line through the text:

Add or change lines displayed against a gray background

~~Delete text shown in strike-through characters~~

The file Disp_sec now needs much work. Here's the new version of DISP_SEC.ASM as shown in Listing 14-5.

Listing 14-5 The New Version of DISP_SEC.ASM (Complete listing in DISP_S14.ASM)

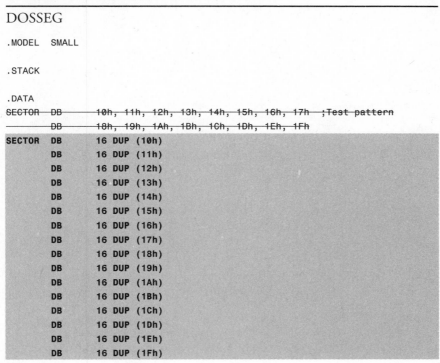

```
DOSSEG

.MODEL  SMALL

.STACK

.DATA
SECTOR  DB      10h, 11h, 12h, 13h, 14h, 15h, 16h, 17h  ;Test pattern
        DB      18h, 19h, 1Ah, 1Bh, 1Ch, 1Dh, 1Eh, 1Fh
SECTOR  DB      16 DUP (10h)
        DB      16 DUP (11h)
        DB      16 DUP (12h)
        DB      16 DUP (13h)
        DB      16 DUP (14h)
        DB      16 DUP (15h)
        DB      16 DUP (16h)
        DB      16 DUP (17h)
        DB      16 DUP (18h)
        DB      16 DUP (19h)
        DB      16 DUP (1Ah)
        DB      16 DUP (1Bh)
        DB      16 DUP (1Ch)
        DB      16 DUP (1Dh)
        DB      16 DUP (1Eh)
        DB      16 DUP (1Fh)

.CODE

        PUBLIC  DISP_HALF_SECTOR
        EXTRN   SEND_CRLF:PROC
;------------------------------------------------------------;
; This procedure displays half a sector (256 bytes)          ;
;                                                            ;
; Uses:         DISP_LINE, SEND_CRLF                          ;
;------------------------------------------------------------;
DISP_HALF_SECTOR        PROC
        MOV     AX,DGROUP               ;Put data segment into AX
```

continues

199

Listing 14-5 continued

```
        MOV     DS,AX                   ;Set DS to point to data

        XOR     DX,DX                   ;Start at beginning of SECTOR
        MOV     CX,16                   ;Display 16 lines
HALF_SECTOR:
        CALL    DISP_LINE
        CALL    SEND_CRLF
        ADD     DX,16
        LOOP    HALF_SECTOR

        MOV     AH,4Ch                  ;Return to DOS
        INT     21h
DISP_HALF_SECTOR        ENDP


        PUBLIC  DISP_LINE
        EXTRN   WRITE_HEX:PROC
        EXTRN   WRITE_CHAR:PROC
;------------------------------------------------------------------------;
; This procedure displays one line of data, or 16 bytes, first in hex,   ;
; then in ASCII.                                                         ;
;                                                                        ;
; On entry:      DS:DX    Offset into sector, in bytes.                  ;
;                                                                        ;
; Uses:          WRITE_CHAR, WRITE_HEX                                   ;
; Reads:         SECTOR                                                  ;
;------------------------------------------------------------------------;
DISP_LINE       PROC
        MOV     AX,DGROUP               ;Put data segment into AX
        MOV     DS,AX                   ;Set DS to point to data

        XOR     BX,BX
        PUSH    BX
        PUSH    CX
        PUSH    DX
        MOV     BX,DX                   ;Offset is more useful in BX
        MOV     CX,16                   ;Dump 16 bytes
        PUSH    BX                      ;Save the offset for ASCII_LOOP
HEX_LOOP:
        MOV     DL,SECTOR[BX]           ;Get 1 byte
        CALL    WRITE_HEX               ;Dump this byte in hex
        MOV     DL,' '                  ;Write a space between numbers
        CALL    WRITE_CHAR
```

```
        INC     BX
        LOOP    HEX_LOOP

        MOV     DL,' '                  ;Add another space before characters
        CALL    WRITE_CHAR
        MOV     CX,16
        POP     BX                      ;Get back offset into SECTOR
        XOR     BX,BX
ASCII_LOOP:
        MOV     DL,SECTOR[BX]
        CALL    WRITE_CHAR
        INC     BX
        LOOP    ASCII_LOOP


        POP     DX
        POP     CX
        POP     BX
        RET


        MOV     AH,4Ch                  ;Return to DOS
        INT     21h
DISP_LINE       ENDP


        END     DISP_HALF_SECTOR
```

The changes are all fairly straightforward. In DISP_LINE, we have added a PUSH BX and POP BX around the HEX_LOOP, because we want to reuse the initial offset in ASCII_LOOP. We have also added PUSH and POP instructions to save and restore all the registers used within DISP_LINE. Actually, DISP_LINE is almost done; the only changes left are to add spaces and graphics characters so you will have an attractive display; those will come later.

When you link the files (after assembling Disp_sec and Cursor), remember that you now have three files: Disp_sec, Video_io, and Cursor. Disp_sec should be first in this list. You should see a display like the one in Figure 14-7 when you run the new Disp_sec.exe.

You will have more files before you are finished. Let's move on to the next chapter, where you will read a sector directly from the disk before dumping half a sector.

```
C>disp_sec
10 10 10 10 10 10 10 10 10 10 10 10 10 10 10 10    ................
11 11 11 11 11 11 11 11 11 11 11 11 11 11 11 11    ................
12 12 12 12 12 12 12 12 12 12 12 12 12 12 12 12    ................
13 13 13 13 13 13 13 13 13 13 13 13 13 13 13 13    ................
14 14 14 14 14 14 14 14 14 14 14 14 14 14 14 14    ................
15 15 15 15 15 15 15 15 15 15 15 15 15 15 15 15    ................
16 16 16 16 16 16 16 16 16 16 16 16 16 16 16 16    ................
17 17 17 17 17 17 17 17 17 17 17 17 17 17 17 17    ................
18 18 18 18 18 18 18 18 18 18 18 18 18 18 18 18    ................
19 19 19 19 19 19 19 19 19 19 19 19 19 19 19 19    ................
1A 1A 1A 1A 1A 1A 1A 1A 1A 1A 1A 1A 1A 1A 1A 1A    ................
1B 1B 1B 1B 1B 1B 1B 1B 1B 1B 1B 1B 1B 1B 1B 1B    ................
1C 1C 1C 1C 1C 1C 1C 1C 1C 1C 1C 1C 1C 1C 1C 1C    ................
1D 1D 1D 1D 1D 1D 1D 1D 1D 1D 1D 1D 1D 1D 1D 1D    ................
1E 1E 1E 1E 1E 1E 1E 1E 1E 1E 1E 1E 1E 1E 1E 1E    ................
1F 1F 1F 1F 1F 1F 1F 1F 1F 1F 1F 1F 1F 1F 1F 1F    ................

C>_
```

Figure 14-7: Output from Disp_sec.

Summary

You know more about the different memory modes for addressing memory and registers in the 80x86 microprocessor. You learned about indirect memory addressing, which you first used to read 16 bytes of memory.

You also used indirect memory addressing in several programs you wrote in this chapter, starting with your program to print 16 hex numbers on the screen. These 16 numbers came from an area in memory labeled SECTOR, which was expanded a bit later so you could display a memory dump for 256 bytes—half a sector.

At last, you have begun to see dumps of the screen as they appear on your display, rather than as they are set in type. We will use these screen dumps to more advantage in the following chapters.

202

Dumping a
Disk Sector

In this chapter you will learn how to use NMake to simplify building your programs (you will just type NMake to rebuild). You will also learn how to read a disk sector, how to refer to variables defined in other files using EXTRN and PUBLIC, and how to load the address of a variable into a register. Finally, you will learn how to keep the size of your EXE file down even when you define large variables.

Files altered: DISP_SEC.ASM, DISK_IO.ASM

Disk files: DISP_S15.ASM, DISK_I15.ASM

15

Topics Covered

Now that you have a program that dumps 256 bytes of memory, you can add some procedures to read a sector from the disk and place it in memory starting at SECTOR. Then, your dump procedures will dump the first half of this disk sector.

Making Life Easier

With the three source files from the last chapter, life becomes somewhat complicated. Did you change all three of the files you were working on, or just two? You probably assembled all three, rather than checked to see if you made any changes since the last assemble. (Of course, if you are using the Programmer's Workbench, you did not have to keep track of which files you changed because it does that for you. This is just one of the advantages of using PWB.

Assembling all of your source files when you have only changed one of them is rather slow and tedious, and will become even slower as Dskpatch grows in size. What you would really like to do is assemble only the files you have changed.

Fortunately, both the assemblers covered in this book (MASM and Turbo Assembler) allow you to do just that. Microsoft and Borland provide programs called Make and NMake, respectively, that do exactly what you want. To use them, you create a file called Makefile that tells NMake, or Make, how to do its work. Then all you have to do is type:

C>**NMAKE**

NMake then assembles only the files you have changed.

> If you are using Borland's Make, you will type MAKE instead of NMAKE.
>
> If you are using MASM 5 or earlier, you will have to type MAKE MAKEFILE because Make did not automatically look for a specific file, whereas both NMake and Borland's Make look for the file MAKEFILE.

The file you create, Makefile, tells NMake what files depend on which other files. Every time you change a file, DOS updates the modify time for this file (you can see this in the DIR display). NMake simply looks at both the ASM and OBJ versions of a file. If the ASM version has a more recent modify time than the OBJ version, NMake knows it needs to assemble that file again.

There is one caveat we need to point out. NMake will work correctly only if DOS' date and time are correct. This may not be the case if your computer's C-MOS clock has a dead battery.

Format of the NMake File

The format for Makefile that we will use with NMake is fairly simple. The format is as follows:

Listing 15-1 The NMake File MAKEFILE

```
disp_sec.exe:    disp_sec.obj video_io.obj cursor.obj
        link disp_sec video_io cursor;

disp_sec.obj:    disp_sec.asm
        ml /c disp_sec.asm

video_io.obj:    video_io.asm
        ml /c video_io.asm

cursor.obj:      cursor.asm
        ml /c cursor.asm
```

Each entry has a file name on the left (before the colon) and one or more file names on the right. If any of the files on the right (such as DISP_SEC.ASM in the first line) are more recent than the first file (DISP_SEC.OBJ), NMake will execute all the indented commands that appear on the following lines. Enter these lines into the file Makefile (without an extension) and make a small change to DISP_SEC.ASM. Then type the following:

`C>`**`NMAKE`**

If you are using a version of Make from MASM 5 or earlier, the first two lines must be at the end of the file, rather than the beginning.

207

If you are using Borland's Make just type MAKE. Type MAKE MAKEFILE if you are using MASM 5 or earlier and you will see something like the following:

```
C>nmake

Microsoft (R) Program Maintenance Utility    Version 1.13
Copyright (c) Microsoft Corp 1988-91. All rights reserved.

        ml /c disp_sec.asm
Microsoft (R) Macro Assembler Version 6.00
Copyright (c) Microsoft Corp 1981-1991. All rights reserved.

 Assembling: disp_sec.asm
        link disp_sec video_io cursor;

Microsoft (R) Segmented-Executable Linker  Version 5.13
Copyright (c) Microsoft Corp 1984-1991. All rights reserved.


C>
```

NMake has done the minimum amount of work necessary to rebuild your program. If you have an older version of the Microsoft Macro Assembler that doesn't include Make, you will find this program worth the price of an upgrade. You will get a nice replacement for Debug, too. It is called CodeView, and it will be covered later in this chapter.

Patching up Disp_sec

Disp_sec, as we left it, included a version of DISP_HALF_SECTOR, which you used as a test procedure and the main procedure. Now, you will change DISP_HALF_SECTOR to an ordinary procedure so it can be called from a procedure named READ_SECTOR. The test procedure to read a disk sector will be in Disk_io.

First, modify Disp_sec to make it a file of procedures, just as you did with Video_io. Change the END DISP_HALF_SECTOR to just END, since your main procedure will now be in Disk_io. Then you will need to remove the

.STACK and DOSSEG directives near the top of Disp_sec.asm, again because you are moving these to a different file.

Since we plan to read a sector into memory starting at SECTOR, there is no need to supply test data. We can replace all the 16 DB statements after SECTOR with two lines which reserves 8,192 bytes for storing a sector.

```
        PUBLIC  SECTOR
SECTOR  DB      8192 DUP (0)
```

Recall our earlier statement that sectors are 512 bytes long. Why, then, do you need such a large storage area? In the old days of DOS, some hard disk companies used large sectors with larger hard disks (300 megabytes, for example) instead of adding more sections, which was needed for versions of DOS before 3.31. These large sector sizes are by no means common these days, but we still want to be certain that you do not read in a sector that is too large to fit into the memory you have reserved for SECTOR. So, in the interest of safety, we have reserved 8,192 bytes for SECTOR. In the rest of this book, with the exception of SECTOR, which we will cover soon, we will assume that sectors are only 512 bytes long.

Now what you need is a new version of DISP_HALF_SECTOR. The old version is nothing more than a test procedure that we used to test DISP_LINE. In the new version, we will want to supply an offset into the sector so you can display 256 bytes, starting anywhere in the sector. Among other things, this means you could dump the first half, the last half, or the middle 256 bytes. Once again, DX supplies this offset. The new, and final, version of DISP_HALF_SECTOR in Disp_sec is as follows:

Listing 15-2 The Final Version of DISP_HALF_SECTOR in DISP_SEC.ASM (Complete Listing in DISP_S15.ASM)

```
        PUBLIC  DISP_HALF_SECTOR
        EXTRN   SEND_CRLF:PROC
;--------------------------------------------------------------------;
;  This procedure displays half a sector (256 bytes)                 ;
;                                                                    ;
; On entry:       DS:DX    Offset into sector, in bytes -- should be ;
;                          multiple of 16.                           ;
;                                                                    ;
```

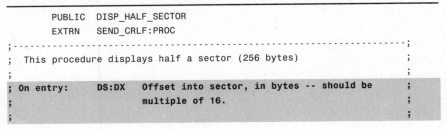

continues

209

Listing 15-2 continued

```
; Uses:          DISP_LINE, SEND_CRLF                                    ;
; - - - - - - - - - - - - - - - - - - - - - - - - - - - - - - - - - - - - - - - - - ;
DISP_HALF_SECTOR        PROC
        MOV     AX,DGROUP                   ;Put data segment into AX
        MOV     DS,AX                       ;Set DS to point to data

        XOR     DX,DX                       ;Start at beginning of SECTOR
        PUSH    CX
        PUSH    DX
        MOV     CX,16                       ;Display 16 lines
HALF_SECTOR:
        CALL    DISP_LINE
        CALL    SEND_CRLF
        ADD     DX,16
        LOOP    HALF_SECTOR
        POP     DX
        POP     CX
        RET

        MOV     AH,4Ch                      ;Return to DOS
        INT     21h
DISP_HALF_SECTOR        ENDP
```

Let's move on to our procedure to read a sector.

Reading a Sector

In this first version of READ_SECTOR we will deliberately ignore errors, such as having no disk in the disk drive. This is not good practice, but this isn't the final version of READ_SECTOR. We won't be able to cover error handling in this book, but you will find error-handling procedures in the version of Dskpatch on the disk that is included with this book. For now we just want to read a sector from the disk. The test version of the file DISK_IO.ASM is as follows:

Listing 15-3 The New File DISK_IO.ASM (DISK_I15.ASM)

```
DOSSEG
.MODEL    SMALL

.STACK

.DATA

          EXTRN     SECTOR:BYTE

.CODE

          EXTRN     DISP_HALF_SECTOR:PROC
;-------------------------------------------------------------------;
; This procedure reads the first sector on disk A and dumps the first  ;
; half of this sector.                                                 ;
;-------------------------------------------------------------------;
READ_SECTOR    PROC
          MOV       AX,DGROUP              ;Put data segment into AX
          MOV       DS,AX                  ;Set DS to point to data

          MOV       AL,0                   ;Disk drive A (number 0)
          MOV       CX,1                   ;Read only 1 sector
          MOV       DX,0                   ;Read sector number 0
          LEA       BX,SECTOR              ;Where to store this sector
          INT       25h                    ;Read the sector
          POPF                             ;Discard flags put on stack by DOS
          XOR       DX,DX                  ;Set offset to 0 within SECTOR
          CALL      DISP_HALF_SECTOR       ;Dump the first half

          MOV       AH,4Ch                 ;Return to DOS
          INT       21h
READ_SECTOR    ENDP


          END       READ_SECTOR
```

There are three new instructions in this procedure. The first moves the *address*, or offset, of SECTOR (from the start of the DGROUP data group created by .DATA) into the BX register; LEA stands for *Load Effective Address*.

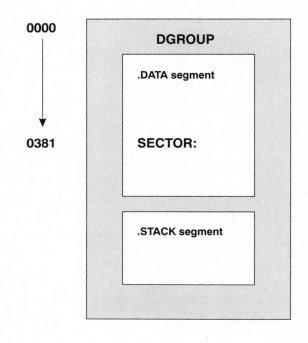

LEA   DX, SECTOR ⟶ MOV   BX, 0381

Figure 15-1: LEA loads the effective address.

```
LEA     BX,SECTOR
```

After this LEA instruction, DS:BX contains the full address of SECTOR, and DOS uses this address for the second new instruction, the INT 25h call, as you will see after a few more words about SECTOR. Actually, LEA loads the offset into the BX register without setting the DS register. You have to ensure that DS is pointing to the correct segment.

SECTOR is not in the same source file as READ_SECTOR. It is over in DISP_SEC.ASM. You tell the assembler where it is by using the EXTRN directive as follows and in Figure 15-2.

```
.DATA, EXTRN, SECTOR:BYTE
```

This set of instructions tells the assembler that SECTOR is defined in the data segment created by .DATA, and that it is defined in another source file, and that SECTOR is a variable of bytes (rather than words). We will be using such

EXTRNs often in following chapters; it is the way we use the same variables in a number of source files. Just be careful to define variables in only one place.

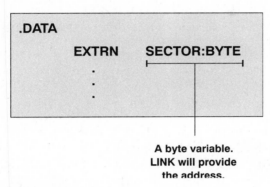

Figure 15-2: The EXTRN directive.

Let's return to the INT 25h instruction. INT 25h is a special function call to DOS for reading sectors from a disk. When DOS receives a call from INT 25h, it uses the information in the registers as follows:

AL	Drive number (0=A, 1=B, and so on)
CX	Number of sectors to read at one time
DX	Number of the first sector to read (the first sector is 0)
DS:BX	Transfer address: where to write the sectors read

The number in the AL register determines the drive from which DOS will read sectors. If AL = 0, DOS reads from drive A.

All versions of DOS since COMPAQ DOS 3.31 and DOS 4.0 support hard disks larger than 32M bytes by changing the way the INT 25h function call works. This isn't a problem for reading from a floppy disk, as we are doing in this book, but it can be if you want to use Dskpatch on a hard disk. You will find the code to read from such hard disks in the advanced version of Dskpatch, included on the disk.

DOS can read more than one sector with a single call, and it reads the number of sectors given by CX. Here, we set CX to one so DOS will read just one sector of 512 bytes.

You set DX to zero, so DOS will read the very first sector on the disk. You can change this number if you want to read a different sector; later on, we will.

DS:BX is the full address for the area in memory where you want DOS to store the sector(s) it reads. In this case, you have set DS:BX to the address of SECTOR so you can call DISP_HALF_SECTOR to dump the first half of the first sector read from the disk in drive A.

Finally, you will notice a POPF instruction immediately following the INT 25h. As mentioned before, the 80x86 has a register called the status register that contains the various flags, like the zero and carry flags. POPF is a special POP instruction that pops a word into the status register. Why do you need this POPF instruction?

The INT 25h instruction first pushes the status registers, then the return address onto the stack. When DOS returns from this INT 25h, it leaves the status register on the stack. DOS does this so it can set the carry flag on return if there was a disk error, such as trying to read from drive A: with no disk in the drive. We won't be checking for errors in this book, but we have to remove the status register from the stack—hence the POPF instruction.

INT 25h, along with INT 24h which writes a disk sector, are the only DOS routines that leave the status register on the stack.

Now you can assemble DISK_IO.ASM and reassemble DISP_SEC.ASM. Then, link the four files Disk_io, Disp_sec, Video_io, and Cursor, with Disk_io listed first. Or, if you have NMake (or Borland's Make), add the following two lines to the end of your Makefile:

```
disk_io.obj:    disk_io.asm
        ml /c disk_io.asm
```

Change the first two lines to the following:

```
disk_io.exe:    disk_io.obj disp_sec.obj video_io.obj cursor.obj
        link disk_io disp_sec video_io cursor;
```

After you create your EXE version of Disk_io, you should see a display something like Figure 15-3 (remember to put a disk in drive A before you run Disk_io).

```
C>disk_io
EB 3C 90 4D 53 44 4F 53 35 2E 30 00 02 01 01 00   δ<ÉMSDOS5.0.....
02 E0 00 60 09 F9 07 00 0F 00 02 00 00 00 00 00   .α.‘.·..........
00 00 00 00 00 00 29 8D 85 1C 19 55 4E 49 4E 53   ......)ìà..UNINS
54 41 4C 4C 20 31 46 41 54 31 32 20 20 20 FA 33   TALL 1FAT12   ·3
C0 8E D0 BC 00 7C 16 07 BB 78 00 36 C5 37 1E 56   └Ä╨╝.|..╗x.6┼7.V
16 53 BF 3E 7C B9 0B 00 FC F3 A4 06 1F C6 45 FE   .S┐>|╣..ⁿ≤ñ..╞E■
0F 8B 0E 18 7C 88 4D F9 89 47 02 C7 07 3E 7C FB   .ï..|êM·ëG.╟.>|√
CD 13 72 79 33 C0 39 06 13 7C 74 08 8B 0E 13 7C   ═.ry3└9..|t.ï..|
89 0E 20 7C A0 10 7C F7 26 16 7C 03 06 1C 7C 13   ë. |á.|≈&.|...|.
16 1E 7C 03 06 0E 7C 83 D2 00 A3 50 7C 89 16 52   ..|...|â╥.úP|ë.R
7C A3 49 7C 89 16 4B 7C B8 20 00 F7 26 11 7C 8B   |úI|ë.K|╕ .≈&.|ï
1E 0B 7C 03 C3 48 F7 F3 01 06 49 7C 83 16 4B 7C   ..|.├H≈≤..I|â.K|
00 BB 00 05 8B 16 52 7C A1 50 7C E8 92 00 72 1D   .╗..ï.R|íP|Φ Æ.r.
B0 01 E8 AC 00 72 16 8B FB B9 0B 00 BE E6 7D F3   ░.Φ¼.r.ï√╣..╛µ}≤
A6 75 0A 8D 7F 20 B9 0B 00 F3 A6 74 18 BE 9E 7D   ªu.ì⌂ ╣..≤ªt.╛₧}
E8 5F 00 33 C0 CD 16 5E 1F 8F 04 8F 44 02 CD 19   Φ_.3└═.^.Å.ÅD.═.

C>_
```

Figure 15-3: Screen dump from DISK_IO.COM.

The .DATA? Directive

If you look back at the definition of SECTOR in Disp_sec.asm, you will see that we reserved 8,192 bytes of zeros, which means that you have to reserve room in the DISK_IO.EXE file on your disk.

```
C>DIR DISK_IO.EXE

 Volume in drive C has no label
 Volume Serial Number is 191C-8737
 Directory of C:\SOURCE\ASM

DISK_IO  EXE      8920 10-17-92   3:28p
        1 file(s)       8920 bytes
                     1310720 bytes free

C>
```

As you can see, Disk_io.exe is 8,920 bytes long, which is mostly filled with zeros. That's a lot of space to reserve just for zeros, especially since you do not care what's in SECTOR before you read a sector into memory. So does SECTOR really need to take space on the disk? Nope.

There is another directive, .DATA?, that allows you to define memory variables that take space in memory, but not on the disk. You can do this by telling the assembler that you do not care what value a memory variable has. Change the three lines in DISP_SEC that define SECTOR to the following:

```
.DATA?

        PUBLIC   SECTOR
        SECTOR  DB        8192 DUP (?)
```

There are two changes here. First, there is a ? after the .DATA directive, which tells the assembler you are about to define variables that do not have initial values and, therefore, do not need to take space in the disk file. Second there is a ? rather than a 0 for the value of each byte in SECTOR. The DUP (?) tells the assembler that you do not care what value each byte has.

> You need to define variables in the .DATA? section with DUP (?). If you define any variables with a value (such as VAR DB 0), or if you use VAR DB ?, the assembler will reserve room in the EXE file for *all* the variables in .DATA?. In other words, put all the variables that have initial values into .DATA, and all variables with DUP (?) in .DATA?.

After making these changes, rebuild Disk_io.exe. It should now be only 727 bytes long. The .DATA? directive allows you to keep your programs quite small on the disk.

We will come back later to add more to Disk_io; we have enough for now. In the next chapter, we will build a nicer sector display by adding some graphics characters to the display, and then adding a few more pieces of information.

Summary

Now that you have four different source files, Dskpatch is becoming somewhat more involved. In this chapter, we looked at the program NMake, which helps make life simpler by assembling only the files you have changed.

We also wrote a new procedure, READ_SECTOR. It is in a different source file from SECTOR, so you used an EXTRN definition in DISK_IO.ASM to tell the assembler about SECTOR, and let it know that SECTOR is a byte variable.

You also learned about the LEA (Load Effective Address) instruction, which you used to load the address of SECTOR into the BX register.

DISK_IO uses a new INT number, INT 25h, to read sectors from a disk to memory. You used INT 25h to read one sector into your memory variable, SECTOR, so you could dump it on the screen with DISP_HALF_SECTOR.

You also learned about the POPF instruction to pop a word off the stack and into the status register. You used this instruction to remove the flags which DOS did not remove from the stack when it returned from INT 25h.

The half-sector display is not very attractive yet. In the next chapter you will use some of the graphics characters available on the PC to make it more aesthetically pleasing.

Enhancing the Sector Display

In this chapter you will continue building the Dskpatch program, adding lines around the display, hex offsets along the left side, and the top. Finally, you will learn two new instructions: LODSB (Load String Byte) and CLD (Clear Direction), which are useful for working with strings of data.

Files altered: DISP_SEC.ASM, VIDEO_IO.ASM, DISK_IO.ASM

Disk files: DISP_S16.ASM, VIDEO_I16.ASM, DISK_I16.ASM

16

Topics Covered

You have come to the last chapter in Part II. Everything covered so far has been applicable to DOS and the 80x86. In Part III, you will begin to write procedures that work more closely with your computer's screen.

But before we move on, we will use this chapter to add several more procedures to Video_io. We will also modify DISP_LINE in Disp_sec. All modifications and additions will be to the display. Most of them will be to improve the appearance of the display, but one will add new information. It will add numbers on the left that act like the addresses in Debug's dump. Let's begin with graphics.

Adding Graphics Characters

The PC has a number of line-drawing characters you can use to draw boxes around various parts of the dump display. You will draw one box around the hex dump and another around the ASCII dump.

Enter the following definitions near the top of the file DISP_SEC.ASM, between the .MODEL directive and the .DATA? directive. Leave one or two blank lines before and after these definitions:

Listing 16-1 Add to the Top of DISP_SEC.ASM
(No Complete Listing on Disk)

```
;-----------------------------------------------------------------------;
; Graphics characters for border of sector.                             ;
;-----------------------------------------------------------------------;
VERTICAL_BAR      EQU     0BAh
HORIZONTAL_BAR    EQU     0CDh
UPPER_LEFT        EQU     0C9h
UPPER_RIGHT       EQU     0BBh
LOWER_LEFT        EQU     0C8h
LOWER_RIGHT       EQU     0BCh
TOP_T_BAR         EQU     0CBh
BOTTOM_T_BAR      EQU     0CAh
TOP_TICK          EQU     0D1h
BOTTOM_TICK       EQU     0CFh
```

These are the definitions for the graphics, line-drawing characters. Notice that we put a zero before each hex number so the assembler will know these are numbers, rather than labels.

We could just as easily have written hex numbers instead of these definitions in the procedure, but the definitions make the procedure easier to understand. For example, compare the following two instructions:

```
MOV     DL,VERTICAL_BAR
MOV     DL,0BAh
```

Most people find the first instruction clearer.

Now, here is the new DISP_LINE procedure to separate the different parts of the display with the VERTICAL_BAR character, number 186 (0BAh). As before, additions are shown against a gray background.

Listing 16-2 Changes to DISP_LINE in DISP_SEC.ASM

```
DISP_LINE       PROC
        PUSH    BX
        PUSH    CX
        PUSH    DX
        MOV     BX,DX               ;Offset is more useful in BX
                                    ;Write separator
        MOV     DL,' '
        CALL    WRITE_CHAR
        MOV     DL,VERTICAL_BAR     ;Draw left side of box
        CALL    WRITE_CHAR
        MOV     DL,' '
        CALL    WRITE_CHAR
                                    ;Now write out 16 bytes
        MOV     CX,16               ;Dump 16 bytes
        PUSH    BX                  ;Save the offset for ASCII_LOOP
HEX_LOOP:
        MOV     DL,SECTOR[BX]       ;Get 1 byte
        CALL    WRITE_HEX           ;Dump this byte in hex
        MOV     DL,' '              ;Write a space between numbers
        CALL    WRITE_CHAR
        INC     BX
        LOOP    HEX_LOOP
```

continues

221

Listing 16-2 continued

```
        MOV     DL,VERTICAL_BAR         ;Write separator
        CALL    WRITE_CHAR
        MOV     DL,' '                  ;Add another space before characters
        CALL    WRITE_CHAR

        MOV     CX,16
        POP     BX                      ;Get back offset into SECTOR
ASCII_LOOP:
        MOV     DL,SECTOR[BX]
        CALL    WRITE_CHAR
        INC     BX
        LOOP    ASCII_LOOP

        MOV     DL,' '                  ;Draw right side of box
        CALL    WRITE_CHAR
        MOV     DL,VERTICAL_BAR
        CALL    WRITE_CHAR

        POP     DX
        POP     CX
        POP     BX
        RET
DISP_LINE       ENDP
```

Use NMake to build the new Disk_io, or assemble this new version of Disp_sec and link your four files (remember to place Disk_io first in the list of files following the LINK command). You'll see nice double bars separating the display into two parts, as you can see in Figure 16-1.

Adding Addresses to the Display

Now try something a bit more challenging. Add the hex addresses down the left side of the display. These numbers will be the offset from the beginning of the sector, so the first number will be 00, the next 10, then 20, and so on.

```
C>disk_io
 ║ EB 3C 90 4D 53 44 4F 53 35 2E 30 00 02 01 01 00 ║ δ<ÉMSDOS5.0..... ║
 ║ 02 E0 00 60 09 F9 07 00 0F 00 02 00 00 00 00 00 ║ .α.`.·.......... ║
 ║ 00 00 00 00 00 00 29 8D 85 1C 19 55 4E 49 4E 53 ║ ......)ìà..UNINS ║
 ║ 54 41 4C 4C 20 31 46 41 54 31 32 20 20 20 FA 33 ║ TALL 1FAT12   ·3 ║
 ║ C0 8E D0 BC 00 7C 16 07 BB 78 00 36 C5 37 1E 56 ║ └Ä╨╝.|..╗x.6┼7.V ║
 ║ 16 53 BF 3E 7C B9 0B 00 FC F3 A4 06 1F C6 45 FE ║ .S┐>|╣..ⁿ≤ñ..╞E■ ║
 ║ 0F 8B 0E 18 7C 88 4D F9 89 47 02 C7 07 3E 7C FB ║ .ï..|êM·ëG.╟.>|√ ║
 ║ CD 13 72 79 33 C0 39 06 13 7C 74 08 8B 0E 13 7C ║ ═.ry3└9..|t.ï..| ║
 ║ 89 0E 20 7C A0 10 7C F7 26 16 7C 03 06 1C 7C 13 ║ ë. |á.|≈&.|...|. ║
 ║ 16 1E 7C 03 06 0E 7C 83 D2 00 A3 50 7C 89 16 52 ║ ..|...|â╥.úP|ë.R ║
 ║ 7C A3 49 7C 89 16 4B 7C B8 20 00 F7 26 11 7C 8B ║ |úI|ë.K|╕ .≈&.|ï ║
 ║ 1E 0B 7C 03 C3 48 F7 F3 01 06 49 7C 83 16 4B 7C ║ ..|.├H≈≤..I|â.K| ║
 ║ 00 BB 00 05 8B 16 52 7C A1 50 7C E8 92 00 72 1D ║ .╗..ï.R|íP|ΦÆ.r. ║
 ║ B0 01 E8 AC 00 72 16 8B FB B9 0B 00 BE E6 7D F3 ║ ░.Φ¼.r.ï√╣..╛µ}≤ ║
 ║ A6 75 0A 8D 7F 20 B9 0B 00 F3 A6 74 18 BE 9E 7D ║ ªu.ì⌂ ╣..≤ªt.╛₧} ║
 ║ E8 5F 00 33 C0 CD 16 5E 1F 8F 04 8F 44 02 CD 19 ║ Φ_.3└═.^.Å.ÅD.═. ║

C>_
```

Figure 16-1: Disk_io with vertical bars added.

The process is fairly simple, since you already have the procedure WRITE_HEX for writing a number in hex. But you do have a problem in dealing with a sector 512 bytes long: WRITE_HEX prints only two-digit hex numbers, whereas you need three hex digits for numbers greater than 255.

Here is the solution. Since your numbers will be between zero and 511 (0h to 1FFh), the first digit will either be a space, if the number (such as BCh) is below 100h, or it will be a 1. So, if the number is larger than 255, simply print a 1 followed by the hex number for the lower byte. Otherwise, you will print a space first. Additions to DISP_LINE that will print this leading three-digit hex number are as follows:

Listing 16-3 Additions to DISP_LINE in DISP_SEC.ASM

```
DISP_LINE       PROC
        PUSH    BX
        PUSH    CX
        PUSH    DX
        MOV     BX,DX                   ;Offset is more useful in BX
        MOV     DL,' '
                                        ;Write offset in hex
        CMP     BX,100h                 ;Is the first digit a 1?
        JB      WRITE_ONE               ;No, white space already in DL
        MOV     DL,'1'                  ;Yes, then place '1' into DL for output
```

continues

Listing 16-3 continued

```
WRITE_ONE:
        CALL    WRITE_CHAR
        MOV     DL,BL                   ;Copy lower byte into DL for hex output
        CALL    WRITE_HEX
                                        ;Write separator
        MOV     DL,' '
        CALL    WRITE_CHAR
        MOV     DL,VERTICAL_BAR         ;Draw left side of box
                  .
                  .
                  .
```

The results are shown in Figure 16-2.

```
C>disk_io
 00 ║ EB 3C 90 4D 53 44 4F 53 35 2E 30 00 02 01 01 00 ║ δ<ÉMSDOS5.0..... ║
 10 ║ 02 E0 00 60 09 F9 07 00 0F 00 02 00 00 00 00 00 ║ .α.`.·.......... ║
 20 ║ 00 00 00 00 00 00 29 8D 85 1C 19 55 4E 49 4E 53 ║ ......)ìà..UNINS ║
 30 ║ 54 41 4C 4C 20 31 46 41 54 31 32 20 20 20 FA 33 ║ TALL 1FAT12   ·3 ║
 40 ║ C0 8E D0 BC 00 7C 16 07 BB 78 00 36 C5 37 1E 56 ║ └Ä╨╝.|..╗x.6┼7.V ║
 50 ║ 16 53 BF 3E 7C B9 0B 00 FC F3 A4 06 1F C6 45 FE ║ .S┐>|╣..ⁿ≤ñ..╞E■ ║
 60 ║ 0F 8B 0E 18 7C 88 4D F9 89 47 02 C7 07 3E 7C FB ║ .ï..|êM·ëG.╟.>|√ ║
 70 ║ CD 13 72 79 33 C0 39 06 13 7C 74 08 8B 0E 13 7C ║ ═.ry3└9..|t.ï..| ║
 80 ║ 89 0E 20 7C A0 10 7C F7 26 16 7C 03 06 1C 7C 13 ║ ë. |á.|≈&.|...|. ║
 90 ║ 16 1E 7C 03 06 0E 7C 83 D2 00 A3 50 7C 89 16 52 ║ ..|...|â╥.úP|ë.R ║
 A0 ║ 7C A3 49 7C 89 16 4B 7C B8 20 00 F7 26 11 7C 8B ║ |úI|ë.K|╕ .≈&.|ï ║
 B0 ║ 1E 0B 7C 03 C3 48 F7 F3 01 06 49 7C 83 16 4B 7C ║ ..|.├H≈≤..I|â.K| ║
 C0 ║ 00 BB 00 05 8B 16 52 7C A1 50 7C E8 92 00 72 1D ║ .╗..ï.R|íP|ΦÆ.r. ║
 D0 ║ B0 01 E8 AC 00 72 16 8B FB B9 0B 00 BE E6 7D F3 ║ ░.Φ¼.r.ï√╣..╛µ}≤ ║
 E0 ║ A6 75 0A 8D 7F 20 B9 0B 00 F3 A6 74 18 BE 9E 7D ║ ªu.ì⌂ ╣..≤ªt.╛₧} ║
 F0 ║ E8 5F 00 33 C0 CD 16 5E 1F 8F 04 8F 44 02 CD 19 ║ Φ_.3└═.^.Å.ÅD.═. ║

C>_
```

Figure 16-2: Disk_io after adding hex addresses on the left.

You are getting closer to the full display. But on the screen, your display is not quite centered. You need to move it to the right by about three spaces. By making this one last change, you have finished your version of DISP_LINE.

You could make the change by calling WRITE_CHAR three times with a space character, but you won't. Instead, you will add another procedure called WRITE_CHAR_N_TIMES, to Video_io. As its name implies, this procedure writes one character N times. That is, you place the number N into the CX register and the character code into DL, and call WRITE_CHAR_N_TIMES to write N copies of the character whose ASCII code you placed in DL. Then you will be able to write three spaces by placing 3 into CX and 20h (the ASCII code for a space) into DL. The procedure to add to VIDEO_IO.ASM is as follows:

Listing 16-4 Procedure Added to VIDEO_IO.ASM

```
            PUBLIC   WRITE_CHAR_N_TIMES
;-----------------------------------------------------------------;
; This procedure writes more than one copy of a character         ;
;                                                                 ;
; On entry:     DL       Character code                           ;
;               CX       Number of times to write the character   ;
;                                                                 ;
; Uses:         WRITE_CHAR                                        ;
;-----------------------------------------------------------------;
WRITE_CHAR_N_TIMES        PROC
        PUSH    CX
N_TIMES:
        CALL    WRITE_CHAR
        LOOP    N_TIMES
        POP     CX
        RET
WRITE_CHAR_N_TIMES        ENDP
```

You can see how simple this procedure is, because you already have WRITE_CHAR. If you are wondering why we bothered to write a procedure for something so simple, it is because the program Dskpatch is much clearer when we call WRITE_CHAR_N_TIMES rather than write a short loop to print multiple copies of a character. In addition, this procedure will be used several times again.

The changes to DISP_LINE to add three spaces on the left of your display are shown in Listing 16-5. Make the changes to DISP_SEC.ASM:

Listing 16-5 Changes to DISP_LINE in DISP_SEC.ASM

```
        PUBLIC  DISP_LINE
        EXTRN   WRITE_HEX:PROC
        EXTRN   WRITE_CHAR:PROC
        EXTRN   WRITE_CHAR_N_TIMES:PROC
;--------------------------------------------------------------------;
;  This procedure displays one line of data, or 16 bytes, first in hex, ;
;  then in ASCII.                                                     ;
;                                                                     ;
; On entry:       DS:DX    Offset into sector, in bytes              ;
;                                                                     ;
; Uses:           WRITE_CHAR, WRITE_HEX, WRITE_CHAR_N_TIMES          ;
; Reads:          SECTOR                                              ;
;--------------------------------------------------------------------;
DISP_LINE       PROC
        PUSH    BX
        PUSH    CX
        PUSH    DX
        MOV     BX,DX                   ;Offset is more useful in BX
        MOV     DL,' '
        MOV     CX,3                    ;Write 3 spaces before line
        CALL    WRITE_CHAR_N_TIMES
                                        ;Write offset in hex
        CMP     BX,100h                 ;Is the first digit a 1?
        JB      WRITE_ONE               ;No, white space already in DL
        MOV     DL,'1'                  ;Yes, place '1' into DL for output
WRITE_ONE:
                    .
                    .
                    .
```

You made changes in three places. First, you had to add an EXTRN statement for WRITE_CHAR_N_TIMES because the procedure is in Video_io, and not in this file. You also changed the comment block, to show that you use this new procedure. The third change, the two lines that use WRITE_CHAR_N_TIMES, is quite straightforward and needs no explanation.

Try this new version of the program to see how the display is now centered. Next we will move on to add more features to the display—the top and bottom lines of the boxes.

Adding Horizontal Lines

Adding horizontal lines to the display is not quite as simple as it sounds, because we have a few special cases to think about. We have the ends, where the lines must go around corners, and we also have T-shaped junctions at the top and bottom of the division between the hex and ASCII windows.

We could write a long list of instructions (with WRITE_CHAR_N_TIMES) to create the horizontal lines, but we won't. We have a shorter way. We will introduce another procedure, called WRITE_PATTERN, which will write a pattern on the screen. Then, all we will need is a small area of memory to hold a description of each pattern. Using this new procedure, we can also add tick marks easily to subdivide the hex window, as you will see when we finish this section.

WRITE_PATTERN uses two entirely new instructions, LODSB and CLD. We will describe them after you see more about WRITE_PATTERN and how you describe a pattern. Right now, enter the following procedure into the file VIDEO_IO.ASM:

Listing 16-6 Add This Procedure to VIDEO_IO.ASM (Complete Listing in VIDEO_16.ASM)

```
         PUBLIC  WRITE_PATTERN
;-------------------------------------------------------------;
; This procedure writes a line to the screen, based on data in the  ;
; form                                                          ;
;                                                              ;
;        DB      {character, number of times to write character}, 0  ;
; Where {x} means that x can be repeated any number of times        ;
;                                                              ;
; On entry:      DS:DX   Address of the pattern to draw            ;
;                                                              ;
; Uses:          WRITE_CHAR_N_TIMES                              ;
;-------------------------------------------------------------;
WRITE_PATTERN   PROC
        PUSH    AX
        PUSH    CX
        PUSH    DX
        PUSH    SI
```

continues

Listing 16-6 continued

```
        PUSHF                               ;Save the direction flag
        CLD                                 ;Set direction flag for increment
        MOV     SI,DX                       ;Move offset into SI register for LODSB
PATTERN_LOOP:
        LODSB                               ;Get character data into AL
        OR      AL,AL                       ;Is it the end of data (0h)?
        JZ      END_PATTERN                 ;Yes, return
        MOV     DL,AL                       ;No, set up to write character N times
        LODSB                               ;Get the repeat count into AL
        MOV     CL,AL                       ;And put in CX for WRITE_CHAR_N_TIMES
        XOR     CH,CH                       ;Zero upper byte of CX
        CALL    WRITE_CHAR_N_TIMES
        JMP     PATTERN_LOOP
END_PATTERN:
        POPF                                ;Restore direction flag
        POP     SI
        POP     DX
        POP     CX
        POP     AX
        RET
WRITE_PATTERN   ENDP
```

Before you see how this procedure works, we will show you how to write data for patterns. You will place the data for the top-line pattern into the file Disp_sec, which is where you will use it. To this end, you will add another procedure called INIT_SEC_DISP to initialize the sector display by writing the half-sector display. Then you will modify READ_SECTOR to call your INIT_SEC_DISP procedure. First, place the following data before the .DATA? where you defined SECTOR (in DISP_SEC.ASM):

Listing 16-7 Additions to DISP_SEC.ASM

```
.DATA

TOP_LINE_PATTERN        LABEL   BYTE
        DB      ' ',7
        DB      UPPER_LEFT,1
        DB      HORIZONTAL_BAR,12
        DB      TOP_TICK,1
        DB      HORIZONTAL_BAR,11
```

```
            DB       TOP_TICK,1
            DB       HORIZONTAL_BAR,11
            DB       TOP_TICK,1
            DB       HORIZONTAL_BAR,12
            DB       TOP_T_BAR,1
            DB       HORIZONTAL_BAR,18
            DB       UPPER_RIGHT,1
            DB       0
BOTTOM_LINE_PATTERN      LABEL    BYTE
            DB       ' ',7
            DB       LOWER_LEFT,1
            DB       HORIZONTAL_BAR,12
            DB       BOTTOM_TICK,1
            DB       HORIZONTAL_BAR,11
            DB       BOTTOM_TICK,1
            DB       HORIZONTAL_BAR,11
            DB       BOTTOM_TICK,1
            DB       HORIZONTAL_BAR,12
            DB       BOTTOM_T_BAR,1
            DB       HORIZONTAL_BAR,18
            DB       LOWER_RIGHT,1
            DB       0
```

```
.DATA?

SECTOR   DB      8192 DUP (?)
```

Note that you put all the new data into .DATA rather than .DATA? because you need to set values for all these variables.

Each DB statement contains part of the data for one line. The first byte is the character to print; the second byte tells WRITE_PATTERN how many times to repeat that character. For example, the top line starts with seven blank spaces, followed by one upper-left-corner character, followed by twelve horizontal-bar characters, and so on. The last DB is a solitary hex zero, which marks the end of the pattern.

We will continue the modifications and show you the result before we discuss the inner workings of WRITE_PATTERN. Here is the test version of INIT_SEC_DISP. This procedure writes the top-line pattern, the half-sector display, and finally the bottom-line pattern. Place it in the file DISP_SEC.ASM, just before DISP_HALF_SECTOR as follows:

229

Listing 16-8 Add This Procedure to DISP_SEC.ASM

```
        PUBLIC  INIT_SEC_DISP
        EXTRN   WRITE_PATTERN:PROC, SEND_CRLF:PROC
;------------------------------------------------------------------------;
; This procedure initializes the half-sector display.                    ;
;                                                                         ;
; Uses:           WRITE_PATTERN, SEND_CRLF, DISP_HALF_SECTOR             ;
; Reads:          TOP_LINE_PATTERN, BOTTOM_LINE_PATTERN                  ;
;------------------------------------------------------------------------;
INIT_SEC_DISP   PROC
        PUSH    DX
        LEA     DX,TOP_LINE_PATTERN
        CALL    WRITE_PATTERN
        CALL    SEND_CRLF
        XOR     DX,DX                   ;Start at the beginning of the sector
        CALL    DISP_HALF_SECTOR
        LEA     DX,BOTTOM_LINE_PATTERN
        CALL    WRITE_PATTERN
        POP     DX
        RET
INIT_SEC_DISP   ENDP
```

By using the LEA instruction to load an address into the DX register, WRITE_PATTERN knows where to find the pattern data.

Finally, we need to make a small change to READ_SECTOR in the file DISK_IO.ASM. This will enable you to call INIT_SECTOR_DISP, rather than WRITE_HALF_SECTOR_DISP, so that a full box will be drawn around the half-sector display.

Listing 16-9 Changes to READ_SECTOR in DISK_IO.ASM (Complete Listing in DISK_I16.ASM)

```
        EXTRN   INIT_SEC_DISP:PROC
;------------------------------------------------------------------------;
; This procedure reads the first sector on disk A and dumps the first    ;
; half of this sector.                                                   ;
;------------------------------------------------------------------------;
READ_SECTOR     PROC
        MOV     AX,DGROUP               ;Put data segment into AX
        MOV     DS,AX                   ;Set DS to point to data
```

```
        MOV     AL,0              ;Disk drive A (number 0)
        MOV     CX,1              ;Read only 1 sector
        MOV     DX,0              ;Read sector number 0
        LEA     BX,SECTOR         ;Where to store this sector
        INT     25h               ;Read the sector
        POPF                      ;Discard flags put on stack by DOS
        XOR     DX,DX             ;Set offset to 0 within SECTOR
        CALL    INIT_SEC_DISP     ;Dump the first half

        MOV     AH,4Ch            ;Return to DOS
        INT     21h
READ_SECTOR ENDP
```

That's all you need to draw the top and bottom lines for the sector display. Assemble and link all these files using NMake (remember to assemble the three files you changed if you are not using NMake) and give it a try. Figure 16-3 shows the output you now have.

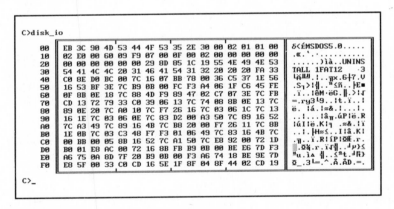

Figure 16-3: The Disk_io display with closed boxes.

Let's see how WRITE_PATTERN works. As mentioned, it uses two new instructions. LODSB stands for *Load String Byte*, which is one of the string instructions—specially designed instructions that work with strings of characters. That is not quite what you are doing here, but the 80x86 doesn't care whether you are dealing with a string of characters or just numbers, so LODSB suits the purposes just fine.

231

LODSB moves (loads) a single byte into the AL register from the memory location given by DS:SI, a register pair you have not used before. You already set DS in READ_SECTOR to point to the data. Before the LODSB instruction, you moved the offset into the SI register with the instruction MOV SI,DX.

The LODSB instruction is somewhat like the MOV instruction, but more powerful. With one LODSB instruction, the 80x86 moves one byte into the AL register and then either increments or decrements the SI register. Incrementing the SI register points to the following byte in memory; decrementing the register points to the previous byte in memory.

Incrementing is exactly what you want to do. You want to go through the pattern, one byte at a time, starting at the beginning. That is what the LODSB instruction does because you used the other new instruction, CLD (*Clear Direction Flag*) to clear the direction flag. If you had set the direction flag, the LODSB instruction would decrement the SI register instead. We will use the LODSB instruction in a few other places in Dskpatch, always with the direction flag cleared, to increment.

Aside from LODSB and CLD, notice that we also used the PUSHF and POPF instructions to save and restore the flag register. We did this just in case we later decide to use the direction flag in a procedure that calls WRITE_PATTERN.

Adding Numbers to the Display

We are almost through with Part II of this book now. We will create one more procedure, then it is on to Part III, and bigger and better things.

Right now, notice that the display lacks a row of numbers across the top. Such numbers—00 01 02 03 and so forth—would allow you to sight down the columns to find the address for any byte. So, let's write a procedure to print this row of numbers. Add the following procedure, WRITE_TOP_HEX_NUMBERS to DISP_SEC.ASM just after INIT_SEC_DISP.

Listing 16-10 Add This Procedure to DISP_SEC.ASM

```
        EXTRN    WRITE_CHAR_N_TIMES:PROC, WRITE_HEX:PROC, WRITE_CHAR:PROC
        EXTRN    WRITE_HEX_DIGIT:PROC, SEND_CRLF:PROC
;----------------------------------------------------------------------;
; This procedure writes the index numbers (0 through F) at the top of   ;
; the half-sector display.                                             ;
;                                                                      ;
; Uses:          WRITE_CHAR_N_TIMES, WRITE_HEX, WRITE_CHAR             ;
;                WRITE_HEX_DIGIT, SEND_CRLF                            ;
;----------------------------------------------------------------------;
WRITE_TOP_HEX_NUMBERS    PROC
        PUSH    CX
        PUSH    DX
        MOV     DL,' '                  ;Write 9 spaces for left side
        MOV     CX,9
        CALL    WRITE_CHAR_N_TIMES
        XOR     DH,DH                   ;Start with 0
HEX_NUMBER_LOOP:
        MOV     DL,DH
        CALL    WRITE_HEX
        MOV     DL,' '
        CALL    WRITE_CHAR
        INC     DH
        CMP     DH,10h                  ;Done yet?
        JB      HEX_NUMBER_LOOP

        MOV     DL,' '                  ;Write hex numbers over ASCII window
        MOV     CX,2
        CALL    WRITE_CHAR_N_TIMES
        XOR     DL,DL
HEX_DIGIT_LOOP:
        CALL    WRITE_HEX_DIGIT
        INC     DL
        CMP     DL,10h
        JB      HEX_DIGIT_LOOP
        CALL    SEND_CRLF
        POP     DX
        POP     CX
        RET
WRITE_TOP_HEX_NUMBERS    ENDP
```

Modify INIT_SEC_DISP (also in DISP_SEC.ASM) as follows so it calls WRITE_TOP_HEX_NUMBERS before it writes the rest of the half-sector display.

Listing 16-11 Changes to INIT_SEC_DISP in DISP_SEC.ASM (Complete Listing in DISP_S16.ASM)

```
; Uses:          WRITE_PATTERN, SEND_CRLF, DISP_HALF_SECTOR         ;
;                WRITE_TOP_HEX_NUMBERS                              ;
; Reads:         TOP_LINE_PATTERN, BOTTOM_LINE_PATTERN             ;
;-----------------------------------------------------------------;
INIT_SEC_DISP    PROC
        PUSH     DX
        CALL     WRITE_TOP_HEX_NUMBERS
        LEA      DX,TOP_LINE_PATTERN
        CALL     WRITE_PATTERN
        CALL     SEND_CRLF
        XOR      DX,DX                   ;Start at the beginning of the sector
        CALL     DISP_HALF_SECTOR
        LEA      DX,BOTTOM_LINE_PATTERN
        CALL     WRITE_PATTERN
        POP      DX
        RET
INIT_SEC_DISP    ENDP
```

Now you have a complete half-sector display, as shown in Figure 16-4.

There are still some differences between this display and the final version. We will change WRITE_CHAR so it will print all 256 characters the PC can display, and then we will clear the screen and center this display vertically, using the ROM BIOS routines inside the PC.

Summary

You have done a lot of work on the Dskpatch program, by adding new procedures, changing old ones, and moving them from one source file to another. From now on, if you find yourself losing track of what you are doing, refer to the complete listing of Dskpatch in Appendix B. The listing there is the final version, but you will probably see enough resemblances to help you along.

```
C>disk_io
         00 01 02 03 04 05 06 07 08 09 0A 0B 0C 0D 0E 0F   0123456789ABCDEF

00    EB 3C 90 4D 53 44 4F 53 35 2E 30 00 02 01 01 00   δ<ÉMSDOS5.0.....
10    02 E0 00 60 09 F9 07 00 0F 00 02 00 00 00 00 00   .α.`.............
20    00 00 00 00 00 00 29 8D 85 1C 19 55 4E 49 4E 53   ......)ìà..UNINS
30    54 41 4C 4C 20 31 46 41 54 31 32 20 20 20 FA 33   TALL 1FAT12   -3
40    C0 8E D0 BC 00 7C 16 07 BB 78 00 36 C5 37 1E 56   └ë╨╝.|..┐x.6╞7.V
50    16 53 BF 3E 7C B9 0B 00 FC F3 A4 06 1F C6 45 FE   .S┐>¦¦..╨⌐.╞E■
60    0F 8B 0E 18 7C 88 4D F9 89 47 02 C7 07 3E 7C FB   .ï..¦êM·ëG.╟.>¦√
70    CD 13 72 79 33 C0 39 06 13 7C 74 08 8B 0E 13 7C   =.ry3└9..¦t.ï..¦
80    89 0E 20 7C A0 10 7C F7 26 16 7C 03 06 1C 7C 13   ë. ¦á.¦≈&.¦...¦.
90    16 1E 7C 03 06 0E 7C 83 D2 00 A3 50 7C 89 16 52   ..¦...¦â╥.ú P¦ë.R
A0    7C A3 49 7C 89 16 4B 7C B8 20 00 F7 26 11 7C 8B   ¦úI¦ë.K¦╕ .≈&.¦ï
B0    1E 0B 7C 03 C3 48 F7 F3 01 06 49 7C 83 16 4B 7C   ..¦.╞H≈.I¦â.K¦
C0    00 BB 00 05 8B 16 52 7C A1 50 7C E8 92 00 72 1D   .┐..ï.R¦íP¦ρ..r.
D0    B0 01 E8 AC 00 72 16 8B FB B9 0B 00 BE E6 7D F3   .øⁿ.r.ï√¦..╛µ}.
E0    A6 75 0A 8D 7F 20 B9 0B 00 F3 A6 74 18 BE 9E 7D   ªu.ìà ¦...≤ªt.R}
F0    E8 5F 00 33 C0 CD 16 5E 1F 8F 04 8F 44 02 CD 19   ρ_.3└=.^.Å.ÅD.=.

C>_
```

Figure 16-4: A complete half-sector display.

Most of the changes in this chapter did not rely on tricks, just hard work. But you did learn two new instructions: LODSB and CLD. LODSB is one of the string instructions that allow you to use one instruction to do the work of several. You used LODSB in WRITE_PATTERN to read consecutive bytes from the pattern table, always loading a new byte into the AL register. CLD clears the direction flag, which sets the direction for increment. Each following LODSB instruction loads the next byte from memory.

In the next part of this book you will learn about the PC's ROM BIOS routines. They will save you a lot of time.

PART III

The IBM PC's ROM BIOS

The ROM BIOS Routines

In this chapter you will learn how to use the INT 10h ROM BIOS routines to clear your screen and move the cursor to any location on the screen. You will rewrite Dskpatch so that it clears the screen before it draws. Then you will rewrite the code so that READ_SECTOR uses memory variables, rather than hard-wired numbers. Finally, you will add a status line to the top of Dskpatch's screen.

Files altered: DSKPATCH.ASM, DISP_SEC.ASM, CURSOR.ASM, VIDEO_IO.ASM, DISK_IO.ASM

Disk files: DSKPAT17.ASM, DISP_S17.ASM, CURSOR17.ASM, VIDEO_17.ASM, DISK_I17.ASM

17

Topics Covered

The ROM BIOS Display Routines

Clearing the Screen

Moving the Cursor

Rewiring Variable Usage

Writing the Header

Summary

Computer chips, or ICs (*Integrated Circuits*), known as ROMs (*Read-Only Memory*) are located inside your computer. One of these ROMs contains a number of routines, very much like procedures that provide all the basic routines for doing input and output to several different parts of your PC. Because this ROM provides routines for performing input and output at a very low level, it is frequently referred to as the BIOS, for Basic Input Output System. DOS uses the ROM BIOS for such activities as sending characters to the screen and reading and writing to the disk, and you are free to use the ROM BIOS routines in your programs.

We will concentrate on the BIOS routines needed for Dskpatch. Among them is a set for video display, which includes a number of functions you couldn't reach without working directly with the hardware.

The ROM BIOS Display Routines

We refer to the elements of the ROM BIOS as routines in order to distinguish them from procedures. Procedures are used with a CALL instruction; whereas you call routines with INT instructions, not CALLs. You will use an INT 10h instruction, for example, to call the ROM BIOS' video I/O routines just as you used an INT 21h instruction to call routines in DOS.

INT 10h calls the video I/O routines in the ROM BIOS; other numbers call other routines, but you won't see any of them. The INT 10h routines provide all the functions you need outside of DOS. (DOS calls one of the other ROM BIOS routines when you ask for a sector from the disk.)

In this chapter, we will use ROM BIOS routines to add two new procedures to Dskpatch: one to clear the screen, and the other to move the cursor to any screen location you chose. Both are very useful functions, but neither is available directly through DOS. Hence, you will use the ROM BIOS routines to do the job. Later, you will see even more interesting things that you can do with these ROM routines. Begin by using INT 10h to clear the screen before you display the half sector.

The INT 10h instruction is your entry to a number of different functions. Recall that, when you used the DOS INT 21h instruction, you selected a particular function by placing its function number in the AH register. You select an INT 10h function in the same way—by placing the appropriate function number in the AH register. A full list of these functions is given in Table 17-1.

Table 17-1 INT 10h Functions

(AH)=0	**Set the display mode.** The AL register contains the mode number.

Text Modes

(AL)=0	40 by 25, black and white mode
(AL)=1	40 by 25, color
(AL)=2	80 by 25, black and white
(AL)=3	80 by 25, color
(AL)=7	80 by 25, monochrome display adapter

Graphic Mode

(AL)=4	320 by 200, color
(AL)=5	320 by 200, black and white
(AL)=6	640 by 200, black and white
(AH)=1	**Set the cursor size.**
(CH)	Starting scan line of the cursor. The top line is 0 on both the monochrome and color graphics displays, and the bottom line is 7 for the color graphics adapter and 13 for the monochrome adapter. Valid range: 0 to 31.
(CL)	Last scan line of the cursor.

The power-on setting for the color graphics adapter is CH=6 and CL=7. The setting for the monochrome display is CH=11 and CL=12.

continues

241

Table 17-1 continued

(AH)=2	**Set the cursor position.**	
	(DH,DL)	Row, column of new cursor position; the upper left corner is (0,0).
	(BH)	Page number. This is the number of the display page. The color-graphics adapter has room for several display pages, but most programs use page 0.
(AH)=3	**Read the cursor position.**	
	(BH)	Page number

	On exit	(DH,DL)	Row, column of cursor
		(CH,CL)	Cursor size

(AH)=4	**Read light pen position.**	
(AH)=5	**Select active display page.**	
	(AL)	New page number (from 0 to 7 for modes 0 and 1; from 0 to 3 for modes 2 and 3).
(AH)=6	**Scroll up.**	
	(AL)	Number of lines to blank at the bottom of the window. Normal scrolling blanks one line. Set to zero to blank entire window.
	(CH,CL)	Row, column of upper left corner of window.
	(DH,DL)	Row, column of lower right corner of window.
	(BH)	Display attribute to use for blank lines.
(AH)=7	**Scroll down.**	

Same as scroll up (function 6), but lines are left blank at the top of the window instead of the bottom.

(AH)=8   **Read attribute and character under the cursor.**

    (BH)   Display page (text modes only).

    (AL)   Character read.

    (AH)   Attribute of character read (text modes only).

(AH)=9   **Write attribute and character under the cursor.**

    (BH)   Display page (text modes only).

    (CX)   Number of times to write character and attribute on screen.

    (AL)   Character to write.

    (BL)   Attribute to write.

(AH)=10   **Write character under cursor** (with normal attribute).

    (BH)   Display page.

    (CX)   Number of times to write character.

    (AL)   Character to write.

(AH)=11 to 13   **Various graphics functions.**

(AH)=14   **Write teletype.** Write one character to the screen and move the cursor to the next position.

    (AL)   Character to write.

    (BL)   Color of character (graphics mode only).

    (BH)   Display page (text mode).

(AH)=15   **Return current video state.**

    (AL)   Display mode currently set.

    (AH)   Number of characters per line.

    (BH)   Active display pages.

Clearing the Screen

We will use the INT 10h function number 6, *Scroll Active Page Up,* to clear the screen. You don't actually want to scroll the screen, but this function also doubles as a clear-screen function. Enter the following procedure into the file CURSOR.ASM.

Listing 17-1 Procedure Added to CURSOR.ASM

```
        PUBLIC  CLEAR_SCREEN
;------------------------------------------------------------------;
; This procedure clears the entire screen.                         ;
;------------------------------------------------------------------;
CLEAR_SCREEN    PROC
        PUSH    AX
        PUSH    BX
        PUSH    CX
        PUSH    DX
        XOR     AL,AL           ;Blank entire window
        XOR     CX,CX           ;Upper left corner is at (0,0)
        MOV     DH,24           ;Bottom line of screen is line 24
        MOV     DL,79           ;Right side is at column 79
        MOV     BH,7            ;Use normal attribute for blanks
        MOV     AH,6            ;Call for SCROLL-UP function
        INT     10h             ;Clear the window
        POP     DX
        POP     CX
        POP     BX
        POP     AX
        RET
CLEAR_SCREEN    ENDP
```

It appears that INT 10h function number 6 needs quite a lot of information, even though all you want to do is clear the display. This function is rather powerful. It can actually clear any rectangular part of the screen (called a window). You have to set the window to the entire screen by setting the first and last lines to 0 and 24 and setting the columns to 0 and 79. The routine can also clear the screen to all white (for use with black characters) or all black (for use with white characters). You want the latter, which is specified with the instruction MOV BH,7. Setting AL to 20, the number of lines to scroll, tells this routine to clear the window, rather than to scroll it.

Now you need to modify the test procedure, READ_SECTOR, to call CLEAR_SCREEN just before it starts to write the sector display. We did not place this CALL in INIT_SEC_DISP, because you will want to use INIT_SEC_DISP to rewrite just the half-sector display, without affecting the rest of the screen.

To modify READ_SECTOR, add an EXTRN declaration for CLEAR_SCREEN and insert the CALL to CLEAR_SCREEN. Make the following changes in the file DISK_IO.ASM:

Listing 17-2 Changes to READ_SECTOR in DISK_IO.ASM (Complete Listing in DISK_I17.ASM)

```
            EXTRN   INIT_SEC_DISP:PROC, CLEAR_SCREEN:PROC
;----------------------------------------------------------------;
; This procedure reads the first sector on disk A and dumps the first  ;
; half of this sector.                                                  ;
;----------------------------------------------------------------;
READ_SECTOR     PROC
        MOV     AX,DGROUP           ;Put data segment into AX
        MOV     DS,AX               ;Set DS to point to data

        MOV     AL,0                ;Disk drive A (number 0)
        MOV     CX,1                ;Read only 1 sector
        MOV     DX,0                ;Read sector number 0
        LEA     BX,SECTOR           ;Where to store this sector
        INT     25h                 ;Read the sector
        POPF                        ;Discard flags put on stack by DOS
        CALL    CLEAR_SCREEN
        CALL    INIT_SEC_DISP       ;Dump the first half

        MOV     AH,4Ch              ;Return to DOS
        INT     21h
READ_SECTOR     ENDP
```

Note where the cursor is located and then run Disk_io. The screen will clear, and Disk_io will start writing the half-sector display wherever the cursor happened to be before you ran the program—probably at the bottom of the screen.

Even though the screen was cleared, we didn't mention anything about moving the cursor back to the top. In BASIC, the CLS command does two things—it clears the screen and then moves the cursor to the top of the screen. Our procedure doesn't do that; you will have to move the cursor yourself.

Moving the Cursor

The INT 10h function number 2 sets the cursor position, which you will use in the GOTO_XY subroutine. You can use GOTO_XY to move the cursor anywhere on the screen (such as to the top after a clear). Enter this procedure into the file CURSOR.ASM:

Listing 17-3 Procedure Added to CURSOR.ASM (Complete Listing in CURSOR17.ASM)

```
        PUBLIC  GOTO_XY
;-------------------------------------------------------------;
; This procedure moves the cursor                             ;
;                                                             ;
; On entry:       DH      Row (Y)                             ;
;                 DL      Column (X)                          ;
;-------------------------------------------------------------;
GOTO_XY         PROC
        PUSH    AX
        PUSH    BX
        MOV     BH,0                    ;Display page 0
        MOV     AH,2                    ;Call for SET CURSOR POSITION
        INT     10h
        POP     BX
        POP     AX
        RET
GOTO_XY         ENDP
```

You will use GOTO_XY in a revised version of INIT_SEC_DISP to move the cursor to the second line just before you write the half-sector display. Modifications made to INIT_SEC_DISP in DISP_SEC.ASM are as follows:

Listing 17-4 Changes to INIT_SEC_DISP in DISP_SEC.ASM

```
        PUBLIC  INIT_SEC_DISP
        EXTRN   WRITE_PATTERN:PROC, SEND_CRLF:PROC
        EXTRN   GOTO_XY:PROC
;-------------------------------------------------------------;
;  This procedure initializes the half-sector display.        ;
;                                                             ;
; Uses:          WRITE_PATTERN, SEND_CRLF, DISP_HALF_SECTOR   ;
;                WRITE_TOP_HEX_NUMBERS, GOTO_XY               ;
; Reads:         TOP_LINE_PATTERN, BOTTOM_LINE_PATTERN        ;
;-------------------------------------------------------------;
INIT_SEC_DISP   PROC
        PUSH    DX
        XOR     DL,DL                   ;Move cursor to beginning
        MOV     DH,2                    ;of 3rd line
        CALL    GOTO_XY
        CALL    WRITE_TOP_HEX_NUMBERS
        LEA     DX,TOP_LINE_PATTERN
                        .
                        .
                        .
```

If you try the new procedure now, you will see that the half-sector display is nicely centered.

It is easier to work with the screen when you have the ROM BIOS routines. In the next chapter, you will use another routine in the ROM BIOS to improve WRITE_CHAR so that it will write any character to the screen. But before continuing, let's make some other changes to your program. After the changes are made, you will finish up by adding a procedure called WRITE_HEADER. This procedure will write a status line at the top of the screen to show the current disk drive and sector number.

Rewiring Variable Usage

There is much that needs to revamped before creating WRITE_HEADER. Many of our procedures as they are now have numbers hard-wired into them; for example, READ_SECTOR reads sector 0 on drive A. We want to place the disk-drive and sector numbers into memory variables, so more than one procedure can read them. You will need to change these procedures so that they will use memory variables.

You will begin by putting all memory variables into one file, DSKPATCH.ASM, to make your work simpler. Dskpatch.asm will be the first file in your program so the memory variables will be easy to find there. The DSKPATCH.ASM, complete with a long list of memory variables is as folows:

Listing 17-5 The New File DSKPATCH.ASM

```
DOSSEG
.MODEL   SMALL

.STACK

.DATA

        PUBLIC   SECTOR_OFFSET
;----------------------------------------------;
; SECTOR_OFFSET is the offset of the half-     ;
; sector display into the full sector. It must ;
; be a multiple of 16, and not greater than 256 ;
;----------------------------------------------;
SECTOR_OFFSET    DW      0

        PUBLIC   CURRENT_SECTOR_NO, DISK_DRIVE_NO
CURRENT_SECTOR_NO        DW      0               ;Initially sector 0
DISK_DRIVE_NO            DB      0               ;Initially Drive A:

        PUBLIC   LINES_BEFORE_SECTOR, HEADER_LINE_NO
        PUBLIC   HEADER_PART_1, HEADER_PART_2
;----------------------------------------------;
; LINES_BEFORE_SECTOR is the number of lines   ;
; at the top of the screen before the half-    ;
; sector display.                              ;
;----------------------------------------------;
```

```
LINES_BEFORE_SECTOR      DB       2
HEADER_LINE_NO           DB       0
HEADER_PART_1            DB       'Disk ',0
HEADER_PART_2            DB       '          Sector ',0

.DATA?

        PUBLIC  SECTOR
;-------------------------------------------------;
; The entire sector (up to 8192 bytes) is         ;
; stored in this part of memory.                  ;
;-------------------------------------------------;
SECTOR  DB      8192 DUP (?)

.CODE

        EXTRN   CLEAR_SCREEN:PROC, READ_SECTOR:PROC
        EXTRN   INIT_SEC_DISP:PROC
DISK_PATCH      PROC
        MOV     AX,DGROUP               ;Put data segment into AX
        MOV     DS,AX                   ;Set DS to point to data

        CALL    CLEAR_SCREEN
        CALL    READ_SECTOR
        CALL    INIT_SEC_DISP

        MOV     AH,4Ch                  ;Return to DOS
        INT     21h
DISK_PATCH      ENDP


        END     DISK_PATCH
```

The main procedure, DISK_PATCH, calls three other procedures. You have seen them all before and soon you will rewrite both READ_SECTOR and INIT_SEC_DISP to use the variables you just placed into the data segment.

Before using Dskpatch, you need to modify Disp_sec to replace the definition of SECTOR with an EXTRN. You also need to alter Disk_io, to change READ_SECTOR into an ordinary procedure you can call from Dskpatch.

249

Let's take SECTOR first. Because you have placed it in DSKPATCH.ASM as a memory variable, you need to change the definition of SECTOR in Disp_sec to an EXTRN declaration. Make the following changes in DISP_SEC.ASM:

Listing 17-6 Changes to DISP_SEC.ASM

```
.DATA?

        EXTRN    SECTOR:BYTE
        PUBLIC   SECTOR
SECTOR  DB       8192 DUP(?)
```

Next you will rewrite the file DISK_IO.ASM so that it contains only procedures and so that READ_SECTOR uses memory variables (not hard-wired numbers) for the sector and disk-drive numbers. The new version of DISK_IO.ASM is as follows:

Listing 17-7 Changes to DISK_IO.ASM

```
DOSSEG
.MODEL  SMALL

.STACK

.DATA

        EXTRN    SECTOR:BYTE
        EXTRN    DISK_DRIVE_NO:BYTE
        EXTRN    CURRENT_SECTOR_NO:WORD

.CODE

        PUBLIC   READ_SECTOR
        EXTRN    INIT_SEC_DISP:PROC, CLEAR_SCREEN:PROC
;-----------------------------------------------------------------;
; This procedure reads one sector (512 bytes) into SECTOR.        ;
;                                                                 ;
; Reads:         CURRENT_SECTOR_NO, DISK_DRIVE_NO                 ;
; Writes:        SECTOR                                           ;
;-----------------------------------------------------------------;
```

```
READ_SECTOR     PROC
        MOV     AX,DGROUP               ;Put data segment into AX
        MOV     DS,AX                   ;Set DS to point to data
        PUSH    AX
        PUSH    BX
        PUSH    CX
        PUSH    DX
        MOV     AL,DISK_DRIVE_NO        ;Drive number
        MOV     CX,1                    ;Read only 1 sector
        MOV     DX,CURRENT_SECTOR_NO    ;Logical sector number
        LEA     BX,SECTOR               ;Where to store this sector
        INT     25h                     ;Read the sector
        POPF                            ;Discard flags put on stack by DOS
        POP     DX
        POP     CX
        POP     BX
        POP     AX
        RET
        CALL    CLEAR_SCREEN
        CALL    INIT_SEC_DISP           ;Dump the first half

        MOV     AH,4Ch                  ;Return to DOS
        INT     21h
READ_SECTOR     ENDP
        END
```

This new version of Disk_io uses the memory variables DISK_DRIVE_NO
and CURRENT_SECTOR_NO as the disk-drive and sector numbers for the
sector to read. Because these variables are already defined in DSKPATCH.ASM,
you won't have to change Disk_io when you start reading different sectors
from other disk drives. If you are using the NMake program to rebuild
DSKPATCH.COM, you will need to make some additions to your Make file
named Makefile. The additions are as follows:

Listing 17-8 The New Version of MAKEFILE

```
dskpatch.exe:   dskpatch.obj disk_io.obj disp_sec.obj video_io.obj cursor.obj
        link dskpatch disk_io disp_sec video_io cursor;
```

continues

251

Listing 17-8 continued

```
dskpatch.obj:    dskpatch.asm
        ml /c dskpatch.asm

disk_io.obj:     disk_io.asm
        ml /c disk_io.asm

disp_sec.obj:    disp_sec.asm
        ml /c disp_sec.asm

video_io.obj:    video_io.asm
        ml /c video_io.asm

cursor.obj:      cursor.asm
        ml /c cursor.asm
```

Remember that if you are using Make from MASM 5 or earlier, the first two lines shown here must be at the end of your Makefile. If you are not using NMake, be sure to reassemble all three files you have changed (Dskpatch, Disk_io, and Disp_sec) and link your five files with Dskpatch listed first:

```
LINK DSKPATCH DISK_IO DISP_SEC VIDEO_IO CURSOR;
```

You have made quite a few changes, so test Dskpatch and make sure that it works correctly before moving on.

Writing the Header

Now that we have converted the hard-wired numbers into direct references to memory variables, we can write the procedure WRITE_HEADER to write a status line, or header, at the top of the screen. The header will look like this:

```
Disk A          Sector 0
```

WRITE_HEADER will use WRITE_DECIMAL to write the current sector number in decimal. It will also write two strings of characters, *Disk* and *Sector* (each followed by a blank space), and a disk letter, such as A. To begin, place the following procedure in DISP_SEC.ASM:

Listing 17-9 Procedure Added to DISP_SEC.ASM (Complete Listing in DISP_S17.ASM)

```
        PUBLIC  WRITE_HEADER
.DATA
        EXTRN   HEADER_LINE_NO:BYTE
        EXTRN   HEADER_PART_1:BYTE
        EXTRN   HEADER_PART_2:BYTE
        EXTRN   DISK_DRIVE_NO:BYTE
        EXTRN   CURRENT_SECTOR_NO:WORD
.CODE
        EXTRN   WRITE_STRING:PROC, WRITE_DECIMAL:PROC
        EXTRN   GOTO_XY:PROC
;------------------------------------------------------------------;
; This procedure writes the header with disk-drive and sector number.   ;
;                                                                  ;
; Uses:         GOTO_XY, WRITE_STRING, WRITE_CHAR, WRITE_DECIMAL   ;
; Reads:        HEADER_LINE_NO, HEADER_PART_1, HEADER_PART_2       ;
;               DISK_DRIVE_NO, CURRENT_SECTOR_NO                   ;
;------------------------------------------------------------------;
WRITE_HEADER    PROC
        PUSH    DX
        XOR     DL,DL                   ;Move cursor to header line number
        MOV  .  DH,HEADER_LINE_NO
        CALL    GOTO_XY
        LEA     DX,HEADER_PART_1
        CALL    WRITE_STRING
        MOV     DL,DISK_DRIVE_NO
        ADD     DL,'A'                  ;Print drives A, B, ...
        CALL    WRITE_CHAR
        LEA     DX,HEADER_PART_2
        CALL    WRITE_STRING
        MOV     DX,CURRENT_SECTOR_NO
        CALL    WRITE_DECIMAL
        POP     DX
        RET
WRITE_HEADER    ENDP
```

The procedure WRITE_STRING doesn't exist yet. As you can see, we plan to use it to write a string of characters to the screen. The two strings, HEADER_PART_1 and HEADER_PART_2, are already defined in DSKPATCH.ASM. WRITE_STRING will use DS:DX as the address for the string.

We have chosen to supply our own string-output procedure so that our strings can contain any character, including the $ which could not be printed with DOS function 9. In places where DOS uses a $ to mark the end of a string, we will use a hex 0. Enter the following procedure into VIDEO_IO.ASM:

Listing 17-10 Procedure Added to VIDEO_IO.ASM (Complete Listing in VIDEO_17.ASM)

```
        PUBLIC  WRITE_STRING
;----------------------------------------------------------------;
; This procedure writes a string of characters to the screen. The ;
; string must end with         DB      0                          ;
;                                                                 ;
; On entry:      DS:DX    Address of the string                   ;
;                                                                 ;
; Uses:          WRITE_CHAR                                       ;
;----------------------------------------------------------------;
WRITE_STRING    PROC
        PUSH    AX
        PUSH    DX
        PUSH    SI
        PUSHF                           ;Save direction flag
        CLD                             ;Set direction for increment
        MOV     SI,DX                   ;Place address into SI for LODSB
STRING_LOOP:
        LODSB                           ;Get a character into AL register
        OR      AL,AL                   ;Have we found the 0 yet?
        JZ      END_OF_STRING           ;Yes, we are done with the string
        MOV     DL,AL                   ;No, write character
        CALL    WRITE_CHAR
        JMP     STRING_LOOP
END_OF_STRING:
        POPF                            ;Restore direction flag
        POP     SI
        POP     DX
        POP     AX
        RET
WRITE_STRING    ENDP
```

As it stands now, WRITE_STRING will write characters with ASCII codes below 32 (the space character) as a period (.), because we don't have a version of WRITE_CHAR that can write *any* character. We will take care of that detail in the next chapter. The advantage of modular design is that you will not have to change WRITE_STRING in the process. Finally, change DISK_PATCH in DSKPATCH.ASM to include the CALL to WRITE_HEADER as follows:

Listing 17-11 Changes to DISK_PATCH in DSKPATCH.ASM (Complete Listing in DSKPAT17.ASM)

```
            EXTRN    CLEAR_SCREEN:PROC, READ_SECTOR:PROC
            EXTRN    INIT_SEC_DISP:PROC, WRITE_HEADER:PROC
DISK_PATCH  PROC
            MOV      AX,DGROUP              ;Put data segment into AX
            MOV      DS,AX                  ;Set DS to point to data

            CALL     CLEAR_SCREEN
            CALL     WRITE_HEADER
            CALL     READ_SECTOR
            CALL     INIT_SEC_DISP

            MOV      AH,4Ch                 ;Return to DOS
            INT      21h
DISK_PATCH  ENDP
```

Dskpatch should now produce a display like the one in Figure 17-1.

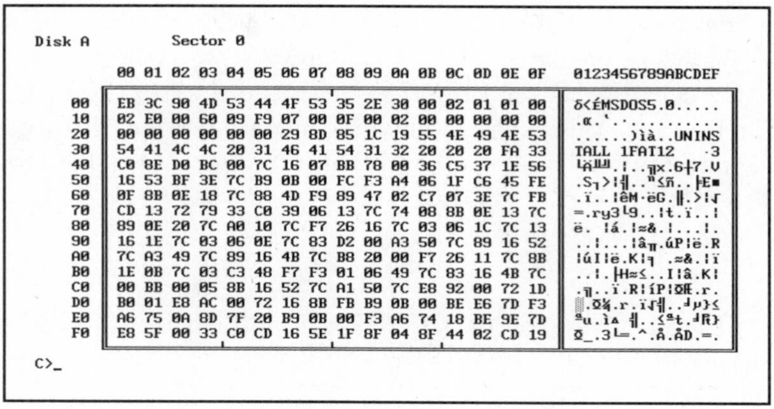

Figure 17-1: Dskpatch with the header at the top.

Summary

At last you have met the ROM BIOS routines inside of your PCs. You have already used two of these routines to help you toward your goal of a full Dskpatch program.

First you learned about INT 10h, function number 6, which you used to clear the screen. You briefly saw that this function has more uses than you will take advantage of in this book. For example, you may eventually find it helpful for scrolling portions of the screen in Dskpatch or in your own programs.

Then you used function 2 of INT 10h to move the cursor to the third line on the screen (line number 2). That is where you started writing the sector dump.

To make programs easier to work with, several procedures were rewritten so that they would use memory variables, rather than hard-wired numbers. Now you will be able to read other sectors and change the way your program works in other ways by changing a few central numbers in DSKPATCH.ASM.

Finally, you wrote the procedures WRITE_HEADER and WRITE_STRING so that a header could be placed at the top of the screen. As mentioned, an improved version of WRITE_CHAR will be written in the next chapter, replacing the dots in the ASCII window of the display with graphics characters. Thanks to modular design, you will do this without changing any of the procedures that use WRITE_CHAR.

The Ultimate
WRITE_CHAR

In this chapter, you will finally change WRITE_CHAR so that it can display any of the 256 characters on your PC. This won't be that difficult, using several new INT 10h functions. You will use function 9 to display a character on the screen, and you will use functions 3 and 2 to read and set the position of the cursor that you will need in order to move the cursor right one position after displaying a character.

Files altered: DISP_SEC.ASM, CURSOR.ASM, VIDEO_IO.ASM

Disk files: DISP_S18.ASM, CURSOR18.ASM, VIDEO_18.ASM

18

Topics Covered

You made good use of the ROM BIOS routines in the last chapter to clear the screen and move the cursor. But there are many more uses for the ROM BIOS, and you will see some of them in this chapter.

Using DOS alone has not enabled you to display all 256 of the characters that the PC is capable of displaying. So, in this chapter, you will write a new version of WRITE_CHAR that displays any character, thanks to another INT 10h function.

Then add another useful procedure, called CLEAR_TO_END_OF_LINE, which clears the line from the cursor to the right edge of the screen. This procedure will be put to use in WRITE_HEADER so that it will clear the rest of the line. Why is this useful? Suppose that we go from sector number 10 (two digits) to sector number 9. A zero would be left over from the 10 after you call WRITE_HEADER with the sector set to 9. CLEAR_TO_END_OF_LINE will clear this zero, as well as anything else on the remainder of the line.

A New WRITE_CHAR

The ROM BIOS function 9 for INT 10h writes a character and its *attribute* at the current cursor position. The attribute controls such features as underlining, blinking, and color as in Figure 18-1. You will use only two attributes for Dskpatch: attribute 7, which is the normal attribute; and attribute 70h, which is a foreground color of 0 and background of 7 and produces inverse video (black characters on a white background). You can set the attributes individually for each character by creating a block cursor in inverse video—we will call it a *phantom* cursor. For now, we will use the normal attribute when we write a character.

The INT 10h, function 9 writes the character and attribute at the current cursor position. Unlike DOS, it does not advance the cursor to the next character position unless it writes more than one copy of the character. This fact will be used later, in a different procedure. For now, you only want one copy of each character, so you will move the cursor yourself.

Here is the new version of WRITE_CHAR, which writes a character and then moves the cursor right one character. Make the following changes to WRITE_CHAR in the file VIDEO_IO.ASM:

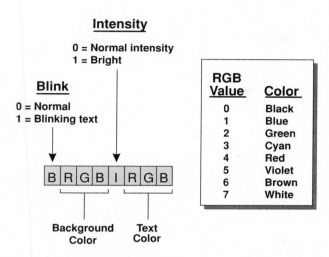

Figure 18-1: How the ROM BIOS specifies character colors.

Listing 18-1 Changes to WRITE_CHAR in VIDEO_IO.ASM (Complete Listing in video_18.asm)

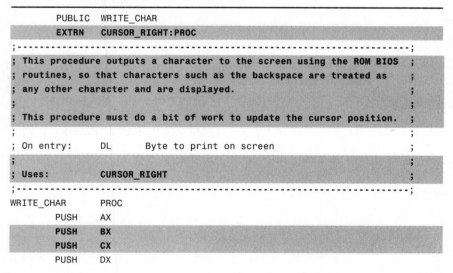

```
        PUBLIC  WRITE_CHAR
        EXTRN   CURSOR_RIGHT:PROC
;--------------------------------------------------------------------;
; This procedure outputs a character to the screen using the ROM BIOS ;
; routines, so that characters such as the backspace are treated as   ;
; any other character and are displayed.                              ;
;                                                                     ;
; This procedure must do a bit of work to update the cursor position. ;
;                                                                     ;
; On entry:     DL      Byte to print on screen                       ;
;                                                                     ;
; Uses:         CURSOR_RIGHT                                          ;
;--------------------------------------------------------------------;
WRITE_CHAR      PROC
        PUSH    AX
        PUSH    BX
        PUSH    CX
        PUSH    DX
```

continues

261

Listing 18-1 continued

```
            CMP     DL,32                      ;Is character before a space?
            JAE     IS_PRINTABLE               ;No, then print as is
            MOV     DL,'.'                     ;Yes, replace with a period
IS_PRINTABLE:
            MOV     AH,2                       ;Call for character output
            INT     21h                        ;Output character in DL register
            MOV     AH,9                       ;Call for output of character/attribute
            MOV     BH,0                       ;Set to display page 0
            MOV     CX,1                       ;Write only one character
            MOV     AL,DL                      ;Character to write
            MOV     BL,7                       ;Normal attribute
            INT     10h                        ;Write character and attribute
            CALL    CURSOR_RIGHT               ;Now move to next cursor position
            POP     DX
            POP     CX
            POP     BX
            POP     AX
            RET
WRITE_CHAR          ENDP
```

In reading through this procedure, you may have wondered why we included the instruction MOV BH,0. If you have a graphics display adapter (as opposed to an ancient Monochrome Display Adapter), your adapter has four text pages in normal text mode. We will only use the first page, page 0; hence the instruction to set BH to 0.

As for the cursor, WRITE_CHAR uses the procedure CURSOR_RIGHT to move the cursor right one character position or to the beginning of the next line if the movement would take the cursor past column 79. Place the following procedure into CURSOR.ASM.

Listing 18-2 Procedure Added to CURSOR.ASM

```
            PUBLIC  CURSOR_RIGHT
;------------------------------------------------------------------;
; This procedure moves the cursor one position to the right or to the  ;
; next line if the cursor was at the end of a line.                ;
;                                                                  ;
```

```
; Uses:          SEND_CRLF                                        ;
;----------------------------------------------------------------;
CURSOR_RIGHT    PROC
        PUSH    AX
        PUSH    BX
        PUSH    CX
        PUSH    DX
        MOV     AH,3                    ;Read the current cursor position
        MOV     BH,0                    ;On page 0
        INT     10h                     ;Read cursor position
        MOV     AH,2                    ;Set new cursor position
        INC     DL                      ;Set column to next position
        CMP     DL,79                   ;Make sure column <= 79
        JBE     OK
        CALL    SEND_CRLF               ;Go to next line
        JMP     DONE
OK:     INT     10h
DONE:   POP     DX
        POP     CX
        POP     BX
        POP     AX
        RET
CURSOR_RIGHT    ENDP
```

CURSOR_RIGHT uses two new INT 10h functions. Function 3 reads the
position of the cursor, and function 2 changes the cursor position. The procedure first uses function 3 to find the cursor position, which is returned in two
bytes, the column number in DL, and the line number in DH. Then
CURSOR_RIGT increments the column number (in DL) and moves the
cursor. If DL was at the last column (79), the procedure sends a carriage-
return/line-feed pair to move the cursor to the next line. You do not need this
column 79 check in Dskpatch, but including it makes CURSOR_RIGHT a
general-purpose procedure you can use in any of your own programs.

With these changes, Dskpatch should now display all 256 characters as shown
in Figure 18-2. You can verify that it does by searching for a byte with a value
less than 20h and seeing whether some strange character has replaced the period that value formerly produced in the ASCII window.

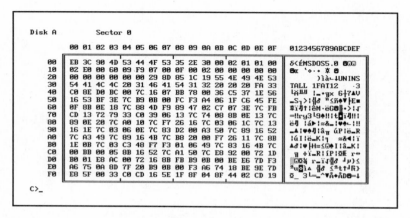

Figure 18-2: Dskpatch with the new WRITE_CHAR.

Now onto something more interesting—writing a procedure to clear a line from the cursor position to the end.

Clearing to the End of a Line

In the last chapter, you used INT 10h, function 6, to clear the screen in the CLEAR_SCREEN procedure. At that time, we mentioned that function 6 could be used to clear any rectangular window. That capability applies even if a window is only one line high and less than one line long, so you can use function 6 to clear part of a line—to the end of the line.

The left side of the window, in this case, is the column number of the cursor, which you get with a function 3 call (also used by CURSOR_RIGHT). The right side of the window is always at column 79. You can see the details in CLEAR_TO_END_OF_LINE; place the procedure in CURSOR.ASM as follows:

Listing 18-3 Procedure Added to CURSOR.ASM (Complete Listing in CURSOR 18.ASM)

```
        PUBLIC  CLEAR_TO_END_OF_LINE
;---------------------------------------------------------------------;
; This procedure clears the line from the current cursor position to  ;
; the end of that line.                                               ;
;---------------------------------------------------------------------;
CLEAR_TO_END_OF_LINE    PROC
        PUSH    AX
        PUSH    BX
        PUSH    CX
        PUSH    DX
        MOV     AH,3                    ;Read current cursor position
        XOR     BH,BH                   ; on page 0
        INT     10h                     ;Now have (X,Y) in DL, DH
        MOV     AH,6                    ;Set up to clear to end of line
        XOR     AL,AL                   ;Clear window
        MOV     CH,DH                   ;All on same line
        MOV     CL,DL                   ;Start at the cursor position
        MOV     DL,79                   ;And stop at the end of the line
        MOV     BH,7                    ;Use normal attribute
        INT     10h
        POP     DX
        POP     CX
        POP     BX
        POP     AX
        RET
CLEAR_TO_END_OF_LINE    ENDP
```

You will use this procedure in WRITE_HEADER to clear the rest of the line when you start reading other sectors (that will be covered soon). You cannot see CLEAR_TO_END_OF_LINE work with WRITE_HEADER until you add the procedures that enable you to read a different sector and update the display. But revise WRITE_HEADER now, just to get it out of the way. Make the following changes to WRITE_HEADER in DISP_SEC.ASM to call CLEAR_TO_END_OF_LINE at the end of the procedure:

Listing 18-4 Changes to WRITE_HEADER in DISP_SEC.ASM (Complete Listing in DISP_S18.ASM)

```
        PUBLIC  WRITE_HEADER
.DATA
        EXTRN   HEADER_LINE_NO:BYTE
        EXTRN   HEADER_PART_1:BYTE
        EXTRN   HEADER_PART_2:BYTE
        EXTRN   DISK_DRIVE_NO:BYTE
        EXTRN   CURRENT_SECTOR_NO:WORD
.CODE
        EXTRN   WRITE_STRING:PROC, WRITE_DECIMAL:PROC
        EXTRN   GOTO_XY:PROC, CLEAR_TO_END_OF_LINE:PROC
;-------------------------------------------------------------------;
;   This procedure writes the header with disk-drive and sector number. ;
;                                                                   ;
; Uses:          GOTO_XY, WRITE_STRING, WRITE_CHAR, WRITE_DECIMAL    ;
;                CLEAR_TO_END_OF_LINE                                ;
; Reads:         HEADER_LINE_NO, HEADER_PART_1, HEADER_PART_2        ;
;                DISK_DRIVE_NO, CURRENT_SECTOR_NO                    ;
;-------------------------------------------------------------------;
WRITE_HEADER    PROC
        PUSH    DX
        XOR     DL,DL                   ;Move cursor to header line number
        MOV     DH,HEADER_LINE_NO
        CALL    GOTO_XY
        LEA     DX,HEADER_PART_1
        CALL    WRITE_STRING
        MOV     DL,DISK_DRIVE_NO
        ADD     DL,'A'                  ;Print drives A, B, ...
        CALL    WRITE_CHAR
        LEA     DX,HEADER_PART_2
        CALL    WRITE_STRING
        MOV     DX,CURRENT_SECTOR_NO
        CALL    WRITE_DECIMAL
        CALL    CLEAR_TO_END_OF_LINE    ;Clear rest of sector number
        POP     DX
        RET
WRITE_HEADER    ENDP
```

This revision marks both the final version of WRITE_HEADER and the completion of the file CURSOR.ASM. You are still missing several important parts of Dskpatch, though. In the next chapter, you will continue by adding the central dispatcher for keyboard commands. You will then be able to press F3 and F4 to read other sectors on the disk.

Summary

This chapter has been relatively easy, without much in the way of new information or tricks. You did learn how to use INT 10h, function number 9, in the ROM BIOS to write any character to the screen.

In the process, you also saw how to read the cursor position with INT 10h function 3 so that the cursor could be moved right one position after you wrote a character. The reason: INT 10h function 9 does not move the cursor after it writes just one character, unless it writes more than one copy of the character. Finally, you put INT 10h function 6 to work by clearing part of just one line. In the next chapter, we will get down to business again as we build the central dispatcher.

The Dispatcher

In this chapter you will build a new version of Dskpatch that can display sectors other than sector 1, using the keyboard for navigation. This chapter contains a lot of code and sets the pace for the rest of the chapters in Part III.

Files altered: DSKPATCH.ASM, DISPATCH.ASM, DISP_IO.ASM, KBD_IO.ASM, DISK_IO.ASM

Disk files: DSKPAT19.ASM, DISP_S19.ASM, DISP_I19.ASM, KBD_IO19.ASM, DISK_I19.ASM

19

Topics Covered

Building a Dispatcher

Reading Other Sectors

Philosophy of the Following Chapters

In any language it is nice to have a well-written program that does something. To really bring a program to life, we need to make it interactive. It is human nature to say, "If I do this, you do that," so we will use this chapter to add some interactivity to Dskpatch.

We will write a simple keyboard-input procedure and a central dispatcher. The dispatcher's job will be to call the correct procedure for each key pushed. For example, when you press the F3 key to read and display the previous sector, the dispatcher will call a procedure called PREVIOUS_SECTOR. To do this, you will be making many changes to Dskpatch. You will start by creating DIS-PATCHER, the central dispatcher, and some other procedures for display for-matting. Next, you will add two new procedures, PREVIOUS_SECTOR and NEXT_SECTOR, which will be called through DISPATCHER.

Building a Dispatcher

The Dispatcher will be the central control for Dskpatch, so all keyboard input and editing will be done through it. DISPATCHER's job will be to read char-acters and call other procedures to do the work. You will soon see how the dispatcher does its work, but first let's see how it fits into Dskpatch.

DISPATCHER will have its own prompt line, just under the half-sector dis-play where the cursor waits for keyboard input. You won't be able to enter hex numbers in the first version of the keyboard-input procedure, but later on you will. Here are the first modifications to DSKPATCH.ASM; these add the data for a prompt line as follows:

Listing 19-1 Additions to DATA_SEG in DSKPATCH.ASM

```
HEADER_LINE_NO          DB      0
HEADER_PART_1           DB      'Disk ',0
HEADER_PART_2           DB      '        Sector ',0
        PUBLIC  PROMPT_LINE_NO, EDITOR_PROMPT
PROMPT_LINE_NO          DB      21
EDITOR_PROMPT           DB      'Press function key, or enter'
                        DB      ' character or hex byte: ',0
```

You will add more prompts later to take care of such matters as inputting a new sector number. Your job will be made simpler by using a common procedure, WRITE_PROMPT_LINE, to write each prompt line. Each procedure that uses WRITE_PROMPT_LINE will supply it with the address of the prompt (here, the address of EDITOR_PROMPT), and then write the prompt on line 21 (because PROMPT_LINE_NO is 21). For example, this new version of DISK_PATCH (in DSKPATCH.ASM) uses WRITE_PROMPT_LINE just before it calls DISPATCHER. The new version is as follows:

Listing 19-2 Additions to DISK_PATCH in DSKPATCH.ASM (Complete Listing in DSKPAT19.ASM)

```
            EXTRN    CLEAR_SCREEN:PROC, READ_SECTOR:PROC
            EXTRN    INIT_SEC_DISP:PROC, WRITE_HEADER:PROC
            EXTRN    WRITE_PROMPT_LINE:PROC, DISPATCHER:PROC
DISK_PATCH  PROC
            MOV      AX,DGROUP              ;Put data segment into AX
            MOV      DS,AX                  ;Set DS to point to data

            CALL     CLEAR_SCREEN
            CALL     WRITE_HEADER
            CALL     READ_SECTOR
            CALL     INIT_SEC_DISP
            LEA      DX,EDITOR_PROMPT
            CALL     WRITE_PROMPT_LINE
            CALL     DISPATCHER

            MOV      AH,4Ch                 ;Return to DOS
            INT      21h
DISK_PATCH  ENDP
```

The dispatcher itself is a fairly simple program, but we do use some new tricks in it. The following listing is the first version of the file DISPATCH.ASM.

Listing 19-3 The New File DISPATCH.ASM
(Complete Listing in DISPAT19.ASM)

```
.MODEL   SMALL

.CODE
        EXTRN    NEXT_SECTOR:PROC                    ;In DISK_IO.ASM
        EXTRN    PREVIOUS_SECTOR:PROC                ;In DISK_IO.ASM
.DATA
;------------------------------------------------------------------;
; This table contains the legal extended ASCII keys and the addresses  ;
; of the procedures that should be called when each key is pressed.    ;
;                                                                   ;
; The format of the table is                                        ;
;              DB        72              ;Extended code for cursor up  ;
;              DW        OFFSET _TEXT:PHANTOM_UP                     ;
;------------------------------------------------------------------;
DISPATCH_TABLE  LABEL    BYTE
        DB       61                          ;F3
        DW       OFFSET _TEXT:PREVIOUS_SECTOR
        DB       62                          ;F4
        DW       OFFSET _TEXT:NEXT_SECTOR
        DB       0                           ;End of the table

.CODE


        PUBLIC   DISPATCHER
        EXTRN    READ_BYTE:PROC
;------------------------------------------------------------------;
; This is the central dispatcher. During normal editing and viewing,  ;
; this procedure reads characters from the keyboard and, if the char  ;
; is a command key (such as a cursor key), DISPATCHER calls the     ;
; procedures that do the actual work. This dispatching is done for  ;
; special keys listed in the table DISPATCH_TABLE, where the procedure ;
; addresses are stored just after the key names.                    ;
;                                                                   ;
; If the character is not a special key, then it should be placed   ;
; directly into the sector buffer—this is the editing mode.         ;
;                                                                   ;
; Uses:        READ_BYTE                                            ;
;------------------------------------------------------------------;
DISPATCHER      PROC
        PUSH     AX
        PUSH     BX
DISPATCH_LOOP:
```

```
        CALL    READ_BYTE               ;Read character into AX
        OR      AH,AH                   ;AX = -1 if no character read, 1
                                        ; for an extended code.
        JS      DISPATCH_LOOP           ;No character read, try again
        JNZ     SPECIAL_KEY             ;Read extended code
; do nothing with the character for now
        JMP     DISPATCH_LOOP           ;Read another character

SPECIAL_KEY:
        CMP     AL,68                   ;F10--exit?
        JE      END_DISPATCH            ;Yes, leave
                                        ;Use BX to look through table
        LEA     BX,DISPATCH_TABLE
SPECIAL_LOOP:
        CMP     BYTE PTR [BX],0         ;End of table?
        JE      NOT_IN_TABLE            ;Yes, key was not in the table
        CMP     AL,[BX]                 ;Is it this table entry?
        JE      DISPATCH                ;Yes, then dispatch
        ADD     BX,3                    ;No, try next entry
        JMP     SPECIAL_LOOP            ;Check next table entry

DISPATCH:
        INC     BX                      ;Point to address of procedure
        CALL    WORD PTR [BX]           ;Call procedure
        JMP     DISPATCH_LOOP           ;Wait for another key

NOT_IN_TABLE:                           ;Do nothing, just read next char
        JMP     DISPATCH_LOOP

END_DISPATCH:
        POP     BX
        POP     AX
        RET
DISPATCHER      ENDP


        END
```

The DISPATCH_TABLE holds the extended ASCII codes for the F3 and F4 keys. Each code is followed by the address of the procedure DISPATCHER should call when it reads that particular extended code. For example, when

READ_BYTE, which is called by DISPATCHER, reads an F3 key (extended code 61), DISPATCHER calls the procedure PREVIOUS_SECTOR.

The addresses of the procedures we want DISPATCHER to call are in the dispatch table, so we used a new directive, OFFSET, to obtain them. The following line, for example, tells the assembler to use the *offset* of your PREVIOUS_SECTOR procedure.

```
DW      OFFSET _TEXT:PREVIOUS_SECTOR
```

The calculation of this offset is relative to the start of your code segment _TEXT, which is why we put the _TEXT: in front of the procedure name. (As it turns out here, this _TEXT: isn't absolutely necessary. Still, in the interest of clarity, we will write OFFSET _TEXT: anyway.)

Notice that DISPATCH_TABLE contains both byte and word data. This raises a few considerations. In the past, we have always dealt with tables of one type or the other: either all words, or all bytes. But here, we have both, so we have to tell the assembler which type of data to expect when we use a CMP or CALL instruction. In the case of an instruction written as follows, the assembler does not know whether you want to compare words or bytes.

```
CMP     [BX],0
```

By writing the following instruction, you tell the assembler that BX points to a byte, and that you want a byte compare.

```
CMP     BYTE PTR [BX],0
```

Similarly, the instruction CMP WORD PTR [BX],0 would compare words. On the other hand, an instruction like CMP AL,[BX] does not cause problems because AL is a byte register and the assembler knows without being told that you want a byte compare.

Remember that a CALL instruction can be either a NEAR or a FAR CALL. A NEAR CALL needs one word for the address, while the FAR CALL needs two. The following instruction tells the assembler, with WORD PTR, that [BX] points to one word, so it should generate a NEAR CALL and use the word pointed to by [BX] as the address. The address is the one we stored in DISPATCH_TABLE.

```
CALL    WORD PTR [BX]
```

For a FAR CALL, which uses a two-word address, you would use the instruction CALL DWORD PTR [BX]. DWORD stands for *Double Word*, or two words.

As you will see in Chapter 22, you can easily add more key commands to Dskpatch simply by adding more procedures and placing new entries in DISPATCH_TABLE. Right now, you still need to add four procedures before you can test this new version of Dskpatch. You are missing READ_BYTE, WRITE_PROMPT_LINE, PREVIOUS_SECTOR, and NEXT_SECTOR.

READ_BYTE is the procedure needed to read characters and extended ASCII codes from the keyboard. The final version will be able to read special keys (such as the function and cursor keys), ASCII characters, and two-digit hex numbers. At this point, you will write a simple version of READ_BYTE—to read either a character or a special key. The first version of KBD_IO.ASM, which is the file where you will store all of your procedures to read from the keyboard, is as follows:

Listing 19-4 The New File KBD_IO.ASM (Complete Listing in KBD_IO19.ASM)

```
.MODEL   SMALL
.CODE

        PUBLIC  READ_BYTE
;--------------------------------------------------------------------;
; This procedure reads a single ASCII character. This is just        ;
; a test version of READ_BYTE.                                       ;
;                                                                    ;
; Returns:       AL      Character code (unless AH = 1)              ;
;                AH      0 if read ASCII char                        ;
;                        1 if read a special key                    ;
;--------------------------------------------------------------------;
READ_BYTE       PROC
        XOR     AH,AH                   ;Ask for keyboard read function
        INT     16h                     ;Read character/scan code from kbd
        OR      AL,AL                   ;Is it an extended code?
        JZ      EXTENDED_CODE           ;Yes
NOT_EXTENDED:
        XOR     AH,AH                   ;Return just the ASCII code
```

continues

275

Listing 19-4 continued

```
DONE_READING:
        RET

EXTENDED_CODE:
        MOV     AL,AH                   ;Put scan code into AL
        MOV     AH,1                    ;Signal extended code
        JMP     DONE_READING
READ_BYTE       ENDP


        END
```

READ_BYTE uses a new interrupt, INT 16h, which is an interrupt that gives you access to the keyboard services in the ROM BIOS. Function 0 reads a character from the keyboard without echoing it to the screen. It returns the character code in AL, and the *scan code* in the AH register.

The scan code is the code assigned to each key on the keyboard. Some keys, such as F3, have not been assigned ASCII codes (which means AL will be 0), but they do have scan codes (you will find a table of scan codes in Appendix D). READ_BYTE puts this scan code into the AL register for special keys, and sets AH to 1. Next, add the new procedure WRITE_PROMPT_LINE to DISP_SEC.ASM as follows:

Listing 19-5 Add This Procedure to DISP_SEC.ASM (Complete Listing in DISP_S19.ASM)

```
        PUBLIC  WRITE_PROMPT_LINE
        EXTRN   CLEAR_TO_END_OF_LINE:PROC, WRITE_STRING:PROC
        EXTRN   GOTO_XY:PROC
.DATA
        EXTRN   PROMPT_LINE_NO:BYTE
.CODE
;------------------------------------------------------------------;
; This procedure writes the prompt line to the screen and clears the  ;
; end of the line.                                                 ;
;                                                                  ;
; On entry:     DS:DX   Address of the prompt-line message          ;
```

```
;                                                              ;
; Uses:          WRITE_STRING, CLEAR_TO_END_OF_LINE, GOTO_XY   ;
; Reads:         PROMPT_LINE_NO                                ;
;-------------------------------------------------------------;
WRITE_PROMPT_LINE        PROC
        PUSH    DX
        XOR     DL,DL                   ;Write the prompt line and
        MOV     DH,PROMPT_LINE_NO       ;move the cursor there
        CALL    GOTO_XY
        POP     DX
        CALL    WRITE_STRING
        CALL    CLEAR_TO_END_OF_LINE
        RET
WRITE_PROMPT_LINE        ENDP
```

There really isn't much to this procedure. It moves the cursor to the beginning of the prompt line, which you set (in DSKPATCH.ASM) to line 21. Then,
it writes the prompt line and clears the rest of the line. The cursor is at the end
of the prompt when WRITE_PROMPT_LINE is done, and the rest of the
line is cleared by CLEAR_TO_END_OF_LINE.

Reading Other Sectors

Finally, you need the two procedures PREVIOUS_SECTOR and
NEXT_SECTOR, to read and redisplay the previous and next disk sectors.
Add the following two procedures to DISK_IO.ASM.

Listing 19-6 Procedures Added to DISK_IO.ASM (Complete Lsting on DISK_I19.ASM)

```
        PUBLIC  PREVIOUS_SECTOR
        EXTRN   INIT_SEC_DISP:PROC, WRITE_HEADER:PROC
        EXTRN   WRITE_PROMPT_LINE:PROC
.DATA
        EXTRN   CURRENT_SECTOR_NO:WORD, EDITOR_PROMPT:BYTE
.CODE
```

continues

277

Listing 19-6 continued

```
;----------------------------------------------------------------;
; This procedure reads the previous sector, if possible.         ;
;                                                                ;
; Uses:         WRITE_HEADER, READ_SECTOR, INIT_SEC_DISP         ;
;               WRITE_PROMPT_LINE                                ;
; Reads:        CURRENT_SECTOR_NO, EDITOR_PROMPT                 ;
; Writes:       CURRENT_SECTOR_NO                                ;
;----------------------------------------------------------------;
PREVIOUS_SECTOR         PROC
        PUSH    AX
        PUSH    DX
        MOV     AX,CURRENT_SECTOR_NO    ;Get current sector number
        OR      AX,AX                   ;Don't decrement if already 0
        JZ      DONT_DECREMENT_SECTOR
        DEC     AX
        MOV     CURRENT_SECTOR_NO,AX    ;Save new sector number
        CALL    WRITE_HEADER
        CALL    READ_SECTOR
        CALL    INIT_SEC_DISP           ;Display new sector
        LEA     DX,EDITOR_PROMPT
        CALL    WRITE_PROMPT_LINE
DONT_DECREMENT_SECTOR:
        POP     DX
        POP     AX
        RET
PREVIOUS_SECTOR         ENDP

        PUBLIC  NEXT_SECTOR
        EXTRN   INIT_SEC_DISP:PROC, WRITE_HEADER:PROC
        EXTRN   WRITE_PROMPT_LINE:PROC
.DATA
        EXTRN   CURRENT_SECTOR_NO:WORD, EDITOR_PROMPT:BYTE
.CODE
;----------------------------------------------------------------;
; Reads the next sector.                                         ;
;                                                                ;
; Uses:         WRITE_HEADER, READ_SECTOR, INIT_SEC_DISP         ;
;               WRITE_PROMPT_LINE                                ;
; Reads:        CURRENT_SECTOR_NO, EDITOR_PROMPT                 ;
; Writes:       CURRENT_SECTOR_NO                                ;
;----------------------------------------------------------------;
NEXT_SECTOR     PROC
        PUSH    AX
```

```
        PUSH    DX
        MOV     AX,CURRENT_SECTOR_NO
        INC     AX                      ;Move to next sector
        MOV     CURRENT_SECTOR_NO,AX
        CALL    WRITE_HEADER
        CALL    READ_SECTOR
        CALL    INIT_SEC_DISP           ;Display new sector
        LEA     DX,EDITOR_PROMPT
        CALL    WRITE_PROMPT_LINE
        POP     DX
        POP     AX
        RET
NEXT_SECTOR     ENDP
```

Now you are ready to build a new version of Dskpatch by assembling all the files you created or changed—Dskpatch, Video_io, Kbd_io, Dispatch, and Disk_io. If you are not using NMake, remember when you Link that there are now seven files— Dskpatch, Disp_sec, Disk_io, Video_io, Kbd_io, Dispatch, and Cursor.

If you are using NMake, you need to make the following additions to the file Makefile are as follows (the backslash at the end of the first line tells Make you are continuing the list of files onto the next line):

Listing 19-7 Changes to the Make File MAKEFILE

```
dskpatch.exe:   dskpatch.obj disk_io.obj disp_sec.obj video_io.obj cursor.obj \
                dispatch.obj kbd_io.obj
        link dskpatch disk_io disp_sec video_io cursor dispatch kbd_io;
                .
                .
                .
cursor.obj:     cursor.asm
        ml /c cursor.asm

dispatch.obj:   dispatch.asm
        ml /c dispatch.asm

kbd_io.obj:     kbd_io.asm
        ml /c kbd_io.asm
```

279

Remember that the first three lines need to be at the end of your file if you are using Make from MASM 5 or earlier. If you don't have Make or NMake, you may wish to write the following short batch file to link and create your EXE file:

```
LINK DSKPATCH DISK_IO DISP_SEC VIDEO_IO CURSOR DISPATCH KBD_IO;
```

As you add more files, you will only need to change this batch file, rather than type this long link list each time you rebuild the EXE program.

This version of Dskpatch has three active keys: F3 reads and displays the previous sector, stopping at sector 0; F4 reads the next sector; F10 exits from Dskpatch. Give these keys a try. Your display should now look something like Figure 19-1.

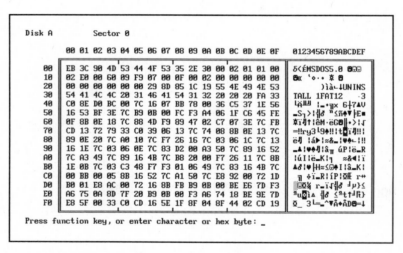

Figure 19-1: Dskpatch with the prompt line.

Philosophy of the Following Chapters

We covered far more ground than usual in this chapter, and in that respect you have had a taste of the philosophy we will be following in Chapters 20 through 27. From now on, we will clip along at a fairly rapid pace so we can get through more examples of how to write large programs. You will also find more procedures that you can use in your own programs.

These chapters are here for you to learn from, hence the rather high density of new procedures. But in the chapters in Part IV of this book, we'll come back to learning new subjects, so hang on, or (if you wish) skip the remaining chapters on Dskpatch until you're ready to write your own programs. When you are ready to come back again, you will find many useful tidbits for programming.

Of course, if you are chomping at the bit and eager to write your own procedures, read the next chapter. Chapter 20 will give you a number of hints you can use if you want to try writing the procedures in the following chapters.

From Chapter 21 on, we will present many different procedures and let you discover how they work. Why? There are two reasons, both related to setting you on your feet and on your way to assembly language programming. First, we want you to have a library of procedures you can use in your own programs; to use them comfortably, you need to exercise your own skills. Second, by presenting this large programming example, we want not only to show you how to write a large program, but also to give you a feel for it as well.

So take the rest of this book in the way that suits you best. Chapter 20 is for those of you eager to write your own programs. In Chapter 21, we will return to Dskpatch and build the procedures to write and move what we call a phantom cursor: a reverse-video cursor for the hex and ASCII displays.

A Programming Challenge

In this chapter we will present a plan for the rest of Dskpatch, which covers Chapters 21 through 27. If you want to try writing some procedures yourself, read this chapter first. You can then read the other chapters if you get stuck, or if you want some hints on how to proceed.

Files altered: None

20

Topics Covered

The Phantom Cursors

Simple Editing

Other Additions and Changes to Dskpatch

This book contains six more chapters of procedures. If you want to try navigating on your own, read this chapter. We will chart a course for you here, and plot your way through Chapters 21 and 22. Then you can try to write the procedures in each chapter before you read it. If you don't wish to try writing pieces of Dskpatch just yet, skip this chapter for now. It is very brief and leaves many details to your imagination.

You may want to make a copy of all your files before you start making changes. Then when you get to Chapter 21, you will have the choice of following along with the changes, or using your own version.

If you decide to read through this chapter, here is a suggestion on how to proceed—read one section and then try to make your own corresponding changes to Dskpatch. When you feel you have made enough progress, read the chapter with the same name as the section title. After you have read the corresponding chapter, then go on to read the next section.

The Phantom Cursors

In Chapter 21 we will place two phantom cursors on the screen: one in the hex window, and one in the ASCII window. A phantom cursor is similar to a normal cursor, but it does not blink and the background turns white, with the characters black, as displayed in Figure 20-1. The phantom cursor in the hex window is four characters wide; the one in the ASCII window is only one character wide.

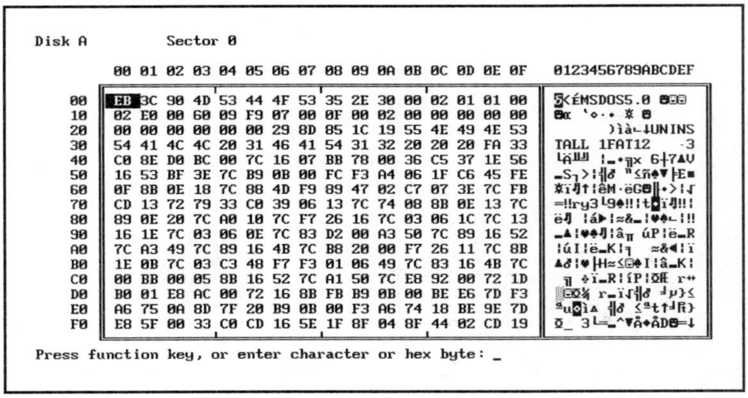

Figure 20-1: A display with phantom cursors.

284

How do we create a phantom cursor? Each character on the screen has an *attribute* byte, which you learned about in Chapter 18. This byte tells your PC how to display each character. An attribute code of 7h displays a normal character, while 70h displays a character in inverse video. The latter is exactly what you want for the phantom cursor, so how can you change the attribute of your characters to 70h?

INT 10h function 9 writes both a character and an attribute to the screen; 10h function 8 reads the character code at the current cursor position. You can create a phantom cursor in the hex window with the following steps:

- Save the position of the real cursor (use INT 10h function 3 to read the cursor position and save this in variables).

- Move the real cursor to the start of the phantom cursor in the hex window.

- For the next four characters, read the character code (function 8) and write both the character and its attribute (setting the attribute to 70h).

- Finally, restore the old cursor position.

You can write a phantom cursor in the ASCII window in much the same way. Once you have a working phantom cursor in the hex window, you can add the extra code for the ASCII window.

Keep in mind that your first try is only temporary. Once you have a working program with phantom cursors, you can go back and rewrite your changes, so you have a number of small procedures to do the work. Look at the procedures in Chapter 21 when you are finished to see one way of doing this.

Simple Editing

Once you have your phantom cursors, you will want to move them around on the screen. You need to pay attention to boundary conditions in order to keep the phantom cursors inside each of the two windows. You also want your two phantom cursors to move together because they represent the hex and ASCII representations of the same thing.

How can you move each phantom cursor? Each of the four cursor keys on the keypad sends out a special function number—72 for cursor up; 80 for cursor down; 75 for cursor left; and 77 for cursor right. These are the numbers you need to add to DISPATCH_TABLE, along with the addresses of the four procedures to move the phantom cursors in each of these four directions.

To actually move each phantom cursor, erase it, then change its two coordinates and write it again. If you have been careful about how you wrote the phantom cursors, the four procedures to move them should be fairly simple.

Whenever you type a character on the keyboard, Dskpatch should read this character and replace the byte under the phantom cursor with the character just read. The steps for the simple editing of characters is as follows:

- Read a character from the keyboard.
- Change the hex number in the hex window and the character in the ASCII window to match the character just read.
- Change the byte in the sector buffer, SECTOR.

Here is a simple hint—you don't have to make many changes to add editing. Dispatch requires little more than calling a new procedure (we have called it EDIT_BYTE) that does most of the work. EDIT_BYTE is responsible for changing both the screen and SECTOR.

Other Additions and Changes to Dskpatch

From Chapters 23 through 27, the changes start to become somewhat trickier and more involved. If you are still interested in writing your own version, consider this—what more would you like to see Dskpatch do than it does right now? We have used the following ideas in the remaining chapters.

You will need a new version of READ_BYTE that will read either one character or a two-digit hex number and wait for you to press the Enter key before it returns a character to Dispatch. This part of our "wish list" is not as simple as it sounds. We will spend Chapters 23 and 24 working on this problem.

In Chapter 25, we will go bug hunting; then in Chapter 26 we will learn how to write modified sectors back to the disk using the DOS INT 26h function, which is analogous to the INT 25h that you used to read a sector from the disk. (In Chapter 26 we won't check for read errors, but you will find such checks in the disk version of Dskpatch that is included with this book.)

Finally, in Chapter 27, we will make some changes to Dskpatch so you can see the other half of the sector display. These changes won't allow you to scroll through the sector display as freely as we would like, but those changes are on the disk version of Dskpatch.

The Phantom Cursors

In this chapter you will learn how to draw two phantom (or bar) cursors on the screen—one in the hex window, and one in the ASCII window.

Files altered: DISP_SEC.ASM, PHANTOM.ASM, VIDEO_IO.ASM

Disk files: DISP_S21.ASM, PHANTO21.ASM, VIDEO_I21.ASM

21

Topics Covered

In this chapter you will build the procedures to write and erase a phantom cursor in the hex window and another in the ASCII window. A phantom cursor is a shadow that inverts a character, turning the background to white and the character to black. The hex window has the room to make this cursor four characters wide so it will be easy to read. In the ASCII window, the phantom cursor will be one character wide, because there is no room between characters.

The Phantom Cursors

INIT_SEC_DISP is the only procedure that changes the sector display. A new display appears when you start Dskpatch and each time you read a new sector. Since the phantom cursors will be in the sector display, you will begin your work by placing a call to WRITE_PHANTOM in INIT_SEC_DISP. That way, you will write the phantom cursors every time you write a new sector display.

The revised—and final—version of INIT_SEC_DISP in DISP_SEC.ASM is as follows:

Listing 21-1 Changes to INIT_SEC_DISP in DISP_SEC.ASM (Complete listing in DISP_S21.ASM)

```
        PUBLIC  INIT_SEC_DISP
        EXTRN   WRITE_PATTERN:PROC, SEND_CRLF:PROC
        EXTRN   GOTO_XY:PROC, WRITE_PHANTOM:PROC
.DATA
        EXTRN   LINES_BEFORE_SECTOR:BYTE
        EXTRN   SECTOR_OFFSET:WORD
.CODE
;-------------------------------------------------------------;
; This procedure initializes the half-sector display.         ;
;                                                             ;
; Uses:     WRITE_PATTERN, SEND_CRLF, DISP_HALF_SECTOR        ;
;           WRITE_TOP_HEX_NUMBERS, GOTO_XY, WRITE_PHANTOM     ;
; Reads:    TOP_LINE_PATTERN, BOTTOM_LINE_PATTERN             ;
;           LINES_BEFORE_SECTOR                               ;
; Writes:   SECTOR_OFFSET                                     ;
```

```
;------------------------------------------------------------;
INIT_SEC_DISP   PROC
        PUSH    DX
        XOR     DL,DL                   ;Move cursor into position
        MOV     DH,LINES_BEFORE_SECTOR
        CALL    GOTO_XY
        CALL    WRITE_TOP_HEX_NUMBERS
        LEA     DX,TOP_LINE_PATTERN
        CALL    WRITE_PATTERN
        CALL    SEND_CRLF
        XOR     DX,DX                   ;Start at the beginning of the sector
        MOV     SECTOR_OFFSET,DX        ;Set sector offset to 0
        CALL    DISP_HALF_SECTOR
        LEA     DX,BOTTOM_LINE_PATTERN
        CALL    WRITE_PATTERN
        CALL    WRITE_PHANTOM           ;Display the phantom cursor
        POP     DX
        RET
INIT_SEC_DISP   ENDP
```

Notice that we have also updated INIT_SEC_DISP to use and initialize variables. It now sets SECTOR_OFFSET to zero to display the first half of a sector.

Let's move on to WRITE_PHANTOM itself. This will take quite a bit of work. Altogether, you have to write six procedures, including WRITE_PHANTOM. First, you will move the real cursor to the position of the phantom cursor in the hex window and change the attribute of the next four characters to inverse video (attribute 70h). This creates a block of white, four characters wide, with the hex number in black. Then you will do the same in the ASCII window, but for a single character. Finally, move the real cursor back to where it was when you started. The procedures for the phantom cursors will be in PHANTOM.ASM, with the exception of WRITE_ATTRIBUTE_N_TIMES, the procedure that will set the attribute of characters. Enter the following procedures into the file PHANTOM.ASM:

Listing 21-2 The new file PHANTOM.ASM (Complete listing in PHANTO21.ASM)

```
.MODEL   SMALL

.DATA

REAL_CURSOR_X            DB      0
REAL_CURSOR_Y            DB      0
        PUBLIC  PHANTOM_CURSOR_X, PHANTOM_CURSOR_Y
PHANTOM_CURSOR_X         DB      0
PHANTOM_CURSOR_Y         DB      0

.CODE

        PUBLIC  MOV_TO_HEX_POSITION
        EXTRN   GOTO_XY:PROC
.DATA
        EXTRN   LINES_BEFORE_SECTOR:BYTE
.CODE
;--------------------------------------------------------------------;
; This procedure moves the real cursor to the position of the phantom ;
; cursor in the hex window.                                           ;
;                                                                     ;
; Uses:          GOTO_XY                                              ;
; Reads:         LINES_BEFORE_SECTOR, PHANTOM_CURSOR_X, PHANTOM_CURSOR_Y ;
;--------------------------------------------------------------------;
MOV_TO_HEX_POSITION     PROC
        PUSH    AX
        PUSH    CX
        PUSH    DX
        MOV     DH,LINES_BEFORE_SECTOR  ;Find row of phantom (0,0)
        ADD     DH,2                    ;Plus row of hex and horizontal bar
        ADD     DH,PHANTOM_CURSOR_Y     ;DH = row of phantom cursor
        MOV     DL,8                    ;Indent on left side
        MOV     CL,3                    ;Each column uses 3 characters, so
        MOV     AL,PHANTOM_CURSOR_X     ; we must multiply CURSOR_X by 3
        MUL     CL
        ADD     DL,AL                   ;And add to the indent, to get column
        CALL    GOTO_XY                 ; for phantom cursor
        POP     DX
        POP     CX
        POP     AX
        RET
MOV_TO_HEX_POSITION     ENDP
```

```
        PUBLIC  MOV_TO_ASCII_POSITION
        EXTRN   GOTO_XY:PROC
.DATA
        EXTRN   LINES_BEFORE_SECTOR:BYTE
.CODE
;------------------------------------------------------------------------;
; This procedure moves the real cursor to the beginning of the phantom  ;
; cursor in the ASCII window.                                           ;
;                                                                        ;
; Uses:          GOTO_XY                                                 ;
; Reads:         LINES_BEFORE_SECTOR, PHANTOM_CURSOR_X, PHANTOM_CURSOR_Y ;
;------------------------------------------------------------------------;
MOV_TO_ASCII_POSITION   PROC
        PUSH    AX
        PUSH    DX
        MOV     DH,LINES_BEFORE_SECTOR  ;Find row of phantom (0,0)
        ADD     DH,2                    ;Plus row of hex and horizontal bar
        ADD     DH,PHANTOM_CURSOR_Y     ;DH = row of phantom cursor
        MOV     DL,59                   ;Indent on left side
        ADD     DL,PHANTOM_CURSOR_X     ;Add CURSOR_X to get X position
        CALL    GOTO_XY                 ; for phantom cursor
        POP     DX
        POP     AX
        RET
MOV_TO_ASCII_POSITION   ENDP


        PUBLIC  SAVE_REAL_CURSOR
;------------------------------------------------------------------------;
; This procedure saves the position of the real cursor in the two       ;
; variables REAL_CURSOR_X and REAL_CURSOR_Y.                            ;
;                                                                        ;
; Writes:        REAL_CURSOR_X, REAL_CURSOR_Y                            ;
;------------------------------------------------------------------------;
SAVE_REAL_CURSOR        PROC
        PUSH    AX
        PUSH    BX
        PUSH    CX
        PUSH    DX
        MOV     AH,3                    ;Read cursor position
        XOR     BH,BH                   ; on page 0
        INT     10h                     ;And return in DL,DH
        MOV     REAL_CURSOR_Y,DL        ;Save position
        MOV     REAL_CURSOR_X,DH
        POP     DX
```

continues

293

Listing 21-2 continued

```
        POP     CX
        POP     BX
        POP     AX
        RET
SAVE_REAL_CURSOR        ENDP


        PUBLIC  RESTORE_REAL_CURSOR
        EXTRN   GOTO_XY:PROC
;-----------------------------------------------------------------------;
; This procedure restores the real cursor to its old position, saved in ;
; REAL_CURSOR_X and REAL_CURSOR_Y.                                       ;
;                                                                        ;
; Uses:          GOTO_XY                                                 ;
; Reads:         REAL_CURSOR_X, REAL_CURSOR_Y                            ;
;-----------------------------------------------------------------------;
RESTORE_REAL_CURSOR     PROC
        PUSH    DX
        MOV     DL,REAL_CURSOR_Y
        MOV     DH,REAL_CURSOR_X
        CALL    GOTO_XY
        POP     DX
        RET
RESTORE_REAL_CURSOR     ENDP


        PUBLIC  WRITE_PHANTOM
        EXTRN   WRITE_ATTRIBUTE_N_TIMES:PROC
;-----------------------------------------------------------------------;
; This procedure uses CURSOR_X and CURSOR_Y, through MOV_TO_..., as the  ;
; coordinates for the phantom cursor.  WRITE_PHANTOM writes this         ;
; phantom cursor.                                                        ;
;                                                                        ;
; Uses:          WRITE_ATTRIBUTE_N_TIMES, SAVE_REAL_CURSOR               ;
;                RESTORE_REAL_CURSOR, MOV_TO_HEX_POSITION                ;
;                MOV_TO_ASCII_POSITION                                   ;
;-----------------------------------------------------------------------;
WRITE_PHANTOM   PROC
        PUSH    CX
        PUSH    DX
        CALL    SAVE_REAL_CURSOR
        CALL    MOV_TO_HEX_POSITION     ;Coord. of cursor in hex window
        MOV     CX,4                    ;Make phantom cursor four chars wide
        MOV     DL,70h
        CALL    WRITE_ATTRIBUTE_N_TIMES
```

```
        CALL    MOV_TO_ASCII_POSITION     ;Coord. of cursor in ASCII window
        MOV     CX,1                      ;Cursor is one character wide here
        CALL    WRITE_ATTRIBUTE_N_TIMES
        CALL    RESTORE_REAL_CURSOR
        POP     DX
        POP     CX
        RET
WRITE_PHANTOM   ENDP


        PUBLIC  ERASE_PHANTOM
        EXTRN   WRITE_ATTRIBUTE_N_TIMES:PROC
;-------------------------------------------------------------------;
; This procedure erases the phantom cursor, just the opposite of     ;
; WRITE_PHANTOM.                                                     ;
;                                                                   ;
; Uses:         WRITE_ATTRIBUTE_N_TIMES, SAVE_REAL_CURSOR            ;
;               RESTORE_REAL_CURSOR, MOV_TO_HEX_POSITION            ;
;               MOV_TO_ASCII_POSITION                               ;
;-------------------------------------------------------------------;
ERASE_PHANTOM   PROC
        PUSH    CX
        PUSH    DX
        CALL    SAVE_REAL_CURSOR
        CALL    MOV_TO_HEX_POSITION       ;Coord. of cursor in hex window
        MOV     CX,4                      ;Change back to white on black
        MOV     DL,7
        CALL    WRITE_ATTRIBUTE_N_TIMES
        CALL    MOV_TO_ASCII_POSITION
        MOV     CX,1
        CALL    WRITE_ATTRIBUTE_N_TIMES
        CALL    RESTORE_REAL_CURSOR
        POP     DX
        POP     CX
        RET
ERASE_PHANTOM   ENDP


        END
```

WRITE_PHANTOM and ERASE_PHANTOM are much the same. In fact, the only difference is in the attribute used: WRITE_PHANTOM sets the attribute to 70h for inverse video, while ERASE_PHANTOM sets the attribute back to the normal attribute (7). Both of these procedures save the old position of the real cursor with SAVE_REAL_CURSOR. This uses the INT 10h function number 3 to read the position of the cursor and then saves this position in the two bytes REAL_CURSOR_X and REAL_CURSOR_Y.

After saving the real cursor position, both WRITE_PHANTOM and ERASE_PHANTOM then call MOV_TO_HEX_POSITION, which moves the cursor to the start of the phantom cursor in the hex window. Next, WRITE_ATTRIBUTE_N_TIMES writes the inverse-video attribute for four characters, starting at the cursor and moving to the right. This writes the phantom cursor in the hex window. In much the same way, WRITE_PHANTOM then writes a phantom cursor one character wide in the ASCII window. Finally, RESTORE_REAL_CURSOR restores the position of the real cursor to the position it was in before the call to WRITE_PHANTOM. The only procedure left unwritten is WRITE_ATTRIBUTE_N_TIMES, so let's take care of it now.

Changing Character Attributes

You are going to use WRITE_ATTRIBUTE_N_TIMES to do three things. First, it will read the character under the cursor position. You will do this because the INT 10h function you use to set a character's attribute, function number 9, writes both the character *and* the attribute under the cursor. Thus, WRITE_ATTRIBUTE_N_TIMES will change the attribute by writing the new attribute along with the character just read. Finally, the procedure will move the cursor right to the next character position, so you can repeat the whole process N times. You can see the details in the procedure itself. Place WRITE_ATTRIBUTE_N_TIMES in the file VIDEO_IO.ASM as follows:

Listing 21-3 Procedure added to VIDEO_IO.ASM (Complete listing in VIDEO_I21.ASM)

```
        PUBLIC   WRITE_ATTRIBUTE_N_TIMES
        EXTRN    CURSOR_RIGHT:PROC
;-------------------------------------------------------------------;
; This procedure sets the attribute for N characters, starting at the   ;
; current cursor position.                                          ;
```

```
;                                                                    ;
; On entry:     CX       Number of characters to set attribute for   ;
;               DL       New attribute for characters                ;
;                                                                    ;
; Uses:         CURSOR_RIGHT                                          ;
;--------------------------------------------------------------------;
WRITE_ATTRIBUTE_N_TIMES PROC
        PUSH    AX
        PUSH    BX
        PUSH    CX
        PUSH    DX
        MOV     BL,DL               ;Set attribute to new attribute
        XOR     BH,BH               ;Set display page to 0
        MOV     DX,CX               ;CX is used by the BIOS routines
        MOV     CX,1                ;Set attribute for one character
ATTR_LOOP:
        MOV     AH,8                ;Read character under cursor
        INT     10h
        MOV     AH,9                ;Write attribute/character
        INT     10h
        CALL    CURSOR_RIGHT
        DEC     DX                  ;Set attribute for N characters?
        JNZ     ATTR_LOOP           ;No, continue
        POP     DX
        POP     CX
        POP     BX
        POP     AX
        RET
WRITE_ATTRIBUTE_N_TIMES ENDP
```

This is both the first and final version of WRITE_ATTRIBUTE_N_TIMES. With it, you have also created the final version of VIDEO_IO.ASM, so you won't need to change or assemble it again.

Summary

You now have eight files to link, with the main procedure still in Dskpatch. Of these, you have changed two files, Disp_sec and Video_io, and created one, Phantom. If you are using NMake or the short batch file we suggested in Chapter 20, remember to add your new file, Phantom, to the list.

When you run Dskpatch now, you will see it write the sector display, just as before, but Dskpatch will also write in the two phantom cursors in Figure 21-1. Notice that the real cursor is back where it should be at the very end.

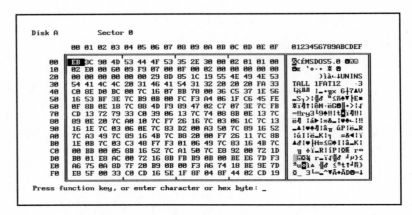

Figure 21-1: Screen display with phantom cursors.

The next chapter covers adding procedures to move your newly formed phantom cursors. It will also cover how to add a simple editing procedure which allows you to change the byte under the phantom cursor.

Simple Editing

In this chapter you will add routines that allow you to move the phantom cursor around on your screen. Then you will add a simple procedure that allows you to input new values into the sector display.

Files altered: DISPATCH.ASM, EDITOR.ASM, PHANTOM.ASM

Disk files: DISPAT22.ASM, EDITOR22.ASM, PHANTO22.ASM

Topics Covered

Moving the Phantom Cursors

Simple Editing

Summary

You have almost reached the point at which you can begin to edit your sector display—change numbers in the half sector display. You will soon add simple versions of the procedures for editing bytes in the display, but before you do, you need some way to move the phantom cursors to different bytes within the half-sector display. This task turns out to be fairly simple, now that you have the two procedures ERASE_PHANTOM and WRITE_PHANTOM.

Moving the Phantom Cursors

Moving the phantom cursors in any direction depends on three basic steps: erasing the phantom cursor at its current position; changing the cursor position by changing one of the variables, PHANTOM_CURSOR_X or PHANTOM_CURSOR_Y; and using WRITE_PHANTOM to write the phantom cursor at the new position. You must be careful not to let the cursor move outside the window, which is 16 bytes wide and 16 bytes high.

To move the phantom cursors, you will need four new procedures, one for each of the arrow keys on the keyboard. DISPATCHER needs no changes because the information on procedures and extended codes is in the table DISPATCH_TABLE. You just need to add the extended ASCII codes and addresses of the procedures for each of the arrow keys. Additions to DISPATCH.ASM that will bring the cursor keys to life are as follows:

Listing 22-1 Changes to DISPATCH.ASM

```
.MODEL   SMALL

.CODE
         EXTRN    NEXT_SECTOR:PROC                       ;In DISK_IO.ASM
         EXTRN    PREVIOUS_SECTOR:PROC                   ;In DISK_IO.ASM
         EXTRN    PHANTOM_UP:PROC, PHANTOM_DOWN:PROC     ;In PHANTOM.ASM
         EXTRN    PHANTOM_LEFT:PROC, PHANTOM_RIGHT:PROC
.DATA
```

```
;-------------------------------------------------------------------;
; This table contains the legal extended ASCII keys and the addresses  ;
; of the procedures that should be called when each key is pressed.    ;
;                                                                      ;
; The format of the table is                                           ;
;               DB        72                  ;Extended code for cursor up  ;
;               DW        OFFSET _TEXT:PHANTOM_UP                       ;
;-------------------------------------------------------------------;
DISPATCH_TABLE  LABEL   BYTE
        DB      61                              ;F3
        DW      OFFSET _TEXT:PREVIOUS_SECTOR
        DB      62                              ;F4
        DW      OFFSET _TEXT:NEXT_SECTOR
        DB      72                              ;Cursor up
        DW      OFFSET _TEXT:PHANTOM_UP
        DB      80                              ;Cursor down
        DW      OFFSET _TEXT:PHANTOM_DOWN
        DB      75                              ;Cursor left
        DW      OFFSET _TEXT:PHANTOM_LEFT
        DB      77                              ;Cursor right
        DW      OFFSET _TEXT:PHANTOM_RIGHT
        DB      0                               ;End of the table
```

As you can see, it is simple to add commands to Dskpatch by placing the procedure names in DISPATCH_TABLE and writing the procedures.

The procedures PHANTOM_UP, PHANTOM_DOWN, and so on are fairly simple. They are also quite similar to one another, differing only in the boundary conditions used for each. We have already described how they work; see if you can write them yourself, in the file PHANTOM.ASM, before you read on. Our versions of the procedures to move the phantom cursors are as follows:

Listing 22-2 Add these procedures to PHANTOM.ASM (Complete listing in PHANTO22.ASM)

```
;-------------------------------------------------------------------------;
; These four procedures move the phantom cursors.                         ;
;                                                                         ;
; Uses:          ERASE_PHANTOM, WRITE_PHANTOM                             ;
; Reads:         PHANTOM_CURSOR_X, PHANTOM_CURSOR_Y                       ;
; Writes:        PHANTOM_CURSOR_X, PHANTOM_CURSOR_Y                       ;
;-------------------------------------------------------------------------;

        PUBLIC  PHANTOM_UP
PHANTOM_UP      PROC
        CALL    ERASE_PHANTOM           ;Erase at current position
        DEC     PHANTOM_CURSOR_Y        ;Move cursor up one line
        JNS     WASNT_AT_TOP            ;Was not at the top, write cursor
        MOV     PHANTOM_CURSOR_Y,0      ;Was at the top, so put back there
WASNT_AT_TOP:
        CALL    WRITE_PHANTOM           ;Write the phantom at new position
        RET
PHANTOM_UP      ENDP


        PUBLIC  PHANTOM_DOWN
PHANTOM_DOWN    PROC
        CALL    ERASE_PHANTOM           ;Erase at current position
        INC     PHANTOM_CURSOR_Y        ;Move cursor down one line
        CMP     PHANTOM_CURSOR_Y,16     ;Was it at the bottom?
        JB      WASNT_AT_BOTTOM         ;No, so write phantom
        MOV     PHANTOM_CURSOR_Y,15     ;Was at bottom, so put back there
WASNT_AT_BOTTOM:
        CALL    WRITE_PHANTOM           ;Write the phantom cursor
        RET
PHANTOM_DOWN    ENDP


        PUBLIC  PHANTOM_LEFT
PHANTOM_LEFT    PROC
        CALL    ERASE_PHANTOM           ;Erase at current position
        DEC     PHANTOM_CURSOR_X        ;Move cursor left one column
        JNS     WASNT_AT_LEFT           ;Was not at the left side, write cursor
        MOV     PHANTOM_CURSOR_X,0      ;Was at left, so put back there
```

```
WASNT_AT_LEFT:
        CALL    WRITE_PHANTOM           ;Write the phantom cursor
        RET
PHANTOM_LEFT    ENDP


        PUBLIC  PHANTOM_RIGHT
PHANTOM_RIGHT   PROC
        CALL    ERASE_PHANTOM           ;Erase at current position
        INC     PHANTOM_CURSOR_X        ;Move cursor right one column
        CMP     PHANTOM_CURSOR_X,16     ;Was it already at the right side?
        JB      WASNT_AT_RIGHT
        MOV     PHANTOM_CURSOR_X,15     ;Was at right, so put back there
WASNT_AT_RIGHT:
        CALL    WRITE_PHANTOM           ;Write the phantom cursor
        RET
PHANTOM_RIGHT   ENDP
```

PHANTOM_LEFT and PHANTOM_RIGHT are the final versions, but you will have to change PHANTOM_UP and PHANTOM_DOWN when you begin to scroll the display.

Test Dskpatch now to see if you can move the phantom cursors around on the screen. They should move together, and stay within their own windows.

As Dskpatch stands now, you can see only the first half of a sector. In Chapter 27, you will make some additions and changes to Dskpatch so you can scroll the display to see other parts of the sector. At that time, you will change both PHANTOM_UP and PHANTOM_DOWN to scroll the screen when you try to move the cursor beyond the top or bottom of the screen. For example, when the cursor is at the bottom of the half-sector display, pushing the cursor-down key again should scroll the display up one line, adding another line at the bottom, so that you see the next 16 bytes. Scrolling is rather messy, however, so we will save these procedures until almost the end. Through Chapter 26, we will develop the editing and keyboard-input sections of Dskpatch by using only the first half sector. Now, let's go on to add editing, so you can change bytes on your display.

Simple Editing

You already have a simple keyboard-input procedure, READ_BYTE, which reads one character from the keyboard without waiting for you to press the Enter key. You will use this old test version of READ_BYTE to develop editing. In the next chapter, you will write a more sophisticated version of the procedure that waits until you press either the Enter key or a special key, such as a function or cursor key.

The editing procedure will be called EDIT_BYTE. It will change one byte both on the screen and in memory (SECTOR). EDIT_BYTE will take the character in the DL register, write it to the memory location within SECTOR that is currently pointed to by the phantom cursor, and then change the display.

DISPATCHER already has a nice niche where you can place a CALL to EDIT_BYTE. The new version of DISPATCHER in DISPATCH.ASM, with the CALL to EDIT_BYTE and the changes to go along with it, is as follows:

Listing 22-3 Changes to DISPATCHER in DISPATCH.ASM (Complete listing in DISPAT22.ASM)

```
        PUBLIC  DISPATCHER
        EXTRN   READ_BYTE:PROC, EDIT_BYTE:PROC
;---------------------------------------------------------------------;
; This is the central dispatcher.  During normal editing and viewing, ;
; this procedure reads characters from the keyboard and, if the character;
; is a command key (such as a cursor key), DISPATCHER calls the        ;
; procedures that do the actual work.  This dispatching is done for    ;
; special keys listed in the table DISPATCH_TABLE, where the procedure ;
; addresses are stored just after the key names.                      ;
;                                                                      ;
; If the character is not a special key, then it should be placed      ;
; directly into the sector buffer—this is the editing mode.           ;
;                                                                      ;
; Uses:          READ_BYTE, EDIT_BYTE                                  ;
;---------------------------------------------------------------------;
DISPATCHER      PROC
        PUSH    AX
        PUSH    BX
```

```
DISPATCH_LOOP:
        CALL    READ_BYTE               ;Read character into AL
        OR      AH,AH                   ;AX = -1 if no character read, 1
                                        ; for an extended code.
        JS      DISPATCH_LOOP           ;No character read, try again
        JNZ     SPECIAL_KEY             ;Read extended code
; do nothing with the character for now
        MOV     DL,AL
        CALL    EDIT_BYTE               ;Was normal character, edit byte
        JMP     DISPATCH_LOOP           ;Read another character

SPECIAL_KEY:
        CMP     AL,68                   ;F10—exit?
        JE      END_DISPATCH            ;Yes, leave
                                        ;Use BX to look through table
        LEA     BX,DISPATCH_TABLE
SPECIAL_LOOP:
        CMP     BYTE PTR [BX],0         ;End of table?
        JE      NOT_IN_TABLE            ;Yes, key was not in the table
        CMP     AL,[BX]                 ;Is it this table entry?
        JE      DISPATCH                ;Yes, then dispatch
        ADD     BX,3                    ;No, try next entry
        JMP     SPECIAL_LOOP            ;Check next table entry

DISPATCH:
        INC     BX                      ;Point to address of procedure
        CALL    WORD PTR [BX]           ;Call procedure
        JMP     DISPATCH_LOOP           ;Wait for another key

NOT_IN_TABLE:                           ;Do nothing, just read next character
        JMP     DISPATCH_LOOP

END_DISPATCH:
        POP     DX
        POP     BX
        POP     AX
        RET
DISPATCHER      ENDP
```

The EDIT_BYTE procedure does a lot of work almost entirely by calling other procedures; this is one feature of modular design. Modular design enables you to write complex procedures by giving a list of CALLs to other procedures that do the work. Many of the procedures in EDIT_BYTE already work with a character in the DL register, so the only instruction other than a CALL (or PUSH, POP) is the LEA instruction to set the address of the prompt for WRITE_PROMPT_LINE. Most of the procedure calls in EDIT_BYTE are for updating the display when you edit a byte. You will see the other details of EDIT_BYTE when you come to the procedure listing.

Because EDIT_BYTE changes the byte on-screen, you need the procedure WRITE_TO_MEMORY to change the byte in SECTOR. WRITE_TO_MEMORY uses the coordinates in PHANTOM_CURSOR_X and PHANTOM_CURSOR_Y to calculate the offset into SECTOR of the phantom cursor. Then it writes the character (byte) in the DL register to the correct byte within SECTOR. The new file, EDITOR.ASM, which contains the final versions of both EDIT_BYTE and WRITE_TO_MEMORY is as follows:

Listing 22-4 The new file EDITOR.ASM (Complete listing in EDITOR22.ASM)

```
.MODEL   SMALL

.CODE

.DATA
         EXTRN    SECTOR:BYTE
         EXTRN    SECTOR_OFFSET:WORD
         EXTRN    PHANTOM_CURSOR_X:BYTE
         EXTRN    PHANTOM_CURSOR_Y:BYTE
.CODE
;-----------------------------------------------------------------;
; This procedure writes one byte to SECTOR, at the memory location ;
; pointed to by the phantom cursor.                                ;
;                                                                  ;
; On entry:      DL     Byte to write to SECTOR                    ;
;                                                                  ;
; The offset is calculated by                                     ;
;   OFFSET = SECTOR_OFFSET + (16 * PHANTOM_CURSOR_Y) + PHANTOM_CURSOR_X ;
;                                                                  ;
; Reads:         PHANTOM_CURSOR_X, PHANTOM_CURSOR_Y, SECTOR_OFFSET ;
; Writes:        SECTOR                                            ;
;-----------------------------------------------------------------;
```

```
WRITE_TO_MEMORY PROC
        PUSH    AX
        PUSH    BX
        PUSH    CX
        MOV     BX,SECTOR_OFFSET
        MOV     AL,PHANTOM_CURSOR_Y
        XOR     AH,AH
        MOV     CL,4                    ;Multiply PHANTOM_CURSOR_Y by 16
        SHL     AX,CL
        ADD     BX,AX                   ;BX = SECTOR_OFFSET + (16 * Y)
        MOV     AL,PHANTOM_CURSOR_X
        XOR     AH,AH
        ADD     BX,AX                   ;That's the address!
        MOV     SECTOR[BX],DL           ;Now, store the byte
        POP     CX
        POP     BX
        POP     AX
        RET
WRITE_TO_MEMORY ENDP


        PUBLIC  EDIT_BYTE
        EXTRN   SAVE_REAL_CURSOR:PROC, RESTORE_REAL_CURSOR:PROC
        EXTRN   MOV_TO_HEX_POSITION:PROC, MOV_TO_ASCII_POSITION:PROC
        EXTRN   WRITE_PHANTOM:PROC, WRITE_PROMPT_LINE:PROC
        EXTRN   CURSOR_RIGHT:PROC, WRITE_HEX:PROC, WRITE_CHAR:PROC
.DATA
        EXTRN   EDITOR_PROMPT:BYTE
.CODE
;-----------------------------------------------------------------;
; This procedure changes a byte in memory and on the screen.      ;
;                                                                 ;
; On entry:     DL      Byte to write into SECTOR, and change on screen ;
;                                                                 ;
; Uses:         SAVE_REAL_CURSOR, RESTORE_REAL_CURSOR             ;
;               MOV_TO_HEX_POSITION, MOV_TO_ASCII_POSITION        ;
;               WRITE_PHANTOM, WRITE_PROMPT_LINE, CURSOR_RIGHT    ;
;               WRITE_HEX, WRITE_CHAR, WRITE_TO_MEMORY            ;
; Reads:        EDITOR_PROMPT                                     ;
;-----------------------------------------------------------------;
EDIT_BYTE       PROC
        PUSH    DX
        CALL    SAVE_REAL_CURSOR
        CALL    MOV_TO_HEX_POSITION     ;Move to the hex number in the
        CALL    CURSOR_RIGHT            ; hex window
```

Listing 22-4 continued

```
        CALL    WRITE_HEX                ;Write the new number
        CALL    MOV_TO_ASCII_POSITION    ;Move to the char. in the ASCII
window
        CALL    WRITE_CHAR               ;Write the new character
        CALL    RESTORE_REAL_CURSOR      ;Move cursor back where it belongs
        CALL    WRITE_PHANTOM            ;Rewrite the phantom cursor
        CALL    WRITE_TO_MEMORY          ;Save this new byte in SECTOR
        LEA     DX,EDITOR_PROMPT
        CALL    WRITE_PROMPT_LINE
        POP     DX
        RET
EDIT_BYTE       ENDP


        END
```

Build this new version and see how it works. By the way, if you see a Link error message about an unresolved external, this probably means you forgot to add EDITOR.ASM to your Makefile. As you type letters in this new version, the byte under the phantom cursor should change instantly. The version of EDIT_BYTE you are using here changes a byte as soon as you type any key. This means that you cannot enter hex numbers, you can only type letters and other symbols on your keyboard. We will show you how to fix this shortcoming in the next chapters.

Summary

Dskpatch now consists of nine files: Dskpatch, Dispatch, Disp_sec, Disk_io, Video_io, Kbd_io, Phantom, Cursor, and Editor. In this chapter, you changed Dispatch and added Editor. None of these files is very long, so they do not take long to assemble. Furthermore, you can make changes fairly quickly by editing one of these files, reassembling it, and then linking all the files together again.

In terms of the current version of Dskpatch, push any key and you will see a change in the number and character under the phantom cursor. Editing works, but it is not very safe yet, since you can change a byte by hitting any key. You need to build in some type of safeguard, such as pressing Enter to change a byte, so you don't make an accidental change by leaning on the keyboard unintentionally.

In addition, the current version of READ_BYTE does not allow you to enter a hex number to change a byte. Chapter 24 will cover rewriting READ_BYTE to allow you to enter a two-digit hex number and to accept a new character by pressing the Enter key. Before rewriting READ_BYTE, you will have to write a hex input procedure. In the next chapter, you will write input procedures for both hex and decimal.

Hex and Decimal Input

In this chapter you will build two subroutines, READ_BYTE and READ_DECIMAL to read hex and decimal numbers. You will build and test these subroutines using a test program, rather than the full Dskpatch program. This makes it easier to test subroutines to make sure they are working properly.

Files altered: KBD_IO.ASM, TEST.ASM

Disk files: KBD_IO23.ASM, TEST23.ASM

23

Topics Covered

You will encounter two new procedures for keyboard input in this chapter: one procedure for reading a byte by reading either a two-digit hex number or a single character, and another for reading a word by reading the characters of a decimal number. These will be the hex and decimal input procedures.

Both procedures are sufficiently tricky that you need to use a test program with them before linking them into Dskpatch. You will be working with READ_BYTE, and a test procedure will be particularly important here because this procedure will (temporarily) lose its ability to read special function keys. Since Dskpatch relies on the function keys, there won't be a way to quit Dskpatch, therefore you will not be able to use the new READ_BYTE with Dskpatch. You will also find out why you cannot read special function keys with the READ_BYTE developed here. In the next chapter, we will modify the file to make function-key problems go away.

Hex Input

Let's begin by rewriting READ_BYTE. In the last chapter, READ_BYTE would read either an ordinary character or a special function key, and return one byte to Dispatch. Dispatch would then call the Editor if READ_BYTE read an ordinary character; EDIT_BYTE would modify the byte pointed to by the phantom cursor. If not, Dispatch looked for special function keys in DISPATCH_TABLE to see if the byte was there; if so, Dispatch called the procedure named in the table.

As mentioned in Chapter 22, the old version of READ_BYTE makes it too easy to change a byte by accident. If you unintentionally hit any key on the keyboard (other than special keys), EDIT_BYTE will change the byte under the phantom cursor. Sometimes people are clumsy, and such an inadvertent change in a sector can lead to disaster.

In this chapter, you will change READ_BYTE so that it won't return the character typed until you press the Enter key. You will add this feature by using the DOS INT 21h function 0Ah to read a string of characters. DOS only returns this string when you press Enter. Along the way, you will lose special function keys, for reasons which become apparent later.

To see exactly how your changes affect READ_BYTE, you need to write a test program to test READ_BYTE in isolation. That way, if anything strange happens you will know it is READ_BYTE and not some other part of Dskpatch. The job of writing a test procedure will be simpler if you use a few procedures from Kbd_io, Video_io, and Cursor to print information on the progress of READ_BYTE. You will use procedures such as WRITE_HEX and WRITE_DECIMAL to print the character code returned and the number of characters read. The details are in TEST.ASM as follows:

Listing 23-1 The test program TEST.ASM

```
.MODEL   SMALL

.STACK

.DATA
ENTER_PROMPT            DB       'Enter characters: ',0
CHARACTER_PROMPT        DB       'Character code: ',0
SPECIAL_CHAR_PROMPT     DB       'Special character read: ',0

.CODE
        EXTRN    WRITE_HEX:PROC, WRITE_DECIMAL:PROC
        EXTRN    WRITE_STRING:PROC, SEND_CRLF:PROC
        EXTRN    READ_BYTE:PROC

TEST_READ_BYTE  PROC
        MOV      AX,DGROUP
        MOV      DS,AX

        LEA      DX,ENTER_PROMPT
        CALL     WRITE_STRING
        CALL     READ_BYTE
        CALL     SEND_CRLF
        LEA      DX,CHARACTER_PROMPT
        CALL     WRITE_STRING
        MOV      DL,AL
        CALL     WRITE_HEX
        CALL     SEND_CRLF
        LEA      DX,SPECIAL_CHAR_PROMPT
```

continues

315

Listing 23-1 continued

```
        CALL    WRITE_STRING
        MOV     DL,AH
        XOR     DH,DH
        CALL    WRITE_DECIMAL
        CALL    SEND_CRLF

        MOV     AH,4Ch                  ;Return to DOS
        INT     21h
TEST_READ_BYTE  ENDP


        END     TEST_READ_BYTE
```

To assemble this file, link it with your current versions of Kbd_io, Video_io, and Cursor (place Test first in the LINK list), and then run Test. If you press any special function key, Test will display the scan code and a 1 to tell you that you typed a special character. Otherwise, it will display 0 (no special key).

The bulk of the instructions in TEST.ASM are for formatting. One thing you may have noticed is that we have used some of the procedures in Kbd_io, Video_io, and Cursor without regard to the other files in our project. We could do this because we were careful to place only general-purpose procedures into these files. In other words, Kbd_io, Video_io, and Cursor are designed to be used by any program you write. It is a good idea to separate your procedures by source file into general-purpose and specific procedures so you can easily reuse general-purpose procedures in new programs you write.

Let's move on to rewriting READ_BYTE to accept a string of characters. Not only will this save you from your clumsiness when you use Dskpatch, it will also allow you to use the Backspace key to delete characters if you change your mind about what you want to type. READ_BYTE will use the procedure READ_STRING to read a string of characters.

READ_STRING is very simple, almost trivial, but we have placed it in a separate procedure so you can rewrite it in the next chapter to read special function keys without having to press the Enter key. To save time, we will also add three other procedures that READ_BYTE uses: STRING_TO_UPPER, CONVERT_HEX_DIGIT, and HEX_TO_BYTE.

STRING_TO_UPPER and HEX_TO_BYTE both work on strings. STRING_TO_UPPER converts all the lowercase letters in a string to uppercase. That means you can type either f3 or F3 for the hex number F3h. By allowing hex numbers to be typed in either lower- or uppercase letters, we add user-friendliness to Dskpatch.

HEX_TO_BYTE takes the string read by DOS, after you call STRING_TO_UPPER, and converts the two-digit hex string to a single-byte number. HEX_TO_BYTE makes use of CONVERT_HEX_DIGIT to convert each hex digit to a four-bit number.

How do you ensure that DOS won't read more than two hex digits? The DOS function 0Ah reads an entire string of characters into an area of memory defined like this:

```
CHAR_NUM_LIMIT  DB      0
NUM_CHARS_READ  DB      0
STRING          DB      80 DUP (0)
```

The first byte ensures that you don't read too many characters. CHAR_NUM_LIMIT tells DOS how many characters, at most, to read. If you set this to three, DOS will read up to two characters, plus the carriage-return character (DOS always counts the carriage return). Any characters typed after that will be discarded, and DOS will beep to let you know you have passed the limit. When you press the Enter key, DOS sets the second byte, NUM_CHARS_READ, to the number of characters it actually read, not including the carriage return.

READ_BYTE and STRING_TO_UPPER both use NUM_CHARS_READ. For example, READ_BYTE checks NUM_CHARS_READ to find out whether you typed a single character or a two-digit hex number. If NUM_CHARS_READ was set to one, READ_BYTE returns a single character in the AL register. If NUM_CHARS_READ was set to two, READ_BYTE uses HEX_TO_BYTE to convert the two-digit hex string to a byte.

The new file KBD_IO.ASM, with all four new procedures is shown in Listing 23-2. (Notice that the old READ_BYTE was kept by renaming it to READ_KEY. This will be used in the next chapter.)

Listing 23-2 The New Version of KBD_IO.ASM

```
.MODEL   SMALL

.DATA

KEYBOARD_INPUT   LABEL   BYTE
CHAR_NUM_LIMIT   DB      0           ;Length of input buffer
NUM_CHARS_READ   DB      0           ;Number of characters read
CHARS            DB      80 DUP (0)  ;A buffer for keyboard input

.CODE

        PUBLIC  STRING_TO_UPPER
;----------------------------------------------------------------------;
; This procedure converts the string, using the DOS format for strings, ;
; to all uppercase letters.                                            ;
;                                                                      ;
; On entry:     DS:DX   Address of string buffer                       ;
;----------------------------------------------------------------------;
STRING_TO_UPPER PROC
        PUSH    AX
        PUSH    BX
        PUSH    CX
        MOV     BX,DX
        INC     BX                  ;Point to character count
        MOV     CL,[BX]             ;Character count in 2nd byte of buffer
        XOR     CH,CH               ;Clear upper byte of count
UPPER_LOOP:
        INC     BX                  ;Point to next character in buffer
        MOV     AL,[BX]
        CMP     AL,'a'              ;See if it is a lowercase letter
        JB      NOT_LOWER           ;Nope
        CMP     AL,'z'
        JA      NOT_LOWER
        ADD     AL,'A'-'a'          ;Convert to uppercase letter
        MOV     [BX],AL
NOT_LOWER:
        LOOP    UPPER_LOOP
        POP     CX
```

```
        POP     BX
        POP     AX
        RET
STRING_TO_UPPER ENDP


;-----------------------------------------------------------------;
; This procedure converts a character from ASCII (hex) to a nibble ;
; (4 bits).                                                        ;
;                                                                  ;
; On entry:     AL      Character to convert                       ;
; Returns:      AL      Nibble                                     ;
;               CF      Set for error, cleared otherwise           ;
;-----------------------------------------------------------------;
CONVERT_HEX_DIGIT       PROC
        CMP     AL,'0'                  ;Is it a legal digit?
        JB      BAD_DIGIT               ;Nope
        CMP     AL,'9'                  ;Not sure yet
        JA      TRY_HEX                 ;Might be hex digit
        SUB     AL,'0'                  ;Is decimal digit, convert to nibble
        CLC                             ;Clear the carry, no error
        RET
TRY_HEX:
        CMP     AL,'A'                  ;Not sure yet
        JB      BAD_DIGIT               ;Not hex
        CMP     AL,'F'                  ;Not sure yet
        JA      BAD_DIGIT               ;Not hex
        SUB     AL,'A'-10               ;Is hex, convert to nibble
        CLC                             ;Clear the carry, no error
        RET
BAD_DIGIT:
        STC                             ;Set the carry, error
        RET
CONVERT_HEX_DIGIT       ENDP


        PUBLIC  HEX_TO_BYTE
;-----------------------------------------------------------------;
; This procedure converts the two characters at DS:DX from hex to one ;
; byte.                                                            ;
;                                                                  ;
; On entry:     DS:DX   Address of two characters for hex number   ;
; Returns:      AL      Byte                                       ;
;               CF      Set for error, clear if no error           ;
;                                                                  ;
; Uses:         CONVERT_HEX_DIGIT                                  ;
;-----------------------------------------------------------------;
```

continues

Listing 23-2 continued

```
HEX_TO_BYTE     PROC
        PUSH    BX
        PUSH    CX
        MOV     BX,DX                   ;Put address in BX for indirect addr
        MOV     AL,[BX]                 ;Get first digit
        CALL    CONVERT_HEX_DIGIT
        JC      BAD_HEX                 ;Bad hex digit if carry set
        MOV     CX,4                    ;Now multiply by 16
        SHL     AL,CL
        MOV     AH,AL                   ;Retain a copy
        INC     BX                      ;Get second digit
        MOV     AL,[BX]
        CALL    CONVERT_HEX_DIGIT
        JC      BAD_HEX                 ;Bad hex digit if carry set
        OR      AL,AH                   ;Combine two nibbles
        CLC                             ;Clear carry for no error
DONE_HEX:
        POP     CX
        POP     BX
        RET
BAD_HEX:
        STC                             ;Set carry for error
        JMP     DONE_HEX
HEX_TO_BYTE     ENDP


;-------------------------------------------------------------------------;
; This is a simple version of READ_STRING.                                ;
;                                                                         ;
; On entry:     DS:DX   Address of string area                           ;
;-------------------------------------------------------------------------;
READ_STRING     PROC
        PUSH    AX
        MOV     AH,0Ah                  ;Call for buffered keyboard input
        INT     21h                     ;Call DOS function for buffered
input
        POP     AX
        RET
READ_STRING     ENDP

        PUBLIC  READ_BYTE
```

```
;------------------------------------------------------------------;
; This procedure reads either a single ASCII character or a two-digit   ;
; hex number.  This is just a test version of READ_BYTE.               ;
;                                                                   ;
; Returns:       AL       Character code (unless AH = 0)             ;
;                AH       0 if read ASCII char                       ;
;                         1 if read a special key                    ;
;                         -1 if no characters read                   ;
;                                                                   ;
; Uses:          HEX_TO_BYTE, STRING_TO_UPPER, READ_STRING           ;
; Reads:         KEYBOARD_INPUT, etc.                                ;
; Writes:        KEYBOARD_INPUT, etc.                                ;
;------------------------------------------------------------------;
READ_BYTE       PROC
        PUSH    DX
        MOV     CHAR_NUM_LIMIT,3        ;Allow only two characters (plus
                                         Enter)

        LEA     DX,KEYBOARD_INPUT
        CALL    READ_STRING
        CMP     NUM_CHARS_READ,1        ;See how many characters
        JE      ASCII_INPUT             ;Just one, treat as ASCII character
        JB      NO_CHARACTERS           ;Only Enter key hit
        CALL    STRING_TO_UPPER         ;No, convert string to uppercase
        LEA     DX,CHARS                ;Address of string to convert
        CALL    HEX_TO_BYTE             ;Convert string from hex to byte
        JC      NO_CHARACTERS           ;Error, so return 'no characters
                                         read'

        XOR     AH,AH                   ;Signal read one byte
DONE_READ:
        POP     DX
        RET
NO_CHARACTERS:
        XOR     AH,AH                   ;Set to 'no characters read'
        NOT     AH                      ;Return -1 in AH
        JMP     DONE_READ
ASCII_INPUT:
        MOV     AL,CHARS                ;Load character read
        XOR     AH,AH                   ;Signal read one byte
        JMP     DONE_READ
READ_BYTE       ENDP


        PUBLIC  READ_KEY
```

continues

Listing 23-2 continued

```
;----------------------------------------------------------------;
; This procedure reads one key from the keyboard.                ;
;                                                                ;
; Returns:        AL       Character code (unless AH = 1)        ;
;                 AH       0 if read ASCII char                  ;
;                          1 if read a special key               ;
;----------------------------------------------------------------;
READ_KEY          PROC
        XOR       AH,AH                      ;Ask for keyboard read function
        INT       16h                        ;Read character/scan code from keyboard
        OR        AL,AL                      ;Is it an extended code?
        JZ        EXTENDED_CODE              ;Yes
NOT_EXTENDED:
        XOR       AH,AH                      ;Return just the ASCII code
DONE_READING:
        RET

EXTENDED_CODE:
        MOV       AL,AH                      ;Put scan code into AL
        MOV       AH,1                       ;Signal extended code
        JMP       DONE_READING
READ_KEY          ENDP


        END
```

Reassemble Kbd_io, by using ML /C KBD_IO.ASM. Link the four files: Test, Kbd_io, Video_io, and Cursor to try this version of READ_BYTE.

At this point, you have two problems with READ_BYTE. You cannot read the special function keys with DOS function 0Ah. Try pressing a function key when you run Test. DOS doesn't return two bytes, with the first set to zero as you might expect. Instead, the test program reports 255 for the special key (1 in AH), which means READ_BYTE didn't read any characters.

You cannot read extended codes with DOS' buffered input, using function 0Ah. This function was used so you could use the Backspace key to delete characters before the Enter key was pressed. Because you cannot read special function keys, you have to write your own READ_STRING procedure. You will have to replace function 0Ah to ensure that you can press a special function key without pressing Enter.

The other problem with DOS' function 0Ah for keyboard input has to do with the line-feed character. Press Control-Enter (line feed) after you type one character, and then try the Backspace key. You will find that you're on the next line, with no way to return to the one above. The new version of Kbd_io in the next chapter will treat the line-feed character (Control-Enter) as an ordinary character; then, pressing line feed won't move the cursor to the next line.

Before moving on to fix the problems with READ_BYTE and READ_STRING, you will write a procedure to read an unsigned decimal number. The procedure will not be used in this book, but the version of Dskpatch on the companion disk does use it so that you can, for example, ask Dskpatch to display sector number 567.

Decimal Input

If you recall, the largest unsigned decimal number that can be put into a single word is 65536. When you use READ_STRING to read a string of decimal digits, you will tell DOS to read no more than six characters (five digits and a carriage return at the end). Of course, that means READ_DECIMAL will still be able to read numbers from 65536 to 99999, even though these numbers don't fit into one word. You will have to keep watch for such numbers and return an error code if READ_DECIMAL tries to read a number larger than 65535, or if it tries to read a character that is not between zero and nine.

To convert our string of up to five digits into a word, you will use multiplication as you did in Chapter 1: You will take the first (leftmost) digit, multiply it by ten, tack on the second digit, multiply it by ten, and so on. Using this method, we could, for example, write 49856 as:

$4*10^4 + 9*10^3 + 8*10^2 + 5*10^1 + 6*10^0$

or, as you will do the calculation:

$10*(10*(10*(10*4+9) +8) +5) +6$

Of course, you must watch for errors as you do these multiplications and return with the carry flag set whenever an error occurs. How do you know when you try to read a number larger than 65535? With larger numbers, the last

MUL will overflow into the DX register. The CF flag is set when DX is not zero after a word MUL, so you can use a JC (*Jump if Carry set*) instruction to handle an error. Here is READ_DECIMAL, which also checks each digit for an error (a digit that is not between 0 and 9). Place this procedure in the file KBD_IO.ASM:

Listing 23-3 Add this procedure to KBD_IO.ASM (Complete listing in KBO_IO23.ASM)

```
                PUBLIC  READ_DECIMAL
;------------------------------------------------------------------;
; This procedure takes the output buffer of READ_STRING and converts    ;
; the string of decimal digits to a word.                          ;
;                                                                  ;
; Returns:      AX      Word converted from decimal                ;
;               CF      Set if error, clear if no error            ;
;                                                                  ;
; Uses:         READ_STRING                                        ;
; Reads:        KEYBOARD_INPUT, etc.                               ;
; Writes:       KEYBOARD_INPUT, etc.                               ;
;------------------------------------------------------------------;
READ_DECIMAL    PROC
        PUSH    BX
        PUSH    CX
        PUSH    DX
        MOV     CHAR_NUM_LIMIT,6        ;Max number is 5 digits (65535)
        LEA     DX,KEYBOARD_INPUT
        CALL    READ_STRING
        MOV     CL,NUM_CHARS_READ       ;Get number of characters read
        XOR     CH,CH                   ;Set upper byte of count to 0
        CMP     CL,0                    ;Return error if no characters read
        JLE     BAD_DECIMAL_DIGIT       ;No chars read, signal error
        XOR     AX,AX                   ;Start with number set to 0
        XOR     BX,BX                   ;Start at beginning of string
CONVERT_DIGIT:
        MOV     DX,10                   ;Multiply number by 10
        MUL     DX                      ;Multiply AX by 10
        JC      BAD_DECIMAL_DIGIT       ;CF set if MUL overflowed one word
        MOV     DL,CHARS[BX]            ;Get the next digit
        SUB     DL,'0'                  ;And convert to a nibble (4 bits)
```

```
        JS      BAD_DECIMAL_DIGIT       ;Bad digit if < 0
        CMP     DL,9                    ;Is this a bad digit?
        JA      BAD_DECIMAL_DIGIT       ;Yes
        ADD     AX,DX                   ;No, so add it to number
        INC     BX                      ;Point to next character
        LOOP    CONVERT_DIGIT           ;Get the next digit
DONE_DECIMAL:
        POP     DX
        POP     CX
        POP     BX
        RET
BAD_DECIMAL_DIGIT:
        STC                             ;Set carry to signal error
        JMP     DONE_DECIMAL
READ_DECIMAL    ENDP
```

To make certain it works properly, you need to test this procedure with all the boundary conditions. A simple test program for READ_DECIMAL that uses much the same approach you used to test READ_BYTE is as follows:

Listing 23-4 Changes to TEST.ASM (Complete listing in TEST23.ASM)

```
.MODEL  SMALL

.STACK

.DATA
ENTER_PROMPT            DB      'Enter decimal number: ',0
NUMBER_READ_PROMPT      DB      'Number read: ',0
CHARACTER_PROMPT        DB      'Character code: ',0
SPECIAL_CHAR_PROMPT     DB      'Special character read: ',0

.CODE
        EXTRN   WRITE_HEX:PROC, WRITE_DECIMAL:PROC
        EXTRN   WRITE_STRING:PROC, SEND_CRLF:PROC
        EXTRN   READ_DECIMAL:PROC

TEST_READ_DECIMAL       PROC
```

continues

Listing 23-4 continued

```
          MOV     AX,DGROUP
          MOV     DS,AX

          LEA     DX,ENTER_PROMPT
          CALL    WRITE_STRING
          CALL    READ_DECIMAL
          JC      ERROR
          CALL    SEND_CRLF
          LEA     DX,NUMBER_READ_PROMPT
          CALL    WRITE_STRING
          MOV     DX,AX
          CALL    WRITE_DECIMAL
ERROR:    CALL    SEND_CRLF
          LEA     DX,SPECIAL_CHAR_PROMPT
          CALL    WRITE_STRING
          MOV     DL,AH
          XOR     DH,DH
          CALL    WRITE_DECIMAL
          CALL    SEND_CRLF

          MOV     AH,4Ch                  ;Return to DOS
          INT     21h
TEST_READ_DECIMAL       ENDP


          END     TEST_READ_DECIMAL
```

Once again, you need to link four files: Test (the preceding file), Kbd_io, Video_io, and Cursor. Try the boundary conditions, using both valid digits and invalid ones (such as A, which is not a valid decimal digit), and with such numbers as 0, 65535, and 65536. When you try a number that isn't valid, Test will exit without displaying a number after you press Enter. It only displays a number when you have typed in a valid number.

Summary

We will return to the two simple test procedures later when we discuss ways you can write your own programs. Then, you will learn how to use a slightly more advanced version of TEST.ASM to write a program that will convert numbers between hex and decimal.

Now, on to the next chapter, where you will write improved versions of READ_BYTE and READ_STRING.

Improved Keyboard Input

In this chapter you will concentrate on keyboard input where you will build a new version of READ_STRING. This new version will be able to read strings as well as special keys, such as cursor and function keys. At the end of this chapter, you will be able to use function and cursor keys in Dskpatch. Dskpatch will also require you to press Enter before it changes any bytes in SECTOR.

Files altered: KBD_IO.ASM

Disk file: KBO_IO24.ASM

24

Topics Covered

A New READ_STRING

User vs Programmer Friendly

Summary

We mentioned that we would present the development of Dskpatch just as we first wrote it—including bugs and clumsily designed procedures, some of which you have already seen. In this chapter, we will write a new version of READ_BYTE, and it will place a subtle bug into Dskpatch. In the next chapter, we will find a can of Raid to exorcise this small bug, but see if you can find it yourself first. (Hint: Carefully check all the boundary conditions for READ_BYTE when it's attached to Dskpatch.)

A New READ_STRING

The modular-design philosophy calls for short procedures so that no single procedure is too difficult to understand. The new version of READ_STRING will be an example of a procedure which is too long. It should be rewritten with more procedures, but we will leave this rewrite to you. Part III of this book is quickly drawing to an end, and you need to write a few more procedures before Dskpatch is a useful program. Right now, you can still edit only the first half of any sector, and you cannot write this sector back to the disk yet.

In this chapter you will give READ_STRING a new procedure, BACK_SPACE, to emulate the function of the Backspace key found in the DOS function 0Ah. When you press the Backspace key, BACK_SPACE will erase the last character typed from both the screen and the string in memory.

On screen, BACK_SPACE will erase the character by moving the cursor left one character, writing a space over it, and then moving left one character again. This sequence will perform the same backspace deletion provided by DOS.

In the buffer, BACK_SPACE will erase a character by changing the buffer pointer, DS:SI+BX, so it points to the next lower byte in memory. In other words, BACK_SPACE will simply decrement BX: (BX = BX - 1). The character will still be in the buffer, but your program won't see it. READ_STRING tells you how many characters it has read; if you try to read more than this number from the buffer, you will see the characters you erased. Otherwise, you won't. You have to be careful not to erase any characters when the buffer is empty. Remember that your string-data area appeared as follows:

```
CHAR_NUM_LIMIT  DB      0
NUM_CHARS_READ  DB      0
STRING          DB      80 DUP (0)
```

The string buffer starts at the second byte of this data area, or at an *offset* of 2 from the start. So BACK_SPACE won't erase a character if BX is set to 2 which is the the start of the string buffer, because the buffer is empty when BX equals 2. Place BACK_SPACE into KBD_IO.ASM as follows:

Listing 24-1 Procedure added to KBD_IO.ASM (Complete listing in KBO_IO24.ASM)

```
        PUBLIC  BACK_SPACE
        EXTRN   WRITE_CHAR:PROC
;-----------------------------------------------------------------------;
; This procedure deletes characters, one at a time, from the buffer and;
; the screen when the buffer is not empty. BACK_SPACE simply returns    ;
; when the buffer is empty.                                             ;
;                                                                       ;
; On entry:     DS:SI+BX        Most recent character still in buffer   ;
; Returns:      DS:SI+BX        Points to next most recent character    ;
;                                                                       ;
; Uses:         WRITE_CHAR                                              ;
;-----------------------------------------------------------------------;
BACK_SPACE      PROC                    ;Delete one character
        PUSH    AX
        PUSH    DX
        CMP     BX,2                    ;Is buffer empty?
        JE      END_BS                  ;Yes, read the next character
        DEC     BX                      ;Remove one character from buffer
        MOV     AH,2                    ;Remove character from screen
        MOV     DL,BS
        INT     21h
        MOV     DL,20h                  ;Write space there
        CALL    WRITE_CHAR
        MOV     DL,BS                   ;Back up again
        INT     21h
END_BS: POP     DX
        POP     AX
        RET
BACK_SPACE      ENDP
```

Let's move on to the new version of READ_STRING. The listing you will see is for only one procedure. READ_STRING is probably the longest procedure (maybe too long) you have written because it is complicated by so many possible conditions.

READ_STRING does so many things because a few more features were added. If you press the Escape key, READ_STRING clears the string buffer and remove all the characters from the screen. DOS also erases all the characters in the string buffer when you press Escape, but it does not erase any characters from the screen. Instead, it simply writes a backslash (\) character at the end of the line and moves to the next line. Our version of READ_STRING will be more versatile than the DOS READ_STRING function.

READ_STRING uses three special keys: the Backspace, Escape, and Enter keys. You could write the ASCII codes for each of these keys in READ_STRING whenever you need them; instead add a few definitions to the beginning of KBD_IO.ASM to make READ_STRING more readable. The definitions are as follows:

Listing 24-2 Additions to KBD_IO.ASM

```
.MODEL  SMALL


BS      EQU     8                       ;Backspace character
CR      EQU     13                      ;Carriage-return character
ESCAPE  EQU     27                      ;Escape character


.DATA
              .
              .
              .
```

Here is READ_STRING. Although it is rather long, you can see from the listing that it is not very complicated. Replace the old version of READ_STRING in KBD_IO.ASM with the following new version:

Listing 24-3 The new READ_STRING in KBD_IO.ASM

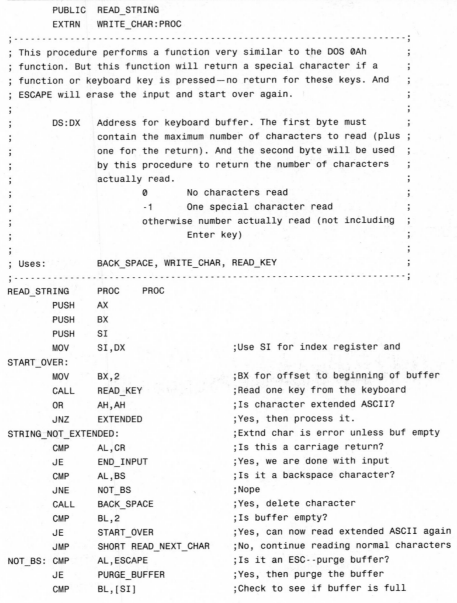

```
        PUBLIC  READ_STRING
        EXTRN   WRITE_CHAR:PROC
;-------------------------------------------------------------------;
; This procedure performs a function very similar to the DOS 0Ah    ;
; function. But this function will return a special character if a  ;
; function or keyboard key is pressed—no return for these keys. And ;
; ESCAPE will erase the input and start over again.                 ;
;                                                                   ;
;       DS:DX   Address for keyboard buffer. The first byte must    ;
;               contain the maximum number of characters to read (plus ;
;               one for the return). And the second byte will be used ;
;               by this procedure to return the number of characters ;
;               actually read.                                      ;
;                       0       No characters read                  ;
;                       -1      One special character read          ;
;               otherwise number actually read (not including       ;
;                       Enter key)                                  ;
;                                                                   ;
; Uses:         BACK_SPACE, WRITE_CHAR, READ_KEY                    ;
;-------------------------------------------------------------------;
READ_STRING     PROC    PROC
        PUSH    AX
        PUSH    BX
        PUSH    SI
        MOV     SI,DX               ;Use SI for index register and
START_OVER:
        MOV     BX,2                ;BX for offset to beginning of buffer
        CALL    READ_KEY            ;Read one key from the keyboard
        OR      AH,AH               ;Is character extended ASCII?
        JNZ     EXTENDED            ;Yes, then process it.
STRING_NOT_EXTENDED:                ;Extnd char is error unless buf empty
        CMP     AL,CR               ;Is this a carriage return?
        JE      END_INPUT           ;Yes, we are done with input
        CMP     AL,BS               ;Is it a backspace character?
        JNE     NOT_BS              ;Nope
        CALL    BACK_SPACE          ;Yes, delete character
        CMP     BL,2                ;Is buffer empty?
        JE      START_OVER          ;Yes, can now read extended ASCII again
        JMP     SHORT READ_NEXT_CHAR ;No, continue reading normal characters
NOT_BS: CMP     AL,ESCAPE           ;Is it an ESC--purge buffer?
        JE      PURGE_BUFFER        ;Yes, then purge the buffer
        CMP     BL,[SI]             ;Check to see if buffer is full
```

continues

333

Listing 24-3 continued

```
        JA      BUFFER_FULL             ;Buffer is full
        MOV     [SI+BX],AL              ;Else save char in buffer
        INC     BX                      ;Point to next free character in buffer
        PUSH    DX
        MOV     DL,AL                   ;Echo character to screen
        CALL    WRITE_CHAR
        POP     DX
READ_NEXT_CHAR:
        CALL    READ_KEY
        OR      AH,AH                   ;An extended ASCII char is not valid
                                        ; when the buffer is not empty
        JZ      STRING_NOT_EXTENDED     ;Char is valid

;-------------------------------------------------;
; Signal an error condition by sending a beep     ;
; character to the display: chr$(7).              ;
;-------------------------------------------------;
SIGNAL_ERROR:
        PUSH    DX
        MOV     DL,7                    ;Sound the bell by writing chr$(7)
        MOV     AH,2
        INT     21h
        POP     DX
        JMP     SHORT READ_NEXT_CHAR    ;Now read next character

;-------------------------------------------------;
; Empty the string buffer and erase all the       ;
; characters displayed on the screen.             ;
;-------------------------------------------------;
PURGE_BUFFER:
        PUSH    CX
        MOV     CL,[SI]                 ;Backspace over maximum number of
        XOR     CH,CH
PURGE_LOOP:                             ; characters in buffer. BACK_SPACE
        CALL    BACK_SPACE              ; will keep the cursor from moving too
        LOOP    PURGE_LOOP              ; far back
        POP     CX
        JMP     START_OVER              ;Can now read extended ASCII characters
                                        ; since the buffer is empty

;-------------------------------------------------;
; The buffer was full, so can't read another      ;
; character. Send a beep to alert user of         ;
```

```
; buffer-full condition.                    ;
;--------------------------------------------;
BUFFER_FULL:
        JMP     SHORT SIGNAL_ERROR    ;If buffer full, just beep


;--------------------------------------------;
; Read the extended ASCII code and place this ;
; in the buffer as the only character, then   ;
; return -1 as the number of characters read. ;
;--------------------------------------------;
EXTENDED:                             ;Read an extended ASCII code
        MOV     [SI+2],AL             ;Place just this char in buffer
        MOV     BL,0FFh               ;Num chars read = -1 for special
        JMP     SHORT END_STRING


;--------------------------------------------;
; Save the count of the number of characters  ;
; read and return.                            ;
;--------------------------------------------;
END_INPUT:                            ;Done with input
        SUB     BL,2                  ;Count of characters read
END_STRING:
        MOV     [SI+1],BL             ;Return number of chars read
        POP     SI
        POP     BX
        POP     AX
        RET
READ_STRING     ENDP
```

Stepping through the procedure, you can see that READ_STRING first checks to see if you pressed a special function key. It allows you to do so only when the string is empty. For example, if you press the F3 key after pressing the *a* key, READ_STRING will ignore the F3 key and beep to tell you that you pressed a special key at the wrong time (we will fix this problem later in the chapter). You can, however, press Escape, then F3, because the Escape key causes READ_STRING to clear the string buffer.

If READ_STRING reads a carriage-return character, it places the number of characters it read into the second byte of the string area and returns. The new version of READ_BYTE looks at this byte to see how many characters READ_STRING actually read.

Next, READ_STRING checks to see if you typed a backspace character. If so, it CALLs BACK_SPACE to erase one character. If the string buffer becomes empty (BX becomes equal to 2—the start of the string buffer), then READ_STRING goes back to the start, where it can read a special key. Otherwise it just reads the next character.

Finally, READ_STRING checks for the ESCAPE character. BACK_SPACE erases characters only when there are characters in the buffer. You can clear the string buffer by calling the BACK_SPACE procedure CHAR_NUM_LIMIT times, because READ_STRING can never read more than CHAR_NUM_LIMIT characters. Any other character is stored in the string buffer and echoed to the screen with WRITE_CHAR, unless the buffer is full.

In the last chapter, READ_BYTE was changed in such a way that it couldn't read special function keys. You need to add only a few lines here to allow READ_BYTE to work with the new version of READ_STRING, which can read special function keys. The changes you need to make to READ_BYTE in KBD_IO.ASM are as follows:

Listing 24-4 Changes to READ_BYTE in KBD_IO.ASM

```
        PUBLIC   READ_BYTE
;------------------------------------------------------------------;
; This procedure reads a single ASCII character of a hex number.   ;
;                                                                  ;
; Returns:       AL      Character code (unless AH = 0)            ;
;                AH      0 if read ASCII char or hex number        ;
;                        1 if read a special key                  ;
;                        -1 if no characters read                 ;
;                                                                  ;
; Uses:          HEX_TO_BYTE, STRING_TO_UPPER, READ_STRING         ;
; Reads:         KEYBOARD_INPUT, etc.                             ;
; Writes:        KEYBOARD_INPUT, etc.                             ;
;------------------------------------------------------------------;
READ_BYTE       PROC
        PUSH    DX
        MOV     CHAR_NUM_LIMIT,3        ;Allow only two characters (plus Enter)
        LEA     DX,KEYBOARD_INPUT
        CALL    READ_STRING
        CMP     NUM_CHARS_READ,1       ;See how many characters
        JE      ASCII_INPUT            ;Just one, treat as ASCII character
        JB      NO_CHARACTERS          ;Only Enter key hit
```

```
            CMP       BYTE PTR NUM_CHARS_READ,0FFh      ;Special function key?
            JE        SPECIAL_KEY                        ;Yes
            CALL      STRING_TO_UPPER                    ;No, convert string to uppercase
            LEA       DX,CHARS                           ;Address of string to convert
            CALL      HEX_TO_BYTE                        ;Convert string from hex to byte
            JC        NO_CHARACTERS                      ;Error, so return 'no characters read'
            XOR       AH,AH                              ;Signal read one byte
DONE_READ:
            POP       DX
            RET
NO_CHARACTERS:
            XOR       AH,AH                              ;Set to 'no characters read'
            NOT       AH                                 ;Return -1 in AH
            JMP       DONE_READ
ASCII_INPUT:
            MOV       AL,CHARS                           ;Load character read
            XOR       AH,AH                              ;Signal read one character
            JMP       DONE_READ
SPECIAL_KEY:
            MOV       AL,CHARS[0]                        ;Return the scan code
            MOV       AH,1                               ;Signal special key with 1
            JMP       DONE_READ
READ_BYTE   ENDP
```

Dskpatch, with the new versions of READ_BYTE and READ_STRING, should be much nicer to use. Unfortunately, there is a bug here. Try to find it by running Dskpatch and by trying all the boundary conditions for READ_BYTE and HEX_TO_BYTE. (Remember that there are nine files that must be linked and converted to an EXE program: Dskpatch, Dispatch, Disp_sec, Disk_io, Video_io, Kbd_io, Phantom, Cursor, and Editor.)

User *vs* Programmer Friendly

We made a design decision in READ_STRING that made Dskpatch easier to write, but it is not friendlier to the user. Run Dskpatch and try the following: type a letter, such as *f,* then press one of the cursor keys. Dskpatch will beep at you because the READ_STRING procedure does not return control once you have started entering a hex number until you press either the Escape or the

Enter key. Unfortunately, the user probably won't know why Dskpatch is beeping at them and that creates a problem. Users also tend to become rather irritated when programs beep at them for no apparent reason.

Programs like this are *Programmer Friendly* since they are simple for the programmer to write. *User Friendly* programs, on the other hand, often require a considerable effort in programming to make them feel simple and natural. A few words of advice on writing user-friendly programs are as follows:

- Avoid beeps except to alert the user of a critical error condition (such as a disk error). There is rarely cause to beep when you press a key that isn't allowed.

- Try to keep in mind what users will want, rather than what is simple to write. Sometimes they will be one and the same, but more often than not, you will find that you have to expend additional effort and development time to write user-friendly programs.

- Try to write modeless programs. By doing so you will eliminate many error conditions such as the one we placed (artificially) into READ_STRING.

- Try out your ideas on real users, not just on other programmers who can easily figure out how your program really works. Users don't want to understand your assumptions; they want your programs to be "obvious." If a user has trouble running your program, try to understand why so you can make it easier to use.

These words of advice just scratch the surface on the issue of writing user-friendly programs. There are a number of books devoted entirely to design; we have recommended a few books in the bibliography that you will find in the last chapter of this book.

The real problem with READ_STRING is that it is modal. As soon as you type one character, you cannot do anything else until you finish typing or press Esc. What READ_STRING should do is only slightly different from what it is doing now. As soon as READ_STRING sees an extended character, it should clear the buffer and return the extended character. That way you won't need to finish entering a string before you can press an extended key. In other words, you can type a letter and then press any of the cursor keys and Dskpatch will move the cursor. A new version of READ_STRING that removes the modal behavior from the previous version is as follows:

Listing 24-5 Changes to READ_STRING in KBD_IO.ASM

```
READ_STRING     PROC      PROC
        PUSH    AX
        PUSH    BX
        PUSH    SI
        MOV     SI,DX               ;Use SI for index register and

START_OVER:
        MOV     BX,2                ;BX for offset to beginning of buffer

READ_LOOP:
        CALL    READ_KEY            ;Read one key from the keyboard
        OR      AH,AH               ;Is character extended ASCII?
        JNZ     EXTENDED            ;Yes, then process it.
STRING_NOT_EXTENDED:                ;No, see what char it is
        CMP     AL,CR               ;Is this a carriage return?
        JE      END_INPUT           ;Yes, we are done with input
        CMP     AL,BS               ;Is it a backspace character?
        JNE     NOT_BS              ;Nope
        CALL    BACK_SPACE          ;Yes, delete character
        JMP     READ_LOOP           ;Read the next character
        JMP     SHORT READ_NEXT_CHAR ;No, continue reading normal characters

NOT_BS: CMP     AL,ESCAPE           ;Is it an ESC--purge buffer?
        JE      PURGE_BUFFER        ;Yes, then purge the buffer
        JNE     NOT_ESC             ;No, put character into buffer
        CALL    PURGE_BUFFER        ;Yes, remove all characters from buffer
        JMP     READ_LOOP           ;Start reading characters again

NOT_ESC:
        CMP     BL,[SI]             ;Check to see if buffer is full
        JA      BUFFER_FULL         ;Buffer is full
        MOV     [SI+BX],AL          ;Else save char in buffer
        INC     BX                  ;Point to next free character in buffer
        PUSH    DX
        MOV     DL,AL               ;Echo character to screen
        CALL    WRITE_CHAR
        POP     DX
        JMP     READ_LOOP           ;Read the next character
```

continues

Listing 24-5 continued

```
READ_NEXT_CHAR:
        CALL    READ_KEY
        OR      AH,AH                   ;An extended ASCII char is not valid
                                        ; when the buffer is not empty
        JZ      STRING_NOT_EXTENDED     ;Char is valid

;-------------------------------------------------;
; Signal an error condition by sending a beep     ;
; character to the display: chr$(7).              ;
;-------------------------------------------------;
SIGNAL_ERROR:
        PUSH    DX
        MOV     DL,7                    ;Sound the bell by writing chr$(7)
        MOV     AH,2
        INT     21h
        POP     DX
        JMP     SHORT READ_LOOP         ;Now read next character

;-------------------------------------------------;
; Empty the string buffer and erase all the       ;
; characters displayed on the screen.             ;
;-------------------------------------------------;
PURGE_BUFFER:
        PUSH    CX
        MOV     CL,[SI]                 ;Backspace over maximum number of
        XOR     CH,CH
PURGE_LOOP:                             ; characters in buffer. BACK_SPACE
        CALL    BACK_SPACE              ; will keep the cursor from moving too
        LOOP    PURGE_LOOP              ; far back
        POP     CX
        JMP     START_OVER              ;Can now read extended ASCII characters
                                        ; since the buffer is empty

;-------------------------------------------------;
; The buffer was full, so can't read another      ;
; character. Send a beep to alert user of         ;
; buffer-full condition.                          ;
;-------------------------------------------------;
BUFFER_FULL:
        JMP     SHORT SIGNAL_ERROR      ;If buffer full, just beep
```

```
;------------------------------------------------;
; Read the extended ASCII code and place this    ;
; in the buffer as the only character, then      ;
; return -1 as the number of characters read.    ;
;------------------------------------------------;
EXTENDED:                               ;Read an extended ASCII code
        CALL    PURGE_BUFFER            ;Remove any chars from buffer
        MOV     [SI+2],AL               ;Place just this char in buffer
        MOV     BL,0FFh                 ;Num chars read = -1 for special
        JMP     SHORT END_STRING


;------------------------------------------------;
; Save the count of the number of characters     ;
; read and return.                               ;
;------------------------------------------------;
END_INPUT:                              ;Done with input
        SUB     BL,2                    ;Count of characters read
END_STRING:
        MOV     [SI+1],BL               ;Return number of chars read
        POP     SI
        POP     BX
        POP     AX
        RET
READ_STRING     ENDP
```

```
;----------------------------------------------------------------;
; This subroutine is used by READ_STRING to clear the contents of the   ;
; input buffer.                                                  ;
;                                                                ;
;       DS:SI   Points to the input buffer for READ_STRING       ;
;----------------------------------------------------------------;
PURGE_BUFFER    PROC
        PUSH    CX
        MOV     CL,[SI]                 ;Backspace over maximum number of
        XOR     CH,CH
PURGE_LOOP:                             ; characters in buffer. BACK_SPACE
        CALL    BACK_SPACE              ; will keep the cursor from moving too
        LOOP    PURGE_LOOP              ; far back
        POP     CX
        RET
PURGE_BUFFER    ENDP
```

341

You will notice that more code was removed than added. This is a good sign because solving a problem by simplifying the code results in more reliable as well as usable programs.

Summary

You wrote a new version of READ_STRING in this chapter that allowed you to read special characters again, in addition to strings. With the exception of the small bug that you will find and fix in the next chapter, READ_STRING works as advertised. This discussion covered several problems with READ_STRING, one being that it is too long and complicated and should be rewritten to be more modular.

Finally, you learned that READ_STRING was not user friendly since it beeped when you tried to move the cursor after you have started to type a hex number. You fixed both of these problems at the end of this chapter. Now it is time to remove the bug that lurks in Dskpatch.

In Search of Bugs

In this chapter you will learn how to fix a small bug that appeared in Dskpatch when you put all the pieces together. See if you can find the bug by trying all the boundary conditions for the hex input prompt.

Files altered: DISPATCH.ASM

Disk file: DISPAT25.ASM

25

Topics Covered

Fixing DISPATCHER

Summary

If you try the new version of Dskpatch with *ag*, which is not a valid hex number, you will notice that Dskpatch does not do anything when you press the Enter key. Since the string *ag* is not a hex number, there is nothing wrong with Dskpatch ignoring it, but the program should, at least, erase it from the screen.

This error is the sort we can find only by thoroughly checking the boundary conditions of a program; not just the pieces, but the entire program. The bug here isn't the fault of READ_BYTE, even though it appeared when you rewrote that procedure. Rather, the problem is in the way we wrote DISPATCHER and EDIT_BYTE.

EDIT_BYTE is designed so it calls WRITE_PROMPT_LINE to rewrite the editor prompt line and clear the rest of the line. This will remove any character you typed. If you type a string like *ag*, READ_BYTE reports that it read a string of zero length, and DISPATCH does not call EDIT_BYTE. What is the solution?

Fixing DISPATCHER

There are actually two ways to solve this problem. The best solution would be to rewrite Dskpatch to be more modular, and to redesign DISPATCHER. We won't do that. Remember: Programs are never complete, but you have to stop somewhere. Instead, you will add a fix to DISPATCHER so it will rewrite the prompt line whenever READ_BYTE reads a string of zero length. Modifications to DISPATCHER (in DISPATCH.ASM) to fix the bug are as follows:

Listing 25-1 Changes to DISPATCHER in DISPATCH.ASM (Complete listing in DISPAT25.ASM)

```
        PUBLIC  DISPATCHER
        EXTRN   READ_BYTE:PROC, EDIT_BYTE:PROC
        EXTRN   WRITE_PROMPT_LINE:PROC
.DATA
        EXTRN   EDITOR_PROMPT:BYTE
.CODE
```

```
;-----------------------------------------------------------------;
; This is the central dispatcher.  During normal editing and viewing,    ;
; this procedure reads characters from the keyboard and, if the character;
; is a command key (such as a cursor key), DISPATCHER calls the          ;
; procedures that do the actual work.  This dispatching is done for      ;
; special keys listed in the table DISPATCH_TABLE, where the procedure   ;
; addresses are stored just after the key names.                         ;
;    If the character is not a special key, then it should be placed     ;
; directly into the sector buffer--this is the editing mode.             ;
;                                                                        ;
; Uses:          READ_BYTE, EDIT_BYTE, WRITE_PROMPT_LINE                 ;
; Reads:         EDITOR_PROMPT                                           ;
;-----------------------------------------------------------------;
DISPATCHER      PROC
        PUSH    AX
        PUSH    BX
        PUSH    DX
DISPATCH_LOOP:
        CALL    READ_BYTE               ;Read character into AX
        OR      AH,AH                   ;AX = -1 if no character read, 1
                                        ; for an extended code.
        JS      NO_CHARS_READ           ;No character read, try again
        JNZ     SPECIAL_KEY             ;Read extended code
        MOV     DL,AL
        CALL    EDIT_BYTE               ;Was normal character, edit byte
        JMP     DISPATCH_LOOP           ;Read another character

SPECIAL_KEY:
        CMP     AL,68                   ;F10--exit?
        JE      END_DISPATCH            ;Yes, leave
                                        ;Use BX to look through table
        LEA     BX,DISPATCH_TABLE
SPECIAL_LOOP:
        CMP     BYTE PTR [BX],0         ;End of table?
        JE      NOT_IN_TABLE            ;Yes, key was not in the table
        CMP     AL,[BX]                 ;Is it this table entry?
        JE      DISPATCH                ;Yes, then dispatch
        ADD     BX,3                    ;No, try next entry
        JMP     SPECIAL_LOOP            ;Check next table entry

DISPATCH:
        INC     BX                      ;Point to address of procedure
```

continues

347

Listing 25-1 continued

```
          CALL     WORD PTR [BX]          ;Call procedure
          JMP      DISPATCH_LOOP          ;Wait for another key

NOT_IN_TABLE:                             ;Do nothing, just read next character
          JMP      DISPATCH_LOOP

NO_CHARS_READ:
          LEA      DX,EDITOR_PROMPT
          CALL     WRITE_PROMPT_LINE      ;Erase any invalid characters typed
          JMP      DISPATCH_LOOP          ;Try again

END_DISPATCH:
          POP      DX
          POP      BX
          POP      AX
          RET
DISPATCHER         ENDP
```

This bug fix does not create any great problems, but it does make DIS-PATCHER slightly less elegant. Elegance is a virtue to strive for. Elegance and clarity often go hand in hand, and the rules of modular design are aimed at increasing elegance.

Summary

DISPATCHER is elegant because it is such a simple solution to a problem. Rather than using many comparisons for each special character you might type, you built a table that can be searched. Doing so made DISPATCHER simpler and more reliable than a program containing different instructions for each possible condition that might arise. By adding the small fix, we complicated DISPATCHER; not by much in this case, but some bugs might require you to really complicate a procedure.

If you find yourself adding fixes that make a procedure too complicated, rewrite whichever procedures you must to remove this complexity. Always check the boundary conditions before and after you add a procedure to your main program. You will save yourself a lot of debugging effort if you do.

We cannot overemphasize the importance of testing procedures with boundary conditions and of following the rules of modular design. Both techniques lead to better and more reliable programs. The next chapter will cover another method for debugging programs.

Writing Modified Sectors

In this chapter you will learn how to build and navigate a road map for your programs. You will also learn how to use the CodeView and Turbo Debugger source-level debuggers to trace through your programs. You will also add a new function to Dskpatch so it can write sectors to the disk.

Files altered: DISPATCH.ASM, DISK_IO.ASM

Disk files: DISPAT26.ASM, DISK_I26.ASM, MAKEFILE, LINKINFO

26

Topics Covered

In this chapter, you will build a procedure to write a modified sector back to disk. In the next chapter, you will write a procedure to show the second half of a sector.

Writing to the Disk

Writing a modified sector back to the disk can be disastrous if it is not done intentionally. All of Dskpatch's functions have depended on the function keys F3, F4, and F10, and on the cursor keys. But any of these keys could be pressed quite by accident. Fortunately, you can use the shifted keys without this happening. We have chosen the shifted F2 key for writing a disk sector because F2 is often used in programs to save changes. This will prevent you from writing a sector back to disk unless you really want to.

The following changes should be made to DISPATCH.ASM to add WRITE_SECTOR to the table.

Listing 26-1 Changes to DISPATCH.ASM (Complete listing in DISPAT26.ASM)

```
.CODE
        EXTRN   NEXT_SECTOR:PROC                        ;In DISK_IO.ASM
        EXTRN   PREVIOUS_SECTOR:PROC                    ;In DISK_IO.ASM
        EXTRN   PHANTOM_UP:PROC, PHANTOM_DOWN:PROC      ;In PHANTOM.ASM
        EXTRN   PHANTOM_LEFT:PROC, PHANTOM_RIGHT:PROC
        EXTRN   WRITE_SECTOR:PROC                       ;In DISK_IO.ASM
.DATA
;--------------------------------------------------------------------;
; This table contains the legal extended ASCII keys and the addresses ;
; of the procedures that should be called when each key is pressed.   ;
;                                                                     ;
; The format of the table is                                         ;
;               DB      72              ;Extended code for cursor up  ;
;               DW      OFFSET PHANTOM_UP                             ;
;--------------------------------------------------------------------;
DISPATCH_TABLE  LABEL   BYTE
        DB      61                              ;F3
        DW      OFFSET _TEXT:PREVIOUS_SECTOR
        DB      62                              ;F4
```

```
        DW      OFFSET _TEXT:NEXT_SECTOR
        DB      72                              ;Cursor up
        DW      OFFSET _TEXT:PHANTOM_UP
        DB      80                              ;Cursor down
        DW      OFFSET _TEXT:PHANTOM_DOWN
        DB      75                              ;Cursor left
        DW      OFFSET _TEXT:PHANTOM_LEFT
        DB      77                              ;Cursor right
        DW      OFFSET _TEXT:PHANTOM_RIGHT
        DB      85                              ;Shift F2
        DW      OFFSET _TEXT:WRITE_SECTOR
        DB      0                               ;End of the table
```

WRITE_SECTOR itself is almost identical to READ_SECTOR. The only change is that you wish to write, rather than read, a sector. Whereas the INT 25h asks DOS to read one sector, its companion function, INT 26h, asks DOS to write a sector to the disk. Place WRITE_Sector into DISK_IO.ASM as follows:

Listing 26-2 Procedure added to DISK_IO.ASM (Complete listing in DISK_I26.ASM)

```
        PUBLIC  WRITE_SECTOR
;-----------------------------------------------------------------;
; This procedure writes the sector back to the disk.              ;
;                                                                 ;
; Reads:      DISK_DRIVE_NO, CURRENT_SECTOR_NO, SECTOR            ;
;-----------------------------------------------------------------;
WRITE_SECTOR    PROC
        PUSH    AX
        PUSH    BX
        PUSH    CX
        PUSH    DX
        MOV     AL,DISK_DRIVE_NO        ;Drive number
        MOV     CX,1                    ;Write 1 sector
        MOV     DX,CURRENT_SECTOR_NO    ;Logical sector
        LEA     BX,SECTOR
        INT     26h                     ;Write the sector to disk
        POPF                            ;Discard the flag information
        POP     DX
```

continues

353

Listing 26-2 continued

```
            POP     CX
            POP     BX
            POP     AX
            RET
WRITE_SECTOR    ENDP
```

Now reassemble both Dispatch and Disk_io, but don't try Dskpatch's write function just yet. Find an old disk you don't need and put it in drive A. Run Dskpatch, which will read the first sector from your scratch disk in drive A. Before you go on, make sure this is a scratch disk you have no qualms about destroying.

Change one byte in your sector display. Make a note of the one you changed and what value it had before. Then press the shifted F2 key. You will see the red drive light come on; you have just written a modified sector back to drive A.

Next, press F4 to read the next sector (sector 1), then F3 to read the previous sector (your original sector, number 0). You should see the modified sector back again. Restore the number you changed in this sector and write it back to Drive A to restore the integrity of your scratch disk.

More Debugging Techniques

What would happen if you had made a small error in the program? Dskpatch is large enough that you might have problems using Debug to find the bug. In addition, Dskpatch is composed of nine different files that must be linked to form DSKPATCH.EXE. How do you find one procedure in this large program found without tracing slowly through much of the program? As you will learn in this chapter, there are two ways to find procedures: by using a road map from LINK, or by using a source-level debugger, such as Microsoft's CodeView or Borland's Turbo Debugger.

When we (the authors) originally wrote Dskpatch, something went wrong when we added WRITE_SECTOR; pressing the Shift-F2 key caused our machine to hang. But we couldn't find anything wrong with WRITE_SECTOR and the only other changes were to DISPATCH_TABLE. Everything appeared to be correct. Finally, we traced the bug to a faulty definition in the dispatcher. The bug turned out to be an error in the DISPATCH_TABLE entry for WRITE_SECTOR. Somehow, we had typed a DW rather than a DB in the table, so WRITE_SECTOR's address was stored one byte higher in memory than it should have been. You can see the bug shown against a gray background as follows:

```
DISPATCH_TABLE  LABEL    BYTE
                  .
                  .
                  .
        DB      77                          ;Cursor right
        DW      OFFSET _TEXT:PHANTOM_RIGHT
        DW      85                          ;Shift F2
        DW      OFFSET _TEXT:WRITE_SECTOR
        DB      0                           ;End of the table
DATA_SEG        ENDS
```

As an exercise in debugging, make this change to your file DISPATCH.ASM (diskfile DISPAT26.ASM), then follow the directions in the next section.

Building a Road Map

Now you will learn how to use LINK to build a map of Dskpatch. This map will help you find procedures and variables in memory. The LINK command you have used in the make file has grown to be fairly long, as follows, and you will add more to it.

```
LINK DSKPATCH DISK_IO DISP_SEC VIDEO_IO CURSOR DISPATCH KBD_IO PHANTOM EDITOR;
```

You will not have to keep typing file after file because LINK allows you to supply an automatic response file containing all the information. We will call the file LINKINFO and type the following:

```
LINK @LINKINFO
```

With the file names used so far, LINKINFO appears as follows:

```
DSKPATCH DISK_IO DISP_SEC VIDEO_IO CURSOR +
DISPATCH KBD_IO PHANTOM EDITOR
```

The plus (+) at the end of the first line tells LINK to continue reading file names from the next line.

You can add more information that tells LINK to create a map of the procedures and variables in the program to this simple Linkinfo file. The entire LINKINFO file is as follows:

```
DSKPATCH DISK_IO DISP_SEC VIDEO_IO CURSOR +
DISPATCH KBD_IO PHANTOM EDITOR
DSKPATCH
DSKPATCH /MAP;
```

The last two lines are new parameters. The first, DSKPATCH, tells LINK you want the .EXE file to be named DSKPATCH.EXE; the second new line tells LINK to create a listing file called DSKPATCH.MAP to create the road map. The /map switch tells LINK to provide a list of all the procedures and variables that you have declared to be public. (Incidentally, the Programmer's Workbench provides these same abilities with a nice user interface. This was covered in Chapter 13.)

Create the map file by relinking Dskpatch with this LINKINFO response file. You will probably want to change your Makefile so it uses LINK @LINKINFO instead of the long link line. The map file produced by the linker is about 140 lines long. The file is too long to be reproduced in its entirety, so we reproduced only the parts that are of particular interest. A partial listing of the map file, DSKPATCH.MAP, is as follows:

```
Start  Stop   Length Name            Class
00000H 005B6H 005B7H _TEXT           CODE
005B8H 006A9H 000F2H _DATA           DATA
006AAH 026A9H 02000H _BSS            BSS
026B0H 02AAFH 00400H STACK           STACK


Origin   Group
005B:0   DGROUP


Address        Publics by Name
```

```
0000:03DB        BACK_SPACE
0000:0274        CLEAR_SCREEN
0000:02B5        CLEAR_TO_END_OF_LINE
0000:033D        CONVERT_HEX_DIGIT
005B:000A        CURRENT_SECTOR_NO
0000:0296        CURSOR_RIGHT
005B:000C        DISK_DRIVE_NO
0000:0010        DISK_PATCH
0000:02E2        DISPATCHER
0000:0127        DISP_HALF_SECTOR
       .
       .
       .

0000:01E1        WRITE_HEX_DIGIT
0000:0255        WRITE_PATTERN
0000:0534        WRITE_PHANTOM
0000:019F        WRITE_PROMPT_LINE
0000:0081        WRITE_SECTOR
0000:01B2        WRITE_STRING
0000:00F0        WRITE_TOP_HEX_NUMBERS
0000:0572        WRITE_TO_MEMORY
005B:00FA        _edata
005B:2100        _end

 Address          Publics by Value

0000:0010        DISK_PATCH
0000:002E        PREVIOUS_SECTOR
0000:004D        NEXT_SECTOR
0000:0068        READ_SECTOR
0000:0081        WRITE_SECTOR
0000:009A        INIT_SEC_DISP
0000:00C4        WRITE_HEADER
0000:00F0        WRITE_TOP_HEX_NUMBERS
0000:0127        DISP_HALF_SECTOR
       .
       .
       .

005B:000D        LINES_BEFORE_SECTOR
005B:000E        HEADER_LINE_NO
005B:000F        HEADER_PART_1
005B:0015        HEADER_PART_2
005B:0026        PROMPT_LINE_NO
005B:0027        EDITOR_PROMPT
005B:00F8        PHANTOM_CURSOR_X
```

```
005B:00F9          PHANTOM_CURSOR_Y
005B:00FA          SECTOR
005B:00FA          _edata
005B:2100          _end
Program entry point at 0000:0010
```

There are three main parts to this load map (so called because it tells you where your procedures are loaded in memory). The first shows a list of segments in the program. Dskpatch has several segments: _TEXT (which contains all your code) and _DATA, _BSS, and STACK, which are grouped together into the group DGROUP, and contain all your data. For those of you interested in more detail, _DATA contains all the memory variables defined in the .DATA segment (such as HEADER_LINE_NO), _BSS contains variables defined in the .DATA? segment (such as SECTOR), and STACK contains the stack defined by .STACK. You may see slightly different numbers in the load map if your procedures are in a different order than our procedures (you can check the order in Appendix B).

The next part of the load map shows the public procedures and variables listed in alphabetic order. LINK lists only those procedures and variables you have declared to be PUBLIC—visible to the outside world. If you are debugging a long program, you may want to declare all procedures and variables to be public, so you can find them in this map.

The final section of the map lists all the procedures and memory variables again, but this time in the order they appear in memory. Both of these lists include the memory address for each PUBLIC procedure or variable. If you check this list, you will find that the procedure DISPATCHER starts at address 2E2h. You will use this address to track down the bug in Dskpatch.

Tracking Down Bugs

If you were to try running the version of Dskpatch with the bug in it, you would find that everything works with the exception of Shift-F2 which caused Dskpatch to hang on our machine. You don't want to try Shift-F2; there is no telling what it will do on your machine.

Since everything worked (and works now) except for Shift-F2, our first guess when we wrote the program was that we had introduced a bug into

WRITE_SECTOR. To find this bug, we could start debugging Dskpatch by tracing through WRITE_SECTOR. Instead, we will take a somewhat different tack.

You know that DISPATCHER works correctly, because everything else (the cursor keys, F3, F4, and F10) all works correctly. That means DISPATCHER is a good starting point to search for the bug in Dskpatch. In other words, start your bug search with code you know works properly. If you look at the program listing for DISPATCHER (in Chapter 25), you will see that the following instruction is the heart of DISPATCHER, because it calls all the other routines.

```
CALL    WORD PTR [BX]
```

In particular, this CALL instruction will call WRITE_SECTOR when you press Shift-F2. Let's start the search here.

For various reasons, the DISPATCHER procedure in your program may be at an address other than 2E2h. Instead of using the addresses below exactly as you see them, you will need to choose the correct address. For DISPATCHER, look in the Dskpatch.map file to find its address. Then in the following code, use the addresses you see in Debug, rather than the addresses shown in this book.

You will use Debug to start Dskpatch with a breakpoint set on this instruction. That means you need the address of this instruction. It can be found by unassembling DISPATCHER which starts at 2E2h. After a U 2E2, followed by another U command, you should see the CALL command as follows:

```
                    .
                    .
                    .
3AC1:0308 EBF2        JMP     02FC
3AC1:030A 43          INC     BX
3AC1:030B FF17        CALL    [BX]
3AC1:030D EBD6        JMP     02E5
                    .
                    .
                    .
```

Now that you know the CALL instruction is at location 30Bh, you can set a breakpoint at this address, then single-step into and through WRITE_SECTOR.

First, use the command G 30B to execute Dskpatch up to this instruction. You will see Dskpatch start up and then wait for you to type a command. Press Shift-F2, since this is the command that is causing problems. You will see the following:

```
-G 30B
```

```
AX=0155  BX=00A1  CX=06AC  DX=0027  SP=03F8  BP=0000  SI=0000  DI=0000
DS=3B1C  ES=3AB1  SS=3D2C  CS=3AC1  IP=030B   NV UP EI PL NZ NA PO NC
3AC1:030B FF17          CALL    [BX] DS:00A1=8100
-
```

At this point the BX register is pointing to a word that should contain the address of WRITE_SECTOR. Let's see if it does.

```
-D A1 L 2
3B1C:00A0      00 81                                              . .
-
```

In other words, you are trying to CALL a procedure located at 8100h (remember the lower byte is displayed first). But if you look at the memory map, you can see that WRITE_SECTOR should be at 81h. In fact, we can also tell from this load map that there aren't any procedures at 8100h; the address is totally wrong.

In your original bug-hunting, once we discovered that this address was wrong, it didn't take us very long to find the error. We knew that DISPATCHER and the table were basically sound because all the other keys worked, so we took a closer look at the data for Shift-F2 and found the DW where we should have had a DB. Having a road map makes debugging much simpler. Now let's look at some more powerful debugging tools.

Source-Level Debugging

Microsoft and Borland have been working hard to provide the ultimate in programming tools. Microsoft's CodeView and Borland's Turbo Debugger are both debuggers of a type called Source-Level Debuggers. In other words, whereas Debug shows you just addresses in CALLs and JMPs, these two debuggers show you the actual source code.

You may only want to read one of the next two sections; since one section covers Microsoft's CodeView and the other Borland's Turbo Debugger, there is some repetition of material between the two sections.

Microsoft's CodeView

CodeView is the older of the two debuggers, having been introduced onto the market in 1986, about two years before Borland's Turbo Debugger. It is now included with every Microsoft Macro Assembler package (we are using version 6.0) as well as most of their other language products. As you will see in this section, CodeView is so useful that you may want to consider upgrading your macro assembler if you don't already have the latest version.

CodeView shares some similarities with Debug, since Microsoft wrote both programs. But there are more differences than similarities. We will use two of the new features here: source-level debugging and screen swapping.

Source-level debugging lets you see the actual source code complete with comments, rather than just instructions and addresses in your display. For example, if you use Debug to unassemble the first line in Dskpatch, you will see the following:

```
3AC1:0010 B81C3B        MOV     AX,3B1C
```

With CodeView, on the other hand, you will see the following (as you can also see in Figure 26-1):

```
MOV     AX,DGROUP             ;Put data segment into AX
```

The second new feature, screen swapping, is handy for debugging Dskpatch. Dskpatch moves the cursor around the screen, writing in different places. In the last section, where we used Debug, Debug started writing to this same screen and eventually the Dskpatch screen was lost.

CodeView, however, maintains two separate screens: one for Dskpatch and one for itself. Whenever Dskpatch is active, you see its screen; whenever

CodeView is active, you see *its* screen. You will get a clearer idea of screen swapping as you run through the following examples.

Before you can use CodeView's symbolic debugging features you need to tell both the assembler and the linker to save debugging information. This can be done with the /Zi switch in the assembler and the /CODEVIEW switch in the linker.

Modify each line in your MAKEFILE (or reassemble each file by hand) so it has the /Zi switch before each file name and modify MAKEFILE so it uses a response file for LINK as follows:

Listing 26-3 Changes made to MAKEFILE

```
dskpatch.exe:   dskpatch.obj disk_io.obj disp_sec.obj video_io.obj cursor.obj \
                dispatch.obj kbd_io.obj phantom.obj editor.obj
        link @linkinfo

dskpatch.obj:   dskpatch.asm
        ml /c /Zi dskpatch.asm

disk_io.obj:    disk_io.asm
        ml /c /Zi disk_io.asm
                .
                .
                .
```

Then change the linker response file LINKINFO as follows:

Listing 26-4 Changes to the response file LINKINFO

```
dskpatch disk_io disp_sec video_io cursor +
dispatch kbd_io phantom editor
dskpatch
dskpatch /CODEVIEW;
```

Finally, delete all the *.obj files and remake Dskpatch.exe (alternatively, you can type NMAKE /A to have NMake reassemble everything). Now you are ready to start CodeView. You should see a display like the one in Figure 26-1 when you type the following:

```
C>CV DSKPATCH
```

Notice that you are viewing the actual source file! This is why CodeView is known as a source-level debugger.

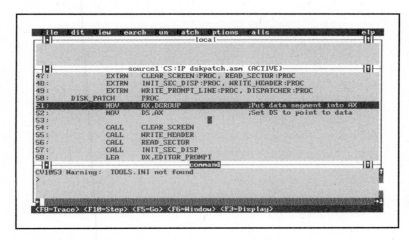

Figure 26-1: The initial view of Dskpatch.exe inside CodeView.

Now that you have CodeView up and running, you can look at the procedure DISPATCHER without knowing where it is. Press Alt-S (to pull down the Search menu), then L (Label/Function...) to search for a label. Next, type *dispatcher* into the dialog box that pops up and press Enter to see the code for DISPATCHER. Finally, use the cursor keys (or the Page Down key) to scroll to the CALL WORD PTR [BX] instruction.

Once you have the cursor on the line with the CALL WORD PTR [BX] instruction, press F7 (which will run the program until it reaches the CALL). You will see Dskpatch draw its screen. You will be returned to CodeView after you press Shift-F2. This time you won't see any of Dskpatch's screen because CodeView swapped screens. To flip back to the Dskpatch screen, press the F4 key. Once you are looking at Dskpatch's screen, pressing any key will return you to CodeView's screen.

363

Press the F2 key to display the register window, on the right side of CodeView's screen as in Figure 26-2, if it is not already visible. If you look on the lower right part of the register screen , you will see two short lines as follows:

```
DS:00A1
  8100
```

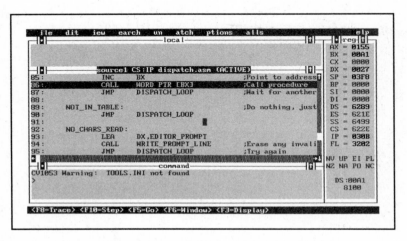

Figure 26-2: CodeView after the F7 (Go) command and then F2 (Register).

This area of the display is used to show the value in memory pointed to by the memory reference in the current instruction. This is the CALL instruction under the inverse-video cursor bar. In this case, the single memory reference is to the value at memory location [BX]. As you can see, 8100 is the value you found by using Debug with the help of Link's memory map. But here you found the value much more quickly.

Type Alt-F (to pull down the File menu) and X (eXit) to exit from CodeView. You may want to skip the next section and go directly to the Summary.

Don't forget to change the DW back to a DB in Dispatch.asm.

You may also want to change back the linkinfo file. You added the /CODEVIEW switch so Link would add the debugging information to the EXE file. But this debugging information makes the .EXE file a bit larger (Dskpatch is about 11K with debugging information, and about 2K without). In any case, you will probably want to remove the /CODEVIEW switch before you give your programs to other people.

Borland's Turbo Debugger

Turbo Debugger shares few similarities with Debug. As you will see in this section, Turbo Debugger uses Borland's multiple-window style of user interface as opposed to Debug's command-line interface. Borland has also added many debugging features that are not present in Debug. You will use two of the new features here: source-level debugging and screen swapping.

Source-level debugging lets you see the actual source code complete with comments, rather than just instructions and addresses, in the display. For example, if you use Debug to unassemble the first line in Dskpatch, you will see the following:

```
3AC1:0010 B81C3B        MOV     AX,3B1C
```

With Turbo Debugger, you will see the following (as you can also see in Figure 26-3):

```
MOV     AX,DGROUP              ;Put data segment into AX
```

The second new feature, screen swapping, is handy for debugging Dskpatch. Dskpatch moves the cursor around the screen, writing in different places. In the last section where you used Debug, it started writing to this same screen and you eventually lost the Dskpatch screen.

Turbo Debugger, however, maintains two separate screens: one for Dskpatch and one for itself. Whenever Dskpatch is active, you see its screen; whenever Turbo Debugger is active, you see *its* screen.

Before you can use Turbo Debugger's symbolic debugging features you need to tell both the assembler and the linker to save debugging information. You do this with the /zi switch in the assembler and the /v switch in the linker.

Modify each line in your Makefile (or reassemble each file by hand) so it has the /zi switch before the file name. And modify Makefile so it uses a response file for TLINK (notice that we are using TLINK):

Listing 26-5 Changes made to Makefile

```
dskpatch.exe:   dskpatch.obj disk_io.obj disp_sec.obj video_io.obj cursor.obj \
                dispatch.obj kbd_io.obj phantom.obj editor.obj
        tlink @linkinfo

dskpatch.obj:   dskpatch.asm
        tasm /zi dskpatch.asm

disk_io.obj:    disk_io.asm
        tasm /zi disk_io.asm
                .
                .
                .
```

Then change the linker response file LINKINFO as follows:

Listing 26-6 Changes to the response file LINKINFO

```
dskpatch disk_io disp_sec video_io cursor +
dispatch kbd_io phantom editor
dskpatch
dskpatch /v;
```

Finally, delete all the *.obj files and remake Dskpatch.exe (or type "make -B" to rebuild everything—the B must be uppercase).

Now you are ready to start Turbo Debugger. Type the following and you should see a display like the one in Figure 26-3:

```
C>TD DSKPATCH
```

Notice that you are viewing the actual source file! This is why Turbo Debugger is known as a source-level debugger.

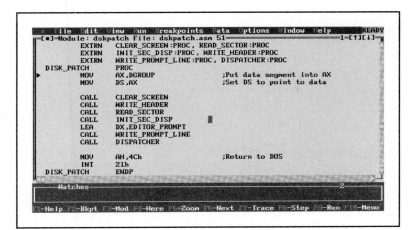

Figure 26-3: The initial view of Dskpatch.exe inside Turbo Debugger.

Now that Turbo Debugger is up and running, you can look at the procedure DISPATCHER without knowing where it is. Press Alt-V to pull down the View menu, followed by V to show the variable window (Figure 26-4). Use the cursor-up and -down keys to move the cursor to dispatcher; press Enter to show the code for DISPATCHER. You can then use the cursor keys to scroll to the CALL Word Ptr [BX] instruction on the second page.

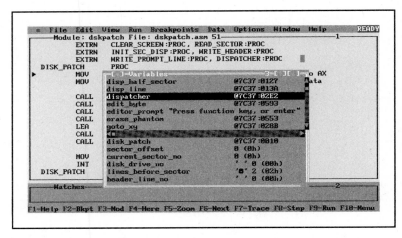

Figure 26-4: Turbo Debugger's variable window allows us to jump to a procedure.

Once you have the cursor on the line with the CALL WORD PTR [BX] instruction, press F4 and follow that with Shift-F2. You will see Dskpatch draw its screen. Then, you will be returned to Turbo Debugger after you push Shift-F2. This time you won't see any of Dskpatch's screen because Turbo Debugger swapped screens. To flip back to the Dskpatch screen, press the Alt-F5 key. Once you are looking at Dskpatch's screen, pressing any key will return you to Turbo Debugger's screen.

At this point you want to see the value of [BX] so you will know which procedure Dskpatch is about to call. For this, add a watch, which allows you to watch a value. Press Ctrl-W to bring up a dialog box that asks for an expression; type in [BX] and press Enter. You will see a screen like the one in Figure 26-5. As you can see in the Watches window, 8100 is the value you found using Debug with the help of Link's memory map. Here you found the value much more quickly.

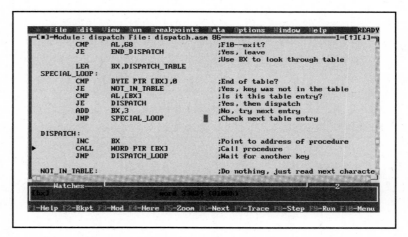

Figure 26-5: Turbo Debugger after executing Dskpatch up to the CALL instruction.

Type Alt-X to exit from Turbo Debugger.

Do not forget to change the DW back to a DB in Dispatch.asm.

You may also want to change back the LINKINFO file. You added the /v switch so Link would add the debugging information to the .EXE file. But this debugging information makes the EXE file quite a bit larger (Dskpatch is about 19K with debugging information, and about 2K without). In any case, you will probably want to remove the /v switch before you give your programs to other people.

Summary

That ends our discussion of debugging techniques. In the next chapter, we will add the procedures to scroll the screen between the two half sectors. Then, in the final part of this book you will learn a number of advanced topics.

By the way, don't forget to fix the bug that you placed in DISPATCH_TABLE.

The Other
Half Sector

In this chapter you will modify Dskpatch so it can show both halves of the sectors.

File altered: PHANTOM.ASM

Disk file: PHANTO27.ASM

27

Topics Covered

Dskpatch should behave like a word processor when you try to move the cursor below the bottom of the half-sector display—the display should move up one line, with a new line appearing at the bottom. The version of Dskpatch on the disk included with this book does that. In this chapter, you will add skeletal versions of the two procedures, SCROLL_UP and SCROLL_DOWN, that scroll the screen. In the disk version of Dskpatch, SCROLL_UP and SCROLL_DOWN can scroll by any number of lines from 1 to 16 (there are 16 lines in our half-sector display). The versions of SCROLL_UP and SCROLL_DOWN that you will add to Dskpatch here scroll by full half sectors, so you will see either the first or second half of the sector.

Scrolling by Half a Sector

The old versions of PHANTOM_UP and PHANTOM_DOWN restore the cursor to the top or bottom of the half-sector display whenever you try to move the cursor off the top or bottom of the display. You will change PHANTOM_UP and PHANTOM_DOWN so that you can call either SCROLL_UP or SCROLL_DOWN when the cursor moves off the top or bottom of the display. These two new procedures will scroll the display and place the cursor at its new position. The modified versions of PHANTOM_UP and PHANTOM_DOWN (in PHANTOM.ASM) are as follows:

Listing 27-1 Changes to PHANTOM.ASM

```
PHANTOM_UP          PROC
        CALL        ERASE_PHANTOM       ;Erase at current position
        DEC         PHANTOM_CURSOR_Y    ;Move cursor up one line
        JNS         WASNT_AT_TOP        ;Was not at the top, write cursor
        MOV         PHANTOM_CURSOR_Y,0  ;Was at the top, so put back there
        CALL        SCROLL_DOWN         ;Was at the top, scroll
WASNT_AT_TOP:
        CALL        WRITE_PHANTOM       ;Write the phantom at new position
        RET
PHANTOM_UP          ENDP
PHANTOM_DOWN        PROC
```

```
        CALL      ERASE_PHANTOM              ;Erase at current position
        INC       PHANTOM_CURSOR_Y             ;Move cursor up one line
        CMP       PHANTOM_CURSOR_Y,16          ;Was it at the bottom?
        JB        WASNT_AT_BOTTOM                ;No, so write phantom
        MOV       PHANTOM_CURSOR_Y,15 ;Was at bottom, so put back there
        CALL      SCROLL_UP               ;Was at bottom, scroll
WASNT_AT_BOTTOM:                           ;Write the phantom cursor
        CALL      WRITE_PHANTOM
        RET
PHANTOM_DOWN  ENDP
```

Don't forget to change the comment header for PHANTOM_UP and
PHANTOM_DOWN to mention that these procedures now use
SCROLL_UP and SCROLL_DOWN as follows:

Listing 27-2 Changes to PHANTOM.ASM

```
;-------------------------------------------------------------------;
; These four procedures move the phantom cursors.                   ;
;                                                                   ;
; Uses:         ERASE_PHANTOM, WRITE_PHANTOM                         ;
;               SCROLL_DOWN, SCROLL_UP                              ;
; Reads:        PHANTOM_CURSOR_X, PHANTOM_CURSOR_Y                   ;
; Writes:       PHANTOM_CURSOR_X, PHANTOM_CURSOR_Y                   ;
;-------------------------------------------------------------------;
```

SCROLL_UP and SCROLL_DOWN are both fairly simple procedures because they switch the display to the other half sector. For example, if you are
looking at the first half sector, and PHANTOM_DOWN calls SCROLL_UP,
you will see the second half sector. SCROLL_UP changes SECTOR_OFFSET
to 256; the start of the second half sector moves the cursor to the start of the
sector display and writes the half-sector display for the second half. Finally it
writes the phantom cursor at the top of this display. You can see all the details
for both SCROLL_UP and SCROLL_DOWN in Listing 27-3. These two
procedures should be added to PHANTOM.ASM as follows:

Listing 27-3 Procedures added to PHANTOM.ASM
(Complete listing in PHANTO27.ASM)

```
        EXTRN     DISP_HALF_SECTOR:PROC, GOTO_XY:PROC
.DATA
        EXTRN     SECTOR_OFFSET:WORD
        EXTRN     LINES_BEFORE_SECTOR:BYTE
.CODE ;---------------------------------------------------------------;
; These two procedures move between the two half-sector displays.     ;
;                                                                     ;
; Uses:         WRITE_PHANTOM, DISP_HALF_SECTOR, ERASE_PHANTOM, GOTO_XY ;
;               SAVE_REAL_CURSOR, RESTORE_REAL_CURSOR                  ;
; Reads:        LINES_BEFORE_SECTOR                                    ;
; Writes:       SECTOR_OFFSET, PHANTOM_CURSOR_Y                        ;
;---------------------------------------------------------------------;
SCROLL_UP       PROC
        PUSH      DX
        CALL      ERASE_PHANTOM           ;Remove the phantom cursor
        CALL      SAVE_REAL_CURSOR        ;Save the real cursor position
        XOR       DL,DL                   ;Set cursor for half-sector display
        MOV       DH,LINES_BEFORE_SECTOR
        ADD       DH,2
        CALL      GOTO_XY
        MOV       DX,256  ;Display the second half sector
        MOV       SECTOR_OFFSET,DX
        CALL      DISP_HALF_SECTOR
        CALL      RESTORE_REAL_CURSOR     ;Restore the real cursor position
        MOV       PHANTOM_CURSOR_Y,0      ;Cursor at top of second half sector
        CALL      WRITE_PHANTOM           ;Restore the phantom cursor
        POP       DX
        RET
SCROLL_UP       ENDP
SCROLL_DOWN     PROC
        PUSH      DX
        CALL      ERASE_PHANTOM           ;Remove the phantom cursor
        CALL      SAVE_REAL_CURSOR        ;Save the real cursor position
        XOR       DL,DL                   ;Set cursor for half-sector display
        MOV       DH,LINES_BEFORE_SECTOR
        ADD       DH,2
        CALL      GOTO_XY
        XOR       DX,DX                   ;Display the first half sector
        MOV       SECTOR_OFFSET,DX
        CALL      DISP_HALF_SECTOR
        CALL      RESTORE_REAL_CURSOR     ;Restore the real cursor position
```

```
        MOV       PHANTOM_CURSOR_Y,15      ;Cursor at bottom of first half sector
        CALL      WRITE_PHANTOM            ;Restore the phantom cursor
        POP       DX
        RET
SCROLL_DOWN       ENDP
```

SCROLL_UP and SCROLL_DOWN both work nicely, although there is one minor problem with them as Dskpatch stands now. Start Dskpatch and leave the cursor at the top of the screen. Press the cursor-up key and you will see Dskpatch rewrite the first half-sector display because Dskpatch rewrites the screen whenever you try to move the cursor off the top or bottom of the half-sector display.

Here's a challenge for you: Modify Dskpatch so that it checks for two boundary conditions. If the phantom cursor is at the top of the first half-sector display and you press the cursor-up key, Dskpatch should do nothing. If you're at the bottom of the second half-sector display and press the cursor-down key, again Dskpatch should do nothing.

Summary

This chapter ends the coverage of Dskpatch (with the exception of Chapter 30, where we will modify Dskpatch for faster screen writing). Our intent was to use Dskpatch as a "live" example of the evolution of an assembly-language program while providing you with a usable program, and a set of procedures you will find helpful in your own programming. But the Dskpatch you have developed here is not as finished as it could be. You will find more features in the disk version of Dskpatch included with this book. You may find yourself changing that disk version, for "a program is never done . . . but there comes a time when it has to be shipped to users."

This book ends with a number of advanced topics: relocation, writing COM programs, writing directly to the screen, writing C procedures in assembly language, TSR or RAM-resident programs, and protected-mode programming under Microsoft Windows.

Advanced Topics

95

96	36

8F	B2	70

23	CF	3F	91

71	A8	43	2E	BD

A9	60	CE	5D	42	C8

63	57	9A	75	B6	D2	FD

Relocation

In this chapter you will learn how EXE programs are relocated when they are run. You will build a program that accomplishes relocation by itself. We will also introduce you to the old-style segment definitions which you may see in some programs.

28

Topics Covered

Writing COM Programs

Using Full Segment Definitions

Relocation

COM vs EXE Programs

Most of the programs in Parts II and III of this book have been EXE programs with two segments, one for code and one for data. The discussion has glossed over one point in dealing with such programs—relocation. This chapter will cover the relocation process, and the steps DOS takes when it loads an EXE program into memory.

In order to show something of the relocation process, you will build a COM program that does its own relocation (since DOS provides no relocation support for COM programs). Since you haven't dealt with using the assembler to build COM programs yet, we will start with a short look at some new directives that you will need to write COM programs.

Writing COM Programs

Throughout this book you have been using the assembler to build EXE programs, which is what you will probably write most of the time. Some programs, however, need to be COM programs (such as some RAM-resident programs like the one we will write in Chapter 32 and our example program in this chapter). Building COM programs is easy: replace the .MODEL SMALL with .MODEL TINY. The tiny memory model supports .COM programs. You also have to remove the code at the start of your program that sets DS to DGROUP. In a COM program all the segment registers point to the same segment and are set when your program loads.

Using Full Segment Definitions

We will not use the simplified segment definitions (such as .CODE). Instead, we will use the full segment definitions so that everything we do will be out in the open. You will also find it useful to be able to read full segment definitions since some programmers still use them. Full segment directives look very much like procedure definitions, as you can see in this example that defines the code segment.

```
_TEXT    SEGMENT
         .
         .
         .
_TEXT    ENDS
```

Rather than start a code segment with .CODE, you need to bracket the code with a SEGMENT and an ENDS (END Segment) directive. You also have to provide the name of the segment (_TEXT in this example).

In addition to the segment definitions, you need to use another directive called ASSUME. When you are using simplified segment directives, the assembler knows from the .MODEL directive which segments the segment registers will point to. With full segment directives, you need to provide this information to the assembler yourself (since you cannot use the .MODEL directive). For this, you use a new directive, ASSUME, as follows:

```
ASSUME  CS:_TEXT, DS:_DATA, SS:STACK
```

This statement tells the assembler that the CS register will be pointing to your code (which is the case when the program starts to run), that the DS register points to the data segment, and that SS points to the stack segment. The .MODEL directive automatically provides this information to the assembler. (By the way, you will have to set up the last two registers yourself.)

Finally, a COM program, being contained entirely in a single segment, begins with the 256 byte PSP. In order to reserve room for the PSP, COM programs must begin with ORG 100h. The ORG tells the assembler to start the program code at 100h (or 256) bytes into the segment. You will see all of these details in the next section, as well as in Chapter 32.

Relocation

Each of our EXE programs begins with the following code that sets the DS register so it points to the data segment which actually consists of a group of segments called DGROUP.

```
MOV     AX,DGROUP
MOV     DS,AX
```

The question is, where does the value for DGROUP come from? If you think about it, programs can be loaded anywhere into memory. This means that the value of DGROUP won't be known until you know where your program is loaded into memory. As it turns out, DOS performs an operation known as relocation when it loads an EXE program into memory. This relocation process patches numbers such as DGROUP so they reflect the actual location of the program in memory.

To understand this process, you will write a COM program that does its own relocation. The goal is to set the DS register to the beginning of the _DATA segment, and the SS register to the beginning of the STACK segment. This can be accomplished with a bit of trickery. First, you need to ensure that your three segments are loaded into memory in the correct order as follows:

```
Code segment (_TEXT)
Data segment (_DATA)
Stack segment (STACK)
```

Fortunately, we have already taken care of this. When you are using the full segment directives, segments are loaded in the order in which they appear in your source file. A word of warning though: If you ever use the following technique to set segment registers, make sure you know the order in which LINK loads your segments (you can use the .MAP file to check the segment order).

How is the value for DS calculated? Let's begin by looking at the three labels we have placed into various segments in the following listing. Those labels are END_OF_CODE_SEG, END_OF_DATA_SEG, and END_OF_STACK_SEG. They aren't exactly where you might have expected them to be because we define a segment like the following (we need to use full segment definitions for COM programs).

```
_TEXT    SEGMENT
```

This statement does not really tell the linker how to stitch together various segments. So, it starts each new segment on a paragraph boundary—at a hex address that ends with a zero, such as 32C40h. Since the Linker skips to the next paragraph boundary to start each segment, there will be a short, blank area between segments. By placing the label END_OF_CODE_SEG at the beginning of _DATA, you include this blank area. If you had put END_OF_CODE_SEG at the end of _TEXT, you would not include the blank area between segments. (Look at the unassemble listing of the program on page 384. You will see a blank area filled with zeros that is 11 bytes long.)

As for the value of the DS register, _DATA starts at 3AB1:0130, or 3AC4:0000. The instruction OFFSET CGROUP:END_OF_CODE_SEG will return 130h, which is the number of bytes used by _TEXT. Divide this number by 16 to get the number we need to add to DS so that DS points to _DATA. We use the same technique to set SS. The listing for the program, including the relocation instructions needed for a COM file, is as follows:

```
CGROUP   GROUP    _TEXT, _DATA, STACK
         ASSUME   CS:_TEXT, DS:_DATA, SS:STACK


_TEXT    SEGMENT
         ORG      100h                        ;Reserve data area for .COM program
WRITE_sSTRING    PROC     FAR
         MOV      AX,OFFSET CGROUP:END_OF_CODE_SEG
         MOV      CL,4                         ;Calculate number of paragraphs
         SHR      AX,CL                        ; (16 bytes) used by the code segment
         MOV      BX,CS
         ADD      AX,BX                        ;Add CS to this
         MOV      DS,AX                        ;Set the DS register to _DATA

         MOV      AX,OFFSET CGROUP:END_OF_DATA_SEG
         SHR      AX,CL                        ;Calculate paras from CS to stack
         ADD      AX,BX                        ;Add CS to this
         MOV      SS,AX                        ;Set the SS register for STACK
         MOV      AX,OFFSET STACK:END_OF_STACK_SEG
         MOV      SP,AX                        ;Set SP to end of stack area

         MOV      AH,9                         ;Call for string output
         LEA      DX,STRING                    ;Load address of string
         INT      21h                          ;Write string

         MOV      AH,4Ch                       ;Ask to Exit back to DOS
         INT      21h                          ;Return to DOS
WRITE_STRING     ENDP

_TEXT    ENDS
```

```
_DATA    SEGMENT
END_OF_CODE_SEG LABEL   BYTE
STRING  DB      "Hello, DOS here.$"
_DATA    ENDS


STACK    SEGMENT
END_OF_DATA_SEG LABEL   BYTE
        DB      10 DUP ('STACK   ')      ;'STACK' followed by three spaces
END_OF_STACK_SEG        LABEL   BYTE
STACK    ENDS


        END     WRITE_STRING
```

Assemble and link this program, just as you would an EXE program, and then type the following to convert writestr.exe into a COM program.

```
EXE2BIN WRITESTR WRITESTR.COM
```

EXE2BIN stands for convert an EXE file into (2) a BINary (COM) file; in other words, EXE to BINary. You can see the results of all this work in the Debug session as follows:

```
C>DEBUG WRITESTR.COM
-U
3AB1:0100 B83001        MOV     AX,0130
3AB1:0103 B104          MOV     CL,04
3AB1:0105 D3E8          SHR     AX,CL
3AB1:0107 8CCB          MOV     BX,CS
3AB1:0109 03C3          ADD     AX,BX
3AB1:010B 8ED8          MOV     DS,AX
3AB1:010D B85001        MOV     AX,0150
3AB1:0110 D3E8          SHR     AX,CL
3AB1:0112 03C3          ADD     AX,BX
3AB1:0114 8ED0          MOV     SS,AX
3AB1:0116 B84600        MOV     AX,0046
3AB1:0119 8BE0          MOV     SP,AX
3AB1:011B B409          MOV     AH,09
3AB1:011D BA0000        MOV     DX,0000
-U
3AB1:0120 CD21          INT     21
3AB1:0122 B44C          MOV     AH,4C
3AB1:0124 CD21          INT     21
3AB1:0126 0000          ADD     [BX+SI],AL
3AB1:0128 0000          ADD     [BX+SI],AL
```

```
3AB1:012A 0000        ADD     [BX+SI],AL
3AB1:012C 0000        ADD     [BX+SI],AL
3AB1:012E 0000        ADD     [BX+SI],AL
3AB1:0130 48          DEC     AX
3AB1:0131 65          DB      65
3AB1:0132 6C          DB      6C
3AB1:0133 6C          DB      6C
3AB1:0134 6F          DB      6F
3AB1:0135 2C20        SUB     AL,20
3AB1:0137 44          INC     SP
3AB1:0138 4F          DEC     DI
3AB1:0139 53          PUSH    BX
3AB1:013A 206865      AND     [BX+SI+65],CH
3AB1:013D 7265        JB      01A4
3AB1:013F 2E          CS:
3AB1:0140 2400        AND     AL,00
```

```
-G 120
AX=0946  BX=3AB1  CX=0004  DX=0000  SP=0046  BP=0000  SI=0000  DI=0000
DS=3AC4  ES=3AB1  SS=3AC6  CS=3AB1  IP=0120    NV UP EI PL NZ NA PE NC
3AB1:0120 CD21        INT     21
```

There are a couple of new things in this program. First, you will notice the following line:

```
CGROUP  GROUP   _TEXT, _DATA, STACK
```

You will recall that a group called DGROUP acts as a single segment, but really holds the _DATA, _DATA?, and STACK segments. What you have done here is create your own group, called CGROUP, that contains all the segments in the program. Creating this group enables you to get the offsets of various labels that are in different segments. You want offsets from the start of the entire program, rather than from the start of any one segment. By defining a group called CGROUP, you can get the offset from the start of the program by asking for the offset from the start of this group as follows:

```
MOV     AX,OFFSET CGROUP:END_OF_CODE_SEG
```

In contrast to this state, the statement

```
MOV     AX,OFFSET STACK:END_OF_STACK_SEG
```

sets AX to the offset of END_OF_STACK_SEG from the start of the segment called STACK.

385

You will almost never need to do this type of relocation yourself since DOS handles this automatically for EXE programs. But it helps to understand what's happening behind the scenes.

COM vs EXE Programs

We will finish this chapter by summarizing the difference between COM and EXE files, and how DOS loads both types of programs into memory.

A COM program stored on disk is essentially a memory image of the program. Because of this, a COM program is restricted to a single segment, unless it does its own relocation, as we did in this chapter.

An EXE program, on the other hand, lets DOS take care of the relocation. This delegating makes it very easy for EXE programs to use multiple segments. For this reason, most large programs are EXE rather than COM programs.

For a final look at COM versus EXE programs, let's examine how DOS loads and starts both of them. This should make the differences between these types of programs clearer and more concrete. We will begin with COM programs.

When DOS loads a COM program into memory, it adheres to the following steps:

- DOS creates the program segment prefix (PSP), which is the 256 byte area you saw in Chapter 11. Among other things, this PSP contains the command line typed.

- DOS next copies the entire COM file from the disk into memory, immediately after the 256 byte PSP.

- DOS then sets the three segment registers DS, ES, and SS to the start of the PSP.

- DOS sets the SP register to the end of the segment, usually FFFE, which is the last word in the segment.

- Finally, DOS jumps to the start of the program, which sets the CS register to the start of the PSP and the IP register to 100h (the start of the COM program).

In contrast, the steps involved in loading an EXE file are somewhat more involved, because DOS does the relocation.

Every EXE file has a header that is stored at the start of the file. This header, or relocation table, is always at least 512 bytes long and contains all the information DOS needs to do the relocation. Microsoft's Macro Assembler includes a program called EXEHDR that you can use to look at some of the information in this header. For example, following is the header we get for the Dskpatch.exe program at the end of Chapter 27:

```
C>EXEHDR DSKPATCH

Microsoft (R) EXE File Header Utility  Version 2.01
Copyright (C) Microsoft Corp 1985-1990. All rights reserved.

.EXE size (bytes)         8fc
Magic number:             5a4d
Bytes on last page:       00fc
Pages in file:            0005
Relocations:              0001
Paragraphs in header:     0020
Extra paragraphs needed:  0241
Extra paragraphs wanted:  ffff
Initial stack location:   0270:0400
Word checksum:            ec2c
Entry point:              0000:0010
Relocation table address: 001e
Memory needed:            11K

C>
```

Near the top of this table, you can see that there is a single relocation entry for the MOV AX,DGROUP instruction. Any time you make a reference to a segment address, as with MOV AX,DGROUP, Link will add a relocation entry to the table. The segment address is not known until DOS loads the program into memory, so you must let DOS supply the segment number.

There are also some other interesting pieces of information in the table. For example, the initial CS:IP and SS:SP values tell you the initial values for Stack and the Entry point. The table also tells DOS how much memory the program needs before it can run (the Memory needed).

Because DOS uses this relocation table to supply absolute addresses for such locations as segment addresses, there are a few extra steps it takes when loading a program into memory. The steps DOS follows in loading an EXE program as follows:

- DOS creates the program-segment prefix (PSP), just as it does for a COM program.

- DOS checks the EXE header to find where the header ends and the program starts. Then it loads the rest of the program into memory after the PSP.

- DOS finds and patches all of the references in the program that need to be relocated, such as references to segment addresses using the header information.

- DOS then sets the ES and DS registers so they point to the start of the PSP. If your program has its own data segment, your program needs to change DS and/or ES so they point to your data segment.

- DOS sets SS:SP according to the information in the EXE header. In the case illustrated, the header states that SS:SP will be placed at 0004:0050. That means DOS will set SP to 0050, and set SS so it is four paragraphs higher in memory than the end of the PSP.

- Finally, DOS jumps to the start of the program using the address provided in the EXE header. This sets the CS register to the start of the code segment, and IP to the offset given in the EXE header.

More on Segments and ASSUME

In this chapter you will learn about segment overrides, which are very useful in real programs. You will use them in Chapter 30 to write characters directly to your computer screen. This is much faster than using the ROM BIOS routines to display characters. You will also learn more about ASSUME statements and full segment definitions.

29

Topics Covered

Segment Override

So far you have read and written data located in the data segment. You have been dealing with a single data segment in this book (which is actually several segments grouped into a single segment called DGROUP), so you have not had any reason to read or write data in other segments.

In some cases you will need more than one data segment. A classic example is writing directly to the screen. Most commercial DOS programs write to the screen by moving the data directly into screen memory and, in the interest of speed, completely bypassing the ROM BIOS routines. Screen memory on the PC is located at segment B800h for color adapters (such as EGA and VGA), and at segment B000h for monochrome display adapters (which are not very common these days). You must write in different segments to write directly to the screen.

In this section you will write a short program that shows you how to write to two different segments by using the DS and ES registers to point to the two segments. In fact, many programs that write directly to screen memory use the ES register to point to screen memory.

In this example, you will use full segment definitions to give you more control over segments than the simplified segment definitions. Most of the time you will be able to use the simplified segment definitions. But we chose to use the full segment definitions in this chapter to give you more examples of how to use them. We also used full segment definitions to give you a better understanding of the ASSUME statement that you will need, along with the full segment definitions.

Our program is an EXE program. It is very short, and you can see that it has two data segments along with one variable in each data segment. The program is as follows:

```
DOSSEG

_DATA    SEGMENT
DS_VAR           DW      1
_DATA    ENDS
```

```
EXTRA_SEG          SEGMENT PUBLIC
ES_VAR             DW      2
EXTRA_SEG          ENDS



STACK     SEGMENT STACK
          DB      10 DUP ('STACK   ')      ;'STACK' followed by three spaces
STACK     ENDS



_TEXT     SEGMENT
          ASSUME  CS:_TEXT, DS:_DATA, ES:EXTRA_SEG, SS:STACK

TEST_SEG           PROC
          MOV      AX,_DATA                 ;Segment address for _DATA
          MOV      DS,AX                    ;Set up DS register for _DATA
          MOV      AX,EXTRA_SEG             ;Segment address for EXTRA_SEG
          MOV      ES,AX                    ;Set up ES register for EXTRA_SEG

          MOV      AX,DS_VAR                ;Read a variable from data segment
          MOV      BX,ES:ES_VAR             ;Read a variable from extra segment

          MOV      AH,4Ch                   ;Ask to Exit back to DOS
          INT      21h                      ;Return to DOS
TEST_SEG           ENDP

_TEXT     ENDS



          END      TEST_SEG
```

This program will help you learn about segment overrides and the ASSUME directive.

Notice that the data segments and the stack segment come *before* the code segment. We have also put the ASSUME directive after all the segment declarations. As you will see in this section, this arrangement is a direct result of using two data segments. Take a look at the two MOV instructions in the program which are as follows:

```
MOV      AX,DS_VAR
MOV      BX,ES:ES_VAR
```

The ES: in front of ES_VAR in the second instruction tells the 80x86 to use the ES, rather than the DS, register for this operation (to read the data from the extra segment). Every instruction has a default segment register it uses when it refers to data. As with the ES register in this example, you can also tell the 80x86 to use some other segment register for data.

The 80x86 has four special instructions, one for each of the four segment registers. These instructions are the *segment-override* instructions. They tell the 80x86 to use a specific segment register rather than the default, when the instruction following the segment override tries to read or write memory. For example, the instruction MOV AX,ES:ES_VAR is actually encoded as two instructions. You will see the following if you unassemble the test program:

```
2CF4:000D 26          ES:
2CF4:000E 8B1E0000     MOV     BX,[0000]
```

This shows that the assembler translated the instruction into a segment-override instruction, followed by the MOV instruction. Now the MOV instruction will read its data from the ES, rather than the DS, segment. If you trace through this program, you will see that the first MOV instruction sets AX equal to 1 (DS_VAR) and the second MOV sets BX equal to 2 (ES_VAR). In other words, you have read data from two different segments.

Another Look at ASSUME

Let's take a look at what happens when you remove the ES: from the program. Change the line

```
MOV     BX,ES:ES_VAR
```

so it reads:

```
MOV     BX,ES_VAR
```

Because you are no longer telling the assembler that you want to use the ES register when you read from memory, you may incorrectly assume that the assembler will go back to using the default segment (DS). Use Debug to look at the result of this change. You will see the ES: segment override is still in front of the MOV instruction. How did the assembler know that it needed to add the segment override? By using the information in the ASSUME directive, the assembler determined that the variable is in the extra segment, rather than in the data segment.

The ASSUME statement tells the assembler that the DS register points to the segment DATA_SEG, while ES points to EXTRA_SEG. Each time you write an instruction that uses a memory variable, the assembler searches for a declaration of this variable to see which segment it is declared in. Then it searches through the ASSUME list to find out which segment register is pointing to this segment. The assembler uses this segment register when it generates the instruction.

In the case of the MOV BX,ES_VAR instruction, the assembler noticed ES_VAR was in the segment called EXTRA_SEG; the ES register was pointing to that segment, so it generated an ES: segment-override instruction on its own. If you were to move ES_VAR into STACK_SEG, the assembler would generate an SS: segment-override instruction. The assembler automatically generates any segment-override instructions needed, provided that the ASSUME directives reflect the actual contents of the segment registers.

Summary

In this chapter you learned more about segments and how the assembler works with them. You learned about segment overrides, which allow you to read and write data in other segments. You will use such overrides in the next chapter when you write characters directly to the screen. Finally, you learned more about the ASSUME directive.

In the next chapter you will learn how to write directly to screen memory. This will dramatically increase the speed of writing characters to the screen.

A Very Fast WRITE_CHAR

In this chapter you will learn about speed and performance. You are going to modify Dskpatch so it displays characters by writing directly to your screen, rather than using the ROM BIOS.

Files altered: DSKPATCH.ASM, KBD_IO.ASM, CURSOR.ASM, VIDEO_IO.ASM

Disk files: DSKPAT30.ASM, KBD_IO.ASM, CURSOR30.ASM, VIDEO_30.ASM

30

Topics Covered

In the beginning of this book we mentioned that many people who write programs in assembly language often do so for speed. Assembly-language programs are almost always faster than programs written in other languages. But you may have noticed that the Dskpatch program does not draw the screen as quickly as many commercial programs. It is slow because we have been using the ROM BIOS routines to display characters on screen. Most programs bypass the ROM BIOS and write characters directly to screen memory in favor of raw speed.

Finding the Screen Segment

Before writing characters directly to screen memory, you need to know where the display memory is and how it stores characters.

Screen memory has its own segment, either B800h or B000h. There are two classes of display adapters: monochrome display adapters and color graphics adapters (CGA, EGA, and VGA). You can have one adapter of each class in your computer at the same time (although not many people do), so IBM gave them non-overlapping screen segments.

Monochrome refers to IBM's monochrome display adapter, Hercules graphics cards, and EGA and VGA cards attached to an IBM monochrome display. Monochrome cards display characters on the screen in green, white, or amber (it depends on the display). They have a limited set of "colors" that can be displayed: normal, bright, inverse, and underlined. Monochrome cards have their screen segment at B000h.

Color graphics adapters can display 16 different text colors at one time, and can be switched to graphics mode. The most common color graphics adapters are EGA and VGA cards, although there are still a few CGA cards from the earlier days. Color graphics adapters have their screen memory at segment B800h.

Users should not need to know which type of display adapter they have. It is up to the program to determine which display adapter is active. For this you can use INT 11h, which returns a list of installed equipment. As you can see in Figure 30-1, bits 4 and 5 tell you if the display is monochrome or color.

The screen segment will be at B000h (monochrome) if both bits are 1, and
B800h (color) if otherwise (we will ignore the case when no display adapter is
installed).

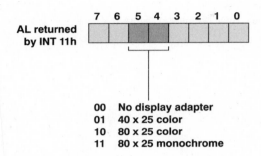

Figure 30-1: The INT 11h equipment flags.

Because you won't know which screen segment to use until you run the program, you will need to call the procedure INIT_WRITE_CHAR, which determines the screen segment, before making any calls to WRITE_CHAR. You
will place this call at the start of DISK_PATCH to make sure it is called before any characters are written on the screen. Changes to DSKPATCH.ASM
to add this call are as follows:

Listing 30-1 Changes to DSKPATCH.ASM (Complete listing in DSKPAT30.ASM)

```
            EXTRN    WRITE_PROMPT_LINE:PROC, DISPATCHER:PROC
            EXTRN    INIT_WRITE_CHAR:PROC
DISK_PATCH  PROC
            MOV      AX,DGROUP              ;Put data segment into AX
            MOV      DS,AX                  ;Set DS to point to data

            CALL     INIT_WRITE_CHAR
            CALL     CLEAR_SCREEN
            CALL     WRITE_HEADER
                         .
                         .
                         .
```

Next, add INIT_WRITE_CHAR to VIDEO_IO.ASM as follows:

Listing 30-2 Procedure added to VIDEO_IO.ASM

```
        PUBLIC  INIT_WRITE_CHAR
;--------------------------------------------------------------------;
; You need to call this procedure before you call WRITE_CHAR since   ;
; WRITE_CHAR uses information set by this procedure.                 ;
;                                                                    ;
; Writes:       SCREEN_SEG                                           ;
;--------------------------------------------------------------------;
INIT_WRITE_CHAR PROC
        PUSH    AX
        PUSH    BX
        MOV     BX,0B800h               ;Set for color graphics display
        INT     11h                     ;Get equipment information
        AND     AL,30h                  ;Keep just the video display type
        CMP     AL,30h                  ;Is this a monochrome display adapter?
        JNE     SET_BASE                ;No, it's color, so use B800
        MOV     BX,0B000h               ;Yes, it's monochrome, so use B000
SET_BASE:
        MOV     SCREEN_SEG,BX           ;Save the screen segment
        POP     BX
        POP     AX
        RET
INIT_WRITE_CHAR ENDP
```

Note that you are saving the screen segment in SCREEN_SEG (which you will add below). WRITE_CHAR will use this variable when you modify it to write directly to screen memory. Now that you know how to find the screen memory, you will learn how the characters and their attributes are stored.

Writing Directly to Screen Memory

If you were to use Debug to look at screen memory when the first line of the screen is

DSKPATCH ASM

you would see the following (for a color graphics card):

400

```
-B800:0
B800:0000  44 07 53 07 4B 07 50 07-41 07 54 07 43 07 48 07    D.S.K.P.A.T.C.H.
B800:0010  20 07 41 07 53 07 4D 07-20 07 20 07 20 07 20 07    .A.S.M. . . . .
           .
           .
           .
```

In other words, there is a 07 between each character on the screen. As you may recall from Chapter 18, 7 is the character attribute for normal text (70h is the attribute for inverse text). Each 7 in the debug display is the attribute for one character, with the character lower in memory. In other words, every character on the screen uses one word of screen memory, with the character code in the lower byte and the attribute in the upper byte. Let's write a new version of WRITE_CHAR that writes characters directly to screen memory. Make changes to VIDEO_IO.ASM as follows:

Listing 30-3 Changes to VIDEO_IO.ASM

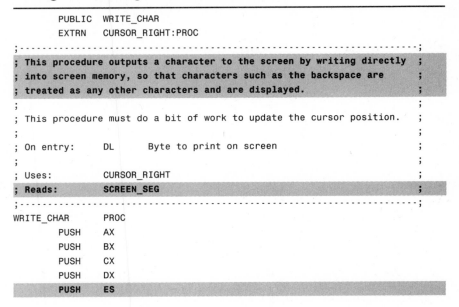

```
            PUBLIC  WRITE_CHAR
            EXTRN   CURSOR_RIGHT:PROC
;------------------------------------------------------------;
; This procedure outputs a character to the screen by writing directly ;
; into screen memory, so that characters such as the backspace are     ;
; treated as any other characters and are displayed.                   ;
;                                                                       ;
; This procedure must do a bit of work to update the cursor position.  ;
;                                                                       ;
; On entry:    DL      Byte to print on screen                         ;
;                                                                       ;
; Uses:        CURSOR_RIGHT                                            ;
; Reads:       SCREEN_SEG                                              ;
;------------------------------------------------------------;
WRITE_CHAR  PROC
            PUSH    AX
            PUSH    BX
            PUSH    CX
            PUSH    DX
            PUSH    ES
```

continues

401

Listing 30-3 continued

```
        MOV     AX,SCREEN_SEG            ;Get segment for screen memory
        MOV     ES,AX                    ;Point ES to screen memory

        PUSH    DX                       ;Save the character to write
        MOV     AH,3                     ;Ask for the cursor position
        XOR     BH,BH                    ;On page 0
        INT     10h                      ;Get row, column
        MOV     AL,DH                    ;Put row into AL
        MOV     BL,80                    ;There are 80 characters per line
        MUL     BL                       ;AX = row * 80
        ADD     AL,DL                    ;Add the column
        ADC     AH,0                     ;Propagate carry into AH
        SHL     AX,1                     ;Convert to byte offset
        MOV     BX,AX                    ;Put byte offset of cursor into BX
        POP     DX                       ;Restore the character

        MOV     DH,7                     ;Use the normal attribute
        MOV     ES:[BX],DX               ;Write character/attribute to screen
        CALL    CURSOR_RIGHT             ;Now move to next cursor position

        POP     ES
        POP     DX
        POP     CX
        POP     BX
        POP     AX
        RET
WRITE_CHAR      ENDP
```

Finally, you need to add a memory variable to VIDEO_IO.ASM:

Listing 30-4 Add DATA_SEG to the start of VIDEO_IO.ASM

```
.MODEL SMALL

.DATA
SCREEN_SEG      DW      0B800h           ;Segment of the screen buffer

.CODE
```

After making these changes, rebuild Dskpatch (you will need to assemble Dskpatch and Video_io) and try the new version. You will see that Dskpatch does not write to the screen any faster than before because you are moving the cursor after you write each character, which slows down the process.

High-Speed Screen Writing

The solution is to rewrite the routines in Video_io and Cursor to keep track of where the cursor should be, instead of moving the cursor (you will move the cursor only when you need to). For this we will introduce two new memory variables: SCREEN_X and SCREEN_Y. This may sound easy, but you will have to change a number of procedures as well as write a few new ones.

There is another optimization you can make. Currently WRITE_CHAR calculates the offset of the cursor into the screen buffer each time you call it. Since you will be keeping track of where the cursor should be, you can also keep track of this offset in the variable SCREEN_PTR.

Listing 30-5 Changes to WRITE_CHAR in VIDEO_IO.ASM

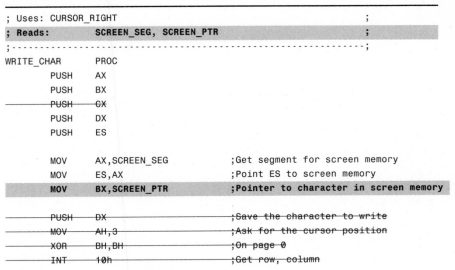

```
; Uses: CURSOR_RIGHT                                     ;
; Reads:         SCREEN_SEG, SCREEN_PTR                  ;
;-----------------------------------------------------;
WRITE_CHAR     PROC
              PUSH     AX
              PUSH     BX
              PUSH     CX
              PUSH     DX
              PUSH     ES

              MOV      AX,SCREEN_SEG      ;Get segment for screen memory
              MOV      ES,AX              ;Point ES to screen memory
              MOV      BX,SCREEN_PTR      ;Pointer to character in screen memory

              PUSH     DX                 ;Save the character to write
              MOV      AH,3               ;Ask for the cursor position
              XOR      BH,BH              ;On page 0
              INT      10h                ;Get row, column
```

continues

Listing 30-5 continued

```
        MOV     AL,DH                   ;Put row into AL
        MOV     BL,80                   ;There are 80 characters per line
        MUL     BL                      ;AX = row * 80
        ADD     AL,DL                   ;Add the column
        ADC     AH,0                    ;Propagate carry into AH
        SHL     AX,1                    ;Convert to byte offset
        MOV     BX,AX                   ;Put byte offset of cursor into BX
        POP     DX                      ;Restore the character

        MOV     DH,7                    ;Use the normal attribute
        MOV     ES:[BX],DX              ;Write character/attribute to screen
        CALL    CURSOR_RIGHT            ;Now move to next cursor position

        POP     ES
        POP     DX
        POP     CX
        POP     BX
        POP     AX
        RET
WRITE_CHAR      ENDP
```

WRITE_CHAR has become quite simple. You must also add three new memory variables to the DATA_SEG in VIDEO_IO.ASM:

Listing 30-6 Changes to .DATA in VIDEO_IO.ASM

```
.DATA
        PUBLIC  SCREEN_PTR
        PUBLIC  SCREEN_X, SCREEN_Y
SCREEN_SEG      DW      0B800h          ;Segment of the screen buffer
SCREEN_PTR      DW      0               ;Offset into screen memory of cursor
SCREEN_X        DB      0               ;Position of the screen cursor
SCREEN_Y        DB      0

.CODE
```

The changes to WRITE_ATTRIBUTE_N_TIMES so it will write directly to the screen are as follows:

Listing 30-7 Changes to WRITE_ATTRIBUTE_N_TIMES in VIDEO_IO.ASM (Complete listing in VIDEO_30.ASM)

```
; Uses:          CURSOR_RIGHT                                           ;
; Reads:         SCREEN_SEG, SCREEN_PTR                                 ;
;--------------------------------------------------------------------;
WRITE_ATTRIBUTE_N_TIMES PROC
        PUSH    AX
        PUSH    BX
        PUSH    CX
        PUSH    DX
        PUSH    DI
        PUSH    ES

        MOV     AX,SCREEN_SEG          ;Set ES to point to screen segment
        MOV     ES,AX
        MOV     DI,SCREEN_PTR          ;Character under cursor
        INC     DI                     ;Point to the attribute under cursor
        MOV     AL,DL                  ;Put attribute into AL
ATTR_LOOP:
        STOSB                          ;Save one attribute
        INC     DI                     ;Move to next attribute
        INC     SCREEN_X               ;Move to next column
        LOOP    ATTR_LOOP              ;Write N attributes

        DEC     DI                     ;Point to start of next character
        MOV     SCREEN_PTR,DI          ;Remember where we are

        POP     ES
        POP     DI
        POP     DX
        POP     CX
        POP     BX
        POP     AX
        RET
WRITE_ATTRIBUTE_N_TIMES ENDP
```

Most of this procedure should be fairly clear, with the exception of a new instruction: STOSB (*STOre String Byte*). Basically, STOSB is the opposite of the LODSB string instruction that loads a byte from DS:SI and increments the SI register. STOSB stores the byte from AL into the address at ES:DI, then increments DI.

All of the other changes you need to make (with the exception of a simple fix in KBD_IO) are to procedures in CURSOR.ASM. First, you will need to change GOTO_XY so it sets SCREEN_X and SCREEN_Y, and calculates the value of SCREEN_PTR.

Listing 30-8 Changes to GOTO_XY in CURSOR.ASM

```
        PUBLIC  GOTO_XY
.DATA
        EXTRN   SCREEN_PTR:WORD ;Pointer to character under cursor
        EXTRN   SCREEN_X:BYTE, SCREEN_Y:BYTE
.CODE
;------------------------------------------------------------------;
; This procedure moves the cursor                                  ;
;                                                                  ;
; On entry:     DH      Row (Y)                                    ;
;               DL      Column (X)                                 ;
;------------------------------------------------------------------;
GOTO_XY         PROC
        PUSH    AX
        PUSH    BX
        MOV     BH,0                    ;Display page 0
        MOV     AH,2                    ;Call for SET CURSOR POSITION
        INT     10h

        MOV     AL,DH                   ;Get the row number
        MOV     BL,80                   ;Multiply by 80 chars per line
        MUL     BL                      ;AX = row * 80
        ADD     AL,DL                   ;Add column
        ADC     AH,0                    ;AX = row * 80 + column
        SHL     AX,1                    ;Convert to a byte offset
        MOV     SCREEN_PTR,AX           ;Save the cursor offset
        MOV     SCREEN_X,DL             ;Save the cursor position
        MOV     SCREEN_Y,DH
```

```
        POP     BX
        POP     AX
        RET
GOTO_XY         ENDP
```

As you can see, this listing moves the calculation of the offset to the character under the cursor from WRITE_CHAR, where it was before, to GOTO_XY. You must also modify CURSOR_RIGHT so it updates these memory variables.

Listing 30-9 Changes to CURSOR_RIGHT in CURSOR.ASM

```
        PUBLIC  CURSOR_RIGHT
.DATA
        EXTRN   SCREEN_PTR:WORD ;Pointer to character under cursor
        EXTRN   SCREEN_X:BYTE, SCREEN_Y:BYTE
.CODE
;-------------------------------------------------------------------;
; This procedure moves the cursor one position to the right or to the ;
; next line if the cursor was at the end of a line.                 ;
;                                                                   ;
; Uses:          SEND_CRLF                                          ;
; Writes:        SCREEN_PTR, SCREEN_X, SCREEN_Y                     ;
;-------------------------------------------------------------------;
CURSOR_RIGHT    PROC
        INC     SCREEN_PTR              ;Move to next character position (word)
        INC     SCREEN_PTR
        INC     SCREEN_X               ;Move to next column
        CMP     SCREEN_X,79            ;Make sure column <= 79
        JBE     OK
        CALL    SEND_CRLF              ;Go to next line
OK:
        RET
CURSOR_RIGHT    ENDP
```

You must also change CLEAR_TO_END_OF_LINE so it uses SCREEN_X and SCREEN_Y rather than the location of the real cursor.

407

Listing 30-10 Changes to CLEAR_TO_END_OF_LINE in CURSOR.ASM

```
        PUSH    CX
        PUSH    DX
        MOV     AH,3                    ;Read current cursor position
        XOR     BH,BH                   ; on page 0
        INT     10h                     ;Now have (X,Y) in DL, DH
        MOV     DL,SCREEN_X
        MOV     DH,SCREEN_Y
        MOV     AH,6                    ;Set up to clear to end of line
        XOR     AL,AL                   ;Clear window
```

The next few steps require an explanation. Because you are no longer updating the position of the real cursor, the real and virtual cursors will often be out of synchronization. Usually this is not a problem. There are a few cases, however, when you have to synchronize both cursors; sometimes you will want to move the real cursor to where you think the cursor is, and sometimes you will want to move the virtual cursor. For example, before asking the user for input, you need to move the cursor to where you think the cursor should be. You will do this with the procedure UPDATE_REAL_CURSOR, which moves the real cursor.

On the other hand, SEND_CRLF moves the real cursor, so you must call UPDATE_VIRTUAL_CURSOR to move the virtual cursor to where the real cursor is after SEND_CRLF. The two procedures you will need to add to CURSOR.ASM are as follows:

Listing 30-11 Procedures added to CURSOR.ASM

```
        PUBLIC  UPDATE_REAL_CURSOR
;---------------------------------------------------------------------;
; This procedure moves the real cursor to the current virtual cursor  ;
; position.  You'll want to call it just before you wait for keyboard  ;
; input.                                                               ;
;---------------------------------------------------------------------;
UPDATE_REAL_CURSOR      PROC
        PUSH    DX
        MOV     DL,SCREEN_X             ;Get position of the virtual cursor
        MOV     DH,SCREEN_Y
```

```
        CALL    GOTO_XY            ;Move real cursor to this position
        POP     DX
        RET
UPDATE_REAL_CURSOR      ENDP



        PUBLIC  UPDATE_VIRTUAL_CURSOR
;-----------------------------------------------------------------------;
; This procedure updates the position of our virtual cursor to agree    ;
; with the position of the real cursor.                                 ;
;-----------------------------------------------------------------------;
UPDATE_VIRTUAL_CURSOR    PROC
        PUSH    AX
        PUSH    BX
        PUSH    CX
        PUSH    DX
        MOV     AH,3               ;Ask for the cursor position
        XOR     BH,BH              ;On page 0
        INT     10h                ;Get cursor position into DH, DL
        CALL    GOTO_XY            ;Move virtual cursor to this position
        POP     DX
        POP     CX
        POP     BX
        POP     AX
        RET
UPDATE_VIRTUAL_CURSOR    ENDP
```

Note that you are using GOTO_XY to update the three variables SCREEN_X, SCREEN_Y, and SCREEN_PTR.

Finally, you must modify several procedures to use the preceding two procedures. The changes to SEND_CRLF are as follows:

Listing 30-12 Changes to SEND_CRLF in CURSOR.ASM (Complete listing in CURSOR30.ASM)

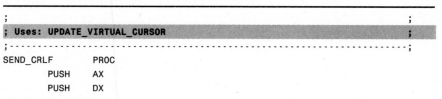

```
;                                                                       ;
; Uses: UPDATE_VIRTUAL_CURSOR                                           ;
;-----------------------------------------------------------------------;
SEND_CRLF       PROC
        PUSH    AX
        PUSH    DX
```

continues

Listing 30-12 continued

```
        MOV     AH,2
        MOV     DL,CR
        INT     21h
        MOV     DL,LF
        INT     21h
        CALL    UPDATE_VIRTUAL_CURSOR    ;Update position of virtual cursor
        POP     DX
        POP     AX
        RET
SEND_CRLF       ENDP
```

This change makes sure that you know where the cursor is after you have moved the real cursor to the next line.

The changes to READ_STRING that keep the virtual and real cursors in synchronization during keyboard input are as follows:

Listing 30-13 Changes to READ_STRING in KBD_IO.ASM (Complete listing in KBD_IO30.ASM)

```
        EXTRN   UPDATE_REAL_CURSOR:PROC
;-----------------------------------------------------------------;
;                       .                                         ;
;                       .                                         ;
;                       .                                         ;
; Uses: BACK_SPACE, WRITE_CHAR, UPDATE_REAL_CURSOR                 ;
;-----------------------------------------------------------------;
READ_STRING     PROC
        PUSH    AX
        PUSH    BX
        PUSH    SI
        MOV     SI,DX                    ;Use SI for index register and

START_OVER:
        MOV     BX,2                     ;BX for offset to start of buffer

READ_LOOP:
        CALL    UPDATE_REAL_CURSOR       ;Move to position of virtual cursor
        CALL    READ_KEY                 ;Read one key from the keyboard
        OR      AH,AH                    ;Is character extended ASCII?
```

Reassemble all three files that you changed (Video_io, Cursor, and Kbd_io) and link Dskpatch. You should notice that screen output is much faster than before.

Summary

Speeding up WRITE_CHAR turned out to be quite a bit of work since you had to change a number of procedures, but the results were well worth the effort. Programs that have snappy screen updates are easier to work with than programs that take longer to paint the screen.

In the next chapter you will learn how to write procedures and functions for the C language in assembly language. For those of you using another language, the next chapter should be a useful starting point.

Using Assembly Language in C and C++ Programs

In this chapter you will learn how to write assembly-language subroutines for C/C++. You will learn about memory models, and how to write your assembly-language subroutines to work with all memory models. Finally, you will learn how to use in-line assembly directly inside your C/C++ programs.

31

Topics Covered

In this chapter we will show you how to use assembly language in C and C++ programs (we will use C from here on to refer to both C and C++, since C++ is a superset of C) both by writing assembly-language subroutines and using in-line assembly. This will enable you to add assembly-language instructions directly to your C programs. Rather than covering languages like Pascal or BASIC, we are concentrating on C because C is the most popular high-level programming language; most commercial programs are written in C, with a sprinkling of assembly language.

C has become quite popular because it is a modern high-level language that provides many assembly-language type functions, such as the ++ increment operator. Because C is a general-purpose programming language, there are times you will want to write parts of your program in assembly language for speed or low-level access to your machine, etc.

A Clear Screen for C

To assemble the programs in this chapter, you will need Microsoft MASM version 5.1 or later or Borland's Turbo Assembler. We are also using the Microsoft C compiler for the examples in this chapter.

We will start by rewriting a fairly simple procedure, CLEAR_SCREEN, so you can call it directly from C. As you will see, writing assembly language programs for use in C programs is actually quite simple.

The .MODEL directive being used allows you to define the memory model of the program you are building. (We have only used the SMALL memory model in this book.) Starting with version 5.1 of MASM, Microsoft added an extension to the .MODEL directive that allows you to write programs to attach to a number of different languages (including C and Pascal). To tell MASM that you are writing a C procedure, you append a ",C" to the end, as follows:

```
.MODEL   SMALL,C
```

Let's start the rewrite of CLEAR_SCREEN by taking another look at the assembly language version written in Chapter 17 of this book.

```
        PUBLIC  CLEAR_SCREEN
;------------------------------------------------------------;
; This procedure clears the entire screen.                   ;
;------------------------------------------------------------;
CLEAR_SCREEN    PROC
        PUSH    AX
```

414

```
        PUSH    BX
        PUSH    CX
        PUSH    DX
        XOR     AL,AL           ;Blank entire window
        XOR     CX,CX           ;Upper left corner is at (0,0)
        MOV     DH,24           ;Bottom line of screen is line 24
        MOV     DL,79           ;Right side is at column 79
        MOV     BH,7            ;Use normal attribute for blanks
        MOV     AH,6            ;Call for SCROLL-UP function
        INT     10h             ;Clear the window
        POP     DX
        POP     CX
        POP     BX
        POP     AX
        RET
CLEAR_SCREEN    ENDP
```

This is a fairly simple assembly language procedure. All you have to do to convert this into a C procedure is remove a number of instructions. The new file, shown in Listing 31-1, will hold all of the C procedures written in assembly language in this chapter.

Listing 31-1 The new file CLIB.ASM

```
.MODEL  SMALL,C

.CODE


;-------------------------------------------------------------------;
; This procedure clears the entire screen.                          ;
;-------------------------------------------------------------------;
CLEAR_SCREEN    PROC
        XOR     AL,AL           ;Blank entire window
        XOR     CX,CX           ;Upper left corner is at (0,0)
        MOV     DH,24           ;Bottom line of screen is line 24
        MOV     DL,79           ;Right side is at column 79
        MOV     BH,7            ;Use normal attribute for blanks
        MOV     AH,6            ;Call for SCROLL-UP function
        INT     10h             ;Clear the window
        RET
CLEAR_SCREEN    ENDP


        END
```

415

(If you are using Turbo Assembler, you will need to add two lines after .MODEL with MASM51 on the first line, and QUIRKS on the second line.) You will notice that we have removed all of the PUSH and POP instructions we used to save and restore registers. These instructions are used in assembly language programs so you do not have to keep track of which registers were changed by procedures you called. This makes programming in assembly language much simpler. C procedures, on the other hand, do not need you to save the AX, BX, CX, or DX registers at all since the C compiler always assumes procedures change these four registers or use them to return values. You are free to use these four registers without saving and restoring them.

You don't need to save and restore the AX, BX, CX, or DX registers in any C procedures you write in assembly language. You do, however, need to save and restore the SI, DI, BP, and segment registers if you change them in your procedures.

Can Change: AX, BX, CX, DX, ES

Must Preserve: SI, DI, BP, SP, CS, DS, SS

Direction flag must be 0 (use CLD)

Following is a very short C program that uses clear_screen(). In fact, that is all this program does.

Listing 31-2 The file test.c

```
main()
{
    clear_screen();
}
```

Use the following steps to assemble CLIB.ASM, compile TEST.C, and link both files together to form TEST.EXE.

```
ML /C CLIB.ASM
CL -C TEST.C
LINK TEST+CLIB,TEST,TEST/MAP;
```

> With some linkers or compilers you may have to tell the linker to ignore case since we have created the assembly-language names in uppercase letters, but we're using lowercase letters in the C code. Alternatively, you could write your assembly-language subroutines in lowercase letters to match your C code.

(The CL -C command compiles a file without linking it.) The last line is a bit more complicated than normal because you have asked Link to create a map file so you will know where to find clear_screen() in Debug. Even though TEST.EXE is a fairly small program, the memory map (TEST.MAP) turns out to be rather long because of some extra overhead present in all C programs. Following is an abbreviated version of this map showing the pieces of information we are interested in.

```
            .
            .
            .

   Address           Publics by Name

0054:00EC         STKHQQ
0000:001A         _clear_screen
0054:01D8         _edata
0054:01E0         _end
0054:00DA         _environ
0054:00B3         _errno
0000:01A2         _exit
0000:0010         _main

            .
            .
            .


Program entry point at 0000:002A
```

As you can see, the procedure is actually called _clear_screen instead of clear_screen. Most C compilers put an underscore in front all procedure names. (C compilers also put an underscore in front of variable names.) Using ",C" in the .MODEL directive tells MASM to add an underscore at the front of all assembly-language procedures in the file.

417

If you don't want a procedure to be public, you can use the PRIVATE keyword to keep a procedure from being declared PUBLIC. For example, this definition creates a private procedure called PrivateProc:

PrivateProc PROC PRIVATE

You will find examples of using the PRIVATE keyword in the library code in Appendix C.

You also may have noticed that we did not include a PUBLIC CLEAR_SCREEN to make CLEAR_SCREEN available to other files. This is another change that ",C" makes for us. The ",C" addition to .MODEL changes the PROC directive so it automatically defines every procedure as a PUBLIC procedure. In other words, if you are writing a C procedure in assembly language (using .MODEL SMALL,C), all of your procedures automatically will be declared PUBLIC for you.

Load TEST.EXE into Debug to see if there are any other changes MASM made for you. Using the address in the load map above (1A, which may be different for your C compiler), the following code is for _clear_screen:

```
C>DEBUG TEST.EXE
-U 1A
4A8A:001A 32C0          XOR     AL,AL
4A8A:001C 33C9          XOR     CX,CX
4A8A:001E B618          MOV     DH,18
4A8A:0020 B24F          MOV     DL,4F
4A8A:0022 B707          MOV     BH,07
4A8A:0024 B406          MOV     AH,06
4A8A:0026 CD10          INT     10
4A8A:0028 C3            RET
      .
      .
      .
```

This is exactly what you have written in CLIB.ASM. In other words, the ",C" at the end of the .MODEL directive only changed the name of the procedure from clear_screen to _clear_screen and declared it as PUBLIC. If this were the only help you got from ",C", we would not be very impressed. Fortunately, there are a number of other areas where MASM helps you to write C procedures in assembly language, specifically in passing parameters to procedures.

Using Clear_screen in C++

C++ adds a slight complication to the picture above as a result of something called *name mangling* or *function-name decorating*. C++ provides extra type-checking for the parameters in subroutines through simple conventions. Names of functions have extra characters added to them that indicate how many and what type of parameters the function defines. For example, if you had a function called

```
some_func(int, double)
```

it might be encoded by your C++ compiler to look something like this:

```
some_func__Fid
```

(In actual practice you will see a different name since different C++ compilers use different schemes for encoding names.) You will notice that the imaginary C++ compiler added __Fid to the end of the name. These extra characters contain information on what some_func refers to. The two underscores separate the subroutine's name from the extra information, which in this example is Fid. The *F* says that some_func is a function, as opposed to a class, and the other letters encode the parameter types, with *i* for the int and *d* for the double.

Each name includes information that uniquely defines the name, as well as the type of all of the parameters in a function. C++ compilers generate such mangled names to ensure that you are using all the correct type of parameters whenever you call an external function.

There are problems, however, with this scheme when you are writing assembly-language subroutines. There is no single standard for name mangling that all compilers use, so you cannot always predict what names a C++ compiler will generate. In addition, you may want to write general-purpose libraries that work both with C and C++ compilers. Since C compilers don't mangle the names, except for adding an underscore at the start of the name, what you need is some way to tell C++ compilers that you want to call an external C function. Fortunately, you can define a function using *extern "C"* to define a function as an external C function. In the example above, you would define some_func as follows in your C++ source file:

```
extern "C" some_func(int, double)
```

You can also define several functions as C functions with the following syntax:

```
extern "C"
    {
    some_func(int, double);
    another_func(int);
    }
```

If you are trying to use the subroutines in this chapter with a C++ compiler using C++ source files, you will have to declare all of the functions as extern "C". This ensures that your compiler does not mangle the names in your function calls.

419

Passing One Parameter

Throughout this book we have used registers to pass parameters to procedures. This has worked well because we never had more than six parameters (which would require the six registers AX, BX, CX, DX, SI, and DI). C programs, on the other hand, use the stack to pass parameters to procedures. This is where the MASM 5.1 .MODEL extensions really come into play. MASM automatically generates much of the code needed to work with parameters passed on the stack.

To see how this works, we will convert several procedures into C procedures. We will start with a procedure to write a string of characters on the screen. We could convert WRITE_STRING, but because it actually uses a number of other procedures (WRITE_CHAR, CURSOR_RIGHT, INIT_WRITE_CHAR, etc.), we will write a new WRITE_STRING that uses the ROM BIOS to write each character to the screen. This new WRITE_STRING uses INT 10h, function 14 to write each character on the screen. This will not be as fast as WRITE_STRING is now, but it is simple enough so you won't get lost in a lot of code.

Listing 31-3 shows our slow, C version of WRITE_STRING that you should add to CLIB.ASM:

Listing 31-3 Procedure added to CLIB.ASM

```
;-------------------------------------------------------------------;
; This procedure writes a string of characters to the screen.  The  ;
; string must end with              DB       0                      ;
;                                                                   ;
;       void write_string(char *string);                           ;
;-------------------------------------------------------------------;
WRITE_STRING    PROC    USES SI, STRING:PTR BYTE
        PUSHF                           ;Save the direction flag
        CLD                             ;Set direction for increment (forward)
        MOV     SI,STRING               ;Place address into SI for LODSB

STRING_LOOP:
        LODSB                           ;Get a character into the AL register
        OR      AL,AL                   ;Have we found the 0 yet?
        JZ      END_OF_STRING           ;Yes, we are done with the string
```

```
        MOV     AH,14               ;Ask for write character function
        XOR     BH,BH               ;Write to page 0
        INT     10h                 ;Write one character to the screen
        JMP     STRING_LOOP

END_OF_STRING:
        POPF                        ;Restore direction flag
        RET
WRITE_STRING    ENDP
```

Most of this code should be familiar because it was taken verbatim from our fast WRITE_STRING. One line, however, is quite different. Notice that we have added two pieces of information to the end of the PROC statement.

The first piece, USES SI, tells MASM that you are using the SI register in the procedure. As mentioned above, C procedures must save and restore the SI and DI registers if they modify them. As you will see, the USES SI causes MASM automatically to generate code to save and restore the SI register.

The second piece is used to pass one parameter to the program, which is a pointer to a string, or bytes of characters. STRING:PTR BYTE says that you want to call the parameter STRING, and that it is a pointer (PTR) to a character (BYTE), which is the first character in the string. By giving this parameter a name, you can use the parameter's value by writing its name, as in MOV SI,STRING.

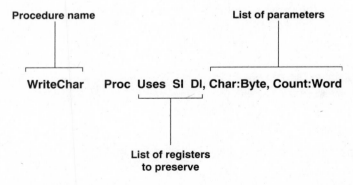

Figure 31-1: The Proc directive allows you to define both parameters that are passed on the stack and which registers will be preserved.

421

The magic of this will become clear as soon as you see the code generated by MASM. Assemble the new CLIB.ASM, then make the following change to TEST.C:

Listing 31-4 Changes to TEST.C

```
main()
{
    clear_screen();
    write_string("This is a string!");
}
```

Recompile TEST.C (with CL -C TEST.C) and link again (with LINK TEST+CLIB,TEST,TEST/MAP;). Looking at the new map file you will see that _write_string is at 33h (you may see a different number depending on the compiler you use).

```
0000:0024          _clear_screen
0056:01EA          _edata
0056:01F0          _end
0056:00DA          _environ
0056:00B3          _errno
0000:01C6          _exit
0000:0010          _main
0000:0033          _write_string
```

Following is the code actually generated by MASM for the write_string we just added to CLIB.ASM (the instructions added by MASM are against a gray background):

```
-U 33
4A8A:0033 55        PUSH     BP
4A8A:0034 8BEC      MOV      BP,SP
4A8A:0036 56        PUSH     SI
4A8A:0037 9C        PUSHF
4A8A:0038 FC        CLD
4A8A:0039 8B7604    MOV      SI,[BP+04]
4A8A:003C AC        LODSB
4A8A:003D 0AC0      OR       AL,AL
4A8A:003F 7408      JZ       0049
4A8A:0041 B40E      MOV      AH,0E
4A8A:0043 32FF      XOR      BH,BH
```

422

```
4A8A:0045 CD10          INT     10
4A8A:0047 EBF3          JMP     003C
4A8A:0049 9D            POPF
4A8A:004A 5E            POP     SI
4A8A:004B 5D            POP     BP
4A8A:004C C3            RET
```

MASM added quite a few instructions to the ones you wrote. The PUSH SI and POP SI instructions should be clear since we said that MASM would save and restore the SI register in response to USES SI. The other instructions require some explanation.

The BP register is a special-purpose register we have not said much about. If you look at the table of addressing modes in Appendix D you will notice that BP is a little different from other registers in that the default segment for [BP] is the SS register rather than the DS register. This is of interest here because C programs pass parameters on the stack rather than in registers. So the instruction

```
MOV     SI,[BP+04]
```

will always read from the stack, even if SS is not the same as DS or ES (which it often won't be for memory models other than SMALL). Because the BP register is so convenient for working with the stack, C procedures use the BP register to access the parameters passed to them on the stack.

In order to use the BP register, you have to set it to the current value of SP, which the MOV BP,SP instruction does for us. But since the C procedure that called us also uses the BP register to access its parameters, we need to save and restore the BP register. So the assembler automatically generates these instructions (without the comments, of course) that allow us to use the BP register to read parameters from the stack:

```
PUSH    BP                      ;Save the current BP register
MOV     BP,SP                   ;Set BP to point to our parameters
        .
        .
        .
POP     BP                      ;Restore the old value of BP
```

Figure 31-2 shows how the stack would look for a procedure, with two parameters, that uses the SI register. The C call, c_call(param1, param2), pushes the parameters onto the stack, from right to left. By pushing the rightmost parameter first, and the leftmost parameter last, the first parameter will always be closest to the "top of the stack"; in other words, closest to SP. Doing so means that param1 will always have the same offset from BP, no matter how many parameters you actually pass to this subroutine.

The CALL instruction created by the write_string( ) statement pushes the return address onto the stack, at which point our procedure gains control. You will notice at this point that the PUSH SI instruction appears *after* the MOV BP,SP instruction. Once you have set the value of BP, you are free to change the stack as much as you want by PUSHing and POPping registers, and by calling other procedures. Because MASM generates all the needed instructions you do not have to concern yourself with writing these instructions in the correct order.

The first parameter will always be at the same offset from BP, which is 4 for the SMALL memory model (it would be 6 for memory models that require a FAR return address, since a FAR return requires both the old CS and IP values to be on the stack). Looking at the unassembled listing above, you will notice that the assembler translated the MOV SI,STRING instruction into MOV SI,[BP+4], see Figure 31-3. If you had used a memory model with FAR procedures, this would be translated into MOV SI,[BP+6].

C passes parameters on the stack in the opposite order from most other high-level languages. Pascal, BASIC, and FORTRAN, for example, push the first parameter onto the stack first, with the last parameter last, which means the last parameter would be closest to the top of the stack (SP). The offset from BP to the first parameter will depend on the number of parameters you pushed onto the stack. This is not a problem in Pascal, BASIC, or FORTRAN where procedure calls *must* have the same number of parameters as defined in the procedure.

In C procedures, however, you can pass more parameters on the stack than are defined in the procedure. The C printf( ) function is a good example. The number of parameters you pass to printf( ) depends entirely on how many % arguments you have in the string. To allow C procedures to have a variable number of parameters, you need to push the parameters in reverse order so the first parameter will always be closest to SP, and not depend on the number of parameters you actually pushed onto the stack.

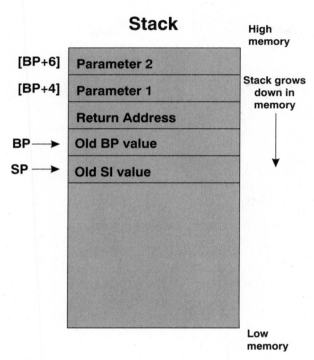

Figure 31-2: How C passes parameters on the stack.

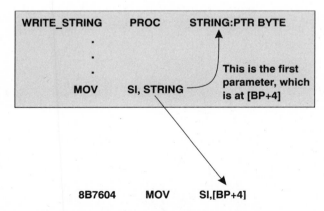

Figure 31-3: The Assembler knows where to find the parameter.

Passing Multiple Parameters

Following is Listing 31-5, another short procedure you will find useful in your C programs.

Listing 31-5 Procedure added to CLIB.ASM.

```
;-------------------------------------------------------------;
; This procedure moves the cursor                             ;
;                                                             ;
;       void goto_xy(int x, int y);                           ;
;-------------------------------------------------------------;
GOTO_XY         PROC      X:WORD, Y:WORD
        MOV     AH,2                    ;Call for SET CURSOR POSITION
        MOV     BH,0                    ;Display page 0
        MOV     DH,BYTE PTR (Y)         ;Get the line number (0..N)
        MOV     DL,BYTE PTR (X)         ;Get the column number (0..79)
        INT     10h                     ;Move the cursor
        RET
GOTO_XY         ENDP
```

Listing 31-6 shows the changes you should make in TEST.C to use goto_xy( ):

Listing 31-6 Changes to TEST.C

```
main()
{
    clear_screen();
    goto_xy(35,10);
    write_string("This is a string!");
}
```

There are two items of interest in goto_xy( ). First, you will notice that we declared the two parameters (X and Y) in the order we wrote them in the procedure call: goto_xy(x, y). We would write these parameters in the same order for a language, like Pascal, which pushes parameters in a different order; MASM handles the differences in order on the stack so you don't have to change your code, or know what order parameters are pushed onto the stack. All you have to do is change the language in the .MODEL from C to, for example, Pascal.

The other change is a bit more subtle. You will notice that we defined X and Y to be words, rather than bytes. We did this because C, and other high-level languages, never push a byte onto the stack, they always push words onto the stack. This occurs because the PUSH instructions push words, and not bytes, onto the stack. In goto_xy, this is not a problem except that you want to move a byte into the DH and DL registers. Writing:

```
MOV     DL,X
```

won't work because the assembler would report an error. Instead, you have to use BYTE PTR X to access X as a byte. But this does not always work in MASM. For example, look at the following line:

```
MOV     DH,BYTE PTR Y        ;Get the line number (0..N)
```

Although this line works correctly in MASM 6, it does not work properly in MASM 5 because of the way the high-level language extensions were implemented before MASM 6.

The X:WORD and Y:WORD definitions in MASM 5's PROC statement are implemented inside the assembler as *macros*. Macros, which we won't cover in this book, are a way to add *features* to the assembler by substituting text for symbols that you type. The parameters X and Y, for example, are actually macros. So when you write MOV DL,X, the X is expanded into the text defined by the macros that MASM created for X, as follows:

```
X       →     WORD PTR [BP+4]
```

If you put BYTE PTR in front of this, you will get something the assembler does not know how to handle, as follows:

```
BYTE PTR X      →      BYTE PTR WORD PTR [BP+4]
```

You can fix this problem by putting parentheses around the X and Y, which tells the assembler that [BP+4] refers to a word, but you wish to treat it as a byte:

```
BYTE PTR (X)      →      BYTE PTR (WORD PTR [BP+4])
```

The parentheses simply tell the assembler to process everything between the parentheses first. In the rest of this chapter, we will write the code specifically for MASM 6.

Returning Function Values

In addition to writing C procedures in assembly language, you will probably want to write C functions in assembly, which is quite simple. C functions return values in the following registers: bytes in AL, words in AX, and long words (two words) in DX:AX, with the low word in AX. If you want to return types with 3 bytes or more than 4 bytes, you will need to consult the *Microsoft Macro Assembler Programmer's Guide*, or the *Turbo Assembler User's Guide* for details.

Here are the registers to use to return values to C programs:

```
Byte      AL
Word      AX
Long      DX:AX
```

The following procedure, which you should add to CLIB.ASM, is a rewrite of READ_KEY that returns the extended key code to C programs.

Listing 31-7 Add this procedure to CLIB.ASM.

```
;--------------------------------------------------------------------;
; This procedure reads on key from the keyboard.                     ;
;                                                                    ;
;       key = read_key();                                            ;
;                                                                    ;
; Returns: ASCII code       For all keys that generate characters    ;
;          0x100 + scan code  For special function keys.             ;
;--------------------------------------------------------------------;
READ_KEY        PROC
        XOR     AH,AH                   ;Ask for keyboard read function
        INT     16h                     ;Read character/scan code from keyboard
        OR      AL,AL                   ;Is it an extended code?
        JZ      EXTENDED_CODE           ;Yes
NOT_EXTENDED:
        XOR     AH,AH                   ;Return just the ASCII code
        JMP     DONE_READING

EXTENDED_CODE:
        MOV     AL,AH                   ;Put scan code into AL
        MOV     AH,1                    ;Signal extended code
DONE_READING:
        RET
READ_KEY        ENDP
```

Listing 31-8 is a version of test.c that will clear the screen, display a string near the center, and wait until you press the space bar before exiting back to DOS.

Listing 31-8 Changes to TEST.C

```
main()
{
    clear_screen();
    goto_xy(35,10);
    write_string("Press space to continue.");
    while (read_key() != ' ')
        ;
}
```

Using Other Memory Models

All of the assembly subroutines we have shown you were designed for the SMALL memory model. In the SMALL model, your program has a single code segment and a single data segment, which means that all calls are NEAR calls and all the data is in the segment pointed to by DS.

Since most real programs use more than 64K for either code or data, how do you write your assembly-language subroutines to work with these other memory models? Part of the answer is easy, and part of the answer is hard.

The easiest way to demonstrate how to handle the different memory models is to first draw a chart that summarizes the different memory models, which you will find in Table 31-1. This chart shows the default type of function calls and pointers used in the different memory models.

Table 31-1 The different memory models

Model	Calls	Data Pointers	DS
TINY	Near	Near	DGROUP
SMALL	Near	Near	DGROUP
COMPACT	Near	Far	DGROUP
MEDIUM	Far	Near	DGROUP
LARGE	Far	Far	DGROUP
HUGE	Far	Far	DGROUP *

* DS does not point to DGROUP in Borland C++'s HUGE memory model.

NEAR calls are the same as all the calls you have seen so far. All of the procedures are in a single segment, so all CALLs change the IP register *without* changing the CS register. On the other hand, FAR calls are used when you have more than one segment for the code in your program, which is typically the case for most programs written in C, since they often have more than 64K of code. In this case, a call needs both an offset and a segment value for the function you are calling (which changes both CS:IP). FAR CALLs push both the return offset and segment onto the stack. Along with FAR CALLs the 80x86 also has FAR Return instructions: RETF.

The same types of ideas also apply to the data in your program. Many programs written in C use more than 64K of data, which means they need to use more than one data segment. All programs have a default data segment which is actually a group called DGROUP where your global variables are stored, but this *NEAR data* is limited to 64K in size. Any data beyond this NEAR data must be stored in other data segments. You then access this data by using both an offset and a segment, as you will see below. Table 31-2 summarizes the segments used by many C/C++ compilers (including Microsoft and Borland).

Table 31-2 Segments used with memory models

Model	Code	Data
TINY	_TEXT	DGROUP (same as _TEXT)
SMALL	_TEXT	DGROUP
COMPACT	_TEXT	DGROUP + other data segments
MEDIUM	*filename*_TEXT	DGROUP
LARGE	*filename*_TEXT	DGROUP + other data segments
HUGE	*filename*_TEXT	DGROUP + other data segments

In most C/C++ compilers, the DS register will always point to the DGROUP data segment, so you can access your NEAR data by using NEAR pointers and references. (NEAR data is any data you define with .DATA or .DATA?.) However, there are cases when this may not be true, such as the HUGE model in Borland's C++ compiler or when you create your own custom memory model. In such cases, you will need to set DS so it points to DGROUP at the start of your assembly-language procedures before you can use any of your NEAR variables. In this chapter we will assume that DS points to DGROUP.

You can see that there are a number of different combinations of NEAR/FAR CALLs and pointers. When you write and assemble a specific library of assembly-language subroutines, it must be built for one of these models. If you build a library for one model, but use it with another, you will almost certainly have problems. For example, if you link some small model assembly-language subroutines with a large model C program, the RET instructions in all your assembly-language code will use NEAR returns, but your C code will make FAR CALLs, which means that the NEAR returns in your assembly-language subroutines won't return properly to your C program since a NEAR return restores the IP register, but *not* the CS register.

What you will need to do is build versions of your libraries for each memory model you want to use. In order to write such libraries, you will have to deal with two separate issues—functions and data references.

Writing NEAR and FAR Functions

Switching between NEAR and FAR subroutines based on which model you are using is trivial. As soon as you change the .MODEL statement in any of your files, MASM will automatically change the RET instruction at the end of your procedures to be either a NEAR or a FAR return, based on the current memory model that you have specified. If you wanted to rewrite all of the functions in CLIB.ASM for the medium model, you would change the first line of CLIB.ASM to read the following:

```
.MODEL  MEDIUM,C
```

Then when you reassemble CLIB.ASM, all the return instructions will be RETF instructions (RETurn Far).

Working with NEAR and FAR Data

Working with FAR data takes more work because you cannot assume, as you have done until now, that the data will be in the segment currently pointed to by the DS register. A FAR pointer contains both an offset *and* a segment since the data could be in any segment. So in order to read a single parameter, you have to use slightly different code than before. For example, the code you have in write_string( ) to retrieve a pointer to STRING in SI (the LODSB instruction retrieves bytes from DS:SI) is as follows:

```
MOV    SI,STRING            ;Place address into SI for LODSB
```

However, in the MEDIUM memory model you need to load both the DS and the SI register, rather than just the SI register. You will use the following form for the MEDIUM model.

```
LDS    SI,STRING            ;Place address into SI for LODSB
```

LDS stands for Load DS, and it loads both the DS register and an index register (SI in this case). To see how this works, let's first look at the machine language generated by this instruction. If you look inside the EXE file at the subroutine write_string, you will find the LDS instruction appears as follows:

```
LDS     SI,[BP+06]
```

As mentioned above, the LDS instruction stands for Load DS because it changes the DS register, as well as an index register. In the instruction above, the name STRING was changed to [BP+06], which is the address of a 2-word pointer on the stack. The first word of this pointer is the offset into the segment, so it is loaded by LDS into the SI register (you can use almost any non-segment register as the second register that LDS uses). The second word, which is the segment value, is loaded by LDS into DS. In other words, LDS SI,STRING loads the FAR pointer represented by STRING into DS:SI.

There is another detail you will need to change. Since LDS changes the value of DS, and since C procedures *must* preserve the value of DS, you will need to change the PROC statement so it will preserve the DS register as follows:

```
WRITE_STRING    PROC    USES SI DS, STRING:PTR BYTE
```

The new USES SI DS tells MASM to generate code to save and restore both SI and DS.

Now we will show you another example that is a little trickier. Say you have a procedure that takes a pointer to an integer that has the following C definition (we will write the procedure in assembly).

```
some_func(int *number)
```

The subroutine in assembly language would then appear as follows for the SMALL memory model.

```
.MODEL  SMALL,C

.CODE

;-----------------------------------------------------------;
; This function modifies the value passed to it.            ;
;                                                           ;
;      some_func(int *number)                               ;
;-----------------------------------------------------------;
SOME_FUNC       PROC    NUMBER:PTR WORD
        MOV     BX,NUMBER
        MOV     [BX],10
        RET
SOME_FUNC       ENDP
```

Since NUMBER is a pointer to the number, rather than the number itself, you need an extra step. The first MOV instruction moves the address of the actual value into the BX register, and the second MOV moves a number into this address.

In the LARGE memory model this same subroutine appears as follows:

```
.MODEL   LARGE,C

.CODE

;------------------------------------------------------------------;
; This function modifies the value passed to it.                   ;
;                                                                  ;
;       some_func(int *number)                                     ;
;------------------------------------------------------------------;
SOME_FUNC        PROC      NUMBER:PTR WORD
         LES     BX,NUMBER
         MOV     ES:[BX],10
         RET
SOME_FUNC        ENDP
```

You will notice that in this case we used the LES (Load ES) instruction instead of LDS. LES and LDS work in the same way, except that LES loads ES:*reg* while LDS loads DS:*reg*. C procedures must preserve DS, but they can change ES. Using the ES register means we don't need to include USES DS, which causes an extra PUSH and POP to be created to preserve the value of DS. But you do need to write ES: in front of [BX] so that you will work with a value in the ES, rather than the DS segment.

The last case we will cover is reading from a global variable. When you are dealing with NEAR data, you can simply refer to the name of the variable. For example, to load NUMBER into the AX register, you will use the following instruction:

```
MOV    AX, NUMBER
```

This assumes that the DS register points to the segment that contains NUMBER, but this may not be the case. Most compilers (C as well as other languages) have a default segment that DS always points to, and this segment contains most of your constants and global variables. But if you have more than 64K of constants and global variables, some of the global variables will have to be in segments other than the default segment. In these cases DS won't point to the segment that contains your global variable, so you will have to set ES so it points to the proper segment and use an ES: in front of the address. The code which does this is as follows:

```
MOV    AX, SEG NUMBER            ;Get NUMBER's segment
MOV    ES, AX                    ;Have ES point to this segment
MOV    AX, ES:NUMBER             ;Read the value of NUMBER
```

The SEG directive gives us the segment of a variable. When the assembler encounters this directive, it creates a relocation-table entry for this number since the actual segment number won't be known until DOS loads your program into memory. By the way, this code will work with any memory model, even when you only have a single data segment. However, this code is slower than a single move statement, since you have three move statements.

The MOV ES, AX command takes only 2 clock cycles to run (3 on the 80486), so it is a very quick command. However, this same command is much slower in protected-mode programs, such as in Windows programs. In these cases, the MOV ES, AX command takes 18 clock cycles on the 80386 and 9 cycles on the 80486. As you will see in Chapter 33, this command does a lot of extra work in a protected-mode program. The bottom line is that as long as you are working with a DOS program, the MOV AX, ES command is very fast.

Table 31-3 summarizes the different types of code you need to read different types of C parameters.

Table 31-3 Code to access C parameters

C Parameter	Small Model Code	Large Model Code
char c	mov al,Byte Ptr c	mov al,Byte Ptr c
int number	mov ax,number	mov ax,number
		(default data segment)

continues

435

Table 31-3 continued

C Parameter	Small Model Code	Large Model Code
int far number	N/A	mov ax, seg number
		mov es, ax
		mov ax, es:number
int *number	**lea** bx,number	**les** bx,number
	mov bx,[bx]	mov bx,**es:**[bx]

Writing General-Model Procedures

All the changes can be rather difficult to keep under control, especially if you need to write procedures that you can use to create code for a number of different memory models. Fortunately, there is a way you can write subroutines that you can reassemble for *any* memory model simply by changing the .MODEL directive at the start of the file. The trick uses something known as *conditional assembly*.

With conditional assembly you can have two versions of code that will be assembled, depending on the outcome of a test. Since you need to generate different code to handle NEAR and FAR pointers, this is a good candidate for conditional assembly. In essence, the kind of code you would write to handle the example SOME_FUNC procedure above is as follows:

```
IF      @DataSize             ;Is this FAR data?
LES     BX,NUMBER             ;Yes, load ES:BX with address
MOV     ES:[BX],10            ;Change value at ES:BX
ELSE
MOV     BX,NUMBER             ;No, load BX with address
MOV     [BX],10               ;Change value at BX
ENDIF
```

The IF, ELSE, and ENDIF directives allow you to control which code will actually be assembled. In this case, @DataSize is a special MASM value that tells you what kind of pointers you have. When @DataSize is 0, it means you have NEAR pointers; otherwise, you have FAR pointers.

436

Although this code works very well, it looks much more complicated than it is. Now we will show you a good trick that you can use in your programs. We will use conditional assembly again, but this time we will use it to define some symbols that make it easy to write two lines, rather than seven lines whenever you want to refer to a pointer.

To see what you need to do, notice that the two sets of assembly-language instructions above differ in two places. In the first instruction, you will use LES rather than MOV to load a FAR pointer; in the second instruction, you use ES: in front of [BX] to refer to the value. We will create two symbols that we will use instead of MOV or LES and instead of the ES:. The definitions you will want to use are as follows:

Listing 31-9 The definitions for creating model-independent code.

```
        IF      @DataSize           ;Are pointers FAR?
lodDS   TEXTEQU <LDS>               ;Yes, use LDS to get DS:pointer
lodES   TEXTEQU <LES>               ;And use LES to get ES:pointer
refES   TEXTEQU <ES:>               ;And put ES: in front of refs
        ELSE
lodDS   TEXTEQU <MOV>               ;No, use MOV to get pointer
lodES   TEXTEQU <MOV>               ;And also for ES case
refES   TEXTEQU <>                  ;And nothing for the references
        ENDIF
```

You can write the code above as follows, no matter which memory model you are using.

```
lodES   BX,NUMBER           ;Get pointer to the value
MOV     refES [BX],10       ;Change the value
```

This is a lot easier to read, and it generates the correct code based on the current memory model.

The TEXTEQU directive is a directive new to MASM 6. It is very much like the EQU directive you learned in Chapter 14. EQU allows you to assign numeric values to a name; TEXTEQU allows you to assign text values to a name. The brackets (< and >) in a TEXTEQU delimit the text that will be substituted whenever MASM sees the name, such as lodDS, that you have defined.

437

The final step you might want to take is to use another TEXTEQU macro to actually define the memory model from the ML command line. You can define any macro before MASM starts to assembly your program by using the following syntax:

```
ML /C /DLANG_MODEL=LARGE CLIB.ASM
```

Your .MODEL directive would appear as follows:

```
.MODEL  LANG_MODEL,C
```

To use a different memory model, simply change the LARGE on the ML command line to any of the other names for memory models.

Table 31-4 summarizes the syntax you will use to read parameters using the macros in Listing 31-9.

Table 31-4 Model-independent code to access C parameters

C Parameter	Model-Independent Code
char c	mov al, Byte Ptr c
int number	mov ax, number
	(default data segment)
int number	mov ax, seg number
	mov es, ax
	mov ax, es:number
	(any data segment)
int *number	lodES bx, number
	mov bx, refES [bx]

Summary on Writing C/C++ Procedures in Assembly

Since we have covered a lot of material about how to write assembly-language procedures for your C/C++ programs, it is useful to summarize all the rules and steps you will want to use.

1. **Register Usage:** Here is a list of registers that you must preserve and can change freely.

   Preserve: SI, DI, BP, SP, CS, DS, SS

   Can Change: AX, BX, CX, DX, ES

2. **C Parameters:** You can access any procedure parameters directly by name, assuming you have defined them in the PROC statement. The compiler will automatically turn all such references into the form [bp+*x*] for you, which will refer to the parameters stored on the stack, by using the SS segment.

3. **Global C Variables:** When you are working with a memory model that uses NEAR pointers, or when global variables are defined in the default data segment (which is a NEAR data segment), you can refer to any global variable directly by name. The DS register will point to the default data segment, which is a NEAR segment, for most C compilers (except for the Huge model in Borland C++). However, if a global variable is in another segment, you will have to load the ES register by first moving SEG *varname* into another register and then by moving this register into ES.

4. **Far C Pointers/Data:** If you are working with Far pointers or with global variables that are not stored in the default data segment, you will need to set the ES register so it points to your data.

5. **Function Return Values:** Just like in assembly-language subroutines, C functions return values in the registers: AL for Char, AX for Int, DX:AX for Long. For returning pointers, you will need to return an offset in AX for NEAR pointers, and a segment:offset pair in the DX:AX registers for FAR pointers.

Writing In-Line Assembly Code

The final subject we will cover in this chapter is *in-line* assembly. Most C and C++ compilers allow you to write code directly in your C files, rather than requiring you to write separate ASM files to do the work. This can often be the most convenient way of adding the power of assembly language to your C programs.

The syntax you will need to use varies very slightly between Borland's Turbo C++, Microsoft's QuickC, and Microsoft's C++ compilers, but only by some underscore characters. Each compiler has a special keyword that indicates when you "turn on" assembly language mode. For Borland, you use asm; for Microsoft's QuickC compiler you use _asm; for Microsoft C/C++ 7 you use __asm.

The reason for the differences in the syntax of the asm keyword is mostly a result of history. The C language began without any real standards, so different companies added their own private keywords (such as asm and _asm). However, there is now a standards committee that defines standards for the C language and for how C compilers should be written; their standard is known as the ANSI C standard.

The ANSI committee now "allows" compiler writers to add their own, private keywords as long as such names begin with two underscores, as in __asm. For this reason, Microsoft's C/C++ compiler (which is more recent than the QuickC compiler we used in this chapter) uses __asm rather than _asm. As an example, we will rewrite GOTO_XY as a C-language subroutine called GotoXY in Microsoft C:

Listing 31-10 A C version of GOTO_XY using in-line assembly.

```
void GotoXY(
        int x,                          // X coordinate, 0..79
        int y )                         // Y coordinate, 0..??
{
    _asm
        {
        mov     ah,2                    // Use Set Cursor Position call
        mov     dl, Byte Ptr x          // Put X, Y into DL, DH
```

```
        mov     dh, Byte Ptr y
        int     10h                     // Call ROM BIOS to move cursor
        }
}
```

You use asm, rather than _asm, in Borland C++; and __asm in Microsoft C/ C++ 7. What you will notice about this new subroutine is that it is a mix between C code and assembly-language code. An assembly-language code is inside the the C subroutine, and some C references are inside the assembly-language code. Now let's look at the code actually generated for GotoXY for the LARGE memory model:

```
PUSH    BP
MOV     BP,SP
PUSH    SI
PUSH    DI
MOV     AH,02
MOV     DL,[BP+06]
MOV     DH,[BP+08]
INT     10
POP     DI
POP     SI
MOV     SP,BP
POP     BP
RETF
```

You will notice that the C compiler automatically converted references to the X and Y parameters into forms like [BP+06], which refers to a value on the stack, at offset 6 above BP. This is the same kind of code that MASM would have generated for you, but it is a lot easier to write a little code with in-line assembly in C rather than firing up MASM with a separate source file.

Using Far Data

As long as you are working with a memory model that uses NEAR pointers for all the data (TINY, SMALL, MEDIUM), reading and writing global variables with in-line assembly is very easy: You simply supply the name of the global variable. An example of reading the global variable *x*: is as folows:

```
int     x;                          // Variable in NEAR segment

main()                              // Program shows how to read
{                                   // NEAR data in in-line assembly
    _asm
        {
        mov     ax, x               // Read NEAR data
        }
}
```

In other words, you can reference the variable directly by name, and everything works without any problems because the variable *x* is in the default segment, DGROUP, and the DS register points to DGROUP.

However, when you are dealing with other memory models (COMPACT, LARGE, HUGE) the DS register may not point to the segment that contains your variable. For example, if you have a large array variable, it may be placed in its own data segment, so the code above won't work. Instead, you will need to set a segment register (ES is a good one to use since you are allowed to change its value in C programs) to point to the segment that contains your variable before you can read or write that variable. An example program which shows you how to read the value from x[0] and x[1] is as follows:

```
int     x[30000];                   // Variable in FAR segment

main()                              // Program shows how to read
{                                   // FAR data in in-line assembly
    _asm
        {
        mov     ax, seg x           // Get the segment for x
        mov     es, ax              // Set ES so it points to x
        mov     ax, es:x            // Read x[0]
        mov     bx, es:x[2]         // Read x[1]
        }
}
```

Let's look at this program in detail. The first assembly-language instruction loads the AX register with the number of the segment that contains the array *x*. The next line then sets the ES register so it points to this segment. The last two lines then read two values from this array. Each of these two instructions uses the ES: segment override to read the value from the segment pointed to by ES, rather than the default segment pointed to by DS. We have also shown you how you can directly read elements from this array. The X[2] actually reads the second element of the array. The 2 here is an offset, in *bytes*, from the start of *x*. Since each element of the *x* array is type bytes long (assuming an int variable is 2 bytes), we wrote es:x[2] to read the array element 1.

When you write in-line assembly code that reads either pointers or global variables, you have two choices—either you can write the code so it works just with NEAR or just with FAR pointers, or you can write general-purpose code that sets the ES register before reading or writing variables. If you write code that sets ES, you will be assured that your code will work with any memory model. However, such code will run slower when you are dealing with NEAR pointers and data. If you want the best of both worlds (general-purpose code, but the fastest code), you could write a set of C macros, just like the assembly-language macros in the previous section, to generate the correct code based on the current memory model.

Summary on In-Line Assembly

In general, there are not many restrictions you need to be aware of when you are writing in-line assembly. The more significant ones are as follows (check your compiler's manual for all the details):

1. **Register Usage:** The same rules applied to in-line assembly are applied to writing external assembly-language procedures.

    Preserve: SI, DI, BP, SP, CS, DS, SS

    Can Change: AX, BX, CX, DX, ES

2. **C Parameters:** You can access any procedure parameters directly by name. The compiler will automatically turn all such references into the form [bp+*x*] for you; this will refer to the parameters stored on the stack by using the SS segment.

3. **Local C Variables:** You can access any local C variables directly by name. All local variables are stored on the stack, so the compiler will generate an address of the form [bp+*x*], which always refers to an address on the stack by using the SS segment.

4. **Global C Variables:** You can refer to any global variable directly by name when working with a memory model that uses NEAR pointers

443

or when global variables are defined in the default data segment (which is a NEAR data segment). However, if a global variable is in another segment, you will have to load the ES register using the method shown above.

5. **Far C Pointers/Data:** If you are working with Far pointers or with global variables that are not stored in the default data segment, you will need to set the ES register so it points to your data.

6. **Function Return Values:** As in assembly-language subroutines, C functions return values in the registers—AL for Char, AX for Int, DX:AX for Long. For returning pointers, you will need to return an offset in AX for NEAR pointers, and a segment:offset pair in the DX:AX registers for FAR pointers.

7. **Comments:** You can use either C or assembly-style comments inside your in-line assembly code. Borland's C++ compiler, however, does *not* allow assembly-style comments using semicolons—you must use C-style comments.

Summary

That wraps up our coverage of using assembly language in C and C++ programs. In Appendix C, and on the disk included with this book, you will find an entire library of assembly-language procedures for writing to the screen, using the mouse, and working with the keyboard, all written using the methods outlined in this chapter. These libraries show how you might put everything together in the real world.

If you want to write procedures for languages other than C or C++, you will need to consult the documentation on your language, or in the assembler that you are using. Not all compilers for the same language (such as Pascal) use the same conventions. So even though MASM (and Turbo Assembler) supports the Pascal conventions, there may be differences if you are not using both an assembler and a compiler from the same company.

The next chapter covers writing RAM-resident programs; the final technical chapter covers protected-mode programming and using assembly-language code in programs for Microsoft Windows.

DISKLITE, a RAM-Resident Program

In this chapter you will write a very simple RAM-resident program called Disklite. This displays a drive letter in the upper-right corner of your screen whenever any program reads or writes to a disk drive.

Disk file: DISKLITE.ASM

32

Topics Covered

RAM-Resident Programs

RAM-resident programs are almost always written in assembly language to allow maximum access to the ROM BIOS and memory and to keep them small. The Disklite program you will build, for example, weighs in at just 247 bytes. Since RAM-resident programs stay in memory until you restart your computer, and since more programs need 512K or more of memory to run, keeping the size down on RAM-resident programs is very important. If a program is too large, users won't be willing to keep a copy in memory, which is the whole point.

RAM-resident programs usually need to work closely with the ROM BIOS or with your computer's hardware to change how existing functions work, or to add new functions. Disklite, for example, watches the ROM BIOS routines that read from and write to disks so it can display a disk drive "light" on the screen.

Many programmers like to watch the disk drive light during compiles to keep track of the compiler's progress. When a compile takes 30 seconds or a minute, there is not much else you can do. Programmers also like to watch the disk drive light when they are testing programs that read from or write to a disk to see if they are actually accessing the disk. But what happens if you place your computer under your desk? In this case, Disklite provides an on-screen drive light that *lights up* whenever you read to or write from a disk. It also tells you which disk you are accessing.

Intercepting Interrupts

As we mentioned above, Disklite displays the drive light by watching the ROM BIOS routines that read to and write from disk. All disk reading and writing is performed by the INT 13h ROM BIOS routine. DOS uses this service by issuing an INT 13h instruction. Interrupts, as you saw in Chapter 11, use a vector table at the start of memory to determine which routine to call. Each interrupt vector in this table is two words long since it holds the FAR address of the routine that will handle the interrupt. The INT 13h instruction will use the address at 0:4Ch (13h times 4) in memory as the address of the routine that will handle the INT 13h function. In other words, you could change this address to point to your routine instead of the ROM BIOS's routine.

Figure 32-1 shows how INT 13h calls the routine in the ROM BIOS. Now imagine that you changed the interrupt vector to point to your procedure. Then the vector will point to you instead of the ROM BIOS. Now you have taken control of the INT 13h function. But this is not quite what you want. If you completely take over INT 13h, you have to write a program that will do everything INT 13h did, as well as the new functions you want to add. What you should use to do most of the work is the existing ROM BIOS INT 13h routines.

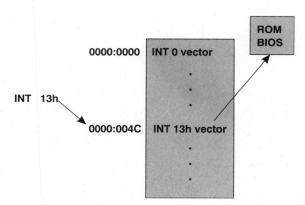

Figure 32-1: INT 13h uses the interrupt vector at 4Ch to determine the address of the routine to call.

Instead of blindly replacing the INT 13h vector, you will save the vector in your own program first, and then you can use the ROM BIOS INT 13h routines by simulating an INT call to the ROM routines. Recall that an INT is like a CALL instruction, but it saves the flags on the stack so they will be restored by an IRET (Interrupt RETurn) instruction. All you need to do is save the address of the INT 13h routines in the variable ROM_DISKETTE_INT, so you can pass control on to the ROM BIOS INT 13h routines with a pair of instructions as follows:

449

```
PUSHF
CAL        ROM_DISKETTE_INT
```

When the ROM finishes accessing the disk, you will receive control again. This means you can execute some code before, as well as after, you call the ROM's disk functions. This is exactly what you need if you are going to display, then remove, a drive letter. Figure 32-2 shows these steps in more detail.

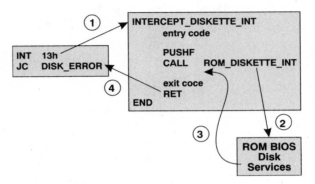

Figure 32-2: Intercepting INT 13h.

The technique we have presented here will work with most ROM BIOS routines. But there is a major caveat. Since DOS is not a multitasking operating system, you cannot make DOS function calls from within an interrupt service routine unless you can be can be absolutely certain DOS was not in the middle of processing a function request. There are ways to ensure this, but they are rather difficult, so we won't cover them in this book. However, you will find some references to this kind of information in the bibliography at the end of the last chapter.

Disklite

Most of the other details of Disklite should either be familiar or documented well enough so you can figure them out. There are a few details, however, that are new or a bit out of the ordinary.

First of all, notice that we are not restoring registers in the procedures of Disklite. Instead, we clearly mark which registers are altered and then we save all the registers that can be altered at the start of INTERCEPT_DISKETTE_INT and nowhere else. We save them only once in order to keep the stack usage to a minimum.

Interrupt service routines generally need to be written so they don't use much of the stack because they are borrowing someone else's stack and there may not be much space left on the stack. You never worried about stack space in your own programs because you gave yourself a large enough stack. You cannot guarantee that everyone will give you a large stack when we get an INT 13h request. For these reasons, many RAM-resident programs set up their own stack.

The procedures GET_DISPLAY_BASE, SAVE_SCREEN, and WRITE_TO_SCREEN should be fairly clear. You have seen GET_DISPLAY_BASE before; the other two should be clear from the last chapter—SAVE_SCREEN saves the two characters in the upper-right corner; WRITE_TO_SCREEN writes two characters in the upper-right corner. WRITE_TO_SCREEN is used both to display the drive letter and to restore the two characters that were on the screen before you displayed the drive letter.

DISPLAY_DRIVE_LETTER is also fairly simple. INT 13h takes a drive number in the DL register. For floppy disk drives, DL will contain 0 for drive A:, 1 for drive B:, and so on. For hard disks, DL starts at 80h. To get the actual drive letter for a hard disk, you subtract 80h and then add the number of floppy disk drives since the first hard disk appears after the last floppy disk.

That leaves you with INIT_VECTORS and GET_NUM_FLOPPIES. INIT_VECTORS shows the details of installing a procedure to intercept an interrupt vector and to keep such a program in memory after you have returned to DOS. First you display an author message, and then you call GET_NUM_FLOPPIES to set NUM_FLOPPIES to the number of floppy disk drives attached to your computer. Next you read and set the INT 13h vector with the INT 21h functions 35h and 25h that read and set interrupt vectors.

You will notice that we put both initialization routines at the very end of Disklite. As it turns out, both these procedures are used only once—when we

451

first load Disklite into memory—so you don't need to keep them in memory after you load Disklite. This is why we have put them at the end. The DOS function call INT 27h, called *Terminate but Stay Resident,* exits your program and keeps most of the program in memory. This function call takes an offset in DX to the first byte you do not want to keep in memory. By setting DX so it points to INIT_VECTORS, you tell DOS to keep all of Disklite in memory *except* for INIT_VECTORS and GET_NUM_FLOPPIES. You could place as much initialization code here as you want without it consuming any memory after Disklite has been installed.

You can enter the following program into a file named DISKLITE.ASM or use the file on disk. Then assemble, link, and convert it into a COM program (you can type ML /AT DISKLITE to create a COM file directly). After you run this program, an inverse X: (where X can be any drive letter) will appear on the very right side of the first line whenever you access a disk drive. To test it, run CHKDSK on any drive.

Listing 32-1 DISKLITE.ASM Program (Disk file DISKLITE.ASM)

```
;-----------------------------------------------------------------;
; Disk Light creates an on-screen version of the disk light that is   ;
; usually on disk drives.  The difference, however, is that this light ;
; will be on only as long as it takes to read or write to the disk.  In;
; other words, it does not stay on while the disk spins without any    ;
; activity.                                                           ;
;                                                                     ;
; This program intercepts the INT 13h vector, which is the entry point ;
; for the ROM BIOS's diskette routine.  On entry, Disklite displays    ;
; the drive letter in the upper-right corner of the screen and         ;
; restores this section of the screen on exit.                         ;
;-----------------------------------------------------------------;


;-----------------------------------------------------------------;
; Here is the DISKLITE's entry point.  It jumps to the initialization ;
; routine which is at the very end so we can throw it out of memory    ;
; after we've used it.                                                ;
;-----------------------------------------------------------------;
CODE_SEG       SEGMENT
       ASSUME  CS:CODE_SEG, DS:CODE_SEG
       ORG     100h                  ;Reserve for DOS Program Segment Prefix
```

452

```
BEGIN:  JMP      INIT_VECTORS

AUTHOR_STRING          DB       "Installed Disklite, by John Socha"
                       DB       0Dh, 0Ah, '$'


ROM_DISKETTE_INT       DD       ?

DISPLAY_BASE           DW       ?
OLD_DISPLAY_CHARS      DB       4 DUP (?)
DISPLAY_CHARS          DB       'A', 70h, ':', 70h
NUM_FLOPPIES           DB       ?              ;Number of floppy drives

UPPER_LEFT    EQU      (80 - 2) * 2           ;Offset to drive light

;-------------------------------------------------------------------;
; This procedure intercepts calls to the ROM BIOS's diskette I/O    ;
; vector, and it does several things:                               ;
;                                                                   ;
;       1. Checks to see if the screen is in an 80-column text mode ;
;          so we can write to the screen.  Disklite won't write any ;
;          characters to the screen if it's not in an 80-column mode.;
;       2. Displays the disk drive letter, "A:" for example, in the ;
;          upper-right corner of the screen.                        ;
;       3. Calls the old ROM BIOS routine to do the actual work.    ;
;       4. Restores the two characters in the upper-right corner of the;
;          screen.                                                  ;
;-------------------------------------------------------------------;
INTERCEPT_DISKETTE_INT  PROC     FAR
        Assume  CS:CODE_SEG, DS:Nothing
        PUSHF                           ;Save the old flags
        PUSH    AX
        PUSH    SI
        PUSH    DI
        PUSH    DS
        PUSH    ES
        CALL    GET_DISPLAY_BASE        ;Calculates the screen's display base
        CALL    SAVE_SCREEN             ;Save two chars in upper right
        CALL    DISPLAY_DRIVE_LETTER    ;Display the drive letter
        POP     ES
        POP     DS
        POP     DI
        POP     SI
```

continues

453

Listing 32-1 continued

```
        POP     AX
        POPF                            ;Restore the old flags

        PUSHF                           ;Simulate an INT call
        CALL    ROM_DISKETTE_INT        ; to the old ROM BIOS routine

        PUSHF                           ;Save the returned flags
        PUSH    AX
        PUSH    SI
        PUSH    DI
        PUSH    DS
        PUSH    ES
        LEA     SI,OLD_DISPLAY_CHARS    ;Point to the old screen image
        CALL    WRITE_TO_SCREEN         ;Restore two chars in upper right
        POP     ES
        POP     DS
        POP     DI
        POP     SI
        POP     AX
        POPF                            ;Recover the returned flags
        RET     2                       ;Leave the status flags intact
INTERCEPT_DISKETTE_INT  ENDP


;--------------------------------------------------------------------;
; This procedure calculates the segment address for the display adapter;
; that we're using.                                                  ;
;                                                                    ;
; Destroys:     AX                                                   ;
;--------------------------------------------------------------------;
GET_DISPLAY_BASE        PROC    NEAR
        Assume  CS:CODE_SEG, DS:Nothing
        INT     11h                     ;Get the current equipment flag
        AND     AX,30h                  ;Isolate the display flags
        CMP     AX,30h                  ;Is this a monochrome display?
        MOV     AX,0B800h               ;Set for a color graphics adapter
        JNE     DONE_GET_BASE           ;Color graphics, base already set
        MOV     AX,0B000h               ;Set for monochrome display
DONE_GET_BASE:
        MOV     DISPLAY_BASE,AX         ;Save this display base
        RET
GET_DISPLAY_BASE        ENDP
```

```
;-----------------------------------------------------------------;
; This procedure saves the two characters in the upper-right corner of ;
; the screen so that we can restore them later.                   ;
;                                                                 ;
; Destroys:    AX, SI, DI, DS, ES                                 ;
;-----------------------------------------------------------------;
SAVE_SCREEN     PROC    NEAR
        Assume  CS:CODE_SEG, DS:Nothing
        MOV     SI,UPPER_LEFT           ;Read chars from the screen
        LEA     DI,OLD_DISPLAY_CHARS    ;Write chars to local memory
        MOV     AX,DISPLAY_BASE         ;Get segment address of screen
        MOV     DS,AX
        MOV     AX,CS                   ;Point to the local data
        MOV     ES,AX
        CLD                             ;Set for auto-increment
        MOVSW                           ;Move two characters
        MOVSW
        RET
SAVE_SCREEN     ENDP


;-----------------------------------------------------------------;
; This procedure displays the drive letter in the upper-right corner of;
; the screen.                                                     ;
;                                                                 ;
; Destroys:    AX, SI                                             ;
;-----------------------------------------------------------------;
DISPLAY_DRIVE_LETTER    PROC    NEAR
        Assume  CS:CODE_SEG, DS:Nothing
        MOV     AL,DL                   ;Get the drive number
        CMP     AL,80h                  ;Is this a hard disk drive?
        JB      DISPLAY_LETTER          ;No, then continue
        SUB     AL,80h                  ;Convert to hard disk number
        ADD     AL,NUM_FLOPPIES         ;Convert to correct disk number
DISPLAY_LETTER:
        ADD     AL,'A'                  ;Convert this into a drive letter
        LEA     SI,DISPLAY_CHARS        ;Point to new char image
        MOV     CS:[SI],AL              ;Save this character
        CALL    WRITE_TO_SCREEN
        RET
DISPLAY_DRIVE_LETTER    ENDP
```

continues

455

Listing 32-1 continued

```
;-------------------------------------------------------------------;
; This procedure writes two characters in the upper-right corner of the;
; screen.                                                           ;
;                                                                   ;
; On entry:    CS:SI   Screen image for two characters              ;
; Destroys:    AX, SI, DI, DS, ES                                   ;
;-------------------------------------------------------------------;
WRITE_TO_SCREEN         PROC    NEAR
        Assume  CS:CODE_SEG, DS:Nothing
        MOV     DI,UPPER_LEFT           ;Write chars to the screen
        MOV     AX,DISPLAY_BASE         ;Get segment address of screen
        MOV     ES,AX
        MOV     AX,CS                   ;Point to the local data
        MOV     DS,AX
        CLD                             ;Set for auto-increment
        MOVSW                           ;Move two characters
        MOVSW
        RET
WRITE_TO_SCREEN         ENDP


;-------------------------------------------------------------------;
; This procedure daisy-chains Disklite onto the diskette I/O vector  ;
; so that we can monitor the disk activity.                          ;
;-------------------------------------------------------------------;
INIT_VECTORS    PROC    NEAR
        Assume  CS:CODE_SEG, DS:CODE_SEG
        LEA     DX,AUTHOR_STRING        ;Print out the author notice
        MOV     AH,9                    ;Display this string
        INT     21h

        CALL    GET_NUM_FLOPPIES        ;See how many floppy drives installed

        MOV     AH,35h                  ;Ask for an interrupt vector
        MOV     AL,13h                  ;Get the vector for INT 13h
        INT     21h                     ;Put vector in ES:BX
        MOV     Word Ptr ROM_DISKETTE_INT,BX
        MOV     Word Ptr ROM_DISKETTE_INT[2],ES

        MOV     AH,25h                  ;Ask to set an interrupt vector
        MOV     AL,13h                  ;Set the INT 13h vector to DS:DX
        MOV     DX,Offset INTERCEPT_DISKETTE_INT
        INT     21h                     ;Set INT 13h to point to our procedure
```

```
        MOV     DX,Offset INIT_VECTORS  ;End of resident portion
        INT     27h                     ;Terminate but stay resident
INIT_VECTORS    ENDP


;--------------------------------------------------------------------;
; This procedure determines how many logical floppy disk drives are in ;
; the system.  The next drive letter will be used for hard disk drives.;
;--------------------------------------------------------------------;
GET_NUM_FLOPPIES        PROC    NEAR
        Assume  CS:CODE_SEG, DS:CODE_SEG
        INT     11h                     ;Get the equipment flag
        MOV     CL,6
        SHR     AX,CL                   ;Right justify num of floppies
        AND     AL,3                    ;Strip all the other flags
        INC     AL                      ;Returns 0 for 1 floppy
        CMP     AL,1                    ;Is this a one-floppy system?
        JA      DONE_GET_FLOPPIES       ;No, then this is the correct number
        MOV     AL,2                    ;Yes, there are 2 logical drives
DONE_GET_FLOPPIES:
        MOV     NUM_FLOPPIES,AL         ;Save this number
        RET
GET_NUM_FLOPPIES        ENDP



CODE_SEG        ENDS

        END     BEGIN
```

Protected-Mode and Windows Programming

In this chapter you will learn the concepts needed to write programs that work in protected-mode environments, such as Microsoft Windows. We will then show you how to write code to test pointers to make sure they are valid, and then show you how to write code to take special advantage of the 80386 instructions in your Windows programs. Please note that you must use MASM 6 to assemble the WINLIB.ASM file in this chapter.

33

Topics Covered

What Is Protected Mode?

The *protected mode* is a special mode on the 80x86 that is designed to provide protection between different programs running in your computer. As you've seen in the DOS world, any program can read or write to any location in memory. However, in protected-mode programs the operating system can divide memory into a number of separate chunks and the *access rights* for these chunks can be controlled independently for every program in the system. This occurs with the help of the 80x86. As you will see when Windows is discussed, the real world isn't quite as pure as it could be.

A Brief History of the 80x86

Let's begin by looking at how the 80x86 deals with protected-mode memory, which is both very much like what you're used to when using segment registers and very different from what you're used to.

First let's look at the individual microprocessors and what their capabilities and limitations are. The 8088 and 8086 microprocessors used by the original IBM PC don't have any support for a protected mode. They can address one megabyte of memory exactly in the way we've been addressing memory throughout this book. In other words, they use the segmented architecture you have learned in this book.

All other microprocessors in the 80x86 family, starting with the 80286, do support protected-mode programs. The original reason for adding the protected mode to the 80286 was to support more than one megabyte of memory. With the segmented architecture of the 8088 there was no easy way to extend the amount of memory you could work with, short of making all the segment registers longer than 16 bits. Intel could have modified the way programs worked with segments to allow more than one megabyte of memory, but they had other plans.

When Intel began designing the 80286, the IBM PC didn't even exist (the 80286 took almost four years to develop and was introduced in 1982, less than a year after the IBM PC reached the market). As far as most experts believed at the time, the UNIX operating system, not DOS, was the wave of the future.

So Intel designed the 80286 really for two totally separate markets—one was as a faster 8088 for the DOS market, and the other was as a good microprocessor for running UNIX, which meant they needed more than just the ability to manage large amounts of memory. They also needed more advanced protection features to allow programmers to write very robust operating systems like UNIX where a program can crash without causing other programs to crash (Windows 3.1 finally has *some*, but not all, of this protection).

As we all know, DOS took the lead in operating systems, and UNIX never caught on in the 80x86 market place. And as a result, most PC users were not able to take advantage of the additional memory potential on their 80x86 computers until protected-mode operating systems, such as Microsoft Windows, came along.

Addressing Extended Memory

Table 33-1 shows the amount of memory you can use with the current microprocessors in the 80x86 family. As you can see, all of the 80x86 microprocessors, except the 808x, support much more than 1 Mb of memory. To get to this extra memory, also known as *extended memory*, you *must* switch to protected mode. In other words, the protected mode of the 80x86 changes the way the 80x86 addresses memory (and it changes other aspects as well, as you will see in this chapter).

Table 33-1 80x86 Memory Address Size

	8088	8086	80286	80386sx*	80386dx	80486
Memory	1 Mb	1 Mb	16 Mb	16 Mb	4 Gb	4 Gb
Protected Mode	No	No	Yes	Yes	Yes	Yes

* The 80386sx is limited to 16 Mb, rather than 4 Gb. In order to make it easy for computer companies to use the 80386 rather than the 80286, Intel built the 80386sx, which only has 24 address pins, just as the 80286 does.

The first change we will look at is how the meaning of segment registers changes when you switch to protected mode. In normal mode, which is called *real mode*, you can calculate the address of any area in memory by multiplying the segment by 4 and adding the offset. In protected mode, however, the segment registers actually contain much more information. As you can see in Figure 33-1, the segment registers contain both a visible part, which is 16 bits long, and a much longer hidden part. The hidden part is where all the work of addressing extended memory takes place.

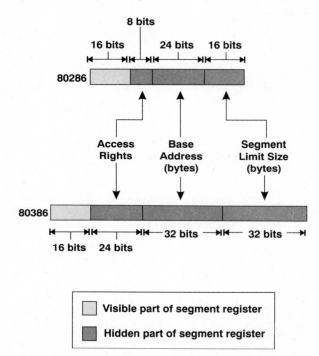

Figure 33-1: In protected mode, the segment registers have a hidden part that contains information on location of a segment, its size, and the access rights.

You will notice that the hidden part of the segment register contains the actual base address of a segment, measured in bytes rather than paragraphs (16 bytes). On the 80286, this field is 24 bits wide, which allows addresses up to 16,772,216, or 16 Mb of memory. The 32-bit field on the 80386 and 80486 allow address up to 4 Gb.

The other two pieces, access rights and the segment limit size, provide some of the protection features we mentioned above. Each segment in protected mode has access rights that control whether you have the right to read from a segment, write to a segment, or run programs in a segment. Segments also have a size, so the 80x86 won't allow you to write or read bytes beyond the end of the segment. If you try to access memory outside these limits, or areas that you don't have the rights to, the 80x86 generates a special type of interrupt known as a *general protection exception*. If you have used Windows 3.1, you have almost certainly heard about and experienced a GPF (general-protection fault), which can be caused by a program attempting to read or write memory that it doesn't own (there are other faults that can also cause a GPF).

The question, then, is how do you load values into these hidden fields? Also, how does the operating system determine which segments you can and cannot access, and where are they located? The answer is that the 80x86 contains one or more tables of such information called descriptor tables.

How Descriptor Tables Work

Whenever you assign a value to a segment register in the protected mode, you are actually using a number, called a *selector*, to look up the actual address and access rights in a table called the *descriptor table* (see Figure 33-2). The descriptor table is a table that maps selector numbers to real addresses in physical memory. The operating system sets up the descriptor table and uses a special protected-mode instruction to tell the 80x86 where to find this table (there are actually two instructions, called LGDT and LLDT, which stand for Load Global/Local Descriptor Table). The hidden part of each segment register is loaded with the values the 80x86 finds in the descriptor table.

The 80x86 allows you to have a number of different descriptor tables. There is a single, *global descriptor table* (GDT), that an operating system generally uses to manage its own private memory. In theory, each program you run should have its own descriptor table, called a *local descriptor table* (LDT). Windows, however, actually uses a single local descriptor table that all programs share, which means Windows programs do not have the kind of protection from each other that they would have if each program had a local descriptor table.

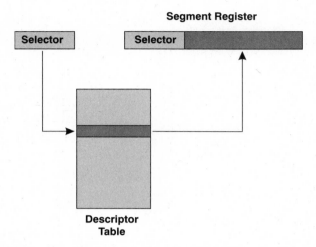

Figure 33-2: When you load a segment register, the 80x86 uses the information in the selector table to load all the hidden fields that tell the 80x86 about the segment.

Each descriptor table has a limit on the number of entries it can contain, which is 8,192. In other words, Windows can never manage more than 8,192 segments at one time. Fortunately, this limit tends not to be a problem for most programs. It does mean, however, that you should be careful not to call GlobalAlloc for many small items since each GlobalAlloc call uses a selector.

Since it takes only 13 bits to address 8,192 selectors, what are the other three bits in the selector used for? It turns out that the lower three bits are used to indicate which descriptor table you should use (local or global) and also privilege information. Since you should never build a selector yourself (you'll always get them from GlobalLock or a similar function), the actual values in these bits aren't very important to you as a programmer.

One interesting side effect of this entire scheme is that Windows, or whatever protected-mode operating system you are using, can move your memory around without your knowledge. Whenever the operating system moves a chunk of memory, all it has to do is update the base address stored in the descriptor table. Your application will continue to use the same selector as if it were a segment, and everything works.

Working in Windows

Let's take a look at how this knowledge, as well as your knowledge of assembly language, can help you write better Windows programs. In this section we will show you some tricks that are very simple using in-line assembly that would be very difficult, if not impossible, to write using straight C code. We will assume here that you have written Windows programs in C, so we won't explain any of the Windows concepts that would be familiar to anyone who has written Windows programs in C.

For our first example, we will show you how to verify that a C-style far pointer (2 words, with a segment and an offset) is legal. As prudent programmers, there are times when it would be nice to test a pointer to see if it is valid before using it. In the DOS world this is typically done by looking at the values referred to by the pointer to see if they are valid. However, you cannot do this in protected mode since you are likely to cause a GPF if the selector is not valid, or if the segment is not large enough. Unfortunately, you cannot protect yourself against these types of problems without some assembly language code. (Windows 3.1 does have a set of functions whose names start with IsBad that you can use to test pointers, but these functions are not available in Windows 3.0.)

Validating Pointers, Part I

Testing a pointer to see if it is valid is easy by using a small amount of assembly language. There are some assembly-language instructions available on the 80x86 that do all the work for you. The VERR and VERW instructions (VERify Read and VERify Write) allow you to test a selector to see if you have read and write privileges. The LSL instruction allows you to retrieve the size of a segment from the descriptor table.

Let's start by looking at the VERR instruction to see how it works. We will use a very short C program to test VERR. This small test program uses a feature you will find in both the Microsoft and the Borland C compilers, which allows you to write simple Windows programs that use the printf( ) function to display output in a window. Microsoft calls this feature QuickWin and Borland calls it EasyWin. The test programs in this section all use printf( ) to

465

display output. Check your documentation on how to use these libraries. In the case of QuickC for Windows, which we used in this chapter, select Project... from the Options menu, then select the QuickWin EXE option in this dialog box.

The VERR instruction uses a single parameter, which is the value of a selector. If the selector is a valid selector and you have read rights to this selector, the VERR instruction sets the zero flag; otherwise it clears the zero flag. Far pointers are always 2 words long in Windows, with the selector in the upper word and the offset in the lower word. The following program checks the selector to see if it is valid:

```
#include        <windows.h>
#include        <stdio.h>

main()
{
    BYTE huge *  lpNum;
    int  valid;                         // -1 if the pointer is valid


    lpNum = (LPBYTE) (5 * 65536);       // This is an invalid selector
    valid = -1;                         // Set to invalid initially

    _asm {
        verr    Word Ptr lpNum[2]       // Is selector valid for reading?
        jz      doneCheck1              // Yes, then we're all done
        mov     valid, 0                // No, report not valid
        }
doneCheck1:

    if (valid)
        printf("Pointer is valid\n");
    else
        printf("Invalid pointer\n");

    return 0;
}
```

This program is not the most elegant. The problem is that the VERR instruction sets or clears the zero flag, but C programs work with variables in memory, rather than flags. So you have to use the variable *valid* to report whether a selector was valid or not, which you can do by setting *valid* to −1 before the VERR instruction. If VERR sets the zero flag, the JZ instruction skips over the instruction that clears *valid*.

You will notice that we had to use a label in the C code to make this test work. If you wanted to check a number of pointers to see if they were valid, you wouldn't want to add this code, with a different label, each time you wanted to test a pointer. Instead, you will probably want to write a function call ValidPtr that tests a pointer to see if it is valid. Such a subroutine appears as follows:

```
//-----------------------------------------------------------------//
// This function tests a pointer first to see if the selector part is   //
// valid.                                                          //
//                                                                 //
// Returns:      0      The pointer isn't valid                    //
//              -1      The pointer is valid                       //
//-----------------------------------------------------------------//
BOOL ValidPtr(
    void FAR *lp )                      // Pointer you want to test
{
    _asm
        {
        mov     ax, 0                   // Return false by default
        verr    Word Ptr lp[2]          // Is selector valid for reading?
        jnz     doneTest                // No, report not valid

        not     ax                      // Pointer is valid, return -1
        }
doneTest:
    ;
}
```

This function does exactly what the in-line code in our previous example did, except that it's now a function. You will notice that this function returns a value in the AX register. We mentioned in Chapter 31 that C functions return word values in the AX register.

Determining the Size of Segments

We are not finished yet, though. The test you have completed so far tested only the selector part of a far pointer. As long as the selector is invalid, the ValidPtr function correctly reports that the pointer is not valid. But what happens if the selector is valid but the offset points past the end of the segment? In this case we need to actually check the size of the segment, which we do using the LSL instruction (Load Segment Limit). This instruction looks up the size of a segment in the descriptor table and returns the size. For example, if you have a selector in the SI register, the following instruction will return the address of the last byte in the segment that you can address:

```
LSL     AX, SI
```

Adding one to this number will give you the size of the segment referred to by SI. By putting this all together, we can write a new version of our test program that tests a selector to see if it is valid, and if it is, it reports the size of the segment. A new version of this test program follows:

```c
#include        <windows.h>
#include        <stdio.h>

//--------------------------------------------------------------------//
// This function tests a pointer first to see if the selector part is //
// valid.                                                             //
//                                                                    //
// Returns:       0        The pointer isn't valid                    //
//               -1        The pointer is valid                       //
//--------------------------------------------------------------------//
BOOL ValidPtr(
    void FAR *lp,                       // Pointer you want to test
    WORD cwSize )                       // Size of object at *pointer
{
    _asm
        {
        mov     ax, 0                   // Return false by default
        verr    Word Ptr lp[2]          // Is this valid for reading?
        jnz     doneTest                // No, report not valid

        not     ax                      // Pointer is valid, return -1
        }
doneTest:
    ;
}


//--------------------------------------------------------------------//
// This function returns the size of a segment pointed to by a far    //
// pointer.                                                           //
//                                                                    //
// Returns:     size    The size, in bytes, of a segment             //
//--------------------------------------------------------------------//
```

```
DWORD SegSize(
    void FAR *lp )                      // Far pointer to some memory
{
    DWORD i = 0;                        // Size of the segment

    _asm
        {
        lsl     ax, Word Ptr lp[2]      // Get size of segment into ax
        mov     Word Ptr i, ax          // Save size in i
        }
    i++;                                // Convert from last byte to size
    return i;
}


main()
{
    HANDLE hmem;
    BYTE huge *  lpNum;
    int   valid;                        // -1 if the pointer is valid


    hmem = GlobalAlloc(GMEM_MOVEABLE, 10L);
    lpNum = (LPBYTE) GlobalLock(hmem);

    if (ValidPtr(lpNum))
        printf("Pointer is valid\nSize = %ld", SegSize(lpNum));
    else
        printf("Invalid pointer\n");

    GlobalUnlock(hmem);
    GlobalFree(hmem);

    return 0;
}
```

When you run this program, it should display the following:

```
Pointer is valid
Size = 32
```

The size returned by this function is actually a little larger than the chunk of memory you asked for (10 bytes) because Windows always returns chunks of memory that are a multiple of 32 bytes in size.

There is a problem with this program, however. Change the size of the segment you allocate from 10L to 66000L.

```
hmem = GlobalAlloc(GMEM_MOVEABLE, 66000L);
```

Then run this program in 386-Enhanced mode. What you will discover is that SegSize( ) now returns the wrong size.

```
Pointer is valid
Size = 480
```

To understand why, we first need to look at how Windows normally works with chunks of data larger than 64 Kb.

Whenever you work with chunks of memory larger than 64 Kb in Windows, you need to use huge pointers. Huge pointers are like far pointers because they contain both a segment and an offset, but unlike far pointers, they can work with data objects larger than 64 Kb. Whenever you reference memory using a huge pointer, it loads the ES register with the segment (selector) part of the pointer and it usually loads the offset into the BX register, so the code to read a word from a far pointer might appear as follows:

```
LES     BX, farPtr
MOV     AX, ES:[BX]
```

The interesting part, however, is the code that handles array indexes or adding a number to a pointer. When you are dealing with a far pointer, these operations simply change the value of the offset. But with huge pointers, you may need to change *both* the offset *and* the segment (selector) value. In other words, memory chunks larger than 64 Kb are actually allocated as more than one selector. For example, you would need 4 selectors for 200,000 bytes of memory (3 * 65536 = 196,608, so you need 4 selectors for 200,000 bytes). So when you call GlobalAlloc to allocate a 200,000 byte chunk of memory, Windows creates 4 contiguous selectors to access all 200,000 bytes of memory. The first selector gives you access to the first 64 Kb of memory, the next selector to the next 64 Kb chunk of memory, and so on. Whenever you cross a segment boundary, your C/C++ compiler effectively adds 8 to the selector (it uses 8 rather than 1 because the lower three bits should not be changed since they are reserved for other uses).

The problem in 386-Enhanced mode is that Windows makes a couple of small changes to this model. Whenever you are in 386-Enhanced mode Windows knows that the 80386 and above can work with segments larger than 64 Kb (segments can be up to 4 Gb). So when you allocate 200,000 bytes of memory, Windows creates 4 contiguous selectors, just as you and your C/C++ compiler would expect. But the first selector will actually have a limited size of 199,999 (the last addressable byte in the segment). The second selector likewise will have a limited size of 199,999 – 65536 = 134,463. In other words, each selector's limited size will reflect the last byte at the end of the large chunk of memory that you allocated (see Figure 33-3).

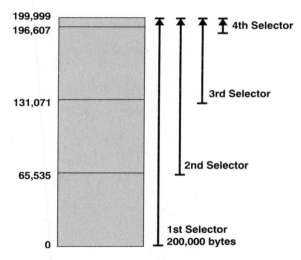

Figure 33-3: This figure shows you how the descriptors created for a large GlobalAlloc cover the memory allocated.

How do you get the actual size of a segment on a 80386 or better processor? For that answer you have to turn back to MASM since you have to use some assembly-language instructions that aren't available in the in-line assembler in most C/C++ compilers.

The 32-Bit Registers

All of the registers we have used in this entire book have been 16 bits long. The 80386 and above processors actually have 32-bit registers that you can use that are longer versions of the 16-bit registers. So just as AX is the 16-bit version of AL, EAX is the 32-bit version of AX (the E stands for Extended). As long as you are writing a program to run on at least the 80386, you can add an E in front of any of the 80x86 registers we've been using. For example, you can add 1 to a 32-bit number by using the following instruction:

```
ADD     EAX, 1
```

To use any of these extended registers in your assembly-language programs you have to first tell the assembler that it can use 80386 instructions (normally the assembler allows only 8088 instructions to ensure that your programs will run on any DOS computer). You turn on 80386 instructions using the .386 directive after the .MODEL directive in your programs:

```
.MODEL  SMALL,C
.386
```

Now you can use the extended registers to get the correct size of a segment larger than 64 Kb. In the next section you will write a set of subroutines in assembly language that you can use to get the correct size of a segment, and to check a pointer to see if it's valid, by checking both the selector and the offset.

Validating Pointers, Part II

In this section we will present three functions that work correctly in all cases when running under Windows. We have written the functions SegSize, ValidReadPtr, and ValidWritePtr as you can see in Listing 33-2. The following listing provides a sample program that both shows you how to use these functions and also shows you the segment sizes for the selectors you get when you allocate objects larger than 64 Kb. Following is the output from Listing 33-1.

```
Selector 0 size = 200000
Selector 1 size = 134464
Selector 2 size = 68928
Selector 3 size = 3392
Invalid pointer
```

When you run the program in 386-Enhanced mode, each selector's size reflects the amount of space to the end of the object you allocated. This is very significant because you can write assembly-language subroutines and functions that work with large chunks of data (larger than 64 Kb) working with just a single segment. You can do this for two reasons: first, Windows sets up the first selector so you can address *all* of the memory you allocated with a single GlobalAlloc call; and second, your assembly-language programs can use the EBX register with 32-bit offsets instead of the usual 16-bit offsets you have used so far. To assemble the WINLIB.ASM file in Listing 33-2, you must use MASM 6.

Listing 33-1 WINTEST.C: A sample program to demonstrate using the SegSize and ValidReadPtr functions

```c
#include <windows.h>
#include <stdio.h>

BOOL  ValidReadPtr(void FAR *lp, WORD cwSize);
DWORD SegSize(void FAR *lp);

main()
{
    HANDLE hmem;
    BYTE huge *  lpNum;
    DWORD size;
    int i;


    hmem = GlobalAlloc(GMEM_MOVEABLE, 200000L);
    lpNum = (LPBYTE) GlobalLock(hmem);

    for (i = 0; i < 4; i++)
        {
        size = SegSize(lpNum);
        printf("Selector %d size = %ld\n", i, SegSize(lpNum));
        lpNum += 65536L;
        }

    if (ValidReadPtr(lpNum, sizeof(BYTE)))
        printf("Pointer is valid\nSize = %ld", SegSize(lpNum));
    else
        printf("Invalid pointer\n");

    GlobalUnlock(hmem);
    GlobalFree(hmem);

    return 0;
}
```

Listing 33-2 WINLIB.ASM: The functions to test a pointer to see if it is valid, and to get the size of a segment

```
;-----------------------------------------------------------;
; This file contains the following functions that you can call from  ;
; C:                                                        ;
;                                                           ;
;       DWORD SegSize(void FAR *lp);                        ;
;       BOOL  ValidReadPtr(void FAR *lp, WORD cwSize);      ;
;       BOOL  ValidWritePtr(void FAR *lp, WORD cwSize);     ;
;-----------------------------------------------------------;

.MODEL  SMALL,C
.386

.CODE


;-----------------------------------------------------------;
; This function tests to see if the processor is an 80286, as opposed  ;
; to an 80386 or above.                                     ;
;                                                           ;
; The 80286 processor always clears the upper four bits when it  ;
; transfers a word from the stack to the status register, while the  ;
; 80386 and above do not, which is how we can tell when we have an  ;
; 80286.                                                    ;
;                                                           ;
; Returns:       ZR      Processor is an 80286 if zero flag set  ;
;                NZ      80386 or above                     ;
;-----------------------------------------------------------;
Is286   proc    private
        pushf                           ; Put flags onto the stack
        pop     ax                      ; And then into AX
        or      ah,0F0h                 ; Set high 4 bits of flags
        push    ax                      ; Put back onto stack
        popf                            ; And back into flag register
        pushf                           ; Then put back into ax
        pop     ax
        and     ah,0F0h                 ; Report if upper bits zero
        ret
Is286   endp
```

```
;-------------------------------------------------------------;
; This function returns the size of the segment whose selector is in   ;
; the upper word of p:                                        ;
;                                                             ;
;       long    SegSize(void FAR *p);                         ;
;-------------------------------------------------------------;
SegSize proc    p:Ptr
        call    Is286               ; Is this a 286 processor?
        je      SegSize286          ; Yes, use 16-bit register version

SegSize386:
        movzx   ebx, Word Ptr p[2]  ; Get the selector into ebx
        lsl     eax, ebx            ; Get last offset in seg into eax
        inc     eax                 ; Add 1 to convert to segment size
        mov     edx, eax            ; Lower word in ax, full in edx
        shr     edx, 16             ; Move upper word into dx
        jmp     doneSegSize         ; We're all done

SegSize286:
        xor     dx, dx              ; Set upper word to 0
        mov     bx, Word Ptr p[2]   ; Get the selector into bx
        lsl     ax, bx              ; Get last offset in seg into ax
        add     ax, 1               ; Add 1 to convert to segment size
        adc     dx, 0               ; Propagate carry to dx

doneSegSize:
        ret
SegSize endp


;-------------------------------------------------------------;
; This function is a private function that checks an offset to see if  ;
; it is inside the allowed range.                             ;
;                                                             ;
; Returns:      AX      0       Offset isn't valid            ;
;                      -1       Valid offset                  ;
;-------------------------------------------------------------;
ValidOffset     proc    private lp:Ptr, cwSize:Word
        INVOKE  SegSize, lp
        sub     ax, cwSize          ; Subtract data size from seg size
        sbb     dx, 0               ; Propagate borrow
        or      dx, dx              ; Is segment > 64 K?
        jmp     IsValidOffset       ; Yes, valid since offset always <= 64K
```

continues

475

Listing 33-2 continued

```
            cmp     Word Ptr lp, ax         ; Is offset too high?
            ja      InvalidOffset           ; Yes, pointer isn't valid

IsValidOffset:
            xor     ax, ax
            not     ax                      ; Return TRUE
            jmp     DoneValidOffset         ; We're all done

InvalidOffset:
            xor     ax, ax                  ; Return FALSE

DoneValidOffset:
            ret
ValidOffset     endp


;------------------------------------------------------------------;
; This function tests a pointer first to see if the selector part is  ;
; valid.  And if so, it makes sure you can read at least cwSize bytes  ;
; starting at *lp.                                                 ;
;                                                                 ;
;       BOOL ValidReadPtr(void FAR *lp, WORD cwSize);             ;
;------------------------------------------------------------------;
ValidReadPtr    proc    lp:Ptr, cwSize:Word
            verr    Word Ptr lp[2]          ; Is the selector valid?
            jnz     InvalidReadPtr          ; No, report this fact

            INVOKE  ValidOffset, lp, cwSize ; Report if offset is valid
            jmp     DoneValidReadPtr

InvalidReadPtr:
            xor     ax, ax                  ; Return FALSE

DoneValidReadPtr:
            ret
ValidReadPtr    endp


;------------------------------------------------------------------;
; This function tests a pointer first to see if the selector part is  ;
; valid.  And if so, it makes sure you can write at least cwSize bytes ;
; starting at *lp.                                                 ;
;                                                                 ;
;       BOOL ValidWritePtr(void FAR *lp, WORD cwSize);            ;
;------------------------------------------------------------------;
```

```
ValidWritePtr    proc    lp:Ptr, cwSize:Word
        verr    Word Ptr lp[2]          ; Is the selector valid?
        jnz     InvalidWritePtr         ; No, report this fact

        INVOKE  ValidOffset, lp, cwSize ; Report if offset is valid
        jmp     DoneValidWritePtr

InvalidWritePtr:
        xor     ax, ax                  ; Return FALSE

DoneValidWritePtr:
        ret
ValidWritePtr    endp

        end_
```

There are a few things in this program that may not be obvious. First, the Is286 function has code to check to see if the processor is an 80286 processor. You need to call this code to see whether or not 32-bit registers will be available. The actual code to test the processors is from an excellent book called *PC Magazine Programmer's Technical Reference: The Processor and Coprocessor,* by Robert L. Hummel, which is the best reference book we know of on the 80x86 processors.

The other thing that may be new to you is the INVOKE directive. This is a special directive added to MASM 6 that makes it very easy to call a high-level language function that expects its parameters to be passed on the stack. Since we wrote SegSize to use the stack for parameters, it was easiest to call it using the INVOKE directive. The INVOKE directive actually creates several assembly-language instructions that push the correct parameters onto the stack by using PUSH instructions, and then uses the CALL instruction to call your function. The advantage of using INVOKE over doing the PUSHes yourself is that the INVOKE directive will always produce the correct code based on the current language you have selected.

Summary

In this chapter we have given you just a glimpse of what you can do using assembly language in your Windows programs. As you have learned from the simple example in this chapter, you can write assembly-language subroutines quite simply for your C/C++ programs. But the interesting part is what you can do when your programs run in 386-Enhanced mode. In this mode you can write very fast assembly-language functions that treat large chunks of memory as a single segment. This is something that you cannot do directly from C/C++ with most of the current batch of compilers. If you need to perform an operation on a large block of data, the fastest code will be written in assembly language.

In this chapter we also provided functions you can use to test pointers to make sure they are valid. These functions will work with any version of Windows, or even in other protected-mode operating systems that run on the 80x86.

This is the last technical chapter in this book. In the next chapter you will find a bibliography of useful books where you can find more advanced information.

Closing Words and Bibliography

By now you have seen many examples of assembly-language programs. Throughout this book we have constantly emphasized programming rather than the details of the 80x86 microprocessor inside your PC. As a result, you have not seen all of the 80x86 instructions, nor all the assembler directives. But most assembly language programs can be written with what you have learned here.

34

Topics Covered

80x86 Reference Books

DOS and ROM BIOS Programming

RAM Resident Programs

Advanced DOS Programming

Windows Programming

Software Design

Other References

Your best approach to learning more about writing assembly language programs is to take the programs in this book and modify them. If you think of a better way to write any part of Dskpatch, by all means try it. This is how we first learned to write programs. We found programs written in BASIC, and began to learn about the language itself by rewriting bits and pieces of those programs. You can do the same with Dskpatch.

After you have tried some of these examples, you will be ready to write your own programs. Don't start from scratch here, either; that is rather difficult for your first time out. To begin, use the programs in this book as a framework. Don't build a completely new structure or technique (your equivalent of modular design) until you feel comfortable with writing assembly language programs.

If you become enthralled by assembly language you will need a more complete book to use as a reference to the 80x86 instruction set. Following is a list of books we have read and liked that you may find useful as references. This list is by no means complete, as the books listed here are only ones that we have read. Also, some of the references are older than you might expect because we learned assembly language programming several years ago. Some of the books may now be out of print; check with your local booksellers.

80x86 Reference Books

The following three books are good programmer's references:

Hummel, Robert L., *PC Programmer's Technical Reference: The Processor and Coprocessor*, Ziff-Davis Press, 1992. This is the best book I have ever seen on the 80x86 processors. In fact, it is probably the only place where you will find all of the bugs in the various processors, as well as ways to work around the bugs. Highly recommended.

Microsoft's 80386/80486 Programming Guide, Microsoft Press, 1991. This book is not as good as Robert Hummel's book (see above), but it does a very nice job describing the protected mode.

iAPX 88 Book, Intel, 1981. This is the definitive sourcebook on the original 8088/8086, and a very good reference.

The following book is an introduction to the 8088 microprocessor, written by a member of the design team at Intel:

Morse, Stephen P., *The 8086/8088 Primer*, Hayden, 1982. As one of the designers at Intel, Morse provides many insights into the design of the 8088 and also talks about some of the design flaws and bugs in the 8088. While not very good as a reference, this book is complete and is readable and informative.

DOS and ROM BIOS Programming

The references in this section are useful to anyone programming the PC.

Norton, Peter and Richard Wilton, *The New Peter Norton Programmer's Guide to the IBM PC & PS/2*, Microsoft Press, 1988. Includes a complete reference to all DOS and BIOS functions, descriptions of important memory locations, and a host of other useful (or at least interesting) information.

Duncan, Ray, *Advanced MS-DOS*, Microsoft Press, 1986. This book covers almost everything you will want to know about using the DOS services in your programs. It also includes a number of sample programs. A nice companion to Peter's *Programmer's Guide*.

Brown, Ralf, and Jim Kyle, *PC Interrupts: A Programmer's Reference to BIOS, DOS, and Third-Party Calls*, Addison-Wesley, 1991. This is probably the best all-around reference to ROM-BIOS and DOS calls.

RAM Resident Programs

There aren't many good references for people who want to write RAM-resident programs because much of the material has not been published in a single place. But there are two good sources for information:

Duncan, Ray, Editor, *The MS-DOS Encyclopedia*, Microsoft Press, 1988. This book has a wealth of information. It covers many of the aspects of writing RAM-resident programs.

PC Magazine, published by Ziff Davis often publishes information on RAM-resident programs, as well as example programs. A subscription to this magazine will provide you with many good assembly-language programs.

Advanced DOS Programming

After you have started DOS programming, you will probably need to branch far beyond this book. The following books should help:

Duncan, Ray, Editor, *Extending DOS: A Programmer's Guide to Protected-Mode DOS*, Addison-Wesley, 1992. If you want to do protected-mode programming from DOS, you want this book. This explains all about EMS memory, extended memory, XMS, VCPI, DPMI, and so on.

Schulman, Andrew, et al, *Undocumented DOS: A Programmer's Guide to Reserved MS-DOS Functions and Data Structures*, Addison-Wesley, 1990. That about says it all for this book. Very interesting.

Windows Programming

There are a number of very good Windows programming books. Following are some of the best ones:

Petzold, Charles, *Programming Windows 3.1*, Microsoft Press, 1992. This is an excellent book that teaches Windows programming.

Norton, Peter and Paul Yao, *Peter Norton's Windows 3.1 Power Programming Techniques*, Bantam, 1992. This is another very good Windows programming book. You will find more advanced material in this book, as well as some good examples of using in-line assembly in Windows programs.

Richter, Jeffrey M., *Windows 3.1: A Developer's Guide*, M&T Books, 1992. This book is considered the standard reference book for more advanced material related to Windows programming.

Schulman, Andrew, et al, *Undocumented Windows*, Addison Wesley, 1992. This is a wonderful book that uncovers many of the previously undocumented parts of Windows.

Software Design

We have a few favorite books when it comes to software design. The books we recommend are a bit out of the ordinary, and well worth the read.

Brooks, Frederick P., Jr., *The Mythical Man-Month: Essays on Software Engineering*, Addison-Wesley, 1982. Everyone who is connected with a software project should read this book, especially your manager.

Normal, Donald A., *The Design of Everyday Things*, Basic Books, 1988. This book provides a lot of useful insight into what does and does not create problems with programs that interact with people.

Heckel, Paul, *The Elements of Friendly Software Design*, Sybex, 1991.

Other References

Startz, Richard, *8087 Applications and Programming for the IBM PC and Other PCs*, Brady Books, 1983 (Out of print). If you need to write programs that use the 8087 math coprocessor, this book should help.

Wilton, Richard, *Programmer's Guide to PC & PS/2 Video Systems*, Microsoft Press, 1987. This is a good book about writing programs for the EGA and VGA display adapters.

Guide to the Disk

The companion disk to this book contains most of the Dskpatch examples you have seen in the preceding chapters, as well as an advanced version of the program that includes a lot of improvements. The files for Dskpatch are in two groups: the chapter examples in the CHAPS directory and the advanced Dskpatch program in the advanced directory. The file for the Disklite program discussed in Chapter 32 is included in the directory DISKLITE. The WINDOWS directory includes the file discussed in Chapter 33. Finally, a special group of assembly procedures written for C/C++ programming is included in the CLIB directory. This appendix will explain what's on the disk, and why.

A

Topics Covered

Chapter Examples

Advanced Version of Dskpatch

DISKLITE Program

Windows Code

C/C++ Libraries

Chapter Examples

All the chapter examples are from Chapters 9 through 27, 30, and 31, and they are in the CHAPS directory. The examples in earlier chapters are short enough so you can type them in quickly. But starting in Chapter 9, we began to build Dskpatch, which, by the end of this book had grown to nine different files. The files are all routines for Dskpatch except CLIB.ASM which is discussed in Chapter 31.

In any one chapter, only a few of these nine files changed. Since they do evolve throughout each chapter, however, there was not enough room on the disk to store each version of each example. So you will find the examples on the disk as they stand after each chapter. If we modify a program several times in, say, Chapter 19, the disk contains the final version.

The table at the end of this appendix shows when each file changes. It also shows the name of the disk file for that chapter. If you want to make sure you are still on course, or you don't feel like typing in the changes for some chapter, just look at this table to find the names of the new files. Then you can either check your work or copy the file(s) to your disk.

The complete list of all the files on the companion disk that cover the chapter-by-chapter changes to Dskpatch is as follows:

```
VIDEO_9.ASM    VIDEO_16.ASM   DISP_S19.ASM   KBD_IO24.ASM
VIDEO_10.ASM   DISK_I16.ASM   KBD_IO19.ASM   DISPAT25.ASM
VIDEO_13.ASM   DSKPAT17.ASM   DISK_I19.ASM   DISPAT26.ASM
TEST13.ASM     DISP_S17.ASM   DISP_S21.ASM   DISK_I26.ASM
DISP_S14.ASM   CURSOR17.ASM   PHANTO21.ASM   PHANTO27.ASM
CURSOR14.ASM   VIDEO_17.ASM   VIDEO_21.ASM   DSKPAT30.ASM
VIDEO_14.ASM   DISK_I17.ASM   DISPAT22.ASM   KBD_IO30.ASM
DISP_S15.ASM   DISP_S18.ASM   EDITOR22.ASM   CURSOR30.ASM
DISK_I15.ASM   CURSOR18.ASM   PHANTO22.ASM   VIDEO_30.ASM
DISP_S16.ASM   VIDEO_18.ASM   KBD_IO23.ASM   CLIB.ASM
DSKPAT19.ASM   DISPAT19.ASM   TEST23.ASM
```

Advanced Version of Dskpatch

As we said, the disk contains more than just the examples in this book. We did not really finish Dskpatch by the end of Chapter 27, and there are many things we should have put into Dskpatch to make it a usable program. The disk contains an almost-finished version in the ADVANCED directory as shown in Figure A-1.

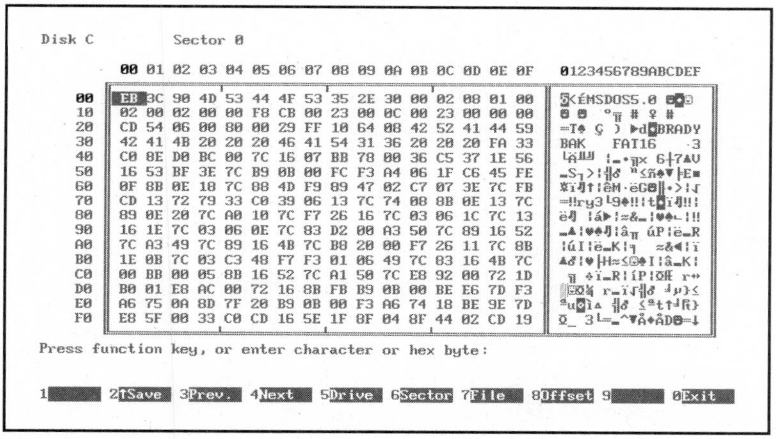

Figure A-1: The Advanced version of Dskpatch.

As it stands (in this book), Dskpatch can read only the next or previous sector. Thus, if you wanted to read sector 576, you would have to push the F4 key 575 times. And what if you wanted to look at sectors within a file? Right now, you would have to look at the directory sector and figure out where to look for the sectors of that file. The disk version of Dskpatch can read either absolute sectors, just as the book version can, or it can read sectors within a file. In its advanced form, Dskpatch is a very usable program.

The advanced version of Dskpatch has too many changes to describe in detail here, so we will take a quick look at the new functions we added to the disk version. You will find many of the changes by exploring Dskpatch and by making your own changes.

The advanced Dskpatch still has nine files, all of which you will find on the disk.

```
DSKPATCH.ASM   DISPATCH.ASM   DISP_SEC.ASM   KBD_IO.ASM
CURSOR.ASM     EDITOR.ASM     PHANTOM.ASM    VIDEO_IO.ASM
DISK_IO.ASM
```

MASM users can assemble the program with the included MAKEFILE and LINKINFO files; TASM users can assemble with the BORLAND. MAK file. You will also find an assembled and linked EXE version ready to run, so you can try out the new version without assembling it.

When you do, you will be able to tell that there are several improvements just by looking at the screen display. The advanced Dskpatch now uses eight function keys. That is more than you can remember if you don't use Dskpatch very often, so the advanced Dskpatch has a "key line" at the bottom of the display. A description of the function keys is as follows:

F2	Press the Shift key and F2 to write a sector back to the disk. We have covered this function in the book.
F3, F4	F3 reads the previous sector, and F4 reads the next sector. We have covered these two functions in the book.
F5	Changes the disk drive number or letter. Just press F5 and enter a letter, such as A (without a colon, :), or enter a drive number, such as 0. When you press the Enter key, Dskpatch will change drives and read a sector from the new disk drive. You may want to change Dskpatch so it does not read a new sector when you change drives. We have set it up so that it is very difficult to write a sector to the wrong disk.
F6	Changes the sector number. Just press F6 and type a sector number, in decimal. Dskpatch will read that sector.
F7	Changes Dskpatch to file mode. Just enter the file name and Dskpatch will read a sector from that file. From then on, F3 (Previous Sector) and F4 (Next

490

Sector) read sectors from within that file. F5 ends file mode and switches back to absolute-sector mode.

F8   Asks for an offset within a file. This is just like F4 (Sector) except that it reads sectors within a file. If you enter an offset of 3, Dskpatch will read the fourth sector in your file.

F10   Exits from Dskpatch. If you accidentally press this key, you will find yourself back in DOS, and you will lose any changes that you have made to the last sector. You may want to change Dskpatch so that it asks if you really want to leave Dskpatch.

A number of other changes are not as obvious as those we just mentioned. For example, Dskpatch now scrolls the screen one line at a time. So, if you move the cursor to the bottom line of the display and press the Cursor-Down key, Dskpatch will scroll the display by one line, putting a new line at the bottom. In addition, some of the other keys on the keyboard also work now:

Home   Moves the phantom cursor to the top of the half-sector display and scrolls the display so you see the first half-sector.

End   Moves the phantom cursor to the bottom right of the half-sector display and scrolls the display so you see the second half-sector.

PgUp   Scrolls the half-sector display by four lines. This is a nice feature when you want to move partway through the sector display. If you press PgUp four times, you will see the last half sector.

PgDn   Scrolls the half-sector display by four lines in the opposite direction from PgUp.

You can modify the advanced Dskpatch to better suit your own needs. That is why the disk has all the source files for the advanced Dskpatch—so you can modify Dskpatch any way you like and learn from a complete example. For instance, you might spruce up the error-checking capabilities. As it stands, if pressing F4 causes you to fall off the end of a disk or file, Dskpatch does not reset the sector to the last sector on the disk or file. If you feel ambitious, see if you can modify Dskpatch so it catches and corrects such errors.

Or, you may want to speed up screen updates. To do this you would have to rewrite some of the procedures, such as WRITE_CHAR and WRITE_ATTRIBUTE_N_TIMES, to write directly to screen memory. Now, they use the very slow ROM BIOS routines. If you are really ambitious, try to write your own character-output routines that send characters to the screen quickly.

DISKLITE Program

The DISKLITE directory included just one file, DISKLITE.ASM. The file contains the complete program for building a RAM resident program that was developed in Chapter 31.

Windows Code

The WINDOWS directory contains two files. WINLIB.ASM contains the code from Chapter 33 that checks pointers to see if they are valid. It also reports the size of segments. WINTEST.C is a sample file used to demonstrate the function. Use MASM 6.

C/C++ Libraries

As mentioned in Chapter 31, you will also find the set of C/C++ libraries on the disk, which are also printed in Appendix C. These libraries provide mouse support, writing to your screen, and some keyboard input routines. They show you how you can write a set of assembly-language subroutines that work with any memory model. MASM 6 is needed to build the library file CLIB.LIB. A list of the files you will find in the CLIB directory is as follows:

```
CURSOR.ASM      FASTWRIT.ASM      HARDWARE.ASM      KBD_IO.ASM
MOUSE.ASM       MAKEFILE          SOCHALIB.INC
```

Number	DSKPATCH	DISPATCH	DISP_SEC	KBD_IO	CURSOR	EDITOR	PHANTOM	VIDEO_IO	DISK_IO	TEST
9								VIDEO_9.ASM		
10								VIDEO_10.ASM		
13								VIDEO_13.ASM		TEST13.ASM
14			DISP_S14.ASM		CURSOR14.ASM			VIDEO_14.ASM		
15			DISP_S15.ASM						DISK_I15.ASM	
16			DISP_S16.ASM					VIDEO_16.ASM	DISK_I16.ASM	
17	DSKPAT17.ASM		DISP_S17.ASM		CURSOR17.ASM			VIDEO_17.ASM	DISK_I17.ASM	
18			DISP_18.ASM		CURSOR18.ASM			VIDEO_18.ASM		
19	DSKPAT19.ASM	DISPAT19.ASM	DISP_19.ASM	KBD_IO19.ASM					DISK_I19.ASM	
21			DISP_S21.ASM				PHANTO21.ASM	VIDEO_21.ASM		
22		DISPAT22.ASM				EDITOR22.ASM	PHANTO22.ASM			
23				KBD_IO23.ASM						TEST23.ASM
24				KBD_IO24.ASM						
25		DISPAT25.ASM								
26		DISPAT26.ASM							DISK_I26.ASM	
27							PHANTO27.ASM			
30	DSKPAT30.ASM			KBD_IO30.ASM	CURSOR30.ASM			VIDEO_30.ASM		

Listing of Dskpatch

This appendix contains the final version of Dskpatch. If you are writing your own programs, you will find many general-purpose procedures in this appendix that will help you on your way. We have included short descriptions of each procedure to help you find such procedures.

B

Topics Covered

Descriptions of Procedures

Dskpatch Make File

Dskpatch Linkinfo File

Program Listings for Dskpatch Procedures

Descriptions of Procedures

CURSOR.ASM

CLEAR_SCREEN Like the BASIC CLS command; clears the text screen.

CLEAR_TO_END_OF_LINE Clears all the characters from the cursor position to the end of the current line.

CURSOR_RIGHT Moves the cursor one character position to the right, without writing a space over the old character.

GOTO_XY Very much like the BASIC LOCATE command; moves the cursor on the screen.

SEND_CRLF Sends a carriage-return/line-feed pair of characters to the screen. This procedure simply moves the cursor to the start of the next line.

UPDATE_REAL_CURSOR Moves the real cursor to the location of the virtual cursor.

UPDATE_VIRTUAL_CURSOR Moves the virtual cursor to the position of the real cursor.

DISK_IO.ASM

NEXT_SECTOR Adds one to the current sector number, then reads that sector into memory and rewrites the Dskpatch screen.

PREVIOUS_SECTOR Reads the previous sector. That is, the procedure subtracts one from the old sector number (CURRENT_SECTOR_NO) and reads the new sector into the memory variable SECTOR. It also rewrites the screen display.

READ_SECTOR Reads one sector (512 bytes) from the disk into the memory buffer, SECTOR.

WRITE_SECTOR Writes one sector (512 bytes) from the memory buffer, SECTOR, to the disk.

DISPATCH.ASM

DISPATCHER The central dispatcher; reads characters from the keyboard and then calls on other procedures to do all the work of Dskpatch. Add any new commands to DISPATCH_TABLE in this file.

DISP_SEC.ASM

DISP_HALF_SECTOR Does the work of displaying all the hex and ASCII characters that appear in the half-sector display by calling DISP_LINE 16 times.

DISP_LINE Displays just 1 line of the half-sector display. DISP_HALF_SECTOR calls this procedure 16 times to display all 16 lines of the half-sector display.

INIT_SEC_DISP Initializes the half-sector display you see in Dskpatch. This procedure redraws the half-sector display, along with the boundaries and top hex numbers, but does not write the header or the editor prompt.

WRITE_HEADER Writes the header at the top of the screen you see in Dskpatch. There, the procedure displays the disk-drive number and the number of the sector you see in the half-sector display.

WRITE_PROMPT_LINE Writes a string at the prompt line, then clears the rest of the line to remove any characters from the old prompt.

WRITE_TOP_HEX_NUMBERS Writes the line of hex numbers across the top of the half-sector display. The procedure is not useful for much else.

497

DSKPATCH.ASM

DISK_PATCH The (very short) main program of Dskpatch. DISK_PATCH simply calls a number of other procedures, which do all the work. It also includes many of the definitions for variables that are used throughout Dskpatch.

EDITOR.ASM

EDIT_BYTE Edits a byte in the half-sector display by changing one byte both in memory (SECTOR) and on the screen. Dskpatch uses this procedure to change bytes in a sector.

WRITE_TO_MEMORY Called upon by EDIT_BYTE to change a single byte in SECTOR. This procedure changes the byte pointed to by the phantom cursor.

KBD_IO.ASM

BACK_SPACE Used by the READ_STRING procedure to delete one character, both from the screen and from the keyboard buffer, whenever you press the Backspace key.

CONVERT_HEX_DIGIT Converts a single ASCII character into its hexadecimal equivalent. For example, the procedure converts the letter A into the hex number 0AH. CONVERT_HEX_DIGIT works only with uppercase letters.

HEX_TO_BYTE Converts a two-character string of characters from a hexadecimal string, such as A5, into a single byte with that hex value. HEX_TO_BYTE expects the two characters to be digits or uppercase letters.

READ_BYTE Uses READ_STRING to read a string of characters. This procedure returns the special function key, a single character, or a hex byte if you typed a two-digit hex number.

READ_DECIMAL Reads an an unsigned decimal number from the keyboard, using READ_STRING to read the characters. READ_DECIMAL can read numbers from 0 to 65,535.

READ_KEY Reads a single key from the keyboard and returns 0 through 255 for ordinary characters, and 100h plus the scan code for special keys.

READ_STRING Reads a DOS-style string of characters from the keyboard. This procedure also reads special function keys, whereas the DOS READ_STRING function does not.

STRING_TO_UPPER A general-purpose procedure; converts a DOS-style string to all uppercase letters.

PHANTOM.ASM

ERASE_PHANTOM Removes the two phantom cursors from the screen by returning the character attribute to normal (7) for all characters under the phantom cursors.

MOV_TO_ASCII_POSITION Moves the real cursor to the start of the phantom cursor in the ASCII window of the half-sector display.

MOV_TO_HEX_POSITION Moves the real cursor to the start of the phantom cursor in the hex window of the half-sector display.

PHANTOM_DOWN Moves the phantom cursor down and scrolls the screen if you try to move past the 16th line of the half-sector display.

PHANTOM_LEFT Moves the phantom cursor left one entry, but not past the left side of the half-sector display.

PHANTOM_RIGHT Moves the phantom cursor right one entry, but not past the right side of the half-sector display.

PHANTOM_UP Moves the phantom cursor up one line in the half-sector display, or scrolls the display if you try to move the cursor off the top.

RESTORE_REAL_CURSOR Moves the cursor back to the position recorded by SAVE_REAL_CURSOR.

SAVE_REAL_CURSOR Saves the position of the real cursor in two variables. Call this procedure before you move the real cursor if you want to restore its position when you have finished making changes to the screen.

SCROLL_DOWN Rather than scrolling the half-sector display, displays the first half of the sector. You will find a more advanced version of SCROLL_DOWN on the disk available with this book. The advanced version scrolls the half-sector display by just one line.

SCROLL_UP Called by PHANTOM_DOWN when you try to move the phantom cursor off the bottom of the half-sector display. The version in this book doesn't actually scroll the screen; it writes the second half of the sector. On the disk, more advanced versions of SCROLL_UP and SCROLL_DOWN scroll the display by 1 line instead of 16.

WRITE_PHANTOM Draws the phantom cursors in the half-sector display: one in the hex window, and one in the ASCII window. This procedure simply changes the character attributes to 70H, to use black characters on a white background.

VIDEO_IO.ASM

Contains most of the general-purpose procedures you will want to use in your own programs.

INIT_WRITE_CHAR Call this procedure before you call any of the other procedures in this file. It initializes the data used by the routines that write directly to screen memory.

WRITE_ATTRIBUTE_N_TIMES A handy procedure you can use to change the attributes for a group of N characters. WRITE_PHANTOM uses this procedure to draw the phantom cursors, and ERASE_PHANTOM uses it to remove the phantom cursors.

WRITE_CHAR Writes a character to the screen. Since it uses the ROM BIOS routines, this procedure does not attach special meaning to any characters. So, a carriage-return character will appear on the screen as a musical note (the character for 0DH). Call SEND_CRLF if you want to move the cursor to the start of the next line.

WRITE_CHAR_N_TIMES Writes *N* copies of one character to the screen. This procedure is useful for drawing lines of characters, such as the ones used in patterns.

WRITE_DECIMAL Writes a word to the screen as an unsigned decimal number in the range 0 to 65,535.

WRITE_HEX Takes a one-byte number and writes it on the screen as a two-digit hex number.

WRITE_HEX_DIGIT Writes a single-digit hex number on the screen. This procedure converts a 4-bit nibble into the ASCII character and writes it to the screen.

WRITE_PATTERN Draws boxes around the half-sector display, as defined by a pattern. You can use WRITE_PATTERN to draw arbitrary patterns of characters on the screen.

WRITE_STRING A very useful, general-purpose procedure with which you can write a string of characters to the screen. The last character in your string must be a zero byte.

Dskpatch Make File

Following is the makefile that you can use to build Dskpatch automatically.

```
dskpatch.exe:   dskpatch.obj disk_io.obj disp_sec.obj video_io.obj cursor.obj \
                dispatch.obj kbd_io.obj phantom.obj editor.obj
        link @linkinfo

dskpatch.obj:   dskpatch.asm
        ml /c /Zi dskpatch.asm
```

```
disk_io.obj:    disk_io.asm
        ml /c /Zi disk_io.asm

disp_sec.obj:   disp_sec.asm
        ml /c /Zi disp_sec.asm

video_io.obj:   video_io.asm
        ml /c /Zi video_io.asm

cursor.obj:     cursor.asm
        ml /c /Zi cursor.asm

dispatch.obj:   dispatch.asm
        ml /c /Zi dispatch.asm

kbd_io.obj:     kbd_io.asm
        ml /c /Zi kbd_io.asm

phantom.obj:    phantom.asm
        ml /c /Zi phantom.asm

editor.obj:     editor.asm
        ml /c /Zi editor.asm
```

Dskpatch Linkinfo File

The linkinfo file is as follows:

```
DSKPATCH DISK_IO DISP_SEC VIDEO_IO CURSOR +
DISPATCH KBD_IO PHANTOM EDITOR
DSKPATCH
DSKPATCH /MAP;
```

Program Listings for Dskpatch Procedures

CURSOR.ASM

```
CR        EQU     13                      ;Carriage return
LF        EQU     10                      ;Line feed

.MODEL    SMALL
.CODE

          PUBLIC  CLEAR_SCREEN
;--------------------------------------------------------------------;
; This procedure clears the entire screen.                           ;
;--------------------------------------------------------------------;
CLEAR_SCREEN      PROC
          PUSH    AX
          PUSH    BX
          PUSH    CX
          PUSH    DX
          XOR     AL,AL                   ;Blank entire window
          XOR     CX,CX                   ;Upper left corner is at (0,0)
          MOV     DH,24                   ;Bottom line of screen is line 24
          MOV     DL,79                   ;Right side is at column 79
          MOV     BH,7                    ;Use normal attribute for blanks
          MOV     AH,6                    ;Call for SCROLL-UP function
          INT     10h                     ;Clear the window
          POP     DX
          POP     CX
          POP     BX
          POP     AX
          RET
CLEAR_SCREEN      ENDP


          PUBLIC  GOTO_XY
.DATA
          EXTRN   SCREEN_PTR:WORD ;Pointer to character under cursor
          EXTRN   SCREEN_X:BYTE, SCREEN_Y:BYTE
```

503

```
        .CODE
;------------------------------------------------------------------;
; This procedure moves the cursor                                  ;
;                                                                  ;
; On entry:     DH      Row (Y)                                    ;
;               DL      Column (X)                                 ;
;------------------------------------------------------------------;
GOTO_XY         PROC
        PUSH    AX
        PUSH    BX
        MOV     BH,0                    ;Display page 0
        MOV     AH,2                    ;Call for SET CURSOR POSITION
        INT     10h

        MOV     AL,DH                   ;Get the row number
        MOV     BL,80                   ;Multiply by 80 chars per line
        MUL     BL                      ;AX = row * 80
        ADD     AL,DL                   ;Add column
        ADC     AH,0                    ;AX = row * 80 + column
        SHL     AX,1                    ;Convert to a byte offset
        MOV     SCREEN_PTR,AX           ;Save the cursor offset
        MOV     SCREEN_X,DL             ;Save the cursor position
        MOV     SCREEN_Y,DH

        POP     BX
        POP     AX
        RET
GOTO_XY         ENDP


        PUBLIC  CURSOR_RIGHT
        .DATA
        EXTRN   SCREEN_PTR:WORD ;Pointer to character under cursor
        EXTRN   SCREEN_X:BYTE, SCREEN_Y:BYTE
        .CODE
;------------------------------------------------------------------;
; This procedure moves the cursor one position to the right or to the ;
; next line if the cursor was at the end of a line.                ;
;                                                                  ;
; Uses:         SEND_CRLF                                          ;
; Writes:       SCREEN_PTR, SCREEN_X, SCREEN_Y                     ;
;------------------------------------------------------------------;
CURSOR_RIGHT    PROC
        INC     SCREEN_PTR                      ;Move to next character position (word)
        INC     SCREEN_PTR
```

```
        INC     SCREEN_X              ;Move to next column
        CMP     SCREEN_X,79           ;Make sure column <= 79
        JBE     OK
        CALL    SEND_CRLF             ;Go to next line
OK:
        RET
CURSOR_RIGHT    ENDP


        PUBLIC  UPDATE_REAL_CURSOR
;------------------------------------------------------------------;
; This procedure moves the real cursor to the current virtual cursor   ;
; position.  You'll want to call it just before you wait for keyboard  ;
; input.                                                               ;
;------------------------------------------------------------------;
UPDATE_REAL_CURSOR      PROC
        PUSH    DX
        MOV     DL,SCREEN_X           ;Get position of the virtual cursor
        MOV     DH,SCREEN_Y
        CALL    GOTO_XY               ;Move real cursor to this position
        POP     DX
        RET
UPDATE_REAL_CURSOR      ENDP


        PUBLIC  UPDATE_VIRTUAL_CURSOR
;------------------------------------------------------------------;
; This procedure updates the position of our virtual cursor to agree   ;
; with the position of the real cursor.                                ;
;------------------------------------------------------------------;
UPDATE_VIRTUAL_CURSOR   PROC
        PUSH    AX
        PUSH    BX
        PUSH    CX
        PUSH    DX
        MOV     AH,3                  ;Ask for the cursor position
        XOR     BH,BH                 ;On page 0
        INT     10h                   ;Get cursor position into DH, DL
        CALL    GOTO_XY               ;Move virtual cursor to this position
        POP     DX
        POP     CX
        POP     BX
        POP     AX
        RET
UPDATE_VIRTUAL_CURSOR   ENDP
```

505

```
        PUBLIC  CLEAR_TO_END_OF_LINE
;-------------------------------------------------------------------;
; This procedure clears the line from the current cursor position to ;
; the end of that line.                                             ;
;-------------------------------------------------------------------;
CLEAR_TO_END_OF_LINE    PROC
        PUSH    AX
        PUSH    BX
        PUSH    CX
        PUSH    DX
        MOV     DL,SCREEN_X
        MOV     DH,SCREEN_Y
        MOV     AH,6            ;Set up to clear to end of line
        XOR     AL,AL           ;Clear window
        MOV     CH,DH           ;All on same line
        MOV     CL,DL           ;Start at the cursor position
        MOV     DL,79           ;And stop at the end of the line
        MOV     BH,7            ;Use normal attribute
        INT     10h
        POP     DX
        POP     CX
        POP     BX
        POP     AX
        RET
CLEAR_TO_END_OF_LINE    ENDP


        PUBLIC  SEND_CRLF
;-------------------------------------------------------------------;
; This routine just sends a carriage return-line feed pair to the   ;
; display, using the DOS routines so that scrolling will be handled ;
; correctly.                                                        ;
;                                                                   ;
; Uses: UPDATE_VIRTUAL_CURSOR                                       ;
;-------------------------------------------------------------------;
SEND_CRLF       PROC
        PUSH    AX
        PUSH    DX
        MOV     AH,2
        MOV     DL,CR
        INT     21h
        MOV     DL,LF
        INT     21h
        CALL    UPDATE_VIRTUAL_CURSOR   ;Update position of virtual cursor
        POP     DX
```

```
            POP       AX
            RET
SEND_CRLF       ENDP


            END
```

DISK_IO.ASM

```
.MODEL  SMALL

.DATA

        EXTRN   SECTOR:BYTE
        EXTRN   DISK_DRIVE_NO:BYTE
        EXTRN   CURRENT_SECTOR_NO:WORD


.CODE

        PUBLIC  PREVIOUS_SECTOR
        EXTRN   INIT_SEC_DISP:PROC, WRITE_HEADER:PROC
        EXTRN   WRITE_PROMPT_LINE:PROC
.DATA
        EXTRN   CURRENT_SECTOR_NO:WORD, EDITOR_PROMPT:BYTE
.CODE
;-------------------------------------------------------------;
; This procedure reads the previous sector, if possible.      ;
;                                                             ;
; Uses:         WRITE_HEADER, READ_SECTOR, INIT_SEC_DISP      ;
;               WRITE_PROMPT_LINE                             ;
; Reads:        CURRENT_SECTOR_NO, EDITOR_PROMPT              ;
; Writes:       CURRENT_SECTOR_NO                             ;
;-------------------------------------------------------------;
PREVIOUS_SECTOR         PROC
        PUSH    AX
        PUSH    DX
        MOV     AX,CURRENT_SECTOR_NO    ;Get current sector number
        OR      AX,AX                   ;Don't decrement if already 0
        JZ      DONT_DECREMENT_SECTOR
        DEC     AX
        MOV     CURRENT_SECTOR_NO,AX    ;Save new sector number
        CALL    WRITE_HEADER
        CALL    READ_SECTOR
```

```
        CALL    INIT_SEC_DISP           ;Display new sector
        LEA     DX,EDITOR_PROMPT
        CALL    WRITE_PROMPT_LINE
DONT_DECREMENT_SECTOR:
        POP     DX
        POP     AX
        RET
PREVIOUS_SECTOR         ENDP


        PUBLIC  NEXT_SECTOR
        EXTRN   INIT_SEC_DISP:PROC, WRITE_HEADER:PROC
        EXTRN   WRITE_PROMPT_LINE:PROC
.DATA
        EXTRN   CURRENT_SECTOR_NO:WORD, EDITOR_PROMPT:BYTE
.CODE
;------------------------------------------------------------------;
; Reads the next sector.                                           ;
;                                                                  ;
; Uses:         WRITE_HEADER, READ_SECTOR, INIT_SEC_DISP           ;
;               WRITE_PROMPT_LINE                                  ;
; Reads:        CURRENT_SECTOR_NO, EDITOR_PROMPT                   ;
; Writes:       CURRENT_SECTOR_NO                                  ;
;------------------------------------------------------------------;
NEXT_SECTOR     PROC
        PUSH    AX
        PUSH    DX
        MOV     AX,CURRENT_SECTOR_NO
        INC     AX                      ;Move to next sector
        MOV     CURRENT_SECTOR_NO,AX
        CALL    WRITE_HEADER
        CALL    READ_SECTOR
        CALL    INIT_SEC_DISP           ;Display new sector
        LEA     DX,EDITOR_PROMPT
        CALL    WRITE_PROMPT_LINE
        POP     DX
        POP     AX
        RET
NEXT_SECTOR     ENDP


        PUBLIC  READ_SECTOR
;------------------------------------------------------------------;
; This procedure reads one sector (512 bytes) into SECTOR.        ;
;                                                                  ;
; Reads:        CURRENT_SECTOR_NO, DISK_DRIVE_NO                   ;
```

```
; Writes:        SECTOR                                              ;
;-------------------------------------------------------------------;
READ_SECTOR     PROC
        PUSH    AX
        PUSH    BX
        PUSH    CX
        PUSH    DX
        MOV     AL,DISK_DRIVE_NO         ;Drive number
        MOV     CX,1                     ;Read only 1 sector
        MOV     DX,CURRENT_SECTOR_NO     ;Logical sector number
        LEA     BX,SECTOR                ;Where to store this sector
        INT     25h                      ;Read the sector
        POPF                             ;Discard flags put on stack by DOS
        POP     DX
        POP     CX
        POP     BX
        POP     AX
        RET
READ_SECTOR     ENDP


        PUBLIC  WRITE_SECTOR
;-------------------------------------------------------------------;
; This procedure writes the sector back to the disk.                ;
;                                                                   ;
; Reads:        DISK_DRIVE_NO, CURRENT_SECTOR_NO, SECTOR            ;
;-------------------------------------------------------------------;
WRITE_SECTOR    PROC
        PUSH    AX
        PUSH    BX
        PUSH    CX
        PUSH    DX
        MOV     AL,DISK_DRIVE_NO         ;Drive number
        MOV     CX,1                     ;Write 1 sector
        MOV     DX,CURRENT_SECTOR_NO     ;Logical sector
        LEA     BX,SECTOR
        INT     26h                      ;Write the sector to disk
        POPF                             ;Discard the flag information
        POP     DX
        POP     CX
        POP     BX
        POP     AX
        RET
WRITE_SECTOR    ENDP


        END
```

DISPATCH.ASM

```
.MODEL   SMALL

.CODE
        EXTRN    NEXT_SECTOR:PROC                        ;In DISK_IO.ASM
        EXTRN    PREVIOUS_SECTOR:PROC                    ;In DISK_IO.ASM
        EXTRN    PHANTOM_UP:PROC, PHANTOM_DOWN:PROC      ;In PHANTOM.ASM
        EXTRN    PHANTOM_LEFT:PROC, PHANTOM_RIGHT:PROC
        EXTRN    WRITE_SECTOR:PROC                       ;In DISK_IO.ASM
.DATA
;-----------------------------------------------------------------------;
; This table contains the legal extended ASCII keys and the addresses   ;
; of the procedures that should be called when each key is pressed.     ;
;                                                                       ;
; The format of the table is                                           ;
;               DB      72                ;Extended code for cursor up   ;
;               DW      OFFSET _TEXT:PHANTOM_UP                          ;
;-----------------------------------------------------------------------;
DISPATCH_TABLE LABEL   BYTE
        DB      61                              ;F3
        DW      OFFSET _TEXT:PREVIOUS_SECTOR
        DB      62                              ;F4
        DW      OFFSET _TEXT:NEXT_SECTOR
        DB      72                              ;Cursor up
        DW      OFFSET _TEXT:PHANTOM_UP
        DB      80                              ;Cursor down
        DW      OFFSET _TEXT:PHANTOM_DOWN
        DB      75                              ;Cursor left
        DW      OFFSET _TEXT:PHANTOM_LEFT
        DB      77                              ;Cursor right
        DW      OFFSET _TEXT:PHANTOM_RIGHT
        DW      85                              ;Shift F2
        DW      OFFSET _TEXT:WRITE_SECTOR
        DB      0                               ;End of the table

.CODE

        PUBLIC  DISPATCHER
        EXTRN   READ_BYTE:PROC, EDIT_BYTE:PROC
        EXTRN   WRITE_PROMPT_LINE:PROC
.DATA
        EXTRN   EDITOR_PROMPT:BYTE
```

```
        .CODE
        ;--------------------------------------------------------------;
        ; This is the central dispatcher. During normal editing and viewing,  ;
        ; this procedure reads characters from the keyboard and, if the char   ;
        ; is a command key (such as a cursor key), DISPATCHER calls the        ;
        ; procedures that do the actual work.  This dispatching is done for    ;
        ; special keys listed in the table DISPATCH_TABLE, where the procedure ;
        ; addresses are stored just after the key names.                       ;
        ;                                                                      ;
        ; If the character is not a special key, then it should be placed      ;
        ; directly into the sector buffer--this is the editing mode.           ;
        ;                                                                      ;
        ; Uses:          READ_BYTE, EDIT_BYTE, WRITE_PROMPT_LINE               ;
        ; Reads:         EDITOR_PROMPT                                         ;
        ;--------------------------------------------------------------;
DISPATCHER      PROC
        PUSH    AX
        PUSH    BX
        PUSH    DX
DISPATCH_LOOP:
        CALL    READ_BYTE               ;Read character into AX
        OR      AH,AH                   ;AX = -1 if no character read, 1
                                        ; for an extended code.
        JS      NO_CHARS_READ           ;No character read, try again
        JNZ     SPECIAL_KEY             ;Read extended code
        MOV     DL,AL
        CALL    EDIT_BYTE               ;Was normal character, edit byte
        JMP     DISPATCH_LOOP           ;Read another character


SPECIAL_KEY:
        CMP     AL,68                   ;F10--exit?
        JE      END_DISPATCH            ;Yes, leave
                                        ;Use BX to look through table
        LEA     BX,DISPATCH_TABLE
SPECIAL_LOOP:
        CMP     BYTE PTR [BX],0         ;End of table?
        JE      NOT_IN_TABLE            ;Yes, key was not in the table
        CMP     AL,[BX]                 ;Is it this table entry?
        JE      DISPATCH                ;Yes, then dispatch
        ADD     BX,3                    ;No, try next entry
        JMP     SPECIAL_LOOP            ;Check next table entry


DISPATCH:
        INC     BX                      ;Point to address of procedure
        CALL    WORD PTR [BX]           ;Call procedure
        JMP     DISPATCH_LOOP           ;Wait for another key
```

511

```
NOT_IN_TABLE:                                   ;Do nothing, just read next character
        JMP      DISPATCH_LOOP

NO_CHARS_READ:
        LEA      DX,EDITOR_PROMPT
        CALL     WRITE_PROMPT_LINE              ;Erase any invalid characters typed
        JMP      DISPATCH_LOOP                  ;Try again

END_DISPATCH:
        POP      DX
        POP      BX
        POP      AX
        RET
DISPATCHER   ENDP


        END
```

DISP_SEC.ASM

```
.MODEL   SMALL


;--------------------------------------------------------------------;
; Graphics characters for border of sector.                         ;
;--------------------------------------------------------------------;
VERTICAL_BAR      EQU      0BAh
HORIZONTAL_BAR    EQU      0CDh
UPPER_LEFT        EQU      0C9h
UPPER_RIGHT       EQU      0BBh
LOWER_LEFT        EQU      0C8h
LOWER_RIGHT       EQU      0BCh
TOP_T_BAR         EQU      0CBh
BOTTOM_T_BAR      EQU      0CAh
TOP_TICK          EQU      0D1h
BOTTOM_TICK       EQU      0CFh


.DATA

TOP_LINE_PATTERN          LABEL    BYTE
        DB        ' ',7
```

```
        DB      UPPER_LEFT,1
        DB      HORIZONTAL_BAR,12
        DB      TOP_TICK,1
        DB      HORIZONTAL_BAR,11
        DB      TOP_TICK,1
        DB      HORIZONTAL_BAR,11
        DB      TOP_TICK,1
        DB      HORIZONTAL_BAR,12
        DB      TOP_T_BAR,1
        DB      HORIZONTAL_BAR,18
        DB      UPPER_RIGHT,1
        DB      0
BOTTOM_LINE_PATTERN     LABEL   BYTE
        DB      ' ',7
        DB      LOWER_LEFT,1
        DB      HORIZONTAL_BAR,12
        DB      BOTTOM_TICK,1
        DB      HORIZONTAL_BAR,11
        DB      BOTTOM_TICK,1
        DB      HORIZONTAL_BAR,11
        DB      BOTTOM_TICK,1
        DB      HORIZONTAL_BAR,12
        DB      BOTTOM_T_BAR,1
        DB      HORIZONTAL_BAR,18
        DB      LOWER_RIGHT,1
        DB      0


.DATA?
        EXTRN   SECTOR:BYTE


.CODE


        PUBLIC  INIT_SEC_DISP
        EXTRN   WRITE_PATTERN:PROC, SEND_CRLF:PROC
        EXTRN   GOTO_XY:PROC, WRITE_PHANTOM:PROC
.DATA
        EXTRN   LINES_BEFORE_SECTOR:BYTE
        EXTRN   SECTOR_OFFSET:WORD
.CODE
;--------------------------------------------------------------------;
; This procedure initializes the half-sector display.                ;
;                                                                    ;
; Uses:          WRITE_PATTERN, SEND_CRLF, DISP_HALF_SECTOR          ;
;                WRITE_TOP_HEX_NUMBERS, GOTO_XY, WRITE_PHANTOM        ;
```

513

```
; Reads:          TOP_LINE_PATTERN, BOTTOM_LINE_PATTERN          ;
;                 LINES_BEFORE_SECTOR                            ;
; Writes:         SECTOR_OFFSET                                  ;
;-----------------------------------------------------------------;
INIT_SEC_DISP   PROC
        PUSH    DX
        XOR     DL,DL                    ;Move cursor into position
        MOV     DH,LINES_BEFORE_SECTOR
        CALL    GOTO_XY
        CALL    WRITE_TOP_HEX_NUMBERS
        LEA     DX,TOP_LINE_PATTERN
        CALL    WRITE_PATTERN
        CALL    SEND_CRLF
        XOR     DX,DX                    ;Start at the beginning of the sector
        MOV     SECTOR_OFFSET,DX         ;Set sector offset to 0
        CALL    DISP_HALF_SECTOR
        LEA     DX,BOTTOM_LINE_PATTERN
        CALL    WRITE_PATTERN
        CALL    WRITE_PHANTOM            ;Display the phantom cursor
        POP     DX
        RET
INIT_SEC_DISP   ENDP


        PUBLIC  WRITE_HEADER
.DATA
        EXTRN   HEADER_LINE_NO:BYTE
        EXTRN   HEADER_PART_1:BYTE
        EXTRN   HEADER_PART_2:BYTE
        EXTRN   DISK_DRIVE_NO:BYTE
        EXTRN   CURRENT_SECTOR_NO:WORD
.CODE
        EXTRN   WRITE_STRING:PROC, WRITE_DECIMAL:PROC
        EXTRN   GOTO_XY:PROC, CLEAR_TO_END_OF_LINE:PROC
;-----------------------------------------------------------------;
; This procedure writes the header with disk-drive and sector number.  ;
;                                                                 ;
; Uses:           GOTO_XY, WRITE_STRING, WRITE_CHAR, WRITE_DECIMAL     ;
;                 CLEAR_TO_END_OF_LINE                            ;
; Reads:          HEADER_LINE_NO, HEADER_PART_1, HEADER_PART_2    ;
;                 DISK_DRIVE_NO, CURRENT_SECTOR_NO               ;
;-----------------------------------------------------------------;
WRITE_HEADER    PROC
        PUSH    DX
        XOR     DL,DL                    ;Move cursor to header line number
        MOV     DH,HEADER_LINE_NO
```

```
        CALL    GOTO_XY
        LEA     DX,HEADER_PART_1
        CALL    WRITE_STRING
        MOV     DL,DISK_DRIVE_NO
        ADD     DL,'A'                  ;Print drives A, B, ...
        CALL    WRITE_CHAR
        LEA     DX,HEADER_PART_2
        CALL    WRITE_STRING
        MOV     DX,CURRENT_SECTOR_NO
        CALL    WRITE_DECIMAL
        CALL    CLEAR_TO_END_OF_LINE    ;Clear rest of sector number
        POP     DX
        RET
WRITE_HEADER    ENDP



        EXTRN   WRITE_CHAR_N_TIMES:PROC, WRITE_HEX:PROC, WRITE_CHAR:PROC
        EXTRN   WRITE_HEX_DIGIT:PROC, SEND_CRLF:PROC
;-------------------------------------------------------------------;
; This procedure writes the index numbers (0 through F) at the top of ;
; the half-sector display.                                          ;
;                                                                   ;
; Uses:         WRITE_CHAR_N_TIMES, WRITE_HEX, WRITE_CHAR           ;
;               WRITE_HEX_DIGIT, SEND_CRLF                          ;
;-------------------------------------------------------------------;
WRITE_TOP_HEX_NUMBERS   PROC
        PUSH    CX
        PUSH    DX
        MOV     DL,' '                  ;Write 9 spaces for left side
        MOV     CX,9
        CALL    WRITE_CHAR_N_TIMES
        XOR     DH,DH                   ;Start with 0
HEX_NUMBER_LOOP:
        MOV     DL,DH
        CALL    WRITE_HEX
        MOV     DL,' '
        CALL    WRITE_CHAR
        INC     DH
        CMP     DH,10h                  ;Done yet?
        JB      HEX_NUMBER_LOOP

        MOV     DL,' '                  ;Write hex numbers over ASCII window
        MOV     CX,2
        CALL    WRITE_CHAR_N_TIMES
        XOR     DL,DL
```

515

```
HEX_DIGIT_LOOP:
        CALL    WRITE_HEX_DIGIT
        INC     DL
        CMP     DL,10h
        JB      HEX_DIGIT_LOOP
        CALL    SEND_CRLF
        POP     DX
        POP     CX
        RET
WRITE_TOP_HEX_NUMBERS   ENDP


        PUBLIC  DISP_HALF_SECTOR
        EXTRN   SEND_CRLF:PROC
;--------------------------------------------------------------------;
;  This procedure displays half a sector (256 bytes)                 ;
;                                                                    ;
; On entry:      DS:DX   Offset into sector, in bytes -- should be    ;
;                        multiple of 16.                             ;
;                                                                    ;
; Uses:          DISP_LINE, SEND_CRLF                                ;
;--------------------------------------------------------------------;
DISP_HALF_SECTOR        PROC
        PUSH    CX
        PUSH    DX
        MOV     CX,16                   ;Display 16 lines
HALF_SECTOR:
        CALL    DISP_LINE
        CALL    SEND_CRLF
        ADD     DX,16
        LOOP    HALF_SECTOR
        POP     DX
        POP     CX
        RET
DISP_HALF_SECTOR        ENDP


        PUBLIC  DISP_LINE
        EXTRN   WRITE_HEX:PROC
        EXTRN   WRITE_CHAR:PROC
        EXTRN   WRITE_CHAR_N_TIMES:PROC
;--------------------------------------------------------------------;
; This procedure displays one line of data, or 16 bytes, first in hex, ;
; then in ASCII.                                                     ;
;                                                                    ;
```

```
; On entry:      DS:DX   Offset into sector, in bytes.                ;
;                                                                     ;
; Uses:          WRITE_CHAR, WRITE_HEX, WRITE_CHAR_N_TIMES            ;
; Reads:         SECTOR                                               ;
;---------------------------------------------------------------------;
DISP_LINE       PROC
        PUSH    BX
        PUSH    CX
        PUSH    DX
        MOV     BX,DX                   ;Offset is more useful in BX
        MOV     DL,' '
        MOV     CX,3                    ;Write 3 spaces before line
        CALL    WRITE_CHAR_N_TIMES

                                        ;Write offset in hex
        CMP     BX,100h                 ;Is the first digit a 1?
        JB      WRITE_ONE               ;No, white space already in DL
        MOV     DL,'1'                  ;Yes, then place '1' into DL for output
WRITE_ONE:
        CALL    WRITE_CHAR
        MOV     DL,BL                   ;Copy lower byte into DL for hex output
        CALL    WRITE_HEX

                                        ;Write separator
        MOV     DL,' '
        CALL    WRITE_CHAR
        MOV     DL,VERTICAL_BAR         ;Draw left side of box
        CALL    WRITE_CHAR
        MOV     DL,' '
        CALL    WRITE_CHAR

                                        ;Now write out 16 bytes
        MOV     CX,16                   ;Dump 16 bytes
        PUSH    BX                      ;Save the offset for ASCII_LOOP
HEX_LOOP:
        MOV     DL,SECTOR[BX]           ;Get 1 byte
        CALL    WRITE_HEX               ;Dump this byte in hex
        MOV     DL,' '                  ;Write a space between numbers
        CALL    WRITE_CHAR
        INC     BX
        LOOP    HEX_LOOP

        MOV     DL,VERTICAL_BAR         ;Write separator
        CALL    WRITE_CHAR
        MOV     DL,' '                  ;Add another space before characters
        CALL    WRITE_CHAR
        MOV     CX,16
        POP     BX                      ;Get back offset into SECTOR
```

```
ASCII_LOOP:
        MOV     DL,SECTOR[BX]
        CALL    WRITE_CHAR
        INC     BX
        LOOP    ASCII_LOOP

        MOV     DL,' '                  ;Draw right side of box
        CALL    WRITE_CHAR
        MOV     DL,VERTICAL_BAR
        CALL    WRITE_CHAR

        POP     DX
        POP     CX
        POP     BX
        RET
DISP_LINE       ENDP


        PUBLIC  WRITE_PROMPT_LINE
        EXTRN   CLEAR_TO_END_OF_LINE:PROC, WRITE_STRING:PROC
        EXTRN   GOTO_XY:PROC
.DATA
        EXTRN   PROMPT_LINE_NO:BYTE
.CODE
;--------------------------------------------------------------------;
; This procedure writes the prompt line to the screen and clears the ;
; end of the line.                                                   ;
;                                                                    ;
; On entry:      DS:DX    Address of the prompt-line message         ;
;                                                                    ;
; Uses:          WRITE_STRING, CLEAR_TO_END_OF_LINE, GOTO_XY         ;
; Reads:         PROMPT_LINE_NO                                      ;
;--------------------------------------------------------------------;
WRITE_PROMPT_LINE       PROC
        PUSH    DX
        XOR     DL,DL                   ;Write the prompt line and
        MOV     DH,PROMPT_LINE_NO       ; move the cursor there
        CALL    GOTO_XY
        POP     DX
        CALL    WRITE_STRING
        CALL    CLEAR_TO_END_OF_LINE
        RET
WRITE_PROMPT_LINE       ENDP


        END
```

DSKPATCH.ASM

```
DOSSEG
.MODEL  SMALL

.STACK

.DATA

        PUBLIC  SECTOR_OFFSET
;-----------------------------------------------;
; SECTOR_OFFSET is the offset of the half-      ;
; sector display into the full sector.  It must ;
; be a multiple of 16, and not greater than 256 ;
;-----------------------------------------------;
SECTOR_OFFSET   DW      0

        PUBLIC  CURRENT_SECTOR_NO, DISK_DRIVE_NO
CURRENT_SECTOR_NO       DW      0               ;Initially sector 0
DISK_DRIVE_NO           DB      0               ;Initially Drive A:

        PUBLIC  LINES_BEFORE_SECTOR, HEADER_LINE_NO
        PUBLIC  HEADER_PART_1, HEADER_PART_2
;-----------------------------------------------;
; LINES_BEFORE_SECTOR is the number of lines    ;
; at the top of the screen before the half-     ;
; sector display.                               ;
;-----------------------------------------------;
LINES_BEFORE_SECTOR     DB      2
HEADER_LINE_NO          DB      0
HEADER_PART_1           DB      'Disk ',0
HEADER_PART_2           DB      '        Sector ',0
        PUBLIC  PROMPT_LINE_NO, EDITOR_PROMPT
PROMPT_LINE_NO          DB      21
EDITOR_PROMPT           DB      'Press function key, or enter'
                        DB      ' character or hex byte: ',0

.DATA?

        PUBLIC  SECTOR
;-----------------------------------------------;
; The entire sector (up to 8192 bytes) is       ;
; stored in this part of memory.                ;
;-----------------------------------------------;
SECTOR  DB      8192 DUP (?)

.CODE
```

519

```
            EXTRN    CLEAR_SCREEN:PROC, READ_SECTOR:PROC
            EXTRN    INIT_SEC_DISP:PROC, WRITE_HEADER:PROC
            EXTRN    WRITE_PROMPT_LINE:PROC, DISPATCHER:PROC
            EXTRN    INIT_WRITE_CHAR:PROC
DISK_PATCH          PROC
            MOV      AX,DGROUP               ;Put data segment into AX
            MOV      DS,AX                   ;Set DS to point to data

            CALL     INIT_WRITE_CHAR
            CALL     CLEAR_SCREEN
            CALL     WRITE_HEADER
            CALL     READ_SECTOR
            CALL     INIT_SEC_DISP
            LEA      DX,EDITOR_PROMPT
            CALL     WRITE_PROMPT_LINE
            CALL     DISPATCHER

            MOV      AH,4Ch                  ;Return to DOS
            INT      21h
DISK_PATCH          ENDP


            END      DISK_PATCH
```

EDITOR.ASM

```
.MODEL  SMALL

.CODE

.DATA
        EXTRN    SECTOR:BYTE
        EXTRN    SECTOR_OFFSET:WORD
        EXTRN    PHANTOM_CURSOR_X:BYTE
        EXTRN    PHANTOM_CURSOR_Y:BYTE
.CODE
;------------------------------------------------------------------------;
; This procedure writes one byte to SECTOR, at the memory location       ;
; pointed to by the phantom cursor.                                      ;
;                                                                        ;
; On entry:     DL      Byte to write to SECTOR                          ;
;                                                                        ;
```

```
; The offset is calculated by                                      ;
;   OFFSET = SECTOR_OFFSET + (16 * PHANTOM_CURSOR_Y) + PHANTOM_CURSOR_X;
;                                                                  ;
; Reads:        PHANTOM_CURSOR_X, PHANTOM_CURSOR_Y, SECTOR_OFFSET  ;
; Writes:       SECTOR                                             ;
;-----------------------------------------------------------------;
WRITE_TO_MEMORY PROC
        PUSH    AX
        PUSH    BX
        PUSH    CX
        MOV     BX,SECTOR_OFFSET
        MOV     AL,PHANTOM_CURSOR_Y
        XOR     AH,AH
        MOV     CL,4                    ;Multiply PHANTOM_CURSOR_Y by 16
        SHL     AX,CL
        ADD     BX,AX                   ;BX = SECTOR_OFFSET + (16 * Y)
        MOV     AL,PHANTOM_CURSOR_X
        XOR     AH,AH
        ADD     BX,AX                   ;That's the address!
        MOV     SECTOR[BX],DL           ;Now, store the byte
        POP     CX
        POP     BX
        POP     AX
        RET
WRITE_TO_MEMORY ENDP


        PUBLIC  EDIT_BYTE
        EXTRN   SAVE_REAL_CURSOR:PROC, RESTORE_REAL_CURSOR:PROC
        EXTRN   MOV_TO_HEX_POSITION:PROC, MOV_TO_ASCII_POSITION:PROC
        EXTRN   WRITE_PHANTOM:PROC, WRITE_PROMPT_LINE:PROC
        EXTRN   CURSOR_RIGHT:PROC, WRITE_HEX:PROC, WRITE_CHAR:PROC
.DATA
        EXTRN   EDITOR_PROMPT:BYTE
.CODE
;-----------------------------------------------------------------;
; This procedure changes a byte in memory and on the screen.      ;
;                                                                  ;
; On entry:     DL      Byte to write into SECTOR, and change on screen;
;                                                                  ;
; Uses:         SAVE_REAL_CURSOR, RESTORE_REAL_CURSOR              ;
;               MOV_TO_HEX_POSITION, MOV_TO_ASCII_POSITION         ;
;               WRITE_PHANTOM, WRITE_PROMPT_LINE, CURSOR_RIGHT     ;
;               WRITE_HEX, WRITE_CHAR, WRITE_TO_MEMORY             ;
; Reads:        EDITOR_PROMPT                                      ;
;-----------------------------------------------------------------;
```

521

```
EDIT_BYTE        PROC
        PUSH     DX
        CALL     SAVE_REAL_CURSOR
        CALL     MOV_TO_HEX_POSITION     ;Move to the hex number in the
        CALL     CURSOR_RIGHT            ; hex window
        CALL     WRITE_HEX               ;Write the new number
        CALL     MOV_TO_ASCII_POSITION   ;Move to the char. in the ASCII window
        CALL     WRITE_CHAR              ;Write the new character
        CALL     RESTORE_REAL_CURSOR     ;Move cursor back where it belongs
        CALL     WRITE_PHANTOM           ;Rewrite the phantom cursor
        CALL     WRITE_TO_MEMORY         ;Save this new byte in SECTOR
        LEA      DX,EDITOR_PROMPT
        CALL     WRITE_PROMPT_LINE
        POP      DX
        RET
EDIT_BYTE        ENDP


        END
```

KBD_IO.ASM

```
.MODEL  SMALL

BS       EQU     8                       ;Backspace character
CR       EQU     13                      ;Carriage-return character
ESCAPE   EQU     27                      ;Escape character

.DATA

KEYBOARD_INPUT  LABEL   BYTE
CHAR_NUM_LIMIT  DB      0                 ;Length of input buffer
NUM_CHARS_READ  DB      0                 ;Number of characters read
CHARS           DB      80 DUP (0)        ;A buffer for keyboard input

.CODE

        PUBLIC  STRING_TO_UPPER
;-----------------------------------------------------------------------;
; This procedure converts the string, using the DOS format for strings,;
; to all uppercase letters.                                            ;
;                                                                      ;
; On entry:     DS:DX   Address of string buffer                       ;
;-----------------------------------------------------------------------;
```

```
STRING_TO_UPPER PROC
        PUSH    AX
        PUSH    BX
        PUSH    CX
        MOV     BX,DX
        INC     BX                      ;Point to character count
        MOV     CL,[BX]                 ;Charac. count in 2nd byte of buffer
        XOR     CH,CH                   ;Clear upper byte of count
UPPER_LOOP:
        INC     BX                      ;Point to next character in buffer
        MOV     AL,[BX]
        CMP     AL,'a'                  ;See if it is a lowercase letter
        JB      NOT_LOWER               ;Nope
        CMP     AL,'z'
        JA      NOT_LOWER
        ADD     AL,'A'-'a'              ;Convert to uppercase letter
        MOV     [BX],AL
NOT_LOWER:
        LOOP    UPPER_LOOP
        POP     CX
        POP     BX
        POP     AX
        RET
STRING_TO_UPPER ENDP

;-------------------------------------------------------------------;
; This procedure converts a character from ASCII (hex) to a nibble  ;
; (4 bits).                                                         ;
;                                                                   ;
; On entry:     AL      Character to convert                        ;
; Returns:      AL      Nibble                                      ;
;               CF      Set for error, cleared otherwise            ;
;-------------------------------------------------------------------;
CONVERT_HEX_DIGIT       PROC
        CMP     AL,'0'                  ;Is it a legal digit?
        JB      BAD_DIGIT               ;Nope
        CMP     AL,'9'                  ;Not sure yet
        JA      TRY_HEX                 ;Might be hex digit
        SUB     AL,'0'                  ;Is decimal digit, convert to nibble
        CLC                             ;Clear the carry, no error
        RET
```

```
TRY_HEX:
        CMP     AL,'A'                  ;Not sure yet
        JB      BAD_DIGIT               ;Not hex
        CMP     AL,'F'                  ;Not sure yet
        JA      BAD_DIGIT               ;Not hex
        SUB     AL,'A'-10               ;Is hex, convert to nibble
        CLC                             ;Clear the carry, no error
        RET
BAD_DIGIT:
        STC                             ;Set the carry, error
        RET
CONVERT_HEX_DIGIT       ENDP

        PUBLIC  HEX_TO_BYTE
;-----------------------------------------------------------------;
; This procedure converts the two characters at DS:DX from hex to one ;
; byte.                                                           ;
;                                                                 ;
; On entry:     DS:DX   Address of two characters for hex number  ;
; Returns:      AL      Byte                                      ;
;               CF      Set for error, clear if no error          ;
;                                                                 ;
; Uses:         CONVERT_HEX_DIGIT                                 ;
;-----------------------------------------------------------------;
HEX_TO_BYTE     PROC
        PUSH    BX
        PUSH    CX
        MOV     BX,DX                   ;Put address in BX for indirect addr
        MOV     AL,[BX]                 ;Get first digit
        CALL    CONVERT_HEX_DIGIT
        JC      BAD_HEX                 ;Bad hex digit if carry set
        MOV     CX,4                    ;Now multiply by 16
        SHL     AL,CL
        MOV     AH,AL                   ;Retain a copy
        INC     BX                      ;Get second digit
        MOV     AL,[BX]
        CALL    CONVERT_HEX_DIGIT
        JC      BAD_HEX                 ;Bad hex digit if carry set
        OR      AL,AH                   ;Combine two nibbles
        CLC                             ;Clear carry for no error
DONE_HEX:
        POP     CX
        POP     BX
        RET
```

```
BAD_HEX:
        STC                              ;Set carry for error
        JMP     DONE_HEX
HEX_TO_BYTE     ENDP


        PUBLIC  READ_STRING
        EXTRN   WRITE_CHAR:PROC
        EXTRN   UPDATE_REAL_CURSOR:PROC
;---------------------------------------------------------------;
; This procedure performs a function very similar to the DOS 0Ah ;
; function.  But this function will return a special character if a ;
; function or keyboard key is pressed--no return for these keys.  And ;
; ESCAPE will erase the input and start over again.              ;
;                                                                ;
;       DS:DX   Address for keyboard buffer.  The first byte must ;
;               contain the maximum number of characters to read (plus ;
;               one for the return).  And the second byte will be used ;
;               by this procedure to return the number of characters ;
;               actually read.                                   ;
;                       0       No characters read               ;
;                       -1      One special character read       ;
;                       otherwise number actually read (not including ;
;                               Enter key)                       ;
;                                                                ;
; Uses: BACK_SPACE, WRITE_CHAR, UPDATE_REAL_CURSOR               ;
;---------------------------------------------------------------;
READ_STRING     PROC    PROC
        PUSH    AX
        PUSH    BX
        PUSH    SI
        MOV     SI,DX                    ;Use SI for index register and

START_OVER:
        MOV     BX,2                     ;BX for offset to beginning of buffer

READ_LOOP:
        CALL    UPDATE_REAL_CURSOR       ;Move to position of virtual cursor
        CALL    READ_KEY                 ;Read one key from the keyboard
        OR      AH,AH                    ;Is character extended ASCII?
        JNZ     EXTENDED                 ;Yes, then process it.
STRING_NOT_EXTENDED:                     ;No, see what char it is
        CMP     AL,CR                    ;Is this a carriage return?
        JE      END_INPUT                ;Yes, we are done with input
        CMP     AL,BS                    ;Is it a backspace character?
```

```
        JNE       NOT_BS                  ;Nope
        CALL      BACK_SPACE              ;Yes, delete character
        JMP       READ_LOOP               ;Read the next character

NOT_BS: CMP       AL,ESCAPE               ;Is it an ESC--purge buffer?
        JNE       NOT_ESC                 ;No, put character into buffer
        CALL      PURGE_BUFFER            ;Yes, remove all characters from buffer
        JMP       READ_LOOP               ;Start reading characters again

NOT_ESC:
        CMP       BL,[SI]                 ;Check to see if buffer is full
        JA        BUFFER_FULL             ;Buffer is full
        MOV       [SI+BX],AL              ;Else save char in buffer
        INC       BX                      ;Point to next free character in buffer
        PUSH      DX
        MOV       DL,AL                   ;Echo character to screen
        CALL      WRITE_CHAR
        POP       DX
        JMP       READ_LOOP               ; Read the next character

;-----------------------------------------------;
; Signal an error condition by sending a beep   ;
; character to the display: chr$(7).            ;
;-----------------------------------------------;
SIGNAL_ERROR:
        PUSH      DX
        MOV       DL,7                    ;Sound the bell by writing chr$(7)
        MOV       AH,2
        INT       21h
        POP       DX
        JMP       SHORT READ_LOOP         ;Now read next character

;-----------------------------------------------;
; The buffer was full, so can't read another    ;
; character.  Send a beep to alert user of      ;
; buffer-full condition.                        ;
;-----------------------------------------------;
BUFFER_FULL:
        JMP       SHORT SIGNAL_ERROR      ;If buffer full, just beep

;-----------------------------------------------;
; Read the extended ASCII code and place this   ;
; in the buffer as the only character, then     ;
; return -1 as the number of characters read.   ;
;-----------------------------------------------;
```

```
EXTENDED:                               ;Read an extended ASCII code
        CALL    PURGE_BUFFER            ;Remove any chars from buffer
        MOV     [SI+2],AL               ;Place just this char in buffer
        MOV     BL,0FFh                 ;Num chars read = -1 for special
        JMP     SHORT END_STRING


;------------------------------------------------;
; Save the count of the number of characters     ;
; read and return.                               ;
;------------------------------------------------;
END_INPUT:                              ;Done with input
        SUB     BL,2                    ;Count of characters read
END_STRING:
        MOV     [SI+1],BL               ;Return number of chars read
        POP     SI
        POP     BX
        POP     AX
        RET
READ_STRING     ENDP




;----------------------------------------------------------------;
; This subroutine is used by READ_STRING to clear the contents of the  ;
; input buffer.                                                  ;
;                                                                ;
;       DS:SI   Points to the input buffer for READ_STRING       ;
;----------------------------------------------------------------;
PURGE_BUFFER    PROC
        PUSH    CX
        MOV     CL,[SI]                 ;Backspace over maximum number of
        XOR     CH,CH
PURGE_LOOP:                             ; characters in buffer.  BACK_SPACE
        CALL    BACK_SPACE              ; will keep the cursor from moving too
        LOOP    PURGE_LOOP              ; far back
        POP     CX
        RET
PURGE_BUFFER    ENDP


        PUBLIC  BACK_SPACE
        EXTRN   WRITE_CHAR:PROC
        EXTRN   UPDATE_REAL_CURSOR:PROC
        EXTRN   UPDATE_VIRTUAL_CURSOR:PROC
```

```
;---------------------------------------------------------------------;
; This procedure deletes characters, one at a time, from the buffer   ;
; and the screen when the buffer is not empty.  BACK_SPACE simply     ;
; returns when the buffer is empty.                                   ;
;                                                                     ;
; On entry:     DS:SI+BX        Most recent character still in buffer ;
; Returns:      DS:SI+BX        Points to next most recent character  ;
;                                                                     ;
; Uses:         WRITE_CHAR                                            ;
;---------------------------------------------------------------------;
BACK_SPACE      PROC                            ;Delete one character
        PUSH    AX
        PUSH    DX
        CMP     BX,2                    ;Is buffer empty?
        JE      END_BS                  ;Yes, read the next character
        DEC     BX                      ;Remove one character from buffer
        MOV     AH,2                    ;Remove character from screen
        MOV     DL,BS
        INT     21h
        CALL    UPDATE_VIRTUAL_CURSOR   ;Update ptrs after moving real cursor
        MOV     DL,20h                  ;Write space there
        CALL    WRITE_CHAR              ;Write, but don't move cursor
        CALL    UPDATE_REAL_CURSOR      ;Cursor moved, update real position
        MOV     DL,BS                   ;Back up again
        INT     21h
        CALL    UPDATE_VIRTUAL_CURSOR   ;Set points back to cursor position
END_BS: POP     DX
        POP     AX
        RET
BACK_SPACE      ENDP


        PUBLIC  READ_BYTE
;---------------------------------------------------------------------;
; This procedure reads either a single ASCII character or a two-digit ;
; hex number.  This is just a test version of READ_BYTE.              ;
;                                                                     ;
; Returns:      AL      Character code (unless AH = 0)                ;
;               AH      0 if read ASCII char                          ;
;                       1 if read a special key                      ;
;                       -1 if no characters read                      ;
;                                                                     ;
; Uses:         HEX_TO_BYTE, STRING_TO_UPPER, READ_STRING             ;
; Reads:        KEYBOARD_INPUT, etc.                                  ;
; Writes:       KEYBOARD_INPUT, etc.                                  ;
;---------------------------------------------------------------------;
```

528

```
READ_BYTE        PROC
        PUSH     DX
        MOV      CHAR_NUM_LIMIT,3        ;Allow only two characters (plus Enter)
        LEA      DX,KEYBOARD_INPUT
        CALL     READ_STRING
        CMP      NUM_CHARS_READ,1        ;See how many characters
        JE       ASCII_INPUT            ;Just one, treat as ASCII character
        JB       NO_CHARACTERS          ;Only Enter key hit
        CMP      BYTE PTR NUM_CHARS_READ,0FFh     ;Special function key?
        JE       SPECIAL_KEY            ;Yes
        CALL     STRING_TO_UPPER        ;No, convert string to uppercase
        LEA      DX,CHARS               ;Address of string to convert
        CALL     HEX_TO_BYTE            ;Convert string from hex to byte
        JC       NO_CHARACTERS          ;Error, so return 'no characters read'
        XOR      AH,AH                  ;Signal read one byte
DONE_READ:
        POP      DX
        RET
NO_CHARACTERS:
        XOR      AH,AH                  ;Set to 'no characters read'
        NOT      AH                     ;Return -1 in AH
        JMP      DONE_READ
ASCII_INPUT:
        MOV      AL,CHARS               ;Load character read
        XOR      AH,AH                  ;Signal read one byte
        JMP      DONE_READ
SPECIAL_KEY:
        MOV      AL,CHARS[0]            ;Return the scan code
        MOV      AH,1                   ;Signal special key with 1
        JMP      DONE_READ
READ_BYTE        ENDP


        PUBLIC   READ_KEY
;-------------------------------------------------------------------;
; This procedure reads one key from the keyboard.                   ;
;                                                                   ;
; Returns:       AL       Character code (unless AH = 1)            ;
;                AH       0 if read ASCII char                      ;
;                         1 if read a special key                  ;
;-------------------------------------------------------------------;
READ_KEY         PROC
        XOR      AH,AH                  ;Ask for keyboard read function
        INT      16h                    ;Read character/scan code from keyboard
        OR       AL,AL                  ;Is it an extended code?
        JZ       EXTENDED_CODE          ;Yes
```

529

```
NOT_EXTENDED:
        XOR     AH,AH                   ;Return just the ASCII code
DONE_READING:
        RET


EXTENDED_CODE:
        MOV     AL,AH                   ;Put scan code into AL
        MOV     AH,1                    ;Signal extended code
        JMP     DONE_READING
READ_KEY        ENDP



        PUBLIC  READ_DECIMAL
;-------------------------------------------------------------------;
; This procedure takes the output buffer of READ_STRING and converts ;
; the string of decimal digits to a word.                            ;
;                                                                    ;
; Returns:      AX      Word converted from decimal                  ;
;               CF      Set if error, clear if no error              ;
;                                                                    ;
; Uses:         READ_STRING                                          ;
; Reads:        KEYBOARD_INPUT, etc.                                 ;
; Writes:       KEYBOARD_INPUT, etc.                                 ;
;-------------------------------------------------------------------;
READ_DECIMAL    PROC
        PUSH    BX
        PUSH    CX
        PUSH    DX
        MOV     CHAR_NUM_LIMIT,6        ;Max number is 5 digits (65535)
        LEA     DX,KEYBOARD_INPUT
        CALL    READ_STRING
        MOV     CL,NUM_CHARS_READ       ;Get number of characters read
        XOR     CH,CH                   ;Set upper byte of count to 0
        CMP     CL,0                    ;Return error if no characters read
        JLE     BAD_DECIMAL_DIGIT       ;No chars read, signal error
        XOR     AX,AX                   ;Start with number set to 0
        XOR     BX,BX                   ;Start at beginning of string
CONVERT_DIGIT:
        MOV     DX,10                   ;Multiply number by 10
        MUL     DX                      ;Multiply AX by 10
        JC      BAD_DECIMAL_DIGIT       ;CF set if MUL overflowed one word
        MOV     DL,CHARS[BX]            ;Get the next digit
        SUB     DL,'0'                  ;And convert to a nibble (4 bits)
```

```
        JS       BAD_DECIMAL_DIGIT      ;Bad digit if < 0
        CMP      DL,9                   ;Is this a bad digit?
        JA       BAD_DECIMAL_DIGIT      ;Yes
        ADD      AX,DX                  ;No, so add it to number
        INC      BX                     ;Point to next character
        LOOP     CONVERT_DIGIT          ;Get the next digit
DONE_DECIMAL:
        POP      DX
        POP      CX
        POP      BX
        RET
BAD_DECIMAL_DIGIT:
        STC                             ;Set carry to signal error
        JMP      DONE_DECIMAL
READ_DECIMAL     ENDP


        END
```

PHANTOM.ASM

```
.MODEL   SMALL

.DATA

REAL_CURSOR_X           DB      0
REAL_CURSOR_Y           DB      0
        PUBLIC   PHANTOM_CURSOR_X, PHANTOM_CURSOR_Y
PHANTOM_CURSOR_X        DB      0
PHANTOM_CURSOR_Y        DB      0

.CODE


;-----------------------------------------------------------------;
; These four procedures move the phantom cursors.                 ;
;                                                                 ;
; Uses:          ERASE_PHANTOM, WRITE_PHANTOM                     ;
;                SCROLL_DOWN, SCROLL_UP                           ;
; Reads:         PHANTOM_CURSOR_X, PHANTOM_CURSOR_Y               ;
; Writes:        PHANTOM_CURSOR_X, PHANTOM_CURSOR_Y               ;
;-----------------------------------------------------------------;
```

```
            PUBLIC    PHANTOM_UP
PHANTOM_UP            PROC
            CALL      ERASE_PHANTOM         ;Erase at current position
            DEC       PHANTOM_CURSOR_Y      ;Move cursor up one line
            JNS       WASNT_AT_TOP          ;Was not at the top, write cursor
            CALL      SCROLL_DOWN           ;Was at the top, scroll
WASNT_AT_TOP:
            CALL      WRITE_PHANTOM         ;Write the phantom at new position
            RET
PHANTOM_UP            ENDP


            PUBLIC    PHANTOM_DOWN
PHANTOM_DOWN          PROC
            CALL      ERASE_PHANTOM         ;Erase at current position
            INC       PHANTOM_CURSOR_Y      ;Move cursor down one line
            CMP       PHANTOM_CURSOR_Y,16   ;Was it at the bottom?
            JB        WASNT_AT_BOTTOM       ;No, so write phantom
            CALL      SCROLL_UP             ;Was at bottom, scroll
WASNT_AT_BOTTOM:
            CALL      WRITE_PHANTOM         ;Write the phantom cursor
            RET
PHANTOM_DOWN          ENDP


            PUBLIC    PHANTOM_LEFT
PHANTOM_LEFT          PROC
            CALL      ERASE_PHANTOM         ;Erase at current position
            DEC       PHANTOM_CURSOR_X      ;Move cursor left one column
            JNS       WASNT_AT_LEFT         ;Was not at the left side, write cursor
            MOV       PHANTOM_CURSOR_X,0    ;Was at left, so put back there
WASNT_AT_LEFT:
            CALL      WRITE_PHANTOM         ;Write the phantom cursor
            RET
PHANTOM_LEFT          ENDP


            PUBLIC    PHANTOM_RIGHT
PHANTOM_RIGHT         PROC
            CALL      ERASE_PHANTOM         ;Erase at current position
            INC       PHANTOM_CURSOR_X      ;Move cursor right one column
            CMP       PHANTOM_CURSOR_X,16   ;Was it already at the right side?
            JB        WASNT_AT_RIGHT
            MOV       PHANTOM_CURSOR_X,15   ;Was at right, so put back there
WASNT_AT_RIGHT:
            CALL      WRITE_PHANTOM         ;Write the phantom cursor
            RET
PHANTOM_RIGHT         ENDP
```

532

```
        PUBLIC  MOV_TO_HEX_POSITION
        EXTRN   GOTO_XY:PROC
.DATA
        EXTRN   LINES_BEFORE_SECTOR:BYTE
.CODE
;----------------------------------------------------------------;
; This procedure moves the real cursor to the position of the phantom  ;
; cursor in the hex window.                                      ;
;                                                                ;
; Uses:        GOTO_XY                                           ;
; Reads:       LINES_BEFORE_SECTOR, PHANTOM_CURSOR_X, PHANTOM_CURSOR_Y;
;----------------------------------------------------------------;
MOV_TO_HEX_POSITION     PROC
        PUSH    AX
        PUSH    CX
        PUSH    DX
        MOV     DH,LINES_BEFORE_SECTOR  ;Find row of phantom (0,0)
        ADD     DH,2                    ;Plus row of hex and horizontal bar
        ADD     DH,PHANTOM_CURSOR_Y     ;DH = row of phantom cursor
        MOV     DL,8                    ;Indent on left side
        MOV     CL,3                    ;Each column uses 3 characters, so
        MOV     AL,PHANTOM_CURSOR_X     ; we must multiply CURSOR_X by 3
        MUL     CL
        ADD     DL,AL                   ;And add to the indent, to get column
        CALL    GOTO_XY                 ; for phantom cursor
        POP     DX
        POP     CX
        POP     AX
        RET
MOV_TO_HEX_POSITION     ENDP


        PUBLIC  MOV_TO_ASCII_POSITION
        EXTRN   GOTO_XY:PROC
.DATA
        EXTRN   LINES_BEFORE_SECTOR:BYTE
.CODE
;----------------------------------------------------------------;
; This procedure moves the real cursor to the beginning of the phantom ;
; cursor in the ASCII window.                                    ;
;                                                                ;
; Uses:        GOTO_XY                                           ;
; Reads:       LINES_BEFORE_SECTOR, PHANTOM_CURSOR_X, PHANTOM_CURSOR_Y;
;----------------------------------------------------------------;
```

533

```
MOV_TO_ASCII_POSITION    PROC
        PUSH    AX
        PUSH    DX
        MOV     DH,LINES_BEFORE_SECTOR  ;Find row of phantom (0,0)
        ADD     DH,2                    ;Plus row of hex and horizontal bar
        ADD     DH,PHANTOM_CURSOR_Y     ;DH = row of phantom cursor
        MOV     DL,59                   ;Indent on left side
        ADD     DL,PHANTOM_CURSOR_X     ;Add CURSOR_X to get X position
        CALL    GOTO_XY                 ; for phantom cursor
        POP     DX
        POP     AX
        RET
MOV_TO_ASCII_POSITION    ENDP


        PUBLIC  SAVE_REAL_CURSOR
;-------------------------------------------------------------------;
; This procedure saves the position of the real cursor in the two   ;
; variables REAL_CURSOR_X and REAL_CURSOR_Y.                        ;
;                                                                   ;
; Writes:       REAL_CURSOR_X, REAL_CURSOR_Y                        ;
;-------------------------------------------------------------------;
SAVE_REAL_CURSOR         PROC
        PUSH    AX
        PUSH    BX
        PUSH    CX
        PUSH    DX
        MOV     AH,3                    ;Read cursor position
        XOR     BH,BH                   ; on page 0
        INT     10h                     ;And return in DL,DH
        MOV     REAL_CURSOR_Y,DL        ;Save position
        MOV     REAL_CURSOR_X,DH
        POP     DX
        POP     CX
        POP     BX
        POP     AX
        RET
SAVE_REAL_CURSOR         ENDP


        PUBLIC  RESTORE_REAL_CURSOR
        EXTRN   GOTO_XY:PROC
;-------------------------------------------------------------------;
; This procedure restores the real cursor to its old position, saved;
; in REAL_CURSOR_X and REAL_CURSOR_Y.                               ;
;                                                                   ;
; Uses:         GOTO_XY                                             ;
; Reads:        REAL_CURSOR_X, REAL_CURSOR_Y                        ;
;-------------------------------------------------------------------;
```

```
RESTORE_REAL_CURSOR     PROC
        PUSH    DX
        MOV     DL,REAL_CURSOR_Y
        MOV     DH,REAL_CURSOR_X
        CALL    GOTO_XY
        POP     DX
        RET
RESTORE_REAL_CURSOR     ENDP


        PUBLIC  WRITE_PHANTOM
        EXTRN   WRITE_ATTRIBUTE_N_TIMES:PROC
;-------------------------------------------------------------------;
; This procedure uses CURSOR_X and CURSOR_Y, through MOV_TO_..., as the;
; coordinates for the phantom cursor.  WRITE_PHANTOM writes this     ;
; phantom cursor.                                                   ;
;                                                                   ;
; Uses:          WRITE_ATTRIBUTE_N_TIMES, SAVE_REAL_CURSOR          ;
;                RESTORE_REAL_CURSOR, MOV_TO_HEX_POSITION           ;
;                MOV_TO_ASCII_POSITION                              ;
;-------------------------------------------------------------------;
WRITE_PHANTOM   PROC
        PUSH    CX
        PUSH    DX
        CALL    SAVE_REAL_CURSOR
        CALL    MOV_TO_HEX_POSITION      ;Coord. of cursor in hex window
        MOV     CX,4                     ;Make phantom cursor four chars wide
        MOV     DL,70h
        CALL    WRITE_ATTRIBUTE_N_TIMES
        CALL    MOV_TO_ASCII_POSITION    ;Coord. of cursor in ASCII window
        MOV     CX,1                     ;Cursor is one character wide here
        CALL    WRITE_ATTRIBUTE_N_TIMES
        CALL    RESTORE_REAL_CURSOR
        POP     DX
        POP     CX
        RET
WRITE_PHANTOM   ENDP


        PUBLIC  ERASE_PHANTOM
        EXTRN   WRITE_ATTRIBUTE_N_TIMES:PROC
;-------------------------------------------------------------------;
; This procedure erases the phantom cursor, just the opposite of     ;
; WRITE_PHANTOM.                                                    ;
;                                                                   ;
; Uses:          WRITE_ATTRIBUTE_N_TIMES, SAVE_REAL_CURSOR          ;
;                RESTORE_REAL_CURSOR, MOV_TO_HEX_POSITION           ;
;                MOV_TO_ASCII_POSITION                              ;
;-------------------------------------------------------------------;
```

535

```
ERASE_PHANTOM   PROC
        PUSH    CX
        PUSH    DX
        CALL    SAVE_REAL_CURSOR
        CALL    MOV_TO_HEX_POSITION       ;Coord. of cursor in hex window
        MOV     CX,4                      ;Change back to white on black
        MOV     DL,7
        CALL    WRITE_ATTRIBUTE_N_TIMES
        CALL    MOV_TO_ASCII_POSITION
        MOV     CX,1
        CALL    WRITE_ATTRIBUTE_N_TIMES
        CALL    RESTORE_REAL_CURSOR
        POP     DX
        POP     CX
        RET
ERASE_PHANTOM   ENDP



        EXTRN   DISP_HALF_SECTOR:PROC, GOTO_XY:PROC
.DATA
        EXTRN   SECTOR_OFFSET:WORD
        EXTRN   LINES_BEFORE_SECTOR:BYTE
.CODE
;--------------------------------------------------------------------;
; These two procedures move between the two half-sector displays.    ;
;                                                                    ;
; Uses:         WRITE_PHANTOM, DISP_HALF_SECTOR, ERASE_PHANTOM, GOTO_XY;
;               SAVE_REAL_CURSOR, RESTORE_REAL_CURSOR                 ;
; Reads:        LINES_BEFORE_SECTOR                                   ;
; Writes:       SECTOR_OFFSET, PHANTOM_CURSOR_Y                       ;
;--------------------------------------------------------------------;
SCROLL_UP       PROC
        PUSH    DX
        CALL    ERASE_PHANTOM             ;Remove the phantom cursor
        CALL    SAVE_REAL_CURSOR          ;Save the real cursor position
        XOR     DL,DL                     ;Set cursor for half-sector display
        MOV     DH,LINES_BEFORE_SECTOR
        ADD     DH,2
        CALL    GOTO_XY
        MOV     DX,256                    ;Display the second half sector
        MOV     SECTOR_OFFSET,DX
        CALL    DISP_HALF_SECTOR
        CALL    RESTORE_REAL_CURSOR       ;Restore the real cursor position
```

```
          MOV      PHANTOM_CURSOR_Y,0        ;Cursor at top of second half sector
          CALL     WRITE_PHANTOM             ;Restore the phantom cursor
          POP      DX
          RET
SCROLL_UP          ENDP


SCROLL_DOWN        PROC
          PUSH     DX
          CALL     ERASE_PHANTOM             ;Remove the phantom cursor
          CALL     SAVE_REAL_CURSOR          ;Save the real cursor position
          XOR      DL,DL                     ;Set cursor for half-sector display
          MOV      DH,LINES_BEFORE_SECTOR
          ADD      DH,2
          CALL     GOTO_XY
          XOR      DX,DX                     ;Display the first half sector
          MOV      SECTOR_OFFSET,DX
          CALL     DISP_HALF_SECTOR
          CALL     RESTORE_REAL_CURSOR       ;Restore the real cursor position
          MOV      PHANTOM_CURSOR_Y,15       ;Cursor at bottom of first half sector
          CALL     WRITE_PHANTOM             ;Restore the phantom cursor
          POP      DX
          RET
SCROLL_DOWN        ENDP



          END
```

VIDEO_IO.ASM

```
.MODEL    SMALL

.DATA
          PUBLIC   SCREEN_PTR
          PUBLIC   SCREEN_X, SCREEN_Y
SCREEN_SEG         DW       0B800h            ;Setment of the screen buffer
SCREEN_PTR         DW       0                 ;Offset into screen memory of cursor
SCREEN_X           DB       0                 ;Position of the screen cursor
SCREEN_Y           DB       0

.CODE
```

```
        PUBLIC  WRITE_STRING
;--------------------------------------------------------------;
; This procedure writes a string of characters to the screen.  The    ;
; string must end with          DB      0                      ;
;                                                              ;
; On entry:    DS:DX   Address of the string                   ;
;                                                              ;
; Uses:        WRITE_CHAR                                       ;
;--------------------------------------------------------------;
WRITE_STRING    PROC
        PUSH    AX
        PUSH    DX
        PUSH    SI
        PUSHF                           ;Save direction flag
        CLD                             ;Set direction for increment (forward)
        MOV     SI,DX                   ;Place address into SI for LODSB
STRING_LOOP:
        LODSB                           ;Get a character into the AL register
        OR      AL,AL                   ;Have we found the 0 yet?
        JZ      END_OF_STRING           ;Yes, we are done with the string
        MOV     DL,AL                   ;No, write character
        CALL    WRITE_CHAR
        JMP     STRING_LOOP
END_OF_STRING:
        POPF                            ;Restore direction flag
        POP     SI
        POP     DX
        POP     AX
        RET
WRITE_STRING    ENDP


        PUBLIC  WRITE_HEX
;--------------------------------------------------------------;
; This procedure converts the byte in the DL register to hex and writes;
; the two hex digits at the current cursor position.           ;
;                                                              ;
; On Entry:    DL      Byte to be converted to hex.            ;
;                                                              ;
; Uses: WRITE_HEX_DIGIT                                        ;
;--------------------------------------------------------------;
WRITE_HEX       PROC                    ;Entry point
        PUSH    CX                      ;Save registers used in this procedure
        PUSH    DX
```

```
            MOV      DH,DL                   ;Make a copy of byte
            MOV      CX,4                    ;Get the upper nibble in DL
            SHR      DL,CL
            CALL     WRITE_HEX_DIGIT         ;Display first hex digit
            MOV      DL,DH                   ;Get lower nibble into DL
            AND      DL,0Fh                  ;Remove the upper nibble
            CALL     WRITE_HEX_DIGIT         ;Display second hex digit
            POP      DX
            POP      CX
            RET
WRITE_HEX           ENDP


            PUBLIC   WRITE_HEX_DIGIT
;-----------------------------------------------------------------;
; This procedure converts the lower 4 bits of DL to a hex digit and  ;
; writes it to the screen.                                        ;
;                                                                 ;
; On Entry:       DL       Lower 4 bits contain number to be printed ;
;                          in hex.                                ;
;                                                                 ;
; Uses:           WRITE_CHAR                                      ;
;-----------------------------------------------------------------;
WRITE_HEX_DIGIT PROC
            PUSH     DX                      ;Save registers used
            CMP      DL,10                   ;Is this nibble <10?
            JAE      HEX_LETTER              ;No, convert to a letter
            ADD      DL,"0"                  ;Yes, convert to a digit
            JMP      Short WRITE_DIGIT       ;Now write this character
HEX_LETTER:
            ADD      DL,"A"-10               ;Convert to hex letter
WRITE_DIGIT:
            CALL     WRITE_CHAR              ;Display the letter on the screen
            POP      DX                      ;Restore old value of DX
            RET
WRITE_HEX_DIGIT ENDP


            PUBLIC   INIT_WRITE_CHAR
;-----------------------------------------------------------------;
; You need to call this procedure before you call WRITE_CHAR since   ;
; WRITE_CHAR uses information set by this procedure.              ;
;                                                                 ;
; Writes:      SCREEN_SEG                                         ;
;-----------------------------------------------------------------;
```

```
INIT_WRITE_CHAR PROC
        PUSH    AX
        PUSH    BX
        MOV     BX,0B800h               ;Set for color graphics display
        INT     11h                     ;Get equipment information
        AND     AL,30h                  ;Keep just the video display type
        CMP     AL,30h                  ;Is this a monochrome display adapter?
        JNE     SET_BASE                ;No, it's color, so use B800
        MOV     BX,0B000h               ;Yes, it's monochrome, so use B000
SET_BASE:
        MOV     SCREEN_SEG,BX           ;Save the screen segment
        POP     BX
        POP     AX
        RET
INIT_WRITE_CHAR ENDP


        PUBLIC  WRITE_CHAR
        EXTRN   CURSOR_RIGHT:PROC
;-----------------------------------------------------------------------;
; This procedure outputs a character to the screen by writing directly  ;
; into screen memory, so that characters such as the backspace are      ;
; treated as any other characters and are displayed.                    ;
;                                                                       ;
; This procedure must do a bit of work to update the cursor position.   ;
;                                                                       ;
; On entry:      DL      Byte to print on screen                        ;
;                                                                       ;
; Uses:          CURSOR_RIGHT                                           ;
; Reads:         SCREEN_SEG, SCREEN_PTR                                 ;
;-----------------------------------------------------------------------;
WRITE_CHAR      PROC
        PUSH    AX
        PUSH    BX
        PUSH    DX
        PUSH    ES

        MOV     AX,SCREEN_SEG           ;Get segment for screen memory
        MOV     ES,AX                   ;Point ES to screen memory
        MOV     BX,SCREEN_PTR           ;Pointer to character in screen memory

        MOV     DH,7                    ;Use the normal attribute
        MOV     ES:[BX],DX              ;Write character/attribute to screen
        CALL    CURSOR_RIGHT            ;Now move to next cursor position
```

```
        POP     ES
        POP     DX                      ;Restore old value in AX and DX
        POP     BX
        POP     AX
        RET
WRITE_CHAR      ENDP



        PUBLIC  WRITE_DECIMAL
;--------------------------------------------------------------------;
; This procedure writes a 16-bit, unsigned number in decimal notation. ;
;                                                                    ;
; On Entry:     DX      N : 16-bit, unsigned number.                 ;
;                                                                    ;
; Uses:         WRITE_HEX_DIGIT                                      ;
;--------------------------------------------------------------------;
WRITE_DECIMAL   PROC
        PUSH    AX                      ;Save registers used here
        PUSH    CX
        PUSH    DX
        PUSH    SI
        MOV     AX,DX
        MOV     SI,10                   ;Will divide by 10 using SI
        XOR     CX,CX                   ;Count of digits placed on stack
NON_ZERO:
        XOR     DX,DX                   ;Set upper word of N to 0
        DIV     SI                      ;Calculate N/10 and (N mod 10)
        PUSH    DX                      ;Push one digit onto the stack
        INC     CX                      ;One more digit added
        OR      AX,AX                   ;N = 0 yet?
        JNE     NON_ZERO                ;Nope, continue
WRITE_DIGIT_LOOP:
        POP     DX                      ;Get the digits in reverse order
        CALL    WRITE_HEX_DIGIT
        LOOP    WRITE_DIGIT_LOOP
END_DECIMAL:
        POP     SI
        POP     DX
        POP     CX
        POP     AX
        RET
WRITE_DECIMAL   ENDP
```

```
        PUBLIC   WRITE_CHAR_N_TIMES
;------------------------------------------------------------------;
; This procedure writes more than one copy of a character         ;
;                                                                 ;
; On entry:     DL      Character code                            ;
;               CX      Number of times to write the character    ;
;                                                                 ;
; Uses:         WRITE_CHAR                                        ;
;------------------------------------------------------------------;
WRITE_CHAR_N_TIMES      PROC
        PUSH    CX
N_TIMES:
        CALL    WRITE_CHAR
        LOOP    N_TIMES
        POP     CX
        RET
WRITE_CHAR_N_TIMES    ENDP

        PUBLIC WRITE_ATTRIBUTE_N_TIMES
        EXTRN CURSOR_RIGHT:PROC
;------------------------------------------------------------------;
; This procedure sets the attribute for N characters, starting at the ;
; current cursor position.                                        ;
;                                                                 ;
; On entry:     CX      Number of characters to set attribute for ;
;               DL      New attribute for characters              ;
;                                                                 ;
; Uses:         CURSOR_RIGHT                                      ;
;------------------------------------------------------------------;
WRITE_ATTRIBUTE_N_TIMES PROC
        PUSH    AX
        PUSH    CX
        PUSH    DI
        PUSH    ES

        MOV     AX,SCREEN_SEG           ;Set ES to point to screen segment
        MOV     ES,AX
        MOV     DI,SCREEN_PTR           ;Character under cursor
        INC     DI                      ;Point to the attribute under cursor
        MOV     AL,DL                   ;Put attribute into AL
ATTR_LOOP:
        STOSB                           ;Save one attribute
        INC     DI                      ;Move to next attribute
        INC     SCREEN_X                ;Move to next column
        LOOP    ATTR_LOOP               ;Write N attributes
```

```
        DEC     DI                      ;Point to start of next character
        MOV     SCREEN_PTR,DI           ;Remember where we are

        POP     ES
        POP     DI
        POP     CX
        POP     AX
        RET
WRITE_ATTRIBUTE_N_TIMES ENDP


        PUBLIC  WRITE_PATTERN
;------------------------------------------------------------;
; This procedure writes a line to the screen, based on data in the   ;
; form                                                               ;
;                                                                    ;
;       DB       {character, number of times to write character}, 0 ;
; Where {x} means that x can be repeated any number of times         ;
;                                                                    ;
; On entry:      DS:DX   Address of the pattern to draw              ;
;                                                                    ;
; Uses:          WRITE_CHAR_N_TIMES                                  ;
;------------------------------------------------------------;
WRITE_PATTERN   PROC
        PUSH    AX
        PUSH    CX
        PUSH    DX
        PUSH    SI
        PUSHF                           ;Save the direction flag
        CLD                             ;Set direction flag for increment
        MOV     SI,DX                   ;Move offset into SI register for LODSB
PATTERN_LOOP:
        LODSB                           ;Get character data into AL
        OR      AL,AL                   ;Is it the end of data (0h)?
        JZ      END_PATTERN             ;Yes, return
        MOV     DL,AL                   ;No, set up to write character N times
        LODSB                           ;Get the repeat count into AL
        MOV     CL,AL                   ;And put in CX for WRITE_CHAR_N_TIMES
        XOR     CH,CH                   ;Zero upper byte of CX
        CALL    WRITE_CHAR_N_TIMES
        JMP     PATTERN_LOOP
```

```
END_PATTERN:
        POPF                            ;Restore direction flag
        POP     SI
        POP     DX
        POP     CX
        POP     AX
        RET
WRITE_PATTERN   ENDP


        END
```

C/C++ Libraries in Assembly

This appendix contains the source listings for the C/C++ libraries mentioned in Chapter 31. These files are included so that you can build a library that will work with any memory model. All you have to change is a single line in the Makefile. Although the assembled library can be used with most C/C++ compilers, you will need MASM 6 to build the CLIB.LIB file.

Topics Covered

Descriptions of Procedures

Descriptions of Procedures

The CLIB directory on the disk included with this book contains five assembly files that include procedures and functions written for C/C++ programs. Using the methods discussed in Chapter 31, calls to the functions can be added to C/C++ files to do fast writes to the screen, change cursor properties, and move a mouse cursor. The included makefile allows you to compile the files into a library called CLIB.LIB that can be linked to your C/C++ files. You will need MASM 6 to assemble the files.

SOCHALIB.INC

This is an include file used by all the other ASM files.

MAKEFILE

This makefile is used to create the CLIB.LIB file.

CURSOR.ASM

The seven functions and procedures in this module control the hardware cursor you see on the screen.

void SetCursor(int size) This procedure allows you to set the size of the hardware cursor. Normally you would use this function along with GetVisibleCursor or GetCursor to save and restore the size of the cursor. For example, at the start of your program you should call GetVisibleCursor and save the return value in a global variable. Then call SetCursor with this value at the end of your program to restore the DOS cursor before your program exits.

int GetVisibleCursor(void) This function returns the size of the hardware cursor. If the cursor is turned off, such as by using CursorOff, this function returns a value that would be visible.

int GetCursor(void) This function is like GetVisibleCursor except that it returns the exact size of the cursor. If the cursor is turned off, you will get a cursor size that will turn the cursor off when you use this value with SetCursor.

void CursorOff(void) This procedure hides the hardware cursor. You can call CursorOn to turn the cursor back on. You cannot nest calls to CursorOff and CursorOn because they use a single value to save the previous state of the cursor.

void CursorOn(void) This procedure turns the cursor back on after you call CursorOff to hide the hardware cursor. You cannot nest calls to CursorOff and CursorOn because they use a single value to save the previous state of the cursor.

void CursorBlock(void) This procedure turns the hardware cursor into a blinking block cursor. This cursor will be the full height of characters. A block cursor is usually easier to see than the normal underscore cursor.

void CursorUnderscore(void) This procedure turns the cursor into the normal underscore cursor.

FASTWRIT.ASM

The 12 procedures in this module support writing characters very quickly to your screen. These procedures also work together with the procedures in MOUSE.ASM to make sure writing to the screen does not interfere with the mouse cursor. In other words, these routines hide the mouse cursor before writing to the screen, so you do not have to worry about hiding the mouse cursor yourself. If you do not hide the mouse cursor, you can write over the mouse cursor, leading to "mouse droppings" when you move the mouse.

void InitFastDisplayModule(void) Call this procedure to initialize the entire module. You will need to call this procedure before you call any other procedures in this module.

void FastFlush(void) Flushes any characters that have not been written to the screen. The procedures in this module put characters in an off-screen buffer, which makes the code extremely fast. You will usually want to call fast flush during your keyboard input code. In fact, you might want to insert calls to FastFlush in KBD_IO.ASM.

549

void FastWriteRawChar(char c) Writes a single character to the screen without special meaning. The other procedure, FastWriteChar, treats some characters as special characters, such as the tab character. But this procedure displays all characters as symbols on the screen rather than giving them special meaning.

void FastWriteChar(char c) Like FastWriteRawChar, this procedure writes a character to the screen. However, it gives special meaning to the following characters: ASCII 7 produces a beep; ASCII 9 is the tab character and moves the cursor to the next tab stop; ASCII 10 moves the cursor down one line; and ASCII 13 moves the cursor to the start of the current line.

int FastReadAttr(void) Returns the character attribute for the character currently under the cursor.

void FastWriteString(char *s) Displays the C-style string on the screen. This procedure uses FastWriteChar to display each character in the string.

void FastWriteUDecimal(int i) Displays the number *i* on the screen as an unsigned decimal number. In other words, the numbers range from 0 to 65535.

void FastWriteNChars(char c, int count) Displays *count* copies of the character *c* on the screen. This procedure uses FastWriteRawChar to display the individual characters on the screen.

void FastWriteSpaces(int count) Displays *count* spaces on the screen.

void FastGotoXY(int x, int y) Moves the cursor to (x, y). This procedure moves both the virtual cursor in FASTWRIT.ASM and the hardware cursor to the new location. You can use CursorOff and CursorOn to hide the hardware cursor when you draw on the screen.

void FastSetCursor(void) Moves the hardware cursor so it matches the position of the virtual cursor. Normally the hardware cursor's position won't be updated after a call to FastFlush.

void FastGetXY(int *x, int *y) Returns the position of the current cursor in (x, y).

HARDWARE.ASM

The three functions in this file report information about your display hardware.

int GetDisplayType(void) Returns information on the type of display card in your computuer: 0 = no cards, 1 = color 40 x 25 card, 2 = color 80 x 25 card, and 3 = monochrome-display card.

int EgaActive(void) Returns true (–1) if you have an EGA or VGA card in your computer and it is currently the active display.

int GetDisplayRows(void) Returns the number of rows on the screen (normally 25, but can be higher numbers).

KBD_IO.ASM

The five functions in this file handle input from the keyboard.

int ReadKey(void) This function uses the ROM BIOS routines to read a single character. It returns the ASCII code for keys that generate an ASCII character. If you push one of the key-pad or function keys, this function returns the scan code in the lower byte and sets the upper byte to 1.

int ReadRawKey(void) This procedure reads one character (or one special function key) from the keyboard and returns the ASCII code, or scan code. It uses the ROM BIOS call so it can read both the character code AND the scan code. The DOS call returns only the ASCII code. On return, the scan code is in the upper byte and the ASCII code (or 0 for non-ASCII keys) is in the lower byte.

void ClearKbdBuffer(void) Clears any characters that are currently in the keyboard buffer. It is a good idea to call this procedure immediately after an error occurs to keep the user from accidently typing the wrong characters.

int KeyWaiting(void) Reports if any characters are waiting to be read from the keyboard buffer, and if so, it returns the same character code that ReadRawChar would return; otherwise, it returns –1.

int ShiftKeys(void) Reports which shift keys are currently down:

80h	Insert state on
40h	Caps Lock on
20h	Num Lock on
10h	Scroll Lock on
08h	Alt key is down
04h	Control key is down
02h	Left shift key is down
01h	Right shift key is down

MOUSE.ASM

The procedures in this module support using a mouse in DOS programs. These procedures are designed to work along with the procedures in FASTWRIT.ASM, but you can easily rewrite them to work without FASTWRIT.ASM. If you do, keep in mind that you will need to hide the mouse cursor before you draw on the screen.

> **void InitMouse(void)** Call this procedure before you call any of the other procedures in this module. This procedure initializes the mouse by calling function 0, which is a full reset of the mouse software AND hardware. In some cases this can take several seconds (a serial mouse or an IBM mouse), which may not be acceptable. Init_mousesw() can be much faster in such cases.

The following rules state which of these two procedures to call:

- Once   Init_mouse() must be called at least to initialize the mouse hardware the first time because not all mouse drivers initialize the mouse properly when you do a software mouse reset.

- After Init_mouse()   From then on you can call Init_mouse_sw() for a fast reset. The Commander calls Init_mouse() once, then Init_mouse_sw() each time you return to the Commander after running a DOS command.

void InitMouseSw(void) This procedure initializes the mouse. It tries to do a software reset first. Only if the software reset doesn't work does it try to do a hardware reset. In some cases (such as a serial mouse or the IBM PS/2 mouse) a hardware reset can take as much as five seconds, which is not an acceptable delay when returning from the Norton Commander.

void UnhideMouse(void) Makes the mouse visible again after a call to HideMouse. You can make nested calls to UnhideMouse and HideMouse.

void HideMouse(void) Removes the mouse cursor from the screen. You can make nested calls to UnhideMouse and HideMouse.

void GetMousePosition(int *x, int *y) Returns the current position of the mouse cursor in character coordinates.

void SetMousePosition(int x, int y) Allows you to set the position of the mouse on the screen, in character coordinates.

int MouseButtons(int *x, int *y) Like GetMousePosition, it returns the current position of the mouse on the screen. It also reports which mouse buttons were pressed:

0 Both buttons up

1 Left button down

2 Right button down

3 Both buttons down

Makefile

Following is the makefile for creating the libraries:

```
#
# This makefile creates the "Socha Libraries".  To change the memory model,
# change the defintion below of MEM_MODEL to one of the valid memory models.
#
MEM_MODEL = LARGE
```

```
#
# The two lines below define how to build an obj file from an asm file.
# I've used the /D switch to define MEM_MODEL, which is used in the .MODEL
# statement to define the memory model to build.  And /Zi includes the
# debugger information in the file.
#
.asm.obj:
        ml /DMEM_MODEL=$(MEM_MODEL) /c /Zi $<
        lib clib -+$*;


#
# This line causes all the files to be assembled and added to the library.
#
clib.lib:      hardware.obj mouse.obj fastwrit.obj cursor.obj kbd_io.obj
```

SOCHALIB.INC

This file is used by all the ASM files in this appendix.

```
;---------------------------------------------------------------;
; I use these macros to write code that works in all memory models.    ;
;---------------------------------------------------------------;
        if      @DataSize               ;Are pointers Far?
lodDS   textequ <lds>                   ;Yes, use LDS to get DS:pointer
lodES   textequ <les>                   ;And use LES to get ES:pointer
refES   textequ <es:>                   ;And put ES: in front of refs
        else
lodDS   textequ <mov>                   ;No, use MOV to get pointer
lodES   textequ <mov>                   ;And also for ES case
refES   textequ <>                      ;And nothing for the references
        endif


        if @CodeSize                    ;Are calls Far?
procRef textequ <far>                   ;Yes, use Far
        else
procRef textequ <near>                  ;No, use Near
        endif
        .
```

CURSOR.ASM

```
.MODEL   MEM_MODEL,C

INCLUDE sochalib.inc


;-------------------------------------------------------------------;
; Copyright © 1992 by John Socha                                    ;
;-------------------------------------------------------------------;


;-------------------------------------------------------------------;
; This file contains a number of procedures that work with the screen   ;
; cursor.                                                           ;
;                                                                   ;
;       SetCursor              Sets the size of the hardware cursor ;
;       GetVisibleCursor       Gets the size of a visible cursor    ;
;       GetCursor              Gets the current size of the cursor  ;
;       CursorOff              Turns the cursor off                 ;
;       CursorOn               Turns the cursor back on             ;
;       CursorBlock            Changes the cursor to a block cursor ;
;       CursorUnderscore       Changes the cursor to an underscore  ;
;                                                                   ;
;       goto_xy                Moves the cursor position            ;
;       get_xy                 Returns the current cursor position  ;
;       get_active_page        Returns the number of the active page ;
;       set_cursor             Sets the size of the hardware cursor ;
;       fix_cursor (private)   Makes sure the cursor size is valid  ;
;-------------------------------------------------------------------;

.CODE


;-------------------------------------------------------------------;
; This procedure moves the cursor to another position on the screen. ;
; It doesn't do any error checking in case you want to do something  ;
; off the screen.  But be careful!                                  ;
;                                                                   ;
; On Entry:     DH      Row (Y)                                     ;
;               DL      Column (X)                                  ;
;                                                                   ;
; Uses:         GET_ACTIVE_PAGE                                     ;
;-------------------------------------------------------------------;
```

```
goto_xy        proc    uses ax bx si di bp
        call    get_active_page         ;Get the number of the active page
        mov     bh,al                   ;Put this page number into BH
        mov     ah,2                    ;Call for SET CURSOR POSITION
        int     10h
        ret
goto_xy        endp
```

```
;-----------------------------------------------------------------;
; This procedure is the reverse of GOTO_XY.  Instead of moving the ;
; cursor to a new position, it returns the current cursor position. ;
;                                                                 ;
; Returns:      AH      Row (Y)                                    ;
;               AL      Column (X)                                 ;
;                                                                 ;
; Uses:         GET_ACTIVE_PAGE                                    ;
;-----------------------------------------------------------------;
get_xy proc     uses bx dx si di bp
        call    get_active_page         ;Return active page in AL
        mov     bh,al                   ;Put this page number into BH
        mov     ah,3                    ;Call for read cursor position
        int     10h
        mov     ax,dx
        ret
get_xy endp
```

```
;-----------------------------------------------------------------;
; This procedure gets the page number for the page shown on the screen ;
; and returns it in the AL register.                              ;
;                                                                 ;
; Returns:      AL      Active page number                        ;
;-----------------------------------------------------------------;
get_active_page        proc    uses bx si di bp
        mov     ah,15                   ;Ask for current video state
        int     10h
        mov     al,bh                   ;Put active page number in AL
        ret
get_active_page        endp
```

556

```
;-----------------------------------------------------------------;
; This variable is used by CursorOn and CursorOff to keep track of the ;
; size of the cursor.                                             ;
;-----------------------------------------------------------------;
.DATA
old_cursor_type         dw      0           ;Old start and end scan lines
.CODE


;-----------------------------------------------------------------;
; This procedure allows you to set the cursor to a new size.  Usually  ;
; you'll use this to restore a cursor that you obtained with      ;
; GetVisibleCursor().                                             ;
;                                                                 ;
;       void SetCursor(int size);                                 ;
;-----------------------------------------------------------------;
SetCursor       proc    cursorSize:Word
        mov     dx, cursorSize
        call    set_cursor
        ret
SetCursor       endp


;-----------------------------------------------------------------;
; This procedure sets the end and start lines of the cursor.      ;
;                                                                 ;
; On entry:      DH      First scan line of cursor.               ;
;                DL      Last scan line of cursor.                ;
;                                                                 ;
; Writes:        OLD_CURSOR_TYPE                                  ;
;-----------------------------------------------------------------;
set_cursor      proc    private uses ax cx si di bp
        call    GetCursor               ;Get the old cursor shape
        mov     old_cursor_type, ax     ;And save it
        mov     ch,dh                   ;Put start line into CH
        mov     cl,dl                   ;Put end line into CL
        mov     ah,1                    ;Set cursor type
        int     10h
        ret
set_cursor      endp
```

557

```
;-------------------------------------------------------------------;
; This procedure gets the start and end scan lines of the cursor.   ;
; If the cursor was not visible, it returns a visible cursor.  Call ;
; GetCursor if you want the exact information on the old cursor.     ;
;                                                                   ;
; Returns:      AH      First scan line of cursor                   ;
;               AL      Last scan line of cursor                    ;
;-------------------------------------------------------------------;
GetVisibleCursor        proc
        call    GetCursor               ;Get cursor size into AX
        cmp     ah,0Fh                  ;Is the cursor off?
        jb      cursor_not_off          ;No, then we're all done
        mov     ax,607h                 ;Yes, set to 607 for CGA
        call    fix_cursor              ;Make sure CX contains a legal value
cursor_not_off:
        ret
GetVisibleCursor        endp



;-------------------------------------------------------------------;
; This procedure gets the start and end scan lines of the cursor.  You ;
; can then use SET_CURSOR to restore the cursor's shape.            ;
;                                                                   ;
; NOTE: There is a bug in the ROM BIOS.  Every time you set the mode, ;
;       it stores 0607h into the cursor type, which is the wrong value ;
;       for a monochrome display.  So...this routine translates 0607h ;
;       into 0B0Ch if the display is a monochrome display.          ;
;                                                                   ;
; Returns:      AH      First scan line of cursor.                  ;
;               AL      Last scan line of cursor.                   ;
;-------------------------------------------------------------------;
GetCursor       proc    uses bx cx dx si di bp
        xor     bh,bh                   ;Make sure page has reasonable value
        mov     ah,3                    ;Get current cursor type
        int     10h                     ;CX = cursor type
        mov     ax,cx                   ;Put cursor type into AX
        call    fix_cursor              ;Make sure CX contains a legal value
        ret
GetCursor       endp
```

```
;------------------------------------------------------------------;
; This procedure "fixes" the cursor start and end scan lines in case ;
; the ROM BIOS gave us bogus information:                           ;
;                                                                   ;
; On entry:     AH        Starting scan line of the cursor          ;
;               AL        Ending scan line of the cursor            ;
;                                                                   ;
;       67h               COMPAQ returns this incorrect result      ;
;       607h              ROM BIOS returns this for monochrome display ;
;                                                                   ;
; Returns:      AX        Valid cursor size                         ;
;------------------------------------------------------------------;
        extrn   GetDisplayRows:procRef
fix_cursor      proc    private
        cmp     ax,67h                  ;Is this a bogus COMPAQ cursor?
        jne     not_bogus_compaq        ;No, then check for monochrome
        mov     ax,607h                 ;Make it a legal type
not_bogus_compaq:
        push    ax
        int     11h                     ;Get the equipment flag
        and     al,30h                  ;Leave only the display type
        cmp     al,30h                  ;Is this a monochrome display?
        pop     ax
        jne     cursor_type_valid       ;No, then accept cursor type

is_monochrome:
        push    ax
        call    GetDisplayRows          ;Get number of lines on screen
        cmp     ax,25                   ;Are we in 43-line mode?
        pop     ax
        ja      cursor_type_valid       ;Yes, keep cursor at 607h

        cmp     ax,607h                 ;Yes, is this a bogus cursor?
        jne     cursor_type_valid       ;No, then continue
        mov     AX,0B0Ch                ;Set to value for underscore cursor
cursor_type_valid:
        ret
fix_cursor      endp



;------------------------------------------------------------------;
; This procedure turns the cursor off.                             ;
;                                                                  ;
; Uses:         SET_CURSOR                                         ;
;------------------------------------------------------------------;
```

559

```
CursorOff       proc    uses ax dx
        mov     dh,0Fh                  ;Set start line for cursor
        mov     dl,0                    ;Set end line for cursor
        call    set_cursor
        ret
CursorOff       endp


;-----------------------------------------------------------------;
; This procedure turns the cursor off.                            ;
;                                                                 ;
; Uses:          set_cursor                                       ;
;                                                                 ;
; Note: This procedure preserves the registers so you can call it from ;
;       assembly language.                                        ;
;-----------------------------------------------------------------;
CursorOn        proc    uses dx
        mov     dx,old_cursor_type      ;Restore old cursor type
        call    set_cursor              ;And set it.
        ret
CursorOn        endp


;-----------------------------------------------------------------;
; This procedure sets the cursor to a block cursor.  Since the color- ;
; graphics and monochrome-display adapter use a different number of   ;
; lines for the character cell, this procedure has to check the display;
; type.                                                           ;
;-----------------------------------------------------------------;
        extrn   GetDisplayType:procRef

CursorBlock     proc    uses ax bx
        xor     dh,dh                   ;Set start line for cursor to 0
        mov     dl,7                    ;Set for color-graphics adapter
        call    GetDisplayType
        cmp     al,3                    ;Is this a monochrome display?
        jne     block_is_graphics       ;No, then don't change CL
        mov     dl,13                   ;Set for monochrome display.
block_is_graphics:
        call    set_cursor              ;Change the cursor's shape
        ret
CursorBlock     endp
```

560

```
;-------------------------------------------------------------;
; This procedure sets the cursor to a block cursor.  Since the color-  ;
; graphics and monochrome-display adapter use a different number of    ;
; lines for the character cell, this procedure has to check the display;
; type.                                                                ;
;-------------------------------------------------------------;
        extrn   GetDisplayType:procRef

CursorUnderscore        proc    uses ax dx
        mov     dh,6                    ;Set start line for cursor to 0
        mov     dl,7                    ;Set for color-graphics adapter
        call    GetDisplayType
        cmp     al,3                    ;Is this a monochrome display?
        jne     underscore_is_graphics  ;No, then don't change CL
        mov     dh,11                   ;Set for monochrome display.
        mov     dl,12
underscore_is_graphics:
        call    set_cursor
        ret
CursorUnderscore        endp

        end
```

_

FASTWRIT.ASM

```
.MODEL  MEM_MODEL,C

INCLUDE sochalib.inc


;-------------------------------------------------------------;
; Copyright © 1992 by John Socha                              ;
;-------------------------------------------------------------;


BELL    equ     7
TAB     equ     9
LF      equ     10
CR      equ     13
```

```
;-----------------------------------------------------------------;
; The procedures in this module are all designed for very fast writes  ;
; to the screen.  DOS is very slow, and so is the ROM BIOS.  So these  ;
; procedures poke characters directly, and very quickly, into memory.  ;
;                                                                 ;
; Because these procedures need special information, and it would be   ;
; ineffecient to constantly update local variables, there is one  ;
; procedure called INIT_FAST_DISPLAY_MODULE that initializes various   ;
; variables.  Call this procedure any time you change the display mode ;
; or screen.                                                      ;
;                                                                 ;
;       InitFastDisplayModule    Call this before calling other procs  ;
;       FastFlush                Flush unwritten chars to the screen   ;
;       FastWriteRawChar         Doesn't check for special characters  ;
;       FastWriteChar            Much faster version of WriteChar  ;
;       FastReadAttr             Returns attribute of char under cursor ;
;       FastWriteString          Much faster version of WriteString ;
;       FastWriteUDecimal        Writes an unsigned-decimal number ;
;       FastWriteNChars          Writes N copies of a character ;
;       FastWriteSpaces          Fills an area with N spaces ;
;       FastGotoXY               Version of GOTO_XY for FAST module ;
;       FastSetCursor            Moves real cursor to screen_x, screen_y ;
;       FastGetXY                Version of GET_XY for FAST module ;
;                                                                 ;
;       move_to_screen           Copies chars in the buffer to screen  ;
;       fast_write_raw_char      The low-level version ;
;       fast_write_char          The low-level version ;
;       calc_display_offset      (private) low-level function ;
;       fast_goto_xy             (private) low-level function ;
;                                                                 ;
; Public variables:                                               ;
;       char_attribute           This is a public variable ;
;       clear_attr               Used for new lines when scrolling ;
;       display_lines            Number of lines on the screen ;
;-----------------------------------------------------------------;


        .DATA
                public  char_attribute, clear_attr, display_lines
char_attribute          db      7, 0    ;Attribute for characters
clear_attr              db      7, 0    ;Attribute for areas to clear
wait_retrace_flag       db      0, 0    ;1 if we should wait for horiz. retrace
topview_flag            db      0, 0    ;If we need to make update calls
```

```
display_base          dw      0B800h   ;For color graphics adapter
display_offset        dw      0        ;The display offset (used for page > 0)
display_page          db      0        ;The currently active page
display_lines         dw      25       ;Number of screen lines

screen_x              dw      0
screen_y              dw      0
screen_ptr            dw      0        ;Points to character under cursor

line_buffer           dw      80 DUP (0)
line_ptr              dw      line_buffer   ;Pointer to next char
line_count            dw      0        ;Number of characters to write
line_start            dw      0        ;Offset in screen memory of line start


max_lines     equ     50               ;Maximum number of screen lines
screen_offset         dw      0,      80,     160,    240,    320
                      dw      400,    480,    560,    640,    720
                      dw      800,    880,    960,    1040,   1120
                      dw      1200,   1280,   1360,   1440,   1520
                      dw      1600,   1680,   1760,   1840,   1920
                      dw      2000,   2080,   2160,   2240,   2320
                      dw      2400,   2480,   2560,   2640,   2720
                      dw      2800,   2880,   2960,   3040,   3120
                      dw      3200,   3280,   3360,   3440,   3520
                      dw      3600,   3680,   3760,   3840,   3920
                      dw      4000,   4080,   4160,   4240,   4320
                      dw      4400,   4480,   4560,   4640,   4720

        .CODE

        extrn   GetDisplayType:procRef       ;In HARDWARE module
        extrn   EgaActive:procRef            ;In HARDWARE module
        extrn   GetDisplayRows:procRef       ;In HARDWARE module
        extrn   get_xy:procRef               ;In CURSOR   module
        extrn   get_active_page:procRef      ;In CURSOR   module
;------------------------------------------------------------------;
; Call this procedure at least once before you call *any* other    ;
; procedures.  This procedure initializes variables that other     ;
; procedures use.                                                  ;
;------------------------------------------------------------------;
InitFastDisplayModule   proc
        push    ax
        push    dx
        mov     display_base,0B000h      ;Set up for monochrome card
```

563

```
        mov     display_lines,25        ;Set to 25 lines on the screen
        mov     wait_retrace_flag,0     ;Don't wait for retraces

        call    GetDisplayType          ;See which card we have
        cmp     al,3                    ;Do we have a monochrome card?
        je      is_monochrome           ;Yes, then we're done
        mov     display_base,0B800h     ;Set up for color graphics card
        call    EgaActive               ;See if we have EGA card (-1)
        or      ax,ax                   ;Is this EGA card?
        jnz     is_ega                  ;Yes, don't wait for retrace
        mov     wait_retrace_flag,1     ;Wait for retraces before writing chars
        jmp     Short finish_init

is_monochrome:
        ;----------------------------------------------;
        ; The display adapter is attached to an IBM    ;
        ; monochrome display, but it could be an EGA   ;
        ; card.                                        ;
        ;----------------------------------------------;
        call    EgaActive               ;See if EGA card (-1)
        or      ax,ax                   ;Is this an EGA/VGA card?
        Jz      finish_init             ;No, then we're done
                                        ;Yes, set display lines

is_ega:
        ;----------------------------------------------;
        ; This section of code gets the number of      ;
        ; screen lines for EGA and VGA monitors.       ;
        ;----------------------------------------------;
        call    GetDisplayRows          ;AX = Number of display lines
        cmp     al,max_lines            ;Too many lines?
        jbe     set_display_lines       ;No, then set
        mov     al,max_lines            ;Yes, set to max_lines
set_display_lines:
        mov     Byte Ptr display_lines,al

finish_init:
        ;----------------------------------------------;
        ; This section of code gets the current page   ;
        ; and calculates the offset.                   ;
        ;----------------------------------------------;
        push    cx
        call    get_active_page         ;Get current page number in AL
        mov     display_page,al         ;Save the display page
        mov     ah,al                   ;Put display page into AH
        xor     al,al                   ;AX = page * 256
```

```
        mov     cl,4                        ;Multiply AX by 16
        shl     ax,cl                       ;AX = page * 4096 (offset to page)
        mov     display_offset,ax           ;Save this page offset
        pop     cx



        ;------------------------------------------------;
        ; Check TopView interface (also windows) for     ;
        ; address of the display buffer.                 ;
        ;------------------------------------------------;
        push    bx
        push    di
        push    es
        mov     bx,display_base             ;Get what we think is the display base
        mov     es,bx
        xor     di,di                       ;ES:DI - where we think display base is
        mov     ah,0FEh                     ;Make call to TopView
        int     10h                         ;Get Video Buffer
        mov     ax,es                       ;Get the new? display base
        cmp     ax,bx                       ;Are we running under TopView?
        je      not_in_topview              ;No, then we're done here
        mov     topview_flag,1              ;Yes we are, set flag
        mov     display_base,ax             ;Save new display base
        mov     display_offset,di           ;Save offset to the buffer
        mov     display_page,0              ;Use page 0 for TopView
        mov     wait_retrace_flag,0         ;No need to wait since TopView updates
not_in_topview:
        pop     es
        pop     di
        pop     bx



        ;----------------------------------------------;
        ; Now read the default character attribute.    ;
        ;----------------------------------------------;
        call    get_xy                      ;Get the current cursor position
        mov     dx,ax                       ;Set up for Fast_goto_xy call
        call    fast_goto_xy                ;Set the character offset
        call    FastReadAttr                ;Read the current attribute
        mov     char_attribute,al           ;Set character attribute to normal
        mov     clear_attr,al               ;And set for cleared regions
        pop     dx
        pop     ax
        ret
InitFastDisplayModule    endp
```

```
;-----------------------------------------------------------------;
; This procedure writes any characters left in the buffer to the  ;
; screen.                                                         ;
;                                                                ;
;       void FastFlush(void);                                    ;
;                                                                ;
; Note: this subroutine preserves all the registers so you can call it ;
;       from assembly language.                                  ;
;-----------------------------------------------------------------;
FastFlush       proc uses ax cx si di es
        mov     cx,line_count           ;Number of characters to display
        jcxz    done_fast_flush         ;If no chars, we're all done

        lea     ax,line_buffer          ;Pointer to off-screen buffer
        mov     line_ptr,ax             ;Reset line_ptr to start of buffer
        mov     si,ax                   ;DS:SI points to line buffer

        mov     ax,line_start           ;Where to start drawing the line
        mov     di,ax
        mov     ax,display_base         ;Segment for the screen buffer
        mov     es,ax                   ;ES:DI points to where we'll draw

        call    move_to_screen          ;Copy the buffer to the screen
        mov     ax,line_start           ;Get the start of the line
        mov     cx,line_count           ;Get num of char/attr pairs in buffer
        shl     cx,1                    ;Convert to number of bytes
        add     ax,cx                   ;Point to first char after line
        mov     screen_ptr,ax           ;Point to next location
        mov     line_start,ax
        mov     line_count,0            ;Reset the line count

done_fast_flush:
        ret
FastFlush       endp


        extrn   HideMouse:procRef
        extrn   UnhideMouse:procRef
;-----------------------------------------------------------------;
; This procedure moves a section of memory directly to screen memory.  ;
; It waits for horizontal retrace periods, where needed, to avoid       ;
; snow.                                                          ;
;                                                                ;
; On entry:     DS:SI           Pointer to data to move to screen  ;
;               DI              Offset in screen of first char     ;
```

```
;                 CX              Number of words to transfer to screen  ;
;                                                                        ;
; Destroys:       CX, SI, DI                                             ;
;------------------------------------------------------------------------;
move_to_screen   proc      private uses ax es
         call     HideMouse               ;Hide cursor while we write
         jcxz     done_move_to            ;CX == 0, we're all done

         mov      ax,display_base         ;Seg register of frame buffer
         mov      es,ax                   ;Set segment to start of frame buffer

         push     cx                      ;Save the character count
         push     di                      ;Save start of screen area
         cld                              ;Set for increment
         test     wait_retrace_flag,1     ;Should we wait for horizontal retrace?
         jnz      move_to_wait            ;Yes.

rep      movsw                            ;No, just move to the screen
         jmp      Short finish_move_to    ;We're all done

move_to_wait:                             ;We need to wait for hoizontal retrace.
         push     bx
         push     dx

         mov      dx,03DAh                ;Status register on color card
move_to_loop:
         lodsw                            ;Get character from off-screen buffer
         mov      bx,ax                   ;Save character in BX register
to_still_in_retrace:
         in       al,dx                   ;Get status byte
         test     al,1                    ;In horizontal retrace?
         jnz      to_still_in_retrace     ;Yes, wait until it's done
         cli                              ;Turn interrupts off for now
to_wait_for_retrace:
         in       al,dx                   ;Get status byte
         test     al,1                    ;In horizontal retrace?
         jz       to_wait_for_retrace     ;Not yet, wait
         mov      ax,bx                   ;Recover character and attribute
         stosw                            ;Save it to the screen
         sti                              ;Turn interrupts back on
         loop     move_to_loop            ;Copy another word.

         pop      dx
         pop      bx
```

567

```
finish_move_to:
        pop     di                      ;Get back start of screen area
        pop     cx                      ;Get back number of characters

        test    topview_flag,1          ;Are we in TopView?
        jz      done_move_to            ;No, we're all done
        mov     ah,0FFh                 ;Tell TopView to update screen
        int     10h

done_move_to:
        call    UnhideMouse             ;Show the mouse again
        ret
move_to_screen  endp


;---------------------------------------------------------------------;
; This procedure provides the C-language interface to the function    ;
; below.                                                              ;
;---------------------------------------------------------------------;
FastWriteRawChar        proc    char:Word
        mov     dl, Byte Ptr char       ; Get the character to display
        call    fast_write_raw_char     ; Display the character
        ret
FastWriteRawChar        endp


;---------------------------------------------------------------------;
; This procedure is like WRITE_CHAR, except that it writes characters ;
; directly to the screen and it doesn't attach special meaning to any ;
; characters, so CR, LF, etc. all appear on the screen as characters  ;
;                                                                    ;
; NOTE: This procedure will set SCREEN_X to 80 if you try to write off ;
;       the right side of the screen.  This way you can tell when you ;
;       tried to write off the screen.                               ;
;                                                                    ;
; Note: This procedure is used by other assembly-language procedures  ;
;       in this file.                                                ;
;                                                                    ;
; On entry:     DL      Character you want to print.                 ;
;                                                                    ;
; Reads:        CHAR_ATTRIBUTE                                       ;
;---------------------------------------------------------------------;
fast_write_raw_char     proc    private uses ax di es
        push    ds
        pop     es                              ;Set ES so it points to data segment
```

```
        cmp     screen_x,79         ;Are we still on screen?
        ja      done_write_raw      ;No, don't write this char
        mov     di,line_ptr         ;Get pointer to the next char
        mov     ah,char_attribute   ;Get current character attribute
        mov     al,dl               ;Get the character to write
        stosw                       ;Save this character
        inc     screen_x            ;Move cursor to next column
        inc     line_count          ;Number of characters in buffer
        mov     line_ptr,di         ;Save new character pointer

done_write_raw:
        ret
fast_write_raw_char     endp



;-----------------------------------------------------------------;
; This procedure provides the C-language interface to fast_write_char: ;
;                                                                 ;
;       void FastWriteChar(int c);                                ;
;-----------------------------------------------------------------;
FastWriteChar   proc    char:Word
        mov     dl, Byte Ptr char   ; Get the character to display
        call    fast_write_char     ; Display the character
        ret
FastWriteChar   endp



;-----------------------------------------------------------------;
; This is a version of WRITE_CHAR that writes characters directly to ;
; the screen.  It uses attribute 7 as the default attribute.      ;
;                                                                 ;
; The following characters all need special treatment:            ;
;       7       Bell                                              ;
;       9       Tab                                               ;
;       10      Line Feed                                         ;
;       13      Carriage Return                                   ;
;                                                                 ;
; On entry:     DL      Character you want to print.              ;
;-----------------------------------------------------------------;
fast_write_char         proc    private
        test    dl,0F0h             ;Special character?
        jz      special             ;Yes, then handle them
```

569

```
        not_special:
                call    fast_write_raw_char     ;No, the write character to screen
                ret

        special:
                cmp     dl,CR                   ;Is it a carriage return?
                je      do_cr                   ;Yes, then take care of CR
                cmp     dl,LF                   ;Is it a line feed?
                je      do_lf                   ;Yes, then take care of LF
                cmp     dl,TAB                  ;Is it a tab?
                je      do_tab                  ;Yes, then take care of tab
                cmp     dl,BELL                 ;Is it a bell?
                je      do_bell                 ;Yes, then sound the bell
                jmp     Short not_special       ;Not a special charcter
                                                ;(It's below all the DO routines)

        do_cr:                                  ;Move the cursor to the left side
                push    dx
                mov     dh,Byte Ptr screen_y
                xor     dl,dl                   ;Move to start of this line
                call    fast_goto_xy
                pop     dx
                ret

        do_lf:
                push    ax
                mov     ax,display_lines        ;Get number of lines on screen
                dec     ax                      ;AX == last line on screen
                cmp     screen_y,ax             ;At or past bottom of screen?
                pop     ax
                jae     passed_bottom           ;Yes, then scroll the screen
                push    dx
                mov     dh,Byte Ptr screen_y
                inc     dh                      ;Move to the next line
                mov     dl,Byte Ptr screen_x    ;But same column
                call    fast_goto_xy            ;Move the cursor
                pop     dx
                ret

        passed_bottom:
                push    ax
                push    bx
                push    cx
                push    dx
                push    si
```

```
        push    di
        push    bp
        mov     ax,0601h                ;Scroll up by one line
        mov     bh,char_attribute       ;Use char. attribute in scrolled lines
        mov     cx,0                    ;Upper left corner at (0,0)
        mov     dh,Byte Ptr display_lines ;Lower right at (display_lines, 79)
        dec     dh                      ;Convert to last screen line
        mov     dl,4Fh
        int     10h                     ; ***Replace with CALL to SCROLL_WINDOW
        pop     bp
        pop     di
        pop     si
        pop     dx
        pop     cx
        pop     bx
        pop     ax
        ret

do_bell:                                ;Ring the bell.
        ret

do_tab:                                 ;Expand the tab into spaces.
        push    cx
        push    dx
        mov     dl,' '                  ;Write out N spaces
        mov     cx,screen_x
        and     cx,7                    ;CX := SCREEN_X MOD 8
        neg     cx
        add     cx,8                    ;CX := 8 - (SCREEN_X MOD 8)
tab_loop:
        call    fast_write_raw_char
        loop    tab_loop
        pop     dx
        pop     cx
        ret
fast_write_char         endp



;-------------------------------------------------------------------;
; This procedure reads the attribute of the character under the cursor ;
;                                                                   ;
; Returns:                                                          ;
;       AX      Attribute of character under cursor                 ;
;-------------------------------------------------------------------;
```

```
FastReadAttr     proc     uses dx di es
        mov      ax,display_base
        mov      es,ax
        mov      di,screen_ptr
        inc      di                      ;Point to the attribute


;-------------------------------------------------;
; This section of code waits for the horizontal   ;
; retrace period before writing characters so     ;
; you won't see snow on an IBM color-graphics     ;
; adapter.  Since the horizontal retrace period   ;
; is only about 2 microseconds, there's only      ;
; time to read one character/attribute.           ;
;-------------------------------------------------;
        test     wait_retrace_flag,1     ;Should we wait for horizontal retrace?
        jz       read_dont_wait          ;Nope

        mov      dx,03DAh                ;Status register on color card
read_still_in_retrace:
        in       al,dx                   ;Get status byte
        test     al,1                    ;In horizontal retrace?
        jnz      read_still_in_retrace   ;Yes, wait until it's done
        cli                              ;Turn interrupts off for now
read_wait_for_retrace:
        in       al,dx                   ;Get status byte
        test     al,1                    ;In horizontal retrace?
        jz       read_wait_for_retrace   ;Not yet, wait
read_dont_wait:
        mov      al,es:[di]              ;Get the attribute
        sti                              ;Turn interrupts back on again
        xor      ah,ah                   ;Return attribute in a word

        ret
FastReadAttr     endp


;------------------------------------------------------------------;
; This procedure writes an ASCIIZ string to the screen.  It uses the  ;
; FAST_WRITE_CHAR so it's very fast, and only a few characters are    ;
; treated specially.                                                  ;
;                                                                     ;
; On entry:     DS:DX   Address of ASCIIZ string.                     ;
; Uses:         FAST_WRITE_CHAR                                       ;
;------------------------------------------------------------------;
FastWriteString proc    uses ax dx si, string:Ptr Byte
        lodES    si,string               ;Get the address of the string
```

```
write_string_loop:
        mov     al,refES [si]          ;Get one character
        inc     si                     ;Point to next character
        or      al,al                  ;Is the end of the string?
        jz      end_of_string          ;Yes, then stop writing
        mov     dl,al                  ;No, then print the character
        call    fast_write_char
        jmp     Short write_string_loop
end_of_string:
        ret
FastWriteString endp



;--------------------------------------------------------------------;
; This procedure writes an unsigned decimal number.                  ;
;                                                                    ;
; On entry:     DX      Number you want to write in decimal          ;
; Uses:         fast_write_char                                      ;
;--------------------------------------------------------------------;
FastWriteUDecimal       proc    num:Word
        mov     ax, num                ;Put number in AX, where we want it
        mov     bx,10                  ;We divide by 10 to pick off digits
        xor     cx,cx                  ;Start with 0 digits on the stack
not_zero:
        xor     dx,dx                  ;Set upper word of 32-bit num to 0
        div     bx                     ;(N mod 10) --> DX, (N div 10) -- AX
        push    dx                     ;Save this digit on the stack
        inc     cx                     ;Keep track of num. of digits on stack
        or      ax,ax                  ;N == 0 yet?
        jnz     not_zero               ;No, put more digits on stack
write_digit_loop:
        pop     dx                     ;Get most recent digit
        add     dl, '0'                ;Convert to '0'..'9'
        call    fast_write_char        ;Display this character
        loop    write_digit_loop       ;Until no more digits on stack
        ret
FastWriteUDecimal       endp



;--------------------------------------------------------------------;
; This procedure writes N characters, starting at the cursor position. ;
;                                                                    ;
;       void FastWriteNChars(int char, int count);                   ;
;                                                                    ;
; Calls:        fast_write_raw_char                                  ;
;--------------------------------------------------------------------;
```

```
FastWriteNChars proc    uses cx, char:Word, count:Word
        mov     dl, Byte Ptr char       ;Get the character to display
        mov     cx, count               ;Number of chars to show
        jcxz    done_fast_write_chars   ;Count == 0, nothing to write
chars_loop:
        call    fast_write_raw_char     ;Write out one character
        loop    chars_loop              ;Keep writing until CX == 0
done_fast_write_chars:
        ret
FastWriteNChars endp



;--------------------------------------------------------------------;
; This procedure writes N spaces, starting at the cursor position.   ;
;                                                                    ;
; On entry:     CX      Number of spaces we should write             ;
; Calls:        FAST_WRITE_N_CHARS                                   ;
;--------------------------------------------------------------------;
FastWriteSpaces proc    count:Word
        INVOKE  FastWriteNChars, ' ', count
        ret
FastWriteSpaces endp



;--------------------------------------------------------------------;
; This procedure calculates the offset into the screen buffer of a   ;
; given character on the screen.  (Note: this procedure handles screen ;
; pages and TopView correctly.)                                      ;
;                                                                    ;
; On entry:     DH      Row     Y                                    ;
;               DL      Column  X                                    ;
; Returns:      Offset, in bytes, from the start of the screen segment ;
;               for the character at (X, Y).                         ;
;--------------------------------------------------------------------;
calc_display_offset     proc    private
        push    bx
        mov     bl,dh                   ;Get the line number
        xor     bh,bh                   ;Convert to a word
        shl     bx,1                    ;Multiply line by 2 for lookup table
        mov     ax,screen_offset[bx]    ;Get character offset for this line

        mov     bl,dl                   ;Get the X position
        xor     bh,bh                   ;Convert to a word
        add     ax,bx                   ;Character offset of cursor
        shl     ax,1                    ;Byte offset of character/attribute
```

574

```
        add     ax,display_offset       ;Add in offset from non-zero page
        pop     bx
        ret
calc_display_offset     endp


;-------------------------------------------------------------------;
; This procedure provides the C interface to fast_goto_xy:          ;
;                                                                   ;
;       void FastGotoXY(x, y);                                      ;
;-------------------------------------------------------------------;
FastGotoXY      proc    x:Word, y:Word
        mov     dh, Byte Ptr y
        mov     dl, Byte Ptr x
        call    fast_goto_xy
        ret
FastGotoXY      endp


        extrn   goto_xy:procRef         ;In CURSOR module
;-------------------------------------------------------------------;
; This is a version of GOTO_XY that works with the other fast screen ;
; procedures.  This procedure moves the cursor to another position on ;
; the screen.  It doesn't do any error checking in case you want to do ;
; something off the screen.  But be careful!                        ;
;                                                                   ;
; On entry:     DH      Row(Y)                                      ;
;               DL      Column (X)                                  ;
; Uses:         GOTO_XY                                             ;
;-------------------------------------------------------------------;
fast_goto_xy    proc    private uses ax bx dx
        call    FastFlush               ;Flush any unwritten characters
        mov     bl,Byte Ptr display_lines ;Temporary storage for Num lines
        dec     bl                      ;Convert to last line on screen
        cmp     dh,bl                   ;Are we off the screen?
        jbe     do_goto_xy              ;No, then move the cursor
        cmp     dh,bl                   ;Are we off the bottom?
        mov     dh,bl                   ; (Set DH to the last line)
        jg      do_goto_xy              ;Yes, then set to last line
        mov     dh,0                    ;No, we're off the top, set to line 0
do_goto_xy:
        call    goto_xy                 ;Move the real cursor
        mov     Byte Ptr screen_x,dl    ;Save coordinates of cursor
        mov     Byte Ptr screen_y,dh
        call    calc_display_offset     ;Get byte offset into AX
        mov     screen_ptr,ax           ;Save this offset
```

575

```
        mov     line_start,ax            ;Remember where next line starts
        ret
fast_goto_xy    endp


;-------------------------------------------------------------------;
; This procedure will move the real cursor to the position of the   ;
; fast cursor, which is just a pair of numbers stored in memory.    ;
;                                                                   ;
; Note: This procedure preserves the registers so you can call it from ;
;       assembly language.                                          ;
;-------------------------------------------------------------------;
FastSetCursor   proc    uses dx
        mov     dl,Byte Ptr screen_x
        mov     dh,Byte Ptr screen_y
        call    goto_xy                  ;Move the real cursor
        ret
FastSetCursor   endp


;-------------------------------------------------------------------;
; This is a version of FAST_GET_XY that works with the fast screen  ;
; module procedures.  It's the reverse of FAST_GOTO_XY.  Instead of ;
; moving the cursor to a new position, it returns the current cursor;
; position.                                                         ;
;                                                                   ;
;       void FastGetXY(int *x, int *y);                             ;
;                                                                   ;
; Returns:      x       Column                                      ;
;               y       Row                                         ;
;-------------------------------------------------------------------;
FastGetXY       proc    x:Ptr Word, y:Ptr Word
        lodES   bx, x                    ; Get pointer to x into es:[bx]
        mov     ax, screen_x             ; Get current x position
        mov     refES [bx], ax           ; Save into C's x variable

        lodES   bx, y                    ; Get pointer to y into es:[bx]
        mov     ax, screen_y             ; Get current y position
        mov     refES [bx], ax           ; Save into C's y variable
        ret
FastGetXY       endp


        if 0
```

```
        PUBLIC  FAST_CLEAR_TO_EOL
        EXTRN   CLEAR_WINDOW:NEAR
;------------------------------------------------------------------;
; This procedure clears the line from the current cursor position to   ;
; the end of the line.                                             ;
;------------------------------------------------------------------;
        PUBLIC  _FAST_CLEAR_TO_EOL
_FAST_CLEAR_TO_EOL      LABEL   NEAR
FAST_CLEAR_TO_EOL       PROC    NEAR
        PUSH    AX
        PUSH    BX
        MOV     BL,BYTE PTR SCREEN_X    ;Get position of cursor
        MOV     BH,BYTE PTR SCREEN_Y
        MOV     AL,79                   ;Last column of the line
        CMP     BL,AL                   ;Was last char on screen?
        JA      DONT_CLEAR_TO_EOL       ;No, then don't try to clear
        MOV     AH,BH                   ;Stay on same line
        CALL    CLEAR_WINDOW
DONT_CLEAR_TO_EOL:
        POP     BX
        POP     AX
        RET
FAST_CLEAR_TO_EOL       ENDP

endif

        end
    .
```

HARDWARE.ASM

```
.MODEL  MEM_MODEL,C

INCLUDE sochalib.inc


;------------------------------------------------------------------;
; JS -- Copyright © 1992 by John Socha                             ;
;                                                                  ;
; This file contains a number of procedures that check or set various  ;
; things having to do with the hardware.                          ;
```

577

```
;                                                                      ;
;          GetDisplayType              Tells you what type of display active  ;
;          is_ega (private)            Checks to see if this is EGA adapter  ;
;          EgaActive                   Checks if EGA is the active card   ;
;          GetDisplayRows              Returns number of rows on screen    ;
;--------------------------------------------------------------------;
rom_seg          segment at 40h
        org      4Ah
crt_cols         DW       ?                    ;Number of columns on the screen

        org      87h
ega_info         DB       ?                    ;Info byte for EGA monitor
rom_seg          ends


        .CODE


;--------------------------------------------------------------------;
; This procedure determines whether the display type is a monochrome  ;
; or color-graphics card.                                             ;
;                                                                     ;
; Returns:        AX       0         No display cards                 ;
;                          1         Color card in 40x25 mode         ;
;                          2         Color card in 80x25 mode         ;
;                          3         If monochrome card               ;
; Destroys:       AH                                                  ;
;--------------------------------------------------------------------;
GetDisplayType   proc     uses cx
        int      11h                           ;Get equipment flags
        mov      cl,4
        shr      ax,cl                         ;Right justify display flags
        and      ax,3                          ;Keep just the display flags
        ret
GetDisplayType   endp


;--------------------------------------------------------------------;
; This procedure checks to see if the display adapter is an EGA card.  ;
; This test is from the IBM Personal Computer Seminar Proceedings     ;
; Volume 2, Number 11 from November 1984                              ;
;                                                                     ;
; Returns:        ZR       If this is an EGA card                     ;
;                 NZ       Otherwise                                  ;
;--------------------------------------------------------------------;
```

```
is_ega   proc    private uses ax bx cx si di bp
         mov     ax,1200h                ;Make an EGA-specific call
         mov     bl,10h                  ;For EGA information
         mov     bh,0FFh                 ;Load BH with invalid info
         mov     cl,0Fh                  ;Load CL with reserved switch settings
         int     10h                     ;Make call to EGA ROM BIOS

         cmp     cl,0Ch                  ;Is switch setting in valid range?
         jae     not_ega                 ;No, this is not an EGA card
         cmp     bh,1                    ;Is this a valid flag?
         ja      not_ega                 ;No, this is not an EGA card
         cmp     bl,3                    ;Is memory value within range?
         ja      not_ega                 ;No, this is not an EGA card
         xor     ax,ax                   ;Set the zero flag for EGA card

done_is_ega:
         ret

not_ega:
         xor     ax,ax
         inc     ax                      ;Clear the zero flag
         jmp     done_is_ega
is_ega   endp


;----------------------------------------------------------------;
; This procedure tests to see if an EGA monitor is the active monitor. ;
;                                                                ;
; Returns:      0       EGA card is not the active card          ;
;              -1       An EGA or VGA card *is* active           ;
;----------------------------------------------------------------;
EgaActive        proc    uses es
         call    is_ega                  ;See if have an EGA card installed
         jnz     ega_not_active          ;No, report EGA not active

         mov     ax,rom_seg              ;Point to ROM BIOS data area
         mov     es,ax
         test    es:ega_info,8           ;Is this card active?
         jnz     ega_not_active          ;No
         xor     ax,ax                   ;Yes, return -1 since EGA card found
         not     ax
         jmp     done_ega_active
```

579

```
ega_not_active:
        xor     ax,ax                           ;Return 0 for no EGA card active

done_ega_active:
        ret
EgaActive       endp


;----------------------------------------------------------------;
; This procedure returns the number of rows on the screen:       ;
;                                                                ;
; Returns:      AX      25              All non-EGA/VGA displays  ;
;                       > 25            EGA/VGA displays with more lines  ;
;----------------------------------------------------------------;
GetDisplayRows  proc uses bx si di bp es
        call    EgaActive               ;Return 0 if no EGA card
        or      ax,ax                   ;Is this an EGA card?
        mov     al,25                   ;Return 25 for non-EGA displays
        jz      done_get_rows           ;No, return 25 lines

        mov     ax,1130h                ;Ask for EGA information
        xor     bh,bh                   ;Return the current information
        int     10h                     ;DL = Number of rows - 1
        inc     dl                      ;DL = Number of rows
        mov     al,dl                   ;Returns result in AX
done_get_rows:
        xor     ah,ah                   ;Set upper byte to 0
        ret
GetDisplayRows  endp


        end
```

KBD_IO.ASM

```
.MODEL  MEM_MODEL,C

INCLUDE sochalib.inc
```

```
;-----------------------------------------------------------------;
; Copyright © 1992 by John Socha                                  ;
;-----------------------------------------------------------------;

;-----------------------------------------------------------------;
; This file contains the following procedures:                    ;
;                                                                 ;
; ReadKey()              Reads a character from the ROM BIOS and returns ;
;                        either an ASCII code, or 0x1?? where ?? is the  ;
;                        scan code of the non-ASCII key.          ;
; scan_to_extended       Converts to extended ASCII code (1xxh)   ;
; ReadRawKey()           Returns scan code in high byte and character ;
;                        code in the low byte.                    ;
; ClearKbdBuffer()       Clears the keyboard buffer               ;
; KeyWaiting()           Returns code of next character if the buffer is ;
;                        not empty, and 0 if it is empty.         ;
; ShiftKeys()            Returns the current state of the shift keys. ;
;-----------------------------------------------------------------;

        .CODE

            public ReadKey
;-----------------------------------------------------------------;
; This procedure uses the ROM BIOS routines to read a single character. ;
; It returns the ASCII code for keys that generate an ASCII character.   ;
; But if you push one of the key-pad or function keys, this procedure    ;
; will return the scan code in the lower byte and set the upper byte     ;
; to 1.                                                           ;
;                                                                 ;
; Returns:      ASCII code for ASCII characters                   ;
;               1xx (hex) where xx is the scan code of the special key ;
;-----------------------------------------------------------------;
ReadKey proc
        xor     ah,ah                   ;Ask for a character from BIOS
        int     16h
        call    scan_to_extended        ;Convert to 1xx for special keys
        cld                             ;Must be cleared for MSC
        ret
ReadKey endp
```

581

```
;--------------------------------------------------------------------;
; This procedure converts a scan-code/ASCII-code pair into an extended   ;
; character.  If the lower byte is 0, this procedure puts the scan        ;
; code into the lower byte and sets the upper byte to 1.  Otherwise, it   ;
; sets the upper byte to 0.                                               ;
;                                                                         ;
; On entry:      AH       Scan code for the key pushed                    ;
;                AL       ASCII code, or 0 for special keys               ;
;                                                                         ;
; Returns:       ASCII code for ASCII characters                         ;
;                1xx (hex) where xx is the scan code of the special key    ;
;                                                                         ;
; Note:          This procedure now works also for the grey keys on the   ;
;                extended keyboard (which have E0h in the lower byte       ;
;                rather than 00h).                                        ;
;--------------------------------------------------------------------;
scan_to_extended        proc      private
        or      al,al                   ;Is this a special key?
        je      special_key             ;Yes, then handle it
        cmp     al,0E0h                 ;Is this a special key?
        je      special_key             ;Yes, then handle it
        xor     ah,ah                   ;No, return the ASCII code
        ret

special_key:
        xchg    al,ah                   ;Put the scan code into AL
        mov     ah,1                    ;And set AH = 1
        ret
scan_to_extended        endp


;--------------------------------------------------------------------;
; This procedure reads one character (or one special function key) from   ;
; the keyboard and returns the ASCII code, or scan code.                  ;
;                                                                         ;
; This procedure uses the ROM BIOS call so it can read both the          ;
; character code AND the scan code.  The DOS call returns only the        ;
; ASCII code.                                                            ;
;                                                                         ;
; Returns:       AH       The scan code of the key you pushed.  This is    ;
;                         useful for special keys that don't have ASCII    ;
;                         codes, like the function and cursor keys.       ;
;                AL       The ASCII code for the key you pushed.          ;
;                         0 for all special keys.                        ;
;--------------------------------------------------------------------;
```

582

```
ReadRawKey      proc
        mov     ah,0                    ;Ask for a character
        int     16h
        cld                             ;Must be cleared for MSC
        ret
ReadRawKey      endp




;------------------------------------------------------------------;
; This procedure clears the keyboard buffer of any characters that may ;
; still be around.                                                 ;
;------------------------------------------------------------------;
ClearKbdBuffer  proc
        push    dx
        mov     ax,0C06h                ;Clear input buffer
        mov     dl,0FFh                 ;Check status of the return
        int     21h
        pop     dx
        cld                             ;Must be cleared for MSC
        ret
ClearKbdBuffer  endp




;------------------------------------------------------------------;
; This procedure checks the keyboard buffer to see if there are any ;
; characters waiting to be read from the ROM BIOS:                 ;
;                                                                  ;
; Returns:      Character code of next character waiting.          ;
;               -1 if there are no characters waiting.             ;
;                                                                  ;
; NOTE: The ROM BIOS returns a scan code and character code of 0 after ;
;       you've hit ^break, so it is possible to detect a ^break by ;
;       checking to see if you read a 0 from the keyboard.         ;
;                                                                  ;
; NOTE: This procedure issues an INT 28h before checking the keyboard ;
;       status to allow background processes more frequent access to ;
;       system resources.                                          ;
;------------------------------------------------------------------;
KeyWaiting      proc
        int     28h                     ;Allow background processes a slice

        mov     ah,1                    ;Check for waiting character
        int     16h
        jnz     done_kbd_hit            ;Return the character code
        xor     ax,ax                   ;Return -1 for no character
```

```
              not     ax
done_kbd_hit:
              cld                              ;Must be clear for MSC compiler
              ret
KeyWaiting    endp


;----------------------------------------------------------------;
; This procedure returns the current state of the shift keys:    ;
;                                                                 ;
; INS_STATE      80h     Insert state is turned on               ;
; CAPS_STATE     40h     Caps lock key is on                     ;
; NUM_STATE      20h     Num lock is turned on                   ;
; SCROLL_STATE   10h     Scroll lock is on                       ;
; ALT_SHIFT      08h     The alt key is down                     ;
; CTL_SHIFT      04h     The control key is down                 ;
; LEFT_SHIFT     02h     The left-hand shift key is down         ;
; RIGHT_SHIFT    01h     The right-hand shift key is down        ;
;----------------------------------------------------------------;
ShiftKeys       proc
        mov     ah,2
        int     16h                      ;Get the current flags
        xor     ah,ah                    ;Set upper byte to zero
        cld                              ;Must be cleared for MSC
        ret
ShiftKeys       endp


        end
```

—

MOUSE.ASM

```
.MODEL  MEM_MODEL,C

INCLUDE sochalib.inc
```

```
;----------------------------------------------------------------;
; Copyright © 1992 by John Socha                                 ;
;                                                                ;
; This file contains some of the mouse interface routines.       ;
;                                                                ;
; InitMouse();            Do a full initlize on mouse hardware and sw. ;
; InitMouseSw();          Initialize the mouse software, and return    ;
;                             -1      Mouse installed               ;
;                             0       No mouse installed            ;
; HideMouser();        Removes the mouse cursor from the screen    ;
; UnhideMouse();       Makes the mouse cursor visible again        ;
;                                                                ;
; Get_mouse_position(&x, &y);        Returns character coords      ;
; Set_mouse_position(x, y);          Returns character coords      ;
; Mouse_buttons(&x, &y);             Which and where buttons pushed ;
;----------------------------------------------------------------;

.DATA
        public  mouse_installed, swap_buttons, mouse_visible
mouse_installed         DB      0               ;TRUE if a mouse is installed
swap_buttons            DW      0               ;TRUE to swap mouse buttons
mouse_visible           DB      0               ;Visible if > 0
                        DB      0               ;Make it a word

mouse_cursor            DW      0               ;Storage for mouse cursor char


.CODE


;----------------------------------------------------------------;
; This procedure tests to see if the mouse driver is installed, or if ;
; some driver is installed on INT 33h.                           ;
;                                                                ;
; Returns:      AX      0       There is no mouse installed       ;
;                       -1      There is a driver on INT 33h      ;
;----------------------------------------------------------------;
check_int_33    proc    private uses bx es
        mov     ax,3533h                ;Get the current INT 33h vector
        int     21h
        mov     ax,es                   ;Put the segment into AX
        or      ax,ax                   ;Is anything installed?
        jz      no_int_33               ;No, then return 0
        or      bx,bx                   ;Is anything installed?
        jz      no_int_33               ;No, then return 0
```

```
            mov     ax,0FFFFh                   ;Return -1, there is INT 33h vector
            jmp     Short done_check_int_33

no_int_33:
            xor     ax,ax
done_check_int_33:
            ret
check_int_33     endp



;------------------------------------------------------------------;
; This procedure initializes the mouse by calling function 0, which is ;
; a full reset of the mouse software AND hardware.  In some cases this ;
; can take several seconds (a serial mouse or an IBM mouse), which may ;
; not be acceptable.  Init_mouse() can be much faster in such cases.   ;
; Here are the rules on which of these two procedures to call:         ;
;                                                                      ;
;       Once                                                           ;
;               Init_mouse() must be called at least to initialize     ;
;               the mouse hardware the first time since not all mouse   ;
;               drivers initialize the mouse proplerly when you do      ;
;               a software mouse reset.                                 ;
;                                                                      ;
;       After Init_mouse()                                             ;
;               From then on you can call Init_mouse_sw() for a fast    ;
;               reset.  The Commander calls Init_mouse() once, then     ;
;               Init_mouse_sw() each time you return to the Commander   ;
;               after running a DOS command.                            ;
;------------------------------------------------------------------;
InitMouse        proc
            mov     bx,0                        ;Ask for a full reset
            call    do_init_mouse               ;Initialize the mouse
            ret
InitMouse        endp



;------------------------------------------------------------------;
; This procedure initializes the mouse.  It tries to do a software  ;
; reset first.  Only if the software reset doesn't work does it try to ;
; do a hardware reset.  In some cases (such as a serial mouse or the  ;
; IBM mouse) a hardware reset can take as much as 5 seconds, which is  ;
; not an acceptable delay when returning from the Commander.          ;
;------------------------------------------------------------------;
```

```
InitMouseSw      proc
        mov      bx,1                    ;Ask for a software reset
        call     do_init_mouse           ;Initialize the mouse
        ret
InitMouseSw           endp


;---------------------------------------------------------------;
; This procedure resets the mouse software, and checks to see if the   ;
; mouse and mouse software are installed.  It returns the following:   ;
;                                                                ;
; On entry:      BX      0       Do a hardware reset             ;
;                        1       Do a soft reset                 ;
;                                                                ;
; Returns:       AX      -1      The mouse and software are installed  ;
;                        0       There is no mouse, driver not installed;
;---------------------------------------------------------------;
        extrn    EgaActive:procRef
do_init_mouse    proc    private uses bx cx dx es bp
        call     check_int_33            ;See INT 33 has vector before we call
        or       ax,ax                   ;Is anything installed?
        jz       no_mouse                ;No, report that there's no mouse

        or       bx,bx                   ;Yes, Is this a full hardware reset?
        jz       do_hardware_reset       ;Yes, do a full hardware reset

do_reset:                                ;No, try to reset the mouse software
        mov      ax,33                   ;Request a software reset
        int      33h                     ;Call the mouse routine
        cmp      ax,33                   ;Did mouse ignore this function?
        je       do_hardware_reset       ;Yes, do a hardware reset
        cmp      ax,-1                   ;Is the mouse installed?
        jne      do_hardware_reset       ;No, then do a hardware reset
        cmp      bx,2                    ;Is the mouse installed?
        je       finish_init             ;Yes, then finish initializing

do_hardware_reset:
        mov      ax,0                    ;Ask for the mouse reset function
        int      33h                     ;Call the mouse routine
        or       ax,ax                   ;Is the mouse installed?
        jz       no_mouse                ;No, report that mouse is not installed

finish_init:
        mov      ax,10                   ;Set the text cursor mask and type
        xor      bx,bx                   ;Select the software text cursor
```

587

```
        mov     cx,0FFFFh               ;Set the mask to all ones
        mov     dx,7700h                ;And set cursor to inverting cursor
        int     33h                     ;Returns -1 if if the mouse installed
        mov     mouse_visible,0         ;The mouse is now hidden

        call    EgaActive               ;See if an EGA card is active
        or      ax,ax                   ;Is EGA active?
        jz      done_init_is_mouse      ;No, then we're all done
        mov     ax,1130h                ;Get EGA information
        xor     bh,bh                   ;Ask for the default information
        int     10h                     ;DL = #rows-1, CX = char height, pixels
        inc     dl                      ;DL = # rows
        cmp     dl,25                   ;Is this normal 25 line mode?
        je      done_init_is_mouse      ;Yes, don't change mouse settings
        mov     al,dl                   ;Put number of rows into AX
        mov     cl,8                    ;Microsoft assumes chars 8 pixels high
        mul     cl                      ;AX = screen height, in pixels
        dec     ax                      ;AX = screen height - 1
        mov     dx,ax                   ;DX = screen height - 1
        mov     ax,8                    ;Set max and min vertical positions
        mov     cx,0
        int     33h

done_init_is_mouse:
        xor     ax,ax                   ;Return -1 to report mouse installed
        not     ax

done_init_mouse:
        mov     mouse_installed,al      ;Save the mouse installed state
        ret

no_mouse:
        xor     ax,ax                   ;The mouse is not installed
        jmp     done_init_mouse
do_init_mouse   endp


;--------------------------------------------------------------------------;
; This procedure puts the mouse cursor back on the screen.  I unhide       ;
; the mouse only when Mouse_visible is 0 when you make this call.  In      ;
; other words, only when you cross the visiblity threshold.                ;
;                                                                          ;
; You can nest calls to Hide and Unhide_mouse_cursor.                      ;
;--------------------------------------------------------------------------;
```

```
UnhideMouse      proc
       test      mouse_installed,0FFh     ;Is the mouse installed?
       jz        done_unhide              ;No, don't do anything
       inc       mouse_visible
       cmp       mouse_visible,1          ;Did mouse just become visible?
       jne       done_unhide              ;No, then don't unhide again
       push      ax                       ;Yes, make the INT 33 call
       mov       ax,1                     ;Ask for the show-cursor function
       int       33h
       pop       ax
done_unhide:
       ret
UnhideMouse      endp


;----------------------------------------------------------------;
; This procedure removes the mouse cursor from the screen.       ;
;----------------------------------------------------------------;
HideMouse        proc
       test      mouse_installed,0FFh     ;Is the mouse installed?
       jz        done_hide                ;No, don't do anything
       dec       mouse_visible            ;Decrement the count
       cmp       mouse_visible,0          ;Did mouse just become invisible?
       jne       done_hide                ;No, then don't hide mouse again
       push      ax
       mov       ax,2                     ;Ask for the hide-cursor function
       int       33h
       pop       ax
done_hide:
       ret
HideMouse        endp


;----------------------------------------------------------------;
; This procedure returns the current mouse position in character ;
; coordinates.                                                   ;
;                                                                ;
;       GetMousePosition(int *x, int *y);                        ;
;----------------------------------------------------------------;
GetMousePosition         proc    x:Ptr Word, y:Ptr Word
       test      mouse_installed,0FFh     ;Is the mouse installed?
       jz        done_get_mouse           ;No, then don't do anything
       mov       ax,3                     ;Ask for get position function
       int       33h                      ;Ask for the mouse position
       lodES     bx,x                     ;Get address of X
```

589

```
            shr     cx,1                    ;Divide result by 8 to get char. coord.
            shr     cx,1
            shr     cx,1
            mov     refES [bx],cx           ;Save X coordinate
            shr     dx,1                    ;Divide by 8 to get char. coord.
            shr     dx,1
            shr     dx,1
            lodES   bx,y                    ;Get address of Y
            mov     refES [bx],dx           ;Save Y coordinate
done_get_mouse:
            ret
GetMousePosition        endp



;---------------------------------------------------------------------;
; This procedure sets the mouse position on the screen in character   ;
; coordinates.                                                        ;
;                                                                     ;
;       SetMousePosition(int x, int y);                               ;
;---------------------------------------------------------------------;
SetMousePosition        proc    x:Word, y:Word
            test    mouse_installed,0FFh    ;Is the mouse installed?
            jz      done_set_mouse          ;No, then don't do anything
            mov     ax,4                    ;Ask for set mouse position function
            mov     cx,x                    ;Get the new X coordinate
            shl     cx,1                    ;Multiply by 8 to get pixel coords
            shl     cx,1
            shl     cx,1
            mov     dx,y                    ;Get the new Y coordinate
            shl     dx,1                    ;Multiply by 8 to get pixel coords
            shl     dx,1
            shl     dx,1
            int     33h
done_set_mouse:
            ret
SetMousePosition        endp



;---------------------------------------------------------------------;
; This procedure checks the status of the mouse buttons:              ;
;                                                                     ;
;       int MouseButtons(int *x, int *y);                             ;
;                                                                     ;
; It returns the following information:                               ;
;                                                                     ;
```

```
;              0         Both buttons up                      ;
;              1         Left button down                     ;
;              2         Right button down                    ;
;              3         Both buttons down                    ;
;                                                             ;
; The X and Y coordinates returned are character coordinates to make  ;
; things easier since my stuff is currently character based.  ;
;                                                             ;
; NOTE: This procedure treats the middle button on three-button mice  ;
;       as the same as both buttons.                          ;
;-------------------------------------------------------------;
        extrn   FastFlush:procRef
MouseButtons    proc    x:Ptr Word, y:Ptr Word
        xor     ax,ax                   ;Return 0 if mouse not installed
        test    mouse_installed,0FFh    ;Is the mouse installed?
        jz      done_mouse_buttons      ;No, then return 0
        call    FastFlush               ;Flush unwritten chars to screen
        mov     ax,3                    ;Ask for button status
        int     33h
        mov     ax,bx                   ;Put button status into AX
        cmp     ax,3                    ;Is center or both buttons down?
        jb      middle_not_down         ;No, then continue.
        mov     ax,3                    ;Yes, set to both buttons
        jmp     Short finish_buttons    ;Now calculate coordinates
middle_not_down:
        or      ax,ax                   ;Are both buttons up?
        jz      finish_buttons          ;Yes, then calculate coordinates
        cmp     swap_buttons,0          ;Should we swap mouse buttons?
        jz      finish_buttons          ;No, calculate coordinates
        xor     ax,3                    ;Swap the mouse buttons
finish_buttons:
        lodES   bx,x                    ;Get address for X
        shr     cx,1                    ;Divide by 8 to return char. coords.
        shr     cx,1
        shr     cx,1
        mov     refES [bx],cx           ;Save X coordinate of mouse
        lodES   bx,y                    ;Get address for Y
        shr     dx,1                    ;Divide by 8 to return char. coords.
        shr     dx,1
        shr     dx,1
        mov     refES [bx],dx           ;Save Y coordinate of mouse
done_mouse_buttons:
        ret
MouseButtons    endp

        end
```

Miscellaneous Tables

The eight reference tables in this appendix provide listings of values used for setting character and keyboard codes, screen display colors, and interrupts.

Topics Covered

ASCII Character Codes

Color Codes

Extended Keyboard Codes

Table of Addressing Modes

INT 10h Functions

INT 16h Functions

INT 21h Functions

Sector Read/Write Functions

Table D-1 ASCII Character Codes

Decimal	Hex	Graphic Character	Decimal	Hex	Graphic Character
000	00	null	028	1C	FS
001	01	☺	029	1D	GS
002	02	●	030	1E	RS
003	03	♥	031	1F	US
004	04	◆	032	20	SP
005	05	♣	033	21	!
006	06	♠	034	22	"
007	07	●	035	23	#
008	08	■	036	24	$
009	09	○	037	25	%
010	0A	■	038	26	&
011	0B	♂	039	27	'
012	0C	♀	040	28	(
013	0D	♪	041	29	)
014	0E	♪♪	042	2A	*
015	0F	☼	043	2B	+
016	10	►	044	2C	'
017	11	◄	045	2D	-
018	12	↕	046	2E	.
019	13	‼	047	2F	/
020	14	¶	048	30	0
021	15	§	049	31	1
022	16	–	050	32	2
023	17	↕	051	33	3
024	18	↑	052	34	4
025	19	↓	053	35	5
026	1A	→	054	36	6
027	1B	←	055	37	7

Decimal	Hex	Graphic Character	Decimal	Hex	Graphic Character
056	38	8	086	56	V
057	39	9	087	57	W
058	3A	:	088	58	X
059	3B	;	089	59	Y
060	3C	<	090	5A	Z
061	3D	=	091	5B	[
062	3E	>	092	5C	\
063	3F	?	093	5D	]
064	40	@	094	5E	^
065	41	A	095	5F	—
066	42	B	096	60	`
067	43	C	097	61	a
068	44	D	098	62	b
069	45	E	099	63	c
070	46	F	100	64	d
071	47	G	101	65	e
072	48	H	102	66	f
073	49	I	103	67	g
074	4A	J	104	68	h
075	4B	K	105	69	i
076	4C	L	106	6A	j
077	4D	M	107	6B	k
078	4E	N	108	6C	l
079	4F	O	109	6D	m
080	50	P	110	6E	n
081	51	Q	111	6F	o
082	52	R	112	70	p
083	53	S	113	71	q
084	54	T	114	72	r
085	55	U	115	73	s

Decimal	Hex	Graphic Character	Decimal	Hex	Graphic Character
116	74	t	146	92	Æ
117	75	u	147	93	ô
118	76	v	148	94	ö
119	77	w	149	95	ò
120	78	x	150	96	û
121	79	y	151	97	ù
122	7A	z	152	98	ÿ
123	7B	{	153	99	Ö
124	7C	¦	154	9A	Ü
125	7D	}	155	9B	¢
126	7E	~	156	9C	£
127	7F	DEL	157	9D	¥
128	80	Ç	158	9E	P$_t$
129	81	ü	159	9F	ƒ
130	82	é	160	A0	á
131	83	â	161	A1	í
132	84	ä	162	A2	ó
133	85	à	163	A3	ú
134	86	å	164	A4	ñ
135	87	ç	165	A5	Ñ
136	88	ê	166	A6	ª
137	89	ë	167	A7	º
138	8A	è	168	A8	¿
139	8B	ï	169	A9	⌐
140	8C	î	170	AA	¬
141	8D	ì	171	AB	½
142	8E	Ä	172	AC	¼
143	8F	Å	173	AD	¡
144	90	É	174	AE	«
145	91	æ	175	AF	»

Decimal	Hex	Graphic Character	Decimal	Hex	Graphic Character
176	B0	▒	206	CE	╬
177	B1	▓	207	CF	╧
178	B2	█	208	D0	╨
179	B3	│	209	D1	╤
180	B4	┤	210	D2	╥
181	B5	╡	211	D3	╙
182	B6	╢	212	D4	╘
183	B7	╖	213	D5	╒
184	B8	╕	214	D6	╓
185	B9	╣	215	D7	╫
186	BA	║	216	D8	╪
187	BB	╗	217	D9	┘
188	BC	╝	218	DA	┌
189	BD	╜	219	DB	█
190	BE	╛	220	DC	▄
191	BF	┐	221	DD	▌
192	C0	└	222	DE	▐
193	C1	┴	223	DF	▀
194	C2	┬	224	E0	α
195	C3	├	225	E1	β
196	C4	─	226	E2	Γ
197	C5	┼	227	E3	π
198	C6	╞	228	E4	Σ
199	C7	╟	229	E5	σ
200	C8	╚	230	E6	μ
201	C9	╔	231	E7	τ
202	CA	╩	232	E8	Φ
203	CB	╦	233	E9	θ
204	CC	╠	234	EA	Ω
205	CD	═	235	EB	δ

Decimal	Hex	Graphic Character	Decimal	Hex	Graphic Character
236	EC	∞	246	F6	÷
237	ED	ø	247	F7	≈
238	EE	∈	248	F8	°
239	EF	∩	249	F9	•
240	F0	≡	250	FA	·
241	F1	±	251	FB	√
242	F2	≥	252	FC	η
243	F3	≤	253	FD	2
244	F4	⌠	254	FE	■
245	F5	⌡	255	FF	

Table D-2 Color Codes

0	Black
1	Blue
2	Green
3	Cyan
4	Red
5	Violet
6	Brown
7	White

Attribute = background color * 16 + foreground color

Add 8 to the foreground color for the bright versions, or add 8 to the background color to turn on blinking.

Table D-3 Extended Keyboard Codes

Many of the keys on the keyboard (such as the function keys) return a two-character code when you read the keys through DOS: a decimal 0 followed by a scan code. The following table shows the scan codes for all the keys that have no equivalent ASCII code.

15	Shift Tab
16-25	Alt keys for Q, W, E, R, T, Y, U, I, O, P
30-38	Alt keys for A, S, D, F, G, H, J, K, L
44-50	Alt keys for Z, X, C, V, B, N, M
59-68	F1 through F10
71	Home
72	Cursor Up
73	PgUp
75	Cursor Left
77	Cursor Right
79	End
80	Cursor Down
81	PgDn
82	Ins
83	Del
84-93	Shift F1 through F10
94-103	Control F1 through F10
104-113	Alt F1 through F10
114	Control PrtSc
115	Control Left Cursor
116	Control Right Cursor
117	Control End
118	Control PgDn
119	Control Home
120-131	Control Alt for 1, 2, 3, 4, 5, 6, 7, 8, 9, 0, -, =
132	Control PgUp

Table D-4 Table of Addressing Modes

Addressing Mode	Format of Address	Segment Register Used
Register	register (such as AX)	None
Immediate	data (such as 12345)	None

continues

Addressing Mode	Format of Address	Segment Register Used
Memory Addressing Modes		
Register Indirect	[BX]	DS
	[BP]	SS
	[DI]	DS
	[SI]	DS
Base Relative*	label[BX]	DS
	label[BP]	SS
Direct Indexed*	label[DI]	DS
	label[SI]	DS
Base Indexed*	label[BX+SI]	DS
	label[BX+DI]	DS
	label [BP+SI]	SS
	label[BP+DI]	SS
String Commands:		Read from DS:SI
(MOVSW, LODSB, *and so on*)		Write to ES:DI

* Label[...] can be replaced by [disp+...], where *disp* is a displacement. Thus, we could write [10+BX] and the address would be 10 + BX.

Table D-5 INT 10h Functions

(AH)=0   **Set the display mode.** The AL registers contains the mode number.

	Text Modes
(AL)=0	40 by 25, black and white mode
(AL)=1	40 by 25, color
(AL)=2	80 by 25, black and white
(AL)=3	80 by 25, color
(AL)=7	80 by 25, monochrome display adapter

Graphics Mode

(AL)=4	320 by 200, color
(AL)=5	320 by 200, black and white
(AL)=6	640 by 200, black and white

(AH)=1 Set the cursor size.

(CH)   Starting scan line of the cursor. The top line is 0 on both the monochrome and color graphics displays, while the bottom line is 7 for the color graphics adapter and 13 for the monochrome adapter. Valid range: 0 to 31.

(CL)   Last scan line of the cursor.

The power-on setting for the color graphics adapter is CH=6 and CL=7. For the monochrome display: CH=11 and CL=12.

(AH)=2 Set the cursor position.

(DH,DL)   Row, column of new cursor position; the upper left corner is (0,0).

(BH)   Page number. This is the number of the display page. The color-graphics adapter has room for several display pages, but most programs use page 0.

(AH)=3 Read the cursor position.

(BH)   Page number

On exit   (DH,DL)   Row, column of cursor

(CH,CL)   Cursor size

(AH)=4 Read light pen position (see Tech. Ref. Man.).

(AH)=5 Select active display page.

(AL)   New page number (from 0 to 7 for modes 0 and 1; from 0 to 3 for modes 2 and 3)

601

(AH)=6   **Scroll up.**

(AL)	Number of lines to blank at the bottom of the window. Normal scrolling blanks one line. Set to zero to blank entire window.
(CH,CL)	Row, column of upper left corner of window
(DH,DL)	Row, column of lower right corner of window
(BH)	Display attribute to use for blank lines

(AH)=7   **Scroll down.**

Same as scroll up (function 6), but lines are left blank at the top of the window instead of the bottom

(AH)=8   **Read attribute and character under the cursor.**

(BH)	Display page (text modes only)
(AL)	Character read
(AH)	Attribute of character read (text modes only)

(AH)=9   **Write attribute and character under the cursor.**

(BH)	Display page (text modes only)
(CX)	Number of times to write character and attribute on screen
(AL)	Character to write
(BL)	Attribute to write

(AH)=10   **Write character under cursor** (with normal attribute).

(BH)	Display page
(CX)	Number of times to write character
(AL)	Character to write

(AH)=11 to 13 **Various graphics functions.** (See Tech. Ref. Man. for the details)

(AH)=14 **Write teletype.** Write one character to the screen and move the cursor to the next position.

        (AL)   Character to write

        (BL)   Color of character (graphics mode only)

        (BH)   Display page (text mode)

(AH)=15 **Return current video state.**

        (AL)   Display mode currently set

        (AH)   Number of characters per line

        (BH)   Active display pages

Table D-6 INT 16h Functions

This table contains the INT 16h functions used in this book to read characters from the keyboard.

(AH)=0 **Keyboard read.** This function waits for you to type a character on the keyboard. It returns the ASCII code in AL and the scan code in AH. For extended keys, AL will be set to 0. See Table D-2 for a list of scan codes for such keys.

        (AL)   ASCII code of the key you press (0 for special keys).

        (AH)   Scan code for the key you pressed.

(AH)=1 **Keyboard status.** This function checks to see if there are any keys waiting to be read.

        ZF   0 if a character is waiting, 1 if there are no characters waiting.

        (AL)   ASCII code of character waiting to be read.

        (AH)   Scan code of character waiting to be read.

(AH)=2   **Shift status.** This function returns a byte with the state of the various shift keys:

(AL)   Status of the shift keys:

     7 6 5 4 3 2 1

     1 . . . . . .   Insert on

     . 1 . . . . .   Caps Lock on

     . . 1 . . . .   Num Lock on

     . . . 1 . . .   Scroll Lock on

     . . . . 1 . .   Alt key down

     . . . . . 1 .   Left shift down

     1   Right shift down

Table D-7 INT 21h Functions

This table contains the INT 21h functions used in this book. For a more complete list, you should buy the IBM *DOS Technical Reference* manual.

(AH)=1   **Keyboard input.** This function waits for you to type a character on the keyboard. It echoes the character to the screen, and returns the ASCII code in the AL register. For extended keyboard codes, this function returns two characters: an ASCII 0 followed by the scan code (see Table D-2).

(AL)   Character read from the keyboard.

(AH)=2   **Display output.** Displays one character on the screen. Several characters have special meaning to this function:

7   Beep: Send a one-second tone to the speaker.

8   Backspace: move the cursor left one character position.

9   Tab: Move to the next tab stop. Tab stops are set to every 8 characters.

0Ah   Line feed: Move to the next line.

0Dh   Carriage return: Move to the start of the
               current line.

(DL)   Character to display on the screen.

(AH)=8   **Keyboard input without echo.** Reads a character from the
keyboard, but doesn't display the character on the screen.

(AL)   Character read from keyboard.

(AH)=9   **Display string.** Displays the string pointed to by the DS:DX
pair of registers. You must mark the end of the string with the
$ character.

DS:DX   Points to the string to display.

(AH)=0Ah   **Read string.** Reads a string from the keyboard. See
Chapter 23 for more details.

(AH)=25h   **Set interrupt vector.** Sets an interrupt vector to point to a
new routine.

(AL)   Interrupt number.

DS:DX   Address of the new interrupt handler.

(AH)=35h   **Get interrupt vector.** Gets the address of the interrupt
service routine for the interrupt number given in AL.

(AL)   Interrupt number.

ES:BX   Address of the interrupt handler.

(AH)=4Ch   **Exit to DOS.** Returns to DOS, like INT 20h, but it works
for both .COM and .EXE programs. The INT 20h function
works only for .COM programs.

(AL)   Return code. Normally set to 0, but you can
               set it to any other number and use the DOS
               batch commands IF and ERRORLEVEL to
               detect errors.

Table D-8 Sector Read/Write Functions

The following two interrupts are DOS calls for reading and writing disk sectors.

INT 25h—Read Disk Sector

On entry:

(AL)	Drive number (0=A, 1=B, and so on)
(CX)	Number of sectors to read at one time
(DX)	Number of the first sector to read (the first sector is 0)
DS:BX	Transfer address: where to write the sectors read

INT 26h—Write Disk Sector

On entry:

(AL)	Drive number (0=A, 1=B, and so on)
(CX)	Number of sectors to write at one time
(DX)	Number of the first sector to write (the first sector is 0)
DS:BX	Transfer address: start of the data we want to write to the disk.

Information Returned by INT 25h, INT 26h

Both INT 25h and INT 26h return the following information in the AX register. They also leave the flags on the stack, so you'll want to use a POP or POPF to remove this word from the stack (see Chapter 15 for an example).

Returns:

Carry Flag	Set if there was an error, in which case the error information will be in AX.
(AL)	DOS error code
(AH)	Contains one of the following:

80h   The drive did not respond

40h   The Seek operation failed

08h   Bad CRC when we read the disk

04h   Could not find the sector we asked for

03h   Tried to write to a write-protected disk

02h   Some other error

Destroys

AX, BX, CX, DX, SI, DI, BP

Index

J

M

W

X-Z

XOR instruction, 131

Zero Flag, 68, 466

zeros
    setting registers to, 131-132
    shifting, 74
ZR status, 68

DISK REPLACEMENT ORDER FORM

In the event that the disk bound in to this book is defective, Prentice Hall Computer Publishing will send you a replacement disk free of charge.

Please fill out the information below and return this card to the address listed below with your original disk. Please print clearly.

BOOK TITLE _____ ISBN _____

NAME _____ PHONE _____

COMPANY _____ TITLE _____

ADDRESS _____

CITY _____ STATE _____ ZIP _____

Prentice Hall Computer Publishing, 11711 North College Avenue, Carmel IN 46032.
ATTN: Customer Service Department.

LIMITED WARRANTY REGISTRATION CARD

In order to preserve your rights as provided in the limited warranty, this card must be on file with PHCP within thirty days of purchase.

Please fill in the information requested:

BOOK TITLE _____ ISBN _____

NAME _____ PHONE NUMBER ( ) _____

ADDRESS _____

CITY _____ STATE _____ ZIP _____

COMPUTER BRAND & MODEL _____ DOS VERSION _____ MEMORY _____ K

Where did you purchase this product?

DEALER NAME? _____ PHONE NUMBER ( ) _____

ADDRESS _____

CITY _____ STATE _____ ZIP _____

PURCHASE DATE _____ PURCHASE PRICE _____

How did you learn about this product? (Check as many as applicable.)

STORE DISPLAY _____ SALESPERSON _____ MAGAZINE ARTICLE _____ ADVERTISEMENT _____

OTHER (Please explain) _____

How long have you owned or used this computer?

LESS THAN 30 DAYS _____ LESS THAN 6 MONTHS _____ 6 MONTHS TO A YEAR _____ OVER 1 YEAR _____

What is your primary use for the computer?

BUSINESS _____ PERSONAL _____ EDUCATION _____ OTHER (Please explain) _____

Where is your computer located?

HOME _____ OFFICE _____ SCHOOL _____ OTHER (Please explain) _____

Prentice Hall Computer Publishing
11711 N. College Avenue
Carmel, IN 46032

Attn: **Order Department**

If your computer uses 5 1/4-inch disks...

While most personal computers use 3 1/2-inch disks to store information, some computers use 5 1/4-inch disks for information storage. If your computer uses 5 1/4-inch disks, you can return this form to Brady to obtain a 5 1/4-inch disk to use with this book. Simply fill out the remainder of this form and mail to:

**Assembly Language
for the PC**

 Disk Exchange
Brady
11711 N. College Ave., Suite 140
Carmel, IN 46032

We will then send you, free of charge, the 5 1/4-inch version of the book software.

Name _____ Phone _____

Company _____ Title _____

Address _____

City _____ St. _____ ZIP _____